China's iGeneration

China's iGeneration

Cinema and Moving Image Culture for the Twenty-First Century

Edited by Matthew D. Johnson, Keith B. Wagner, Tianqi Yu and Luke Vulpiani

BLOOMSBURY
NEW YORK • LONDON • NEW DELHI • SYDNEY

Bloomsbury Academic
An imprint of Bloomsbury Publishing Inc

1385 Broadway	50 Bedford Square
New York	London
NY 10018	WC1B 3DP
USA	UK

www.bloomsbury.com

Bloomsbury is a registered trade mark of Bloomsbury Publishing Plc

First published 2014

© Matthew D. Johnson, Keith B. Wagner, Tianqi Yu, Luke Vulpiani and Contributors 2014

All rights reserved. No part of this publication may be reproduced or transmitted in any form or by any means, electronic or mechanical, including photocopying, recording, or any information storage or retrieval system, without prior permission in writing from the publishers.

No responsibility for loss caused to any individual or organization acting on or refraining from action as a result of the material in this publication can be accepted by Bloomsbury or the author.

Library of Congress Cataloging-in-Publication Data
China's iGeneration : cinema and moving image culture for the twenty-first century / edited by Matthew D. Johnson, Keith B. Wagner, Tianqi Yu, and Luke Vulpiani.
 pages cm
Includes bibliographical references and index.
ISBN 978-1-62356-595-4 (hardback : alk. paper) 1. Motion pictures--China--History--21st century. I. Johnson,, Matthew D., editor of compilation. II. Wagner, Keith B., 1978- editor of compilation. III. Yu, Tianqi, editor of compilation. IV. Vulpiani, Luke, editor of compilation.
 PN1993.5.C4C44219 2014
 791.430951'09051--dc23
 2013049431

ISBN: HB: 978-1-6235-6595-4
ePub: 978-1-6235-6847-4
ePDF: 978-1-6235-6312-7

Typeset by Fakenham Prepress Solutions, Fakenham, Norfolk NR21 8NN
Printed and bound in the United States of America

Contents

Foreword: China's iGeneration: From Film Studies to Screen Studies *Chris Berry*　vii
Acknowledgements　xi
Notes on Transliteration　xiii
List of Figures and Tables　xv

　Introduction: China's iGeneration Cinema *Keith B. Wagner, Tianqi Yu*
　with *Luke Vulpiani*　1

Part One Technologies

1　Toward a Communicative Practice: Female First-Person Documentary in
　Twenty-first Century China *Tianqi Yu*　23

2　Quasi-Documentary, Cellflix and Web Spoofs: Chinese Movies' Other
　Visual Pleasures *Paola Voci*　45

3　Individuality, State Discourse and Visual Representation:
　The Imagination and Practices of the iGeneration in Chinese
　Animation *Weihua Wu*　57

4　Cinema of Exhibition: Film in Chinese Contemporary Art
　Dong Bingfeng　73

Part Two Aesthetics

5　Goodbye to the Grim Real, Hello to What Comes Next: The Moment of
　Passage from the Sixth Generation to the iGeneration *Luke Vulpiani*　89

6　Digitizing City Symphony, Stabilizing the Shadow of Time: Montage and
　Temporal–Spatial Construction in *San Yuan Li* *Ling Zhang*　105

7　From Pirate to Kino-eye: A Genealogical Tale of Film Re-Distribution in
　China *Dan Gao*　125

8　Xue Jianqiang as Reckless Documentarian: Underdevelopment and
　Juvenile Crime in post-WTO China *Keith B. Wagner*　147

Part Three Social Engagement

9   Of Animals and Men: Towards a Theory of Docu-ani-mentary *Yiman Wang*   167

10 Working with Rubble: Montage, Tweets and the Reconstruction of an Activist Documentary *Ying Qian*   181

11 Provincializing the Chinese Mediascape: Cantonese Digital Activism in Southern China *Jia Tan*   197

Part Four Platforms and Politics

12 Interpreting *ScreenSpaces* at the Shanghai Expo and Beyond *Jeesoon Hong with Matthew D. Johnson*   215

13 Regarding the Grassroots Chinese Independent Film Festivals: Modes of Multiplicity and Abnormal Film Networking *Ma Ran*   235

14 Bringing the Transnational Back into Documentary Cinema: Wu Wenguang's *China Village Documentary Project*, Participatory Video and the NGO Aesthetic *Matthew D. Johnson*   255

15 The Cinematic Deng Xiaoping: Scripting a Leader or a 'Traitor'? *Xiaomei Chen* 283

Part Five Online Audiences

16 Zhang Yimou's Sexual Storytelling and the iGeneration: Contending *Shanzhashu Zhi Lian* (*Under the Hawthorn Tree*) on *Douban* *Ralph Parfect*   301

17 From the Glaring Sun to Flying Bullets: Aesthetics and Memory in the 'Post-' Era Chinese Cinema *Xiao Liu*   321

Notes on Contributors   337
Index   341

Foreword: China's iGeneration: From Film Studies to Screen Studies

Chris Berry

It is a great honour to be asked to write a preface to *China's iGeneration: Cinema and Moving Image Culture for the Twenty-First Century*. This is an exciting and fresh, new collection of material. First, it focuses on contemporary work in the new century – the 'post-Sixth Generation' period. Second, edited by four young scholars and featuring a cohort of fresh faces (as well as some more established names!), it marks a changing of the guard in terms of who is writing as well as the material covered.

However, the book is more than just a collection. It is also an active and self-conscious intervention into the field of Chinese Cinema Studies, and perhaps Cinema Studies as a whole. In the range of topics and approaches covered, it marks out a different understanding of what Chinese cinema is in the new century. In their introduction, the editors clearly mark out the specificity of the conjuncture that holds their interest and makes the volume cohere. They write of 'iGeneration cinema' as a 'cinema of dispersion' in China today, characterized by: the eclipse of the centralized command economy by a burgeoning and multi-polar market economy along with the emergence of public discourse not directed by the state; the consumption of moving image works across many different platforms with ever-declining distinction between television programmes, videos and movies; and viewers who are increasingly mobile and individual yet internet-connected, even in collective environments. In the Chinese context, perhaps we must also add the social factors beyond globalized neoliberalism that have produced an increasingly I-focused and monadic culture: the one-child policy and the rise of a national labour market and a vast 'floating population' of people living away from family and which numbers in the hundreds of millions.

'iGeneration cinema' is Chinese cinema in the age of the digital. Importantly, in this book digital cinema is not in material and technological terms alone, although of course it does not neglect the importance of these technological changes as both pre-conditions and factors that actively shape the new cinema of dispersion. The materiality of digital cinema as technology has been the centre of concern for so many writers and theorists concerned about the significance of a shift from the analogue to the digital and away from the indexical imprint that light leaves on celluloid.[1] Instead, the approach in this volume is one that I would characterize as based in a cultural understanding of cinema as a culture.[2] I want to use this foreword to point out that this approach marks a shift away from the understanding of Chinese cinema in terms of Film Studies and towards a re-framing of it in terms of Screen Studies.

What does this reconfiguration mean and why is it so marked in contemporary Chinese cinema and this collection? I would like to start out my consideration of some of the reasons for this shift at some remove from this actual collection, by describing a question that occurred to me a couple of years ago. *China's iGeneration* has brought that question back into my mind and helped me to understand it better.

In 2011, two artists who work with moving images in gallery environments had simultaneous exhibitions in London. The Chinese artist Yang Fudong, who is having a mid-career retrospective at the Berkeley Art Museum and Pacific Film Archive as I write this,[3] had a solo exhibition, entitled 'One Half of August,' in London at Parasol Unit.[4] The works were black-and-white, often with velvety night settings. Some were single channel and some multi-channel. Many were shot on 35mm and transferred to high definition video. One in particular drew attention to its own virtuoso production. *Fifth Night* consists of seven screens stretched across a long wall, on which carefully synchronized long takes of a scene from various different angles play. You can tell all the shots were filmed at the same time, because an actor might appear doing exactly the same thing in two shots at the same time. The cameras track and pan but never actually appear in each other's frames, making the viewer feel a frisson of excitement at the sheer risk and high degree of difficulty in executing the work. The ersatz 1930s Shanghai setting evokes the first 'Golden Age' of Chinese cinema. But, although it may have been shot on 35mm, it would be impractical if not impossible to project seven separate films simultaneously using seven separate 35mm film projectors. So, while it invokes celluloid, its display was distinctly and necessarily digital.

Meanwhile, on the other side of the Thames, Tacita Dean's 'Film' was the Turbine Hall work at the Tate Modern that year. An 11-minute 35mm film, it was projected onto a huge column of a screen at the end of the hall. As the Tate's announcement states, 'It is the first work in The Unilever Series devoted to the moving image, and celebrates the masterful techniques of analogue filmmaking as opposed to digital.'[5] Indeed, anxiety about the digital and the possible death of celluloid featured frequently in Dean's own statements about her work. For example, an audio talk recorded for the *Guardian*'s online website is captioned with a statement saying the work 'is a love letter to a disappearing medium,' and noting that in her talk, 'she explains how she hopes to create something magical and spectacular to carry her message: film is beautiful – let's keep it.'[6]

This anxiety about the transition to the digital is something I have never run across in the Chinese context, and it is not there at all in Yang Fudong's *Fifth Night* (or any of his other work that I am aware of). Yang just gets on with it, using celluloid for what he likes about it, then transferring it and adding the crisp shine of high definition video to the smooth quality of celluloid, and being able to project the result more effectively. There is no hand-wringing here. Yang is clearly part of the 'iGeneration.'

Around the same time, I was teaching a core module for an M.A. course at Goldsmiths, University of London, in Screen Studies. We had a small cohort of students from the Department of Film and Television at Shanghai University on the programme. One week, I asked students to keep a diary of what moving image materials they watched and where. In the ensuing in-class discussion, it soon became clear that some of my British and European students were very attached indeed to watching movies in the cinema, as we call movie theatres in the UK. On the other hand, my Chinese students watched nearly everything on their computers and iPads, and never thought twice about it until it became a seminar topic.

I do not want to ask here whether this new cinema culture that has emerged so strongly in China and is the object of this collection is a good or a bad thing. But I do wonder why it is that Chinese moving image cultures seem to have moved so smoothly into the digital age, while it has been the subject of so much anxiety in Europe and North America? I cannot offer any definitive answer, but I can make some suggestions. First, and perhaps most obviously, the English word 'film' and most European equivalents make direct reference to the material medium of celluloid. As is well known, the Chinese 'dianying' simply means 'electric shadows,' with no more specific material referent than electricity and instead an emphasis on the idea of movement. So, in some sense, 'cinema' in China has never had a specific association with celluloid, even before the advent of the digital.

Second, as many of my Chinese students frankly told me, the cinema scene in the People's Republic is characterized by strong censorship of theatrically released films and a very limited range of titles in release, due to the box office stranglehold of a small number of commercial exhibition chains and the absence of independent theatres. In these circumstances, few young people who have a genuine interested in 'electric shadow' culture are motivated to go to the movie theatres. Unlike my other students, perhaps it is the case that the more of a cinephile you are in China, the less likely you are to be attached to the movie theatre or to celluloid.

The diversity of the essays in this volume cohere to begin mapping this 'iGeneration cinema' culture that is emerging so quickly in China. Ranging in coverage from micro-movies made for cell phones to independent film practices, internet fandom, moving image screens in public spaces, informal distribution and first-person filmmaking, they add up to a brave new cinematic world. The result is distinctively Chinese, but also may well presage new directions and tendencies that will affect us all in the very near future.

Whatever mixed feelings of excitement and disquiet this new cinema culture may inspire, it challenges us intellectually to develop new theories, methods and approaches. Many of those particular innovations are developed to address the specific phenomena considered in the individual essays here. But taken as a whole, what we see in *China's iGeneration* is a radical re-framing that takes us from Film Studies to what might be called Screen Studies. As I have tried to point out here, this approach to moving image culture is grounded in more than a technological shift from the analogue to the digital, although it might be underpinned by that change. As a cultural approach, it is fully attendant to the transformations in patterns of production, consumption and discourse around cinema that result when it appears across all manner of different screens in different environments and socio-historical situations.

It is because *China's iGeneration* effects the shift from Film Studies to Screen Studies in both its conception and execution that I believe this collection is an intervention not only in Chinese Cinema Studies but in Cinema Studies more generally.

The cutting-edge quality of Chinese culture makes this possible, but it is a tribute to the foresight and insight of the editors and authors that they have been able to capture this moment so successfully in the book.

However, I must also acknowledge that only an optimist would expect the rest of our larger field to pick up on the value of this book for all of them. Those of us working on non-Western cinemas in English – in other words, the vast bulk of global cinema production and consumption by any definition and measure – have long become resigned to the determination of our other colleagues to relegate our work to a 'minority interest' assumed to be derivative rather than at the leading edge. Again and again, I hear tales from authors dealing with publishers who insist that they will only publish their work if this 'minority interest' is clearly tagged by identifying the niche that the book is destined for in its title, even if it has far wider significance. But that should not deter us from noting and claiming the importance of what is going on in this collection both for Chinese Cinema Studies and Cinema Studies as a whole. Perhaps I might end by allowing myself not only to hope that *China's iGeneration* heralds a time in the very near future when more and more cinema scholars can see how China is changing our understanding of cinema in general, but also to acclaim the collection for making that new perception possible.

Notes

1 Examples might include Sean Cubbitt, *The Cinema Effect*. Cambridge: MIT Press, 2004; and D. N. Rodowick, *The Virtual Life of Film*. Cambridge: Harvard University Press, 2007.
2 Janet Harbord, *Film Cultures*. London: Sage Publications, 2002.
3 http://www.bampfa.berkeley.edu/exhibition/yangfudong (accessed 5 November 2013).
4 http://parasol-unit.org/yang-fudong-one-half-of-august (accessed 2 November 2013).
5 http://www.tate.org.uk/whats-on/tate-modern/exhibition/unilever-series-tacita-dean-film (accessed 3 November 2013).
6 See, for example, http://www.theguardian.com/culture/video/2011/oct/12/tacita-dean-film-tate-video (accessed 4 November 2013).

Acknowledgements

This anthology began as a conversation among three of the editors at 'Contemporary Chinese Film,' a screening event curated by Tianqi Yu at *Cinéphilia West*, Notting Hill Gate, London. That intial, inspiring dialogue led to the first conference on contemporary Chinese cinema organized in England, 'New Generation Chinese Cinema: Commodities of Exchange,' held at King's College London in May 2011. From these two signal events many of the chapters and critical formations presented in this collection took shape. Subsequent rounds of discussion among the collaborators led to expansion of the volume's original themes to include work by leading Chinese film studies scholars around the world. Theoretical and empirical dimensions of the project expanded as a result; we are grateful to all of the contributors and to one another for their willingness to engage in this lengthy and illuminating process of exchange.

This volume would not have been possible without the generous support of numerous institutions, colleagues and intellectual benefactors. We would particularly like to thank: Sarah Cooper at King's College London and the Department of Film Studies; the Roberts Fund Open Competition Award from King's College London; Sylvain Levy at DSL Collection in Paris; and Rosie Thomas at the University of Westminster. We are also grateful to the keynote speakers at the original 'New Generation Chinese Cinema' conference: Chris Berry, Yomi Braester, Zhang Zhen and Julian Stringer. Their expansive and erudite talks highlighted important new vantage points from which to analyse contemporary Chinese cinema. As this volume and its central 'iGeneration' concept began to take shape, we benefitted from the additional and timely support of: at Grinnell College, the Committee for Support of Faculty Scholarship and the Jack ('39) and Lucile Hanson ('40) Harris Faculty Fellowship; at Hongik University, the Graduate School of Film and Digital Media, New Faculty Research Fund, Dean Jongdeok Kim, Dean Hyunsuk Kim and the dedicated research assistance of Haejeong Yoon, Haeyoon Chang and Sohyoung Roh. We are also grateful for the intellectual contributions and support of fellow scholars: Davido Caputo, Ying Xiao, Soyoung Kim, Michael Unger, Jiyoung Lee, Alex Zahlten, JungBong Choi, Julian Ward, Song Hwee Lim, Mark Betz and Dudley Andrew.

Throughout the publishing process, invaluable insight and oversight was provided by Katie Gallof, Laura Murray, Claire Cooper, and Mary Al-Sayed at Bloomsbury Press. We appreciate their patience and exceptional acumen in matters of organization and promotion. From Grinnell, Iowa, John Grennan provided sure-handed and stylistically superb copy-editing in the zero hour prior to submission. Kim Storry, Moira Eagling and Robert Bullard at Fakenham Prepress Solutions made truly heroic efforts to improve the quality of the manuscript at every stage of its production. We are indebted to all of them.

Additional thanks are due to filmmaker Wu Haohao for giving us permission to use images from his work in the production of our cover, and to Miao Hui for delivering a laudable English-language translation of Dong Bingfeng's chapter.

Finally, each of the *iGeneration* editors – Matthew D. Johnson, Keith B. Wagner, Tianqi Yu and Luke Vulpiani – want to thank one another for time and energy devoted to this shared project, as well as their respective families and friends for sustenance and intellectual encouragement along the way.

We are grateful to *Senses of Cinema* for permission to reproduce the following copyrighted material: Paola Voci. 'Quasi-Documentary, Cellflix and Web Spoofs: Chinese Movies' Other Visual Pleasures.' *Senses of Cinema*, no. 41 (October–December 2006).

Notes on Transliteration

The book uses the pinyin system to romanize Chinese characters. Chinese-language names and phrases first appear in English translation followed by Chinese pinyin. Chinese-language film titles all appear in their English translations and pinyin in brackets. Names of Chinese authors, filmmakers and individuals appear according to the Chinese convention, with surname followed by first name.

List of Figures and Tables

Figure 1.1. Yang asks the mother to persuade the father in *Home Video* (2001). 31
Figure 1.2–1.4. The three interviews are cross-cut in *Home Video* (2001). 32–3

Figure 2.1. Surrounded by a dark background, the close-up of her face kissing the panda is strikingly bright and her skin is exposed in piercing detail. While softly addressing him, she strokes him with both sensuality and sorrow. The mocking tone is gone; Bai's deep sadness and solitude fill the screen. *Ying and Bai* (2002). 47

Figure 3.1. *Talk*, directed by Meng Jun. BlackAnt Animation Studio, 2001. 61
Figure 3.2. *Pond*, directed by Huang Ying. 2003. 62
Figure 3.3. 'May Fourth Movement,' *Mr. Lu Xun*, directed by Jiang Jianqiu, 2001. 66

Figure 7.1. Shen Ming watching a pirated DVD in *Pirated Copy* (2004). 135
Figure 7.2. Mada watching a pirated VCD in *Suzhou River* (2000). 135
Figure 7.3. Mada and Mudan looking into the TV screen in *Suzhou River* (2000). 136

Figure 11.1. Still of an aerial shot of Guangzhou's cityscape in online video *Rap Cantonese* (2010). 204
Figure 11.2. Still of men carrying a dragon boat in online video *Rap Cantonese* (2010). 205
Figure 11.3. Still of a smiling woman in online video *Rap Cantonese* (2010). 205

Figure 12.1 The National Pavilion at the 2010 Shanghai Expo. Source: Lucia Wang, 2010. Available from: Wikimedia Commons. 216
Figure 12.2 *ScreenSpace* along Nanjing Road, Shanghai. Source: tayloranddayumi, 2008. Available from: Wikimedia Commons. 219
Figure 12.3 Images from Zhang Zeduan, 'Riverside Scene at Qingming Festival', early eleventh century. Available from: Wikimedia Commons. 221
Figure 12.4 The digitally enhanced and animated 'Riverside Scene at Qingming Festival' scroll, located in the National Pavilion. Source: AlexHe34, 2010. Available from: Wikimedia Commons. 222
Figure 12.5 Long queues and human crowds in the National Pavilion. Available from: Wikimedia Commons. 223
Figure 12.6 Bund, bank, lions and man in Jia Zhangke's *I Wish I Knew* (2010). 226

Figure 12.7 Reverse shot: surveying urban development and debris, *I Wish I Knew* (2010). 226
Figure 12.8 A ghostly Zhao Tao haunts the rubble-strewn Bund ... 227
Figure 12.9 ... and is figuratively juxtaposed against the Shanghai Expo, *I Wish I Knew* (2010). 228

Figure 16.1. Screenshot of the review 'Great Master, The People Present You with a Pair of Pants' on douban.com. 310

Figure 17.1. The amorous screen of revolutionary ballet in *Let the Bullets Fly* (2010). 326
Figure 17.2. Paving the street with gold and silver in *Let the Bullets Fly* (2010). 332

Table 8.1. 14 to 25 Year Olds as Percentage of Total Youth Offenders, 1975–89. 157

Introduction

China's iGeneration Cinema: Dispersion, Individualization and Post-WTO Moving Image Practices

Keith B. Wagner, Tianqi Yu with Luke Vulpiani

Chinese cinema is moving beyond the theatrical screen. While the country is now the world's second-largest film market in addition to being the world's second-largest economy, visual culture in China is increasingly multi-platform and post-cinematic.[1] Digital technology, network-based media and portable media player platforms have contributed to the creation of China's new *cinema of dispersion* or 'iGeneration cinema,' which is oriented as much toward individual, self-directed viewers as toward traditional distribution channels such as the box office, festival, or public spaces. Visual culture in China is no longer dominated by the technology and allure of the big screen, if indeed it ever was. While China's film industry still produces 'traditional' box-office blockbusters and festival-ready documentaries, their impact and influence is increasingly debatable.

This volume of essays captures the richness and diversity of China's contemporary moving image culture, while suggesting that familiar notions of 'cinema' must be reconceptualized as just one of many platforms and experiences available within that broader culture. In the process, each essay contributes to the larger project of mapping out where this moving image culture exists within the context of China's individualizing, consumption-oriented, urban and technologically mutable post-WTO society.

Cultural dispersion in a WTO era

One of the ways we can conceptualize the *dispersion* of Chinese cinema and moving image culture in the new millennium period is to understand it in relation to sociological and economic changes ushered in by the country's accession to the World Trade Organization (WTO) in 2001. This climactic moment signalled not only China's official integration into the global economic system of expanding capitalism, but also a moment of significant financial and cultural rescaling. For more than a decade, China's new forms of cinema and moving image practices have been capturing this new neoliberal reality in ways that cannot be neatly portioned into the standard regional, national and transnational perspectives. Rather, this book shows how individual aspirations expressed through post-WTO digital and new media can be classified as appraisals of cultural realities and possibilities that were either unthinkable or untenable one decade earlier. Examples of the new ground broken by Chinese visual culture include: documentary exposés, based on found footage of the 2008 Sichuan earthquake, about substandard construction and the death of thousands of schoolchildren; multimedia artists' films exhibited in upmarket galleries and purchased by collectors for large sums of money; filmmakers' digital activism in preserving Cantonese language through videos like *Rap Guangzhou*; and personal documentaries individually produced by subaltern villagers, marginalized juveniles and self-realizing women.

This volume examines the great upheaval that Wang Hui has described as 'neoliberalism with Chinese characteristics,' while paying special attention to what these characteristics mean for new forms of moving image culture. In other words, we do not posit a dichotomy between economics and culture in China. In reality, this dichotomy should be superceded by analyses that interrogate the intersection of both realms. In furthering this goal, this volume examines a wide array of sources, ranging from blockbuster movies to individual auteur films to experimental documentaries. Our contributors draw on reception theory, neo-formalism and sociological methodologies to unpack depictions of China's cultural transformation in the past decade. Neoliberalism, as an increasingly visible/powerful governing ideology in China, has come under significant scrutiny as filmmakers have had more freedom to criticize a party-state which still intervenes in individuals' cultural lives through censorship in film, TV and art production, distribution and exhibition.[2] The chaotic task of keeping up with these changes inspires much reflection and critical assessment, as is the case with almost everything new in the post-WTO era.

Following the further implementation of neoliberal policies since 2001, the Communist Party continues to eviscerate social programmes, neglect wage–price factors and deny the internal antagonisms that exist because of these changes – mainly 'industrial democracy versus corruption'[3] – all to ensure the survival of this political–economic system. The rationale is that because of Chinese neoliberalism, social welfare institutions and local governments remain in perilous fiscal health, while consumption soars along with profits derived from the state-owned enterprises and entrepreneurial sectors of the economy. It is also this rise in consumption that frames the debate in China over 'individualization' (*geren hua*), a thesis suggested by Yan Yunxiang, and one developed from the 'contemporary individualization thesis' found in the Western social theory, proposed earlier by Ulrich Beck, Anthony Giddens, Zygmunt Bauman and others. While the discourse of neoliberalism promotes the absence of external interference on individuals' lives, the individualization thesis emphasizes the ongoing negotiation between the individual and the state, whereby public interventions and modern social institutions can promote individual autonomy and self-determination.[4] In the context of postsocialist China, Yan Yunxiang argues that the individualization thesis is not only central to, but also a development away from, the earlier neoliberal model, as both ideologies emphasize the importance of promoting and protecting individual rights and freedoms.[5]

A post-WTO transition, of course, continues to impact the cultural sphere beyond just the question of individual choice. As Rob Wilson and Wimal Dissanayake have argued, '[In] the creative–destructive dynamic driving contemporary phases of global capitalism, the local goes on being micromapped and micromined into so many consumer zone(s).'[6] We find this 'micromapped' and 'micromined' local culture in China, which is connected to the cross between privatization and socialism that Li Zhang and Aihwa Ong call 'socialism from afar.'[7] With this confluence in mind, we observe that China's politico-cultural and consumer spheres have experienced dramatic changes since 2001. New developments include more hedonistic revelry (including frank discussions about sexuality and sex acts); more cosmopolitan travel for business, leisure and educational opportunities (including mobility in and out of the country); more concern on personal happiness (ie. food safety, air pollution, environmental issues, real-estate market); self realisation as the heated public discussion on the marriage issue of high income, highly educated women); outspoken activism (and repression, in the case of Ai Weiwei); neo-nationalism (in positions *vis-à-vis* Tibet, Japan and the United States); more black market criminality (and its growing consumer base); greater levels of migration (as a result of shrinking job opportunities in rural areas and the eroding of familial bonds); and greater social flexibility around questions of gender identity (as more LGBT (lesbian, gay, bisexual, transgender) organizations in metropolises and more queer personalities online and on the ground than ever before), to name a few. These examples of 'multiple private choices' and new expressions show an 'increased latitude to pursue self-interest that are at the same time variously regulated or controlled by the party-state.'[8]

Regardless of how amorphous this regulation of choice may sometimes seem, the Chinese government continuously censors external internet content via the Great Fire Wall, its cancellation of gay rights parades and film festivals (YunFest in 2007 and 2013), its detainment of foreigners who speak out 'politically' in the country (as happened after Elton John's so-called controversial support of Ai at a concert in Beijing in 2013). All of these developments ultimately point to the existence of several different dichotomies in contemporary China: between media access and suppression, material acquisition and deprivation, middle-class mobility and enduring poverty – dichotomies which are all depicted across official, semi-official and unofficial media platforms.

iGeneration cinema: Scene, technologies, global contexts

China's 'iGeneration cinema' began sometime in the first decade of the twenty-first century, when digital image-making technologies and internet connectivity made more dispersed modes of production, distribution and consumption possible. In this sense, the iGeneration continues to overlap with what film studies scholars call China's

'Sixth/Urban Generation' and with the country's contemporary commercial film market. When we speak of iGeneration *cinema*, we are speaking specifically of three key developments in cinematic and moving image culture: (1) the emergence of new, non-industry producers and venues as key 'nodes' within the Chinese cinema and moving image scene; (2) the ubiquity of digital and internet-based technologies; and (3) the globalization of individualization and experience under conditions of 'neoliberalism with Chinese characteristics,' as we have described previously. Taken together, we argue, these developments have ushered in a new period of cinematic culture that is significant precisely because it threatens to displace the 'old' cinema, much as digital and on-demand technologies have corresponded with a drop in US movie attendance to mid-1990s levels.[9]

Why use the term 'iGeneration'? One answer is that it has become an accepted practice in studies of Chinese cinema, and particularly of mainland Chinese cinema, to mark major shifts in cinematic practice by referring to each discrete stage as a 'generation' (Fifth Generation, Sixth Generation and so on). We have two reasons for naming the most recent major shift 'the iGeneration.' First, the 'i' indicates an emphasis on 'individuals,' or what we have termed 'individualization.' It stands for an increasing concern with individual self-expression and self-realization, 'relying on oneself' (*kao ziji*) in uncertain times, and the prevalence of an increasingly solipsistic directorial style among independent film practitioners. While previous studies distinguish one cinematic generation from another primarily according to chronology and socioeconomic structures, we also take technological change into account – in this case, the emergence of digital technology as an essential factor changing filmmaking around the globe.[10] Therefore, the other 'i' dimension of the 'iGeneration' is the use of information technology – the internet, personal computers and personal media technologies (cameras, players, smartphones) – for audiovisual image-making and image distribution. Adobe Flash, iPhones, blogs or microblogs (*weibo*) and mobile social media applications have given rise to a post-cinematic culture of amateur production and transformed cinema into yet another form of online experience for the hundreds of millions of Chinese citizens with access to the internet. Personal modes of consumption have triumphed over theatrical modes. The 'i' is now ascendant.

Whereas 'cinema' once referred to production for, and experience of, the communal screen, in the post-cinematic era of moving image culture *cinema is increasingly another form of televisual or online content for personalized screens*. On the commercial end of the spectrum, this transition is marked by the fact that television-based media enterprises, not film companies, are the most economically vibrant producers of cultural content in East Asia.[11] Visual *aides-mémoires* on Chinese television currently range from programmes devoted to celebrated philosophers to the cultural legacy of Deng Xiaoping. In her chapter on these visual *aides-mémoires* films shown on television and in movie theatres since the late 1990s and 2000s, Chen Xiaomei tries to tease out contradictory representations of Deng, the initiator of China's post-socialist reform, as he is now re-represented in different filmic and televisual manifestations. She examines what is indispensable to Deng's legacy and what is not, and in the process questions the 'cultural logic' that these visual *aides-mémoires* serve in the greater cine-media nexus found in twenty-first-century China. Personal modes of consumption have triumphed over theatrical modes.

Our focus on this new group of filmmakers and practitioners is not to say that moving image culture has become completely individualized or private. Digital formulations are always *communal* – that is to say, shared and collectively discussed – even as velocity and intensity of personal media consumption reaches startling magnitudes. (For more on this phenomenon, see Paola Voci's chapter in this volume.)[12] One example of this communal aspect of film production and consumption in contemporary China is the posting and tweeting of content links online – for example, to humourous parody films (e.g. Hu Ge's 'Wheat Bun,' an internet sensation from 2007). In addition, the increasingly popular format of *wei dianying*, which literally means 'mini films' or 'short films', relies almost exclusively on online circulation. Moreover, professional filmmakers have begun to submit to a culture of constant online exposure. For example, starlet Zhou Dongyu's efforts to create an internet persona through online publication of gossip and personal statements directed at her fans, or film studios' internet marketing of new film releases through online events, adhere to the marketing of the self and of cultural products as new *icommodities* in China. All of these developments indicate that audiences expect content to be delivered *to them*, rather than consumed as part of a public, shared event. This 'me culture' (*ziwo wenhua*) is particularly noticeable among young Chinese, iGeneration media consumers, as expressed through their creation and unceasing calibration of online identities through posted 'selfies' (*zipai*) – pictures taken of and by one's self using a phone or laptop camera – microblog (*weibo*) Wechat profiles and Facebook-style status updates.[13] Updating an older film media theory in light of this intense internet activity in China, Ralph Parfect's chapter in this volume deploys reception theory to analyse online responses to Zhang Yimou's *The Love of the Hawthorn Tree* (2010). Here the aging auteur and his film have found new life – not in movie theatres, but rather through online chat rooms where people prosaically, and sometimes poetically, discuss the film's nostalgic treatment of Maoist-era sexual politics.

What are the consequences of all these changes for Chinese cinema – or, as we have termed it, moving image culture – in the new millennium? For starters, a growing individualized culture is an increasingly pluralistic culture, in the sense that creators *strive* to create discrete, individual points of view. Again, some would refer to such work as solipsistic, but such critiques can become tricky when iGeneration work reveals individual image-makers' perspectives on 'big' issues, such as familial, societal and environmental change. Tianqi Yu, in her chapter, explores first person documentary practice by a cohort of women filmmakers, including Yang Lina, Wang Fen, Liu Jiayin and Song Fang. While some of these films investigate hidden familial trauma, Yu regards this practice of filming oneself and one's closely related as a form of communicative practice, a practice that proactively builds the bridge of the broken communications and re-negotiates their position as daughters in their families and women in society at large. Their work blends the virtues of the family with experimental aesthetics that emphasize, unabashedly, the 'i' in individual immediacy and intimacy (see Tianqi Yu's chapter on female first-person documentary).

Another big issue for the iGeneration is the forging of a digital activism, which illuminates the participatory use of the internet and electronic devices for the articulation of group identity (see, for example, Jia Tan's chapter on digital activism and Cantonese identity). Elsewhere, Ai Xiaoming's documentary film *Our Children* brings to life the toppled edifices after the 2008 Sichuan earthquake as a testimony to the 'visual wreckage preserved by ordinary people with whatever recording devices they have'. Ying Qian studies this film, which examines the concrete and steel rubble of the earthquakes as sites of remembrance and also documents the results of hasty urban planning and its disastrous consequences in China (see Ying Qian's chapter). Another significant new area of documentary film involves films devoted to animals as primary documentary subject. *Three Sisters/San jiemei* (Wang Bing 2012) and *My Himalayan Vulture/Wo de gaoshan tujiu* (Tashi Sang'e, Zhou Jie 2009) go beyond their 'ostensibly fringe, auxiliary and/or dependent life conditions/roles and permeate into the very texture of the documentaries' – creating a 'humanimal' documentary genre, as explored by Yiman Wang in her chapter on docu-ani-mentary cinema.

The subjective 'i' in contemporary China has become more visible and more engaged with the wider world through access to, and visual commentary on, the world's ever-growing sea of digitally transmitted information. In no small measure, technology has collapsed the distinction between direct and indirect experience. Indeed, as Shu-mei Shih contends, 'it is no wonder that the relationship between the eye and the "I," and increasingly between the camera and the "I," has emerged as one of the major theoretical issues in studies of visuality.'[14] Moving image technology has become, in a sense, more 'micro,' in terms of permeating and mediating the space of individual interactions. This change is not unique to China, but it is nonetheless new in Chinese cinema. The many 'i's of China's visual- and techno-literate population are rapidly transforming the cultural sphere. How is this happening? And how is it different from the post-cinematic culture elsewhere in the world?

The iGeneration scene

Pluralism at the level of individuals is not political pluralism, but it nonetheless offers a certain freedom and autonomy of self-expression. Individualized subjects in China are becoming unmoored from – or are detaching themselves from – communal social institutions such as production teams, work units, kinship networks and hometowns. State policies emphasize that individuals should become consumers and pursue aspirational notions of 'quality' (*suzhi*), while at the same time denying the importance of 'Western-style' human rights, constitutionalism and democracy.[15] The editors see Wu Wenguang's influence and support for civic action and decades-long commitment to Chinese documentary as central to publicizing human rights suffering in China, especially his ideological and creative treatment of the issue since the first screening of his seminal documentary *Bumming in Beijing* in 1990. Commenting on the evolution of Wu's docu-style, what we refer to as an 'NGO-aesthetic,' Matthew D. Johnson's chapter discusses the wider appeal of Wu's films to international audiences, ensuring that human rights concerns/advocates in China maintain visibility and receive support from transnational networks of humanitarian aid, NGO funding and global awareness campaigns. Yet Wu composes these films without losing their local appeal and constructs a critique of fledgling government involvement in rural areas with his trademark flair for politicizing the banality of neglect.

Moving in a different direction from Wu and Johnson's assessment of him, Keith B. Wagner discusses the less politically committed films that he calls 'reckless documentaries.' Wagner outlines the loose faction of filmmakers behind these documentaries, individuals who are striving to abandon the rules and convictions typically associated with issue-based filmmaking, characteristics best exhibited by the truculent newcomer Xue Jianqiang and his film *Three Small Animals II* (2009). Xue's approach (and the approach of other kindred documentary filmmakers) is marked by the abolition of so-called ethics for an approach that one might see as heedless and at times boorish, as well as by visual characterizations of the *here and now* of China's peripheral cities and populations; these films cast a critical eye on the Chinese government's neoliberal policies and its 'two nation strategy' – one fixed on hyper-development and the other with unchecked underdevelopment.[16]

In the case of the film industry, China's deregulation and compliance with WTO rules have largely eliminated barriers to domestic and foreign investment. Marketization has become sustainable and the state's role in film production has diminished. New policies issued through the State Administration of Radio, Film, and Television (SARFT) have led to the privatization of formerly state-owned and state-operated industries – not just film studios, but also distributors. Beginning in 1993, these developments forced the 16 remaining state-owned studios to find ways of marketing and selling their films in the absence of guaranteed government support. By 1997, China's neoliberal economic reformers had turned their attention to film production, and state-funded ventures were replaced by local, privately controlled operations backed by foreign capital, while overhauled state-owned film groups represented government interests via a new model of public–private joint management. China's WTO accession in 2001 ushered in a new period of reduced barriers to foreign investment and market entry, though the state maintains a guiding (sometimes heavy) hand.

Within the domestic private sector, SARFT has made it possible for private companies with as little as one million RMB in assets to engage in film production and distribution.[17] In 2010, for example, the central government officially urged support for the further development of the cultural industry, including regular capital infusions to the film industry from the financial sector.[18] More recently, private equity funds have become a new force in the film industry, investing massively in the construction of exhibition sites (such as IMAX or luxury cinema chains in shopping complexes) and in film production (usually involving co-production within the Greater China region and with foreign capital or film professionals). Many of these high-tech theatres or IMAX super-theatres were relatively unknown to Chinese consumers two decades ago. Jeesoon Hong and Matthew D. Johnson's chapter probes the impact of what they label 'New ScreenSpaces in China,' particularly those found at the Shanghai Expo in 2010. Reflecting on the impact of ScreenSpaces, they suggest moving beyond the

Manovich/Bolter school of thought regarding the aesthetics of technology or remediation paradigms, and find instead greater rapport with Alexander Galloway's notions of interactivity and interface.

As for co-productions in 'Greater China,' the Beijing government's 'Closer Economic Partnership Arrangement' with Hong Kong in 2003 facilitated more rapid absorption of Hong Kong's remaining film production resources into the Chinese movie industry. With respect to other foreign investors, SARFT encourages Chinese film companies to pursue investment-seeking – including the recruitment of human capital – mainly in co-production, and less in the more profitable sites of film exhibition and distribution, which are still strictly controlled by the state. Foreign investors, such as Hollywood studios, are encouraged to co-produce with Chinese companies in order to bypass China's film quota system on imported films and gain access to the mainland Chinese market.[19]

Thus, a major consequence is that in 2013, the mainland Chinese film industry has far more participants than was the case just a decade ago. State, private and foreign investors commingle and compete like never before. As critic Dai Jinhua has discussed, 80 per cent of films produced in China rely on non-state or overseas capital.[20] Nevertheless, the state remains dominant. The trinity of the state-owned China Film Group, Shanghai Film Group and Xi'an Film Group ensures that a steady stream of 'main melody' ideological films and hagiographies enters the market, seemingly in defiance of popular taste's drift away from top-down political art. The state's dominance over the film sector, however, is primarily reflected in what is and is not approved for production or exhibition. As is well known, independent filmmaking devoted to a range of subjects, some of them quite taboo by state standards, took off in the 1990s simply by circumventing the state-regulated system. Fifth Generation 'renegades' like Zhang Yimou took Chinese cinema to international markets on the strength of iconoclastic styles and exotic subject matter. The so-called New Documentary Movement of Zhang Yuan, Wu Wenguang and other proponents of observational cinema also burst onto the international festival, university and arts scenes during this period, giving rise to a whole cohort of documentary filmmaking 'amateurs' with their own stories to tell. In the new millennium, Fifth Generation allegorists gave way to the gritty realists of the Sixth/Urban Generation. New directors such as Jia Zhangke largely repeated the internationally focused pattern established by their predecessors, but with enough innovation in production and aesthetics to qualify for their own generational moniker.

iGeneration filmmakers have thus come of age in an era when many filmmakers of the Fifth Generation, Sixth/Urban Generation and New Documentary Movement were and are still active cinema and media producers. As we have begun to show, China's iGeneration moving image scene is increasingly diverse. The growth of the private sector has brought with it new industry developments, particularly a keen sense of competition. Meanwhile, joint ventures between domestic and foreign enterprises have added new financial channels and opportunities for producers. Political rules (spoken and unspoken) and SARFT regulations still apply, in part to muzzle government critics and historical revisionists, and in part to manage the threat to

China's domestic film industry posed by foreign film imports. The latter has been partially contained through imposition of a quota system and revenue-sharing scheme currently allowing for the exhibition of 20 foreign films per year, and the number was raised to 34 in 2011, 14 of which must be in IMAX or 3D. This system[21] has been less successful in limiting the flow of pirated (recorded and bootlegged) and downloaded (streaming and P2P) films into China, as evidenced by frequent Motion Picture Association of America complaints.[22] Other measures to curtail Hollywood's influence include periodic 'blackouts' of foreign films during holidays and the manipulation of release schedules to reduce head-to-head competition between domestic and foreign blockbusters.

In addition to a competitive and internationalized cultural marketplace, iGeneration image-makers must also contend with the power of filmmakers from previous generations over cultural trends. These 'main-melody' filmmakers, based in the state studios, produce mainstream propaganda films for popular consumption via block booking and political education. Many main-melody films produced or co-produced by the state-owned film groups employ classic Hollywood narrative and characterization methods, and feature regional superstars to achieve the effect of 'blockbusterization' of propaganda drama,[23] such as in the production of *The Funding of a Republic* (*Jianguo daye*, 2012). Commercially oriented filmmakers, such as superstar director Feng Xiaogang, specialize in entertainment films (such as comedy, drama, martial arts and crime thrillers) as well as hyperkinetic genre mash-ups which have recently captivated domestic audiences, such as the domestic hit *If You Are the One I&II* (*feicheng wurao I & II*, 2008, 2010), and historical event blockbuster[24] *Back to 1942* (2012). Support for this commercial sector comes primarily from domestic private film companies, but such distinctions are blurred by investment from state-owned and foreign corporations. In addition, internationally well-known directors from the Fifth Generation have begun to produce commercial Chinese blockbusters for regional and global release. Of these films – *Hero* is perhaps the most obvious example – and is typically characterized by exotic 'oriental' settings, stories of ancient empires, elaborate production, musical soundtracks featuring Chinese instrumentation, and simulated feats of martial arts daring reminiscent of earlier 'knight-errant' (*wuxia*) films and novels. Sixth/Urban Generation directors, such as Jia Zhangke and Wang Xiaoshuai, have cashed in as well, continuing to court international audiences while simultaneously reaching out directly, through films licensed for domestic release, to China's growing urban bourgeoisie.

Music or sound theory has often been neglected by film critics and more generally in the disciplines of film and cultural studies. To *bring back in the aural* as central to the moving image itself, city films are back as a genre of film, in and beyond China. From platforms of expression to new metropolitan dissections of urbanity in China, Ling Zhang's chapter on digitizing city symphony films explores the early twentieth-century German-themed city symposium film *Berlin: Symphony of a Metropolis* (1929) and how several Chinese filmmakers have paid homage to it by exploring the seemingly endless construction of new urban centres in China during the new millennium, making films with delicate musical scores and new, visual expressions.

What is surprising about Zhang's analysis is the careful attention she places on the scoring of the sequences, explicating the harmony of rhythm between architecture and music as it is composed visually.

If we have now established a dozen or so films associated with the iGeneration, who else, then, also falls under this categorization? In our view, this label should not refer to filmmakers born during a specific time period – for instance, those who came of age during the 1990s – but instead describes directors and moving image-makers whose work has been determined by the digital (i.e., the use of digital and networked technologies is prevalent in its production, distribution and consumption); is no longer correlated with the experience of postsocialism; and depicts a China that is globalized, individualized and shares features of neoliberal globalization with the world beyond China's borders (i.e., is not predominantly self-orientalizing or auto-chthonic). As we have argued, some of these filmmakers possess a strongly solipsistic streak, but others use personal technologies to create interpersonal amateur works or engage in documentary-based social advocacy. In addition, not all iGeneration directors are anti-commercial, art-for-art's sake underground practitioners. Directors with notable box office successes include Xu Zheng, director of *Lost in Thailand* (*Tai Jiong*, 2013), and writer-turned-director Guo Jingming, whose debut *Tiny Times I & II* (*Xiao shidai*, 2013) attracted both derision and applause with its depictions of unbridled upper-class consumption.

iGeneration filmmakers also openly question where commodities and capital figure in the country, at a time when money itself seems to be what is on a lot of Chinese minds. Yet how do filmmakers deal with money cinematically, when it is not venerated like it is in the West (at least not publicly)? In Xiao Liu's chapter, money is more than just currency – it is a thing that obtains its own life, energy and seductive power as postmodern filmic object (capital as a visible thing) and filmic subject (capital as commodifiable in its cultivated status as a new cultural thing, post-Mao). Money thus becomes reified and its mythical or magical power is articulated in a film like Jiang Wen's *Let the Bullets Fly* (2010) and its narrative and visual terms that allude to the extraordinary economic times enveloping the country.

In addition to releases via the theatre and, via piracy on the internet, iGeneration work has emerged in the context of a concomitant proliferation of *minjian* (grassroots, nongovernmental) film festivals devoted to the exhibition of amateur work, as well as by the increasing number of screening spaces devoted to independent and experimental moving image culture. Piracy is often linked to the country's market structures, including a '"freemium" business model' that violates, 'erodes'[25] or 'diffuse[s] the values of creativity.'[26] The problem with capital-intensive infrastructures in the music, telecommunication, film and new media industries in China is that it fosters rampant file sharing, copycatting and bootlegging. This leads to non-contractual reproductions, and such reproductions are then sold by unlicensed vendors or accessed and then downloaded from the internet.[27] It is these very copyright and piracy issues that Dan Gao's chapter 'From Pirate to Kino-eye' expands and deepens with a view toward this practice being fictionalized as a trope in contemporary Chinese film. Yet what is at stake in these fictive portrayals of pirate culture? What does it mean to act as an appropriator, and is this a new mode of expression? For one thing, Gao sees piracy as a new digital cinephilia, one which violates distribution networks in order to create new modes of expression. To put it in her own words: 'What kind of customs, tastes, sensibilities, and knowledge are being produced and accompany this subject formation of the digital "pirate?" Or, what kind of techniques do "pirates" used to posit themselves within the fissure between postsocialist reality and the pirated, informal media worlds?'

These spaces of critical public discourse on piracy and independent filmmaking, though mainly limited to communities of practitioners, scholars and enthusiasts, are sufficiently dispersed throughout China to have created an interconnected independent scene.[28] Prominent venues include the China Documentary Film Festival (Beijing), Chinese Independent Film Festival (Nanjing), and Yunnan Multi Culture Biannual Visual Festival (Kunming), or 'Yunfest.' In her chapter, Ma Ran analyzes the impact of these independent festival networks, especially more 'fringe' venues such as the Chongqing Independent Film and Video Festival (CIFVF, since 2007) and the *minjian* film festivals. To this list must be added screenings in universities, cafes, bars and art galleries. On the official side, state-owned central and regional television stations, such as CCTV Channel 9 and the Shanghai Documentary Channel, have also begun airing independently produced documentaries. This latter move is perhaps tantamount to recognition of public demand for more independent voices within the state media, despite the fact that the works are inevitably 'censored' – pre-screened and, in some cases, edited to remove politically sensitive content.[29]

iGeneration technologies

Finally, and most importantly, the rise of iGeneration filmmaking is supported by digital technologies such as DV cameras and social media. These technologies make the production and sharing of moving images considerably easier than was the case under prior technological conditions and, we argue, have enabled new forms of information-sharing and individual empowerment. New technologies have also given rise to new genres and formats, such as increasingly popular 'micro films' (*wei dianying*), which are exclusively shown via video sharing sites, internet protocol television (IPTV) and mobile applications. They have also facilitated artists' films and multiscreen moving image installations, now a familiar sight in upmarket galleries and contemporary art museums.

Digital film- and image-making is everywhere in China today. Since many iGeneration figures began their careers during the 2000s, very few have ever shot or recorded on anything but digital cameras, or edited on anything but computers. The iGeneration genealogy of camera technology begins with clunky camcorders and currently ends with compact, handheld, memory-rich Sony cameras – or with camera phones and Flash. D. N. Rodowick, speaking about the digital turn more generally, argues that the new technologies are primarily distinguished from – and can come into conflict with – the old technologies by virtue of their attendant ideology of simulation:

Narrative conflict with the digital reasserts the aesthetic value of analogue images as somehow more real than digital simulation, not only at the cinema but also in computer gaming and other new media. *The Matrix* is a marvelous example of how Hollywood has always responded ideologically to the appearance of new technologies. Incorporated into the film at the level of both its technology of representation and its narrative structure, the new arrival is simultaneously demonized and deified, a strategy that lends itself well to marketing and spectacle.[30]

This is partly true of contemporary cinema in China – simulation has become spectacle, particularly in the commercial realm. At the same time, digital cameras have also given rise to a vibrant culture of amateur realism and self-representation, so we cannot wholly concur that authenticity lies solely with analogue technologies or low-resolution images. We do, however, concur with Rodowick that moving image studies must take account of the digital evolution, and 'navigate the rapid flows and directions of technological change.'[31] In our view, the most significant impact of digital and networked technology on Chinese cinema is the creation of a *post-cinematic moving image culture, or affect*. Cinema – whether as industry or culture – can no longer be distinguished from broader configurations of media, and entertainment can no longer be distinguished from contemporary dynamics of high-volume data or information 'flow.'

This post-cinematic condition allows for the mixing of moving images with an ever-widening variety of agendas and expressive modes via the digital spaces which all of these elements – technologies, individuals and aesthetics – inhabit. One of the main theorists of the post-cinematic condition, Steven Shaviro, has described the origins of the concept thusly: 'Digital technologies, together with neoliberal economic relations, have given birth to radically new ways of manufacturing and articulating lived experience.'[32] Moreover, according to Shaviro, the post-cinematic condition is defined by the rapidity with which new subjectivities and perceptions can be deployed across the globe via moving image culture and data networks:

> Films and music videos, like other media works, are *machines for generating affect*, and for capitalizing upon, or extracting value from, this affect. As such, they are not ideological superstructures, as an older sort of Marxist criticism would have it. Rather, they lie at the very heart of social production, circulation, and distribution. They generate subjectivity and they play a crucial role in the valorization of capital. Just as the old Hollywood continuity editing system was an integral part of the Fordist mode of production, so the editing methods and formal devices of digital video and film belong directly to the computing-and-information-technology infrastructure of contemporary neoliberal finance.[33]

Admittedly, Shaviro's analysis – focused on the nature of affect in the United States – may not wholly align with China's realities, particularly the nature of public and private culture since 1978. But the basic point seems valid. The technology employed by the iGeneration was not created for the specific purpose of creating an entertainment or ideological 'superstructure' – its functional uses are far more open-ended. And yet the technology is unified by the same basic design goal, which is to capture attention (in the context of competing information sources) through their insistence and ubiquity.

What iGeneration image-makers employ digital technology *for* is thus wholly dependent on the maker's intentions. Some seek to inhabit global theatrical or virtual spaces as entertainers, artists and advocates. Among the more socially engaged image-makers, some 'netizens' choose to be identified (even if by *noms de plume*), others remain anonymous. Representations are fantastic or real, identities blurred or concrete. Some combine several of these qualities at once. Genres include spoofs, documentaries, narratives, or 'pure' spectacles that recall the very birth of cinema. The political is not always present, but neither has it been abandoned. Exposé-style documentaries depict the failures of the party-state to protect its citizens, while downloaded propaganda may be subjected to 're-mixing' that ranges from the ironic to the scathingly satirical. Some iGeneration filmmakers rely intensively on animation or the editing of found footage. Others are less interested in conventional narrative techniques and focus instead on punkish provocation through audience-abusing, 'in-your-face' images of violence, degradation and raunch. A common denominator in all of these newer forms of image-making is the phenomenon that Haidee Wasson calls 'networked screens' – the fusion of the digital camera with high-speed telecommunications and social media. Images are rapidly produced, digested, commented on, and recombined to form new images.[34] Substance, meaning and truth are in the eye of the beholder, as has always been true of cinema.

The networked screen is also changing the very nature of exhibition space. At a micro level, images are proliferating in social space through the ubiquity of theatres, political displays, advertising, personal media players, smartphones, computers, television, and the falling price of LCD- and plasma-screen technology. Like the sea of data it swims in, moving image content is everywhere. The saturation of public, semi-public and private or personal space with these networked interfaces is hard to miss, even if individual responses remain difficult for researchers to access. Nevertheless, personal computers, smartphones and social media have likewise moved reception into the digital arena, where blogs and response columns fill with audience opinion and planted buzz.

Animation continues to be an understudied genre. Some critics misidentify it as children's media, indelibly connected to lowbrow sensibilities from Sunday morning cartoons. Others even disavow more serious-minded animated films from Pixar (such as *WALL-E,* an animated film about environmental degradation, recycling and cinephilia that has received scant critical attention despite its incorporation of these important themes). Because cartoon culture is not taken as seriously as it should be, studies on the subject are rare, especially articles that provide an accurate picture of the animation industry today – both in commercial and amateur production. Perhaps this is because of the dynamics of East Asia's regional animation development and the dominance of its production juggernaut – Japan. More significantly, the expansion of Chinese animation can be traced to the 'missing period' and has grown in popularity from the early Reform Era to the current post-WTO moment. In this volume, Weihua Wu sheds light on the very recent happenings in the world of Chinese animation by building on his previous research regarding the political economy of China's animation industry and the country's amateur, fan-driven Flash animation scene.

The iGeneration in global context(s)

It is difficult to define the iGeneration in terms of aesthetics. As China's moving image culture has grown substantially in its diversity of producers and reproducers in the past decade, it now defies easy characterization. As the breadth of this volume indicates, digitally driven multiplicity of representational modes is one of the iGeneration's defining features. Coupled with China's economic growth, post-Deng reforms in the country's cultural industries have also played an important role in supporting the emergence of new players – a theme that we have touched upon frequently. With the amendment of China's constitution in 2004, the call to the development of creative and cultural industries by the then Hu-Wen Leadership, China's leaders are now charged with creating an 'advanced culture' by:

> deepening cultural restructuring, improving the system of the market for cultural products, deepening the internal reform of cultural enterprises and institutions, gradually establishing a management system and operational mechanism favorable to arousing the initiative of cultural workers, encouraging innovation and bringing forth top-notch works and more outstanding personnel.[35]

These reforms have resulted in the increased circulation of ideas, goods and media, while creating larger markets for monetary and intellectual exchange. At the same time, they have also accompanied a wider process of globalization that has transformed China's culture industries irrevocably.

It is difficult to miss the tide of international media, and particularly cinema, that has reached China's shores in theatrical or bootlegged form in China's post-WTO era. At the same time, this globalization of visual media has been a two-way street, as Chinese directors have been a presence on the international festival scene as far back as the 1980s. More recently, domestic international film festivals, such as the A-list Shanghai International Film Festival and the Beijing International Film Festival, invite international film professionals into China to embrace this growing hotspot of international co-production and collaboration. International art circuits, university campuses, as well as expatriate- and bourgeois class-frequented cultural 'contact zones' (e.g. Beijing's 798 Art District, Shanghai M50 Art District, Shenzhen OCT LOFT), have provided a complementary infrastructure to cultivate domestic and international cultural consumption. The conversation with Dong Bingfeng by Tianqi Yu in this volume reveals some first-hand reflections on how the increasingly interconnected film world and art scene in China is changing how we conceive of 'cinema' and is pushing the disciplinary boundaries between film studies and art history. Tracing the curatorial history of how art films have been included in 'experimental sections' of China's domestic independent festivals and exhibited in art spaces as film installations, Dong discusses the special features of 'cinema as exhibition' in the context of Chinese contemporary art and independent cinema, and how it reflects the *intertwined and interconnected nature* of 'iGeneration' cinematic production.

To be sure, not all filmmakers embrace globalizing trends, and there has been a distinct 'local turn' in iGeneration image-making that focuses solely on specific geographic, personal or digital communities, such as animal documentary and first-person documentary. For this reason, it is unlikely that future surveys of cinema and moving image culture in China will ever be as complete as those produced during the heyday of the Fifth Generation. If anything, the promise of cinematic *terra incognita* is now stronger than ever before, in part due to the diversity of cultural artefacts to be uncovered, and in part due to broader international interest in China's media culture – the latter a testament to China's rising significance within international political, commercial and academic circles.

The growing international prominence of China's national image is apparent in venues and forums across the globe – whether in international public spaces (e.g. Times Square in New York), art fairs (e.g. La Biennale di Venezia), academic programmes, or in any business or cultural institution with a credible global strategy. Chinese art, scholarship, insider analysis, expertise and investment are in high demand worldwide, including in other emerging markets that are eager to emulate China's growth rates (or, as China's official rhetoric under new President Xi Jinping would have it, to share in the 'China dream'). Much of this admiration can be connected to China's economic stability since the 1997–8 East Asian Financial Crisis and the improvement in its international position relative to the European Union, Japan and the United States since the 2008 Global Financial Crisis. Such economic good fortune (linked, at least in theory, to prudent macroeconomic policy) has helped create a cosmopolitan Chinese upper class that is able to afford luxury brands, real estate, and other markers of elite status in ever-greater quantities. Such elites have always existed in China; their numbers, however, are now far greater than they were a decade ago. Greater parity in international economic and political relations, and even the re-establishment of a 'Sinocentric' world order, once again appear as real possibilities, as does irreversible First-World decline.

This narrative, however, conceals the existence of considerable inequalities in Chinese society. The country's per capita GDP, even adjusted for purchasing-power parity, is 92nd among the world's 195 countries[36] and is $3,000 below the global average.[37] iGeneration films have often captured this internal economic unevenness in images that reflect affluence, poverty, and much in between. These films also address the sense that China is experiencing both an unprecedented and contradictory moment in its history. How long will the good times last? And have they even arrived? Many of iGeneration filmmakers, like their Fifth and Sixth/Urban counterparts, sometimes seem torn between admiration for China's changes and scepticism concerning the future, and even the present, as is illustrated in Ying Liang's *Good Cats* (*Haomao*, 2008).

Finally, while this volume does not posit a complete break between the iGeneration and earlier generations such as the Fifth Generation and the Sixth/Urban Generation, it does argue for a reconsideration of the use of the generational taxonomy. Although the director remains a key figure in film studies, the changes wrought by new technologies and post-WTO market regimes have by now made it impossible to understand the 'generation' marker as referring to a shared set of personal experiences in Chinese society as expressed through filmic texts and other elements of moving image culture. Personal experiences of visual culture are now inscribed via media such as experimental and amateur documentaries, animation, artists' films, 3-D and IMAX image configurations, all of which are as much about ambiguous cultural positions as they are about market success. Therefore, we are asserting that future studies of Chinese film 'generations' will be shaped by a newer, and in our view more accurate, paradigm – one that understands moviemaking and cine-media practices as embodying a range of agendas (such as the pursuit of nation-building, profit, cultural capital, social justice), and functions (such as state didacticism, commodified leisure, surveillance, self-expression, identity construction, activism and transnational connoisseurship). While these agendas and functions frequently overlap, chapters in this volume represent an attempt to capture how Chinese cinema and moving image culture has been reinvigourated, reinvented and even recycled by iGeneration practitioners and audiences.

Structure of the volume

iGeneration cinema is a multifaceted phenomenon that exists in and through different systems. Accordingly, we have organized this volume into sections devoted to: (1) technologies, (2) aesthetics, (3) social engagement, (4) platforms and politics; and (5) online audiences. In our view, each of these systems represents a key node of scholarly and critical inquiry. The five-part formulation owes something to the classical division of film studies into production, content and reception, but emphasizes – as we have done throughout this Introduction – the importance of technology, and the ways in which iGeneration film- and moving image-making overlaps with other social practices in contemporary China.

Works cited

Castells, Manuel and Gustavo Cardoso. 'Piracy Cultures: Editorial Introduction' in *International Journal of Communication* 6 (2012), 826.
Chan, A. and L. T. Chuen (eds). 'The impact of the WTO on workers in China, Part I' in *The Chinese Economy*, vol. 34:3 (2001).
Curtin, Michael. *Playing to the World's Biggest Audience: The Globalization of Chinese Film and TV*. Berkeley, CA: University of California Press, 2007.
Dai, Jinhua. 'Celebrity Screens: Chinese Cinema in the New Millennium' in Olivia Khoo and Sean Metzger (eds), *Futures of Chinese Cinema: Technologies and Temporalities in Chinese Screen Cultures*. Bristol: Intellect, 2009, 53.
Deleuze, Gilles. *Essays Critical and Clinical*, translated by D. W. Smith and M. A. Greco. Minneapolis, MN: University of Minnesota Press, 1997.
Gold, Thomas 'Youth and the State' in Brian Hook (ed.), *The Individual and the State in China*. Oxford: Clarendon Press, 1996, 16–42.

Hasen, Mette Halskov and Svarverud, Rune (eds). *iChina, the Rise of the Individual in Modern Chinese Society*, Nias Press, 2010.

Howard, Cosmo. 'Three Models of Individualized Biography' in Cosmo Howard (ed.), *Contested Individualization: Debates about Contemporary Personhood*. New York: Palgrave Macmillan, 2007.

Jessop, Bob, Kevin Bonnett, Simon Bromley and Tom Ling (eds). *Thatcherism*. Oxford: Polity, 1988.

Kaufman, Amy. 'Movie attendance falls to 16-year low', Jan 3, 2012, http://articles.latimes.com/2012/jan/03/entertainment/la-et-box-office-20120103

Liu, Xiao. 'Small videos, Hu Ge impact: parody videos in postsocialist China' in *Journal of Chinese Cinemas*, 4:3 (2010).

Manovich, Lev. *The Language of New Media*. Cambridge, MA: MIT Press, 2001.

Massumi, Brian. *Parables for the Virtual: Movement, Affect, Sensation*. Durham, NC: Duke University Press, 2002.

McGrath, Jason. *Postsocialist Modernity: Chinese Cinema, Literature, and Criticism in the Market Age*. Stanford: Stanford University Press, 2008, 4.

McKenna, A. T. 'Beyond National Humiliation: Han Sanping and China's Historical Event Blockbusters' in *Beyond the Bottom Line: The Role of the Film Producer* (ed.) Andrew Spicer, A. T. McKenna, Christopher Meir (London and New York: Bloomsbury 2014), pp. 229–48.

Nakajima, Seio. 'Watching Documentary: Critical Public Discourses and Contemporary Urban Chinese Film Clubs' in Chris Berry, Xinyu Lu and Lisa Rofel (eds), *The New Chinese Documentary Film Movement: For the Public Record*. Hong Kong: Hong Kong University Press, 2010, 117–34.

Pang, Laikwan. 'The Transgression of Sharing and Copying: Pirating Japanese Animation in China' in Jonathan D. Mackintosh, Chris Berry and Nicola Liscutin (eds), *Cultural Studies and Cultural Industries in Northeast Asia: What a Difference a Region Makes*. Hong Kong: Hong Kong University Press, 2009, 119.

Prince, Stephen. 'The emergence of filmic artifacts: cinema and cinematography in the digital era' in *Film Quarterly*, vol. 57, no. 3 (Spring 2004).

Pye, Lucian W. 'The State and the Individual: An Overview Interpretation' in Brian Hook (ed.), *The Individual and the State in China*. Oxford: Clarendon Press, 1996.

Rodowick, D. N. *Reading the Figural, or, Philosophy After the New Media*. Durham, NC: Duke University Press, 2001, 209.

—*The Virtual Life of Film*. Cambridge, MA: Harvard University Press, 2007, 5.

Rofel, Lisa. *Desiring China: Experiments in Neoliberalism, Sexuality, and Public Culture*. Durham, NC: Duke University Press, 2007.

Rosen, Larry. 'Understanding the iGeneration – Before the Next Mini-Generation Arrives', http://www.nieman.harvard.edu/reports/article/102405/Understanding-the-iGenerationBefore-the-Next-Mini-Generation-Arrives.aspx

Shaviro, Steven. *Post Cinematic Affect*. Zero Books, 2010.

—'Post-cinematic affect: on Grace Jones, Boarding Gate and Southland Tales', *Film Philosophy*, 14.1 (2010), 2.

Shih, Shu-mei. *Visuality and Identity: Sinophone Articulations Across the Pacific*. Berkeley, CA: University of California Press, 2007, 17.

Simanowski, Roberto. *Digital Art and Meaning: Reading Kinetic Poetry, Text Machines, Mapping Art, and Interactive Installations*. Minneapolis, MN: University of Minnesota Press, 2011.

Voci, Paola. *China on Video: Smaller-Screen Realities*. London: Routledge, 2010.
Wang, Ban and Jie Lu (eds). *China and New Left Visions: Political and Cultural Interventions*. Lexington Books 2012.
Wasson, Haidee. 'The Networked Screen: Moving Images, Materiality, and the Aesthetics of Size' in Janine Marchessault and Susan Lord (eds), *Fluid Screens, Expanded Screens*. Toronto: University of Toronto Press, 2007, 74.
William, Darell Davis and Emily Yueh-yu Yeh (eds). *East Asian Screen Industries* London: British Film Institute, 2008, 64–84.
Wilson, Rob and Wimal Dissanayake, 'Introduction: Tracking the Global/Local' in Wilson and Dissanayake (eds), *Global Local: Cultural Production and the Transnational Imaginary*. Durham, NC: Duke University Press, 1996, 2.
Xiao, Ying. 'Leitmotif: State, Market, and Postsocialist Chinese Film Industry under Neoliberal Globalization' in Jyotsna Kapur and Keith B. Wagner (eds), *Neoliberalism and Global Cinema: Capital, Culture, and Marxist Critique*. London: Routledge, 2011, 157–79.
Yan, Yunxiang. *The Individualization of Chinese Society*. London School of Economics Monographs on Social Anthropology, 2009, 274.
Yangzi, Sima and Peter C. Pugsley. 'The rise of a "me culture" in postsocialist China: youth, individualism and identity creation in the blogosphere', *The International Communication Gazette* vol. 72:3 (2010), 287.
Zhang, Li and Aihwa Ong. 'Introduction' in Zhang and Ong (eds), *Privatizing China: Socialism from Afar*. Durham, NC: Duke University Press, 2007, 2.
Zhu, Ying and Chris Berry (eds). *TV China*. Bloomington, IN: University of Indiana Press, 2009.

Notes

1 Michael Curtin, *Playing to the World's Biggest Audience: The Globalization of Chinese Film and TV*. Berkeley, CA: University of California Press 2007. On the 'post-cinematic,' see Steven Shaviro, *Post Cinematic Affect*. Zero Books, 2010.
2 Ban Wang and Jie Lu (eds), *China and New Left Visions: Political and Cultural Interventions*. Lexington Books, 2012.
3 Chan, A. and L. T. Chuen (eds), 'The impact of the WTO on workers in China, part I' in *The Chinese Economy*, vol. 34:3, 2001.
4 Howard, 'Three Models of Individualized Biography' in Howard, Cosmo (ed.) *Contested Individualization: Debates about Contemporary Personhood*. New York: Palgrave Macmillan, 2007.
5 Yunxiang Yan, *The Individualization of Chinese Society*. London School of Economics Monographs on Social Anthropology, 2009, 274.
6 Rob Wilson and Wimal Dissanayake, 'Introduction: Tracking the Global/Local' in Wilson and Dissanayake (eds), *Global Local: Cultural Production and the Transnational Imaginary*. Durham, NC: Duke University Press, 1996, 2. Also see Lisa Rofel, *Desiring China: Experiments in Neoliberalism, Sexuality, and Public Culture*. Durham, NC: Duke University Press, 2007.
7 Li Zhang and Aihwa Ong, 'Introduction' in Zhang and Ong (eds), *Privatizing China: Socialism from Afar*. Durham, NC: Duke University Press, 2007, 2.
8 Ibid., p. 4.

9 Amy Kaufman, 'Movie attendance falls to 16-year low,' 3 January 2012, http://articles.latimes.com/2012/jan/03/entertainment/la-et-box-office-20120103 (accessed 9 January 2014).
10 Larry Rosen, 'Understanding the iGeneration – Before the Next Mini-Generation Arrives,' http://www.nieman.harvard.edu/reports/article/102405/Understanding-the-iGenerationBefore-the-Next-Mini-Generation-Arrives.aspx (accessed 9 January 2014). As this article notes, the main criterion used in distinguishing one generation from another is not age, but technological change.
11 See Darrell William Davis and Emily Yueh-yu Yeh, *East Asian Screen Industries*. London: British Film Institute, 2008, 64–84. Also see Ying Zhu and Chris Berry (eds), *TV China*. Bloomington, IN: University of Indiana Press, 2009.
12 See Paola Voci, *China on Video: Smaller-Screen Realities*. London: Routledge, 2010; and Xiao Liu, 'Small videos, Hu Ge impact: parody videos in postsocialist China' in *Journal of Chinese Cinemas*, 4:3, 2010.
13 Yangzi Sima and Peter C. Pugsley, 'The rise of a "me culture" in postsocialist China: youth, individualism and identity creation in the blogosphere,' *The International Communication Gazette*, vol. 72:3, 2010, 287. Also see Hasen, Mette Halskov and Rune Svarverud (eds), *iChina, the Rise of the Individual in Modern Chinese Society*, Nias Press, 2010.
14 Shu-mei Shih, *Visuality and Identity: Sinophone Articulations Across the Pacific*. Berkeley, CA: University of California Press, 2007, 17.
15 For more, see Lucian W. Pye, 'The State and the Individual: An Overview Interpretation'; and Thomas Gold, 'Youth and the State' in Brian Hook (ed.), *The Individual and the State in China*. Oxford: Clarendon Press, 1996, 16–42.
16 See Bob Jessop, Kevin Bonnett, Simon Bromley and Tom Ling (eds), *Thatcherism*. Oxford: Polity, 1988.
17 'No. 20 Regulation of SARFT,' *The Central People's Government of The People's Republic of China*, Oct 29, 2003 http://www.gov.cn/gongbao/content/2004/content_62744.htm
18 'The guidance of Financial Support to the revitalization and development of cultural industry,' *SARFT*, 8 April 2010, http://www.sarft.gov.cn/articles/2010/04/08/20100408153315910460.html
19 'No. 20 Regulation of SARFT,' *The Central People's Government of The People's Republic of China*, Oct 29, 2003, http://www.gov.cn/gongbao/content/2004/content_62744.htm
20 Dai Jinhua, 'Celebrity Screens: Chinese Cinema in the New Millennium' in Olivia Khoo and Sean Metzger (eds), *Futures of Chinese Cinema: Technologies and Temporalities in Chinese Screen Cultures*. Bristol: Intellect, 2009, 53.
21 China is now MPAA members' largest market. '2012 Global Boxoffice Results'. http://www.mpaa.org/resources/29dfd830-8e9d-4ed2-be67-b1881ca91c03.pdf
22 See, most recently, 'IIPA Details Significant Copyright Piracy and Market Access Barriers in Key Markets; Requests Designation of Ukraine as a Priority Foreign Country.' http://www.mpaa.org/resources/dff1f22b-d6a0-4648-b967-3d31b05027bb.pdf
23 Ying Xiao, 'Leitmotif: State, Market, and Postsocialist Chinese Film Industry under Neoliberal Globalization' in Jyotsna Kapur and Keith B. Wagner (eds), *Neoliberalism and Global Cinema: Capital, Culture, and Marxist Critique*. London: Routledge, 2011, 157–79.

24. A. T. McKenna, 'Beyond National Humiliation: Han Sanping and China's Historical Event Blockbusters' in *Beyond the Bottom Line: The Role of the Film Producer* (ed.) Andrew Spicer, A. T. McKenna, Christopher Meir (London and New York: Bloomsbury 2014), 229–48.
25. Michael Curtin, *Playing to the World's Biggest Audience: The Globalization of Chinese Film and TV.* Berkeley, CA and Los Angeles: University of California Press, 2007, 68.
26. Laikwan Peng, 'The Transgression of Sharing and Copying: Pirating Japanese Animation in China' in Jonathan D. Mackintosh, Chris Berry and Nicola Liscutin (eds), *Cultural Studies and Cultural Industries in Northeast Asia: What a Difference a Region Makes.* Hong Kong: Hong Kong University Press, 2009, 119.
27. Manuel Castells and Gustavo Cardoso, 'Piracy cultures: editorial introduction' in *International Journal of Communication* 6, 2012, 826.
28. Seio Nakajima, 'Watching Documentary: Critical Public Discourses and Contemporary Urban Chinese Film Clubs' in Chris Berry, Xintu Lu, and Lisa Rofel (eds), *The New Chinese Documentary Film Movement: For the Public Record.* Hong Kong: Hong Kong University Press, 2010, 117–34.
29. This is through Yu's interviews with some independent documentary filmmakers whose works have aired on such TV channels.
30. D. N. Rodowick, *The Virtual Life of Film.* Cambridge, MA: Harvard University Press, 2007, 5. For more on the 'digital turn' in film studies please also see Lev Manovich, *The Language of New Media.* Cambridge, MA: MIT Press, 2001; Stephen Prince, 'The emergence of filmic artifacts: cinema and cinematography in the digital era' in *Film Quarterly,* vol. 57, no. 3, Spring 2004.
31. D. N. Rodowick, *Reading the Figural, or, Philosophy After the New Media.* Durham, NC: Duke University Press, 2001, 209.
32. Steven Shaviro, 'Post-cinematic affect: On Grace Jones, Boarding Gate and Southland Tales', *Film Philosophy,* 14.1, 2010, 2. For more on affect, see Gilles Deleuze, *Essays Critical and Clinical,* trans. D. W. Smith and M. A. Greco. Minneapolis, MN: University of Minnesota Press,1997; Brian Massumi, *Parables for the Virtual: Movement, Affect, Sensation.* Durham, NC: Duke University Press, 2002.
33. Shaviro, 'Post-Cinematic Affect,' 3.
34. Haidee Wasson, 'The Networked Screen: Moving Images, Materiality, and the Aesthetics of Size' in Janine Marchessault and Susan Lord (eds), *Fluid Screens, Expanded Screens.* Toronto: University of Toronto Press, 2007, 74. Also see, Roberto Simanowski, *Digital Art and Meaning: Reading Kinetic Poetry, Text Machines, Mapping Art, and Interactive Installations.* Minneapolis, MN: University of Minnesota Press, 2011.
35. Jason McGrath, *Postsocialist Modernity: Chinese Cinema, Literature, and Criticism in the Market Age.* Stanford: Stanford University Press, 2008, 4.
36. World Bank, International Comparison Program database. http://data.worldbank.org/indicator/NY.GDP.PCAP.PP.CD?order=wbapi_data_value_2012+wbapi_data_value+wbapi_data_value-last&sort=desc
37. World Bank, International Comparison Program database. http://data.worldbank.org/indicator/NY.GDP.PCAP.PP.CD/countries/1W-CN?display=graph

Part One

Technologies

1

Toward a Communicative Practice: Female First-Person Documentary in Twenty-first Century China

Tianqi Yu

Communication is truth; communication is happiness. To share is our duty; to go down boldly and bring to light those hidden thoughts which are the most diseased; to conceal nothing; to pretend nothing; if we are ignorant to say so; if we love our friends to let them know it.

Virginia Woolf

This chapter explores the changing features of the individual self in China as demonstrated through first-person filmmaking by women around the beginning of the twenty-first century, a time when China has been going through a process of decollectivization and individualization. I centre my analysis on Wang Fen's *They Are Not the Only Unhappy Couple* (*Bu Kuaile de buzhi yige*, 2000) and Yang Lina's *Home Video* (*Jiating Luxiang*, 2001), and also include readings of other examples such as Liu Jiayi's *Oxhide I* (*niupi*, 2005) & *II* (*niupi*, 2009) and Song Fang's *Memories Look At Me* (*jiyi kanzhe wo*, 2012). As both aesthetic and social pioneers, these women have been experimenting with a new documentary language to express their subjectivity and thus depart from earlier Chinese independent documentary practices in the 1990s for two key reasons. First, unlike many documentaries traditionally made by male filmmakers, the women who make these films tend to highlight a personalized vision, by bringing their own intimate familial spaces to wider audiences and reflexively turning themselves into key characters in their own films. Second, their first-person documentary practice often arises from a subversive impulse: namely, it departs from the political economy of the mainstream film industry, connecting a new strand of film practices to the iGeneration canon; and at the same time it challenges these filmmakers' traditional role as women constrained by patriarchal expectations and the burdens of institutional and familial persecution. It is here that they negotiate their position in the still largely male-dominated film world, as well as their personal position as daughters in these families.

First-person filmmaking in China emerged around the start of the twenty-first century, within ten years of Deng Xiaoping's Southern Tour in 1992, which marked a new intensification in development of the socialist market economy 'with Chinese characteristics.' Along with fostering rapid economic growth, China's post-Mao reform has also stimulated what the anthropologist Yan Yunxiang observes as an 'individualization process,' in which individuals have been largely untied from previous social institutions, and have gained more space and autonomy to develop their own lifestyle choices.[1] Alongside China's colossal economic boom and rapid mass urbanization, individuals are quietly transforming their social roles, often in subversive ways. Through various eco-political and cultural practices, individuals are consciously and unconsciously examining and reconstructing their individual subjectivities. These practices have included women's first-person filmmaking, which has demonstrated some features of contemporary women's lives in the individualizing China of the post-Mao era. In fact, the increasing number of female filmmakers and the focus on personal narratives regarding memory, family and private spaces are in many respects at the centre of what we deem here 'iGeneration' production. There are considerably fewer female directors among the so-called Fifth and Sixth Generation filmmakers, and those relatively well known to the public include Ning Ying, for her Beijing Trilogy *For Fun* (*zhaole*, 1993), *On the Beat* (*minjing gushi*, 1995), and *I Love Beijing* (*Xiari guan yangyang*, 2001), and documentary *Railroad of Hope* (*xiguang zhilü*, 2002); Li Yu for her *Buddha Mountain* (*guanyin shang*, 2011); and Li Hong for her documentary *Huido Fenghuang Qiao* (1994). These filmmakers have become the leading female directors to emerge in this past decade. Some of them have also produced films in innovative genres for theatrical release, such as Wang Fen's debut thriller *Suitcase* (*xiangzi*, 2008). In addition to these female directors, established Sixth Generation filmmakers, such as Jia Zhangke, also explore personal narratives about memories and family. For example, both of Jia's innovative documentary films *24 City* (*24 chengji*, 2008) and *I Wish I Knew* (*haishang chuanqi*, 2010) exclusively reconstruct their narrated histories through personal memories of the past. This theme is also explored in Luke Vulpiani's chapter in the next section of this volume.

In this chapter, I will combine a close inspection of these filmmaking practices with textual analysis of the films. One the one hand, I analyse how the filmmaker's self is represented on her own camera, through what Catherine Russell calls the four layers of self-inscription in autoethnographic film: (1) the self – that is, the speaker in the first-person voice-over; (2) the seer, the 'origin of gaze'; (3) the seen, the 'body image,' the subject in the film; and (4) the editor, who constructs a certain aesthetic style.[2] On the other hand, I read this practice as an art practice, as well as a form of socio-political participation. I will situate my analysis of women's first-person documentary practice in the debates over China's path toward individualization discussed by influential anthropologist Yan Yunxiang[3] and further elaborated by others.[4] The debates on China's individualization process are largely influenced by the contemporary individualization thesis, developed from the theories of Zygmunt Bauman, Anthony Giddens, Ulrich Beck and Elisabeth Beck-Gernsheim.[5] This thesis arose in an attempt to understand individualization as a social phenomenon that emerged in the second half of the twentieth century, or the so-called second modernity,[6] where individuals tend to be nomadic, non-linear, fluid, reflexive, and have lots of choices.

Yan[7] recognizes four features of contemporary life demonstrated by the 'European individualization thesis,' two of which also describe the traits of the individualizing society in contemporary China. The first one is 'disembedment,' or what Giddens regards as 'detraditionalization' [8] from external social constraints, including cultural traditions and encompassing categories such as family, kinship, social classes, ethnic groups and local and national communities. The second one is what Bauman refers to as a paradoxical phenomenon of 'compulsive and obligatory self-determination,' in order to search for 're-embeddedness'.[9] This means individuals under the modern social structure have to take full responsibility for their own issues and be more proactive to develop their lives. This process requires a new set of social institutions to enable and structure individual choices and to provide resources, techniques, security and incentives for individuals to develop their own way of life.[10] However, while individual freedom is rather flexible and uncertain in contemporary Western society, individual rights and freedoms in China are largely at the discretion of the state. Under these circumstances, the traditional institution of family still plays an important role in providing individuals with a sense of security and identity.

In this sense, proactive first-person filmmaking by women can be read as an action of their 're-embedding' themselves back into the family. By reconnecting themselves with the traditional collective institution, they are consciously searching for their sense of self, and also examining how family has been transformed in the broader 'detraditionalization' process. Instead of passively performing the conventional image of their 'given' identity of obedient daughter, these women take a dual role of both daughter and independent outsider. In negotiating this contradictory role of playing both observer and subject, these filmmakers use the camera as a mediator, whereby their practice bridges a conversation with their parents – and, by extension, with the audience – on the renegotiation of the parent–child relationship and the role of women in contemporary Chinese society.

In the first part of this chapter, I will discuss how first-person filmmaking practices initially developed in the West, and then situate this type of filmmaking into the sociopolitical and historical contexts of contemporary China, especially regarding issues related to women and individualization in the post-Communist epoch. I will then analyze how Wang and Yang position themselves as strong authorial voices, but also as relational subjects. Lastly, I will probe the reception of the films, the ethics they have challenged, and how these challenges have been carried on by other women filmmakers in recent years. I argue that the women's first-person documentary filmmaking that I study here can be seen as a form of 'communicative practice' between children (daughters) and parents, generating what Harriet Evans regards as 'a new ethics of mutual recognition and exchange between parents and children.'[11] In my observation, Wang's and Yang's authorial voices do not just speak for themselves, but for the family as a larger collective. This echoes what Yan identifies as the tension between the increasing demands for freedom imposed on individuals and the unavoidable and re-dependence of the individuals on social institutions – in this case, the family. Nevertheless, the women's first-person films that explore familial traumas have not been widely shown to audiences in public spaces outside the film community, and have received criticism for being narcissistic and solipsistic. They are also seen as challenging the relational and collective-centred social ethics that dominated traditional Chinese society as well as Mao's China, cultural forces that are still influential today. These criticisms suggest that the individualizing society in China seems not to have accepted women who openly challenge parental and patriarchal power. Their position in society and communicative practices have remained the subject of an ongoing negotiation in China since the beginning of the twenty-first century.

Defining first-person filmmaking in the West

To understand first-person filmmaking as a form of film and art practice, I will first provide a review of how it originated and developed in the West. We can trace its emergence to North America and Western Europe during the late 1960s and 1970s, a time when the politics of identity dominated the general cultural sphere.[12] Filmmakers and artists came to document their own engagement with society, reflecting the multi-layered nature of fragmented self-identities, in terms of sociocultural practices, ethnicity and sexuality, all of which were seen as categories constantly in flux. The advance of video technology in the 1970s then played a compelling role, as the influential documentary film theorist Michael Renov explains that, '[v]ideo can be seen as a format historically joined to the private and the domestic, a medium capable of supplying inexpensive sync sound images, a vehicle of autobiography in which the reflexive gaze of the electronic eye can engender an extended, even obsessive, discourse of the self.'[13] The presence of digital video cameras in China since the late 1990s has had a similar effect to that of video in North America in the 1970s. In addition, the epistemological critique of postmodernism and poststructuralism also had a strong impact on the emergence of a more reflexive documentary form, or what Bill Nichols postulates as the 'reflective mode' and 'performative mode,'[14] which has been further explored by film scholar Stella Bruzzi.[15]

Since the 1980s, first-person documentary filmmaking has been the subject of a small but highly significant number of scholarly studies in traditional Anglo-European film studies.[16] In particular, Catherine Russell's appropriation of Mary Louise Pratt's term 'autoethnography' to the field of filmmaking is instructive. For Russell, '[a]utobiography becomes ethnographic at the point where the film or videomaker understands his or her personal history to be implicated in larger social formations and historical processes. Identity is no longer a transcendental or essential self that is revealed, but a "staging of subjectivity" – a representation of the self as a performance.'[17] Chris Marker's *San Solei* (1984) and American filmmaker Ross McElwee's *Six O'Clock News* (1994) can be seen as autoethnographic examples in their inwards exploration on the maker's own self, even if it is a fictional self, as was the case in *San Solei*. Nevertheless, the term autoethnography still emphasizes an Orientalist division of 'Self and Others' that is outmoded today.

Michael Renov prefers to use 'filmic autobiography'[18] to describe this autobiographic mode of nonfiction and emphasizes the genre's confessional features. These confessional elements are present in the work of Jonas Mekas, Wendy Clarke, Alan Berliner and Michelle Citron, all of whom explore the personal, often familial, issues to promote self-understanding, emotional repair or memory reconstruction. Elsewhere, Laura Rascaroli's highly inspiring monograph *Personal Camera* adopts the umbrella term 'personal cinema' to refer to films that explicitly document issues directly relating to the first-person self, including the sub-genres of diary films, self-portrait films and notebook films. Closely engaged with Renov's analysis, Alisa Lebow prefers to use the term 'first-person documentary'. Instead of stating a singular self, she claims that first-person expression always belongs to 'the first person plural,' which embeds the history, memory and identity of a much larger entity.[19]

Here I take the concept of first-person documentary to describe the films I analyse, while also taking inspiration from the scholarly discussions of autoethnography, filmic autobiography and personal cinema. This is to avoid overt separation of self and other in 'autoethnography,' and these films are not necessarily all about the maker's self as in autobiography. I understand the concept of 'first person' to have a strong connotation with the self as an individual subject. 'First-person filmmaking,' according to this view, is a practice where filmmakers point the camera inward to film the self and milieu, and choose to inscribe their first-person voice through revealing elements of the filmmaking process, interacting with the subjects, and reflexively commenting on their filmmaking. This genre also includes the creative use of home movies, animation, found footage, graphics, re-enacted scenes and even theatrical performance. Elements of reflexivity, subjectivity and performativity are often interwoven together to deliver a hybridization of documentary modes and formats. Films of this type that have gained significant commercial and/or critical success include Marlon Riggs' *Tongues Unties* (1989), Ari Forman's *Waltz with Bashir* (2008), Michael Moore's *Fahrenheit 9/11* (2004), and more independent productions such as Alisa Lebow's *Tref* (1994) and Andrés Di Tella's *Fotografías* (2007). Such films articulate – through first-person narration – a subjective interpretation of one's world or one's vision of the world for the viewer.

Women's first-person documentary in individualizing China

Pioneered by women filmmakers, first-person documentary film ought to be seen as a groundbreaking mode of intimate documentation in postsocialist individualizing China, which has experienced a transformation of social structures through decollectivization or '*songbang*' – which literarily means to untie (or loosen control of) individuals.[20] Individuals are emancipated from 'the ascribed, inherited and inborn determination of his or her social character'[21] and have to rely more on themselves. This has consequently encouraged the rise of a 'me culture' (*ziwo wenhua*).[22] However, this does not mean individuals have been totally unencumbered by social structures and norms.²³ Instead, human identities have been transformed 'from a "given" into a "task," and [being charged] with the responsibility for performing that task and for the consequences (also the side-effects) of their performance.'²⁴ Two key women filmmakers under investigation in this chapter actively challenge their 'given' identity through their filmmaking practice. In this sense, they are a crucial part of the 'iGeneration' – proactively deconstructing their 'given' identity and using a new alternative amateur documentation tool – the digital video camera – to negotiate a new way of communication. Both women filmmakers, as daughters, view filmmaking as a way to renegotiate their gendered identity.

One of these women is Yang Lina. Born in 1972, Yang was trained as a dancer and worked at the People's Liberation Army Theatre in her 20s. During these formative years, she felt increasingly uncomfortable, as the environment was very socially and aesthetically rigid. Eager to express her true self, Yang left her military work unit and went to Beijing to start a new life.²⁵ From 1996 to 1999, she used a mini DV (digital video) camera to film the daily lives of a group of old men in a Beijing residential area. This work formed the basis of her first documentary *Old Men* (a.k.a. *Lao Tou*, 1999), which won her much public attention. *Home Video* is her second film, and investigates her parents' divorce.

The other filmmaker I discuss here is Wang Fen. Born in 1978 when China had just started its economic reform, she attended a drama and performance school starting at the age of nine. Unlike Yang, Wang has never worked in a state-owned work unit, partly because the state no longer allocated compulsory jobs by the time Wang reached working age in the late 1990s. Wang first worked as a freelance actress, then she realized that she wanted to be a director. She borrowed a video camera, went back to her hometown in Jiangxi province, and made her first documentary about her parents.²⁶

Ten years after making her first film, *They Are Not the Only Unhappy Couple*, Wang was sitting with me in a modern restaurant in Wangjing, a recently developed middle-class district in Northeast Beijing. Looking out on a set of glitzy modern apartment blocks and newly erected skyscrapers that reflect the country's economic success over the last two decades, we started to chat about personal stories of living through China's dramatic social transitions. Wang recalled the experience of making her inaugural first-person documentary in her early 20s, a personal journey that investigated her own parents' unhappy marriage.

> At that time, I was only about twenty-one years old, but already an adult. I was eager to know myself, my emotions, and how I became who I was…These were some things I did not understand and really wanted to know… Before that, it is usually the parents who take care of the children, but by making this film, I start to care about them.²⁷

It was the desire for self-understanding and parent-child communication that compelled Wang to take a digital video camera back home just as these cameras were becoming available on the Chinese consumer market for the first time. She regards the making of *They Are Not the Only Unhappy Couple* as the starting point of her adulthood, when she was willing to display emotional concern for her parents. As a filmmaker, Wang also believed that the film could raise wider social awareness about marital problems and domestic issues in contemporary Chinese society.[28] However, traditional Confucian family ethical relations tend to construct women as powerless and voiceless. To a large extent, the woman plays the role of the daughter and the wife, subject to the father, the husband and the eldest son respectively, which is indicated in the 'Three Obediences.'[29] Rather than simply following the conventional ethical norms, however, the two women filmmakers inscribed themselves as strong authorial voices in their films, constantly asking questions from behind the camera.

Resistance to the ethics of female obedience as a discursive process has gone through various changes in China, dating back to the country's modern individualization process in the late nineteenth century. During the May Fourth period in the 1910s and 1920s, a group of modern, educated, intellectual 'new women' emerged and actively challenged traditional perceptions of Chinese womanhood.[30] However, the Nationalist Government repressed these 'new women' during the 'New Life Movement' in the 1930s, seeing them as a challenge to political uniformity and social stability.[31] After the establishment of the People's Republic of China, gender inequality was strongly countered through a series of legislation, such as the new Marriage Law and the establishment of the Women's Federation or 'Fulian'. The empowered new strong female figure was largely used for the construction of the socialist collective ideology, signifying that the Communist Party would liberate the female victims of traditional Chinese feudal society and help them become active members of the proletarian class. However, in the period from 1950 to 1980, and despite assertions to the contrary by the Communist Party,[32] a gendered hierarchy continued to exist.[33] Nevertheless, the status of women rose significantly in Mao's China, as compared to their role in traditional Chinese society.

Even with all the social changes that have accompanied Chinese economic reform since 1980, popular discourse in China still maintains a focus on the importance of women's re-emphasizing their own familial obligations. As Evans states, '"soft and gentle" images of a supportive femininity topped the rankings for desirable wives. Treating love and sex as key constituents of a happy and stable marriage rapidly became crucial criteria of China's new claims to being a "modern society." Though these images were sometimes disturbed by others of the "strong woman" (*nüqiangren*) and the ambitious female entrepreneurs, the dominant popular message is one of a naturalized and emotional female and connotes the attributes of gentleness, sympathy and care.'[34] Confronting this mainstream discourse, women's personal writings, as 'an act, a negotiation of selves and identities in history'[35] emerged in the 1980s, unconventionally exposing personal emotions, desires and sexuality from women's perspective. These writings have faced strong criticism and been denounced as 'privacy literature' (*yinsi wenxue*).

In the face of this denunciation, public opinion towards personal writing has changed during the 1990s, which marks an age of 'privacy fever.'[36] Such (semi-)autobiographical women's 'individualized writing' (*gerenhua xiezuo*)[37] is now enjoying a re-proliferation, however, and has been packaged as a seductive popular cultural commodity[38] to satisfy the rapidly globalizing market society, as well as the hedonistic and narcissistic consumer culture [in China].[39] Though such women's personal writing has carved out a space for women's own voices, the mass consumption of it has made women's personal voice subject to market forces, problematizing the traditionally oppositional relationships between women's culturally prescribed roles and their newly independent voices, as well as between the private and the public sphere.

Turning the camera inward to explore filmmakers' familial aspects in a fast-transforming society, female first-person documentaries can be read as 'DV individualized writing'. Judith Butler highlights the role of iterability in performativity in cultural construction, which means 'a regularized and constrained repetition of norms'.[40] As women filmmakers, Yang and Wang are 'performing' – but also challenging – the stereotyped 'given' role of the passive obedient daughter. By reconnecting to their parental history, they are actively producing a new understanding of a parent–daughter relationship. It is in this sense that I regard these two women's proactive first-person filmmaking about their parents' marriages as a kind of active communication (*goutong*). Their work can also been seen as a mode of 'communicative practice,' a term used by Harriet Evans, developed from Jürgen Habermas's theory of communicative action. While Evans uses this term to describe the changing pattern of mother–daughter communication, as daughters of the younger generation in her ethnographical studies long for emotional relatedness with their parents,[41] the women filmmakers in my study also aim for a reconnection with their parents and are proactively altering the communication pattern they used to have with their elders. Unabashedly rebellious, first-person filmmaking by women also serves as means of social/cultural construction, as they subversively generate a new set of ethics for communication between parents and children, through the medium of the DV camera.

A strong authorial voice

Both Yang and Wang approach their parents not just from the viewpoint of a daughter, but more as an 'outsider' – an independent individual who shows responsibility towards her family, and renegotiates the filial duties expected of a daughter. While Yang uses handheld point-of-view shots to create a subjective gaze at her parents, and uses off-screen first-person voice to lead the narrative, Wang does something quite different, in that she creates a formal 'objective' look and speaks calmly to her parents, trying to maintain her position as an 'outsider.'

In *Home Video*, Yang aims to dig out the unspoken secret that has caused the break between her divorced parents and between her father and her brother. She inscribes herself as *the seer*, equating her own eyes with the lens of the camera, and *the speaker*, who speaks from behind the camera. And her film subjects also speak directly to her camera in close-up. Such cinematographic techniques demonstrate a more intimate relationship between the filmmaker and the subjects, and are very different from the conventional fly-on-the-wall observational documentary mode that had a significant impact on earlier Chinese independent documentaries in the 1990s. Yang's personal relationship with her family members enables her camera to enter the private familial space. She conducts interviews in a very casual way, interrogating her parents almost like an arbiter. When talking to her mother or her father, Yang's camera sometimes looks at them from above. Her voice coming behind the camera sounds very firm, almost in an aggressive manner.

The film opens with a medium-close up of Yang's mother lying on the bed and wearing only her underwear. Yang's off-screen voice states persistently: 'I want to make an investigation into the divorce of my parents. If you think it is boring or too intrusive, I will stop.' Her voice is the first one we hear in the film, making it clear it is 'I' who is holding the camera and investigating 'my' parents' divorce. Yang then cuts away from these personal interviews and moves to three family members, to compare their different attitudes toward the divorce and its subsequent effects on the whole family. It is interesting to note the mother seems not care about disclosing the family scandal to the public. In contrast, even though her father and her brother are on opposite sides in this dispute, neither was willing to participate on camera in the beginning. After gaining support from the mother, the film cuts to Yang's father lying in bed in a different bedroom. The camera zooms in on his face, as he addresses the viewfinder: 'Your mum has no idea about anything. She's just happy that she's going

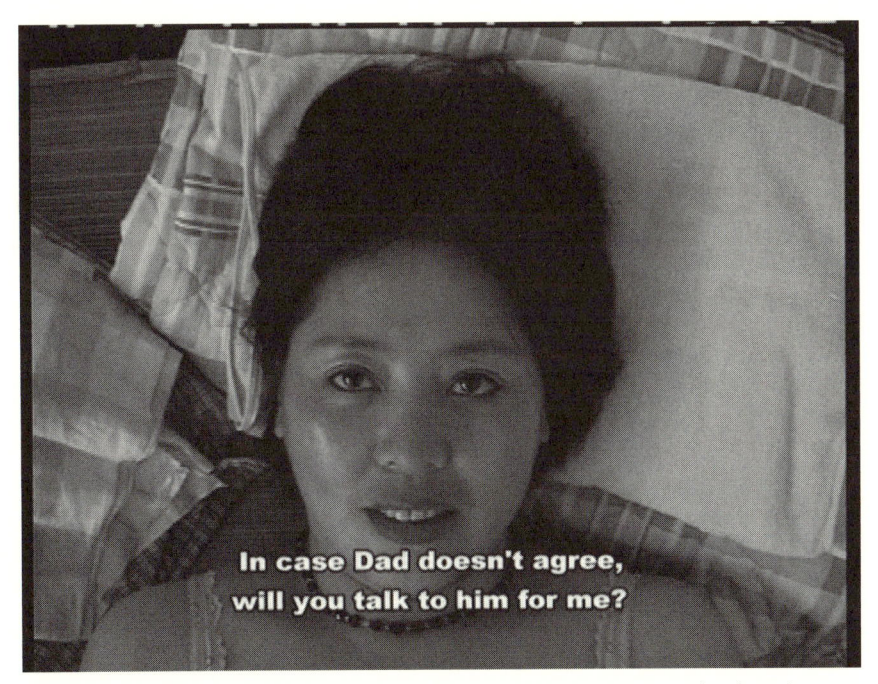

Figure 1.1 Yang asks the mother to persuade the father in *Home Video* (2001).

to be an actress, right?' Yang laughs while replying: 'No way. How can you think of her like that?' It cuts back to the mother looking up at the camera, saying: 'Tell him to think about it carefully.' Then the camera follows the father walking around, while Yang's off-screen voice speaks: 'If you don't agree, I'll keep following you around.'

While the father's rejection may come from self-censorship, feeling ashamed about talking about the divorce, the brother thinks remembering the 'broken past' will hurt them again. In another shot, the camera reveals the brother sitting in a darkened living room facing the camera in a medium close-up as he says: 'I cannot support this.' As Yang insists, the brother replies: '…If we all just speak from our own points of view, it will turn into a family war…This is not just an average event from our past…You are hurting people…Stop talking, turn that thing off….' Similarly, the father tries to cover up the lens, asking Yang to stop filming: 'It's best not to do anything that you will regret.' Despite this warning, Yang firmly replies: '…No, I will be very fair.' At this moment, she does not simply act in the role of a daughter, but like a judge, with the ability to make her own independent decision on this issue. Though challenged in this way by the two male figures in the family, Yang does not give up. She even shows how her brother criticizes her on camera. In a shot of the brother sitting in living room in medium close-up, he tells Yang, 'I think you are a little shameless.' Yang does not feel guilty; instead, she admits it and playfully says from behind the camera, 'Yes, yes, you are right. I'm beginning to feel very shameless…' Nevertheless, the father and the brother finally agreed to participate.

Figure 1.2-4 The three interviews are cross-cut in *Home Video* (2001).

Toward a Communicative Practice

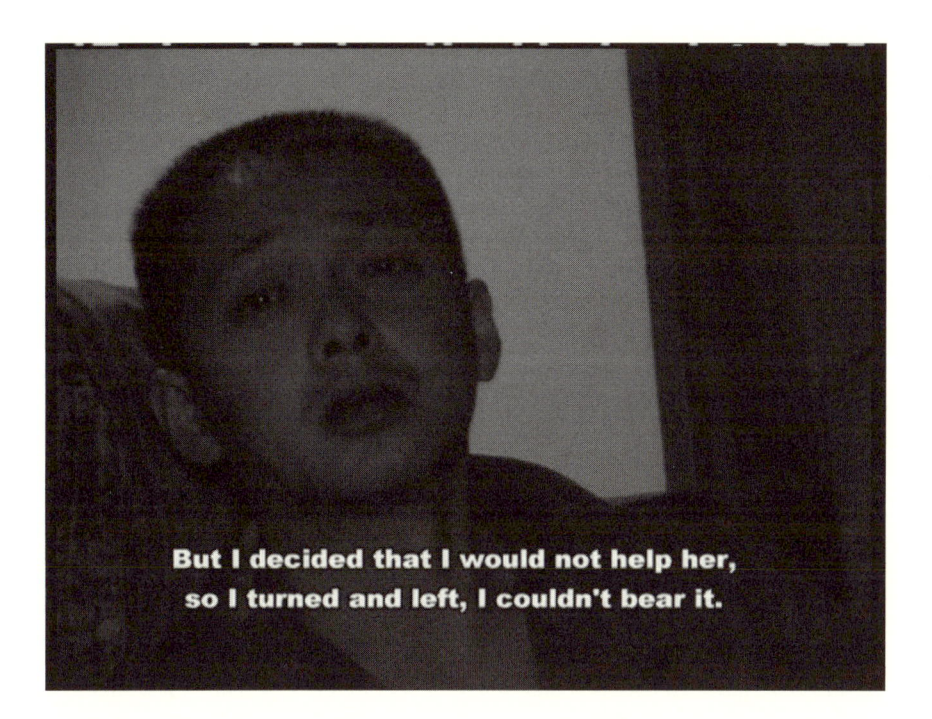

But I decided that I would not help her, so I turned and left, I couldn't bear it.

He was to get much in return for providing evidence.

After the interviews, Yang invites the mother and the brother to watch the film together and records their responses. It is the first time we see the mother and the brother together, and for them to see what the father thinks. Then, despite Yang's mother's warning not to show the film to her father, Yang insists on doing so. The father figure is challenged not only through encouraging him to remember the hidden family history and tell it in front of the camera, but also through the filmmaker's use of the mother's and brother's subjective memories to disturb the father's own memory and judgement. Toward the end, Yang says she hopes the film can bridge the long-term misunderstanding among these three traumatized family members.

In *They Are Not the Only Unhappy Couple*, Wang's first-person influence is articulated strongly through her self-inscription as the 'seer' and the 'editor.' Wang creates a look that is less personal and more objective. She puts the camera on a tripod to achieve a stable view, constructing the interview setting in a more formal way. The father and the mother each sit in the middle of the frame in medium close-up, and address the camera directly, rather than looking at Wang behind the camera. As in the film about Yang's parents, the close relationship between Yang's parents and their daughter makes the parents reveal themselves to the camera without much worry. For them, it is more like their daughter's amateur home movie practice than a new mode of documentary filmmaking.

Like Yang, Wang edits the material and constructs her parents' confessions according to her own personal interpretation. In the opening sequence, Wang uses some experimental elements, having her parents to 'perform themselves.' Wang accomplishes this by starting in fast-forward, as we see close-ups of two pairs of hands cutting out phrases like 'marriage,' 'love' and 'family' from magazines. Then we see one set of hands throw the paper cutouts into a bin, and another set of hands pick them out of the rubbish. The film moves next to an establishing shot, as the camera zooms in and we see a couple standing side by side, who we will later realize are Wang's parents. In this sequence, Wang introduces us to the relationship of her parents through a performance she directed. It is a construction of how she wants to present her parents.

Wang's off-screen voice only appears a few times from behind the camera, speaking in a very calm and unemotional tone. She neither argues with her parents loudly nor laughs nor cries with them, as Yang does in her film. This neutral tone of questioning reinforces her position as someone who tries to stand outside her own familial relationship, and creates a space for her parents to confess, to speak out about their pain.

Still a relational self

Even though both Yang and Wang take on a transgressive role in their films that challenges the traditional image of the daughter, their authorial voices do not just speak for themselves, but for the sake of their family as a larger collective.

In *Home Video*, Yang's interviews with her mother, father and younger brother are shot via a consecutive and cross-cut technique, producing the appearance of a face-to-face conversation between the three, with the central focus on the family. While one person recalls an event, the other two immediately respond. As their conversation reveals, the violent family history is that the mother had an affair, which the brother witnessed and then later told the father. The father consequently began beating the mother for her infidelity, and they divorced because of these irreconcilable spousal difficulties. The brother also witnessed the domestic violence, and therefore has a complex set of feelings towards the parents. The film reveals that the relationship between the mother and father, as well as the relationship between the father and the son, are in fact strained.

Yet Yang is not the only person who cares about the family as a whole. Her mother insists that Yang should not show the film to her father, as it would ruin the relationship among the family members that has just been rebuilt again in recent years. The mother is especially afraid that the younger brother would lose his inheritance from the father. However, in the end Yang still shows the film to the father. In the last shot of the film, Yang asks what the father thinks. Her father responds by asking his daughter the same question: 'What do *you* think?' Film scholar Yomi Braester argues that this moment indicates that Yang is the ultimate protagonist of the film.[42] However, as I see it, what Yang cares about most is the family appearing as a collective, which is the central focus of her film. Yang believes that this filmmaking activity has indeed created a chance for the family members to re-examine their relationships, and to engage in a deeper level of communication than they have had in a long time.[43]

In *They Are Not the Only Unhappy Couple*, Wang's camera focuses on examining the relationship between the husband and the wife. The majority of the film is made of two separate confessional interviews with the mother/wife and the father/husband, cross-cut and organized like a dialogue of the two. The film presents the couple's dissatisfaction towards each other. The father starts with revealing his promiscuous love life and affairs with other women, followed by the mother saying, 'I never really trusted him.' The film cuts back to the father complaining about his wife, then back the mother who is frank about her animosity towards the man she married. The couple speaks to the camera, to their daughter, and it seems like they do not know these interviews would be shown to the public.

As the conversations continue, we realize that the traditional ethical relationship between husband and wife is seriously strained in Wang's portrait of her family. In Chinese culture, the 'Three Cardinal Guides' request that the husband guide his wife, showing her affection and protecting her from harm, while the 'Three Obediences' request that the wife obey the husband. Even when socialist ideology replaced traditional family ethics in Mao's China, the new morality of socialist 'command-ership' required an equal relationship and mutual respect. However, Wang's parents' confessions to her personal camera have somehow destroyed the stereotyped image of a good harmonious couple. As the film continues, it reveals that Wang's parents' unhappy marriage might be a result of China's changing sociopolitical climate during the Maoist era, when the father could not marry another woman because of class differences. In one scene, Wang leaves her father alone with the camera on and asks him to say whatever he wants to say. The father appears to be a little uncomfortable at first, gazing at the camera, but then he starts to confess:

> On the issue of marriage, I have been tortured my whole life. Why? Because I cannot be with the one I love. The society did not allow it. But the one I don't like at all becomes my real wife, then I do not experience a single happy day ever since...

It is interesting to analyse whom the father is addressing in this segment when he is by himself. Is he addressing his daughter, as he knows that she will eventually watch this? Is he addressing himself, revealing the pain in his heart? Is he addressing other potential viewers and does he knows that this confession will be watched by a larger audience? The father reveals that he attributes his unhappy marriage at least partially to the Communist class struggle during the Cultural Revolution, when people were grouped strictly according to their class labels and when personal affections toward a member of a different class were not encouraged.

This scene of the father's personal confession stands in sharp contrast with the last scene, where Wang's parents are standing happily together side by side, waving goodbye to the camera. This 'happy together' moment is a conscious performance in front of the camera, which can be read in several ways. Is it a performance directed by Wang, who imposes her own romantic wish on to her parents? Is the performance happening because her parents want to present a happy image when they are together facing the camera, not knowing what each other has said? Or is it actually part of their daily life, as they both reveal that they do not want to divorce, because they wish to give their children a unified family? In all of these possible interpretations, the family members, both Wang and her parents, still show considerable care for the family as a collective unit.

Ethics of screening

Filming oneself and one's family is an important self-understanding process. Wang Fen regards the investigation in her film as valuable guidance for her to understand the meaning of marriage. She states that, even if she had not made the film, she would have understood the problem later. The filmmaking accelerated the process, at a time when she had just started a relationship herself.[44] Now Wang does not choose the traditional path of marriage for herself, but instead has given birth to a son with Ai Weiwei, China's most politically outspoken contemporary artist (who is also already married to another woman). It would be an oversimplification to judge Wang's choice of her unconventional unification of partnership as a direct response to her parents' unhappy marriage, but it nevertheless shows her rebellious attitude towards traditional marriage. As for Yang Lina, the criticism she received from her brother and father, as well as from her audience, has made her reflect on her own ethical relations with her family and the audience.[45]

While writing is a process limited to a space of one's own, at least until publication, these women have moved their process of discovery a step further. By using a DV camera instead of a pen, they create new avenues of communication – reconnecting with their parents on the one hand and directly challenging the problematic familial relations (and the expectations of women) in Chinese society on the other. Their work draws attention to a re-examination of the institution of the family, which has become heavily layered and more complicated in China's period of transition. Their films illustrate the fact that family, as a traditional institution that has historically defined the individual self in an ethical relational society, still plays an important role in the construction of the individual self. Presenting themselves in the complex relations, these women still think highly of the family as a collective group, which can provide individuals with a sense of identity and security. However, unlike the May Fourth new women of 1920s China and the post-Mao individual women writers who built up a collective power and social awareness, these female filmmakers have not yet formed a broader alliance.

Even though Yang and Wang have only interacted with a limited number of people through their filmmaking and screenings, these two women have been regarded as highly transgressive and have received strong criticism. Their filmmaking has not only challenged their parents, but has also provoked their audience in serious ways and disrupted conventional Chinese expectations of passive obedient women. Their capturing of their family members' stories on film has drawn attention to ethical questions. As Yang's mother says in the film: 'A movie like this will have a huge impact, but it will make us all look very bad, Yang Lina.' *Home Video* has only been shown three times in ten years – once at the Leipzig Film Festival in Germany, and twice inside China. Similarly, *They Are Not the Only Unhappy Couple* was first shown at Yamagata International Documentary Film Festival (YIDFF) in Japan, then it was shown twice in Beijing. Wang Fen recalls that some domestic journalists seriously criticised her as being shameless.[46] To some extent, such responses reflect the societal taboo regarding public discussion of personal familial issues in contemporary China.

It cannot be denied that both Yang Lina and Wang Fen hoped to make a 'film as a film.' In *Home Video*, Yang's mother's response to Yang's idea of filming the family as 'fashionable' and a 'good topic' somehow also reflects her own intention. As Yang reveals, 'I've been listening to my mother talking about the issue several times, and think maybe I can make a film out of it, and investigate how others think of the issue.'[47] However, by making a film out of it and showing it to a wider audience, the familial issue is no longer a personal one. The strong criticism these filmmakers received made them question their own motivations, and they have not made similar documentaries since. Wang was funded to make a domestic commercial fiction feature in 2008 before editing some documentaries for Ai Weiwei, the father of her son. And while Yang Lina keeps making documentaries, she treats it as a profession, has done some commissioned work for foreign broadcasters, and has avoided personal topics.

Their self-censorship says something about the complex construction of the individual self. Gendered expectations of obedience and filiality, as well as family obligations, still play a crucial role in the individual constrcution of self in contemporary

China. While the individualizing society of post-reform China has offered these women more autonomy to pursue their selves outside of the traditional familial space, society seems not to have accepted women who openly challenge parental power and their conventional roles as a way to renegotiate the communication patterns between parents and children. It also indicates that society has not yet opened up public spaces for individuals to examine their selves in the context of unstable, uncommunicative familial relations that were, to a great extent, created by the dramatic transitions occurring in society.

To challenge the still highly patriarchal structure of contemporary Chinese society (as well as the patriarchal nature of the independent film world itself), Yang Lina recently finished her debut feature fiction *Longing For the Rain* (2013), which deals openly with women's sexuality by representing the sexual desire of a newly affluent urban middle-class woman. Yang aims to represent the innermost desires and emotions of women living in today's China, a topic that is rarely portrayed even in Chinese independent cinema.[48] The film, according to Yang, was not submitted for censorship and will mainly be shown internationally at film festivals and to a small audience in independent domestic screenings. Touching on a topic that is little represented in Chinese cinema, even by women filmmakers, Yang hammers at the invisible 'taboo' in the still largely patriarchal society. Moving from the documentary genre to the fiction genre is also a way to avoid the sensitive ethics of documentary filmmaking.

More women first-person documentaries

Following pioneer women filmmakers Yang Lina, Wang Fen, Tang Danhong, more filmmakers are exploring their private familial issues as well as their engagement in the public spaces through a first-person approach. These include Shu Haolun (*Nostalgia*, 2006), the amateur filmmaker Hu Xinyu (*The Man*, 2001, *Sister*, 2003, and *Family Phobia*, 2010), the younger iGeneration filmmakers Wu Haohao (*Criticising China*, 2008 and *Kun1: Action*, 2008) and Xue Jianqiang (*I Beat the Tiger when I was Young*, 2010 and *Martian Syndrome*, 2010). Similar to the first women filmmaking pioneers, these filmmakers have explicitly depicted the self in family or public spaces, challenging existing social conventions and ethical relations. Keith B. Wagner's chapter in this volume offers a fresh and in-depth analysis of the subversive nature of Xue's practice, which he reads as part of small faction of 'reckless documentaries' from a marginalized social class in China's regions. Apart from these relatively unknown filmmakers, the internationally recognized artist and activist Ai Weiwei has also produced a number of highly controversial first-person political documentaries with his volunteers.

In addition, more women filmmakers are starting to make personal documentaries by presenting themselves on camera. For example, Beijing Film Academy graduate Liu Jiayin has made two award-winning first-person docu-dramas, *Oxhide I* (2005), and *Oxhide II* (2009) with his/her family members playing themselves. Similarly, Song

Fan's *Memories Look at Me* (2012) also portrays her and her parents in their domestic setting, as they casually dig up shared memories from mundane family life in the past. It is interesting to note that neither of these filmmakers describes their work as documentary, as it involves real-life characters playing themselves and the filmmakers also taking part. Liu's and Song's films, as well as the two films studied here by Wang and Yang, are all dialogue-based, and the conversations are usually unscripted, with individuals speaking in their home dialects. Nevertheless, it is worth noting that such parent–daughter conversations, no matter how casual they seem, are all carefully staged for the purpose of filming, as if a communication between the two generations is only possible through a deliberate arrangement. Another woman's first-person film that deals with generational communication is Zhang Mengqi's *Self Portrait: Three Women* (2010). Solely focusing on the women of the filmmaker's family, the film explores different values of love and marriage among Zhang's grandmother, mother and herself. Different from other dialogue-based productions, this film includes elements of on-stage performance, as the filmmaker/dancer Zhang uses her own body as a communicative tool, performing in front of the camera as a way to communicate to her mother, and to herself.

Furthermore, a few women in China's subaltern classes are also beginning to create first-person documentary films with DV cameras. They use the camera both as a communicative tool and as a constructive engine to build a new identity. Guo Lifen's *My Name is Fenfen* (2008) documents her personal experience as a rural-to-urban migrant worker in China's nationwide urbanization and decollectivization process. Familial conflicts, especially her challenges to patriarchal authority, are inevitably part of her transitional life. Shao Yuzheng, one of the amateur villager filmmakers in Wu Wenguang's 'Villager Documentary Project,'[49] has also made first-person documentaries since 2005. Unlike other female filmmakers, who predominantly focus on familial issues or their personal emotions, Shao is more like an independent journalist, as she keeps a record of the daily events in her village, even documenting her own interaction and confrontation with the state media and legal bureaucracy.[50] By doing so, she has not only challenged the stereotypical image of the peasant class, but also the image of an illiterate domestic peasant woman who has little interaction with the public and wider society.

In all these films, the construction of self, especially with regard to gender, has been further complicated in a society that is undertaking a dramatic decollectivization, urbanization and marketization processes. While these women filmmakers raise their strong authorial voice, confronting the conventional expectations of women, they still care about the family as a collective unit. Utilizing different devices of cinematic representations to inscribe themselves in their films, these women filmmakers are searching for a new voice, and new ways to communicate with their families and the society. The complicated and problematic family relations explored in these films also reflect the multi-layered and still largely relational dynamics in wider sociopolitical spaces in China today.

Works cited

Beck, Ulrich. *Risk Society: Towards a New Modernity*, trans. Mark Ritter. London: Sage Publications, 1992.
Beck, Ulrich and Elisabeth Beck-Gernsheim. *Individualization: Institutionalised Individualism and its Social and Political Consequences*. London and Thousand Oaks: Sage Publications, 2003.
—Foreword. 'Varieties of Individualization' in M. Halskov Hansen and Rune Svarverud (eds), *iChina: The Rise of the Individual in Modern Chinese Society*. Copenhagen: Nias Press, 2010, 1–38.
Berry, Chris. 'Getting Real: Chinese Documentaries, Chinese Postsocialism' in Zhang Zhen (ed.), *China's Urban Generation*. Duke University Press, 2007, 115–34.
Berry, Chris and Mary Farquhar. *China on Screen – China and Nation*. New York: Columbia University Press, 2006.
Braester, Yomi. 'Excuse Me, Your Camera Is in My Face: Auteurial Intervention in PRC New Documentary' in Chris Berry, Xinyu Lü and Lisa Rofel (eds), *The New Chinese Documentary Film Movement: For the Public Record*. Hong Kong: Hong Kong University Press, 2010, 195–216.
Butler, Judith. *Bodies That Matter: On the Discursive Limits of 'Sex.'* New York: Routledge, 1993.
Dirlik, Arif. 'The Ideological Foundation of the New life Movement: A Study in Counterrevolution', *The Journal of Asian Studies*, 34:4 (August), 945–80.
Evans, Harriet. *Women and Sexuality in China*. Cambridge: Polity Press, 1997.
—*The Subject of Gender: Daughters and Mothers in Urban China*. Lanham, BO, New York, Toronto and Plymouth: Rowman & Littlefield Publishers, Inc, 2008.
—'The gender of communication: changing expectations of mothers and daughters in urban China,' *China Quarterly* 204 (2010): 980–1000.
Jaffee, Valerie. '"Every Man a Star": The Ambivalent Cult of Amateur Art in New Chinese Documentaries' in Paul G. Pickowicz and Yinjing Zhang (eds), *Underground to Independent*. Lanham, MD: Rowman & Littlefield Publishers, 2006, 77–108.
Lebow, Alisa. *First Person Jewish*. London: University of Minnesota Press, 2008.
Liang, Shuming. 'Zhongguo Wenhua Yaoyi (The essentials of Chinese Culture)' in *Liang Shuming Quanji*, vol. 3. Jinan: Shangdong People's Press, 1990.
Liu, Lydia H. *Translingual Practice: Literature, National Culture, and Translated Modernity – China, 1900–1937*. Stanford, CA: Stanford University Press, 1995.
Lü, Xinyu. 'Rethinking China's New Documentary Movement', trans. Tan Jia and Lisa Rofel, in Chris Berry, Xinyu Lü and Lisa Rofel (eds), *The New Chinese Documentary Film Movement: For the Public Record*. Hong Kong: Hong Kong University Press, 2010, 15–48.
Rascaroli, Laura. *The Personal Camera – Subjective Cinema and the Essay Film*. London and New York: Wallflower Press, 2009.
Renov, Michael. *The Subject of Documentary*. Minneapolis: University of Minnesota Press, 2004.
—'First-person Films. Some Theses on Self-inscription' in Thomas Austin and Wilma de Jong (eds), *Rethinking Documentary. New Perspectives, New Practices*. Berkshire: Open University Press, 2008, 39–50.
Renov, Michael and Erika Suderberg (eds). *Resolutions: Contemporary Video Practice*. Minneapolis and London: University of Minnesota Press, 1996.

Russell, Catherine. *Experimental Ethnography – the Work of Film in the Age of Video*, Durham, NC and London: Duke University Press, 1999.
Wang, Lingzhen. *Personal Matters: Women's Autobiographical Practice in Twentieth-Century China*. Stanford, CA: Stanford University Press, 2004.
—'Reproducing the Self: Consumption, Imaginary, and Identity in Women's Autobiographical Practice in the 1990s' in Charles A. Laughlin (ed.), *Contested Modernities in Chinese Literature*. New York: Palgrave Macmillan, 2005, 173–92.
Wang, Qi. *'Writing Against Oblivion: Personal Filmmaking from the Forsaken Generation in Postsocialist China.'* PhD diss., University of California, LA, 2008.
Wolf, Margery. *Revolution Postponed: Women in Contemporary China*. Stanford: Stanford University Press, 1985.
Wedell-Wedellsborg, Anne. 'Between Self and Community: The individual in Contemporary Chinese Literature' in M. Halskov Hasen and Rune Svarverud (eds), *iChina, the Rise of the Individual in Modern Chinese Society*. Copenhagen: Nias Press, 2010, 164–92.
Yan, Yunxiang. *The Individualization of Chinese Society*. London School of Economics Monographs on Social Anthropology, 2009.
—'Introduction: Conflicting Images of the Individual and Contested Process of Individualization' in M. Halskov Hansen and Rune Svarverud (eds), *iChina: The Rise of the Individual in Modern Chinese Society*. Copenhagen: Nias Press, 2010, 1–38.

Notes

1 Yan Yunxiang, *The Individualization of Chinese Society*, xxvii.
2 For more, see Catherine Russell, *Experimental Ethnography*. Durham, NC and London: Duke University Press, 1999, 277–8.
3 Yan, *Private Life Under Socialism*. Stanford University Press, 2003; Yan, 'Introduction' (2008); Yan, *The Individualization of Chinese Society*. Bloomsbury Academic, 2009; Yan, Introduction to M. Halskov Hasen and Rune Svarverud (eds), *iChina: the Rise of the Individual in Modern Chinese Society*. Copenhagen: Nias Press, 2010.
4 For more see *iChina*.
5 Bauman, *The Individualised Society*; Giddens, *Modernity and Self-Identity*; Beck, *Risk Society*, translated by Mark Ritter, London: Sage Publications, 1992; Beck and Beck-Gernsheim, *Individualization*. London and Thousand Oaks: Sage Publications, 2003; 'Varieties of Individualization' in M. Halskov Hansen and Rune Svarverud (eds), *iChina: The Rise of the Individual in Modern Chinese Society*. Copenhagen: Nias Press, 2010.
6 Elliott, 2002, 1–38.
7 Yan, *The Individualization of Chinese Society*, xvii; Yan, Introduction to *iChina*.
8 Giddens, *Modernity and Self-Identity*.
9 Bauman, *The Individualised Society*, 32 and 145.
10 Giddens, *Modernity and Self-Identity*; Beck and Beck-Gernsheim, *Individualization*.
11 Evans, 'The Gender of Communication,' 986.
12 Michael Renov observes that 'the displacement of the politics of social movement by the politics of identity…The women's movement changed all that and helped to

usher in an era in which a range of "personal" issues – race, sexuality, and ethnicity – became consciously politicised... In all cases, subjectivity, a grounding in the personal and the experiential, fueled the engine of political action.' See Michael Renov, *The Subject of Documentary*. Minneapolis: University of Minnesota Press, 2004, 176–7.
13 Renov, *The Subject of Documentary*. Minneapolis: University of Minnesota Press, 2004, 203.
14 Nichols, *Introduction to Documentary* 1991, *Representing Reality* 2001.
15 Bruzzi, *New Documentary: A critical Introduction*, 2006.
16 Michael Renov and Erika Suderberg, Resolutions. Mineapolis and London: University of Minnesota Press, 1996; Michael Renov, *The Subject of Documentary,* Minneapolis: University of Minnesota Press, 2004; Michael Renov, 'First-person Films' in Austin, Thomas and Wilma de Jong (eds), *Rethinking Documentary. New Perspectives, New Practices*. Berkshire: Open University Press, 2008, 39–50; Catherine Russell, *Experimental Ethnography*. Durham, NC and London: Duke University Press, 1999, 275–314; Alisa Lebow, *First Person Jewish*. London: University of Minnesota Press, 2008; Laura Rascaroli, *The Personal Camera*. London and New York: Wallflower Press, 2009.
17 Russell, 'Autoethnography,' 276.
18 Renov, *The Subject of Documentary*, 2004.
19 Lebow, *First Person Jewish*, 2008, xv.
20 Yan, *The Individualization of Chinese Society*.
21 Bauman, *The Individualised Society*, 144
22 Sima and Pugsley, 'The rise of a "me culture" in postsocialist China: youth, individualism and identity creation in the blogosphere' in *The International Communication Gazette*, vol. 72.3 (2010), 287.
23 Howard, 'Three Models of Individualized Biography.'
24 Bauman, *The Individualised Society*, 144.
25 Yang Lina, interviewed by the author, July 2010. All English translations by the author unless otherwise indicated.
26 Wang Fen, interviewed by the author, July 2010.
27 Ibid.
28 Ibid.
29 Wolf, *Revolution Postponed*. Stanford: Stanford University Press, 1985.
30 New women including journalists, novelists, playwrights, poets and critics, such as Ding Ling, Bing Xin, Xiao Hong, Qiu Jin and Zhang Ailing.
31 This conservative view rejected Western individualism, and tried to reconstruct traditional Confucian morality centering on principles of 'orderliness, cleanliness, frugality, simplicity, promptness, precision, harmoniousness, and dignity.' For more, see Tani Barlow, *The Question of Women in Chinese Feminism*, 2004, and Arif Dirlik, 'The ideological foundation of the new life movement' in *The Journal of Asian Studies*, 34:4 (August), 965–6.
32 Harriet Evans, *Women and Sexuality in China*. Cambridge: Polity Press, 1997, 8.
33 Wolf analyses the reasons why gender equality was not achieved during Mao's China. 'Although sexual equality as a principle has not been vacated, it has been set aside at each economic downturn or show of rural resistance without recognition that such casual treatment will in time devalue a principle until it is but a hollow slogan. I do not think this was a conscious effort on the part of CCP to keep women

subordinated, but rather a consistent failing on the part of an all-male leadership to perceive their own sexist assumptions.' See Margery Wolf, *Revolution Postponed*. Stanford: Stanford University Press, 1985, 26.

34 Harriet Evans, 'The gender of communication' in *China Quarterly* 204 (2010), 998–9.
35 Lingzhen Wang, *Personal Matters*. Stanford: Stanford University Press, 2004, 175.
36 Wang, *Personal Matters*, 12.
37 Anne Wedell-Wedellsborg, 'Between Self and Community' in *iChina*. Copenhagen: Nias Press, 2010, 174.
38 This includes work by younger writers such as Wei Hui, Mian Mian and Mu Zimei.
39 Lingzhen Wang, 'Reproducing the Self' in Charles A. Laughlin (ed.), *Contested Modernities in Chinese Literature*. New York: Palgrave Macmillan, 2005, 182.
40 For Butler, 'this repetition is not performed by a subject; this repetition is what enables a subject and constitutes the temporal condition for the subject. This iterability implies that "performance" is not a singular "act" or event, but a ritualized production, a ritual reiterated under and through constraint, under and through the force of prohibition and taboo, with the threat of ostracism and even death controlling and compelling the shape of the production, but not… determining it fully in advance.' For more, see Butler, *Bodies That Matter*. New York: Routledge, 1993, 95.
41 Harriet Evans, 'The gender of communication' in *China Quarterly* 204 (2010), 986.
42 Yomi Braester, 'Excuse Me, Your Camera Is in My Face' in Chris Berry, Lü Xinyu and Lisa Rofel (eds), *The New Chinese Documentary Film Movement*. Hong Kong: Hong Kong University Press, 2010, 211.
43 Yang Lina, interviewed by the author, July 2010.
44 Wang Fen, interviewed by the author, July 2010.
45 Yang Lina, interviewed by the author, July 2010.
46 Wang Fen, interviewed by the author, July 2010.
47 Yang Lina, interviewed by the author, July 2010.
48 See also http://www.hollywoodreporter.com/news/chinese-director-yang-lina-china–431966 (accessed May 2013).
49 The 'Villager Documentary Project' is a series of first-person documentaries made by selected villagers from different regions of China. It was originally an EU–China Village Governance Project in 2005, in which ten villagers were chosen to film their own villages with a portable DV camera. Some of them have continued making documentaries on a yearly basis, under the mentorship of Wu Wenguang. Shao Yuzheng is the only female director to continue her DV documentary work.
50 Locally well-known as a villager filmmaker, Shao has attracted interest from state journalists wishing to interview her. However, when asked her to rehearse her responses, she has used her camera to document these efforts to manage and control the image of rural filmmakers.

2

Quasi-Documentary, Cellflix and Web Spoofs: Chinese Movies' Other Visual Pleasures

Paola Voci

In China, as elsewhere, new locations and new media have redefined the experience of watching a moving image, beyond just the cinematic experience.[1] The visual works that one can view outside movie theatres differ greatly in scope and style. Some explore alternatives to classic Hollywood narratives; others engage with the documentary idea, but reposition themselves away from realism and, in fact, might offer surreal and even distorted representations of the real. Often crossing the fiction and nonfiction divide, these *movies* simply fall under the broad category of non-feature films.[2] The producers often embrace the cheaper, more manageable and far-reaching DV technology and rely on distribution channels as different as television, the internet and galleries.[3] Among non-feature films, Chinese video art and experimental videos have attracted most of the scholarly attention, while much less academic interest has been given to *other* movies.

In this chapter, I begin to look at these other movies and explore some recent developments in Chinese moviemaking beyond the silver screen and outside art galleries, such as the quasi-documentary, the *e gao* (or spoofs) and the cell/DV flicks. I argue that their *lightness* contributes to establishing a new relationship between movies and pleasure.[4] In my analysis, lightness refers to a self-reflective and often humorous mode of representation, but also relates to issues of production and distribution. Superfluous and often volatile cultural products, these movies are unlikely to be seen as generating either commercial or intellectual capital, and thus effectively locate themselves beyond the duality of popular and élite culture.

The sensual panda: *Ceci n'est pas un documentaire*

An intriguing example of lightness is *Ying he Bai* (*Ying and Bai*, Zhang Yiqing, 2002), a quasi-documentary in which irony goes hand in hand with sensuality.[5] *Ying and Bai* is an unusual take on the national icon: the panda bear. The movie revolves around a panda, Ying, and his relationship with Bai, his trainer and caretaker, but, from the start, it displaces our expectations about what a panda story is generally about.⁶ Not only are pandas among the most widely recognized symbols of China, they are also linked to a variety of controversial issues, from China's commitment to wildlife preservation to so-called panda diplomacy.⁷ Yet, the movie deals with none of the above and, in fact, at the end of the documentary one has a hard time describing what 'the story' is really about. In *Ying and Bai*, authenticity seems to be displayed in the recording of the everyday routine of a panda and his caretaker. However, the shots are often edited and explicitly manipulated to comment on the unusual *ménage à deux*. In fact, editing and camera angles change the relation between Ying and Bai into a *ménage à trois*, as the woman and the panda's enclosed reality is invaded by broadcasts on a television set with which they both share their lives. The staging of an artificial viewing relationship between the panda and the television set upsets the idea of authenticity in the film even further.

The opening shot of the film is framed upside-down. Shown through a set of iron bars that clearly indicate that the camera is located behind a cage, one can see a little television set with a window in the background. A news programme is on. A woman enters the shot, hangs a picture on the wall, moves towards the camera, opens the cage, gets out a bowl, and exits the frame. At this point, the movie cuts to a medium-shot of a panda sitting on its head, revealing the source of the previous point-of-view shot. The next shot is a close-up of the upside-down television screen with a news journalist who is reporting on President Bill Clinton's potential impeachment. As we realize that the panda is actually watching the news, the tone becomes humorous. The scene suggests that the documentary is going to be an exploration of the life of a panda captured from his perspective, with some sardonic comments on the human beings who surround him.

As the video introduces Bai, a sad-looking single woman whose life has been dedicated to the training and care of Ying, an odd love story unfolds. The relationship between the woman and the panda is shown in its most intimate and almost sensual details. The intensity of Bai's physical connection complicates the documentary at the levels of both form and content. In one scene, Bai strokes Ying through the bars of the cage. The camera's point of view is once again placed inside the cage, but, unlike the scenes where the panda is shown as if he is watching television, the panda's reaction (or, in fact, lack of reaction) in this case is not exposed. The absence of the shot-reverse-shot structure keeps the focus on the woman's agency in this interaction with the panda. Surrounded by a dark background, the close-up of her face kissing the panda is strikingly bright and her skin is exposed in piercing detail. While softly addressing Ying, Bai strokes him with both sensuality and sorrow. The mocking tone is gone; Bai's deep sadness and solitude fill the screen.

Sexuality, its repression, and its outlets eventually become the unexpected focus of the documentary. In one scene, the panda is shown rolling on his back while seemingly looking into the camera; a laconic subtitle helps us decode his movements: 'Masturbation.' Off screen, a female voice talking over a fast-paced music soundtrack encourages viewers to move up, left, and right. The soundtrack already suggests what the next shot – a medium-shot of the television screen – reveals: the panda is

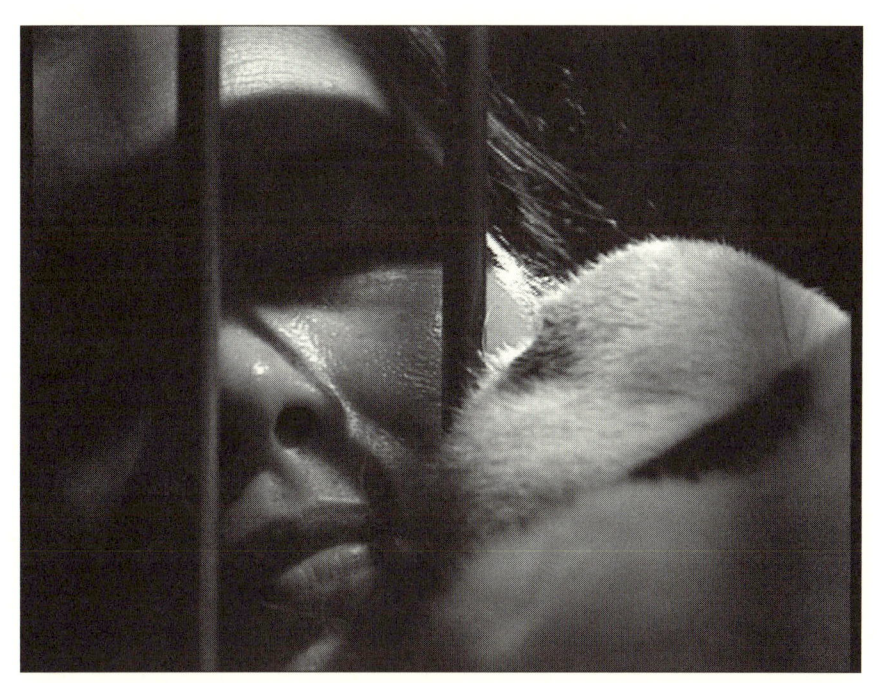

Figure 2.1 Surrounded by a dark background, the close-up of her face kissing the panda is strikingly bright and her skin is exposed in piercing detail. While softly addressing him, she strokes him with both sensuality and sorrow. The mocking tone is gone; Bai's deep sadness and solitude fill the screen. *Ying and Bai* (2002).

watching television, again. At least this is what the narrative shows, but does not ask us to believe. On television, three women in aerobic shorts are stepping up and down. As the blonde who is leading the exercise in the front asks, 'Aren't you feeling your body getting hot?', the camera returns to the panda rolling in the cage. While the scene clearly invites laughter, the joke is not so obvious. Are we laughing at the masturbating panda or at the women on the screen? The documentary does not provide time to intellectualize the rapid mockery into a structured message as the following fragment of Bai's life shifts again.

However, Bai never becomes a real protagonist. We only receive very scattered information about her life through short inter-titles. For instance, we learn that she is half-Chinese and half-Italian, used to be a well-conditioned dancer, and left China to live for a long period of time in Canada. However, many pieces are missing from the mosaic. Rather than expanding on Bai's unusual life story and engaging in a serious exploration of her solitude, subsequent scenes revert to lightness and instead go back to illustrate the everyday routine of her life with Ying (e.g. his defecation, his baths, his eating habits) and their physical connection.

Ying and Bai ends with no real conclusion, and ultimately challenges not only the idea of a linear narrative, but the notions of genre and mode as well. The video evokes elements of nature shows, docudrama and mockumentary, while also shifting from satirical to empathetic tones. Its mode of representation of the real relies on manipulative shots rather than the 'on-the-spot-realism' typical of the move towards authenticity initiated by the 'new documentary movement' and its subjective conjectures about reality.[8] Disguised as a documentary on a panda, *Ying and Bai* is better described as an exploration into trans-gendered and trans-species sexualities and unfulfilled desires. The panda and his trainer both share a life behind bars where the outside world is out of reach and only accessible through a television. On screen, old films, news and morning fitness programmes are the only markers of time in the unchangeable and timeless routine of Ying and Bai. For example, we know that one year has elapsed because of the television news's references to Clinton's sexual scandal, the bombing of the Chinese embassy in Belgrade, and the Y2K scare. But on almost every occasion, each piece of mediated reality is shown as either remote (shown through the cage bars), absurd (displayed upside-down), or laughable (as seen through a panda's perspective). The only tangible, compelling and authentic moments are the small and intense pleasures the two prisoners can offer to each other when the television is off.

Lightness and internet movies

Self-reflexivity and irony have also been recurrent traits of online movies. Unlike their feature-film counterparts, which can only be downloaded either illegally or at a cost, cellflix (mobile phone movies) and *e gao* (spoofs) are mostly legal and free.[9] While cellflix are rarely longer than a minute, spoofs are much longer, generally ten to 20 minutes long.[10] Both phenomena have generated widespread discussions on Chinese blogging sites and, recently, Hu Ge's spoofs have also attracted the attention of Western media. The free, creative flow of online movies is likely to be further regulated in the near future by the Chinese government, which for now continues to focus on word-based filtering for its censorship. In the meantime, cellflix and web spoofs are enjoying relative freedom.

For instance, in January 2006, the Shanghai-based magazine *Metroer* launched a cellflix online competition, where the submissions could (and can still) be viewed and downloaded from small windows within the larger *Metroer* webpage.[11] Mostly entertaining and light, these movies, with their hypershort format, fulfil both artists' desire to exhibit their fast-created visual work and web visitors' desire for a quick fix to satisfy their curiosity. The 'one click' easiness of the cellflix distribution and reception is certainly an important factor in defining both the quality and the aims of these movies. However, upon a second, more attentive look, these movies show more than their average 40-second format seems to allow. Most of these flix contain explicit references to films, parodies of famous events and people, or more implicit commentaries on urban isolation.

For instance, despite its travel-diary layout, the cellflick *Zai Xizan* (*In Tibet*) frames itself within the larger context of cinematic representations of Tibet. Its superimposed titles mimic that of the film *Kekexili* (*Kekexili: Mountain Patrol*, Lu Chuan 2004) and some shots evoke Tian Zhuangzhuang's *Delamu* (2004). *Yige zai zumujiade xiawu* (*An Afternoon at Grandma's*) goes beyond the home-video format and uses three simple but carefully framed shots to expand its 63 seconds into a long, silent, slow afternoon which manages to capture the increased marginality of old age by glancing at a mah-jong game, a window opened onto a narrow alley, a sleeping old man, and the final medium close-up of a grandma's direct look in the camera. Even more captivating are the short experimental narratives of the quasi-MTV video *Shanghai Freak* (no Chinese title), which shows elliptic images of Shanghai accompanied by Carla Bruni's 'La Dernière Minute,' or the surreal *Tango on the Fingers* (no Chinese title), a 31-second dance of two fingers and their long shadows on a table, accompanied by the notes of a tango.[12]

Lightness becomes parody and explicit satire in web spoofs. The most famous example is *Yige mantou yinfade xue an* (*The Bloody Case that Started from a Steamed Bun*, a.k.a. *A Murder Caused by a Mantou*), a spoof of Chen Kaige's *Wuji* (*The Promise*, 2006). The video began to circulate on the web in February 2006, just weeks after the official release of Chen's *Wuji*. The producer, Hu Ge, declared that he decided to create this spoof because he was extremely disappointed by Chen's film, and was mad about having wasted his money and time to watch such a bad movie. Hu Ge had also previously produced a spoof of *The Matrix* (Wachowski Brothers, 1999), but it was only when he successfully parodied *The Promise* and was threatened by a lawsuit that he became a big hit among netizens inside and outside China. The spoof originated its own sequels, like *Yige mantou fayinde mafan* (*The Troubles Caused by a Bun*), which relies on clips from Hong Kong films starring Stephen Chow, and *Yigen kuaizi fayinde ming'an* (*The Murder Caused by a Chopstick*), which spoofs Zhang Yimou's *Yingxiong* (*Hero*, 2002) while also making some references to Osama Bin Laden.[13] Hu went on to produce his first self-produced mini-feature film, *Niaolong shan jiao fei ji* (*Annihilate the Gangsters on Niaolong Mountain*), a parody of famous films (although this time no original footage was used to avoid copyright problems). The movie was released as a web video on 6 June 2006.

Parodies of famous films go together with parodies of real life. In April 2006, *Bashi Ashu* (*Bus Uncle*), a video showing an old man and a young man quarrelling on a bus, attracted the attention of more than a million viewers.[14] Evidence of its success is the fact that the video exists in multiple versions. Besides its original Cantonese version, on YouTube one can find a censored edition (where all the obscenities are blanked out) and Chinese-language and English-language subtitled versions. Other 'hot remixes' (with added music, captions and animation) have also been added in the following months.[15]

While circulating widely among the netizens, spoofs are very limited as a popular culture phenomenon because of their medium and the required computer literacy required for viewing or downloading web-based videos. Furthermore, although produced for entertainment, their commercialization beyond the usual association with internet advertising (e.g. Google ads) remains unlikely.

Quasi-conclusions: Popular culture and unpopular movies

In the Chinese context, moviemaking and screening environments still remain under the control of the state, although whether such control is factual rather than nominal has increasingly become a source of debate. Independent movies have become the privileged location for exposing the constrictions and the limits of such control. Sixth Generation filmmakers working outside the film bureau's approval have been regarded as either champions of an underground resistance to censorship in China or de facto allies of the system that initially banned them but ultimately allowed them to gain first an international reputation and then even a domestic audience. In both cases, the implied assumption has been that in Chinese cinema, dissent is a *serious* matter, either an issue to debate and fight for or one to condemn and attack. On the other end of the spectrum, one finds those working with the blessing of the system. Among these commercially successful filmmakers, one finds the new practically minded like Feng Xiaogang, as well as established filmmakers like Zhang Yimou and Chen Kaige, who have also put their creative efforts towards the production of the ultimate blockbuster.

The movies that are discussed in this essay, meanwhile, are still largely unknown. Produced by moviemakers ranging from professional documentarians to amateur videomakers, these *other* movies belong neither to the world of movie theatres nor to the world of art galleries. Rarely broadcast on television, they have very little or no commercial potential. They are far from being mainstream, but they do not claim to represent any *serious* dissent. They are popular culture products that are not likely to actually become popular. Being *unpopular* is not the same as being controversial. While some of these movies deal with delicate social issues such as prostitution or homosexuality, many are simply not suitable for television broadcast – not because of censorship's problems, but rather because of their unusual length or format. Furthermore, even though political and social concerns are not necessarily rejected, they are often dealt with in an unserious or even frivolous tone. In most cases, such lightness is not a sign of superficiality, but rather reflects the moviemaker's own self-reflective and often ironic agenda.

My brief exploration of visual pleasures offered by independent movies circulating outside of movie theatres in China shows that connection with cinema remains an important cultural reference. Even though many movies have almost completely abandoned film as a medium and the silver screen as an outlet, the connection with cinema has not been disengaged, but complicated instead. Not only are films the main inspiration sources for spoofs, but films remain the archetype against which videos (DV or cellflix) variations are developed. Yet, the critical discourse surrounding Chinese cinema is still mostly constructed around the supremacy of full-length feature films, which has defined as marginal all other genres. What makes the study of movies like *Ying and Bai* even more peripheral to film studies is that not only do they depart from what Christian Metz has defined as a 'king's highway of filmic expression' (i.e. 'the feature-length film of novelistic fiction'), but, in doing so, they also engage with means of production and distribution outside film studios and movie theatres.[16] Given these circumstances, it is no surprise that, with very few exceptions, discussions regarding the role of film within new media and multimedia in China have occurred separately from discussions regarding cinema.[17] A more inclusive and interdisciplinary approach to moviemaking that acknowledges the centrality – rather than peripherality – of the relationship between film and new media is a necessary and long-overdue addition to Chinese film studies.

When discussing the relevance of movies produced thanks to the introduction of new technologies, a note of caution is warranted. The possibilities offered by the introduction of DV, cyberspace and mobile phones should not be overemphasized and need to be understood in relation to the new media environment developed in what Chris Berry has appropriately defined as *postsocialist* China.[18] Since the early 1990s, cinema, television and the internet have all experienced important reforms and changes.[19] Currently in China, an impressive number of television stations run their programmes with different degrees of autonomy, but arguably have less editorial freedom than the state-run China Central TV (CCTV). Film production and distribution has also undergone some major reforms during this period. As the case of the Sixth Generation has shown, it is now possible to shoot a film without the Film Bureau's official approval. In addition, even if a film is not released in movie theatres, it can still be legally distributed and purchased as a DVD.[20] While one should not overestimate the power of the internet, web posting (e.g. file transfer protocols, peer-to-peer file-trading systems, blogging and moblogging) has also managed to create new spaces for the distribution of films and videos. In sum, the availability of cheaper and more manageable means of film production would not have had the same significance without the innovations that have occurred regarding different channels of distribution.

While new media have brought about radical changes in access to and circulation of information in China, one also needs to acknowledge the restrictions set in place by the Chinese cyber police with the complicity of the Western corporate world. For instance, in January 2006, Google announced the launch of google.cn, a limited and censored version of the popular search engine that was specifically tailored for Chinese users according to the Chinese government's requirements.[21] Furthermore, cyber filters are only a relatively small obstacle for those who are already privileged enough to browse the internet. Many other factors (e.g. the country's major rural–urban divide and, more broadly, the deeply unequal distribution of China's new wealth) limit access to new media to an even greater extent.[22] In sum, unless we historicize and contextualize the advent of new media in political and economic terms, Marshall McLuhan's vision of a global village or Pierre Levy's utopian dream of a new democratic and collective intelligence created thanks to the all-encompassing power of the internet can only lead to a distorted image of the actual power of technological innovation.[23]

Thus, the relevance of 'non-feature film' independent movies does not lie in their technological novelty *per se*, but rather in how they are contributing to the redefinition of the visual medium in China and how they are de-intellectualizing the discourse on dissent and avant-garde. Their most provoking feature is not their use of new means of production and distribution, but their deployment of *lightness* and their exploration of mockery, sarcasm, paradox and insincerity as evocative and disobedient visual pleasures.

Works cited

Berry, Chris. 'Facing Reality: Chinese Documentary, Chinese Postsocialism' in Hung Wu, Huangsheng Wang and Boyi Feng (eds), *The First Guangzhou Triennial Reinterpretation: A Decade of Experimental Chinese Art 1990-2000*. Guangzhou: Guangdong Museum of Art, 2000, 121-31.
Donald, Stephanie Hemelryk, Michael Keane and Yin Hong (eds), *Media in China*. New York: Routledge Curzon, 2002.
Hong, Junhao. *The Internationalization of Television in China: the Evolution of Ideology, Society, and Media Since the Reform*. Westport, CT: Praeger, 1998.
Levy, Pierre. *Collective Intelligence*. New York: Plenum Publishing Corporation, 1997.
Lu, Sheldon. *China, Transnational Visuality, Global Postmodernity*. Stanford: Stanford University Press, 2001.
Lü, Xinyu, *Jilu Zhongguo: Dangdai Zhonguo xin jilupian yundong* (*Recording China: Contemporary Chinese new documentary movement*). Beijing: Shenghuo, dushu, xinzhi sanlian shudian, 2003.
Mallaby, Sebastian. 'Google and My Red Flag,' *Washington Post*, 30 January 2006.
Magnier, Mark. 'Attack of the Pandas: Will Taiwan's wary, pro-independence government succumb to a pair of China's most adorable ambassadors? History says yes,' *LA Times*, 21 March 2006.
McLuhan, Marshall. *Understanding Media: The Extensions of Man*, London: Ark, 1987.
Metz, Christian. 'From Film Language. Some Points in the Semiotics of the Cinema' in Gerald Mast, Marshal Cohen and Leo Brady (eds), *Film Theory and Criticism*, fourth edition. New York: Oxford University Press, 1992, 68-78.
Reynaud, Bérénice. 'New Visions/New Chinas: Video-Art, Documentation, and the Chinese Modernity in Question' in Michael Renov and Erika Suderburg (eds), *Resolutions: Contemporary Video Practices*. Minneapolis: University of Minnesota Press, 1996, 229-57.
—'Cutting Edge And Missed Encounters: Digital Short Films By Three Filmmakers,' *Senses of Cinema*, no. 20, May-June 2002.
Rosen, Stanley and Gary Zou (eds). 'The Chinese Television Documentary 'River Elegy' (part I),' *Chinese Sociology and Anthropology*, vol. 24, no. 2, Winter 1991-2, 3-90.
Wu, Hung, *Transience: Chinese Experimental Art at the End of the Twentieth Century*, revised edition. Co-published with the David and Alfred Smart Museum of Art, 2004.

Notes

1 Art historians, critics and curators have been quite active in the debate over the new experimental art. See Wu Hung, *Transience: Chinese Experimental Art at the End of the Twentieth Century*, revised edition (co-published with the David and

Alfred Smart Museum of Art, 2004). Chris Berry and Bérénice Reynaud have helped pioneered the discussion on documentary filmmaking, but much work is yet to be done in this area. Scholars working on cinema have not yet given enough attention to the recent development of video-making and its significance in changing film culture at large.

2 By using the term movie, I wish to emphasize that, increasingly, 'film' is no longer the main medium for these type of works.

3 In China (as elsewhere), digital technology has impacted on almost all visual arts, from feature films to video arts. For instance, director (screen writer and novelist) Cui Zi'en has exclusively used this type of medium to produce his videos. The winner of the 63rd Venice Film Festival was Jia Zhangke's *Sanxia Haoren* (*Still Life*, 2006), which was entirely shot on a high-definition digital camera.

4 I borrow and adapt the notion of lightness from Milan Kundera's association between the multiplicity of insignificant events and their deep (unbearable) meaning in defining human existence.

5 The movie is distributed as *jilupian* (documentary) by Channel Zero Media (CZM). According to CZM's viewing data, *Ying and Bai* was broadcast only once on 11 April 2002 on *Yangguang weishi* channel.

6 *Ying and Bai* was awarded Best Documentary, Best Director, Most Innovative Documentary and Best Sound Effects at the Sichuan Television Festival in 2001. It won Best Director at the 19th China 'Golden Eagle Awards'. It was also selected for the FIPA in France, as well as the Shanghai International TV Festival. *CZM* website, filmmakers: www.bjdoc.com/english1/makers-yiqingzhang.htm (accessed 9 January 2014).

7 In line with a long tradition of using pandas as a gift to support diplomatic relations (a tradition that is well-exemplified by the donation of a pair of pandas following President Richard Nixon's 1972 visit to China), in March 2006 the Chinese government offered to send two pandas to Taiwan. The offer was viewed by many as an attempt 'to destroy Taiwan's psychological defences.' Huang Shi-cho of the Taiwan Solidarity Union party, quoted in Mark Magnier, 'Attack of the Pandas: Will Taiwan's wary, pro-independence government succumb to a pair of China's most adorable ambassadors? History says yes,' *LA Times*, 21 March 2006.

8 Chris Berry's translation of *jishizhuyi* as 'on-the spot-realism' well captures the close link to a very specific temporality that characterized most of the works that are generally referred to as part of the 'new documentary movement' of the 1990s. Lü Xinyu was the first scholar to use the term '*xinjilupian yundong*' in her book, the first book-length analysis of the renewal of Chinese documentary. Chris Berry, 'Facing Reality: Chinese Documentary, Chinese Postsocialism,' in Hung Wu, Huangsheng Wang and Boyi Feng (eds), *The First Guangzhou Triennial Reinterpretation: A Decade of Experimental Chinese Art 1990–2000* (Guangzhou: Guangdong Museum of Art, 2000), 121–31. Lü Xinyu, *Jilu Zhongguo: Dangdai Zhonguo xin jilupian yundong* (*Recording China: Contemporary Chinese new documentary movement*) (Beijing: Shenghuo, dushu, xinzhi sanlian shudian, 2003).

9 The term cellflix is used as the English equivalent to *shouji dianying* (cell phone movies) on the *Metroer* website and explained as the merging of 'cellphone + films.' One wonders if the creators of this term wanted to reference the Australian-based Film Lovers of Independent Cinema (FLICs) or the controversy surrounding copyright violation and companies like Clean Flicks, Flick's Club and Family Flix, which re-edit and then rent 'clean' versions of films.

10   Most of the videos that populate video sites like *YouTube.com* are made with cell phones rather than DV cameras; blogging has increasingly turned into moblogging (mobile blogging).
11   A link to the *Cellflix* page is on the main *Metroer* page. A complete list of the submissions also includes DV short movies.
12   *Tango on the fingers* was posted by kfotoe on 2 April 2006 and won the first prize. *Metroer* decided to start a second competition in July, as submissions continued to arrive.
13   Both videos were available for free download on several sites.
14   'The film was uploaded on YouTube.com and then seen by the whole wide world. As of 19 May, 1.2 million people have watched the video clip! (Update: 1.9 million as of 26 May; ETTV cited a 5.9 million figure on 27 May, which probably combines all the editions)'. EastSouthWestNorth, www.zonaeuropa.com/20060524_1.htm (accessed 6 March 2014).
15   The original video is available on YouTube (accessed on 20 August 2006), where one can also find links to all the other versions.
16   Christian Metz, 'From Film Language. Some Points in the Semiotics of the Cinema', in Gerald Mast, Marshal Cohen and Leo Brady (eds), *Film Theory and Criticism*, fourth edition. New York: Oxford University Press, 1992, 68–78.
17   In particular, traditionally Chinese television has been studied separately from film, mostly from a communication studies perspective: e.g. Junhao Hong, *The Internationalization of Television in China: the Evolution of Ideology, Society, and Media Since the Reform* (Westport, CT: Praeger, 1998). Specific television events have been analysed from an anthropological perspective: e.g. Stanley Rosen and Gary Zou (eds), 'The Chinese Television Documentary "River Elegy" (part I)', *Chinese Sociology and Anthropology*, vol. 24, no. 2, Winter 1991–2, 3–90. Among the exceptions (i.e. comparative studies which bring together film and other media), one finds Bérénice Reynaud, 'New Visions/New Chinas: Video-Art, Documentation, and the Chinese Modernity in Question,' in Michael Renov and Erika Suderburg (eds), *Resolutions: Contemporary Video Practices* (Minneapolis: University of Minnesota Press, 1996), 229–57, and 'Cutting Edge And Missed Encounters: Digital Short Films By Three Filmmakers,' *Senses of Cinema*, no. 20, May–June 2002. See also Sheldon Lu's studies on television included in his *China, Transnational Visuality, Global Postmodernity* (Stanford: Stanford University Press, 2001).
18   While many contested the use of Western theoretical categories in the Chinese context, I believe that 'postsocialism' is a useful framework of analysis because it does not position itself as a linear, temporally consequential development from a previously accomplished socialism, but rather points to a new awareness of its unstable meanings.
19   For an overview on the recent developments in Chinese media industry and a critical analysis of its changed scope and reception, see Stephanie Hemelryk Donald, Michael Keane and Yin Hong (eds), *Media in China* (New York: Routledge Curzon, 2002).
20   For instance, Zhang Yuan's *East Palace West Palace* was released on authorized DVD even though the film had not been approved for movie theatre distribution.
21   Google was just the last in a long list of big software providers and internet routers (e.g. Microsoft, Yahoo and Cisco) that all reached commercial agreements with China by giving in to certain restrictions. 'Internet router firm Cisco had no qualms about building a great cyberwall around China, which blocks Chinese surfers from

"subversive" foreign Web sites. Thus Yahoo has obliged the Chinese government by tracing pro-democracy e-mails to one of its users. The e-mailer has been jailed, and Yahoo has effectively become a Chinese police auxiliary." Sebastian Mallaby, 'Google and My Red Flag,' *Washington Post*, 30 January 2006.

22 According to a state-sponsored study, Chinese internet users are estimated to number more than 130 million (about 8 to 10 per cent of the total Chinese population). *China Internet Network Information Center* (CNNIC), 16th Statistical Survey Report on the Internet Development in China, July 2005.

23 Marshall McLuhan, *Understanding Media: The Extensions of Man*. London: Ark, 1987, and Pierre Levy, *Collective Intelligence*. New York: Plenum Publishing Corporation, 1997.

3

Individuality, State Discourse and Visual Representation: The Imagination and Practices of the iGeneration in Chinese Animation

Weihua Wu

The past two decades have witnessed dynamic technological and cultural changes in China's animation industry and its cinematic representation, developments that have converged with the arrival of the new iGeneration filmmakers and audiences in the twenty-first century.

Chinese animation has been historically termed *Meishu* film (literally, fine arts film) in Chinese film studies vocabulary. The earliest examples of animation in China were the Wan Brothers'[1] patriotic shorts of 1930s, which were distinguished by their artistic experimentation, strong nationalism and protest against the Japanese invasion and occupation of China. Later, the first Chinese Animation Conference was held in 1962 in order to address the animation film industry and its impact – not only as a specifically Chinese genre related to Chinese classical painting and with the ability to 'educate children' but also to entertain. In the 1960s and 1970s, the Chinese government regarded Chinese animation as an ideologically 'established, national film genre' that is 'represented as a cinematic linkage between Chinese modern art history and the socialist literary canon.'[2] This link between animation and ideology has deteriorated since the mid-1980s, and the widely accepted term *Meishu* film has also fallen into decline.

More recently, during the 2000s, animation has embraced digitally drawn animation practices and the immersive internet experience, while managing to throw a farewell party to the traditional socialist animation discourse found across the 1990s. This chapter historicizes the past two decades in which China's animation industry has faced two main challenges: (1) a struggle to relocate itself among the state discourse of animation culture; and (2) the opening-up to the global market to circulate and compete with other expressive cartoon mediums. Throughout this period, younger Chinese individuals can be seen as fighting against the visual hegemony of established Chinese animation culture by creating a unique virtual space for dialogue through the practice of web-based Flash animation.

Among the flourishing forms of animation in the new millennium, I analyse three different genres of Chinese animation: (1) commercial television series; (2) independent and academic animation; and (3) web-based Flash animation. These three categories are interrelated on some levels, as each intervenes and creates new cultural spaces to respond to the changing spectatorship of Chinese animation. The rise of the animation series for commercial television has suited the Chinese government's attempts to develop domestic cultural industries in China. The emergence of independent and Flash animation, meanwhile, has demonstrated how computer-mediated technology encourages individual expression that encapsulates the iGeneration prerogative of 'relying on oneself' (*kao ziji*), a prerogative that has consequences which state discourses are struggling to control. Young artists and amateurs from the iGeneration openly represent their desires, dreams and fantasies about living within the glories of global economy and pop culture, expressions that the Chinese Communist Party tolerates more than ever before. These animators have grown accustomed to creating content that takes advantage of greater visual autonomy in China. As such, Chinese animation represents a unique genre not only in the realm of global cinema, but also in the field of Chinese film studies.

The rejuvenation of animation on Chinese television – a historical review

The *People's Daily Overseas* newspapers published a front-page article on 23 November 2005 headlined '"China-made" Called for in Cultural Products'. The article argued passionately that the Chinese animation industry should contribute to the state-directed ideological discourse within the burgeoning creative industries. The article placed animation in a key position within film and television culture and the wider industry. It also argued that Chinese animation should be oriented toward commercial and market-driven priorities rather than ideological ones. The author argued that Chinese animation needs to brand its own creative industry by borrowing from foreign animation industries, which should serve as important models to drive new cultural production in China.

> [...] Japan's animation industry, which accounts for 63 percent of the world's market, is now worth more than US$170 million. Disney's animated feature *Mulan* has been seen around the world, earning more than US$400 million and becoming one of the company's most profitable movies. [...] China has time-honored cultural traditions, profound cultural resources and immense reserves of creative energy, all of which will be needed to develop an international culture industry with Chinese characteristics.[3]

Of particular interest here is a belief that Chinese animation has the potential to be a dominant player in the country's creative industries, yet such precedence rests on the achievements of Chinese animation in the 1990s and their development of several successful television series. At the end of the 1980s, there were only seven animated series produced in China, with only 47 episodes in production by all animation studios combined. This low level of production was addressed through the launch of nine National Animation Industry Bases across mainland China by the middle of the 2000s. The annual gross from animated television series increased by 20 per cent from 2005 to 2012 due to this new infrastructure and government support. More than 73 per cent of the newly produced animation series saw distribution from these national bases. From 1995 to 2012, the dominant call by defining animation as a commercial product, as well as the expectations highlighted by the state's cultural policy, have attributed to a year-on-year increase in the domestic production of animation. By 2011, the local animation studios produced a total of 435 episodes (about 261,224 minutes in length) of youth-oriented animated series; and in 2012 there were 395 episodes (222,938 minutes) repeated on air in mainland China.[4] Significant productions in 2011 and 2012 include: *Blue Cat's Three Thousand Questions* (424 episodes), *Star Wars* (384 episodes), *The Dinosaur Era* (264 episodes), *Seaworld* (312 episodes), *Sports* (226 episodes), *Cosmic Aviation* (400 episodes),[5] and *Pleasant Goat and Big Bad Wolf* (1,050 episodes).[6]

China's animation industry has shown its cultural power by taking a leading role in the development of the country's rising creative industry. In light of this productivity, new animation series are aesthetically sophisticated and have high production values, and are based either on simple storytelling models for a child-oriented demographic or provide scientific and moral education narratives for a more adult demographic. These works also often adopt classic plots from sources such as Chinese myths, folklore and moral fables with animal characters. Here the aesthetic authority of the Chinese School had been destabilized and frequently translated as a kind of visual parody which marked a pragmatic farewell to the mimicry of Chinese traditional animation culture.

To better understand Chinese animation, it is crucial to analyse the contradictory relationships between the state, the audience and the domain of digitized visual production. Chinese scholars have yet to develop a historical and theoretical model to examine both the hegemony of the Chinese School and the range of cultural consequences that have resulted from the aesthetic interactions between computer technology and Chinese animation. Animators and Chinese audiences were convinced that computerization and a mutual exchange between traditional visual culture and digital technology would lead to the production of China's own animated blockbusters. Assumptions about the ideological power of animation suddenly assumed a reflective, flag-waving position from which to pursue the renaissance of a decaying glory of the past generation of Chinese animation.

Much of the problem lies in separating the techno-cultural machine of the animation industry, which is influenced by official state discourse and the visual narratives that are generated by it. The former became entangled within the metaphors of state discourse and adopted systematic procedures to enhance Chinese notions of an animation industry, while the latter faced the danger of being trapped in a wonderland of Oriental spectacles that constitute 'not simply feelings of nostalgia' but also, as Rey

Chow notes, 'involve a coeval, co-temporal structure of representation at moments of cultural crisis.'[7]

The coming of age of independent animation

Following the widespread desire for a shift in the production of animation – and coupled with the rise in state discourse to redefine the cultural industry in China – more and more of the country's universities and arts academies promised to lead animation to the forefront of creative innovation in the People's Republic of China (PRC). Two leading animation schools in China, the Animation School of the Beijing Film Academy and the Animation and Digital Arts School at the Communication University of China, both contributed significantly to the empowerment and diversification of independent animation filmmaking in China, especially as more and more students enrolled in these schools' degree courses. As the direct consequence of this engagement, one began to see independent animation reappear after a 60-year absence in China's film history, caused by advances in digital technology.

The term 'independent animation' was introduced to Chinese animators and scholars in 2002, when Rebecca Jean Bristow gave a speech at the Chinese Cartoon Industry Forum entitled 'Animation Education in China,' where she explained that independent animation in the United States had broadened its creative practices and would be helpful to Chinese animation education.[8] The term was then used in 2003 to name the Chinese Independent Animation Festival, which was organized by the UltraGirl Animation Studio – a venture co-founded in 2000 by the band New Pants, which sold albums to support its work in clay animation. The small festival was held at the Beijing 22 Film Café and exhibited the works of independent animators (mostly students).

Independent Chinese animation in its present form has flourished owing to computer technology, with the internet providing a platform on which individual animated works could be made and distributed both nationally and globally without the intervention of industry professionals. This independent animation is not homogenous, and can be divided into three broad groups. The first group is the researchers in computer graphics and students of animation who help the mainstream Chinese media update their skills in visual effects. The second group comprises individual animators (usually industry insiders) with backgrounds in professional animation making; this group usually works for non-government run studios or commercial animation companies. The third group includes self-taught animators, most of whom have little or no previous experience in making or producing animation works and who relate to the rise in amateurism in China's cultural sphere.

In the late 1990s, Chinese animation experienced a subversive revolution in its visual narratives following the spread of independent animation and computer graphic activities such as computer game animation, special effects in film and television, and animated messages for mobile phones. At the same time, the mainstream Chinese animation industry struggled to compete with the popularity of its Western counterparts – such as Pixar in the United States and Aardman in the United Kingdom. Most animators who had either worked for government-run animation studios, or been employed by Western or Japanese animation companies, began to establish or co-found animation studios to challenge domestic cultural stagnation and the frenzy of downloading blockbuster film animation from California (particularly *Toy Story* (1995)) and from Bristol, England (particularly *Wallace and Gromit: The Wrong Trousers* (1993)). For instance, Jun Meng, the director of *Talk* (2001),[9] joined the team of BlackAnt Studio (which focuses on hand-drawn animations) when he left an animation company in Shenzhen and returned to Beijing to move back to pre-digital animation. Jun had become dissatisfied with the decline of traditional animation and the emergence of the Western and Japanese animation industry in China, and finally began to explore the creative possibilities of independent animation, which meant that he could at least make something he wanted to be seen publicly.

Talk was one of two independent animated films shown at the Unrestricted New Image Festival in 2001; the other was UltraGirl Studio's clay animation *I Love You*.[10] The festival also featured 104 digital documentaries and live-action fiction shorts that were produced between 1996 and July 2001. *Talk* was a hit among internet users and gained attention from both animators and animation fans. The animation draws on cultural memory through the lens of a boy's old camera, as it captured the Cultural Revolution, his first love, and inspired his passion for photography.

Since the release of these two seminal animated films in 2001, the everyday life of Chinese people is now a common narrative trope in independent animations such

Figure 3.1 *Talk*, directed by Meng Jun. BlackAnt Animation Studio, 2001.

as *Snow*[11] and *Life*.[12] *Snow* draws a vivid picture of the urban life of young students, while *Life* comes to narrate a one-day story of the romantic but simple life of suburban Chinese lower classes. These animated films offered a fresh perspective on the lives of ordinary Chinese people, but the opportunities to take this kind of creative approach to social reality are so limited that only a few independent animators work in this area today.

This dialectic between new technology and older storytelling techniques is encapsulated in many scenes in recent animated films where digital technology opens a window for independent animators to construct the storylines and characters they want, while still occupying, in a nostalgic mode, the grand narrative space fashioned by classical elite literature in China. Two examples of this digital/traditional binary are *Pond*[13] and *Ode to Summer*.[14] These animation films borrow conventions and iconography from traditional Chinese landscape paintings: 'yellowing' the background to mimic ancient canvas and using line-typed characters to flatten the pictorial plain. Since the mid-1980s, the main Chinese animation studios, Shanghai Animation Studio and Changchun Film Studio, have not produced traditional water and ink animations due to the expense and complicated nature of the process. Water and ink animated practices can be used to evoke nostalgia, but use of technologies that mimic water and ink effects can potentially narrate another story of cultural nostalgia, a story focusing on a commercialized souvenir of a traditional process rather than on the process itself.

Without the Academic Awards, many independent animators would not have the opportunity to display their work in China. Flash animation can gain a wide audience on the internet, but non-Flash independent animation often malfunctions on the internet, due to the challenges related to transforming file formats. Indeed, many

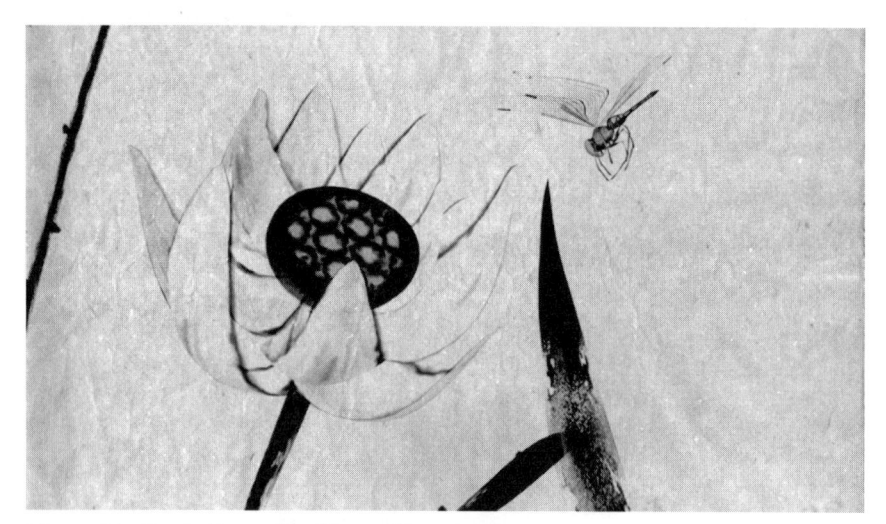

Figure 3.2 *Pond*, directed by Huang Ying, 2003.

independent animation websites have disappeared due to evolutions in technique, technology and animators' lack of interest in maintaining their sites. Even websites with up-to-date information have many links that are out of date. For example, on the *Animation Kitchen* clay animation website of Chen Zhang, Xinning Xie and Bo Cai, the demonstration links on the 'Introduction to our Work' page is no longer connected to a URL. This is also the case on UltraGirl Studio's website, tintoon.com. Nonetheless, the Animation Sky Studio – operated by Yihui Chui, Da Li, Xiaoping Zhou, Yue Wu and others – launched anisky.com to distribute their creative and commercial projects, create an animators' community, and build up an independent channel for Chinese clay animation. While independent animation does not have much of an online presence, there are a few internet sites that offer stable channels for uploading independent animations. For instance, chinanim.com, the website of the Chinese Animation Association, includes all fields of animation in China. Although most of its content comes from state-sponsored media/animation companies, it also offers a space for experimental, independent animation. Before this site went live, Chinese audiences did not get a chance to watch *Talk* or *Ode to Summer* until they were released on this website.

Animated shorts like *The Butterfly Lovers* benefited from China's cultural tradition of unlimited expression afforded by the shadow play of the pre-industrialized era, the cinema/television screen of classical animation from different modernist periods, and the digital interface of trans-media animation in the computer era. Even with the difficulties involved in making and distributing animation, independent work still paved the way for an effective usage of digital technology for creativity ingenuity.

Independent Chinese animation emerged in the 1990s concurrently with independent live-action films from Sixth Generation filmmakers, digital video and the newly formed cyberculture. Global digitization altered the cultural interface so that style became even more important than essence in contemporary China, leaving animators to busily reconfigure the visual style of Chinese culture. This transformation, however, created a remarkable opportunity to see the world and Chinese animation anew.

The rise and fall of flash animation during the 2000s

As dramatic cultural changes swept through China in the 1990s, Chinese audiences witnessed a new form of independent animation practice online, the Flash animation short. Flash is a software program designed by the US-based Adobe company that was initially regarded primarily as a web-based design tool in China. It has proven resilient and popular, with applications for practical forms of web design and development, as well for creating autonomous works of animation. Flash had a considerable impact on animation in China, accumulating an astounding 50,000 animated works produced online, by mostly anonymous animators. The popularity of Flash among Chinese animators and fans is part of a trend involving the global expansion and the redefinition of visual narrative storytelling beyond the realm of traditional moving image works and into the various regions of cyberspace.

The histories of animation, computing and cyberculture in China are quite distinct from those of the West in important ways. Important differences include: the more recent emergence of China as a global economic power; the fact that the state's control and monitoring of the internet is much more heavy-handed and overt in China; and the presence of both statutory and unofficial mechanisms of censorship in China on a large scale. These factors have meant that the first Chinese animators who used Flash were independent artists, designers and hobbyists who had no connection with the official, state-sponsored and state-regulated animation industry. For some animators, Flash was appealing in no small measure because it provided a means of developing a form of unofficial, alternative popular expression. Consequently, as a social phenomenon, Flash encouraged new areas and intensities of involvement with the world of digital culture in general, taking Chinese animators and fans at least obliquely into the midst of discussions about the relationship between globalization and national culture, not to mention those involving dimensions of personal expression. Thus Flash culture in China is part of a much wider trend incorporating all forms of creative expression, from painting, sculpture and fiction-writing to filmmaking and popular music.

In pursuit of this new Flash visuality and by the beginning of the 2000s, we must admit that these two areas of social development are comparatively immature in China. The Flash dream draws on a range of often interlocking motivations: on the one hand, there is a desire for personal expression in a society that is becoming increasingly integrated into a global popular culture where techno-fetishism has value; and on the other hand, knowledge of this program benefits those eager to find work in creative or tech fields of employment now that China is more integrated into the global economy. Flash animation, arguably, has a strong symbolic resonance in China, especially in relation to a burgeoning youth subculture that is closely aligned with consumerism and some of the most visible aspects of the expanding digital realm. The popularity of Flash as a do-it-yourself medium of self-expression for non-professional animators (and their fans) is quite logical in an evermore media-saturated environment that increasingly favours vivid visual imagery over the printed word (although online bulletin boards, blog-writing, podcasting are quite popular in China, too). Many users associate Flash with the idea of self-expression, which also helps to explain the comparative importance of the Flash aesthetic in China – it is a tool not just for building eye-catching websites, but also for contributing to the construction of a new self-identity in post-WTO China.

On 21 November 1999, FlashEmpire.com posted its first list of the 40 most popular Chinese Flash animations (measured by click count).[15] As a constantly updated chronicle of activity, this 'top forty' list has become crucially important to the development of Flash culture in China. During the first 12 months of the list's existence, 533 different animations made the list, including 373 independently produced animations, 133 website demos and 27 commercial advertisements. One of the first milestones of Chinese Flash animation to appear on the list was Jiang Jianqiu's[16] (known online as

Lao Jiang) 'Rock 'n' roll on the New Long March' (*Xin changzheng lu shang de yaogun*), a visual interpretation of one of the most famous songs of Cui Jian. The success of Jiang's animated music video led to a September 2000 feature in the magazine *Sanlian Life Weekly* entitled 'Big Talk with Flash animators,' which gave an overview of Flash technology and an introduction to three Flash animators – Jiang Jianqiu, Qi Zhaohui (known online as *BBQI*) and Zhu Zhaoxi (known online as *Baiding*). This marked the domestic mainstream media's first acknowledgement of Chinese Flash animation.

The most prominent indication of the growing importance of this new medium occurred between 18 April and 15 August 2001, when the First Chinese Pentium 4 Computer Game and Flash Animation Festival was held. Mainstream media outlets started to report regularly on new developments in Flash animation, and 2001 was officially designated as the year of Chinese Flash. But for many Chinese pop culture junkies who had not yet climbed onto the Flash bandwagon, the turning point was Xuecun's online music video, 'People from the Northeast Are All Living Lei Fengs' (*Dongbeiren doushi huo LeiFeng*),[17] produced by Tu Liyi (known online as Babylon, and in Chinese as *Beibeilong*). This video got the ball rolling, and Flash-animated music videos were soon all the rage in China. This was a dramatic change for Chinese flash animators, whose popularity was previously confined to an online subculture of fellow true believers; now, though, their work was celebrated by fans and critics who had only recently learned what Flash animation was. The first significant mainstream television exposure for Flash came on the employment-counselling programme *Choose* (*Xuanze*), broadcast on CCTV–10 on 9 September 2001. Subsequently, in late 2001 and early 2002, Qi Zhaohui and Jiang Jianqiu created nine animated segments for a special feature entitled 'Showing Marvelous Ability' (*Shengong jiemi*) on the CCTV talk show *Tell the Truth* (*Shihua shishuo*). The assimilation of Flash by the mainstream media seemed complete by 6 June 2002, with the CCTV–7's broadcast of the first of 85 all-Flash episodes of the animated children's series *Bang Bang English*, created by Beijing River Culture Development Ltd. Still, despite this surge of mass media acceptance, the tools and styles associated with the Flash phenomenon, not to mention its subcultural origins, have led some Chinese scholars to regard the form and its independent practitioners as a welcome, utterly 'modern' challenge to traditional pictorial and literary forms with the potential to break through the limitations of 'old media' forms and pave a digital path to the new media with Chinese characteristics.

Meanwhile, Chinese avant-garde artists, drama directors and independent filmmakers began to adopt the visual elements of Flash animation into their works by incorporating the previously marginalized web-based animation style into the avant-grade artistic spaces. In May 2001, the Chinese musical drama director Zhang Guangtian invited two well-known flash animators, Jiang Jianqiu and Qi Zhaohui, to create four animations for his new stage drama *Mr. Lu Xun*. This was the first attempt to transfer Flash animation to 16mm film in China, and it was an indication of the degree of cultural and artistic capital the form was now enjoying. Under such conditions, Chinese popular culture critics and fans alike began to recognize Flash as a genuine phenomenon. The form contained several ingredients that marked it as a significant element within the 'new' cultural scene: unusual visual rhythms and styles,

Figure 3.3 'May Fourth Movement,' Mr. Lu Xun, directed by Jiang Jianqiu, 2001.

irreverent themes, nonsensical humour, and the unmistakable presence of genuinely idiosyncratic, individual imaginations.

Besides the original, self-identified Flash animators, there are other individuals in loose creative alliances that are also devoted to the theory and practice of Flash, with enthusiasts often gathering in cyber forums to share production techniques and story ideas. These are mostly animators or younger fine artists who are dissatisfied with the lingering state belief that animation is a medium only suitable for children. The fact that Flash is relatively easy to learn has allowed people to begin to quickly create their own work, and as the latest converts gain expressive ability and confidence, some of them begin to identify themselves as professional animators. A number of the animation films by these artists are well-crafted and have shown commercial potential. These include Bu Hua's *Maomao's Summer, Cat* and *Heart*;[18] Yang Ge's *Paradise Garden, Imagination* and *One Day*;[19] Ma Lin's *New Youth*;[20] Doupi's *Nostalgia Series* and *Western Liang Series*;[21] and Shi Huang's *Pobaby Series*.[22] Most of these works are, to borrow from Maureen Furniss's description of aesthetic intensity in the thematic structure of compilation films, '…meditative or poetic in nature, exploring experience, emotion or other abstract concepts in depth. They also tend to be highly subjective to and rely on abstract concept imagery, which might provide the only means of expressing an ineffable notion.'[23] Meanwhile, a number of Flash animators have developed pictorial methods that simulate traditional Chinese animation's self-conscious allegiance with forms of fine art painting and folk expression, as well as styles associated with the Western avant-garde.

The Flash animator Bu Hua's works simulate the modernist woodcut style in an act of commemorating a lost (and more idealistic) world, and through stories that focus on subjects such as love, emotion, family relationships and childhood fables. One key work, entitled *Maomao's Summer*,[24] combines film, woodcut printing and Manga influences to construct a commentary on the destruction of Beijing's *hutongs* (and their replacement by pre-fabricated and anonymous apartment complexes that reflect China's neoliberal turn) seen from the perspective of the main character.[25] The activity that is so lyrically chronicled in this animation is not only a contemporary reality, but the work seems to be a commentary on the confusing nature and destruction of childhood in postsocialist China, as Maomao constructs her memorial to the past with the waste products of modern consumer culture.

Chinese Flash animators can be seen as facing a contradictory dilemma similar to Maomao's. The mass commercialization of their once-marginal creative form looms large: the influence of Western fine art and popular culture tendencies and styles is ubiquitous, and the connections to indigenous forms and aesthetics appear to be fading. For instance, Yang Ge's work looks like a post-Impressionist painting. Yang's *Paradise Garden*[26] opens with an illustrator's daydream, expressed in bold, hypersaturated colours, of the dichotomy between the world of reality and a New Age fantasyland (accompanied by an Enya song) that is a refuge for fatigued and lonely souls. At the end of the story, a visualization of the 'real world' is replaced by the animator's daydream, and the protagonist enters a fairyland dreamspace to enjoy a series of hyperreal illusions. As this description suggests, Yang Ge's work is also marked by a strong use of symbolism and elements of mysticism.

Such an overt embracing of highly subjective motifs is significantly at odds with the historically realist basis of Chinese animation. Some animators have self-consciously created works based on earlier popular and folk culture styles, including the four-frame comic strip, paper-cut, Chinese shadow puppetry and Spring Festival paintings (*Nianhua*). Ma Lin's *New Youth*, for instance, adapts the four-frame strip cartoon and features a figure wearing a Chinese cap, accompanied by background music played on an *erhu* (a Chinese stringed instrument that resembles a violin). Doupi's *Western Liang Series* combines a muted colour palette dominated by browns and grays with Flash emulations of watercolour painting and Chinese shadow puppets in order to illustrate the animator's personal philosophical sketches (which appear as onscreen text). Doupi also experiments with a simulation of the paper-cut style to create the *Nostalgic Series*. Her work is rather introspective and non-narrative, with animations that provide impressionistic visual accompaniments to her poetic musings. One distinctive element of her style is the use of an onscreen signature in the form of a traditional Chinese seal. Shanke typically include their personal Web URLs and online names in the credits of their animations, but Doupi's seal is unusual in that it explicitly combines the technology of the digital interface with an element of classical Chinese representation. This 'flattening two-dimensionality' of temporal factors is itself a frequently cited postmodernist trope, a situation characteristic of many forms of contemporary audiovisual culture in which the component parts of a work are appropriated from a variety of historical sources, both temporally and spatially. Many Flash animators, in China and elsewhere, operate within this digital cultural logic.

The global diffusion of the key technological tools, as well as some kinds of animation products, mean that Chinese artists can draw from both the traditional aesthetic principles of indigenous animation and all relevant Western artistic genres. Flash has built up a commercial visibility, based initially on the individual and collaborative pioneering of such techniques and then on the aesthetic and stylistic refinements by more skilled animators. This led, in the space of less than three years, to the emergence of an identifiable commercialized studio system working on Flash animation. This group includes independent animators such as Gan Tao (known online as *Labi X*), Tan Beilin (known online as *Zhouye*, a partner of *Ziyou kongqi*), He Dihe (known online as *Ranfang hu*), He Yi, Cheng Tao (known online as *Shanke Taotao*), Yang Yue (known online as *Piaomiao chenfeng*) and Li Mingming (known online as *Yila guan*); and animation studios including E-TOON Creation Co., Ltd, XOYTO Comic, Snail Studio, Miaoyin Motion Pictures, B&T Studio, Pacoo, Sinodoor Animation,[27] and others. At this point, the cultural location and significance of Flash in China is still evolving, and some of its most talented purveyors have decided to take their talents mainstream, caught up in China's consumerist fever.

In the short span of ten years, the Flash phenomenon has contributed significantly to the transformation of animation in China. Critics of the form are often alarmed by the potential of Flash (and other primarily visual forms of digital narrative) to displace 'acceptable' modes of expression, especially given the degree to which these new forms are infected with the twin viruses of consumerism and individualism. Along these lines, Flash might be seen as one of several popular contemporary styles that have generated an immersive crash course on the tropes of postmodernity for Chinese users and audiences.

Flash animation has been a significant factor contributing to the breakdown of boundaries between independent and mainstream animation culture and has provided audiences with a vehicle for expressing and sharing complex sentiments. It has given them a means to simultaneously embrace and ridicule pop mythologies; deconstruct the social structures of an acutely immediate, often painful present; immerse themselves in liberating nonsense; and give themselves the luxury of relaxing with slackly cute and clichéd humour and sentiment.

Chinese Flash animation's heyday ended with the rise of online video making and sharing around 2010. Flash empire.com closed its business of hosting Flash animators and their work, and most of these brilliant animators have all but disappeared. Even though the state-sponsored independent animation festival and animation-industry support helped create a cultural scene for Flash animators, it is still hard for them to find large audiences. Animated television series are once again the dominant form of Chinese animation consumed on a national scale in series such as *Pleasant Goat and Big Bad Wolf* (*xiyangyang yu huitailang*) and *Watch out for the Bear* (*xiong chu mo*).

Conclusion: Individuality, state discourse and visual representation

In recent years, Chinese animators have faced difficult aesthetic and cultural dilemmas that have been common to innovative Chinese artists in all media since the early twentieth century: how to articulate (and rearticulate) the narrative of China's modernization into artistic language, and how to nurture the aesthetic development of animation arts. Since the mid-1980s, China's Fifth and Sixth Generation film directors and reform era avant-garde visual artists have explored avenues of self-expression and artistic experimentation in ways that were seen as taboo since at least 1949. Animators have explored similar thematic subtexts, both in industry and in independent contexts, and their journeys of discovery have taken place in a public arena far closer to the centre of contemporary popular cultural trends and aspirations than most Chinese fine artists and art filmmakers have been able to enter. In a very real sense, Chinese animation – especially independent animation – is at the heart of the iGeneration's changes of cultural identity in the digital era.

In recent decades, Chinese animation has navigated between state-framed discourse and individual artistic representation. Through this process, Chinese animation filmmakers have drawn a sophisticated map to show their audience the linkages between ideology, individuality and creativity. Chinese animation has reflected both the historical changes of the socialist cultural policy and the postsocialist market-driven industrialization, and paved a path for independent animators, amateur filmmakers and spectators of today's iGeneration.

Works cited

Bristow, Rebecca Jean. 'Animation Education in China' in *Chinese Cartoon Industry Forum*. Hangzhou, China, 2002.
Chow, Rey. *Primitive Passions: Visuality, Sexuality, Ethnography, and Contemporary Chinese Cinema*. Film and Culture. New York: Columbia University Press, 1995.
Dolphin, Laurie and Stuart Shapiro. *Flash Frames: A New Pop Culture*. New York: Watson-Guptill Publications, 2002.
Furniss, Maureen. *Art in Motion: Animation Aesthetics*. London: John Libbey, 1998.
Jin, Delong. 'Animation Industry Takes the Leading Role of Cultural Industry in China' in *The 2012 China Animation Industry Annual Conference*, Hangzhou, China, 2012.
Li, Fang. '"China-Made" Called for in Cultural Products (Zhong Guo Zhi Zao Hu Huan Wen Hua Chan Pin),' *People's Daily Overseas Edition*, 2005, 1.
Shi, Jiaoying and Zhigeng Pan. 'China: computer graphics education available at universities, institutes and traning centers,' *Computer Graphics* 3 (August 1996): 31.
Tan, Fei. 'Computer Special Effects: Give Wings to the Cinematic Imagination (Dian Nao Te Ji, Gei Dian Ying Cha Shang Huan Xiang De Chi Bang),' *Beijing Youth*, August 1, 1995, 7.
Wu, Weihua. 'In memory of meishu film: catachresis and metaphor in theorizing Chinese animation.' *Animation: An Interdisciplinary Journal* 4, no. 1 (2009): 53–76.

Notes

1 Wan Brothers, namely Wan Guzhan, Wan Laiming, Wan Chaochen and Wan Dihuan were the first generation of Chinese animation filmmakers in 1930s; they produced some shorts, such as such as *Citizen, Wake Up!* (Shanghai Lianhua Film Company, 1931), *Sincere Solidarity* (Shanghai Lianhua Film Company, 1932), *Detective Dog* (Mingxing Film Company, 1933), *Price of Blood, Painful Story of the Nation, The Year of Chinese Goods* and *Motherland Is Saved by Aviation* (all Mingxing Film Company, 1934) etc., and the first feature animation *The Princess of Iron Fan* (Shanghai Lianhe Film Company, 1941) .
2 Wu, Weihua. 'In memory of meishu film: catachresis and metaphor in theorizing Chinese animation.' *Animation: An Interdisciplinary Journal* 4, no. 1 (2009): 53–76.
3 I borrowed this translation from *People's Daily Online*. For more information, see http://english.people.com.cn/200511/23/eng20051123_223463.html (accessed 6 March 2014).
4 Jin, Delong. 'Animation Industry Takes the Leading Role of the Cultural Industry in China' in *The 2012 China Animation Industry Annual Conference*. Hangzhou, China, 2012.
5 *Blue Cat's Three Thousand Questions* [*Lanmao taoqi sanqianwen*]. Hunan Sunshine Cartoon Group, 1999 till now. It was first aired on Beijing Television's Channel 8 in October 1999. The broadcasting network included 700 local and overseas television stations in 2000. It was once aired simultaneously on 1,012 television stations, with 13 local satellite television stations.
6 Produced by Creative Power Entertaining. The show is about a group of goats fighting against a clumsy wolf that wants to eat them, which has been becoming enormously popular with Chinese school children since its debut in 2005. It is aired on over 50 local TV stations, including Hong Kong's TVB, BTV Animation Channel and CCTV. As of 2011, an English dub has been aired in Taiwan. In 2010 Disney gained the licence to broadcast the popular children's show on their Disney Channels.
7 Chow, Rey. *Primitive Passions: Visuality, Sexuality, Ethnography, and Contemporary Chinese Cinema*. Film and Culture. New York: Columbia University Press, 1995.
8 Bristow, Rebecca Jean. 'Animation Education in China' in *Chinese Cartoon Industry Forum*. Hangzhou, China, 2002.
9 *Talk* (*Liaotian*). Directed by Mengjun. BlackAnt Animation Studio, 2001.
10 *I Love You* (*Wo ai ni*). Directed by Peng Lei. Beijing, UltraGirl Clay Animation Studio, 2001.
11 *Snow* (*Xue*). Directed by Sun Tian. 2003.
12 *Life* (*Shenghuo*). Directed by Han Bo. 2003.
13 *Pond* (*Tang yun*). Directed by Huang Ying. Beijing, Beijing Film Academy, 2003, DVD.
14 *Ode to Summer* (*Xia*). Directed by Xu Wei. Shenzhen, IDMT Ltd., 2003, DVD.
15 The list was regularly updated before 2006.
16 His information was available at http://www.heaventown.com/ before 2007. Some of Jiang's Flash animations were also available at http://flash.tom.com before 2007.
17 Lei Feng, a People's Liberation Army soldier who died in the line of duty, became a famous quasi-folk hero on the basis of his diary, in which he chronicled many instances of selfless service for the glory of the motherland.

18 Bu Hua. *Maomao's Summer* (*Maomao de xiatian*), 2002; Cat (*Mao*), 2003; Heart (*Xin*), 2003. Bu Hua's works are available at http://www.buhua.com (accessed October 2004.)
19 Yang Ge. *Paradise Garden* (*Tiantang huayuan*), 2002; Imagination (*Huangxiang*), 2002; One Day, 2005. Yang Ge's works are available at http://www.yangge.com (accessed October 2004.)
20 Ma Lin. *New Youth* (*Xin qingnian*), 2002.
21 Doupi. *Nostalgia Series* (*Huaijiu xilie*), 2002–3; Western Liang Series (*Xiliang Xianhua*), 2002–3. The Western Liang was a short-lived (400–421 AD), northern kingdom of the 16 Kingdoms Era. Its capitals were Dunhuang and Jiuquan in Gansu. Doupi's animations are available at: http://doupi.com/xl_download.htm (accessed October 2004).
22 Shihuang. Pobaby (*Xiao pohai*), 2002–6. The name Pobaby was translated by Shihuang from a form of Chinese northern slang that often was used to scold naughty kids. Available at http://www.shihuang.com/ (accessed October 2004).
23 Furniss, Maureen. *Art in Motion: Animation Aesthetics*. London: John Libbey, 1998.
24 Available at http://www.buhua.com/flash/maomao.html (accessed October 2004).
25 The onscreen titles read (the approximate syntax is in the original English translation): 'Maomao is an ordinary child, one day she found the beauty of the dismantling of old Beijing houses, For the first time, she noticed there are *chai* (a character marking a building for demolition) everywhere. She knows the saying "Out with the old and in with the new." But who else would bother to look back at those dismantled houses like looking back on old times? Maomao decided to build a "city" to memorize the disappearing old houses. All the materials would come from the old houses. She goes to collect all the materials. Ten days later…'
26 Listed in the sub-category of 'New Media Art', http://www.yangge.com/yangge.htm (accessed October 2004). Also available at http://flash.tom.com/flash_show.php?user=flash_yangge&id=30719 (accessed October 2004).
27 See http://www.e-toon.com.cn/; http://www.xoyto.com/; http://www.snailcn.com/; http://www.miaoyin.org/; http://www.xxbt.com/; http://www.pacoo.net/; http://www.sinodoor.com/

4

Cinema of Exhibition: Film in Chinese Contemporary Art

Dong Bingfeng

In conversation with Tianqi Yu
Translated by Hui Miao

Dong Bingfeng is regarded as one of the most active curators and art critics working on Chinese contemporary art and visual culture in mainland China today. In the past eight years he has worked at several different contemporary art museums, including the Guangdong Art Museum, Ullens Center for Contemporary Art and Iberia Center for Contemporary Art. At these leading art institutions, he explored the nature and ontology of the 'moving image' in its various forms – video art, new media art, video and film installations – pushing the boundaries of the various forms and deconstructing the moving image culture. Currently, Dong is the artistic director at the Li Xianting Film Fund, where he has implemented an intensive exploration into artists' films shown in gallery spaces, or what has been recently referred to as 'cinema of exhibition.' *China's iGeneration* co-editor Tianqi Yu interviewed Dong Bingfeng on the emerging field of 'cinema of exhibition,' and in the interview Dong shares some of his views on cinema and moving image culture, particularly among China's current iGeneration.

****

> *Tianqi Yu: As a curator, art critic, and the current artistic director at Li Xianting Film Fund, can you please introduce the kinds of projects Li Xianting Film Fund is involved in, and what your engagement with moving image curation is at this organization?*
>
> Bingfeng Dong: Since taking over at Li Xianting Film Fund, my work is naturally integrated with the agenda of the Film Fund in the area of independent films and documentaries, especially in terms of research and film festival curation. Chinese contemporary art and independent film have been purposefully

put together as an important combination through which to explore the interrelatedness and differences of these two moving image cultures.

In China's specific social and political environment, the Li Xianting Film Fund mainly focuses on four areas of work: film archiving, research and publications, developing our film academy, and promotion of film festivals. In recent years, the Film Fund has been under great pressure from official state control. Recently, a large number of the established public film events have been either called off or prohibited from taking place, which has forced us to consider focusing our future work on two main areas: film archiving, and research and publications. These seemingly static and interior areas can in fact be a very effective way to support the Film Fund's academic direction and influence, especially in terms of expanding the space and nature of the exhibition, as well as attracting new resources to foster international cooperation, which remains very important for the future existence of the Film Fund. In 2012, the Film Fund published a book series on film directors, showcasing works by moving image artists who have experience in multiple creative fields in film and contemporary art, such as Tsai Ming-liang from Taiwan, Yang Fudong from China, and Raqs Media Collective from India. This will become our primary research focus and theme for the year 2013.

Yu: *How is the artist film being accepted by young Chinese filmmakers today?*

Dong: Currently in China – apart from the Yunnan Multi Culture Visual Festival, which focuses on documentaries – experimental films have been introduced to major independent film festivals in Beijing, Chongqing and Nanjing. The idea is to encourage and attract more artist films and short films with a stronger artistic quality to participate in these platforms each year. In 2010, the China Independent Film Festival in Nanjing invited me to plan a display unit on the subject of creation and presentation of Chinese contemporary art and film. Artists such as Wang Jianwei, Cao Fei, Zhou Xiaohu, Sun Xun, and other important moving image artists were invited to attend the event. Such an event was not a coincidence. In 2001, a few *minjiang* (grassroots) film groups in China jointly organized and launched China's First Unrestricted New Image Festival. The winner of the experimental film category was Yang Fudong who was, and still is, a famous moving image artist, rather than a director active in theatrical film like Jia Zhangke. Similarly, the film festivals that were initiated by our Film Fund specifically include artist films within the competition in the experimental film category, outside traditional documentary and feature film categories.

Yu: *As an emerging visual practice, cinema of exhibition has been attracting attention from a growing number of artists, curators, critics and scholars. How do you define the concept of cinema of exhibition? When was it first accepted in China and how long has it been practised by Chinese artists? Can you trace the development in the past ten years for us?*

Dong: The earliest discussions of cinema of exhibition can be traced to Taiwan rather than the mainland of China. In 2006, Pompidou Arts Centre organized an exhibition in Taiwan, showcasing a large collection of new media art. In this exhibition, the concept of cinema as an important concept for moving image practice was translated into Chinese and introduced to the Chinese language world. In 2007, after Taiwanese director Tsai Ming-Liang's filmic installation work, *It is a Dream*, was submitted to the Venice Biennale, the concept of 'cinema of exhibition' was explored by some critics in Taiwan. In mainland China, four curators – Huang Chienhong from Taiwan, Du Qingchun and Zhu Zhu from mainland China, and myself – co-sponsored and planned the project 'Looking Through Film: Traces of Cinema and Self-constructs in Contemporary Art' at Shenzhen's OCT Contemporary Art Theatre in 2010. It was the first time in China that the 'artists' film' was included in the discussion of the historical context of contemporary art in China and Taiwan in the last three decades.

In recent years, cinema of exhibition has become a very important form of creative expression and an innovative display of moving image in galleries and biennials in China. Compared to 'video art' and 'new media art' that have been accepted and integrated by museums and art critics, cinema of exhibition embraces a broader research level and thematic framework in terms of history, culture, politics and aesthetics. It is like a new subject in the creative production and exhibition of contemporary art. It is at this cultural crossroad that 'cinema of exhibition' has come into being. For example, in Luc Vancheri's study of 'contemporary film,' the obvious focus is the transformation of a concept from 'film' to 'installation.' But for Chinese contemporary art, the way films enter the space of art museums and galleries not only symbolizes a new combination of temporality and aesthetics, but also breaks the viewing experience that is led by other forms of visual art on display at art galleries. On a second level, the major shift from the screening of films at cinemas to the projection of moving images in exhibition spaces has liberated images from the confines of the theatre and offers more possibilities of future film. Just as Godard said, 'Film is no longer the prisoner of the movie theatre.'

Yu: What is the connection between cinema of exhibition and video art and independent film? In other words, what kind of different positions does the artists' 'cinema of exhibition' have in Chinese moving image creative production and Chinese contemporary art?

Dong: The emergence of Chinese video art occurred almost in the same period of the early 1990s as Chinese independent film. Furthermore, artists and film directors insisted upon strict distinctions in each other's work, which was an important phenomenon in the 1990s. In addition to making standard video art, many artists were also making documentaries and even working on fiction films, while some independent film directors also began to explore a more open-ended filmmaking that is clearly indebted to artistic experimentation. The 1990s was a very open period for moving image creation. One could say that there was an endless stream of styles and genres that were influencing and interacting with each other.

Performance art, video art and installation art are increasingly the central mainstay of Chinese contemporary art, compared to more traditional artistic media, including painting and sculpture. The emergence of video art started as a challenge to the museum classification principle. In the trend of 'internationalization' of Chinese contemporary art after the 1990s, contemporary video art and artist films became more well-known within the international art world.

Yu: *Can you give us some examples of Chinese artist films shown at international art biennales or on film festival circuits?*

Dong: For example, in Kassel, Germany, the Documentary series in 1997 and 2002 saw three Chinese artists invited to participate, whose main creative approach was the melding together of moving image, documentary and film to great effect and critical acclaim: Wang Jianwei (documentary 'Living Elsewhere'), Feng Mengbo (multimedia interaction work 'Family Album'), and Yang Fudong (film 'An Estranged Paradise').

Yu: *What key feature defines the artist film in China?*

Dong: Compared to installation art, performance art, and other artistic concepts that were greatly influenced by Western art, Chinese video art and the artist film have the distinctive qualities of being 'local' and recording Chinese social reality and history, and are not subject to the traces of 'impact-acceptance' response doctrine under the context of Western history of art. The rapid internationalization, globalization and marketization of Chinese contemporary art since the 1990s is clearly a response to the logic of the global market and cultural politics rather than a consequence of local consciousness and transformation. However, current Chinese moving image culture, both independent films and documentaries, and cinema of exhibition, have a stance of radical aesthetic transformation and social participation, such as the 'citizen documentary' series by artist Ai Weiwei.

Yu: *In this volume, we specifically focus on cinema and moving image culture since 2000, and advocate the notion of 'iGeneration' – here the little "i" can be seen as denoting the 'individual,' 'internet,' and the 'intertwined and interconnected nature of film.' What do you make of our neologism? Please anchor your response by way of your experience as a curator. How might this term be emblematic to what is happening with the artist filmmaking practice?*

Dong: In fact, my view is not very optimistic. On the one hand, more and more artist films are restricted by the mechanisms of the museum system and the art market. On the other hand, the so-called independent film and independent art productions have become self-institutionalized. By saying 'self-institutionalized,' I mean filmmakers and artists operate with a preconceived notion before they produce work, particularly for what is acceptable by the museums or market. The artwork or films are therefore produced for that purpose rather than being pure creative acts, or experiments in form.

> Yu: Regarding the collection of work: we know that the mechanism of 'art collection' in the art world has to a great extent challenged the way that film is distributed – through theatrical release and more recently through DVDs and then online streaming. However, the codified reproduction of digital media is also challenging the conventional way that art is being collected. Or should the meaning of 'collection' in contemporary art change, facing this new form of art practice? What do you think?

Dong: In mainland China, the emergence of cinema of exhibition or artist film is a form of resistance to discourses and commercial tendencies found within the mechanisms of the museum system and the art market. Just as we spoke about before, the 'self-institutionalization' of video art or new media, the emergence of exhibition film must be based on a form of resistance to certain commercial purposes or the art exhibition system itself. Naturally, it should be a response to theoretical issues or themes of practice that are not covered or discussed in the history of art and film. What it aims for should not be a fixed art form, but to go beyond the constraints of contemporary moving image practices and exhibition patterns, and constantly throw up more questions and issues for the viewer, or the potential revolutionary.

The birth of Chinese video art

However, its (the combination of video and installation) target audience is not the viewer in front of the television, rather it is the visitor at the scene of the installation. – Lin Zhonglu[1]

The main concern in cinema of exhibition is how to imagine the relationship with the mass public from the art works. – Jean-Christophe Royoux[2]

From the perspective of curating, divergent opinions surrounding 'the origin myth' of Chinese video art are clearly articulated through four research and exhibition projects that took place consecutively in mainland China. These four cases are: *New Media Archaeology* at the 2009 Shanghai eArts Festival; *Looking Through Film: Traces of Cinema and Self-constructs in Contemporary Art* at Shenzhen's OCAT Contemporary Art Centre in 2010; *Out of the Box: The Threshold of Video Art in China 1984–1988* at Guangzhou's Times Art Museum in 2011; and *Moving Image in China 1988–2011* at Shanghai's Minsheng Art Museum. More recently, *Chinese*

Realities/Documentary Vision 1988–2013 at the Museum of Modern Art (MoMA) in New York in May 2013 further confirmed the narrative of how Chinese video art came into being.

In November 1988, Zhang Peili, an artist from Hangzhou, introduced and presented one of his moving image productions (called *30x30*) at the 'Huangshan Meeting,' which is considered to be the inaugural meeting that led to the 'China Avant-Garde' exhibition in 1989. *30x30* was at the time, and is still today, regarded as the first Chinese video art work by many art critics and historians. Its content and production process were very simple; but the films in the exhibition are very powerful in compositional arrangement and use the video format to play simultaneously with materiality and spatiality. To accomplish this effect, Zhang began by holding a 30cm square piece of glass at a height of 40cm from the ground and then dropped it, shattering the plate glass on the floor. The broken pieces were glued back together with '502 glue,' a strong adhesive widely used in China at the time. The same process was then repeated until the videotape ran out. The original version of *30x30* was 180 minutes in length, which was the longest available running time for Beta videotapes in this period. Many leading art historians, critics and now film scholars view this production process and the content of this video art work as a form of clever assemblage. In many ways, Zhang's practice was closely linked with the so-called '85 New Wave' of Chinese contemporary art.[3] Video art came into being in China not in response to Western art history or to the development of video art in the West. Rather, it was an unconscious 'action' that started from performance art in China. In fact, the early stage of Chinese video art was filled with this kind of 'image of concept' which places an emphasis on the recording of artistic behaviour.

It was not until two key events in 1990 and 1996 that video art entered into the canon of Chinese contemporary art and became widely discussed by both Chinese and international theorists. According to many Chinese artists and critics, the story goes like this: in 1990, Professor Mijka from the Hamburg Academy of Fine Arts systematically introduced and demonstrated the techniques from Western 'video art' at the China Academy of Art in Hangzhou. Then in September 1996, the *Phenomenon/Moving Image* exhibition was held at the China Academy of Art, which for the first time comprehensively and systematically focused on and introduced research and exhibition projects on Chinese video art. The significance of *Phenomenon/Moving Image* lies in its translation of the important arguments about video art from the West. It was this theoretical platform for discussion and analysis of work that encouraged Chinese critics to submit articles and practitioners to present their own creative works in a wider context. The same happened in the early 1990s. The dramatic social changes in 1989, on the one hand, deepened the rupture between contemporary art and official art, which represented tradition and the egalitarian spirit of the proletarian class. On the other hand, these social changes accelerated the internationalization and integration of Chinese contemporary art and efforts to seek alternative spaces of production. In other words, the birth of Chinese video art was a consequence of the constant innovation and the intrinsic motivation for experimentation in Chinese contemporary art-making in the 1990s. Simultaneously, through external forces, it was advanced into dialogue and exchange in the developing global system of cultural commodity exchange. For example, several Chinese artists participated collectively in the Venice Biennale in 1993 and the Sao Paulo Biennale in 1994, which serve as two obvious examples of the internationalization of Chinese video art.

Independent film, the new documentary movement and new media art

The birth of video art in China in 1988 was not accidental, nor was it an isolated experiment in unapproved creative innovation. It is linked to another watershed moment in Chinese moving image culture that also occurred in 1988: Wu Wenguang's decision to start shooting his now-canonical independent documentary, *Bumming in Beijing*. Wu, who is considered one of the most important filmmakers of the Chinese documentary movement, started filming his debut independent documentary between 1988 and 1990. Around the same time, China's first independent film practitioner Zhang Yuan was also preparing to produce his first film, *Mama*. His previous attempt at film, *Solar Tree*, had been aborted while it was still in the planning stages. The screenplay of *Solar Tree* was from the essay 'Curved Poplar' written by the famous writer Dai Qing, who was an activist in the student movement in 1989.[4] Chinese independent art and film was dynamic and community-centred during this period. This was largely due to filmmakers' resistance against the official system and the persistence of creative freedom.

Wu Wenguang also raised his doubts over using the term 'movement' to describe his and his colleagues' work when he retrospectively examined the independent documentaries of the 1990s after a lapse of ten years. He argues that:

> So far, I still hold my doubt towards the so-called "New Documentary Movement" (including towards DV which emerged later and has been named as "DV movement," I have the same feeling of suspicion). Perhaps there have been some new ideas and ways gradually entering into the practice of these documentary makers. However, this is only contrary to the propaganda products from official TV stations. In other words, this only returns to the due concern of the documentary about people and about the existence behind the real social life.[5]

Looking back at the social atmosphere and creative production in film and art, the term 'New Documentary Movement' obviously exaggerated what was a personal and underground experiment and practice. Lü Xinyu, who coined the phrase 'New Documentary Movement,' argued that the emergence of these new documentary films in China was a move against the 'special topic films' that were produced by official TV stations before the 1990s and could be regarded as 'propaganda.' She states:

> This term was obtained in rebellion against the old established customs in the Chinese historical context in the 1980s and 1990s. It made the pursuit of documentary begin as a consensus. Consensus implied a sense of alliance because

of mutual point of reference. Rebellion then emerged as a collective behavior. The term "movement" then came into being.[6]

There are certain overlaps in the concepts and forms of production between video art, independent film and the New Documentary Movement. Some video artists produced independent documentaries, and some film directors participated in the creation of contemporary art. The artist Wang Jianwei began his documentary production in the early 1990s. His *Production* (1993) and *Living Elsewhere* (1998) are standard examples of independent documentaries. They were submitted to the Yamagata Documentary Film Festival in Japan 1999. However, the creative concepts and central themes in these works are closer to the forms of what would become known as 'artists' films.' Artists reject a seemingly objective recording of a live scene. Instead, they reconsider the interdisciplinary and cross-field propositions during the process of their artistic practice, such as the 'grey zone' that has been mentioned repeatedly by the artists. For example, artist Yang Fudong started looking for sites for filming in Hangzhou in 1997 to shoot his first black-and-white feature film *Strange Paradise* (1997–2002). The single screen works and interactive moving image works of artist Feng Mengbo were officially named as 'Feng Mengbo film.' By the late 1990s, films had undeniably entered into Chinese contemporary artists' sphere and became a major form and concept for their creative works through the emergence of the 'independent film movement' and 'New Documentary Movement.' Consequently, independent film, documentary, video art and the more complex concept of 'artists' films' together constituted a substantial part of the landscape of Chinese moving image culture.

In 2001, a few folk film groups sprung up in China, namely the 'Practice Communities' in Beijing, 'Free Cinema' in Shenyang, '101 Film Studio' in Shanghai, and 'U-thèque' in Shenzhen. Together, these groups organized and launched China's 'First Unrestricted New Image Festival.' The festival was the first major non-governmental moving image exhibition. It reviewed and concluded the overall trend for independent production in the 1990s. The short film *Backyard-Hey! Sun is Rising* (2001) by Yang Fudong won the award for Best Experimental Film.

The emergence of new media art in China was accompanied by introductions and translations of Western theories, technological developments, exhibitions and art students training at university level. Later new media art became the 'engine' in China's official art system and part of the country's process of cultural industrialization. For example, in the late 1990s, the China Academy of Art began establishing the Department of New Media Art. After the *Phenomenon/Moving Image* exhibition, Qiu Zhijie compiled *The Maturity of New Media Art 1997–2001*, in which he illustrated the phenomenon of creative production in new technologies such as CD-ROM, Flash internet art and other new multimedia formats that seemed to supersede video art. In 2001, the launch of the Loft New Media Art Centre provided an important platform and space for discussing and developing multimedia moving image practices. However, it was not until the First Beijing International New Media Arts Exhibition and Symposium in 2004 that Chinese new media art was formally recognized as a sustainable and major platform for international collaboration, dialogue and exchange.

Art galleries and biennials

As the title of this chapter indicates, there is no doubt that the concept and form of cinema of exhibition could not arise without the multimedia art practices that were first initiated in the 1980s. In 2002, the feature film *An Estranged Paradise* (1997–2002) by artist Yang Fudong was officially included in the 11th Documenta in Kassel, Germany. In his article, 'Art and Film: Some Critics and Reflections,' one of the Documenta curators, Mark Nash, argued that 'film has redefined the way that we understand contemporary art.'[7] Meanwhile, as was apparent at the first triennial *Representation: Chinese Experimental Art 1990–2000* in Guangzhou in 2002, moving image production from film, documentary and video art from the 1990s had become an important point of reference and a significant topic among the invited exhibition works.

Since 2000, both official art galleries (such as the Shanghai Art Museum and Guangdong Art Museum) and privately run art museums (such as the Chengdu Upriver Gallery, Tianjin Teda Art Museum and Shenyang Dongyu Art Museum) have been actively promoting and supporting the creation and exhibition of Chinese contemporary art. For example, in 2000, Chinese contemporary art was included for the first time as a theme in the exhibition at the Shanghai Biennale at the government-run Shanghai Art Museum. The biennale also employed an international curator system. Some critics suggest that this exhibition was the beginning of 'legitimacy' for Chinese contemporary art. Indeed, the Chinese authorities started adopting more open and more flexible policies toward art in the context of the rise of the market economy and the upcoming 2008 Olympic Games. This was in distinct contrast to the situation during the 1990s, when the authorities strictly prohibited and suppressed the practice of contemporary art. However, this is not the whole story. The partially open policy toward artistic expression was also accompanied by a coexisting ban. Censorship regarding art and film was not abolished completely – instead, it was controlled by official guidance, permission and at times tolerance.

The organization of increasingly internationalized large-scale biennial/triennial exhibitions in China has advanced the development of contemporary art even further. Differing quite remarkably from the awkward environment of artistic production and underground exhibition in the 1990s, contemporary art is becoming increasingly open in China. More art galleries and exhibition organizations are adopting organizational forms that are more cosmopolitan and experimental in nature. Multimedia art and moving image art have increasingly become the theme of major exhibitions, such as the continuous 'Beijing International New Media Arts Exhibition and Symposium' and 'Techniques of the Visible: 2004 Shanghai Biennale,' which are important representative exhibitions in terms of promoting discussion about moving image art.

If we say that 'video art' in the 1990s was the initial stage or the meaningful start of moving image art practice in China, then 'video art' or 'new media art' must be considered in relation to the creation of alternative spaces in art galleries and museums that have emerged since the 1990s. The 'Black Box'[8] has increasingly become the theme of art museums, similar to developments in the West. In these museum spaces, the technology for projectors and moving image display equipment has been updated constantly. In addition, moving image art has gradually expanded and penetrated the entire exhibition hall. In the future, perhaps the content of the moving image and audience could all become the main content of an exhibition rather than the video art that is restricted to a TV screen. In other words, the installation of video art and the new image–space relationship have greatly expanded the negotiation and tension between the exhibition works of the art galleries and the autonomy of their audiences. Art galleries no longer succumb to the static, closed artistic aesthetic and intellectual activities (such as traditional painting or sculpture exhibitions); instead, they become 'a public sphere to enter without special qualification.'[9] Video installation or cinema of exhibition are in some ways a breakthrough and are compelling Chinese contemporary art galleries to make changes.

As this discussion of art galleries and biennales has demonstrated, video installation art or the phenomenon of 'film at the art galleries' have played a significant role at Chinese art galleries since 2000. Different from cinema in the traditional sense, 'cinema' shown at art galleries must present a completely new theme and achieve breakthroughs in some aesthetic forms and narrative experiments. Perhaps cinema as exhibition should first be considered in the context of the design arts and visual arts, instead of through the discursive link between film art and film history. Song-Yong Sun states that cinema as exhibition has escaped the dimension of continuous narrative and representation and has stepped forward towards 'style,' the pure 'visual,' and the 'picture' nature of the image.'[10] According to Sun, 'film is not only a representation of knowledge and theories, but is also a combination of new technology and contemporary cultural and visual practice.'[11]

Themes explored in cinema of exhibition are not entirely irrelevant to the 'democratic' and 'public' thinking occurring at contemporary art museums in China. Some of the themes are even more intensively targeted. Without a doubt, there is a sufficient correlation between the fields of cinema as exhibition and independent cinema. Since 1989, 'independent cinema' has greatly promoted and influenced the creative production of personal auteur film. This includes the breakthroughs in the traditional film industry, such as films by the Sixth Generation directors or the 'independent films' and 'underground films' at international film festivals that have not yet passed government censorship. It also includes the 'artist film' that is the film production for certain artistic themes. This genre includes work by artists such as Zhao Liang, Wang Jianwen, Wang Fei, Jiang Zhi, as well as the series of feature films *Seven Intellectuals in Bamboo Forest* (2003–7) by Yang Fudong. In order to somehow avoid the ubiquitous form of political or ideological censorship in China, the 'artist film' or 'cinema of exhibition' at art galleries and art museums become forms of subtle and symbolic 'micro-resistance,' or images of artistic action. Especially in the forms of some exhibitions, such as multi-screening movie devices, these works of art have integrated image narrative/non-narrative ambiguity with viewers' spatial experience, suggesting and implying the coming of some democratic consciousness.

The cinema of the future

In my opinion, the question of how to face and answer the future of film is the central theme of Luc Vancheri's book *Contemporary Cinema: From Film to Installation* (*Cinémas contemporains: Du film à l'installation*).[12] From theatrical cinema to art galleries, from big screen to small screen, film has become one of the intrinsic driving forces of contemporary art. This is especially true with regard to the film in Chinese contemporary art. Yang Beichen suggests that,

> The significance of film is that it starts with the most pristine light, however, it carries out some open and changing works in efforts to achieve the eternal guarantee of 'multiple.' It allows us to face the things outside this totally blank border and those hidden outside the sole projector light and dormant in mysterious shadow during the film. We probably can call these 'the upcoming images.'[13]

If the question of film is the question of *cinématographicité*, then 'film in the future' should be emphasizing the redeployment of the film (in other words, *dispositif cinématographique*) rather than certain aesthetic forms or provisions.

One Half of August (2011) was a very interesting transitional work for Yang Fudong. In the film, he emphasized the relationship between architectural space and image, attempting to break the limitations of the moving image. Yang projected his film series *Seven Intellectuals in Bamboo Forest* onto buildings or architectural models to achieve a kind of live theatrical experience. He then filmed these scenes as they were projected on the buildings and architectural modules. The scenes in the film and the scenes projected on buildings construct an architectural experience.[14] This reminds me of some moving image installation works by Taiwanese director Tsai Ming Liang. His film *Ghost* and installation work *Erotic Space2* place the same focus on dealing with multilayered relationships between moving image and architecture, space and viewing, rather than on the organization of a traditional sense of story and theatrical experience.

Since 2000, cinema of exhibition has expanded from being focused on a single theme to a reflection on the sites of exhibition. In terms of site layout and space planning, these installations are still largely casual and random. Viewers can freely decide how long they would like to stop for and walk among the many film screens. They have no intention to organize a possible narrative or story. Instead, these installations are a completely new experience of moving image and space. A film that is outside of traditional theatre must face this new experience and challenges, to obtain subjective liberation. These works are not only projections in art space, they also strongly encourage spectators to participate. For example, many large pieces of animation by the artist Sun Xun (such as his *Magician Party and Dead Crow* that was shown from 30 April to 8 May 2013) are presented as open work sites. Ready-made items, footage, set-ups and the visual experience of the animation can be freely transformed.

Finally, I would like to turn to a personal topic of interest: how to carry out active and effective artistic practices in the particular social situation and reality of China today – that is, the post-WTO epoch of the iGeneration. It is true that the discussion over 'film in the future,' no matter whether this is proposed at an aesthetic or political level, unavoidably touches on the urgent propositions and strategic responses that are raised by 'activism' in contemporary Chinese society. That is to say, in any aesthetic and political dimension, the biggest theme that is faced by cinema of exhibition is to restore political passion and space for the imagination. The key reason why the future can become the future is because of its current attitude and awareness. Or, as the Raqs Media group declared, 'The future is waiting – the future will be self-organized.'[15]

Works cited

Chakrabarty, Dipesh. *Dipeishi chakalabati duben* (*Dipesh Chakrabarty Reader*). Nanfang ribao Press, First Edition, 2010.

Dong, Bingfeng, Qingchun Du, Jianhong Huang and Zhu Zhu (eds). *Cong dianying kan: dangdai yishu de dianying henji yu ziwo jiangou* (*Looking Through Film: Traces of Cinema and Self-Constructs in Contemporary Art*). Xinxing Press, first edition, 2010.

Lü, Xinyu. *Jilu zhongguo: dangdai zhongguo xinjilu yundong* (*Documentary China: Contemporary Documentary Movement in China*). Beijing: Sanlian chubanshe (Joint Publishing Group), first edition, 2003.

Obrist, Hans Ulrich. *Guanyu cezhan de yiqie* (*Everything You Always Wanted to Know About Curating*). Jincheng Press, first edition, 2013, 6.

Qiu, Zhijie (ed.). *Xianxiang/yingxiang: yishu yu lishi yishi* (*Phenomenon/Image: Art and the Historical Consciousness*), Exhibition catalogue, 1996.

Vancheri, Luc. *Cinémas contemporains: Du film à l'installation*. Paris: Aleas, 2009.

Van Assche, Christine. *Conception et direction d'ouvrage, Pangbidu zhongxin: xinmeiti yishu 1965–2005* (*New Media Collection 1965–2005: Centre Pompidou*). Taipei: Taipei Fine Arts Museum and Art & Collection Group, 1 (2005).

Wu, Wenguang. '*Ganggang zai lushang – fasheng zai jiushi niandai de geren yingxiang jilu fangshi de miaoshu*' (*Just on the Road: A Description of Modes of Personal Image Recording in the 1990s*). http://blog.sina.com.cn/s/blog_8203e0da0101aau6.html (accessed 9 January 2014).

Yang, Beichen. '"*Dianyingxing*" wenti: shilun jijiang daolai de yingxiang gongtongti' (*Questions on the Nature of Film: on the Upcoming Image Community*). See Chinese website of Artforum. http://www.artforum.com.cn/film/4989

Zhang, Yuan. '*Wenyi fuxing jiushi rang yishujia fuwu yu "ren" er bushi "zhuyi"*' (*Renaissance is When the Artists Serve 'People' instead of 'Doctrine'*). http://www.douban.com/note/249579106/

Zhang, Zhen. 'Yishu, gandongli he xingdong zhuyi jilupian' (Art, Affect and Activist Documentary) in *Zhongguo dudi yingxiang* (*Chinese Independent Cinema*). *Chinese Independent Cinema*, issue 11, 2012.

Notes

1 Lin Zhonglu, 'Lishi de kunjing yu jiyu: guonei luxiang yishu zhuangkuang' (Historical Dilemma and Opportunity: The Condition of Video Art in China) in *Xianxiang/yingxiang: yishu yu lishi yishi* (*Phenomenon/Image: Art and the Historical Consciousness*). Please see the catalogue for the same name exhibition, 1996, 33.
2 Jean-Christophe Royoux, 'Yizhong zhanshi de dianying' (Pour un cinéma d'exposition) in *Pangbidu zhongxin: xinmeiti yishu 1965–2005* (*New Media Collection 1965–2005: Centre Pompidou*). Taipei: Taipei Fine Arts Museum and Art & Collection Group, 1 (2005), 94.
3 '85 New Wave' is regarded as the first contemporary art movement in China and the most important one in the twentieth century, which brought Chinese art into an international context. It is generally believed that much of the ethos and trends of contemporary Chinese art is based on the influence of the '85 New Wave.'
4 Zhang Yuan, 'Wenyi fuxing jiushi rang yishujia fuwu yu "ren," er bushi "zhuyi"' (Renaissance is When the Artists Serve 'People' instead of 'Doctrine'). http://www.douban.com/note/249579106/ (accessed 6 March 2014).
5 Wu Wenguang, 'Ganggang zai lushang – fasheng zai jiushi niandai de geren yingxiang jilu fangshi de miaoshu' (Just on the Road: A Description of Modes of Personal Image Recording in the 1990s). http://blog.sina.com.cn/s/blog_8203e0da0101aau6.html (accessed 9 January 2014).
6 Lü Xinyu, *Jilu zhongguo: dangdai zhongguo xinjilu yundong* (*Documentary China: Contemporary Documentary Movement in China*). Beijing: Sanlian chubanshe (Joint Publishing Group), first edition, 2003, 13.
7 Mark Nash, 'Yishu yu dianying: yixie piping fansi' (Art and Cinema: Some Critical Reflections) in *Pangbidu zhongxin: xinmeiti yishu 1965–2005* (*New Media Collection 1965–2005: Centre Pompidou*). Taipei: Taipei Fine Arts Museum and Art & Collection Group, 2 (2005), 40.
8 Black Box is analogous to 'White cube.' While 'white cube' refers to an exhibition space constructed by white walls in museums and galleries, 'Black Box' means a screening room surrounded by curtains or walls built inside museum gallery spaces.
9 Dipesh Chakrabarty, 'Wanjin minzhu zhidu zhong de bowuguan' (Museum in Late Democracies) in *Dipeishi chakalabati duben* (*Dipesh Chakrabarty Reader*). Nanfang ribao chubanshe, first edition, 2010, 121.
10 Song-Yong Sing, 'Zhanshi dianying jiyi de meishuguan' (Meseum Exhibiting the Memories of Film) in *Cong dianying kan: dangdai yishu de dianying henji yu ziwo jiangou* (*Looking Through Film: Traces of Cinema and Self-Constructs in Contemporary Art*). Xinxing chubanshe, first edition, 2010, 121.
11 Ibid., 128.
12 Luc Vancheri, *Cinémas contemporains: Du film à l'installation*. Paris, Aleas, 2009.
13 Yang Beichen, '0"Dianyingxing" wenti: shilun jijiang daolai de yingxiang gongtongti'

(Questions on the Nature of Film: on the Upcoming Image Community). See Chinese website of Artforum. http://www.artforum.com.cn/film/4989 (accessed 6 March 2014).
14 Li Zhenhua, Interview on *The Nightman Cometh*. Please see ShanghART Gallery website. http://www.shanghartgallery.com/galleryarchive/texts/id/4621 (accessed 6 March 2014).
15 Hans Ulrich Obrist, 'Weilai shi tiao gou' (The Future is Dog) in *Guanyu cezhan de yiqie* (*Everything You Always Wanted to Know About Curating*). Jincheng chubanshe, first edition, 2013, 6.

Part Two

Aesthetics

5

Goodbye to the Grim Real, Hello to What Comes Next: The Moment of Passage from the Sixth Generation to the iGeneration

Luke Vulpiani

The origins of China's iGeneration can be found through an examination of two films by two Sixth Generation directors: *24 City* (*Ershi si chengji*, 2008) by Jia Zhangke and *Summer Palace* (*Yíhé Yuán*, 2006) by Lou Ye. In this chapter, I argue that these two films represent the end of the Sixth Generation as a configuration and are evidence of the transition to a new mode of film in China in the latter part of the 2000s called the iGeneration. In describing these two movies as 'transition films,' I mean that they retain many elements of the Sixth Generation, but also contain new elements that signal the passage to a different film style in China, particularly in terms of the representation of subjectivity and history.

The Sixth Generation emerged in the early 1990s, with the 1993 film *Beijing Bastards* (*Běijīng Zázhǒng*), directed by Zhang Yuan, commonly considered the first Sixth Generation film. The Sixth Generation constituted, as with other films of the early 1990s, an urban turn in Chinese film. Zhang Zhen aptly describes the films of the period as having 'a singular preoccupation with the destruction and reconstruction of the social fabric and urban identities of post-1989 China.'[1] My analysis focuses on the Sixth Generation in terms of its aesthetics and film-style, and I posit two key concepts that I view as the unique aspects of the Sixth Generation. These two concepts are intertwined and work in dialogue with each other. The first concept is a realist film aesthetic called '*xianchang*,' best translated as 'on-the-scene,' a term coined by the Chinese documentary filmmaker Wu Wenguang (b. 1956) that describes the re-establishing of the physical body in urban space.[2] The Sixth Generation films combine *xianchang* with fictional narratives, not only to capture the impact of urban change in 1990s China, but also to explore urban subjectivity in moments of great transformation. The second key concept that I identify is that of a detached specular gaze, which I argue is bound up with fantasy and the commodity form. This specular gaze, often counterpointed to *xianchang*, serves to create a subject who is unstable, fragmentary and opaque.

By the middle of the 2000s, China was a very different country from that of the early 1990s, when the Sixth Generation had emerged. China joined the World Trade Organization in 2001, a demonstration of the country's importance to the global economy and its complete turn away from Maoist economics. China's economy continued to grow, and in 2010 China became the world's second biggest economy, overtaking Japan and ranking behind only the United States.[3] Li Minqi goes as far as to argue that China's economic power is of such significance that it represents the end of the established capitalist powers and a new global order.[4] It is important to place the iGeneration within this changed economic and social situation. Cultural production is part of the wider economy in which it operates, and therefore it is important to consider the relationship between economics and aesthetic style, without intending to suggest that aesthetics in a particular society are simply a reflection and consequence of the economic base. Yomi Braester, in his book *Paint the City Red*, argues that Chinese cinema in the 1950s and 1960s, as well as wider urban aesthetics such as architecture, reflected the economic mode of production at the time:

> The cinema shares the plight of urban design, which is subject to a double-tier centralised control – state-level 'economic planning' (*jingji jihua*, handled after the Soviet model by the State Planning Commission) as well as municipal-level spatial planning (*chengshi guihua*, literally 'urban planning,') under the Ministry of Construction.[5]

While the Sixth Generation had an aesthetic defined by the changing space of the city, the iGeneration is more influenced by the signifiers of commerce and marketing.

In my view, the iGeneration has two defining features that differentiate it from the Sixth Generation. The first is the iGeneration's organic relationship with the digital and its correlate the internet. The iGeneration cannot be thought or divorced from digital technology or culture, which is a condition of its existence. The digital covers all aspects of film in the iGeneration, from production (the use of digital cameras and software editing packages) to distribution (the use of the internet to circulate and market films on both a high-budget and low-budget scale) and reception (the computer screen or mobile phone increasingly are the places where films are watched, discussed and consumed). The second defining feature of the iGeneration is its relationship to the wider economic realm of China in the late 2000s. In particular, the iGeneration is in part a consequence of the Chinese state's desire to create a domestic cultural industry that has global reach, while at the same time maintaining control over creative and imaginative works. In this chapter, I focus on aesthetic considerations to examine the changing representation of time and the subject during the transition from the Sixth Generation to the iGeneration. However, it is also important to bear in mind the factors that determine, affect and shape aesthetics.

24 City – directed by one of the key directors of the Sixth Generation, Jia Zhangke – signals the shift to a different mode of film style in Chinese film in the latter half of the 2000s, owing to its manner of representating the subject and history. The film is structured around the story of Factory 420 – an armaments factory built in Chengdu at the beginning of the 1950s during the Korean War. In 2007, the year in which the film is set, Factory 420 is being decommissioned and the land it occupies converted into luxury housing. To appreciate the cultural significance of Factory 420, it has to be understood in the Chinese context as not just a factory but a *danwei* (work unit) of over 100,000 people, including 30,000 employees and their families.[6] The *danwei* in Mao's China was the fundamental social and political structure that organized work and everyday life, including housing, education, health care and policing.[7] The size and nature of *danweis* meant they were almost miniature cities within a city. For Robin Visser, the *danwei* and the local street committee (*jiedao banshichu*) were 'the socialist organizational mechanisms that had once circumscribed nearly all forms of urban life.'[8] Thus, the significance of Factory 420 being mothballed is that it represents not just the loss of a place of employment, but also the loss of the very institution that organized life and served as the dominant social structure of Communist China. While China has retained a formally Communist government, the changes to property laws and the restructuring of urban space during the 1990s and beyond have represented not only an economic transformation, but a social and political one also. The Sixth Generation emerged during these changes and in this regard, *24 City* is a typical Sixth Generation film, retaining the visual tropes of the transformation of the urban space, demolition and the city as a ruin.

24 City presents a range of characters connected to Factory 420, mainly as talking heads in isolated segments. The film uses a pseudo-documentary style and some of the characters are based on real interviews conducted by Jia Zhangke. The talking heads are intercut with interludes from the characters' lives and scenes of Factory 420 being gradually demolished. From the very beginning, *24 City* creates the sense of a different relationship to time and history than is typical of Sixth Generation films. While Sixth Generation characters are caught in the intensity of the present moment, *24 City* places its characters within a much longer temporal arc. The shift to a focus on reflection and memory is evident in the first character in the film, Xiao He – an old man who recounts his memories of coming to work in Factory 420 as a young man and of his workteam leader, old Master Wang. Xiao He is shown in plain mid-shot, sitting on a chair in the empty factory, with only the sound of traffic in the background, as if he is being interviewed for a documentary about the factory. At one point, a voice off-screen joins in the conversation, prompting him like an interviewer. Xiao He's memories of Master Wang are interrupted by a black screen with writing that reads '*Xiao He, born 1948 in Chengdu, apprenticed in Factory 420 in 1964, to work group 61. Later was in the army.*' The next shot is of Xiao He's worker's card, which contains his photo as a young man. The use of dates is crucial in *24 City* and marks a shift from the Sixth Generation, where time appears only as an eternal present, to a representation of time as movement. The shot of the worker's card serves to create a sense of the film as a historical document and places the old Xiao He in the film within a wider history.

24 City is not primarily focused on narrative, but on the relationship in and between the characters, the factory and the city. The film uses a multiplicity of voices, characters and viewpoints to create a non-linear narrative that focuses on memory and the past. Despite the multiplicity of characters in the film, *24 City* actually creates a much more coherent temporal arc than is typical of Sixth Generation works. It is easy for the viewer to locate the characters within the wider historical arc presented in the film, with Factory 420 serving as an anchor to a common point of reference. The sense of historical movement created in *24 City* is a development away from other Sixth Generation works, where such a concept of temporal movement is largely absent. *24 City* indicates the passage of the Sixth Generation by taking a different stance toward events, unfolding the narrative and stories in the film primarily through memories of the past rather than moments in the present. The important point is not that the past can be re-thought in the imagination, but that the now of the present is materially related to a real historical development.

The representation of characters and subjectivity in *24 City* constitute two other ways the film moves away from the Sixth Generation, a movement that I argue is away from portrait and toward biography. The Sixth Generation's presentation of its characters is that of the portrait – a representation or impression of character that focuses on mood and emotions as opposed to experience and understanding. A Sixth Generation protagonist is often ambiguous in motive, without a contextual history or with only a very sparsely drawn one. Portrait is an effective means in the Sixth Generation to capture the young, urban, marginal subjects caught in the frenetic whirl of the present, people who are unable to articulate a coherent narrative of the self. The characters in *24 City* by contrast are presented as biographies linked to both Factory 420 and the wider historical arc that the film constructs. Similarly, in *Summer Palace*, there is an attempt to present the characters within a continuum of the biographical, as a means to explore how the characters are affected by events. This transition from portrait to biography, I argue, is one key distinguishing feature of the passage of the Sixth Generation to the iGeneration.

There is an interesting counterpoint created in *24 City* between scenes of individual characters (particularly their presentation as talking heads) and scenes of more collective activity in the form of song, dance, or play. A good example of collective activity occurs near the beginning of the film, in a moment when the workers sing together. After a few establishing exterior longshots of the factory gates as workers arrive, the film moves to an interior shot of a crowd of workers, all dressed in virtually identical drab work-overalls, filing up some stairs into a meeting hall. The sequence continues with the workers seated in a large hall, as they listen to the announcement that Factory 420 is to be closed and converted into luxury housing. The scene ends with a collective patriotic song, a scene that can be read in numerous ways. The underplayed solemnity of the singing, despite the fact that the workers have in effect just been told that they will all lose their jobs, could be read as a biting satire of the Chinese people's compliant behaviours or a subtle critique of the extent to which propaganda has so permeated the Chinese population that they sing about the glory of the motherland even while the land is being sold from under them. However, the scene also functions as one of the few uplifting moments in *24 City*, that overall is characterized by a downbeat sense of inevitability that I call the 'grim real.'[9] The term 'grim real' was coined by Alain Badiou to characterize the period from the 1970s, after the end of political revolutionary movements. I utilize it here in aesthetic terms to describe presentation of an eviscerated bleak real. There are a number of other scenes of collective activity in *24 City*, such as the performance of a Chinese opera and groups playing Mah-Jong, that provide a sense of shared communality absent from much of the rest of the film where the grim real persists.

24 City, although it appears to be realist in style as it utilizes aspects of the documentary form, actually has a highly structured aesthetic. The film, like other Jia films, is very studied and controlled, with meticulous shot composition, framing and *mise-en-scène*. Xudong Zhang describes Jia's filmic style as 'a systematic and methodical sociological approach',[10] and sees it as a means to interrogate competing versions of reality rather than an attempt to present reality as a totality. The constructed artificiality and formalism of the aesthetic style in *24 City* plays against the other signifiers in the film that codify it as realist – the long-take shots, the interviews and the use of diegetic sound. This aesthetic style creates the sense of a sociological study, but one that is ambiguous. *24 City* creates a sense of elegy, in part through careful pacing and the use of long-take shots, in part through a musical score that uses slow-tempo *sostenuto* string compositions in minor keys. The film brings history to the fore through a series of different voices, intending to follow the postmodern problematic of avoiding grand narratives. *24 City* presents not just a visual history, but also an oral/auditory history, mixing the stories recounted by the characters with poems and songs – not only to signal changes in time, but also to create a multilayered fabric of history. The demolition of the factory exists alongside these multilayered memories and lives.

The changes in the representation of subjectivity and urban space evident in *24 City* are especially prominent in the character of Su Na, who bookends the film. Su Na is a young 20-something woman who is intended, no doubt, to be an image of China in the late 2000s. She is presented as enterprising, ambitious and savvy. She is aware of the importance of the way she looks and is first shown meticulously applying make-up. A thread that runs throughout the Su Na segment of the film is her awareness of the importance of consumption and the presentation of the self within the cycle of consumption – from her carry-case to her stylish, foreign-made Volkswagen Beetle car. Su Na works as a personal shopper for rich Chengdu women and travels to Hong Kong to purchase fashion and other consumer items on their behalf. Her job is, of course, a huge contrast with the life offered to the workers in Factory 420 and evidence of the shift toward a more consumption-oriented economy in China in the 1990s. Su Na is also presented as an atomized individual; she is never shown with other people and the only interaction she has is via a hands-free phone in her car, where she talks to her clients (inevitably about money).

The presentation of Su Na is typical of the style of *24 City* more generally, favouring slow, static, carefully composed shots and studied camera movements that seem weighty with significance. The Su Na sequence begins, after a brief introduction to the character driving in her car and talking to her client, with a long-shot of fields with buildings in the background. In the left foreground of the shot is a young couple – the woman poses while the man takes a photograph. Bright yellow flowers run horizontally across the middle of the frame and the camera pans slowly to the right, to where two middle-aged women dressed in agricultural workers' clothes walk down a path in the centre of the screen with their implements. As the camera begins to pan slowly to the right, Su Na's car is revealed in the right foreground, on a slight diagonal. She is seated in the car, posed with her arms folded, looking out of the window. In the right background are a number of dark tower blocks, perhaps ready to be demolished.

The camera continues to pan right, bringing Su Na's car into the centre of the shot, as the two agricultural workers walk in front of her car and out of shot to the right. The slow pan brings Su Na to the centre of the frame with the buildings in the background. There is a constant low-level rumble of traffic noise heard throughout this scene and many others in *24 City*, as if a constant reminder of the persistent presence of the city even in this seeming rural location. A counterpoint is created between the bright colours of the flowers, the car and the darker buildings in the background. The next shot is a close mid-shot of Su Na in her car looking out of the window on the right of the image; the left of the image is filled with the vivid yellow flowers. The words 'Su Na, born 1982 in Chengdu' appear on the screen.

The counterpoint created in this scene purposefully encompasses the young couple, the two women workers, and Su Na. Even the very posing of a car in a field seems to mimic familiar images from American cinema that treats the car as an emblem of consumption and liberation. The shot is carefully composed and highly complex, as with many of the shots in *24 City*, containing numerous layers of reference that are dense with information and significance. It provides a comment on different social roles in its contrast between Su Na, the young couple and the older agricultural workers. At the same time, it is tinged with humour – the incongruity of Su Na posing in her car in the countryside, seemingly out of place with the rest of the scene around her, cannot but strike the viewer as comically odd. Su Na, as with many of the characters in *24 City*, knows that she is posing for the camera. In this way, the film constructs a sense of realism by acknowledging the presence of the camera, but counterpoints this sense of realism with the highly composed and structured nature of the shot, indicating that what is presented is artificial and not a verisimilitude.

The Su Na sequence continues with two shots of her in the interior of the desolate Factory 420, as she slowly wanders through the now empty building and, in a voiceover, recounts her memories of her school days in the factory. There is then an eight-minute monologue with a static shot of Su Na framed mid-shot inside the factory between two large windows. The cityscape of Chengdu is visible through the windows, with its tower blocks and expressways busy with traffic. Su Na's monologue is interrupted twice by a fade to black, which seems to indicate the passing of time as it becomes gradually darker outside. The monologue concludes with Su Na crying, as she talks about the hard life her parents endured working in Factory 420 and how she wants to make lots of money to be able to buy them a house in the new housing development.

The final shot of *24 City* is an exterior mid-shot of Su Na. She is framed in profile as she looks out to the left over Chengdu's buildings and expressways from a high vantage point at the top of the now desolate Factory 420. The camera slowly pans left to reveal more of the Chengdu cityscape, which gradually fills the screen as Su Na disappears from the right edge of the frame. The camera continues to pan slowly over the vast cityscape, while the sound of traffic and city life in the background becomes louder. The film ends with the words of a poem by Wan Xia appearing on the screen, as the image fades to black and music rises. What is left at the end of *24 City* is the 'grim real': the bare autonomous life of the city that subsumes the subject. *24 City* leaves the Sixth Generation at an impasse, stuck in the grim real without escape. Stylistically, the film feels exhausted, with a representational inarticulacy that seems to be smothered by the monstrous all-consuming city. Interestingly, Jia did not make a feature film for five years after *24 City* and, when he did with *A Touch of Sin (Tian zhu ding)* in 2013, he would turn to the *wuxia* martial arts genre.

In the iGeneration, the grim real disappears, replaced by a brutal realism or by more commercially oriented filmmaking. The brutal realism, seen in the hooligan films, conveys a savagely violent, almost anthropological vision of China – the underbelly of neoliberal development. The more commercially oriented cinema celebrates China's newfound economic power, even if sometimes appearing uneasy about the rising inequality that has been a consequence of economic growth. In *24 City*, Su Na can be read as a transitional figure from the Sixth Generation to the iGeneration: she is not a marginal character and she embraces the new economy and cycle of consumption against which many Sixth Generation characters stand. Su Na's tears, her sadness as she tells how she wants a better life than her parents, should be read not as tears for her parents' wasted past but for the grim real of Su Na's present, where the only ethics is money. What disappears in the character of Su Na is the embodied collective once at the very heart of Chinese life, which has been replaced by the atomized consumer.

Like *24 City*, *Summer Palace* ends with tears, but of a different kind, tears that I argue seek to bypass the grim real and open historical events to thought. The film tells the story of Yu Hong, a young girl from a provincial city, who comes to study at university in Beijing in the late 1980s and becomes involved in the tumultuous political protests in China in 1989. The protests have the name Tiananmen in the West, after the square in central Beijing that became the protests' focal point.[11]

The film is two hours and 22 minutes long and split into three parts, largely defined by the locales featured in each part. The first and shortest part, almost a prologue, lasts 15 minutes and is set in Yu Hong's hometown Tumen, a nondescript city on the China–Korea border. The second part, approximately an hour, takes place in Beijing, where Yu Hong discovers a world of art, politics and sex, and forges the key relationships in the film, with her friend Li Ta and her lover Zhou Wei. The Beijing section culminates with Yu Hong and her friends going to join the protests at Tiananmen and Yu Hong learning of Zhou Wei's infidelity with Li Ta. With their university suffering a government crackdown following the Tiananmen protests, Yu Hong returns to Tumen with her old boyfriend, and the friends remain separated for the rest of the film. The final part of *Summer Palace*, also approximately an hour, takes place nine years later and deals with the characters in their adult lives. Yu Hong, who lives in China, is consumed by memories of Zhou Wei and drifts between jobs, cities and unfulfilled sexual relationships, as the country undergoes rapid economic and social change. Meanwhile, Li Ta, Zhou Wei and Li Ta's partner, Ruo Gu, live as exiles from China in Berlin. Li Ta's suicide is the catalyst for Zhou Wei to return to China, where he eventually has a meeting with Yu Hong in the coastal city of Beidaihe. The encounter is a failure, and Zhou Wei drives off without saying goodbye.

Summer Palace represents a transition from the Sixth Generation to the iGeneration, as it explores a more expansive temporal and spatial canvas, as well as creating a different relationship to the historical. Xudong Zhang characterized the Sixth Generation as a 'vanishing cinema,'[12] and *Summer Palace* is about revealing a vanished moment in China's political and social history. While *24 City* retains the key Sixth Generation trope of the city as a site of ruin, *Summer Palace* turns the city into the site of a political ruin. The first section of *Summer Palace*, set in Yu Hong's hometown, is typically Sixth Generation in terms of theme and aesthetic style. The focus on anonymous provincial city life, the pared-down realist aesthetic and muted palette bring to mind films such as Jia Zhangke's 2002 *Unknown Pleasures* (*Rèn xiāo yáo*, literally *Free from all constraint*). However, *Summer Palace* shifts registers in the Beijing section, using long steadicam tracking shots and elliptical editing to create a sense of energy and vibrant life. In *Suzhou River* (*Sūzhōu Hé*, 2000), an earlier Lou Ye Sixth Generation film, rapid montage shots of Shanghai were used to represent Shanghai as an unstable physical entity, which paralleled the film's representation of ambiguous and disappearing subjects. *Summer Palace*'s use of montage is not focused on the representation of Beijing but on unspoken political events of a traumatic past.

The enunciating positions in *Summer Palace* are more complex and the switch between registers is more fluid and less clearly signalled than in *24 City*. The narrative viewpoint in *Summer Palace* has at least three layers or enunciating positions: the point of view of Yu Hong, expressed most directly via her voiceovers and shots which appear to signal her memories; short passages of real footage, such as documentary shots of the Tiananmen protests and historical events such as the fall of the Berlin Wall and the return of Hong Kong to Chinese rule; and the narrative eye of the camera, which shows events at which Yu Hong is neither present nor a witness. The complex and multiple enunciating positions should be read as an indication of the move away from realist representation, or *xianchang*, to a more layered enunciating position that seeks to create a sense of history and memory and explore the relationship between the two. *Summer Palace* does not construct an omniscient narrative perspective; instead, it approaches the historical through the personal, able to create a clear enunciating position for the viewer without taking a didactic or polemical approach to Tiananmen.

A scene in *Summer Palace* that exemplifies the style of the Beijing section is the one in which Yu Hong and Zhou Wei get together for the first time. The scene takes place in the kind of Western-style bar that was becoming popular in the late 1980s in China's major cities. The scene is not only a narrative device to bring the two characters together, but also a means of representing Beijing in the late 1980s as a place of liberalizing energy and possibility. The sequence begins with a steadicam tracking shot of Yu Hong and Li Ta facing the camera as they walk down a street at night past lit doorways – perhaps Sanlitun, Beijing's famous bar street renowned for its bars and Western influence. As the two friends walk with Yu Hong's arm draped over Li Ta, the American song 'You're Just Too Good to be True' by Andy Williams plays in the background. The song could be diegetic music from a bar or non-diegetic music, but either way it emphasizes the shift in the film to a more cosmopolitan and externally directed space that contrasts sharply with the first section of *Summer Palace* in Tumen. The camera turns left as the two friends walk through a doorway into a bar and the camera follows them from behind as they enter the busy interior. A sequence of cuts then shows various groups within the bar: a seated woman reading a Chinese poem in front of an abstract painting, a number of shots of a group having a political discussion and a shot of a man singing, accompanied by a girl drumming on the bar and someone playing a guitar off-screen. The camera remains mobile throughout these shots, as if a curious onlooker exploring an unfamiliar space. The sequence creates the sense of a liberal, communal, shared space of creativity and openness.

The sequence continues with a cut to a mid-shot of Yu Hong alone as she takes a seat at the bar, while the American song 'Seven Little Girls Sitting in the Backseat' by Paul Evans begins to play in the background. The choice of the song seems rather comical, as if to emphasize the innocence and even naïvety of the characters at this stage of the film. There is then a series of complex cuts between Yu Hong as she sits at the bar and Li Ta, Ruo Gu and Zhou Wei, who appear to be sitting across the room. Li Ta and Ruo Gu move onto the busy dance floor as the steadicam shot tracks behind them, and Zhou Wei comes over to Yu Hong, to try and persuade her to join him on the dance floor. Zhou Wei is at first unsuccessful, until Li Ta and Ruo Gu come over and help to cajole Yu Hong onto the dance floor. Yu Hong and Zhou Wei dance apart at first, but eventually move closer together. The use of editing in this sequence creates an interesting dynamic for the viewer, who is led to identify with Yu Hong through a number of angles appearing to signal her viewpoint. At the same time, the use of elliptical editing creates a sense of incompleteness, as if the events are being imperfectly remembered. Interestingly, the scene recurs at the end of the film as a coda, with the viewer told in writing what happened to the characters after the film ends. The music in the coda is no longer the breezy lines of 'Seven Little Girls,' but the *Summer Palace* theme, composed by Peyman Yazdanian, that appears throughout the film. The theme features an insistent bass line overlaid with a slow piano line that is suggestive of loss.

The Tiananmen protests serve as the central pivot in *Summer Palace* and divide the film in half. Despite the fact that much is alluded to and remains off-screen, the sequence represents, as Michael Berry comments, 'the single most extensive portrayal of the incident to yet appear (or disappear) on the Chinese screen.'[13] Tiananmen is, in many ways, the event that is the unspoken core of the Sixth Generation – the structural cause that conditions their films, yet always existing as an absence. The trauma of Tiananmen and its aftermath can account for the turn away from any direct social or political engagement by the Sixth Generation and the intense, sometimes almost narcissistic, focus on the individual who seeks an island of refuge from the world. I read the irruption of Tiananmen in *Summer Palace* as the culmination of the Sixth Generation – the moment it exhausts itself by saying the unspeakable and representing the unrepresentable.

It is in the Tiananmen sequence that the combination of steadicam shots and elliptical editing has its greatest effect. The sequence begins with the sound of running feet, excited chatter and non-diegetic music in the form of the song 'Oxygen' by Lei Hao[14] beginning to play, as a series of quick shots with shaky framing shows groups of students rushing to a truck and climbing on board. The song 'Oxygen' plays throughout the Tiananmen sequence and is crucial to its overall impact. 'Oxygen' contrasts moments of building anticipation through a pulsing, insistent bass line and quiet, almost-whispered lyrics to moments of climax where the female vocals reach a soaring crescendo accompanied by swelling strings in the background. The crescendos fall with the emergence of a fragile piano line that suggests the impossibility of sustaining the intense moments. The lyrics of 'Oxygen' are Chinese and can be interpreted as a meta-commentary on the sequence, particularly the chorus, which speaks of a moment of intense climax of overwhelming proportions: 'All rays of light rush into me / I inhale all of the oxygen / All objects lose their weight / My love proceeds to the end of all roads.'[15]

The Tiananmen sequence continues with a series of shots of a larger group of students, including Li Ta, running to the truck. The movement of the students, quick editing, mobile-framing and music create the sense of a rush of energy and pressing urgency, as well as the excited optimism of the students. There is a sense of being caught in the moment, of *xianchang* pushed to its most chaotic extreme – of being on-the-scene and desperately trying to capture what is happening. The viewer is left unsure whether he or she is being implicated in the events or being asked to observe them, and this oscillation creates an interesting position for the viewer. For example, the next shot is a low-angle shot zoom-in on Yu Hong at her dormitory window looking down at the students climbing into the truck. There are then two other quick shots of the students climbing onto the truck, but not from Yu Hong's perspective, and the next shot is again of Yu Hong as she turns away from the window. The next shot swivels 180 degrees in a whip-pan from the students on the truck to Yu Hong and her friend Dongdong running to the truck and clambering aboard, as the sound of the truck's engine being started is heard.

The vocals of 'Oxygen' reach the first crescendo over a number of shots of the students on the now-moving truck with banners flying. A mid-shot frames Yu Hong, Zhou Wei and Li Ta centrally as part of the group of students on the truck and they begin to sing and cheer together. The next shot is of the truck as part of a convoy of trucks presumably entering the area around Tiananmen Square and the students waving to crowds of supporters off-screen, as cheering and beeping horns are heard. A virtual match-on-action cut then moves from the fictional truck to a shot of real documentary footage of a truck from the Tiananmen protests. A sequence of 13 shots of real footage of the Tiananmen protests follows, lasting 32 seconds in total. The real documentary shots include images of the protestors at a packed Beijing railway station and crowds of demonstrators carrying placards and banners.[16] The final two shots show Tiananmen Gate with the famous portrait of Mao almost hidden behind the demonstrators' flags and a long shot of Chang'an Avenue (Cháng'ān Jiē), the long road in Beijing that leads to Tiananmen Square, packed with demonstrators. At this point, the film cuts back to the fictional world, with Yu Hong, Li Ta and Zhou Wei running down a road in a state of euphoria, presumably having just left the protests at

Tiananmen, although their mood quickly dampens, as if they already fear what is to come.

The use of the documentary footage represents an irruption of the Real, in the Lacanian sense, into the fictional narrative of *Summer Palace*. The Real in Lacan is the thing that the symbolic (in the form of discourse) and the imaginary (in the form of fantasies) come up against but against which they ultimately fail.[17] The real footage has the effect of bringing the fictional events into collision with the historical real and forces the viewer to confront the images on the screen as not simply fictional. For a Chinese viewer, the scenes are likely to be deeply shocking and also for some no doubt intensely liberating, as Tiananmen is one of the great unspoken black holes in Chinese political and social history. Even in 2013, 4 June proved to be a sensitive date for the Chinese authorities, with the anniversary of Tiananmen being censored in the news in China as well as on the internet.[18] Perhaps unsurprisingly, this provocative sequence led Chinese authorities to ban Lou Ye from filmmaking.[19] The consequence of this irruption of the Real is a breakdown of the symbolic order: in film terms, of the fictional images; for the characters, the breakdown of their world. In *Summer Palace*, the events of Tiananmen cannot be integrated into the symbolic order by the friends and remain an open wound throughout the rest of the film.

Zhou Wei and Li Ta's infidelity adds a secondary layer to the overall catastrophic breakdown. As the university is thrown into chaos – which the viewer is left to conjecture is a result of the government/military crackdown – a student tells Yu Hong about Zhou Wei and Li Ta's infidelity. Shortly afterwards, Zhou Wei is told by Dongdong that Yu Hong knows of his infidelity and that their relationship is over. As Zhou Wei and Dongdong look for Yu Hong at night, they stumble across violent scenes of a burning car, students throwing rocks and soldiers with guns slowly advancing. Although the film does not show any direct confrontation between the students and soldiers, it is easy to make the chilling connection to the government-authorized crackdown on the Tiananmen demonstrators. The infidelity between Zhou Wei and Li Ta is no doubt a means of expressing the catastrophe of Tiananmen without being able to show events directly. However, it should not be read as simply a clever mask through which the film can indirectly approach the political dimension of the bitter defeat of Tiananmen. The creation of a dual breakdown works in both a literal and metaphorical sense, and serves to emphasize the trauma, betrayal and destruction the characters, particularly Yu Hong, experience. The attempt to represent and thus reflect on the events of Tiananmen is in contrast to earlier Sixth Generation works, which turn to the grim real as an escape from any direct representation of the political sphere. *24 City*, for example, separates the personal and political, seeking to navigate an uneasy path between the two spheres; however, this runs the risk of suggesting the two can be compartmentalized and hides the inter-relationship between the two spheres.

The final section of *Summer Palace* explores the consequences of the past and highlights the move from portrait to biography that I argue is a symptom of the transition from the Sixth Generation to the iGeneration. It is through Yu Hong's sexual relations that *Summer Palace* most clearly moves to the biographical, exploring the changes to her character during the various stages of her life. *Summer Palace* uses sex scenes in part to stir controversy, but more fundamentally to explore adult characters who have complex needs of intimacy, love and pleasure. Yu Hong's first sexual encounter, both in the film and in her character's life, is with her boyfriend in Tumen, and the scene emphasizes the tentativeness of the experience by the virtual quiet maintained throughout the sequence and the characters' awkwardness. Yu Hong's character and sexual development blossom in Beijing through her relationship with Zhou Wei. The relationship is intense and loving, as well as volatile and passionate. Romantic scenes of them riding bikes around Kunming Lake (*Kūnmíng Hú*), the famous lake around Beijing's Summer Palace, are mixed with scenes of their love-making and contrasted with scenes of violence between the two. The heightened personal feelings, of course, correspond with the amplified political events presented in the Beijing section. In the final section, Yu Hong has a number of relationships, which appear as intense moments of pleasure and release, but which are detached from true feelings of intimacy and express her character's sense of emptiness in the grim real of 2000s China.

It will be sex in the form of a second infidelity between Zhou Wei and Li Ta, who is still partnered with Rou Gu, that drives *Summer Palace* to its conclusion. After Zhou Wei and Li Ta have sex in his Berlin apartment, the next scene sees the two characters with Rou Gu on the streets of Berlin, where the friends come across a left-wing demonstration while out walking. During the scene, the friends go onto a rooftop, presumably at a friend's house, and Li Ta commits suicide by jumping from the building. As Michael Berry points out, the two key events, the personal and political, mirror those from the Beijing section. He describes the demonstration as follows: 'The spectral return of these socialist deities in an age of liberal economic reform and material prosperity is a reminder of the lingering power of the state to discipline, punish and regulate.'[20]

However, it is not the state that *Summer Palace* endows with libidinal force; rather, it is the emancipatory power of the collective that the film celebrates, seen in the earlier scenes in Beijing. The true moments of pleasure in the film are collective – sports, dancing, discussions, demonstrations – or intimate sexual relations. The prominence of the red flags on the streets of Berlin during the left-wing demonstration is not an echo of the power of the state, but of the optimism of the friends as they rode on the truck to Tiananmen. The idea is reinforced in a shot, shortly after Li Ta has committed suicide, of Zhou Wei standing alone on a Berlin street as he listens to a street-band play 'Suliko' – an old Georgian folk song popular in the Soviet Union under Stalin.[21] The sense of sadness Zhou Wei expresses in this scene is not the fear of the lingering power of the state, but the sense of lost love, lost possibilities and lost comradeship as suggested by the song. *Summer Palace* cuts from Zhou Wei listening to 'Suliko' in Berlin to Yu Hong back in China in a restaurant, listening to an accordionist, which reinforces the idea of separation. Li Ta's suicide is not caused by her renewed infidelity; rather, the infidelity is a futile attempt to recapture the past and escape from the grim real. The sight of red flags at the demonstration in Berlin proves unbearable for Li Ta, the most vibrant, artistic character in the film, and her suicide is a mourning for the lost emancipatory possibilities offered by the red flag.

Following Li Ta's death, Zhou Wei returns to China for the final, failed encounter with Yu Hong. The two former lovers meet at the coastal city Beidaihe in a small hotel room and appear to be about to rekindle their love. However, when Yu Hong leaves to get some drinks, Zhou Wei, sensing that the relationship is over and cannot be resurrected, drives off without saying goodbye. I read the scene as an attempt to refuse both the grim real and any easy resolution that would close the events of the film. *Summer Palace* wants to leave an open wound to challenge the viewer and to open memory out into the historical real, and thus allow the events of Tiananmen and their impact to be considered. At the end of *24 City*, the grim real smothers the screen, leaving nothing except for a song: an abstract, rather weak residue. *Summer Palace*, by contrast, opens new avenues of thought to a new generation, allowing them to think about their origins and how the defeat of Tiananmen conditioned the grim real of 'the brave new capitalist world' in which China and the iGeneration are left stranded.

In this chapter, I have traced the origins of the iGeneration through an examination of two Sixth Generation films that display symptoms of the transition to a new configuration. Both the iGeneration and the Sixth Generation must be read as conditioned by the economic and social factors prevalent at the time in which they emerged. The Sixth Generation draws on a vernacular of the city and utilizes *xianchang*, as well as a specular gaze, to create an intense focus on notions of reality and truth. The iGeneration is in many ways a more carefree configuration, conditioned by digital culture and Chinese neoliberalism – an economic mode that mixes global capitalism with autocratic state control. It is polymorphous as an aesthetic, heterogeneous and universal, it reflects the diversity (and inequality) of China as a major world power. The Sixth Generation followed the familiar model of minor national cinemas gaining recognition through distribution and visibility at international (mainly Western) film festivals and the international art film circuit. The iGeneration, by contrast, is marked by the dispersion of the internet – infinitely accessible to anyone with a computer, and yet at the same time frequently ghettoized to those who know where to access the relevant material. The Sixth Generation is fundamentally a cinematic movement, while the iGeneration marks the arrival of the post-cinematic moment in China explored in this volume.[22]

Works cited

Badiou, Alain. *Handbook of Inaesthetics*, translated by Alberto Toscano. Stanford: Stanford University Press, 2005.
—*The Century*, translated, with commentary and notes, by Alberto Toscano. Cambridge: Polity, 2007.
Berry, Michael. *A History of Pain: Trauma in Modern Chinese Literature and Film*. New York: Columbia University Press, 2011.
Braester, Yomi. *Paint the City Red*, Durham, NC: Duke University Press, 2010.
Bray, David. *Social Space and Governance in Urban China: The Danwei System From Origins to Urban Reform*. Stanford: Stanford University Press, 2005.

'China Overtakes Japan as World's Second-Biggest Economy,' Bloomberg News, 16 August 2010, http://www.bloomberg.com/news/2010-08-16/china-economy-passes-japan-s-in-second-quarter-capping-three-decade-rise.html

Fink, Bruce. *The Lacanian Subject: Between Language and Jouissance*. Princeton, NJ: Princeton University Press, 1996.

Lei Hao, myspace https://myspace.com/leihaosummerpalace

Li, Minqi. *The Rise of China and the Demise of the Capitalist World Economy*. London: Pluto Press, 2008.

Robinson, Luke. *Independent Chinese Documentary: From the Studio to the Street*. London: Palgrave Macmillan, 2013.

Shaviro, Stephen. *Post-Cinematic Affect*. Hampshire: Zero Books, 2010.

'US call for full Tiananmen massacre disclosure angers China' BBC News, 1 June 2013, http://www.bbc.co.uk/news/world-asia-china-22744242

Visser, Robin. *Cities Surround the Countryside*. Durham, NC: Duke University Press, 2012.

Wikipedia contributors. 'Suliko,' *Wikipedia, The Free Encyclopedia*, http://en.wikipedia.org/wiki/Suliko

Zhang, Xudong. 'Market Socialism and its Discontents: Jia Zhangke's Cinematic Narrative of China's Transition in an Age of Global Capital' in Jyostnsa Kapur and Keith B. Wagner (eds), *Neoliberalism and Global Cinema: Capital, Culture and Marxist Critique*. London: Routledge, 2011, 135–56.

Zhang, Zhen. *The Urban Generation: Chinese Cinema and Society at the Turn of the Twenty-First Century*. Durham, NC: Duke University Press, 2007.

Notes

1 Zhang Zhen, *The Urban Generation: Chinese Cinema and Society at the Turn of the Twenty-First Century*. Durham, NC: Duke University Press, 2007, 2.

2 For an overview of *xianchang* in Chinese documentary film see Luke Robinson, *Independent Chinese Documentary: From the Studio to the Street*. London: Palgrave Macmillan, 2013.

3 http://www.bloomberg.com/news/2010-08-16/china-economy-passes-japan-s-in-second-quarter-capping-three-decade-rise.html (accessed 8 September 2013).

4 See Minqi Li, *The Rise of China and the Demise of the Capitalist World Economy*. London: Pluto Press, 2008.

5 Yomi Braester, *Paint the City Red*. Durham, NC: Duke University Press, 2010, 16.

6 Zhang Xudong, 'Market Socialism and its Discontents: Jia Zhangke's Cinematic Narrative of China's Transition in an Age of Global Capital' in Jyostnsa Kapur and Keith B. Wagner (eds), *Neoliberalism and Global Cinema: Capital, Culture and Marxist Critique*. London: Routledge, 2011, 135–56.

7 For a history of the Danwei's role in China see David Bray, *Social Space and Governance in Urban China: The Danwei System From Origins to Urban Reform*. Stanford: Stanford University Press, 2005.

8 Robin Visser, *Cities Surround the Countryside*. Durham, NC: Duke University Press, 2012, 7.

9 I take the concept of the grim real from Alain Badiou's *The Century*. Cambridge: Polity Press, 2007. I discuss its relevance to the Sixth Generation in my forthcoming thesis.

10 Zhang Xudong, 138.
11 In China, the events are known as the June 4th incident, I retain the Western designation of Tiananmen here to refer to all of the national protests that took place in China in 1989 while recognizing the focal point Tiananmen Square in Beijing.
12 Zhang Xudong, 148.
13 Michael Berry, *A History of Pain: Trauma in Modern Chinese Literature and Film*. New York: Columbia University Press, 2011, 342.
14 https://myspace.com/leihaosummerpalace (accessed 28 August 2013).
15 Thanks to Hui Liu for the translation.
16 The shots are as follows: (1) Long-shot of truck driving down Beijing city street; (2) Close-up of male on truck carrying flag; (3) Track out over packed Beijing railway station; (4) Close-up of student climbing out of train carriage window; (5) Mid-shot of marching demonstrators; (6) Demonstrators pouring out of Beijing railway station with one red flag prominent; (7) Demonstrators dressed all in white holding placards including 'I love free press' in English; (8) Red flags filling the screen; (9) Long-shot of demonstrators in Tiananmen square; (10) Shot of red, black and white flags filling the screen; (11) Right-panning shot of protestors' placards; (12) Tiananmen Gate with the famous portrait of Mao almost hidden behind the demonstrators' flags; (13) Long-shot of demonstrators filling Chang'an Avenue.
17 Bruce Fink, *The Lacanian Subject: Between Language and Jouissance*. Princeton, NJ: Princeton University Press, 1996.
18 http://www.bbc.co.uk/news/world-asia-china-22744242 (accessed 20 August 2013).
19 Michael Berry, 342.
20 Michael Berry, 348.
21 http://en.wikipedia.org/wiki/Suliko (accessed 28 August 2013).i
22 For an introduction to post-cinema see Stephen Shaviro, *Post-Cinematic Affect*. Hampshire: Zero Books, 2010.

6

Digitizing City Symphony, Stabilizing the Shadow of Time: Montage and Temporal–Spatial Construction in *San Yuan Li*[1]

Ling Zhang

As an audiovisual medium that developed amid advances in modern technology and sensitivity, cinema from its inception formed an intimate affinity with changing urban cityscapes. With their ability to capture urban images, reconstruct urban time–space and represent urban experience, the 'city symphony' films from the 1920s and 1930s[2] constitute a film mode that has been investigated by numerous film and cultural critics, social theorists and urban geographers, leading to diverse historical, theoretical and geographical accounts.[3] City symphony films deploy a combination of everyday images and complex montage, an avant-garde artistic practice and documentary impulse, in order to articulate the new intensity of speed and excessive sensory stimulations that define experience in the rapidly and incessantly changing modern city.[4] The cinematic portraits of modern metropolises such as Berlin, Paris, New York[5] and Moscow culminate in two exemplary aesthetically sophisticated films during the interwar years: Walther Ruttmann's *Berlin, Symphony of a Metropolis* (Berlin: Die Sinfonie der Großstadt 1927) and Dziga Vertov's *Man with a Movie Camera* (*Chelovek s kinoapparatom* 1929), which highlight the significance of the montage aesthetic in conveying the modern mentality of city life and giving it new prominence.[6]

In Alexander Graf's view, montage, as an expression of urban modernity, played an essential role in defining film as a 'modern' art form. The representation and reconstruction of the pace and rhythm of urban life, as expressed through editing techniques, is the overriding concern of the city symphony film genre.[7] Montage reconstructs fragmented time by reassembling individual shots taken in various locations, simultaneously or consecutively. It also spatializes time and creates intricate rhythms within a filmic text. Thus, the city symphony film is striving to become the most appropriate form for audiovisually representing the modern urban experience, while at the same time revealing the urban subject's unconscious experience or fantasy of modern urban life. The standard metrical editing rhythm at the formal level in city symphony films, together with an exploration of the dynamics of a global space – time continuum on the level of content,⁸ embody the modernist impulse, the ideal of visual transparency, and the ordering of chaos. By surmounting the human eye's limitations with the omniscient camera eye and non-linear montage synthesis,⁹ city symphony films create a totalizing and abstracting vision – one that is stylized, provocative and socially critical. Regarding the city as a significant site of empowerment and resistance, cultural critics and urban scholars have intensively discussed the problems of urban spatial segregation, social and cultural inequality each based on class, gender, race and ethnicity; academics also work within the same broad tradition, seeking to celebrate lived urban rhythms, anonymity and the differences found in city films.¹⁰

In this chapter, I examine the employment of montage and the temporal-spatial construction in the contemporary Chinese city symphony film *San Yuan Li* (Ou Ning and Cao Fei, DV format, 40 minutes, 2003), in order to explore how the montage aesthetic in city symphony films has undergone temporal, spatial and medium/material displacement and transformation, from the 1920s in the West to twenty-first century China, and from celluloid to digital video. This case study also allows a closer look at the ways in which cinematic time–space and its representation of social time–space have been constructed within the city symphony film tradition, while maintaining its own stylistic and thematic uniqueness, as well as local specificity, entrenched in the Chinese sociopolitical context of urbanization and the third-world country's interactions with neoliberal globalization. As a spatialization of global power and located on global circuits, the third-world city Guangzhou is both a generic, global city, one transcending locality and temporality, and a city with stubborn local and temporal anchors. And it is Guangzhou's rapid urban development that most likely intrigued the directors of *San Yuan Li* to envisage this twenty-first century bustling 'workshop of the world' – not unlike Ruttmann's frenetically paced Berlin of the twentieth century.

As a 'city symphony' film¹¹ paying homage to Dziga Vertov's *Man with a Movie Camera* (1929), *San Yuan Li* can be put into the genealogy of the city symphony film tradition via world film history. However, with an almost 70-year gap between the films, the contemporary city symphony in *San Yuan Li* displays considerable modifications¹² and distinguishing characteristics that make it distinct from other early 'city symphony' films – not only in terms of form, content and social contexts, but also in term of medium. The digital video format that *San Yuan Li* deploys is imbued with some ontological and material differences from the conventional city symphonies, which are made with silver-based film stock.¹³

The intricate spatio-temporal configuration in *San Yuan Li* is achieved and enhanced by its ingenious deployment of cinematic techniques like rapid montage, dynamic camera movements, and extreme camera angles, as well as the manipulation of time and speed through fast motion, slow motion and group photos with temporal duration.¹⁴ The rhythm and temporality constructed in the film are interdependent and intertwined with the social time and actual space in San Yuan Li, the village within Guangzhou city where the film is set.¹⁵ Guangzhou is the capital of Southern coastal Guangdong Province, regarded as the frontline of Chinese economic reform, a basin of production, and a window opening onto the outside world since the 1980s.

'San Yuan Li' is an urban village (*chengzhongcun*), literally 'village encircled by the city,' characterized by large-scale rural–urban migration and the radical expansion of built-up urban areas. The rapid expansion of Chinese cities has been encroaching into surrounding villages since the 1990s. In Guangzhou, the metropolitan area expanded from 136 to 287 square kilometres between 1980 and 1999; it now contains 277 *chengzhongcun* with approximately 1,000,000 indigenous villagers. Losing their farmland due to land requisition by the city government, while maintaining property rights over their own houses and their housing plots (*zhaijidi*), local villagers have built houses and leased these properties to rural migrant workers from all over the country at a premium rate. This new type of urban neighbourhood is considered transitional under China's rapid urbanization because of the influx of new tenants from far-flung provinces.

Chengzhongcun are generally perceived, from the policymaker's perspective, as undesirable in terms of urban planning and governance because of their association with inappropriate land use, poor housing construction, severe infrastructural deficiencies, exacerbated social disorder and the deterioration of the urban environment. Some Chinese sociologists argue that *chengzhongcun* in fact contribute significantly to Chinese urbanization by offering a feasible solution to the housing problem of massive numbers of rural migrants, allowing city governments to take advantage of cheap and flexible rural labour without bearing the extra costs associated with labour relocation.[16] Large portions of these urban villages have little connection to the city, even though they are physically proximate: they represent the 'local' within the 'local' and the global city of Guangzhou in globalization. The almost claustrophobic density of architecture and population in *San Yuan Li* contributes to the specificity of the space and the mentalities of its inhabitants. It also reveals social and historical problems related to urban expansion, urban planning, and the inevitable process of globalization that are continued themes from the Urban Generation to the iGeneration.[17]

The displacement of the 'city symphony' film genre not only implies temporal and spatial fluidity, but also provokes some contemplation on the imbricated relations between tradition, memory, modernity and urban experience. In *San Yuan Li*, tradition and modernity do not appear as a conventional dichotomy; they coexist peacefully and infiltrate each other. Local tradition and collective memory are embedded in contemporary cosmopolitan texture and experience, evoking a sense of 'alternative modernity' with a specific vernacular characteristic in perceiving and experiencing time and space in the globalization era, due to the uneven development and temporality between the West and China. To a certain extent, the urban village San Yuan Li is a dynamic site of autonomy resisting the hegemonic power of globalization through its own way of allocating and manipulating time and space. Not only are there uneven landscapes and sites of powerful symbolism in contemporary cities, but such places are capable of generating and maintaining robust and active communities; places where collective memory and local meaning shape the social and physical landscape.[18] I see David Harvey and Michel de Certeau's insightful accounts of urban time and space, as well as theories and observations of urban studies, as valuable frameworks for conceptualizing and contextualizing temporal–spatial constructions in *San Yuan Li*.[19]

In the process of creating compelling city audio-imagery and a cinematic promenade in *San Yuan Li*, the cameramen traverse and observe the urban space from a privileged position, like the Baudelairian city *flâneur* who is 'secure in his distance from the scenes he observes, and empowered by his ability to penetrate the "labyrinthine" spaces of the city.'[20] Mediated by a detached and aestheticized view with a mechanical 'camera eye', the city *flâneurs* resist the 'blasé attitude' of the urban dwellers which Georg Simmel elaborates[21] and instead produce defamiliarized images facilitated by the flexibility, spontaneity and immediacy of the digital medium, enhanced by the lightness of the digital camera and the sense of a de-historicized black and white digital image. With the film showing the act of walking, cartographic space is transformed into a place of meaning and memory. Thus, within a single urban landscape, multiple places defined through use, imagination and a range of cultural practices will emerge. De Certeau argues that it is in the act of walking that a 'myriad' of uses write and rewrite the city as 'their' place – creating fragmentary stories that link and intersect with other fragmentary stories.[22] Cities are comprised of multiple histories and a web of coexisting and contesting presents. In Giuliana Bruno's words, 'Different temporalities are spatially mapped as different sites are revisited in different bodies.'[23] Thus time, space and the rural–urban experience of San Yuan Li village in 2002 have been preserved, enriched and immortalized in the filmic tapestry of *San Yuan Li*, as a mobile cityscape and urban memory archive. *San Yuan Li* is both an homage to, and instantiation of, the early city symphony film tradition, and an updating of this genealogy, in response to both globalization's interaction with the local village and to technological and aesthetic shifts within the film medium.

Metrical montage and the manipulation of cinematic time

Like music, film is a time-based medium and art form. As a 'city symphony' film, *San Yuan Li* is endowed with punctuality and precision, adhering to principles of balance and formal discipline in order to achieve dynamic coherence in its aural and visual composition.[24] The composition is accentuated by both the visual layout and movement in an individual frame and the construction of rhythmic montage. In Alexander Graf's view, rhythmic montage involves the precise calculation of duration, which can be compared to musical composition.[25] *San Yuan Li* privileges graphic qualities and rhythm over the chronology of the footage through the extensive use of metrical montage, and relinquishes the dawn-to-night temporal format that prevailed in early city symphony films.[26] This configuration allows it to build up a more unrestricted narrative and spatio-temporal structure dependent exclusively on visual and aural rhythm.

As a 40-minute long visual symphony, *San Yuan Li* consists of seven episodes.[27] The first act lasts nine minutes and 23 seconds, and functions as a prelude, depicting the process of approaching and traversing Guangzhou city by boat, motorcycle, automobile, and finally entering San Yuan Li village by subway.[28] The second act is about four minutes and 33 seconds long, and depicts the dense and unoccupied architectural space in San Yuan Li village in silence. The third section lasts slightly less than three minutes, and explores the spatial relationship between mobile airplanes and the stationary village in Guangzhou's cityscape. The fourth episode is around five minutes, and portrays street life and performance in public space in the urban village.[29] The fifth episode lasts about ten minutes, and illustrates nightlife, workshops, service and leisure in the village. The sixth segment is three minutes and 23 seconds, and consists of 18 group photos with temporal duration of local people in different vocations. The final act serves as a postscript, containing two parts: 32 seconds of subtitles briefly explaining the significant time markers in the official history of San Yuan Li village, and a four-minute outtake of the self-reflexive images of U-thèque members'[30] location shooting, accompanied by a lyrical song.

The seven episodes are connected by themes and rhythm rather than any chronological order. This structure takes the spectator on a journey that approaches and penetrates the main protagonist of the film – San Yuan Li, the village within the city – layer by layer, locating it at the centre of Guangzhou and indicating its intimate yet distant relationship to the city.[31] The film gradually focuses more on San Yuan Li's residents, who are the essence of the space and who energize silent, uninhabited architecture into a bustling, vigorous urban village. The increasing vitality and dynamism that people bring into the concrete physical space resonate with the intensified tempo of the film. In addition, with the 'music video' style outtake in the final part, *San Yuan Li* echoes the demystification of the filmmaking process and self-referentiality of the camera as apparatus in Vertov's *Man with a Movie Camera*, which is achieved by incorporating footage of shooting, editing and screening the film within the film itself.[32]

The narrative structure and audiovisual diegesis of *San Yuan Li* are complemented by the dynamic, speedy montage, which corresponds to the filmmakers' (and the audience's) perception of urban time and space, and which reassembles fragmentary images into an elaborate interpretation of San Yuan Li from a fresh perspective. In *San Yuan Li* editor Cao Fei's words, 'In editing [the film], [I attempted to] highlight visual density and speed. [These two elements] are also the conspicuous features in the development of the city; the almost frantic growth oppresses us and intrudes into our lives, and we have to be forced to accept it.'[33] As the embodiment of a spectacular acceleration in the city's life circle, the dazzling patterns of montage (including single-frame editing in some sequences) in *San Yuan Li* cut back and forth across time and space and intertwine disjointed and unruly themes and fragments simultaneously, providing an excess of sensory stimuli and unrestrained rhythm.

The alternating audiovisual acceleration and deceleration of rhythm underscored by montage creates a rich pattern of pace in *San Yuan Li*. The strategy and theory of 'interval,' borrowed from musical terms and extolled by Dziga Vertov[34] as the basis of his aesthetic project, also plays a significant role in transitioning from one movement, act, or theme to another. Between each two episodes in the film, there are intervals: images and music slow down, halt for a moment, and cross-fade before the next section starts, communicating through music or ambient sound. In this sense, cinematic time seems to repose briefly, forming an effective contrast with the speed of the previous and subsequent parts and highlighting a pulsing rhythm.

In addition to the use of intervals, the film's aesthetic experimentation with radical temporal acceleration and deceleration involves a manipulation of speed as well as the reconstruction of cinematic time. The extensive deployment of fast motion[35] and slow motion in *San Yuan Li* alters customary ways of representing actual time versus normative spectatorial perceptions of time, creating temporal elasticity. Moreover, these techniques generate a tension between the images in different speeds since there is only 'relative speed'; alternating between images in various frame compositions, shot lengths and ranges also contributes to the effect. For example, in a 20-second sequence (7:33–7:55) in episode one, there is an intercut between fast-motion long shots of people entering a building or exercising in the street in comparison to standard-speed medium shots of an old woman having breakfast and pouring herself a cup of tea. Since the former group of images is in fast motion, the audience will likely have the illusion that the later group of standard-speed images are in slow motion. Cinematic time is not an absolute concept, but one that depends on contexts within the film and on the spectator's perception; it can be understood as shortened or extended,[36] even though its duration does not alter.

Yuri Tsivian relates image speed and cinematic time with shot range in a metaphorical way: he regards slow motion as a 'close-up' of time.[37] Slow motion affords the audience more time to scrutinize details in the frame, thus spatializing and visualizing time and creating the illusion of an extended and enlarged 'now' image. Since the time of an individual shot has been stretched with slow motion, a given amount of cinematic time contains fewer images. The fast-paced short film *San Yuan Li* does not utilize slow motion very frequently, which greatly increases the capacity of incorporating a large number of shots by employing fast motion and rapid montage. Two conspicuous examples of using slow motion, however, appear at 25:01 and 28:29 in the film; these sequences feature some security guards walking away from the camera and a ball that some boys are using to play soccer in the back alley dashing toward the camera. There are other slow-motion images, in close-up, of people laughing and of crowds flowing in the street. In these sequences, the motion slows down and the moving subjects or shifting facial expressions are endowed with a subtle poetic resonance that exceeds everyday life and realistic representation, especially when accompanied by music.

When the film presents images in fast motion, the information presented is so overwhelming and transient that it becomes impossible for the spectator to examine the details carefully. This illusion of shortening cinematic time increases the image capacity in a given time range. However, like slow motion, fast motion also represents warped time and distorted motion, in this case through excessive dynamism. Moving human bodies in fast motion appear mechanical and almost burlesque, as exemplified by the shot of many people exercising in Act One. The human bodies with exaggerated speed of motion in this scene seem to be mechanized, performing like androids for the audience. However, *San Yuan Li* does more than involuntarily invoke Vertov's fascination with the creation of a machine-man;[38] in general, the film embraces a model of unregulated human energy.

The mechanization of the human body is redressed, in a manipulated, artificial way, in Act Six, with the group photos of San Yuan Li residents/inhabitants statically posing for the camera in various geometrical patterns. At first glance, these group photos seem to be faithful to recorded time (real time in normal speed). However, they serve to probe the interstices between recorded time and playback time, employing slightly slow or fast motion that can only be discerned when one subject in the frame changes facial expression (smiling or blinking), or when another subject traverses the foreground of the frame.[39] Since people are supposed to maintain a still position when taking photographs, which makes slight shifts difficult to detect, it is only in these moments that the cinematic time can be seen to be fluid and not frozen. In Ou Ning's words, 'The static shooting combines still photography and moving image; the images seem still, but in fact some tiny moving details are discernible, that will invoke an interesting viewing experience.'[40] In spite of manipulations of speed, the spatio-temporal continuities within these roughly 11-second shots mostly remain uninterrupted.

The tension between photographic mimesis and dynamic motion in these group portraits is embodied by the carefully grouped human bodies, which are reminiscent of a *tableau vivant*, a popular spectacle of the eighteenth and nineteenth centuries that exhibited mimesis in the form of 'living pictures,' in which live 'actors' adopted immobile poses in imitation of artworks or historical and literary scenes.[41] Devoid of the imitation dimension in *tableau vivant* here, these live bodies in this sequence of the film are made to freeze (though not strictly, as in *tableau vivant*) and the corporeal landscape turns the body itself into a 'site' of exhibition. However, the bodies in exhibition are not simply passive objects of viewing; they confront the viewer and the camera unflinchingly and even produce self-reflective images if we consider the camera lens as a mirror. Furthermore, the four-dimensional temporal-spatial configuration of these animated group photos conveys a sense of uncanniness or uneasiness at the moment of confrontation, while the extra-diegetic music and ambient sounds seem to hamper this sense[42] through acoustic mediation and aestheticization. This type of 'bodily experience of affectivity'[43] is also related to the representation and perception of time in the digital media age, as Mark Hansen has argued: 'Insofar as new media art invests in the bodily experience of affectivity, intensifying it and enlarging its scope, it might be said to embody time consciousness and, indeed, to embody the being of time itself.' The shift from an abstract consciousness of time to an embodied affectivity allows for a fuller and more intense experience of subjectivity and intimacy.[44] The importance of affect is also acknowledged by Ou Ning: '[...] Taking group photos is a way of expressing emotions for Chinese people; I want to denote my identification with them by shooting the footage as group portraits because they have inconceivable wisdom and energy in facing harsh reality. There is a kind of poetics transcending reality.'[45]

Temporalizing visual and acoustic space

In addition to still human bodies in group photos, *San Yuan Li* foregrounds human bodies navigating and mapping space. This is true both of the human subjects in the film and of the cameramen as they convey a mobile and subjective vision with their 'mechanical eye.' The film attempts to construct a three-dimensional audio-visual space (however fragmented) by combining metrical montage, innovative camera movements, unusual camera angles and sophisticated extradiegetic music and ambient sound. The mixture of abstract architectural photography and figurative, documentary-style sequences presents both a tranquil architectural space devoid of human activity and a human-scape which energizes that physical space. These spatial continuities persist through rapid successions of disparate and incoherent images that suggest sharply discontinuous temporal associations.

Elusive cinematic space is interdependent with the particularities of the physical space of the urban village San Yuan Li. Located at the fringe of Guangzhou city a decade ago, San Yuan Li has now found itself in the centre of the city after decades of urban expansion. It is surrounded by gleaming high-rise buildings and stands in great proximity to the Guangzhou railway station and Baiyun airport.[46] San Yuan Li has become a besieged urban village, an encircled neighbourhood with porous spatial boundaries preserving its own life rhythms, administrative system and rural social structure in contrast with the rest of the city. The village has assumed an aberrant extra-territoriality that outstrips the clutch of 'normal' urban life. As Michel de Certeau's *Concept City*, which endeavours to render the city transparently, explains, 'Rational organization must thus repress all the physical, mental and political pollutions that would compromise it.'[47]

Some of the rural-rooted low-income migrant populations in San Yuan Li are considered 'deviant' by the government and mainstream media, as well as by a large number of urban residents; crimes and unlawful activities occurring in the area are regarded as social 'pathologies.' Many global cities have endured slum clearance and gentrification, in the name of rehabilitation and redevelopment, in order to control the urban spatial power agenda and turn an unruly space into areas for the middle class and their residential and recreational priorities and to rid the areas of the poor and the criminal.[48] Cities are becoming more sharply divided into ghettos of homogeneity based on capital, class, ethnicity, sexual orientation and so on. People are actively seeking to avoid encounter and contact with difference, the (threatening) 'Other,' fostering and giving visual expression to greater imbalance of power and social, cultural and economic inequality. This inequality in turn leads to urban partitioning and enclaves of homogeneity. However, San Yuan Li's complexity and vitality resist the government's attempts at rationalized, standardized appropriations of time–space. The village strives to sustain its chaotic but vigorous autonomy, a combination (and juxtaposition) of global capitalist modes with socialist and agricultural traces.

The term 'urban village' was coined by Taylor (1973) as a response to the bland and monotonous developments of the 1960s, 1970s and 1980s; the UVF (Urban

Villagers Forum) developed the concept as an urban settlement which is small and of neighbourhood size; combines residential with work, retail and leisure units; aims to be self-sustaining; mixes different social and economic groups; has efficient transportation; and is well designed and managed. Despite criticism, the urban village has been recognized as a valuable way to encourage social interaction, create a balanced community, and unravel the complexities of urban sustainability from a systemic point of view.[49] China's urban village shares some similarities with the Western concept – such as pedestrian-oriented spaces, accessibility, self-containment, mixed land use, and neighbourhood interaction. Nonetheless, these are largely contingent and spontaneous similarities rather than the results of conscious urban planning and management: for example, local villagers who lose their farmland build up rental houses that shelter members of the rural–urban low-income migrant community. Despite unruliness and disorder, security and social problems, the urban village alleviates urban poverty to a certain extent and provides rural migrants who lack social cohesion with a sense of belonging. This village-style of self-organization has preserved social and cultural traditions and played a large role in easing the pressure of urbanization in China.[50]

Because of its horizontal spatial constraints, San Yuan Li has grown through vertical extension.[51] The result is an extraordinary enclave of crowded, well-worn tenements, a maze of narrow winding lanes, a thin strip of sky and a hodge-podge of shops, eateries and service outlets, all surrounded by modern skyscrapers. In this context, architecture can be perceived as a mode of expression and communication. As the congestion of construction leaves only a small gap for light[52] between adjacent structures, there is a serious erosion of privacy among the densely packed inhabitants, who, ironically, may never make acquaintance with one another or exchange a word. Therefore, as Georg Simmel puts it, 'The bodily proximity and narrowness of space makes the mental distance only the more visible.'[53] The physically intimate environments foster an anxious, claustrophobic and estranged existence, as well as an instrumental, blasé and reserved urban attitude, as a protective response to the relentless bombardment of stimuli that one experiences in the modern city.[54] Ever since Western-style industrial capitalism and urbanization has taken root (in China), life in the cities is represented as the 'unnatural setting for the anonymous interaction of an alienated population.'[55] However, these rational and calculating factors also make liberation possible: they have freed people from the constraints and obligations that are a feature of communal country life. This temporary, transitional community of rural migrants is in many ways discursive, but linked to a specific site and embedded in a larger matrix of socioeconomic relations, forming a place-bound collective identity.

Various temporalities coexist in what we might call a 'temporal fusion' within these intricate spaces, as well as in the relationship between these spaces and the rest of the city. The antique, traditional ancestral temples that epitomize the rural dwelling styles of southern China, together with the relics of a religious and patriarchal kinfolk system, coexist with new rental dwellings illegally constructed by villagers to maximize incomes during the latest economic boom.[56] The village lifestyle and social network will not easily meet its demise with the local villagers' changes in *hukou* registration status and occupation. The effervescent modern urban street life that has infiltrated San Yuan Li is also juxtaposed with the agrarian lifestyle on the village's interconnected rooftops. Dispossessed of their agricultural lands, the villagers-turned-landlords repurpose their rooftops as sanctuaries and retrace their pastoral past by turning them into small farms where they grow plants and vegetables and raise poultry. This practice generates a conspicuous aerial landscape in the city scene, especially when airplanes constantly fly over these rooftop farms; the mobile modern technological invention accentuates the tranquil, traditional agricultural lifestyle both temporally and spatially, fusing the linear time of technological progress with the cyclical time of nature and agricultural convention. In David Harvey's words, 'cyclical and repetitive motions (such as daily routines and seasonal rituals) provide a sense of security in a world where the general thrust of progress appears to be ever onwards and upwards into the firmament of the unknown.'[57] However, the film's employment of dynamic montage and jittery images of airplanes flying over the urban village reinforces a pervasive sense of insecurity and uncertainty.

The airplanes also engage closely with local history and tradition through their spatial relationship with the city's anti-British monument and with a traditional local performance (the lion dance). This is demonstrated in two scenes, both of which appear in Act Four: (1) a long-shot of an airplane gliding over a soaring monument; and (2) a long-shot of an airplane flitting across the frame while a lion-dancing performance takes place on a terrace (18:59 and 20:49, respectively). The juxtaposition of the horizontal vector and fluttering noise of the plane with the silent, vertical immobility of the monument corresponds to the relationship between the ephemeral and fleeting and the eternal and immutable. History and memory are embedded in contemporary daily life through monument and ritual.

As a landmark with emblematic meaning, the monument is imbued with a quality of permanence and bears the trace of suspended time. Time is stabilized by the fixed points of the monument, which incorporate and preserve a 'mysterious' sense of collective memory: the monument is dedicated to the civil insurrection of San Yuan Li villagers against British military forces 160 years ago – a rebellion against imperialist invaders that has been written into Chinese historical textbooks as an important part of local and national heroic anti-colonial history. The preservation of myth through ritual[58] constitutes a key to understanding the meaning of monuments and, moreover, the implications of the founding of cities and of the transmission of ideas in an urban context.[59] The place of singular local significance acts as repository of collective memory, with communal or shared architectural and spatial symbols; however, history itself is not a sufficient condition for generating memorials. The past does not inhere in places, but is fused and brought out by groups of actors and sequences of events. These sites seem to have a sacred quality about them, in the sense of their having been set apart from the mundane and infused with unusual powers of instruction and remembrance.[60] The civic or public realm – the sites of ceremonies, parades and imposing public architecture, and the sites of movement and congregation, of urban density and diversity – advocates a celebration of heterogeneity.

As a particular locality situated in a zone of intensive global–local negotiations, San Yuan Li is a place that is too complicated and unruly to be disciplined. It both relies on and resists globalization.[61] It eludes or diverts control with its own rhythm, lifestyle and particular constructions of time–space. In San Yuan Li, there is neither a clear demarcation between work, leisure and entertainment time, nor a clear division between living and business space within some small workshops and factories. Unlike some early city symphony films, which underline the significance of the clock in embodying standardized time and regulating social life in the modern city,[62] *San Yuan Li* does not highlight clocks showing exact time. Instead, it emphasizes quotidian scenes of the urban village in action over a 24-hour period as a way of suggesting its resistance to the regulated urban schedule and the partitioning of day and night. The creative energy permeating the village is partly due to the diverse and changing demographic mix of its inhabitants. The population consists mostly of migrant workers from other provinces seeking opportunities in the coastal city of Guangzhou, since living in an urban village is relatively inexpensive. They bring their local culture, habits, dialects and accents to this congested space, and experience a sense of linguistic heterogeneity and spontaneous self-diversification. San Yuan Li's tradition and memory are diluted, and its culture is dynamically re-composed and rendered plural.

The film language deployed in *San Yuan Li* reflects the cramped space, the chaotic yet vigourous atmosphere and the exuberant affectivity of the village. The spatial structure in the urban village is so dense that it makes a panorama nearly impossible, but the immense 'sky plaza' formed by the interconnected rooftop verandas provides a vantage point to display an omniscient view in high-angle shots. The formally and thematically associated montage and the graphic contrast between images in the film create a visual rhythm. The graphic match is constituted through analogous or contrasting shapes, lines, camera angles, viewpoints, light/shadow contrasts and other visual themes.[63] The orderly perspective from above and the disorienting fragmentation of living experience from below also create a compelling visual and sensory contrast. With these purposeful motifs, the disparate images and fragments of time–space, though devoid of inherent correlations, are logically assembled to produce meaning and order.

Moreover, multiple layers of movement – including camera movements, object movements within a single frame and double movements of both the camera and the vehicle on which the camera has been mounted – suggest the passage of time by traversing space and creating spectacular visual cadences. Elsewhere, Andrew Webber argues that transportation and motion pictures are coupled in the experience of the 'image rush' of location in transit and a heightened experience of space through time. The city is understandable both as a spatial structure (a more or less fixed system of spaces and places) and as the motions or transitions that traverse that structure.[64] Both the fixed and mobile sides of the city are explored and reinforced in the film, through elaborate camera movements and the manipulation of lenses, including rapid panning shots (horizontal movement), zooming shots (both inward and outward) and tracking shots (in-depth or lateral). These techniques penetrate perspectival space, creating an unstable, mobile and spatial depth and an evocative sensory experience.[65] Through associative montage, a sequence of rapid zooms in and out of rooftops (12:17 into the film) intensifies these dazzling and vertiginous effects. The intercutting between moving and static shots of the architectural space in Act Two[66] puts moments of motion and stillness in constant contrast. It also represents movement through the mobilization of the abstract, geometric forms of architecture. The mobile vehicles[67] navigating among the motionless urban structures not only travel on the city's skin-like surface (as in the case of the automobile, bus and train), but also underneath (subway) and above (airplane), thus constructing a vertical space that cuts across the three horizontal levels. On the one hand, the traversing vehicles oppose insularities and traverse spatial barriers; on the other hand, they confirm these barriers through the same actions. The unrestrained liberty suggested by the flowing, subjective view from a fast-moving boat, taxi or subway train augments and multiplies the camera's own movement.[68]

The acoustic space constructed by the film's music and ambient sounds resonates with the vivid visual space created by elaborate metrical montage and camera movements, stimulating the viewer's auditory sense. Alexander Graf points out the decisive role that music plays in city symphony films, as the mathematical abstraction of musical aesthetics endeavours to establish a film language intrinsic to the film medium in the city symphonies.[69] In *San Yuan Li*, music determines the structure, creates and reinforces the rhythm and shapes the montage pattern[70] through its tonal variations and tempo shifts. The images that are deprived of diegetic sound seem insubstantial and without depth, as if silent pictures were being assembled together; synchronized sound magically crystallizes the image and enables it to represent a realistic three-dimensional space. In *San Yuan Li*, most images are accompanied by music and added sounds; only a few sequences feature synchronized ambient sound. This indicates that the film does not intend to represent the urban village in a realistic documentary mode, but in an impressionistic, experimental way. Echoing the heterogeneous cityscape, the film emphasizes this urban plurality of sounds, by turning a cacophony and euphony with pulsating, extra-diegetic music and boisterous, ambient sound. We hear the diegetic sounds of a man playing *gaohu*,[71] miscellaneous voices from television, various provincial dialects and accents emerging from a public telephone booth, sounds from walkie-talkies, mahjong playing, car horns, street noise and so on. People are conspicuously involved in creating a sophisticated soundscape that plays a significant role in evoking an unruly, vibrant atmosphere. The spatial density of San Yuan Li village also exerts an influence on the quality, transmission and perception of sound: the noise can either be sealed off or amplified into tremendous echoes.[72] In addition, musical metaphors visualize and spatialize sound. At the beginning of Act Two, for instance, the music sounds like bells and symbolizes the footsteps of invincible time; in this sense, the onomatopoeic music auralizes the concept of time instead of visualizing it, thus departing from early city symphony films that utilize images of clocks as a corollary device.

Conclusion

San Yuan Li inherits some vibrant characteristics from the tradition of the city symphony films. Its efforts to vividly portray the spatial distinctiveness of an urban village in specific historical time and to construct an intricate cinematic time–space are particularly indebted to Vertov's *Man with a Movie Camera*, with its ingenious deployment of metrical montage, black-and-white imagery and sensitivity to rhythm and tempo. However, as a contemporary digital video work made in a distinct cinematic, geographical and social context, *San Yuan Li*'s aesthetic experimentation in cinematic time (fast motion, slow motion and the semi-static group photo) and its manipulation of the spectatorial experience of time (shifts in recording speed, camera angle and soundtrack) distinguish it from early city symphony films and reflect the seemingly uncontrolled acceleration of temporal processes and a more fragmented reality of the current era. As Ou Ning explains, the film 'chronicles the fragments of a Chinese city shattered by incessant waves of globalization.'[73] Taken together, the manifold, fragmentary nature of visual impressions, intensified by rapid montage, profoundly alters the perception of discontinuous urban time and space in *San Yuan Li*.

Furthermore, *San Yuan Li* develops a sense of time–space distinct from early city symphonies because of the new medium of digital video it employs. A delicate, grainy texture usually enriches the surface of silver-based film; in the digital image, however, the smooth, shiny surface constituted by layers of pixels facilitates an 'urban-cinematic pellicle,'[74] since the city as digital image is insistently experienced as face or skin. Additionally, in terms of the perception of time, Babette Mangolte claims that the difference between 'real time' and 'screen time' is not clear in digital viewing,[75] whereas the variation in projection speed and the halting motions of silver-based film make it possible in that medium to distinguish between 'real time' and 'screen time'. In digital media, however, electronic recording and the persistence of vision ensure a direct correspondence between the two. In this sense, time has been preserved on standardized digital images: the colours never fades and the time is timeless. Consequently, 'time is fixed as in a map in digital and is totally repeatable with no degradation due to copying loss, while silver-based film is structured by time as entropy, therefore, unrepeatable. The unpredictability of time passing and time past, the slippage between one and the other, and the pathos of their essentially ineluctable difference are lost.'[76] In William C. Wees's view, the highly standardized version of 'visual life' composed by standardized digital images is focused and stable, constructing unambiguous representations of familiar objects in three-dimensional space.[77] However, *San Yuan Li* plays with recorded time and playback time, uncertainty and certainty, and the unpredictable and predictable, using alterations of speed in an attempt to subvert the standardization of the digital medium.

San Yuan Li exemplifies the empowering potential of new digital video technologies and their alternative modes of production, distribution and exhibition. With the immediacy and democraticization of digital image-making, digital video works consist of more selective images (though they do not necessarily employ *better* selection or quality): the ratio of shooting to finished film in *San Yuan Li* is 90:1,[78] compared to a ratio of 20:1 for Vertov's *Man with a Movie Camera*.[79] *San Yuan Li* was commissioned by the 'Z.O.U' (*Zone of Urgency*) exhibition, curated by Hou Hanru as part of the Fiftieth Venice Biennale in 2003 and screened in an open, metaphorical space designed to resemble a train.[80] Thus, *San Yuan Li* experienced double displacements in its initial setting: the shift of the city symphony film genre from the 1920s West to contemporary China; and the shift of a digital video work depicting a Chinese urban village to an exhibition in the West, thus breaking away from the constraints of its original temporal–spatial context. To counterbalance an inevitable tendency to reduction, *San Yuan Li* was supplemented, as a part of a multimedia project, by a display of print publications in the screening space. The open screening space, the itinerant spectators and the screening mode of recurrence and repetition all differentiate *San Yuan Li*'s spectatorial experience and perception of time–space from that of early city symphony films, which are usually shown in the dark and enclosed space of a theatre.

Finally, *San Yuan Li* also crafts an alternative understanding and practice of urban time–space and modernity, foregrounding the more than 70-year time lag from the flourishing age of modernity and cinema in the West.[81] The film attempts to represent the quickly changing alternative reality of Chinese urban experience in an increasingly homogeneous yet fragmented world. By emphasizing the ambiguity and contradictions of this experience, the film cultivates a cinematic form with specificity, authenticity and singularity that resists the homogenizing forces of globalization in historically and geographically distinct ways, even as it remains a result of these forces.[82] However, *San Yuan Li* 'aimed at preserving an archive of an alternative history that registers the urbanization process of the city of Guangzhou.'[83] The temporal–spatial significance of the visual archive as repository of collective memories and experiences has been acknowledged by David Harvey: 'If it is true that time is always memorialized not as flow, but as memories of experienced places and spaces, then history must indeed give way to poetry, time to space, as the fundamental material of social expression. The spatial image (particularly the evidence of the photograph) then asserts an important power over history.'[84] Thus, the cinematically excavated and reconstructed space of the village in *San Yuan Li* represents histories, memories and belongings, exerting a power that transcends historical time.

Works cited

AlSayyad, Nezar. *Cinematic Urbanism: A History of The Modern From Reel to Real*. New York and London: Routledge, 2006.
Benjamin, Walter. *Charles Baudelaire: A Lyric Poet in The Era of High Capitalism*, trans. Harry Zohn. New York: Verso, 1992.
—Marcus Bullock and Michael W. Jennings (eds). *Selected Writings*. Cambridge, MA: Belknap Press, c. 1996–2003.

Bruno, Giuliana. *Atlas of Emotion: Journeys in Art, Architecture, and Film*. New York: Verso, 2002.
Chen, Daiguang. *History of the Development of Guangzhou City*. Guangzhou: Jinan University Press, 1996.
de Certeau, Michel. *The Practice of Everyday Life*. Berkeley, CA, Los Angeles and London: University of California Press, 1988.
Donald, James. 'The City, The Cinema: Modern Spaces' in Chris Jenks (ed.) *Visual Culture*. London and New York: Routledge, 1993.
Frisby, David and Mike Featherstone (eds). *Simmel on Culture: Selected Writings*. London and Thousand Oaks, CA: Sage Publications, 1997.
Graf, Alexander. 'Paris-Berlin-Moscow: On the Montage Aesthetic in the City Symphony Films of the 1920s' in Alexander Graf and Dietrich Scheunemann (eds), *Avant-Garde Film*. Amsterdam and New York: Rodopi, 2007.
Hansen, Mark. 'The time of affect, or bearing witness to life,' *Critical Inquiry* 30 (Spring 2004).
Harvey, David. *The Condition of Postmodernity*. Cambridge and Oxford: Blackwell, 1990.
Krause, Linda and Patrice Petro (eds). *Global Cities: Cinema, Architecture, and Urbanism in a Digital Age*. New Brunswick, NJ and London: Rutgers University Press, 2003.
Liu, Yuting, Shenjing He, Fulong Wu and Chris Webster. 'Urban villages under China's rapid urbanization: unregulated assets and transitional neighborhoods,' *Habitat International*, 34 (2010), 135–44.
Mangolte, Babette. 'Afterward: A Matter of Time, Analog Versus Digital, the Perennial Question of Shifting Technology and Its Implication for an Experimental Filmmaker's Odyssey' in Richard Allen and Malcolm Turvey (eds), *Camera Obscura, Camera Lucida: Essays in Honor of Annette Michelson*. Amsterdam: Amsterdam University Press, 2003.
Ou Ning and Cao Fei. *San Yuan Li* booklet.
Roberts, Graham. *The Man with the Movie Camera*. London and New York: I. B. Tauris Publishers, 2000.
Shiel, Mark and Tony Fitzmaurice (eds). *Screening the City*. London and New York: Verso, 2003.
Stevenson, Deborah. *Cities and Urban Cultures*. Maidenhead and Philadelphia: Open University Press, 2003.
Webber, Andrew and Wilson Emma (eds). *Cities in Transition: the Moving Image and the Modern Metropolis*. London and New York: Wallflower Press, 2008.
Wees, William C. *Light Moving in Time, Studies in the Visual Aesthetics of Avant-Garde Film*. Berkeley, CA: University of California Press, 1992.
Zhang, L., Simon X. B. Zhao and J. P. Tian. 'Self-help in housing and chengzhongcun in China's urbanization,' *International Journal of Urban and Regional Research*, vol. 27, 4 December 2003, 912–37.

Notes

1 The author wants to thank Keith B. Wagner, Paola Iovene, Ou Ning, Xie Wen, Miriam Hansen, James Lastra, Adam Hart, Nathan Holmes, Thomas Kelly, Cordell Green, and members of 'mass culture workshop' at the University of Chicago, for their generous support and insightful comments.

2 Including Alberto Cavalcanti's *Rien que les Heures* (1926), Walther Ruttmann's *Berlin, Symphony of a Metropolis* (1927), Dziga Vertov's *Man with a Movie Camera* (1929), Joris Ivens' *Rain* (1929), László Moholy-Nagy's *Impressionen vom alten Marseiller Hanfen* (*vieux port*) (1929), Jean Vigo's *Propos de Nice* (1930), Herman Weinberg's *City Symphony* (1930), Liu Na'ou's *The Man Who Has a Movie Camera* (1933), as well as some other early avant-garde films picturing New York City in the 1920s such as Charles Sheeler and Paul Strand's *Manhatta* (1920), Jay Leyda's *A Bronx Morning* (1931), and so forth.
3 See, for example, Georg Simmel, *Simmel on Culture: Selected Writings* (eds David Frisby and Mike Featherstone. Sage Publications, 1997); Walter Benjamin, *Charles Baudelaire: A Lyric Poet in The Era of High Capitalism* (translated by Harry Zohn. Verso, 1992); Walter Benjamin, *Selected Writings* (eds Marcus Bullock and Michael W. Jennings. Cambridge, MA: Belknap Press, c. 1996–2003); David Harvey, *The Condition of Postmodernity* (Cambridge and Oxford: Blackwell, 1990); James Donald, *The City, The Cinema: Modern Spaces*, in *Visual Culture* (ed. Chris Jenks. London and New York: Routledge, 1993); Giuliana Bruno, *Atlas of Emotion: Journeys in Art, Architecture, and Film* (New York: Verso, 2002), among others.
4 Mark Shiel, Introduction in Mark Shiel and Tony Fitzmaurice (eds), *Screening the City*. London and New York: Verso, 2003, 2.
5 Charles Sheeler and Paul Strand's *Manhatta* (1920) was shot in New York City and René Clair's *Paris qui dort* (1925) was shot in Paris.
6 More examples from other cinematic traditions and non-Western countries are worth exploring, such as private film experiments in 1930s Japan, Taiwan and China. 'Neo-Sensationist' writer, translator and film critic Liu Na'ou's city film *The Man Who Has a Movie Camera* (1933), paying explicit tribute to Vertov's film, is an inspiring resonance in this cinematic tide.
7 Alexander Graf, 'Paris-Berlin-Moscow: On the Montage Aesthetic in the City Symphony Films of the 1920s' in Alexander Graf and Dietrich Scheunemann (eds), *Avant-Garde Film*. Amsterdam and New York: Rodopi, 2007, ix.
8 Ibid., 78.
9 Carsten Strathausen argues that the modernist ideal of absolute vision shifts power from the 'I' of man to the 'eye' of the camera so that cinematic vision as such gains control in and of these films. 'Uncanny Spaces: The City in Ruttmann and Vertov,' in Mark Shiel and Tony Fitzmaurice (eds), *Screening the City*. London and New York: Verso, 2003, 18.
10 Deborah Stevenson, *Cities and Urban Cultures*. Maidenhead, PA: Open University Press, 2003.
11 Or more accurately, a cinematic document that is referred to as a video installation instead of a film.
12 Other later city or city symphony films could include Patrick Keiller's *London* (1994) and American experimental filmmaker Godfrey Reggio's *Koyaanisqatsi* (1982).
13 I will elaborate on this point later.
14 In my email interview, Ou Ning admits that his work had been influenced by *Koyaanisqatsi* (1982). One of Cao Fei's later experimental works, and Jia Zhangke's *24 City* (2008), which is a mixture of fiction film and documentary, both employ the same strategy.
15 As a result of rampant urban expansion, San Yuan Li, which was located in the outskirt of Guangzhou, now finds itself in the centre of the city even as it preserves its rural social structures and lifestyles.

16 L. Zhang, Simon X. B. Zhao and J. P. Tian, 'Self-help in Housing and Chengzhongcun in China's Urbanization,' *International Journal of Urban and Regional Research*, vol. 27, 4 December 2003, 912–37; Yuting Liu, Shenjing He, Fulong Wu and Chris Webster, 'Urban Villages under China's rapid urbanization: Unregulated assets and transitional neighborhoods,' *Habitat International*, 34 (2010), 135–44.

17 The social phenomena related to urbanization and globalization presented in the film include the government's requisition of farmland in San Yuan Li in the 1980s and 1990s, the emergence of manual workshops in back alleys and migrant workers swarming into the city. See Ou Ning, Cao Fei and Hou Hanru's essays on the *San Yuan Li* project in the book *San Yuan Li*. I will discuss the problem of 'globalization' in more detail in the following pages.

18 Jennifer Jordan, 'Collective Memory and Locality in Global Cities' in Linda Krause and Patrice Petro (eds), *Global Cities: Cinema, Architecture, and Urbanism in a Digital Age*. New Brunswick, NJ and London: Rutgers University Press, 2003, 32.

19 See, David Harvey, *The Condition of Postmodernity*. Cambridge and Oxford: Blackwell, 1990; Michel de Certeau, *Practice of Everyday Life*. Berkeley, CA, Los Angeles and London: University of California Press, 2002; Linda Krause and Patrice Petro (eds), *Global Cities: Cinema, Architecture, and Urbanism in a Digital Age*. New Brunswick, NJ and London: Rutgers University Press, 2003; Deborah Stevenson, *Cities and Urban Cultures*. Maidenhead, PA: Open University Press, 2003.

20 Nezar AlSayyad, *Cinematic Urbanism: A History of The Modern From Reel to Real*, New York and London: Routledge, 2006, 5–6.

21 Georg Simmel, 'The Metropolis and Mental Life,' in David Frisby and Mike Featherstone (eds), *Simmel on Culture: Selected Writings*. Sage Publications, 1997, 176.

22 Stevenson, 8; 68.

23 Giuliana Bruno, *Atlas of Emotion: Journeys in Art, Architecture, and Film*. New York: Verso, 2002, 185.

24 Alexander Graf, 80.

25 Ibid.

26 *Berlin, Symphony of a Metropolis*, *Man with a Movie Camera*, and *Manhatta* all employ this format.

27 Alternatively, one could divide it into eight episodes by considering the epilogue as two sections: subtitles and music video.

28 There is a narrative and stylistic continuity with earlier city symphony films: *Berlin* introduces the city from an approaching train and *Manhatta* portrays New York City from a boat in the river.

29 For example, women walking, Muslims strolling, the juxtaposition of 'Anti-British' monument and ancestral temples, local Cantonese opera and lion-dancing performance (staged for the film). In this compact space, the traditional and the contemporary, the ideological/political and the rural clan system, the official history and non-official local past, all coexist.

30 'U-thèque' is an unofficial cinephile organization that curator and filmmaker Ou Ning founded in 1999 in Guangzhou and Shenzhen; they screened and discussed foreign and Chinese art films and published independent film magazines. *San Yuan Li* can be considered as a collaborative work shot by some U-thèque members, with Ou Ning and Cao Fei as director and editor. One of the cameramen, Huang Weikai,

is an independent filmmaker who has made documentary and experimental works such as 'Floating' (2005) and 'Disorder' (2009).
31 Geographically intimate, but socially, economically and politically marginal and distant from the rest of the city due to its rural social structure and migration culture.
32 In *Man with a Movie Camera*, the narrative structure and temporal continuity are broken deliberately in order to construct a more complicated structure. Ou Ning explained in an interview that they would disperse and integrate the outtake footage in the film to break its enclosed narrative structure if they had more time for editing.
33 Cao Fei, *San Yuan Li* book, 315.
34 Vertov claims 'intervals are the transitions from one movement to another.' Graham Roberts, *The Man with the Movie Camera*. London and New York: I. B. Tauris Publishers, 2000, 35.
35 This prevails in *San Yuan Li*, especially in sections one and four, with the images of cityscape and street crowds; here the hectic montage is much faster than that in early city symphony films, reflecting a contemporary urban experience of speed.
36 This is also related to whether it is a mobile or stationary shot; if it is a mobile shot, or with moving subjects in a static shot, the audience perceives them as shorter than that of still subjects in a stationary shot.
37 Graham Roberts, *The Man with the Movie Camera*. London and New York: I. B. Tauris Publishers, 2000, 79.
38 Carsten Strathausen, 'Uncanny Spaces: The City in Ruttmann and Vertov' in Mark Shiel and Tony Fitzmaurice (eds), *Screening the City*. London and New York: Verso, 2003, 30.
39 See examples: 33:17 into the film, fast motion can only be detected when someone passing by in the foreground and people in the centre blinking rapidly; 35:04 into the film, a chef gives a gesture of 'V', showing in slow motion.
40 Ou Ning, interview via email, November 2008 [my translation].
41 Giuliana Bruno, *Atlas of Emotion: Journeys in Art, Architecture, and Film*, New York: Verso, 2002, 149. Derek Jarman in his film *Caravaggio* (1986), and Pier Paolo Pasolini in his segment 'La Ricotta' in *Ro. Go. Pa. G.* (1963), deploy the technique of 'tableau vivant'. Andy Warhol made *Blow Job* (1963) and a series of '*Screen Test*' (1965-6) that portray people in the fashion of 'tableau vivant' in temporal duration. Jia Zhangke's *24 City* utilizes a similar way in portraying some factory workers and their families. This stylistic experimentation also appears pervasively in contemporary video art works.
42 Jia Zhangke's *24 Cities* reinforces the uncanniness and tension with synchronized sound.
43 Mark Hansen, 'The Time of Affect, or Bearing Witness to Life,' *Critical Inquiry* 30 (Spring 2004), 589
44 Hansen is discussing Bill Viola's video work *Anima* (2000), ibid., 589.
45 Ou Ning, interview via email, November 2008 [my translation].
46 Baiyun airport, the once-unique opening of China towards to the outside world, now sees itself as a bizarre void inside the urban density of high rises; it has been abandoned and obsolete since another new airport was constructed.
47 Michel de Certeau, *The Practice of Everyday Life*. Berkeley, CA, Los Angeles and London: University of California Press, 1988, 94.
48 Stevenson, 45.
49 Liu, He, Wu and Webster, 136.
50 Ibid, 142-3.

51 Cao Fei points out that, 'there is a limit to the amount of available land for new buildings. Hungry for more space to increase rental income, the villagers have no choice but to contrive ingenious ways of reaching up to the sky, digging underground, as well as stretching out sideways in every conceivable direction…the insatiable craving to expand into more space is responsible for this most grotesque dwelling style…'. Cao Fei, 'A Wild Side of Guangzhou,' *San Yuan Li* book, 52.
52 Described as 'one strip of sky' by local residents.
53 Georg Simmel, 'The Metropolis and Mental Life,' in David Frisby and Mike Featherstone (eds), *Simmel on Culture: Selected Writings*. Sage Publications, 1997, 181.
54 Stevenson, 24.
55 Ibid., 25.
56 Ou Ning, 'Shadows of Times,' in *San Yuan Li* book, 40.
57 David Harvey, *The Condition of Postmodernity*. Cambridge and Oxford: Blackwell, 1990, 202.
58 See, for example, the sequence in which schoolchildren offering paper flowers in front of the monument are juxtaposed with a woman and a boy who are burning incense in an ancestral temple, suggesting the diversity of San Yuan Li's culture and the coexistence of national and local, collective and private pasts.
59 Harvey, 85.
60 Durkheim, quoted from Jordan, 44.
61 Most migrant workers living in San Yuan Li benefit from globalization because they work primarily for factories making products for export and the service professions now booming in the new density of the population.
62 There are scenes of the city waking up or falling asleep in both *Berlin* and *Man with a Movie Camera*, which connote a rationalized schedule and the disciplining of social life by controlling time.
63 See, for instance, the collage of images of straight or tangled lines (vertical, horizontal, diagonal) of telephone wires at 13:20 in part two; the round wheels and duct cutting together in act one; a group of images of differently sized windows at 10:10 in section two; associative editing of a group of images with television screens (29:32–29:55); close-ups of smiling faces (30:49–31:50); and the 18 group photos (31:51–35:11).
64 Andrew Webber, 'Introduction: Moving Images of Cities,' in Andrew Webber and Emma Wilson (eds), *Cities in Transition: the Moving Image and the Modern Metropolis*. Wallflower Press, 2008, 2.
65 The jittery camera movement in narrow back alleys with vertiginous space and perspectives conveys subjective experience of disorientation and uneasiness.
66 See, for example, 10:57 to 11:30 (33 seconds). There are 14 shots, half-moving shots and half-static, with an average shot length of 2.35 seconds; the moving shots are longer at about three seconds, the static ones are shorter (some only last one second). The alternation between mobility and stillness creates a compelling rhythm.
67 The transportation vehicles appearing in *San Yuan Li* include boats, automobiles, motorcycles, trains, buses, subway trains, airplanes and bicycles. Walking is also treated as a mode of movement, especially in tracking shots.
68 Bruno, 24.
69 Graf, 81.
70 Ou Ning, in a question and answer section at the University of Chicago, October 2008.

71 A traditional string musical instrument in the Guangdong area; its tonal quality is similar to that of *Erhu*.
72 On the deafening sound of the airplane, Cao Fei describes that 'the densely packed office buildings and dwellings around the village have sealed up every niche from the ground up, leaving no cracks and crannies for the jet noise to seep down onto the heedless crowds below…The tiniest of sounds created in such claustrophobic surroundings, be that the turn of a key, or a jangle of the bicycle bells, is instantly amplified into tremendous echoes.' Cao Fei, 50 and 53.
73 Ou Ning, 43.
74 Andrew Webber, 'Introduction: Moving Images of Cities,' in Andrew Webber and Emma Wilson (eds), *Cities in Transition: the Moving Image and the Modern Metropolis*. Wallflower Press, 2008, 3.
75 Babette Mangolte, 'Afterward: A Matter of Time, Analog Versus Digital, the Perennial Question of Shifting Technology and Its Implication for an Experimental Filmmaker's Odyssey' in Richard Allen and Malcolm Turvey (eds), *Camera Obscura, Camera Lucida: Essays in Honor of Annette Michelson*. Amsterdam: Amsterdam University Press, 2003, 265.
76 Ibid., 264.
77 William C. Wees. *Light Moving in Time, Studies in the Visual Aesthetics of Avant-Garde Film*. Berkeley, CA: University of California Press, 1992, 3.
78 In other words, 60 hours of footage was made into a 40-minute final film. Ou Ning, 43.
79 Graham Roberts, *The Man with the Movie Camera*. London and New York: I. B. Tauris Publishers, 2000, 26.
80 Interview with Ou Ning via email, November 2008.
81 The time lag is also related to artists' belated knowledge of world film history and practice, as Ou Ning explains: 'My interest of film comes from the pirate DVDs… which helped me complete a study of film history by myself.' Ou Ning, in http://www.alternativearchive.com/ouning/article.asp?id=576 (accessed November 2008).
82 Besides Venice, *San Yuan Li* has been exhibited in various film festivals, art galleries and museums in many countries – a result of globalization and the advance of information and communication technology.
83 Ou Ning, 42.
84 David Harvey, 218.

7

From Pirate to Kino-eye: A Genealogical Tale of Film Re-Distribution in China

Dan Gao

In recent years, the problem of piracy has become an ever more prevalent part, and contested practice, of cultural communication and consumption around the world, due in large part to both globalization and digital technology. With a proliferation of news stories about copyright infringement lawsuits and government crackdowns on piracy in China, it is no longer a secret to the rest of the world that piracy has constituted a thriving and stubbornly persistent black-market 'profession' and a 'culture' in the country for more than three decades. Since the Economic Opening-up [*gaige kaifang*], starting in the early 1980s, China's piracy practice has already been studied heavily in academe, drawing scholarly interest in the fields of critical legal studies, sociology and communication studies.[1]

In terms of film piracy, two in-depth book-length studies written almost a decade ago have laid the groundwork for empirical research and theoretical contemplation – Shujen Wang's *Framing Piracy: Globalization and Film Distribution in Greater China* (2003) and Laikwan Pang's *Cultural Control and Globalization in Asia: Copyright, Piracy, and Cinema* (2005). Both works approach film piracy in China from a transnational perspective, with a shared emphasis on the post-VCD era (the technology of VCD became obsolete fairly fast in the West after the rise of DVD, but in China's case, VCD remained an effective format from the mid-1990s to the early 2000s). While Pang ultimately reaffirms piracy's viral effect upon the transnational creative industry in general, Wang is one of the earliest media scholars to move the spotlight away from the right/wrong moral–legal debate on piracy to its actual practices (i.e. distribution and consumption of pirated film) in East Asia – 'in the hope of knowing the actual experiences consumers had when using pirated products.'[2] Yingjin Zhang advocates the kind of switch of attention made by Wang, pointing to the significant cultural role that piracy has played in China. Zhang has gone even further, embracing the study of piracy as a whole new area of audience research, suggesting that we may better understand contemporary moviegoers by looking back at the history of film piracy, given the fact that illegitimate copies (in the formats of LD, VHS, VCD, DVD, CD-ROM, online streaming video, etc.) have been and continue to be one of the major means through which films are viewed in China.[3]

In this chapter, I will expand and at times depart from Zhang and Wang's lines of thought, arguing that it is important to keep in mind that piracy, as a mode of economic and cultural practice, is a dialectical process. In other words, as people participate in illegitimate copying and viewing of media products, they are also subjected to the transformation and construction brought about by piracy culture. This naturally makes one ask: what kind of new subjects does piracy produce? This question can lead to further questions. For instance, what kind of customs, tastes, sensibilities and knowledge are being produced alongside this subject formation of the digital 'pirate?' What kind of techniques do 'pirates' use to posit themselves within the fissure between postsocialist reality and the pirated, 'informal' media worlds? (Here, I am referring to both the *shadowy* 'underground world' of piracy commerce and 'the rest of the world' – i.e. the world beyond China – encapsulated in the pirated foreign media products, which the pirates consume and sometimes uneasily seek to identify with). How do they live with or resist the postsocialist civic order of things and the neoliberal culture in post-WTO China, to which piracy is at once an alleged enemy and a secret accomplice, by constituting part of the 'shadow economies of cinema,' as Ramon Lobato calls it?[4] To me, these questions are no less important than the ones about the so-called 'new people' [*xinren*] (i.e. postsocialist subjects), which featured prominently in popular literary and filmic imaginations in the 1980s and 1990s.[5] Indeed, the 'pirate' may be a close kin or subspecies of the 'new people,' whose legacy has been fleshed out more saliently in the new millennium.

The participants in the piracy culture I describe here do not only refer to the audience/consumer of piracy, but also include the producers (smugglers, owners of the reproduction factories, ordinary viewers-turned-bootleggers), distributors (wholesalers, storekeepers, street vendors, file-sharing netizens) and other possible constituent subjects; even scholars and cultural critics who are sympathetic with piracy culture (Zhang, myself and many others) can be counted among these informal distribution provocateurs. Indeed, in practice, participants in piracy are not locked within one single identity, but usually morph from one form to another, depending on their given activity and predilection. For instance, a person who goes by a pseudonym when publishing reviews in online film discussion boards such as 'Rear Window' [*houchuang kan dianying*] (named after a well-known film BBS in China in the early 2000s) may, once he goes offline, reveal his other identity as the owner of a 'DVD theatre' in the corner of the street, enthusiastically changing his persona from a serious petty intellectual to boisterous informal street merchant.[6] If I may use the signifier 'pirate' to bracket all the morphologies of this subject, then the focus of this chapter will be on two of them, whom I call the 'pirate-cinephile' and the 'pirate-eye' (a term inspired by Dziga Vertov's idea of 'kino-eye'). Of course, due to the limited space, it is not realistic for me to deal with all of the questions about the pirates that are stated above. As the metaphor 'from pirate to kino-eye' from this chapter title suggests, my major goal here is to narrate the transformation certain pirates undergo and look at how they reconstruct their experience with film piracy in their writings and audiovisual works. To be more precise, my question is: how has the genealogical trope – 'transforming from a pirate to a kino-eye' – become a narrative that plays into so many recent independent films?

In the first half of this chapter, I will give a brief account of the piracy film culture that has developed in China in the past three decades, in order to explain the transformative nature of the subjects whom I call the 'pirate-cinephile' and the 'pirate-eye.' This step of analysis is informed by Walter Benjamin's theory of 'mimetic faculty,' Dziga Vertov's ideal of the 'kino-eye,' and recent theoretical reconsideration of 'cinephilia' as a desirable mode of film culture in China. Then, I will closely examine several fiction films (such as *Platform* [*Zhan Tai*, Jia Zhangke 2000], *Suzhou River* [*Suzhou He*, Lou Ye 2000], and *Pirated Copy* [*Man Yan*, He Jianjun 2004]), which represent archetypal 'pirate-eye' characters. I will finish my analysis with a discussion of two documentaries about pirated DVD vendors (who are transmuted by the practice of piracy).

A generation of pirate-cinephile

It is almost self-evident that one of the most historically significant aspects of piracy film culture in China is that it has nurtured and shaped a considerable portion of the consumers and creators of Chinese film in the new millennium. Right at the beginning of China's Economic Reform, the Chinese government started to allow the entry of non-state economic elements (individually owned economic enterprises in particular) into the market.[7] The field of media production, however, was still generally kept in the hands of the state. The rights to publish and reproduce print publications (*yinshua chubanwu* – books, magazines, journals and newspapers) and audiovisual publications (*yinxiang chubanwu* – tapes, videocassettes and optical discs) were exclusively entitled to a small number of state-owned presses,[8] whose production capacities (in terms of both the variety of titles and the quality of the output) were quite incompatible with the citizens' enormous appetite for cultural products, which was recognized at that time as a new form of 'cultural fever' (*wenhua re*). A 'book famine' (*shu huang*) soon swept China.[9]

Similar problems plagued the field of film during this period. In the early stage of the Reform Era, film and TV were still financed and tightly controlled by the state at every step of production and distribution. In 1979, 65 fiction films were produced in mainland China, while the country's moviegoing audience in that year was 29.3 billion – meaning the average citizen had watched an estimated 28 films that year.[10] These striking numbers clearly point to a severe imbalance between demand and supply, and are simultaneously indicative of Chinese audiences' rising passion for film. Unfortunately, domestic film output remained low throughout much of the 1980s (only 82 to 158 fiction films were produced per year; in comparison, two decades later, this number has tripled – the film output in 2009 was 456).[11] In addition, film imports were heavily restricted, due to the notoriously small quota imposed by the government and stringent censorship throughout the 1980s and 1990s.

Outside of these formal chains of cultural production for government-sanctioned films, an increasing flow of illegal audio and visual products made in foreign countries (as well as Taiwan) began to make its way into China. This material had been quietly smuggled into the PRC and spread quickly. In cottage factories in many cities near the national border (such as Shishi in Fujian Province, Wenzhou in Zhejiang and Haikou in Hainan), popular music cassettes from Hong Kong, erotic Taiwanese poker cards, Japanese *manga* and posters of nude or semi-nude Hollywood stars were widely copied and bootlegged. Videocassettes of Hong Kong films were among the most popularly disseminated merchandise at that time. They were sold to myriads of newly emerging and privately owned video halls (*luxiang ting*) all over China, as well as to movie theatres, where screening booths equipped with video projection systems had just opened up as an additional attraction to catch up with the new fad of *luxiangdai* (VHS tapes). According to *China Radio & TV Yearbook*, the *luxiang ting* culture started to exert its presence in 1983 and reached its heyday at the end of the 1980s,[12] becoming a powerful competitor with cinema and television.

Indeed, in addition to *luxiang ting*, there were other venues where films not officially released through the government and commercial genre films were made accessible to the general public. In certain public libraries – especially larger ones, such as the National Library (NLC) in Beijing – any reader could request to watch foreign films from their catalogue. For example, a friend of mine – who is an independent film director – told me that in the 1990s, he spent several whole days in the NLC, watching European art films such as *Last Tango in Paris*. In many urban centres some local cinemas and theatres affiliated with cultural institutions would rent copies of the so-called '*neican pian*' (internal reference films) and '*guolu pian*' (passerby films) from national archives or libraries and arrange a couple of 'internal' screenings for each film.[13] Special privileges were also enjoyed in certain coastal regions, due to their geopolitical advantages and cross-cultural demography. For instance, film critic Lie Fu recalled, 'In the 1950 and 1960s, Guangzhou was the only city where public screening of Cantonese films could be allowed; at the same time, Mandarin productions by Hong Kong studios like Changcheng and Fenghuang were also put onto screen.' For Lie Fu and his contemporaries, Guangzhou was already the 'film special zone' (*dianying tequ*) *de facto* at that time.[14] Guangzhou also had access to a variety of Hong Kong entertainment on TV after the Reform Era, thanks to Yagi antennas (well known as the *yugu tianxian* – fishbone antennas), commonly installed by many households in Guangdong Province. However, this type of accessibility to imported or banned films remained quite limited in China – this resource was not readily available to the general public; at the same time, there was a large population with a burning passion for cinematic experiences. In this context, the rise of piracy cinephilia began, as described by Jia Zhangke: 'When *implausible* (*bu heli de*) film policy was broken through by *illegal* (*bu hefa de*) piracy practice, we were falling into a discomforting paradox. However, it is a cultural fact that moving [sic] eventually came into the lives of *ordinary* people,' so that Chinese film lovers were, thanks to piracy, finally able to 'watch' film rather than 'read' films from fanzines and newspapers.[15]

Like other public entertainment businesses (karaoke booths, disco halls and music cafes) of the early Reform Era, *luxiang ting* were soon subjected to the discursive regulation of the state. Most of the films taped and screened at *luxiang ting* were not only illegally brought into China, but censors and commentators deemed much of the content morally decadent, ideologically inadequate, and sexually explicit. Many laws and regulations were initiated to stop the spread of this viral culture based on smuggling and piracy.[16] Massive nationwide enforcement to '*sao huang*' (sweep the Yellow publications) has occurred annually since 1989, with illegal films screened in video halls always a major target. However, rather than disappearing completely, film smuggling, illegal copying and *luxiang ting*-style screenings submerged into the underground, merging into the enormous body of China's shadow economy.[17]

On the one hand, as the price for video recorders and cassettes dropped in the 1990s, many film lovers chose to buy or rent tapes, and consequently retreated from the public space of *luxiang ting* and into the private spaces of their homes. This more internalized and privatized mode of piracy film consumption persists today, with magnetic cassettes soon being replaced by optical discs, and then by compressed-digitized data. On the other hand, publicly participatory piracy culture has developed into new forms. Since the end of the 1990s, as digital technologies and equipment such as LCD projecting systems and personal computers became more widespread, films that were once only available through 'grey' channels entered new types of public spaces – they were talked about via online discussion forums, introduced and analyzed in fanzines, and screened on college campuses and in hip bars. These films were viewed by a new species of film-loving collectives – i.e. cine-clubs, student communities, editorial teams and column writers, as well as fansubbing groups.[18] This new wave of film culture in China became quite culturally autonomous and grabbed many observers' and critics' attention. Piracy's impact – popularizing otherwise expensive and hard-to-get copies of films – was readily recognizable during this period.

There are so many ways to look at the pirate-film lovers. A lot has been written on who they are, where they come from, or what they are doing now. They are said to have constituted part of 'the urban generation' that revived a 'cinephile culture' in China using '"primitive" or "pirated" form of postmodern technology of the VCD.'[19] They are identified as the 'saw-gashed generation' (*dakou yidai*) – a new breed of cultural producers who acquired a certain independent spirit through piracy practices and have played it into Chinese rock music.[20] Others call them the 'D-generation' (the all-encompassing 'D' stands for disc (*die*), *daoban* (media piracy), and digital), who have now graduated from a 'pirate film school' and become creative media workers themselves.[21] Many fans and cinephiles cultivated by *daoban die* become directors, critics and scholars, who 'initiated film websites, entered editorial office of fanzines, or published monographs because of their love for film.'[22] It is fair to argue that it was through and only through intimate emotional and bodily engagement with pirated film that the pirate-cinephiles acquired a certain *transformative agency* – to transform themselves as much as to transform the social space they reside in (turning a dingy attic into lucrative *luxiang ting*; or transmuting a bar or classroom into a mini 'art cinema').

'Cinephile,' in its most rigorous definition, usually refers to a middle-class educated European male movie-goer-writer-cineaste who was active between 1950 to 1980.

The term 'cinephilia' used to be associated with a certain specific historical period and a European identity. Cinephilia, as defined by Susan Sontag, 'is not simply love of but a certain *taste* in films (grounded in a vast appetite for seeing and re-seeing as much as possible of cinema's glorious past).'[23] For many of its renowned interpreters (such as Sontag, Antoine de Baecque, and more critically, Paul Willemen), cinephilia should be historicized as a phenomenon that appeared after the Second World War on the European (mainly French) cultural scene and generally withered away by the 1980s. However, some more recent scholarly interpretations suggest that rather than quietly dying out in the 1980s, cinephilia has actually expanded its territory and thrived in multiple geographic regions other than Europe. This scholarship has explored alternative conceptualizations, uses and techniques of cinephilia, especially in the digital age, with a more global and less nostalgic vision.[24] For these scholars, it is still meaningful to continue using this word and moulding it into a much broader umbrella term to signify the 'simultaneity of different technological formats and platforms, subject positions, and affective encounters that characterizes the current practice referred to as "cinephilia"' from all over the world.[25]

Piracy-cinephilia in China certainly falls under this rubric. Like any other type of cinephilia, Chinese piracy-cinephilia is characterized by temporal and geographic 'deferral.'[26] One form of deferral reflects how Chinese piracy-cinephiles usually tend to feel a connection with films that are made outside of their country and are recuperated and displaced from a near or distant past. Another form of deferral reflects the belated '(re)discovery' of cinephilia (*yingchi, miying*, or *dianying milian* when translated into Chinese) itself as a mode of film culture. After reintroducing a new pantheon of European cinephiles to a renewed standard of this concept, young film scholar Li Yang announces at the end of his book *Cinephilia: The History of A Culture* that '... this is the real reason why I wrote about cinephilia culture. I want to tell the young film lovers in China, your passion and frenzy for film is not alone in the world. Your cinephilia has a tradition – you are standing along with many legendary figures of the film history.'[27]

In such a light, pirate-cinephiles in China view producing and using pirated film as much more than just copyright infringement or even resistance against global capitalism; rather, it is more about reclaiming what is repressed, rarely seen, or forbidden under a conservative (if not xenophobic) cultural regime. For them, pirated film is not only an exhibit window through which the ordinary Chinese consumer 'shops' (and inevitably fetishizes) exotic merchandises or a reflective screen where local desire gets projected and absorbed at the same time. It is also a viewfinder, through which an 'audience-hunter' (similar to the reader-hunter de Certau describes[28]) gazes at and 'preys' his/her game. The pirate-cinephile is always simultaneously a greedy consumer subjected to manipulation and a political dissent ready to take action, however benign.

Kino-eye, pirate-eye

Before analysing mimesis and the formation of the pirate-cinephile turned kino-eye, it is helpful to first explain the concept of 'kino-eye' (movie camera as the machine eye), or the historically complicated connotation of *kinok* (man with movie camera). Kino-eye and kinok are two neologisms created by Soviet filmmaker and theorist Dziga Vertov, who led an experimental film group designed to deliver a cinematic ideal where human and machine are harmoniously merged in the post-October Revolution (1917) context. Indeed, it is a common notion that the apparatus of the movie camera can be seen as an extension of the human body and, in fact, human life. For example, Béla Balázs suggested that once a camera is set up at a certain angle and starts rolling, it is as if the machine acquires its own life. At this time, even if the cinematographer (in his case, a war journalist) cannot carry out his mission because, say, his life reaches its end, the camera will take over this task. In the famous experimental work by the kino-eye group, *Man with a Movie Camera* (1929), the filmmakers went even further. The movie camera is endowed with a morphological quality and, more importantly, a 'capability of mimicry' – which usually only belongs to live beings – through the magic of montage. By constructing such an image, Vertov was trying to promote a cinematic form in which the human being and the mechanical apparatus of camera can extend and 'learn from' each other harmoniously. In other words, the kino-eye ideal not only envisions elongating the perceptual spectrum of human eye via the machine, but also expects the perfection of the human itself, through establishing certain 'kinship with the machine'[29] – to mimic, cooperate with and 'love' the machine as well as the moving image created in their co-production. Inspired by Walter Benjamin, Malcolm Turvey suggests that Vertov's kino-eye ideal can be understood as a playful mimetic game, pointing out that a two-way mimesis[30] lies at the fundamental heart of it, through which both cinema and human being may achieve a sense of liberation.[31]

Kino-eye started as a dialectical yet also idealist vision clearly inflected by communism and industrial modernism – two consequential outcomes of monopoly capitalism. Nevertheless, after moving beyond its Soviet origins, it has been revitalized, reinterpreted and recast many times. Vertov used to claim that the kino-eye 'lives and moves in time and space.'[32] This statement originally intended to underscore the mobility of the machine and the constructive power of cinematic montage; however, we can also read it as a prophecy about the kino-eye movement's recurring life cycles in diverse historical and cultural locales. During the century since kino-eye's initial appearance, this notion had been undertaken, translated and further theorized by proponents of film and video practices such as *cinéma vérité* and direct cinema. The camera-eye approach has been gradually transmuted into a documentary and epistemological tool for filmmakers to come closer to or penetrate deeper into the alleged 'truth' of reality, and hence has lost its original dose of mimetic magic and idealist zest. This seems to be an inevitable result of modernization, as Benjamin astutely points out, in modern time, as mimetic faculty experiences 'increasing decay,' so that 'the observable world of the modern man contains only minimal residues of the magical correspondences and analogies that were familiar to ancient people.'[33] This still seems to hold true in our information age when everyone is constantly struck by twisted strands of messages transmitted via sophisticated new-age machines (TV, PC, smartphone and touchscreen pads). For those who seek to shrug off potential manipulation of these media and get closer to the 'truth' buried underneath mediated 'realities,' mimetic faculty – the gift of seeing resemblance – may only induce yet another layer of illusion one wants to resist, rather than bringing antidotes.

As a faculty intrinsic to human beings, mimesis still functions as usual in every unattractive corner of our life, even though it has lost its past glory as a ritualistic practice infused with transcendental power and prestige. For me, the kind of two-way mimesis established between man and his camera (and by extension, other human–media interfaces) presented in Vertov's ideal of kino-eye is coming back now with significant cultural implications where film piracy is concerned. As suggested at the end of the last section, the notion of kino-eye (or pirate-eye, in order to make it more specific to piracy film culture) provides an interesting analytical angle for us to understand how the pirate-cinephiles interact with their object of frenziness, in often playful and 'primitive' ways.

My analysis is not based on fieldwork or ethnographic accounts about individual pirate-cinephiles or their community. Rather I choose to establish my entry point with certain self-reflexive cinematic representations of figures that I define as pirate, pirate-cinephile, kino-eye, or pirate-eye. (Of course, most of the filmmakers discussed in this section are either sympathetic with the pirates or belong to the generation of pirate-cinephile themselves.) In the films, we do not see direct connection between kino-eye and truth value. Instead, camera and screening devices such as television, once again, function in more primitive ways on the users' affective and bodily experience. In these cinematic representations, a ritualistic sensibility is present. It is also clear that the characters do believe in the magical power of mimesis, or its 'schooling' function, to use Benjamin's word,[34] as a workable way to modify, or even alter, their relationship with the world. Moreover, pirated discs and digital video cameras are represented in these films as mimetic object/subject, just like the camera in *Man with the Movie Camera*. It is as if access to these moving images and machines offers a certain empowering force, as Vertov claimed decades ago, and this technological upgrade makes possible an expansion of the imaginative and practical horizons of Chinese postsocialist subjects.

After watching several fiction and documentary films that put piracy culture or a pirate-cinephile at the textual centre, I was surprised by three things. First, the representation of pirate as cinephilic amateur looms large in all these sample texts. Second, in recent documentaries, the symbolizing quality of the pirates, which has been made quite prominent in fiction films, is replaced by flesh-and-blood, individualized life experience crisscrossed with the person's social status. Third, either textually or contextually in all these films, the filmmaker is associated with the pirate in one way or another, implicating the various kinds of kinships between them. In *Suzhou River*, a viewfinder is installed for audiences to separate out as well as mirror the pirate and the videographer simultaneously; in the case of *Pirated Copy*, one finds an ambiguous inter-textual amalgamation of the two which is visible in the diegetic world; eventually, in *DVD Boys* and *Toto* (dir. Huang Weikai, preproduction), the two subjects merge together in both films' visualities, whereby two personal histories are conflated when TV screen transmutes into viewfinder, in an aesthetic move by Huang that may or may not be perceived as successful. It is fair to claim that these images and stories, driven by self-reflexive and documentary impulses, have told us a genealogical tale in which the pirate turns into the kino-eye. For either the filmmaker or his audience as the postsocialist subjects in China, this metanarrative is certainly constitutive in forming new concepts and knowledge about piracy.

DVD culture

One of the earliest visual memoirs that vividly captured this mimetic relationship between illegitimate cultural objects and the postsocialist subjects is Jia Zhangke's film *Platform*. Jia is well known for his affective attachment to popular cultures of the early Reform period, including *luxiang ting*, Chinese rock, disco halls, touring troupes and pirated discs, to which he has devoted many nostalgic writings and audiovisual works.

In the film *Platform*, we see waves of foreign fads – flared jeans, Bollywood films, smuggled tape recorders and cassettes, Hong Kong pop songs, perms and breakdancing – flooding into a small and conservative inner land town, Fenyang, as the Reform deepens. Nevertheless, the younger generation of residents there soon embraces them all and is inspired to change its way of life. Some of the kids join a travelling troupe later in the film and wander beyond the city wall that symbolizes the limit of old cultural life. They perform breakdances and pop songs on the stage for an unknown, yet engaging and longing audience, as if they are the embodied and lived 'pirated copies' themselves. Using their bodies as the medium, these young social performers enliven, exhibit, vernacularize, spread, and finally grow the new cultural seeds.

If piracy culture is only implicitly referenced in *Platform* as a natural component of the 'new era,' *Pirated Copy*, a DV feature film by He Jianjun made between 2002 and 2004, has offered the most frank representation of piracy culture in fiction films to date. Piracy is placed at the central nodal point of the film's 'network narrative'.[35] A sexually repressed college film lecturer, a desperate laid-off couple, a prostitute, an AIDS-infected drummer and two phony policemen are linked together through their encounters with a cinephilic street vendor, Shen Ming, and the pirated DVDs he and his fellow vendors bring to every corner of the cityscape. For many reasons, the film juxtaposes piracy consumption with human desire (especially sexual desire). They mirror and channel into each other on material, psychic and social levels, which further drives the image flow and motivates diegetic actions. The film thus becomes a perfect text for us to read the mimetic transgression symbolized by piracy culture.

We are not formally introduced to Shen Ming – the male protagonist as well as the nexus of the networked diegetic world – until the fifteenth minute of the film, when he sits in a dark corner against a whole bookshelf of DVDs. Only part of his face is lit by the cold fluorescence emitted from the TV screen, which is at the centre of his attention (Figure 7.1). This scene is reminiscent of how we are introduced to Mada in *Suzhou He* (*Suzhou River*, 2000), an emblematic work of the Sixth Generation (Figure 7.2). Of course, *mise-en-scène* is but one element that makes an analogy of these two characters interesting. As we know, *Suzhou River*, the Shanghai version of *The Double Life of Veronique* (Kieslowski, 1991), is already a tale about 'optical twins' in itself. Therefore, before getting into the analogy between Shen and Mada, I suggest that we read the two mirroring male protagonists of *Suzhou River* ('I' and Mada) as prototypes of kino-eye and pirate-eye respectively. In these two delicately laid-out and paralleled love stories of *Suzhou River*, one of the male characters (hereafter 'I') – who is also the first-person narrator of the film – never reveals his identity in a frontal shot. 'I' is a freelancing videographer who seems to be always shouldering his camera. We enter the diegetic world through his hand-held, documentary point-of-view shots from the very start. In other words, he is the man with the movie camera; he is the kino-eye. In addition, 'I' claims that his camera doesn't lie, although we are soon invited to enter a love story he makes up, in which all kinds of imaginations and uncertainties abound.

The second story in the film also revolves around a man, who is named Mada. The girlfriend of 'I' reads a romantic but sad story about Mada and his lover Mudan from a newspaper. Being cynical about the story's authenticity, 'I' fills in the skeleton with abundant life details, which merge the two men's lives in a mystical fashion. The first quality 'I' gives Mada is that he loves watching pirated discs (meaning he is a pirate-cinephile). 'I' narrates: 'He may often pass by my balcony to deliver stuff, and then go home every day, watching the pirated VCDs he likes for the whole night, usually until daybreak. This is how he lives.' In other words, Mada is different from a kino-eye like 'I' – he is down on the street, a manual labourer, a passive 'receiver' of vulgar popular culture. This description invites us to read Mada as the double of 'I' – his mirror image who resides in an opposite space, probably a fictive and romantic world – someone he can observe and consume from a distance. Moreover, the girlfriend of 'I' and Mada's lover look exactly the same, which further indicates the ambiguous correspondence between the two couples. 'I' travels back and forth between two lives, unravelling love and lie, as well as made-up romantic story and reality. It is not difficult for the audience to sense the filmmaker's uncertainty about history, fiction and the camera-eye, through an allegorical play enacted by two pairs of 'optical twins.' The camera, as Vertov suggests, plays the role of a mimetic apparatus here. When reading *Suzhou River* and several other popular filmic texts which put the 'phantom sisters' at the centre, Zhang Zhen points out that it is 'the presence of camera… on a metanarrative level' that 'mediates or triggers the magical transformation of virtual twinhood.'[36] In a half-realistic and half-fairytale diegesis, the film sets out a two-way mimetic tunnel between Mada and 'I' using the device of camera.

This argument appears to be more interesting when we juxtapose *Suzhou River* with *Pirated Copy*, since on a metanarrative level, we can further see Shen Ming as yet another *double* of Mada in a different diegetic world. Like *Suzhou River*, *Pirated Copy* unfolds its narrative around the male lead's amorous relationship. Obsession with

Figure 7.1 Shen Ming watching a pirated DVD in *Pirated Copy* (2004).

Figure 7.2 Mada watching a pirated VCD in *Suzhou River* (2000).

pirated film in both films can readily be read as the substitute of unfulfillable romantic desire. In a sense, like the camera, the TV screen showing pirated films functions as the consensual medium that motivates desire and affect of the subject who sits in front of it, magically transforming him or her. For instance, in *Suzhou River*, 'I' falls for Meimei the mermaid performer at the time when his video camera captures her

Figure 7.3 Mada and Mudan looking into the TV screen in *Suzhou River* (2000).

swimming in the water tank; Mada and Mudan also consummate their love (though represented implicitly) after watching a pirated film (see Figure 7.3).

This point is enlarged and brought even closer to the foreground in *Pirated Copy*. Shen Ming and Mei Xiaojing are two sexually repressed subjects criminalized or victimized by repressive social structures of sexuality (Shen is expelled from high school because of his love affair with a classmate; Mei was married to a homosexual man without knowing his identity). Like Shen, Mei is a fervent cinephile who also chooses a film-related profession. She teaches film in college. The difficulty in acquiring legitimate copies of foreign art films, which are 'mistaken' for porn by the police earlier in the film, leads Mei to Shen. We soon find that Mei's favourites are the erotic tales told by Spanish auteur Pedro Almodóvar. These films are not only taught in class, but also 'used' at home by Mei to channel her unfulfilled desire. Again, like in *Suzhou River*, the flickering TV screen (where sensual scenes from *Bullfighter* and random porn excerpts are shown back to back) and erotic images on DVD covers (passed from Shen to Mei), rather than verbal flirtation or physical touches, serve as the consensual medium for the two persons to grow the seeds of yearning and to cope with their pathologies. Indeed, Shen and Mei are only two figurines among the ensemble of 'pirate-eyes' depicted in the film. All characters enjoy the companionship of the TV screen and pirated discs. The dark corner in which each person consumes these 'banned' images is also where their suppressed libidos are unleashed. The film constantly switches between its own plot and sequences taken out of film classics. It is as if the two kinds of moving images serve as the point-of-view shots of each other. It is as if each character's life and the pirated films are commenting on, or even conversing with, one another. By 'staring' at 'each other,' the character and the TV both find playfulness and empowerment in a practice of mimetic nature. Furthermore, the filmmaker goes as far as to pair each of his characters with a film or a film genre he or she loves. We usually see the sound or image of the film first, and are then cued to the character, whose diegetic life trajectory further 'mimics' the 'fiction' he or she watches. Therefore, these pirate-eyes not only associate themselves more closely with their objects through watching and imagining. They are like the primitives discussed by Benjamin, who get to know the world through the magic of mimetic performances and expect to modify their lives via such spontaneous practices or recurring rituals.

For example, the prostitute in the film likes to do her 'business' while playing Wong Kar-wai's *In the Mood for Love* on the TV screen, as if doing so endows the ongoing sex trade with a gloss of secret romance and ironic dignity. In another instance, 'inspired' by *Pulp Fiction*, a laid-off couple plans an armed robbery so they can pay for their son's book fees. They follow the prostitute into a deserted warehouse, only to witness her being sexually coerced by two phony policemen. Out of sincere respect for Jules, the hit man in *Pulp Fiction*, the laid-off man in *Pirated Copy* takes out his pistol, recites the same Bible passage as Jules does, and then shoots and kills the two policemen. This 'heroic' act, however, eventually pushes the couple to the extreme of desperation. The story ends with their suicides. In these ways, poaching and imitating the 'stolen' plots indeed end up making these 'modern primitives' (to be more precise, 'postsocialist primitives') into certain embodied 'copies' of the pirated film copies they watch. Of course, the process of mimesis and its social consequences may make one's sensorium excited and self-pride soar for a moment. Nevertheless, these playful acts eventually exert enormous performative power on the characters, overwhelming their 'reel' lives. They do not necessarily jump out of traps and dilemmas as the result, but end up stepping into another *degenerated* carnival which is destined to be saw-gashed or eliminated.

Post-WTO pirate filmmakers: Documenting pirate-eyes

Both *Suzhou River* and *Pirated Copy* invoke questions about the interrelations between the independent filmmaker and the pirate; between Chinese independent cinema and the 'stolen' popular culture; and between the TV screen which shows the pirated film, the viewfinder in the hands of the filmmaker and the story or life on both sides of these mediating planes. If identification or sympathy still seems to be oblique or kept at arm's length in these two fiction films made in the first half of the 2000s, two recent documentaries have disposed with romantic fantasies about the pirates. In these documentaries, the filmmakers refrained from abusing their discursive privilege to appropriate (if not exploit) the pirate's image to make the film's own statement, and expressed another kind of concern about marginal and grassroots subjects through documentary forms of representation. It is interesting that in these two documentaries, the identities of pirate and cinephile no longer stick together. Even though screen and camera lens still appear to possess a certain magic power, which ignites mimetic impulse and passion, they only constitute one facade of the petty disc vendor's life. The rest is filled with love, friendship, familial relationships, emotional attachment to their career, and constant struggle to make ends meet. If in the fiction films (including *Platform*) I discussed earlier, there is always a phantom of the filmmaker himself that is projected onto the figure of the pirate-eye, now this self-reflexive identity seems to have moved to the other side of the viewfinder. He or she becomes a quietly documenting observer behind the camera.

Both the protagonists of *Paigu* (dir. Liu Gaoming, 2006) and *DVD Boy* (Dang Li Ge Dang, dir. Li Ruihua and Fan Qipeng, 2009) became pirated DVD vendors because they were migrant workers who did not have many career choices in the city, as they came from underdeveloped towns and had no higher education. Nevertheless, both end up finding a sense of belonging and attachment to their illegitimate 'profession.' In *Paigu*, the vendor named Paigu claims: 'I like this business.' This definitive statement is placed at the very beginning of the film, hence serves as part of the foundational address of both the vendor and the documentarian. Similarly, *DVD Boy* also unfolds and revolves around its protagonist Huang Liyin's profession. The zigzagged 'career' path Huang wanders along also becomes a journey of the boy's searching for himself. Huang starts off as the shopkeeper of a video store located at the entrance of Beijing Film Academy. Recounting the genesis of this business, he successfully associates it to the glorious past of Chinese art cinema, the Fifth Generation: 'My boss was Tian Zhuangzhuang's *mazai* [sidekick]; and I am his.' Rather than benefitting from this 'nepotism,' however, he is fired one-third of the way through the film. He also fails to pull together the DV footage he shoots in his spare time into a short film. And when he opens an online virtual DVD store, that does not work out either. His career (at least as presented in the film) looks like a chain of failures. In comparison, Paigu appears to be quite 'professional' in his job and has no difficulty in feeding himself, and sustains a regular income by attracting a group of loyal customers. Despite his own preference for popular cultural products, Paigu makes every effort to maintain a catalogue filled with hard-to-find and high quality art films 'just because of these loyal customers.' He loves the feeling when the customers find what they need and has trained himself to be ultra-knowledgeable about internationally hailed directors and film titles, with the help of DVD buyer's guides. At one point, he says, 'If I ever have enough money in the future, I want to sell legal copies.' But for now, he hangs a foreign filmmaker's newspaper article defending pirated DVDs on the wall in his room, in order to 'encourage' himself. The filmmaker follows Paigu deeper into his personal world: visiting his family in a small town, sharing his disturbing moments in dealing with romantic relationships, and finally witnessing how he has to give up his business. As the documentarian points out, the film revolves around pirate vendors as flesh and blood persons rather than trying to prove that piracy is a lucrative and exploitative business.

The tangible texture of vendors' real lives in these two documentaries poses great challenge to any mythic shell (no matter villainous or heroic) piracy has been put into by popular discourses. For those who deem piracy sales as a career alternative, piracy becomes 'a locus of political resentment toward the failure of the state and state elites,' as Brian Larkin points out in his extensive study of the Nigerian video industry and its root in piracy culture.[37] A pirate's life just resembles the pirated copies he makes a living with, which may contain inherent defects or frauds, with no guarantee of quality. While trying one's best to mend the holes, the pirates still inevitably encounter rupture, anxiety and frustration. Among these broken pieces of the chain of life, these 'systematic failures' of piracy signify and amplify the state or ideological infrastructure's potential for collapsing.

These two films driven by the 'documentary impulse' are more conscious about the power imbalance induced by the apparatus of camera, and offer a different kind of cinematic identification between the kino-eye and the pirate. They did not indulge the filmmaker's power of shooting and representation; instead, they adopted certain techniques in order to pursue visual equality. For instance, many sequences in *DVD Boy* are shot by Huang Liyin of himself (Huang is credited as one of the film's cinematographers). These parts are presented in black-and-white and crosscut with other scenes shot by the two documentarians. Moreover, the film ends with Huang narrating his own story in the form of folk rap (*kuai ban*) – '*dang li ge dang*' – this is also where the film's Chinese title comes from – as if the kino-eye is handing over his or her discursive (or ever historiographical) power to the pirate. Huang uses a chopstick and a bowl to strike a rhythm, facing the camera with a big smile. The lyrics tell his personal history in third-person: 'He quit high school at 15 ... He wanted to make film but obviously failed ... However, man's morality cannot be disgraced, so that his grand dream will eventually be realized someday.' As the lyrics predict, when I saw Huang at DOChina in 2009, he did continue to work with the filmmakers of *DVD Boy* on other projects, anticipating further self-transformation through both piracy and amateur film practices.

Conclusion

In this chapter, I have attempted to theorize an under-explored film culture in China's postsocialist era. I argue that piracy is not only a social problem that is of economic and moral significance, but also an intriguing object of study for cultural historians and social scientists. The history of contemporary piracy in China is of even greater importance, given the special political, economic and cultural condition of this transitional society. In the past three decades, piracy has manifested as a unique mass cultural formation and given shape to new postsocialist subjectivities. It is clear that I have only set out one small aspect of this cultural history here, by looking at the cultural practices of pirate-cinephiles and pirate-eyes since the 1980s. As I pointed out earlier, these people are only some of the many kinds of cultural participants in piracy. Pirate, as I define it, consists of a much broader range of subjects, including: the first wave of private publishers who 'plunged into the sea' (*xia hai*) at the beginning of the Reform Era; certain intellectuals who abandoned scholarly writing and became commercial writers; students who admired Western thoughts and turned to pirated books for enlightenment; dissidents who resisted the status quo by consuming bootlegs and underground media; and cottage factory-owners who make copycat products. In one way or another, they have made various connections with the transitional social reality of postsocialist China through piracy and moulded themselves into the historical actors of their age.

In conclusion, I want to borrow the on-the-go nature of an unfinished fiction film project by Huang Weikai to indicate the open-endedness of this chapter, and also to highlight, once again, the road on which many pirates are continuing to transform into kino-eye. At the end of 2010, I met Huang Weikai, a young independent filmmaker from Guangzhou, and got involved in the project he was initiating at that moment. Huang has recently become known for his film *Disorder*, aka, *Now is the Future of the Past* (*Xianshi shi Guoqu de Weilai*, 2008) – a short compilation documentary made from a thousand hours of footage he collected from the hands of a group of DV amateurs. Recognizing amateur and grassroots media production as an important medium through which Chinese citizens connect with their seemingly alienating and ridiculous social reality, Huang decided to make a fiction film which would carry on and expand the main concern of his previous documentary works. This new film – *Toto*, now still in preproduction – is exactly a new incarnation of the tale about the cinephilic pirate in transformation: a pirated DVD vendor, overwhelmed by the potential power of documentary, steals a DV camera and begins to shoot whatever his 'machine-eye' captures. Eventually, he becomes a 'kino-eye' – a videographer and a caring documentarian. Although Huang's project may keep evolving in the future, I am quite certain that the tale 'from pirate to the kino-eye' has constituted one way for many of us to narrate our own history.

Works cited

Alford, William P. *To Steal a Book Is an Elegant Offense: Intellectual Property Law in Chinese Civilization*. Stanford: Stanford University Press, 1995.
Benjamin, Walter. 'Doctrine of the Similar (1933),' *New German Critique*, no. 17 (Spring 1979): 65–9.
—'On the Mimetic Faculty', trans. Edmund Jephcott, in Peter Demetz (ed.) *Reflections: Essays, Aphorisms, Autobiographical Writings*, New York: Harcourt Brace Jovanovich, 1978, 333–6.
Bordwell, David. *Poetics of Cinema*. London: Routledge, 2008.
Dai, Jinhua. *Wu Zhong Fengjing: Zhongguo Dianying Wenhua 1978–1998* [Landscape in the Mist: Chinese Film from 1978–1998]. Beijing: Peking University Press, 2000.
de Certeau, Michel. *The Practice of Everyday Life*. Berkeley, CA: University of California Press, 1984.
Entgroup. 'China Film Industry Report 2009–10.' Entgroup Inc., 2010.
Gao, Dan. 'Chinese Independent Cinema in the Age of "Digital Distribution"' in Angela Zito and Zhen Zhang (eds), *DV-Made China*. Durham, NC: Duke University Press, forthcoming.

Jia, Zhangke. 'Wei Yingxiang Shidai De Daolai Er Huanhu.' [Hooray for the Arrival of an Age of Images] in Yunlei Li. Nanchang (ed.) *Tao Die*. Baihuazhou Literature and Art Press, 2003.

—'Wufa Jinzhi De Yingxiang' [The Images that Cannot be Banned: Chinese Film since 1995] in Zhangke Jia (ed.), *Jiaxiang 1996–2008: Jia Zhangke Dianying Shouji*. Beijing: Peking University Press, 2009, 122–33.

—'Wufa Jinzhi De Yingxiang' [Images that Cannot be Banned] in Teri Chan and Xiaoyi Li (eds), *Jia Zhangke Dianying Shijie Teji*. All About the World of Jia Zhangke. Hong Kong: Hong Kong Art Center, 2005.

Kloet, Jeroen de. *China with a Cut: Globalisation, Urban Youth and Popular Music*. Amsterdam: Amsterdam University Press, 2010.

Lobato, Ramon. *Shadow Economies of Cinema: Mapping Informal Film Distribution*. London: Palgrave Macmillan, 2012.

Larkin, Brian. *Signal and Noise: Media, Infrastructure, and Urban Culture in Nigeria*. Durham, NC: Duke University Press, 2008.

Li, Dongyu. 'Chongsheng: Zhongguo Dianying Chanye Baogao.' *Shiting Jie*, no. 3 (2005): 12–17.

Li, Jinying. 'From "D-buffs" to the "D-generation": piracy, cinema, and an alternative public sphere in urban China', *International Journal of Communication* (2012): 542–63.

Li, Yang. *Miying Wenhua Shi* [Cinephilia: the History of a Culture]. Shanghai: Fudan University Press, 2010.

Li, Yufeng. *Qiangkou Xia De Falv: Zhongguo Banquan Shi Yanjiu* [Law Making at the Gunpoint: A Study of the History of Chinese Copyright law]. Beijing: Intellectual Property Press, 2006.

Lie, Fu. 'Kan Xianggang, Jian Zhongguo' [Looking at Hong Kong, Seeing China] in Weixiong Zhang (ed.), *Wo He Dianying De Ersan Shi* [My Own Private Cinema]. Hong Kong: Hong Kong Film Critics Society, 2004.

Liu, Yuzhu. *Wenhua Shichang Shiwu Quanshu* [Practical Guide of Chinese Cultural Market]. Beijing: Xinhua Press, 1999.

Nakajima, Seio. 'Film Clubs in Beijing: The Cultural Consumption of Chinese Independent Films.' Chapter 8 in Paul Pickowicz and Yingjin Zhang (eds), *From Underground to Independent : Alternative Film Culture in Contemporary China*. Lanham: Rowman & Littlefield, 2006.

National Bureau of Statistics. *Zhongguo Tongji Nianjian. 2008* [China Statistical Yearbook 2008]. Beijing: Zhongguo tongji chuban she, 2008, 161–208.

Pang, Laikwan. *Cultural Control and Globalization in Asia: Copyright, Piracy, and Cinema*. London and New York: Routledge, 2006.

Ren, Ke. *'Saohuang' Zai 1989* ['Sweeping the Yellow' in 1989]. Beijing: People's University of China Press, 1989.

Rosenbaum, Jonathan. *Goodbye Cinema, Hello Cinephilia: Film Culture in Transition*. Chicago: University of Chicago Press, 2010.

Shu, Fanghou and Weiyu Shan. *Zhongguo Chuban Tongshi 9: Zhonghua Renmin Gongheguo Juan* [General History of Publication in China, vol. 9: People's Republic of China]. Beijing: China Press of Books, 2008.

Sontag, Susan. 'A Century of Cinema' in Susan Sontag (ed.), *Where the Stress Falls: Essays*. New York: Picador, 2002, 117–22.

Statistics, National Bureau of. *Zhongguo Tongji Nianjian 2008* [China Statistical Yearbook 2008]. Beijing: China Statistics Press, 2008.

Sun, Yuemu and Xusheng Wu. *Sanshi Nian Zhongguo Changxiao Shu Shi* [Bestselling Books of the Past 30 Years in China]. Beijing and Nanchang: China Translation & Publishing Corporation and Jiangxi Education Press, 2009.
Turvey, Malcolm. 'Can the Camera See? Mimesis in *Man with a Movie Camera*,' October 89 (Summer 1999): 25–50.
de Valck, Marijke and Malte Hagener (eds). *Cinephilia: Movies, Love and Memory*. Amsterdam: Amsterdam University Press, 2005.
Vertov, Dziga. 'Kinoks: A Revolution,' trans. Kevin O'Brien, in Annette Michelson (ed.), *Kino-Eye: The Writings of Dziga Vertov*. Berkeley, CA: University of California Press, 1984, 11–21.
—'We: Variant of a Manifesto,' trans. by Kevin O'Brien, in Annette Michelson (ed.), *Kino-Eye: The Writings of Dziga Vertov*. Berkeley, CA: University of California Press, 1984, 5–9.
Wang, Shujen. *Framing Piracy: Globalization and Film Distribution in Greater China*. Lanham, MD: Rowman & Littlefield, 2003.
Wei, Junzi and Pingguozhu. *Xianggang Zhi Zao: Yi Meng Shi Nian* [Made in Hong Kong A Dream for Ten Years]. Tianjin Shi: Tianjin jiao yu chu ban she, 2011.
Wu, Angela Xiao. 'Broadening the Scope of Cultural Preferences: Movie Talk and Chinese Pirate Film Consumption from the Mid–1980s to 2005,' *International Journal of Communication* 6 (2012): 501–29.
Xia, Xingyuan. *Zhongguo Dixia Jingji Wenti Yanjiu* [Studies of Chinese Underground Economy]. Zheng zhou: Henan People's Press, 1993.
Yan, Chunjun 'Jianguo Yilai Dianying Chuanbo De Jizhong Tcahu Xingtai.' *Modern Communication*, no. 5 (2011): 75–80.
Yan, Jun. 'Zhongguo 'Daoban Shiye' He "Saw-Gash Generation".' [Piracy Enterprise and the Saw-gash Generation of China] in Guanzhong Chen, Weitang Liao and Jun Yan (eds), *Bohemian China*. Hong Kong: Oxford University Press, 2004.
Zhang, Xiaoqi. 'Hun Zai Luntan De Rizi,' *Cinema World 2011*, no. 9 (2011): 24–9.
Zhang, Yingjin. 'Zhongguo Dianying Daoban De Yujing: Yinmou, Minzhu, Haishi Youxi?,' *Twenty-first Century*, no. 107 (2008): 112–18.
Zhang, Zhen. 'Bearing Witness: Chinese Urban Cinema in the Era of "Transformation" (Zhuanxing)' in Zhen Zhang (ed.), *The Urban Generation: Chinese Cinema and Society at the Turn of the Twenty-First Century*. Durham, NC: Duke University Press, 2007, 1–45.
—'Urban Dreamscape, Phantom Sisters, and the Identity of an Emergent Art Cinema' in Zhen Zhang (ed.), *The Urban Generation: Chinese Cinema and Society at the Turn of the Twenty-First Century*. Durham, NC: Duke University Press, 2007, 344–87.
Zheng, Chengsi. *Banquan Fa* [Copyright Law]. Beijing: China People's Literature Press, 1990.
Zhongguo Guangbo Dianshi Nianjian 1988. [China Radio and TV Yearbook]. Beijing: Beijing Broadcasting Institute Press, 1988.
Zhu, Yue and Fengxu Wu. *Zhongguo Diyidai Getihu* [The First Generation of Self-employed Entrepreneur in China]. Beijing: China Ethnic Photography Press, 2006.

Notes

1. For a survey of the major forms of piracy film consumption that existed in China from c. 1985 to 2005, see Angela Xiao Wu, 'Broadening the Scope of Cultural Preferences: Movie Talk and Chinese Pirate Film Consumption from the Mid-1980s to 2005,' *International Journal of Communication* 6 (2012): 501–29. Book-length critical legal studies include William P. Alford, *To Steal a Book is an Elegant Offense: Intellectual Property Law in Chinese Civilization* (Stanford, CA: Stanford University Press, 1995); Chengsi Zheng, *Banquan Fa* [Copyright Law] (Beijing: China People's Literature Press, 1990); Yufeng Li, *Qiangkou xia de Falv: Zhongguo Banquan Shi Yanjiu* [Law Making at the Gunpoint: A Study of the History of Chinese Copyright law] (Beijing: Intellectual Property Press, 2006).
2. Yingjin Zhang, 'Zhongguo Dianying Daoban de Yujing: Yinmou, Minzhu, haishi Youxi?' [The Context of Chinese Film Piracy: Conspiracy, Democracy, or Play?], *Twenty-first Century*, no. 107 (2008): 114.
3. Yingjin Zhang, 'Zhongguo Dianying Bijiao Yanjiu de Xinshiye' [New Horizon of the Comparative Studies of Chinese Cinema.] *Wenyi Yanjiu*, no. 8 (2007): 79–88.
4. Ramon Lobato, *Shadow Economies of Cinema: Mapping Informal Film Distribution* (London: BFI, 2012). Lobato's book calls for attention to 'informal systems of film circulation,' to which piracy networks constitute one crucial part. By 'shadow economies' he refers to the 'unmeasured, unregulated and extra-legal audiovisual commerce' that indeed underpin any international film culture.
5. In an essay about Chinese 'city film' in the 1980s and 1990s, Dai Jinhua invokes Gramsci's thesis about 'cultural revolution' (via Frederick Jameson) to analyse the emergence of 'new human' [*xinren*] in a series of popular films such as *Heipao Shijian* (*The Black Cannon Incident*, 1986), *Fengkuang de Daijia* (*The Price of Frenzy*, 1988), and *Wanzhu* (*The Troubleshooters*, 1988), addressing the effort these films have made to 'relocate' the *xinren* subject – 'the master and habitant of the new modern and urban life' – back into adequate places after the revolution. Jinhua Dai, *Wu zhong Fengjing: Zhongguo Dianying Wenhua 1978–1998* [Landscape in the Mist: Chinese Film from 1978–1998] (Peking University Press, 2000), 196.
6. Such kind of switch of persona is described in *Made in Hong Kong*, a compilation of old posts and new essays by veteran writers on a film BBS 'Made in Hong Kong,' at Netease. See especially Ziwen Song's essay '*Shuiren Zhi, na Yichang Fenghua Xueyue de Shi*' [Who Knows, that Affair with Spring, Blossoms, Snow and the Moon], *Xianggang Zhizao: Yimeng Shinian* [Made in Hong Kong: A Dream for Ten Years] (Tianjin: Tianjin Education Press, 2011), 208–15.
7. At the year end of 1980, the first privately owned business [*geti gongshang hu*] was born in Wenzhou, Zhejiang, a wholesaler of buttons and women's purses. Yue Zhu and Fengxu Wu, *Zhongguo Diyidai Getihu* [*The First Generation of Self-employed Entrepreneur in China*] (Beijing: China Ethnic Photography Press, 2006), 1.
8. In terms of distribution, however, the government started to allow enterprises under collective ownership [*jiti qiye*] or self-employers [*geti hu*] to register as book retailers (though wholesaling is still forbidden) at the year end of 1980. See Fanghou Shu and Weiyu Shan, *Zhongguo Chuban Tongshi 9: Zhonghua Renmin Gongheguo Juan* [General History of Publication in China Volume 9: People's Republic of China] (Beijing: China Press of Books, 2008), 287.

9 The end of the 1970s to the early 1980s is commonly called 'the time of book famine' [*shuhuang shidai*]. It was described as a period of absolute seller's market. The well-known scholar Xu Youyu recalls, 'There was always a huge line of awaiting buyers in front of Xinhua Bookstore. A book travelled among the hands of so many people that its pages were soon worn out.' Sales of classics such as *The Count of Monte Cristo* and *Le Rouge et le Noir* exceeded a million each. Even foreign theory books were best-sellers. Both *Being and Nothingness* [*cunzai huo xuwu*] by Sartre and *Interpretation of Dreams* [*meng de shiyi*] by Freud sold 150,000 copies. Yuemu Sun and Xusheng Wu, *Sanshi Nian Zhongguo Changxiao Shu Shi* [Bestselling Books of the Past 30 Years in China] (Beijing and Nanchang: China Translation & Publishing Corporation and Jiangxi Education Press, 2009), 2, 214–5.
10 Data comes from National Bureau of Statistics, *Zhongguo Tongji Nianjian 2008* [China Statistical Yearbook 2008] (Beijing: China Statistics Press, 2008), accessed via cnki.net (National Knowledge Infrastructure Project); also see Dongyu Li, 'Chongsheng: Zhongguo Dianying Chanye Baogao' [Rebirth: A Report on the Industrialization of Chinese Film], *Shiting Jie*, no. 3 (2005): 16.
11 National Bureau of Statistics, *Zhongguo Tongji Nianjian 2008*. Entgroup, 'China Film Industry Report 2009–10,' (Bejing: Entgroup Inc., 2010), 9.
12 The number of *luxiang ting* in China reached 25,000. *Zhongguo Guangbo Dianshi Nianjian 1988*, [China Radio and TV Yearbook] (Beijing: Beijing Broadcasting Institute Press, 1988), 15.
13 The so-called *neican pian* [internal reference film] and *guolu pian* [passerby film] are two film categories known between the 1950s and 1970s. They were the result of the 'privilege to enjoy non-publicly released films to be screened at small scale' by 'certain people,' i.e. party/political leaders and cultural specialists, even 'at the time when ideological control was rather heavy-handed.' See Chunjun Yan, 'Jianguo yilai Dianying Chuanbo de Jizhong Teshu Xingtai' [An Analysis of some Special Forms of Film Communication in China after 1949], *Modern Communication*, no. 5 (2011). The film copies for these internal screenings came from various sources, including old Chinese and foreign films which had been released before 1949; a foreign film collection compiled at the China Film Archive; Russian Revisionist films submitted to the Chinese cultural bureau for the sake of criticizing (such as *The Cranes are Flying* and *Ballad of a Soldier*); and a series of Hollywood commercial films which were dubbed to entertain the Culture Revolution Group [*wenge xiaozu*]. After 1976, these films were no longer reserved only for the members of the central government and specialists. Many of them were lent to various institutions and even certain enterprise units to consult with or arrange public screenings with. Therefore a small number of ordinary citizens started to gain access to these rarely seen films. Most of these screenings did not bother with the right clearance at all and are therefore essentially copyright infringements too.
14 Fu Lie, 'Kan Xianggang, Jian Zhongguo' [Looking at Hong Kong, Seeing China] in Weixiong Zhang (ed.) *Wo he Dianying de Ersan Shi* [My Own Private Cinema]. Hong Kong: Hong Kong Film Critics Society, 2004, 73.
15 Zhangke Jia, 'Wei Yingxiang Shidai de Daolai er Huanhu' [Hooray for the Arrival of an Age of Images] in Yunlei Li (ed.), *Tao Die*. Nanchang: Baihuazhou Literature and Art Press, 2003, 1.
16 Rules and regulations include 'Luyin Luxiang Zhipin Guanli Zanxing Guiding' [Provisional Regulations on Audio and Video Products] (1982), 'Yinxiang Zhipin

Pifa, Lingshou, Chuzu he Fangying Guanli Fangfa' [Administrative provisions on A/V Product Wholesale, Retail, Rental, and Screening] (1996); 'Guanyu Qudi Bianxiang Yingyexing Luxiang Fangying Huodong de Tongzhi' [Circular Concerning the Annulment of Disguised Forms of Commercial Video Screening] (1997), etc. See Ke Ren, *'Saohuang' zai 1989* ['Sweeping the Yellow' in 1989]. Beijing: People's University of China Press, 1989, 2–7. Yuzhu Liu, *Wenhua Shichang Shiwu Quanshu* [Practical Guide of Chinese Cultural Market]. Beijing: Xinhua Press, 1999, 679, 702.

17 According to statistics and calculation, during the early stages of the Reform Era, the size of China's underground economy (including the grey economy and shadow economy) was around 20 per cent of the national economy. It reached the highest point of 33.8 per cent in 1988. Xingyuan Xia, *Zhongguo Dixia Jingji Wenti Yanjiu* [Studies of Chinese Underground Economy]. Zheng zhou: Henan People's Press, 1993, 110–12.

18 For some more detailed descriptions of these collectives, see Seio Nakajima, 'Film Clubs in Beijing: the Cultural Consumption of Chinese Independent Films' in Paul Pickowicz and Yingjin Zhang (eds), *From Underground to Independent: Alternative Film Culture in Contemporary China*. Lanham: Rowman & Littlefield, 2006. Dan Gao, 'Chinese Independent Cinema in the Age of "Digital Distribution"' in Angela Zito and Zhen Zhang (eds), *DV-Made China*. Honolulu: University of Hawaii Press, forthcoming. Xiaoqi Zhang, 'Hun zai Luntan de Rizi' [The Days When We Commingled on the Forums], *Cinema World 2011*, no. 9.

19 Zhen Zhang, 'Bearing Witness: Chinese Urban Cinema in the Era of "Transformation" (Zhuanxing)' in Zhen Zhang (ed.), *The Urban Generation: Chinese Cinema and Society at the Turn of the Twenty-First Century*. Durham, NC: Duke University Press, 2007, 27.

20 Musician and critic Jun Yan is among the earliest ones who reveal the genealogical root of Chinese independent rock, or even independent cultures at large, within a 'saw-gashed culture' [*dakou wenhua*] which encompasses consumption of *dakou*, *zousi luxiangdai* (smuggled video tape), and pirated discs. *Dakou* literally refers to audio tape or CD with a punched dent on it. This kind of deformed media product was originally surplus in the West. Instead of simply being dumped, they were punched and sold to developing countries as recyclable plastic. However, while missing a couple of songs, these tapes and discs actually could still be listened to, hence were turned into rare merchandises among a generation of young music lovers in China in the 1980s. Jun Yan, 'Zhongguo "Daoban Shiye" he "Saw-gash Generation"' [Piracy Enterprise and the Saw-gash Generation of China] in Guanzhong Chen, Weitang Liao and Jun Yan (eds), *Bohemian China*. Hong Kong: Oxford University Press, 2004. Jeroen de Kloet, *China with a Cut: Globalisation, Urban Youth and Popular Music*. Amsterdam: Amsterdam University Press, 2010, 19–22.

21 See Jinying Li, 'From "D-buffs" to the "D-generation": piracy, cinema, and an alternative public sphere in urban China', *International Journal of Communication* (2012). Her examples include independent filmmakers Zhang Yue and Chen Tao.

22 Yang Li, *Miying Wenhua Shi* [Cinephilia: the History of a Culture]. Shanghai: Fudan University Press, 2010, 9.

23 Susan Sontag, 'A Century of Cinema,' in Susan Sontag (ed.), *Where the Stress Falls: Essays*. New York: Picador, 2002, 122.

24 For example, see Marijke de Valck and Malte Hagener (eds), *Cinephilia: Movies, Love and Memory*. Amsterdam University Press, 2005; Jonathan Rosenbaum, *Goodbye*

Cinema, Hello Cinephilia: Film Culture in Transition. Chicago: University of Chicago Press, 2010. Li Yang also elongated Sontag's historical spectrum for cinephilia to encompass a spiritual legacy of a near-religious faith in movie (not only film, but also motion pictures carried by other media such as DVD and internet stream) which existed in figures from Méliès, Truffault, to the cinephile-turned-critics/filmmakers in China today. *Cinephilia: The History of a Culture* (2010).

25 Valck and Hagener, 'Down with Cinephilia? Long Live Cinephilia? And Other Videosyncratic Pleasures,' *Cinephilia: Movies, Love and Memory* (2005), 22.
26 Thomas Elsaesser names three kinds of deferrals inherent in cinephilia: 'a detour in place and space, a shift in register and a delay in time.' 'Cinephilia or the Uses of Disenchantment,' *Cinephilia: Movies, Love and Memory* (2005), 30.
27 Li, *Cinephilia: The History of a Culture* (2010), 313.
28 Michel de Certeau, *The Practice of Everyday Life*. Berkeley, CA: University of California Press, 1984.
29 Dziga Vertov, 'We: Variant of A Manifesto,' in Annette Michelson (ed.), *Kino-eye: the Writings of Dziga Vertov*. Berkeley, CA: University of California Press, 1984.
30 Mimesis, as defined by Benjamin, is the human 'ability to see resemblances,' coupled with an underlying impulse to 'become and behave like something else.' Walter Benjamin, 'On the Mimetic Faculty,' in Peter Demetz (ed.), *Reflections: Essays, Aphorisms, Autobiographical Writings*. New York: Harcourt Brace Jovanovich, 1978. 'Doctrine of the Similar,' *New German Critique*, no. 17 (Spring 1979).
31 Malcolm Turvey, 'Can the Camera See? Mimesis in *Man with a Movie Camera*,' *October* 89 (Summer 1999).
32 Vertov, 'Kinoks: A Revolution,' 15.
33 Benjamin, 'On the Mimetic Faculty,' 334.
34 Ibid., 331.
35 Network narrative is also known as the 'converging fate plot.' It is a term coined by David Bordwell in order to categorize film plots that involve parallel or sequential unfolding of multiple (usually gradually converging) narratives. David Bordwell, *Poetics of Cinema*. Routledge, 2008.
36 Zhang, 'Urban Dreamscape, Phantom Sisters, and the Identity of an Emergent Art Cinema,' 370.
37 Brian Larkin, *Signal and Noise: Media, Infrastructure, and Urban Culture in Nigeria*. Duke University Press, 2008, 220.

8

Xue Jianqiang as Reckless Documentarian: Underdevelopment and Juvenile Crime in post-WTO China

Keith B. Wagner

Standing in front of Wu Wenguang's Beijing studio in 2010, young documentarian Xue Jianqiang is found violently knocking at his predecessor's door. Armed with his DV camera in his film, *I Beat Tiger When I Was Young/Wo nianqing shi ye da laohu* (2010), Xue points the camera aggressively at Wu, zeroing in on his target and pressing the father of the New Documentary Movement about his legacy. We hear Xue shouting at Wu to leave Chinese documentary film to the now more capable – presumably, Xue himself. The implications of such a demand are obvious, if we take this moment in the film as an example: the time has come to break the limitations of the still-restrictive Chinese documentary form and content, and to do so with unrelenting artistic and political conviction.

Despite the poisonous impression one may gather after watching *I Beat Tiger When I Was Young*, Xue's debasement of Wu's career (and other filmmakers in this documentary) in some ways stages the debate[1] between an older generation documentarian and an enthusiastic newcomer. Culturally speaking, Wu's *Bumming in Beijing* (1990) remains a hugely influential film in China today due to its portrait of five self-marginalized artists in the capital that draws attention to a 'kind of independence from dominant structures and ideologies that shape mainland Chinese life,' and the 'ways in which these directors, and their works, might serve as catalysts of sociocultural transformation' for the 1990s.[2] Matthew D. Johnson has argued that Wu's representation of a postsocialist reality is 'specific to these individuals' "actual lives" (*zhenshi shenghuo*), with particular emphasis on both hardships and "rich experiences" that downward mobility paradoxically provide.'[3] And this remains a central critique in *Bumming in Beijing*. Here Wu's 'spirited critique' is somewhat compatible with Xue's own documentary trailblazing in the post-WTO period; though Xue's trailblazing is also quite different from Wu's, whereby he hopes to provide a unique documentary vision for the twenty-first century – a method of making that is both vainly expressive and socially conscious – a paradox of expression worth exploring in the pages to come.

This paradox in writing about Xue and others' work is what Paul Pickowicz calls the 'self-indulgent to the extreme' phase of independent Chinese film and documentary.[4] Yet I would like to proceed anyway and look at the implications of excessiveness to hopefully arrive at the other side of this characteristic by detecting the socially conscious elements that are sometimes concealed by iGeneration solipsism. To think about Xue's new documentary vision, we must start with questions of methodology. As such, the boundaries and methods for documentary operation in China have been newly drawn and discussed in divisional terms by Yingjin Zhang, who cites Taiwanese film scholar Wang Weici for methodological guidance. Wang provides a standard interpretation of Chinese documentary film, delineating 'four modes of documentary in contemporary China: (1) conventional voiceover (straightforward propaganda), which characterizes the mainstream media; (2) observation, which emphasizes non-interference and derives from Euro-American direct cinema and cinéma vérité; (3) interviews, which became popular with CCTV *Living Space*; and (4) self-reflection, which is still rare in China.'[5] In more theoretical terms, Chinese documentary film has been in its own categorical context up until 1990, if we think of Bill Nichols's six documentary categories – poetic, expository, observational, participatory, reflexive and performative. Despite their limitations, these presiding categories are a necessary evil in film studies because they hold together the disparate patterns of documentary filmmaking, in China and in the West.[6]

In light of these methods of analysis, the modes categorized by Wang and reappropriated by Zhang are accurate; however, I would add a fifth mode to the list – 'reckless documentaries,' films that catapult their viewers into extreme realities or viewing positions. Reckless documentary is a method whereby the observational mode, with its *cinéma vérité* influence, is taken in a new direction, driven by a forceful, even combustible look at lower-class subjects who are often encouraged to act badly, even violently, for the camera. This combustible mode is derived through an approach that is careless of consequence and filmmakers who provoke their subjects to act irresponsibly and behave with little regard for personal safety or ethics, toward themselves or others around them. Indeed, this reckless instigation caught on film is arguably a new approach in the field of documentary filmmaking in post-WTO China. I see Xue living up to this approach in how he targets his subjects on the margins of Chinese society, often disregarding ethical or practical precision for a no-holds-barred approach. And despite the enfant terrible label, his flippant documentary style also underpins a crude dissection of Chinese underdevelopment via a sensational visuality.

Xue's tongue-in-cheek attitude

I read Xue's reckless approach as more in line with contemporary visual artists in England than traditional documentary filmmaking in China. The feel of *I Beat Tiger When I Was Young* resonates as incendiary in a postmodern sense, making me think of the Young British Artists (YBA) of the 1990s, particularly the work of Jake and Dinos Chapman and their reputation for satirizing other artistic movements, practitioners and even patrons in creating artistic pieces that are at their core both sensational and polemical in nature. In particular, their sculptural installation titled 'Hell' (2000), where hundreds of nude and bloodied miniature figurines are encased in a plexi-glass purgatory, conjures up scenes from Dante's *Inferno*, or even from Dutch medieval painter Hieronymus Bosch and his unsettling triptychs.

Like the Chapman brothers' 'Hell' as grotesque allegory for British (even Western) unbridled consumer culture, Xue's postsocialist configuration of underdevelopment is both political and apolitical simultaneously – visually arresting as well as contentious in sociocultural terms. This tongue-in-cheek attitude by the Chapman brothers is a commonality I see Xue sharing, and it is refreshing because it signals a paradigm shift in the larger Chinese documentary scene the last ten years. Furthermore, Xue's undisciplined attack demonstrates, among other things, a refusal to conform to ivory tower standards. This refusal is exemplified by Xue's challenging of Wu Wenguang's uncontested status in artistic and intellectual circles in *I Beat Tiger When I Was Young*. In fact, Wu's status is a major issue for newer documentarians to grapple with in China: do they challenge, embrace, or ignore his legacy? One imagines Wu to be like John Grierson in the influence Grierson had as the British and European father of documentary practice in the 1930s. Faced with this creative shadow, Xue shows there is indeed something beyond the institutional mosaic of documentary film Wu has shaped in China, and at the same time provides a new mode in Wang's and Zhang's documentary taxonomy.[7]

In this chapter, I conceive of Xue's work as assessing the harm to weaker sectors of Chinese society, though admittedly not a new vantage point, an important film among others because it continues to structure the steady neoliberal creep in the country. And it is a filmic timeline we can trace from Wu's *Bumming in Beijing* to Xue's corpus of work. This is so, I argue, because neoliberal policies have left behind many areas in China in what Wang Hui describes as China's Rust Belt; his thoughts guide much of my theorizations of underdevelopment in lower-order cities discussed in this chapter. I will also question the so-called ethics involved (or not involved) in Xue's and others' 'reckless documentary' films. This approach will draw on Yingjin Zhang's and Yiman Wang's research on the changing nature of documentary film in China. Thus, in synthesizing these three scholars' ideas with my own, I hope to legitimate how Xue captures the rise in delinquency among young nomadic types in contemporary China in an unsophisticated, bottom-up vision.

A reckless approach to Chinese documentary film

Is the reckless documentary a new niche in contemporary documentary film culture in China? *I Beat Tiger When I Was Young* seems to parallel the tactics of British documentary film from the last decade. For instance, Xue's approach is reminiscent of the British *kamikaze* filmmaker Nick Broomfield, who also uses a no-holds-barred approach to shadow his documentary subjects. His most memorable film, *Tracking Down Maggie* (1990), audaciously follows Margaret Thatcher in her private life after her fall from power as British Prime Minister in the early 1990s. Broomfield's pursuit of Thatcher sees him zigzag across the country, from heckling her at a book signing in London to a British Naval ceremony in Plymouth – while Xue takes a more direct approach and ambushes Wu Wenguang at his Beijing studio. Here both directors are unrelenting and cross traditional lines of documentary production by literally chasing their subjects. In effect, these two unorthodox approaches in documentary film come to overexpose, aggravate and taunt their respective subjects, and are seen as a new mode of documentary filmmaking in England in the 1990s, and a newer approach in China in the 2000s.

In another short documentary, peculiarly titled *Martian Syndrome*, Xue shapes a story about a deranged homeless man with whom he strikes up a conversation, and proceeds to analyse and then antagonize from the inside of his own apartment in Beijing. Interestingly, the documentary uses practically zero light and switches from a darkened interior to a reverse negative of the apartment, whereby the talking head shots of the homeless man produce a ghostly effect, even a Martian sci-fi aesthetic in its greenish glow – hence the film's title – and these elements provide a sinister distance to Xue's exploited subject. In addition, *Martian Syndrome* is strikingly amateurish in its formal style, where one is puzzled by the use of a reverse negative but amused by the frightening aesthetic it produces. First screened internationally in 2011 at the New Generation Chinese Cinema Conference in London, *Martian Syndrome* drew notice from established and young Chinese film scholars.

Yet before the arrival of Xue's work in official Anglo-American academic circles, I had the privilege of seeing an earlier work of his, in 2010, at the now defunct Cinephilia West, in Notting Hill Gate, London. Chinese film scholar and documentarian Tianqi Yu screened Xue's *Three Small Animals II* (2009), which will be the focus of the remainder of this chapter.[8] Not only is Xue's 17-minute-long experimental documentary an illustrative example of neoliberal underdevelopment in China's Rust Belt, but it also focuses on three delinquent teenage boys who commit crimes against other youths, capturing a hostility that undercuts the film's reckless style. This, in my view, signals something more alarming, and challenges the showmanship and recklessness Xue portends in the earlier films I mention – *I Beat Tiger When I Was Young* and *Martian Syndrome*. Indeed, *Three Small Animals II* focuses on the negative components of China – impoverishment, exclusion and criminalization of both China's regions and its youth – that on a visual level blurs the boundaries of the experimental documentary, toward my notion of a reckless style. Thus, the Janus-faced methodology for making *Three Small Animals II* for Xue is both excessive and churlish in terms of its subject matter in the portrayal of juvenile crime, but also unapologetic and regionally specific. And by critiquing China as a partition society, Xue exposes the allusiveness of more refined and developed Chinese culture.

Taiyuan

Despite the 17-minute length of *Three Small Animals II*, one gets an immediate sense of the dilapidated post-industrial landscape Xue hones in on and where the film is based. The imagery of Taiyuan comes to foreground an uncosmetic set of spaces in the northern Chinese city: derelict housing estates and crumbling industrial buildings off in the distance of the frame. This uncosmetic set of spaces is Xue's drab cityscape in *Three Small Animals II*. It is replete with filthy alleyways, cramped inner-city roads, rusty mining equipment and scruffy apartment interiors, all drenched by constant acid rain – it is a documentary that highlights the now almost-clichéd images of *xiancheng*, a term defined as 'county-level city'. The term provincializes urban decay and slow urban renewal, which is bundled up with many fictional and documentary films from China. During the last decade and a half, we have encountered the *xiancheng mise-en-scène* in the works of Wang Bing, Jia Zhangke, Li Yang, Lu Chuan, Cui Jian, and more recently, in the quasi-documentary work of Xue, Xu Tong and Wu Haohao among others.

However, the difference in Xue's style if we compare him to other young experimental documentarians is sizeable. Take Xue's aesthetic experimentation. In *Three Small Animals II*, he incorporates a simple-looking computer-generated clock-type calendar, blue and white and half-circular in shape, to accompany his real *xiancheng* footage. This clock-type calendar template comes to break these bleak *xiancheng* images within the filmic frame. Here, we see the hand of the clock display the birth year of the three hooligan boys that Xue follows, which acts as a type of marker; the significance of the calendar clock is to chronicle how transformation is economically and socially attached to these teenage boys. It becomes a 'translation machine', to echo Henri Bergson and Flaubert before him, where the apparatus addresses a simultaneous time outside the cheerful economic reforms felt in other parts of the country, but not enjoyed by these teenage boys in Taiyuan. We find in Xue's and others' films the exploration not of construction sites where cities are erected overnight or places that await gentrification. Instead, we see blatant neglect, deindustrialization and groups of people with nothing to lose – acting wildly and destructively – given the destitution they face.

Beyond the emphasis on time, or its elapse, the documentary provides other unusual visual motifs. For example, camera angles are quite haphazard. We see in one scene a close-up of a card table with *mah jong* titles stacked on its surface and a pan-out to one child being trained how to gamble on the game with adults looking on. In another scene, the filmmaker records one of the teenage boys speeding through a run-down area of Taiyuan on a three-wheeled motorcycle, filming over his subject's shoulder as he rides on the back. The composition is intriguing because it parallels the circular calendar clock template, which works to gauge large blocks of time. We see another circular device in this scene, a speedometer, gauging the motorcycle's speed as it records the three teenage boys carelessly joyriding through Taiyuan. Here Xue's focus on framing the speedometer seems to signify, in some respect, the rapid decomposition of his young subjects. These reckless teenagers express themselves through daredevil acts on their motorcycle, unconcerned for their own safety or the public's.

Most interesting of all, in terms of this documentary's aesthetic composition, is *Three Small Animals II*'s focus on small-screen displays. In another scene in the reckless documentary, the three teenage boys surround a fourth boy and then begin to strike him in the head with an umbrella. Their violent actions become just another form of stimulation for them to pass time in Taiyuan. We see this dynamic in another scene in the film, where there is a cut to a long-shot of them beating another unidentified young boy, then a cut-away that puts us hovering over the three delinquent teenage boys who are engrossed in watching their assault as it is played back on one of their mobile phones. All the time, Xue shoots them holding the mobile phone as they laugh at their recent crime, unfazed by their violent offence. The scene ends with them screening this content over and over again. Aesthetically speaking, it becomes a documentary *mise-en-abyme* mode of framing, strikingly original in its visual adeptness, yet also sinister in its ability to address the impact of economic conditions and the fate of its delinquent teenagers committing this senseless, or perhaps necessary, crime to survive.

If *Three Small Animals II* is a reckless documentary, it shares a political and aesthetic link to other recent Chinese documentary and docudramatic films that conform to my notion of a reckless mode of filmmaking. These films, defined by a loose aesthetic approach that complements a self-affirmed identification with regionally based realities, now include themes of criminal activity, usually involving jobless males, animal cruelty, natural disasters, dangerous situations and drug use – particularly egregious are dog fight videos from Guangzhou and portraits of heroin addicts from Shanghai. For instance, many of the dog fight videos that are posted anonymously (given their disturbing content) personify this reckless mode of filmmaking. Elsewhere, Du Haiban's hasty decision to film the Sichuan earthquake's devastation a day or so after it happens in *1428* (2009) is another type of reckless filmmaking, chasing after danger (much like Huang Weiai's *Disorder* from 2007 that records urban accidents on Chinese streets). In addition, *Shanghai Panic* (Andrew Cheng, 2002), adapted from Mian Mian's writings, tells the story of rampant drug use and prostitution by young urbanites with nothing to lose. These depraved activities caught on camera thus form another, less socially conscious reckless approach and point viewers to other uncosmetic environments in China: grubby alleyways, toppled architecture, unnamed streets and run-down apartments where these tragedies occur.

Scenes in these films can also be read in two ways. On the one hand, they focus on dangerous situations and illegal recreations we come to understand as the subjects (and sometimes the filmmakers themselves) trying in vain to articulate their endless lust for empty pleasures (wagers on bloodthirsty dogs to exhibiting human fatalities to scoring drugs). On the other hand, these same films, reflexive in format, reflect an amateurish style and embrace sloppy editing techniques, which are chalked up to rookie mistakes and are a distinct modality of the younger generation's amateurism. The larger phenomenon of amateur filmmaking has been discussed elsewhere by Ying Qian, who finds 'a poverty of aesthetic imagination and artistic vision' that in some way unites directors like Du, Huang, Cheng, Xue and countless other filmmakers in contemporary China.[9] Their films – including Xue's *Three Small Animals II* – confront/feature subjects no longer enamoured (or never enamoured) with neoliberal reform.

These films come to undermine government discourses of a cosmopolitan life in China by going in the opposite direction: visualizing heinous acts of animal cruelty, carnage, hedonistic pleasure and juvenile offences.

Another elusive question remains, and I need to return to *Three Small Animals II* directly to answer it: is it possible to untangle the objectification of Xue's youth in this film from its murky sociocultural critique? And is there an ethical problem if Xue refrains from humanizing these troubled teenage boys? And what are the consequences of remaining caught in such a paradox, even aporia? One answer might be found in Yingjin Zhang's recent work, where he posits a new appoach not only to thinking about Chinese documentary films but also what these newer films are saying to the Chinese public. This is important to bear in mind, as Zhang argues that 'Owing to its marginalization [*bianyuan*] in contemporary China – a deplorable fact sometimes attributed in part to irresponsible dismissals by self-designated mainstream intellectuals – independent documentary has consistently pursued alternative, oppositional, even subversive functions.'[10] If I understand Zhang correctly, my point of inquiry into these films, however debased they may be, should be with how this group of filmmakers – particularly Xue – lacks an allegiance to an ethical position (instead they glorify reckless acts, presenting, perhaps too excessively, killer dogs, earthquakes and road hazards, drug addicts, and troubled youth to a Chinese public), and also with what these subversive functions veil – depressed living standards, in all different narrative and visual scales of reference. Therefore, some of the subversive elements often dismissed by Western and at times mainland scholars, particularly the way in which teenage violence and crime have come to contravene traditional ethical values, seem redeemable, in an academic sense, if we think less about the ethical questions and more about the social context many of these films expose. At least this is the position I have been taking thus far in this chapter. In what follows, my Marxist-sociological critique will be fused to several close textual analyses to explicate the rise in regional unemployment and lack of family support, which we find Xue's criminalized teenage boys inherit as citizens living in Taiyuan.

Contextualizing underdevelopment and crime

Central to Xue's original, if subversive, approach is of course the question of how the rules for making and interpreting newer documentary films remain in flux, a question the filmmakers themselves are beginning to rethink. *Three Small Animals II*, for instance, questions documentary film's traditional notion of ethical distance from its subject. Because of their extreme approach, we can view Xue's and others' films that focus on socioeconomic problems as a distillation of neoliberalism's effects on China's most marginalized. I therefore extract from Xue's reckless documentary the plain face of neoliberal underdevelopment. Here I see a newer expression of the limits of Chinese neoliberalism in territories that are seen less often, with imagery hardly found on CCTV or other private media content circulating China. Instead, *Three Small*

Animals II delineates an uncosmetic projection of parochial life in China's hinterlands. Focusing on the features of Taiyuan – the capital city of Shanxi province, a remote city not benefiting as other cities have from complete architectural or structural redesign – *Three Small Animals II* shows its audience a worn and dilapidated set of spaces that backdrops Xue's teenage subjects, and this backdrop lacks the shimmering glow that is depicted in much mainstream cinema.

Speaking about the economic state of Taiyuan, prosperity has all but passed it by. It lacks what the 'coastal belt cities' have, especially if we follow Xiangming Chen's prognosis, that 'early developers like Shenzhen and other cities in Guangdong and Fujian provinces, which were fairly small and marginal in the past, have raced ahead of the more established port cities like Shanghai and Tianjin, which have since picked up pace and regained their earlier glory. This sequence and pattern of growing inter-local differentiation stems from the state's policies of targeting and favouring sets of cities in different regions for fast and focused growth in a staged and incremental fashion.'[11] In fact, this follows the historical trajectory for neoliberal development in regard to city policies in China, where by the mid-1980s, 'its northeastern and southwestern border regions fell much behind.' Taiyuan is not a city given central consideration by the state, as we can gather from the discordant images on view in this film. Thus, *Three Small Animals II* comes to disentangle the familiar logic of neoliberalism's ability to supersede territorial constraints, via its small-scale analysis of three marginal teenagers and the dilapidated city they call home.

In much of its depiction of parochial life, *Three Small Animals II* stands in diametric opposition to Wu Wenguang's citizen activism captured in his later work – especially *Dance with Peasant Workers* (2001). In that film, Wu presents a polished documentary treatment of lower-class misfortune, and its optimistic social message can be seen to counterpoise the stark vision we find in Xue's *Three Small Animals II*. Indeed, in ragged formal terms, *Three Small Animals II* does not wrap its subjects in the warmth of a cosmopolitan amelioration. Instead, it illustrates the instabilities many Chinese face. Of course, this is not meant to denigrate Wu Wenguang's important film, but rather suggests a bleaker portrait of Chinese lower-class society that is now present throughout the country. I therefore would stress the social context of Xue's film – which is about struggle, tragedy and poverty for Chinese citizens, yet never willing to profess a direct political or activist stance against these realities. The events that unfold in front of Xue's viewfinder provide the viewer with a sense of China's developmental problems in this region of the country, or, more dubiously, a penchant for lowly characters and their deplorable behaviour. To put it in the words of another young documentarian named Qiu Jiongjiong: 'Shoot films like an animal. Criticize [films] like an animal. Animals of a different species [*sic*].'[12] Lu Xinyu argues that low-budget documentarians with an affinity for depravity come to view their own 'social responsibility as an oppressive concept,' a conundrum most marginalized Chinese filmmakers must face.[13]

Despite the rejection of so-called 'social responsibility' in Xue's and others' work, many of these reckless films hint at, whether implicitly or explicitly, the scarcity of social services in the country with no remedies to fix these social problems, at least in the near future. Barriers to a better life are presented by the intensification of deindustrialization and underdevelopment in smaller cities, which often trigger social problems that continue to haunt China.[14] As Wang Hui argues:

> ...we must respect the deep relationship between cultural pluralism and the problem of development; we must also investigate rural problems alongside urban ones. The free movement of labor, public management, and government intervention are all necessary conditions for the market system; but how to limit its destruction of the environment, traditions, customs, rituals and other aspects of life and values is a major problem for the study of development today.[15]

More generally, Xue depicts not only an unprivileged urban condition for his delinquent teenagers, but also espouses an anti-establishment lifestyle, one that Chris Berry explains only became 'possible in the People's Republic with the development of a non-State sector in the 1980s.'[16] *Three Small Animals II* thus crystallizes the dispersal and evisceration of citizens and their sites of origin, a genuine embedded feature in this documentary film. Moreover, its portrait of these delinquent teenage boys is not colonized by a mainstream reality, insofar as it clues its audiences in to the disconnectedness and push toward neoliberal nomadism that Xue's delinquent teenagers face. They wander the streets day in and day out in search of excitement and distraction, not caught up with typical Chinese activities found at their age: education, family and social responsibility. These boys also lack employment to guide them, and ultimately the codes of the streets inform their truculent behaviour in Taiyuan. Unemployment is in fact common to this region, where production-based services were eclipsed by service-sector activities long ago. 'After 2001, growth rate of labour productivity is also higher in service industry than manufacturing industry and the average level is 20.1 per cent and 11 per cent respectively.'[17] Unsurprisingly, unemployment in Taiyuan is coupled with weak capital investment from foreign investors, waning state subsidies to its lagging manufacturing industries, and no visible tourism industry that would otherwise offset the city's continued underdevelopment.

The notion that environment dictates social behaviour is not too far-fetched if we apply these bleak socioeconomic variables to Xue's teenage boys, who almost wholly lack community or family support to share in their burdens of daily life in Taiyuan. These social conditions can be considered as one of many causes of their deviant behaviour, and in another scene, we see Xue recording them smashing a factory window late at night to steal tanks of compressed air to sell on the black market. Once they move the stolen items to the back of their three-wheeled motorcycle and flee the scene, one of the boys proudly declares their robbery a success. This scene of the theft from the factory is presented in a matter-of-fact, detached style, as Xue passes no judgement on the boys for their crime. Therefore, as *Three Small Animals II* blurs the line between a reckless documentarian and a documentarian building a visual record of social deviance in an uncosmetic place like Taiyuan, a question emerges: is social responsibility relieved of its implication for a better life, when a better life was never an option in the first place? To explain this, I have deployed a macro-intuitive approach to neoliberal neglect found in regional cities like Taiyuan, which I see this film able to articulate in its focalization on a Chinese underclass – young delinquents, who are beneath migrant workers, both in larger cities and in their hometown – and below, too, the largely uneducated peasant classes. These jobless and orphaned subjects constitute the most marginal group found in the discursive modes of documentary filmmaking.

Though we should avoid calling these teenage boys' acts of criminal mischief a form of 'gang' violence, their behaviour does warrant a reflection on recent sociological studies in China, particularly studies of individuals who are exposed to criminal activity. In a final scene of violence, we see the three teens beating another boy on the street. This violent incident occurs when the three teenage boys form a semicircle around a fourth boy, whom they then start to taunt. Initially, the fourth boy reacts timidly and takes their abuse. But after he does not react, Xue's three teenage boys begin to push him until he starts to cry. This sign of weakness then incites the three teenage boys to push the fourth boy more violently, eventually resulting in his being struck in the arms and head repeatedly. Though this appears more like bullying than first-degree assault, one finds a complete absence of social restraint in this world of neoliberal nomadism, where the three teenage boys lurk about and 'commit crimes basically by chance.' One might say their temptation to 'prove themselves' or just to 'act tough' thus culminates in this public attack and later, I assume, more deviant behaviour, beyond these criminal incidents caught on camera. We could call this in sociological terms 'co-offence' (*gongtong fanzui*), which refers to the commission of a crime jointly by at least two people.[18]

This blunt perspective on life in Taiyuan, in a more profound sense, visualizes one aspect of underdevelopment and a reality not contested by the Chinese government.[19]

> Unlike other countries that have experienced rapid modernization and industrialization, China, and the Asian-Pacific nations in general, have had relatively moderate increases in their rates of delinquency. Still, it can be said that shifts in economic conditions in these societies have had an impact on the volume of youth crime…In addition, unemployment has risen at an unprecedented rate; in 1990, the number of urban unemployed was projected to be 6 million, a rate of 3.5% versus 2% a year earlier (China News Analysis 1989). More significantly, in 1991, it was estimated that 100 million peasants were unemployed, and projected that the number may approach 300 million by the end of the century.[20]

For example, one can trace the upswing of unemployed to crime and this follows China's move toward neoliberalization. Picking up on this social trend toward crime, Manzhi Cao provides the following statistical data from the 1970s through 1989 to reflect this troubling economic problem.[21]

By 1989, and before the crackdown in Tiananmen Square, the rise in crime committed by youth offenders is astounding – an estimated 74.1 per cent of youth crime was perpetrated by youths aged 14–25 years. In more recent reports, the numbers have remained practically the same, with a slight increase in the 1990s and a dip of 2 per cent in the 2000s. Of course, to link all crime to neoliberalization in China would be preposterous, but levels of corruption, theft, gambling, unemployment,

Table 8.1 14 to 25 Year Olds as Percentage of All Youth Offenders, 1975–89

Year	Percentage
1975	37.0
1976	N.A.
1977	N.A.
1978	N.A.
1979	47.6
1980	61.2
1981	64.0
1982	65.9
1983	67.0
1984	63.3
1985	71.2
1986	72.5
1987	74.4
1988	75.7
1989	74.1

vagrancy, nomadism, and the elimination of social programmes have all increased under China's market flexibility programmes. These undeniable realities are linked to underdevelopment, which seems hard to contest when we see hypermodernity in Shanghai and Beijing and deindustrialization in Taiyuan and other lower-order cities. Correspondingly, such a transformation of the socioeconomic fabric in China has led to higher rates of concern, particularly in juvenile crime committed. No stranger to this reality, Wang Hui postulates that Chinese labourers based in more rural areas face unique problems and connects this underdevelopment to neoliberalism in China.

> …the expansion of the market system brings with it the entry of circulation activities and its values into all aspects of life, which breaks apart all preexisting social structures (such as communities and their values), and brings all communal life formations (such as minority formations) down to their lowest common denominator. In this sense, to merely discuss development from the perspective of the freedom to contract labor while ignoring the relationship between development and social conditions could indeed lead to the disintegration of society.[22]

Indeed, in Wang's view social disintegration is an integral factor to underdevelopment, and is reproduced in what Xue's three disenchanted teenage boys come to face: no alleviation of social problems, which means no respect for those problems they encounter in Taiyuan. They become reactionary in spirit and rebel to survive and be heard like other oppressed youth. While daily routines captured in the film show the three teenage boys spending their days with no structure to their schedule, one could assume that petty crime like this is brought on by boredom and degeneracy. In this regard, I believe the time template is suggestive in *Three Small Animals II* and signifies a type of stasis for these unruly teenage boys, where social, cultural, demographic and, most importantly, economic growth has been petrified in time, well before their births. The three teenage boys in Xue's film are bound to no moral or economic systems – systems that would otherwise regiment how they keep their time, and what rewards are reaped in following a path to neoliberal self-sufficiency and sociocultural compliance. If we zoom out to view this phenomenon as connected to China's rapid economic growth, such social exclusion relates, to some degree, to the breakdown of the familial and fraternal bonds found outside large cities like Shanghai and Beijing. These problems are widespread – not just for Xue's three orphaned delinquents, but also for migrant labourers, prostitutes and ethnic minorities, who all struggle to make ends meet.

With the steady disintegration of the domestic sphere in China's Rust Belt, this documentary critiques neoliberal underdevelopment, which can be read through the *associative patterns* of neglect and crime. Taiyuan is thus shown to audiences as worn down, with children left behind and a free-for-all mood indulged in by many operating at the edge of Chinese society. Moreover, as China's neoliberal policies have continued to weaken the economies of remote small cities like Taiyuan during the last 20 years, Xue shows us these changes in less discernible ways via his flippant documentary style. Here the dichotomy found in *Three Small Animals II* is similar to Yiman Wang's witnessing concept.[23] I see Wang's theory as a way to interpret whether Xue is literally 'one of them' (as he lives in the same city and is related to one of the teenage delinquents), while also allowing his 'actors to co-author' his production. Wang's concept calls into question the usefulness of hanging onto civic principles (i.e. critiquing Chinese social decline) in documentary films such as this one. In other words, I believe *Three Small Animals II* proposes an 'against the grain' critical approach and does not question whether we actually need to exempt the violent juvenile behaviour in the film; on the contrary, *Three Small Animals II* rejects being 'irreconcilably split into stable categories of the powerful and the powerless…'.[24] To me, the film plays with 'the powerful and the powerless,' but in its reckless approach defies the often lopsided position in which the documentarian usually finds himself or herself. Instead, these reckless films contest such a binary in the first place.

Essentially, *Three Small Animals II* records the existence of three marginalized teenage boys, vulgar as they may be. It represents them as a type of regional citizen in China's Rust Belt, worthy of filmic attention in the post-WTO moment. But the documentary's fatalism is something we cannot ignore either. Wang has argued that many grassroots documentary filmmakers develop a double-edged sword in their films' predilection to depict a reality, and due to the need to be close to their subjects, it is said, a filmmaker violates a perceived documentary ethics in not keeping an objective distance. Wang explains this double-edged sword mentality as follows:

> …the act of penetrating into the subjects' private space leads to objectification, voyeurism, and exhibitionism, or whether it generates genuine concern for grassroots interests and thereby delivers a humanist (*renwen*) "thick description" of the subject's existential life experience. In other words, the issue of documentary

ethics is ultimately bound up with effective presentation and articulation of grassroots reality from a humanist, sympathetic perspective.[25]

Whether considered exploitative or not, Xue's violation of documentary ethics does all of what Wang proposes simultaneously – 'penetrating into the subjects' private space [that] leads to objectification, voyeurism, and exhibitionism' – but the violation also allows a 'concern for grassroots interests,' though not in a manner I, or most theorists, are comfortable with.[26] Instead, *Three Small Animals II* visualizes a rather brutish reality, and if we cut through the reckless approach, we find neglect and underdevelopment as *associative patterns* of documentary critique. These *associative patterns* locate neoliberalism's inability to penetrate regional cities such as Taiyuan, and are a visual testament to underdevelopment; moreover, *Three Small Animals II*'s unsympathetic presentation of further grassroots problem in China – particularly juvenile crime and violence – have evolved to such an extent that many of the aggressive and reckless stances taken by the filmmakers now can be seen as a backlash against the unsympathetic policies of neoliberal reform being implemented by the state. Right or wrong, these are problems that China must face and what we will continue to see produced from iGeneration filmmakers.

Conclusion

It is undeniable that regionally based DV practices such as Xue's have increased due to the affordability of digital cameras. Likewise, the most unskilled filmmakers can now chronicle and archive what the state calls the most negative of content, so that the once-alienated resident is replaced by growing groups of film practitioners, of not only the benign variety, but also young hooligan types, eager to document their violent deeds. A reckless approach that was incomprehensible to a Chinese public one decade ago is now on the rise. More than a latent problem for scholars of documentary practice in China, the reckless Chinese documentary represents a new category in the 'polyphonic'[27] multitude of styles, politics and preferences that embrace brutish figurations of petty crime on film (textual) that in the process disguise the territorial fixity of underdevelopment (contextual). I have tried to demonstrate that a Marxist-sociological approach is one way to not completely dismiss these reckless filmmakers and their rough-acting and rough-talking subjects. Such a reckless approach for making these films reflects the petty criminality as a consequence of accelerated marketization in Chinese society, and it is a culture that must not be ignored by scholars, especially in the context of China's 'pragmatic' experiment with neoliberalism.[28]

In terms of the film's level of objectivity (or lack thereof), *Three Small Animals II* supplies its audiences with a vernacular present, a present unconcerned with audience approval or with following the provisions set forth by the state. As such, this film offers a glimpse of a small segment of the Chinese population – youth offenders – and by doing so consciously violates ethical considerations to bring viewers a no-holds-barred approach to oppositional (and unlawful) lifestyles. Through a complete rejection of traditional modes of Chinese documentary filmmaking, Xue has shown the country's most Dickensian subjects through his reckless approach, while coming to grasp their spirit to get at the severity of underdevelopment in China's Northern Rust Belt. In the end what we get is a form of anomie, caught between shocking depravity and maverick class depictions, and in this episodic accomplishment, it is uncertain whether we may or may not see more of it from China.

Works cited

Bergson, Henri. *Le Rire. Essai sur la signification du comique*. Paris: Alcan, 1924.
Berry, Chris. 'Wu Wenguang: an introduction' in *Cinema Journal*, vol. 46, no. 1 (2006), 135.
Berry, Chris, Lu Xinyu and Lisa Rofel (eds). *The New Chinese Documentary Film Movement: For the Public Record*. Hong Kong: Hong Kong University Press, 2010.
Chen, Xiangming. 'Beyond the Reach of Globalization: China's Border Regions and Cities in Transition' in Fulong Wu (ed.), *Globalization and the Chinese City*. London: Routledge, 2006.
Chu, Yingchi. *Chinese Documentaries: From Dogma to Polyphony*. London: Routledge, 2007.
Curran, Daniel J. and Sandra Cook. Quoting data from Cao Manzhi's anthology, *Zhongguo qingshaonian fanzuixue/The Criminality of Chinese Juvenile Delinquency*. Beijing: Qunzhong chubanshe, 1988.
—'Growing Fears, Rising Crime: Juveniles and China's Justice System' in *Crime & Delinquency*, vol. 39:3 (1992).
Johnson, Matthew. 'Wu Wenguang and New Documentary Cinema's Politics of Independence' in Paul Pickowicz and Yingjin Zhang (eds), *From Underground to Independent: Alternative Film Culture in Contemporary China*. Lanham, MD: Rowman & Littlefield, 2006.
Liu, Fu-Kuo. 'A Critical Review of East and Northeast Asian Regionalism' in Christopher M. Dent and David W. F. Huang (eds), *Northeast Asian Regionalism: Learning from the European Experience*. London: Routledge, 2002.
Nichols, Bill. *Introduction to Documentary Film*. Indianapolis: Indiana University Press, 2001.
Pickowicz, Paul. 'Social and Political Dynamics of Underground Filmmaking in China' in Pickowicz and Zhang (eds), *From Underground to Independent: Alternative Film Culture in Contemporary China*. Lanham, MD: Rowman & Littlefield, 2006.
Qian, Ying. 'Just images: ethics and documentary film in China' in *China Heritage Quarterly*, no. 29 (March 2012).
Qiao D. P. and Y. C. Chan. 'Child abuse in China' in *Child and Family Social Work*, 10 (2005).
Wang, Hui. *The End of the Revolution: China and the Limits of Modernity*. London and New York: Verso, 2009.
Wang, Yiman. '"I am One of Them" and "They Are My Actors": Performing, Witnessing, and DV Image-Making in Plebeian China' in Chris Berry, Lu Xinyu and Lisa Rofel (eds), *The New Chinese Documentary Film Movement: For the Public Record*. Hong Kong: Hong Kong University Press, 2010, 219.

Xinyu, Lu. *Jilu Zhongguo: dangdai Zhongguo xin jilu yundong*. Beijing: Sanlian shudian, 2003.
—'Rethinking China's New Documentary Movement: Engagement with the Social' in Chris Berry, Lu Xinyu and Lisa Rofel (eds), *The New Chinese Documentary Film Movement: For the Public Record*. Hong Kong: Hong Kong University Press, 2010.
Zhang, Lening, Steven F. Messner, Zhou Lu and Xiaogang Deng. 'Gang crime and its punishment in China,' *Journal of Criminal Justice* 25, no. 4 (1997): 291–2.
Zhang, Yingjin. 'Of Institutional Supervision and Individual Subjectivity: The History and Current State of Chinese Documentary' in Ying Zhu and Stanley Rosen (eds), *Art, Politics, and Commerce in Chinese Cinema*. Hong Kong: Hong Kong University Press, 2010.
Zheng, Jianghuai, Lili Zhang and Yu Wang.'The underdevelopment of service industry in china: An empirical study of cities in Yangtze River Delta' in *Frontiers of Economics in China*, vol. 6, no. 3 (2011).

Notes

1 At the level of production, Xue's output is admirable. He has already directed several other documentaries in addition to *I Beat Tiger When I Was Young*, namely: *The Little Worker's Six Daughters/Lingqi quiyi* (2007), *Three Small Animals I/San zhi xiao dongwu I* (2007), *Three Small Animals II/San zhi xiao dongwu II* (2009), and *Martian Syndrome/Houxing zonghezheng* (2009) – with several others in post-production according to an interview at 'Get It Louder – Shanghai Independent Moving Screening' in 2010. These five films in a four-year period poise Xue as a workhorse compared to Wu's more paced release of documentary films, six in total since *Bumming in Beijing* in 1990. Moreover, given their age gap and Xue's focus on more destitute subjects in Chinese society – delinquent teenagers and the mentally ill from metropolitan areas of China – at the very least, I believe, Xue is one of China's more intriguing documentary figures to emerge in the last few years.
2 Matthew D. Johnson, 'Wu Wenguang and New Documentary Cinema's Politics of Independence' in Paul Pickowicz and Yingjin Zhang (eds), *From Underground to Independent: Alternative Film Culture in Contemporary China*. Lanham, MD: Rowman & Littlefield, 2006, 49–50.
3 Ibid., 53.
4 Paul Pickowicz, 'Social and Political Dynamics of Underground Filmmaking in China' in Pickowicz and Zhang (eds), *From Underground to Independent: Alternative Film Culture in Contemporary China*. Lanham, MD: Rowman & Littlefield, 2006, 17.
5 Yingjin Zhang, 'Of Institutional Supervision and Individual Subjectivity: The History and Current State of Chinese Documentary' in Ying Zhu and Stanley Rosen (eds), *Art, Politics, and Commerce in Chinese Cinema*. Hong Kong: Hong Kong University Press, 2010, 139.
6 See Bill Nichols, *Introduction to Documentary Film* and *Representing Reality*. These methodological hierarchies are disputed by many of China's documentary practitioners, with the 'Doc. Filmmakers vs. Doc. Critics' squabble at the CIFF in Nanjin in 2011 as a case in point.
7 See the most timeless work on Wu, for example Lu Xinyu's *Jilu Zhongguo: dangdai*

Zhongguo xin jilu yundong (Beijing: Sanlian shudian, 2003). Matthew D. Johnson, 'Wu Wenguang and New Documentary Cinema's Politics of Independence' in Paul Pickowicz and Yingjin Zhang (eds), *From Underground to Independent: Alternative Film Culture in Contemporary China*. Lanham, MD: Rowman & Littlefield, 2006. Or more recently, the anthology largely dedicated to Wu and his legacy on documentary film in China, Chris Berry, Lu Xinyu and Lisa Rofel (eds), titled *The New Chinese Documentary Film Movement: For the Public Record*. Hong Kong: Hong Kong University Press, 2010.

8   The film had such an effect on me at the time, that while I was preparing an essay on Wu Wenguang, I realized my conceptualization over what I saw as Wu's anti-neoliberal filmmaking was more representative in Xue's *Three Small Animals II*. This film, with its anarchic atmosphere and pauper-like subjects, also fits an anti-neoliberal theoretical framework, without me having to stretch it to fit the visual and ideological parameters found in *Bumming in Beijing*.
9   Ying Qian, 'Just images: ethics and documentary film in China' in *China Heritage Quarterly*, no. 29 (March 2012).
10 Yingjin Zhang, 140.
11 Xiangming Chen, 'Beyond the Reach of Globalization: China's Border Regions and Cities in Transition' in Fulong Wu (ed.), *Globalization and the Chinese City*. London: Routledge, 2006, 21–46.
12 See the following website: http://screenville.blogspot.kr/2011/12/doc-filmmakers-vs-doc-critics-ciff.html (accessed 6 March 2014).
13 Lu Xinyu, 'Rethinking China's New Documentary Movement: Engagement with the Social' in Chris Berry, Lu Xinyu and Lisa Rofel (eds), *The New Chinese Documentary Film Movement: For the Public Record*. Hong Kong: Hong Kong University Press, 2010, 18.
14 D. P. Qiao and Y. C. Chan, 'Child abuse in China,' *Child and Family Social Work*, 10 (2005), 25.
15 Wang Hui, *The End of the Revolution: China and the Limits of Modernity*. London: Verso, 2009, 41.
16 Chris Berry, 'Wu Wenguang: an introduction,' *Cinema Journal*, vol. 46, no. 1 (2006), 135.
17 Jianghuai Zheng, Lili Zhang and Yu Wang,'The underdevelopment of service industry in china: an empirical study of cities in Yangtze River Delta' in *Frontiers of Economics in China* vol. 6, no. 3 (2011), 413–46.
18 Leng Zheng, Steven Messner, Zhou Lu and Xiangang Deng 'Gang Crime and its punishment in China,' *Journal of Criminal Justice* 25, no. 4 (1997), 291–2.
19 Ibid., 292.
20 Daniel J. Curran and Sandra Cook, 'Growing Fears, Rising Crime: Juveniles and China's Justice System' in *Crime & Delinquency*, vol. 39:3 (1993), 307–8.
21 Daniel J. Curran and Sandra Cook quoting data from Cao Manzhi's important anthology, *Zhongguo qingshaonian fanzuixue/The Criminality of Chinese Juvenile Delinquency*. Beijing: Qunzhong chubanshe, 1988.
22 Wang Hui, 31–2.
23 Yiman Wang, '"I am One of Them" and "They Are My Actors": Performing, Witnessing, and DV Image-Making in Plebeian China' in Chris Berry, Lu Xinyu and Lisa Rofel (eds), *The New Chinese Documentary Film Movement: For the Public Record*. Hong Kong: Hong Kong University Press, 2010, 219.

24 Ying Qian, 'Just Images: Ethics and Documentary Film in China' in *China Heritage Quarterly*, no. 29 (March 2012).
25 Yiman Wang, 219.
26 Ibid., 219.
27 See Yingchi Chu, *Chinese Documentaries: From Dogma to Polyphony*. London: Routledge, 2007.
28 Fu-Kuo Liu, 'A Critical Review of East and Northeast Asian Regionalism' in Christopher M. Dent and David W. F. Huang (eds), *Northeast Asian Regionalism: Learning from the European Experience*. London: Routledge, 2002, 16–33.

Part Three

Social Engagement

9

Of Animals and Men: Towards a Theory of Docu-ani-mentary

Yiman Wang

This chapter explores the implications of animal presence and performativity as captured, enhanced and induced by the act of documentation in four contemporary Chinese documentaries that showcase variegated animal–human interactions. The animals that appear in these documentaries can be *preliminarily* described as (1) work animals, as depicted in *Sand and Sea* (*Sha yu hai*, dir. Kang Jianning 1990), (2) domestic/food animals, as depicted in *Three Sisters* (*San Zimei*, dir. Wang Bing 2012), (3) wild, endangered animals, as depicted in *My Himalayan Vulture* (*Wo de gaoshan tujiu*, dir. Tashi Sang'e, Zhou Jie 2009), and (4) show animals, as depicted in *Ying and Bai* (*Ying he Bai*, dir. Zhang Yiqing 1999). These categories, however, will be questioned in my analysis below. Challenging the understanding that animals play only fringe and auxiliary roles in relation to the human world, I argue that these animals permeate the very texture of the documentaries, forging a co-implicating relationship between the animal and the human that defies anthropocentrism and compels a 'humanimal' perspective. The imbrication of the animal and the human instigated through the act of ground-level documentation leads to what I theorize as 'docu-ani-mentary' – a new approach to studying contemporary Chinese documentary in relation to global environmentalism, especially as articulated in eco-criticism and ecocinema.

The notion of docu-ani-mentary highlights the continuous animal presence in contemporary Chinese documentary-making, despite the filmmakers' different training, affiliations, documentary poetics and socio-cultural-political concerns. As such, it allows us to renegotiate the 'generational' discourse (that has defined post-1980s Chinese film history) by underscoring sites of inter-generational dialogue across divergences.

Furthermore, this concept enables us to probe the ramifications of the (oftentimes contingent, inadvertent and marginal) animal presence mediated through film documentation by raising questions concerning sustainable economy, ethics and biodiverse ecocommunity in the face of China's developmentalism and neoliberal policies that contribute to various forms of environmental degradation. It contributes to nurturing what Masao Miyoshi terms as 'planetarianism' – i.e. the 'planet-based totality' that leads humanity to 'agree in humility to devise a way to share with all the rest our only true public space and resources.'[1] Such planetarianism based on humility and resource-sharing offers powerful theoretical support for recently spotlighted public campaigns against China's rampant animal exploitation networks that enable large-scale bear-farming, ivory trade, as well as a dog- and cat-meat industry. My concept of docu-ani-mentary, therefore, participates in campaigns of animal and eco-preservation in the face of anthropocentric capitalism both within and outside China.

Importantly, I use docu-ani-mentary in contradistinction to wildlife cinema or ecocinema. Wildlife film, according to Cynthia Chris, mobilizes 'the strategy of minimizing human presence,' and 'seems to invite viewers to forget that their view of nature is mediated.'[2] Implicit in this genre is the fundamental split between the human and the wildlife, hence the irresolvable tension between the attempt to conceal human mediation one the one hand, and the persistent anthropocentrism and anthropomorphism on the other.

If wildlife film ultimately signals human spectators' *consumption* (albeit distanced and obscured) of nature, Scott MacDonald's notion of 'ecocinema' offers a different perspective on the imbrication between human practices (including filmmaking) and the ecosystem. According to MacDonald, ecocinema has as its fundamental job 'a retraining of perception, … a way of offering an alternative to conventional media-spectatorship, or … a way of providing something like a *garden* – an "Edenic" respite from conventional consumerism – within the machine of modern life, as modern life is embodied by the apparatus of media.'[3] The task of retraining perception and countering commercial media can be accomplished through long-duration takes and other avant-garde techniques by artist-makers, who not only foreground ecological concerns, but also strive to minimize the footprint on the ecosystem by their own filmmaking.

Following the burgeoning field of Western language ecocinema, Sheldon Lu has introduced this concept into Chinese film studies in a timely fashion. In his *Chinese Ecocinema*, co-edited with Jiayan Mi, Lu defines 'Chinese ecocinema' as 'a critical grid, an interpretive strategy,' and 'a description of a conscious film practice.' He especially encompasses 'individual, independent film initiatives that often stand in opposition to the prevalent cultural climate at the time.'[4] Lu's affinity with MacDonald's emphasis on the anti-commercial, avant-garde filmmaking practice is obvious.

In my study, I shift gears and refocus on a set of films in which the oppositional stance and the consciousness of the animal-ness (or of the ecosystem in general) are not unanimously explicit or thematized. And yet, it is precisely through documenting animal presence (ranging from its un-thematized mere existence to its centrality in the entire project) that these films contribute to the new framework of docu-ani-mentary that de-metaphorizes animality, and debunks anthropocentrism and anthropomorphism.[5] Furthermore, docu-ani-mentary imagines a humanimal perspective by drawing on what Donna Haraway calls the 'becoming with' of the human and their companion species, and by attending to the sense of responsibility and ethics such worlding calls for.[6]

In my analysis below, I trace the ways in which animals exist and persist in the interstice of domestication and wildness. It is in this interstice that the anthropocentric hierarchies are disrupted, yielding to a humanimal and Haraway-ian 'natureculture' perspective premised on non-mimetic and non-anthropomorphic sensibilities.[7] By showing animals in the domestic setting, juxtaposed with humans out of or stripped of their conventional domesticity, these documentaries challenge us to fathom the extent to which human history has impacted and reshaped the non-human animal existence – and conversely, the ways in which the animal presence significantly constitutes, while also pushing beyond, the human history. In this sense, the animal-ness is never just a natural, history-less phenomenon, nor a metaphorical symbol reducible to human concerns. Rather, its deictic materiality and performativity, as captured, elicited and constructed by the documentary lens, constitute the very basis of the humanimal and natureculture nexus.[8]

The work animal

Sand and Sea (*Sha yu hai*, 1990), a TV documentary co-directed by Kang Jianning (director of the International Division at the Ningxia TV station) and Gao Guodong (senior journalist at the Liaoning TV Station), was one of the first documentaries from within the official media system to capture human and animal codependence as experienced by ordinary people living in remote, isolated Chinese regions. The documentary is symmetrically structured, interweaving the stories of a settler pastoralist family in the northwestern Tengger Desert and a fishing family on a small northeastern island in the Yellow Sea. Director Kang describes the feeling of helplessness in extremely secluded environments, as depicted in the documentary, and characteristic of the Chinese population in general. Specifically, his ruminations on the families' seclusion and desire to reach out accurately capture the pulse of China in the early 1990s – poised for full-scale economic reform that results in major population migration.

Examined from a humanimal perspective, however, this documentary yields an ecological narrative. The adversaries that the families face, especially the unpredictable desert and sea, are also the basis of their livelihood. Their heavy dependence on natural resources (seafood, camels, plants and water) stitches the human drama into the larger ecosystem. Thus, it is not surprising that animals are omnipresent as part of the landscape, and that their presence is taken for granted and treated as what Carol Adams calls the 'absent referents,' or metaphors of human persistence. Yet, more importantly, they also erupt into the foreground with little narrative justification, thus compelling an ecological reading.

To take the pastoralist family as an example, independent of shots depicting the camels under human care and camels reciprocating by offering wool, meat, and the means of transportation (and consequently, becoming tightly sutured into the human economic system), the film also shows that the camels seem to break free from the human-centred narrative, and that visual documentation and composition supersede voiceover description. By gesturing toward an ecological and humanimal perspective, this documentary not only demonstrates how human and animal work cooperatively, but also articulates the significance of understanding the humanimal cohabitation of the screen space.

Here is an example on this point. A sequence opens with a wide shot capturing the expanse of the desert, with a minute human figure in the distant background and a string of white objects in the medium ground. The camera then zooms onto the middle part of the white objects, revealing cleanly picked rib bones in close-up. The next close-up shot shows a hairy hoof sticking out of the sand, with a fly crawling around it. This is followed by two more close-up shots of the skull and ribs and another hoof. The film then cuts to a second set of close-up shots showing the pastoral father, the mother and their youngest child. The voiceover then narrates the family's efforts to retrieve the camels lost in the desert sandstorm before the animals die of weakness.

Before the voiceover kicks in, the concatenated close-up shots suggest the humanimal affinity through similar tight framing and a consistent, emphatic rhythm of editing. Presented as (mostly) still and stranded objects/subjects against the background of sand, the animal skeletal pieces and the human faces become eerily analogous, for they share the same perseverance and transience in the permanent desert. As death and life are equalized through the camerawork and editing, the human and the animal reach a new rapport, not based on the interdependent owner-property relationship, but rather on their comparable material existence that is both enabled and circumscribed by the larger ecosystem. Here the camel (in its solemnly silent, disassembled state) is no longer a work animal or a piece of property; or, perhaps it is never *just* a work animal in its relation to the human. And the humans, sitting face to face with their dead and living camels, are no longer just the owners. Rather, they share each other's fragility as well as tenacity in the wide landscape. This new humanimal communion echoes Haraway's 'non-mimetic shared suffering' and other experiences.

Importantly, the non-mimetic sharing takes place when the human and the animal both occupy the interstice of domesticity and wildness. The camel is domesticated in the sense that it is converted into a vehicle of economic gain for the pastoral family. Yet, its inextricable linkage with the desert (as poignantly signalled by the skeletal remains buried in the sand) ensures its wildness rooted in the larger ecosystem. On the human side, the pastoralist family adheres to domestic values to an extent. The father attempts to keep the children around by offering to buy a TV as well as an electric generator. Yet, his decision to give up farming 20 years before and switch to animal husbandry in the Tengger Desert signals a step away from conventional domesticity.

In the interstice and oscillation between domesticity and wildness, the human and the animal acquire a new relationality to each other and to the ecosystem. This relationality exceeds the owner–property dynamic to involve both the human and the animal as equal participants in the wider eco-landscape. In this sense, the non-narrativized close-up juxtaposition of the camel bones and human faces suggests a diverse eco-community with multiple temporalities (of life and death). From this perspective, the feeling of isolation and helplessness – from the human perspective – can be reinterpreted as a necessary humbling process that opens up a vista of much wider relationality and 'becoming with.'

The domestic animal

If Kang Jianning's *Sea and Sand* offers us a glimpse of the burgeoning humanimal and natureculture perspective, Wang Bing's recent documentary, *Three Sisters* (*San Zimei*, 2012) foregrounds the present-tense, material existence of animals, compelling us to rethink the meaning of the future for a sustainable eco-community. A leading figure in contemporary Chinese independent documentary, Wang Bing, contrary to Kang Jianning, avoids everything that aims to bring out human drama, including aesthetic landscape shots, heavy-handed editing, the use of interview, voiceover and extra-diegetic music track. Instead of aestheticization and dramatization, Wang's documentary poetics cast an unflinching and contemplative gaze at the most mundane everyday life and toil as experienced by ordinary Chinese people.

In *Three Sisters*, winner of the 2012 Venice Horizons Award, the ordinary Chinese people are represented by three young girls left behind in a Yunnan village, while their father goes to work in the city. In documenting the three sisters' everyday chores, play and caring for each other, the film unpretentiously and unsurprisingly fleshes out the experience of growing up in what is commonly perceived as extreme material deprivation. What intrigues me, however, is that the girls' apparently monotonous, even miserable, house chores are enlivened by the ever-present domestic animals – dogs, goats, ducks, pigs and a constantly meowing cat. Left in the care of family relatives, the girls, in their turn, care for the animals. Their daily schedule is significantly determined by the responsibility of feeding and herding the animals.

These animals, ordinary and domestic, can be easily dismissed as part of a common rural scene that hardly warrants special attention. And the film makes no explicit attempt to focalize or narrativize the animals' omnipresence, other than documenting their matter-of-fact, material existence in the three sisters' everyday life. Yet, a closer analysis reveals an interesting phenomenon. While the three sisters barely have the necessities of life, the animals are well provided for. Pigs and goats are herded in the open air. Ducks and pigs eat from the same fully stocked trough. Dogs follow the sisters around. Unlike their human owners, the animals live a seemingly sumptuous life with fresh air, healthy food and ample space for roaming.

This contrast also significantly recasts the meaning of domesticity. From the human perspective, the sisters' material deprivation is easily attributed to their lack of domestic protection, resulting from the larger social problem of the collapse of rural economy, the exploitation of cheap labour from the countryside, and the disintegration of the family structure. All of these are set into relief by the ironic existence of a TV set in the aunt's home, which barely attracts any attention and fails to make a home (contrary to what the pastoral father expects in *Sand and Sea*). While the children's decreased domesticity is treated as a disadvantage, the animals become less domestic with the happy result of thriving in the unconstrained rural landscape.

Yet, for both the sisters and the animals, living in the interstitial space between domesticity and autonomy entails the disruption of their preconceived futurity. The children's schooling is no longer emphasized as a means of self-fulfilment or improvement that might lead to a more enriched material or intellectual life. The domestic animals are also somewhat dislodged from their 'future' as assigned by the humans – namely, being converted into financial profit or consumed for meat (except in the one feast scene held by the extended family in a different village). In the absence of predetermined futurity, both the human and the non-human animals live in the thick materiality of the present and the now. Thus, the film ends up (inadvertently) qualifying its professed humanist concern with the sisters' future. It exposes our (well-intentioned) pity for the sisters as originating from the ideological assumption of the universal value of modern urban amenities and institutionalized education. Furthermore, it deploys fully fledged animal-ness (contrary to industrialized animal husbandry or animals as an auxiliary appendage of human life) to invite humanimal perspective.

As such, Wang's documentary becomes a docu-ani-mentary that presents the rooted metabolism between human labour and the ecosystem not as a sign of backwardness or deficiency, nor as a simple utopia of human–nature harmony, but rather as an ecocommunity premised upon localized everyday contact, care, labour and other non-mimetic shared experiences. Needless to say, this ecocommunity is under increasing threat from global capitalism and its Chinese manifestations (as illustrated in peasants' dislocation into the cities as cheap mobile labour). Yet, the layered materiality of the docu-ani-mentary shows that such an ecocommunity may turn out to be more vibrant than we think. In the interstitial space between staying in one's hometown and becoming homeless (for the three sisters), between domesticity and free-range autonomy (for the animals), the preconceived 'future' becomes suspended for both the younger generation and the domestic animals. From this suspension arise the questions of what kinds of 'future' matter, and how we may envision other futures that can best foster a humanimal ecocommunity.

The wild animal

These questions are explicitly tackled in *My Himalayan Vulture* (*Wo De Gaoshan Tujiu*, 2009), an eco-film that offers a glimpse into the possibility of non-human-centred ecocommunity. Made by two Tibetans, Tashi Sang'e, a 'bird-watching Lama' with a PhD in Buddhist Studies, and Zhou Jie, a Tibetan monk who helped found a local ecosystem protection society, the documentary is part of the Yunnan Qinghai Rural Moving Image Project (*Yunnan Qinghai xiangchun yingxiang jihua*), launched by the Baima Mountain Cultural Research Center of the Yunnan Academy of Social Sciences, in collaboration with Beijing's Shanshui Conservation Center and three environmental protection associations in Qinghai. Sponsored by the EU–China biodiversity programme, the Rural Moving Image Project yielded eight documentaries in 2009, all made by local villagers and monks with DV cameras in their respective dialects. They represent a range of ethnicities in southwest China; many of these groups were already participating in eco-protection programmes.

Unsurprisingly, their documentaries all promote the preservation of local natural resources and traditional sociocultural practices in face of the onslaught of profit-driven developmentalism. To convey this message, *My Himalayan Vulture* opens with Tashi Sang'e identifying himself and stating his commitment to vulture preservation. Toward the end, he again speaks to the audience in direct address about his project. The main body of the film follows him and Zhou Jie helping vultures survive the worsening food shortage. They present the problem as one of encroaching commercialization. More specifically, the local merchants sell dead livestock to city people for profit, instead of leaving the carcasses in the open air for vultures (as has traditionally been done). This disrupted food chain causes the vultures to starve. The documentary then shows Tashi and Zhou trekking into the mountains, visiting bird nests and delivering animal carcasses they have purchased from the herdsmen and merchants to the vultures. Toward the end, Tashi sums up his conservation endeavour, only to then raise a crucial doubt regarding its ultimate effectiveness. This prompts us to ask exactly which strategies should be developed to preserve not only a certain species, but more broadly, the sustainable ecocommunity.

To start understanding the filmmakers' scepticism, we may turn to the ambivalent effects of the DV technology. On the one hand, the DV camera's portability and easy operation makes it a most powerful tool of cutting into the concrete, located situations and issues. It contributes to what Ban Wang calls 'a zero degree' of constructedness, with the documentary being 'embedded in daily living and works at the grassroots level'.[9] Furthermore, it significantly connects the local villagers and monks with the outside world by bridging the local eco-preservation efforts with global environmentalism, and thus contributes to fostering local–global coalitions.

On the other hand, however, DV also potentially threatens the very integrity of the ecosystem the film seeks to preserve, as demonstrated in the film's DV aesthetics. During the filmmakers' harsh trekking trips into the vultures' habitat, DV's close miking foregrounds the howling wind and the heavy breathing, enabling us to vicariously experience the filmmakers' physical exertion. Furthermore, the DV camera's fast zooming in and out alternately makes us privy to extreme close-up shots of the eggs and the chicks in the hidden nests, *and* repositions us far away to survey the adult vultures gliding across the vast sky in various directions. At one moment, the filmmakers' closely miked breathing is matched with a close-up framing of the chick's wide-open eyes. The audio-visual syncing creates a haptic effect as if *our* heavy breathing really touched the vulnerable chick. Such DV-mediated intimacy crystallizes both the conservationist desire to approach and care for the endangered species *and* the dilemma that such proximity inevitably impinges on the space of the wild animal.

Indeed, in the tug-of-war between conservationists–filmmakers and merchants, the vultures become the 'subaltern' animal whose wild scavenging ability is no longer sufficient for survival, and who is rendered dependent on human providers. Whereas humans and non-human animals have always coexisted and cohabited in a mutually adaptive and constitutive manner, the drastic shift in the food chain takes place within such a short time span that the wildness and autonomy of the animal species are compromised with little chance of re-adaptation. Thus, despite the good intention of preservation, the ecological project may turn out to be a double-edged sword that potentially compromises the species' capacity for self-sufficiency.

Given DV's significance in facilitating human control over (as well as interaction with) the wild species, the documentary risks making the wild species 'our own "technological creations," rather than "real" animals.'[10] Here, 'technologization' of the vultures goes hand in hand with their domestication through the filmmakers' care, which results in what Jennifer Ladino terms as the 'species-ed' perspective that 'privileges an anthropocentric, often androcentric, way of seeing whereby nonhuman animals are depicted as humans see and understand them and often, perhaps more problematically, simply *as humans*.'[11]

This 'species-ed' perspective comes under scrutiny when the filmmakers reflect on the efficacy of their conservationist endeavour toward the end. It is here we may discern a subtle hint of humanimal 'becoming with.' After Tashi finishes his didactic message with a question, the film fades out, then fades back into an ostensibly disconnected coda. In this sequence, a wide long-shot covers two red-robed Tibetan monks (presumably the two filmmakers) treading on snow-covered hills toward the horizon. Another long-shot shows one monk approaching a group of vultures on top of the hill in the background. Then, all of a sudden, he unfolds his head cover, running with the fluttering cover over his head, causing the vultures to take off. For a moment, his head cover flutters like the birds' wings. The film ends with various angle shots of the birds flying in the sky, skimming over the tiny tents on the grassland.

The human–bird co-fluttering suggests a sensation of aviation, which the human can feel only vicariously through the collective feathery body of the bird flock. The moment the human flutters into the flock evokes what Gilles Deleuze and Félix Guattari term as 'becoming-animal,' when the self becomes 'a threshold, a door, a becoming between two multiplicities.... A fibre stretches from a human to an animal, from a human or an animal to molecules, from molecules to particles and so on to the imperceptible.'[12] Cryptic and ahistorical as the language may sound, becoming-animal dissolves the anthropocentric notion of human subjectivity, rejects the fixation on individuated animal characteristics, and opens the individual up to the *contagion* of a pack or multiplicity of animals. The result of becoming-animal is to become uprooted from humanity, and to metaphorically 'scrape at one's bread like a rodent' or to see with 'the yellow eyes of a feline.'[13] The stress on the pack and multiplicity, the contagion and affect, makes becoming-animal a 'fearsome involution' that undermines the anthropocentric perspective and blurs the human–animal boundaries.

Instead of seeing the human as the reference point – being either the enemy or the saviour of the vultures depending on how the human economic system impacts on the vultures' food source – becoming-animal enables us to reconsider biodiversity from the other side of the lens so that we may recognize the vultures' infectious wild animal-ness itself as an active agent in instigating an affective economy. This affective economy is undoubtedly connected to the human economy of production, distribution, consumption and redistribution. Yet, it also resists the logic of quantitative calculation and the associated human power of control. Instead, it compels the human to yield and to become, rather than just to share, so as to forge a mutually infective and inter-subjective humanimal ecocommunity.

With this, the on-the-spot, grassroots DV aesthetics can also hope to take on new features such as aerial mobility, wild animality and a non-anthropocentric perspective. In the next section, I turn to a TV documentary, *Ying and Bai* (*Ying he bai*, 1999), to study how we may simulate and visualize a non-anthropocentric perspective, and in what ways this may reshape human society in relation to deep ecology.

The show animal

Directed by Zhang Yiqing for Hubei TV Station, *Ying and Bai: A Chronicle of 1999* took three years to complete. It was an award-winning documentary praised for its humanist spirit conveyed through incisive depiction of profound loneliness shared between Ying, the world's only show panda, and Bai, his half-Italian, half-Chinese caregiver. The sentiment of loneliness is in turn seen as a pathological symptom of modern human civilization as a whole. To foreground the existential situation of non-communication and solitude, director Zhang deploys a TV set as a structural device. As the TV blasts apparently momentous domestic and international news (echoing the film's subtitle: 'A Chronicle of 1999'), Ying and Bai watch nonchalantly as if from another world where the news is nothing more than a jumble of sound bites and colour blotches.[14] Remarking on their asociality, mutual dependence and ultimate existential dis-communication, Bai observes (in a third-person title): 'Nobody could understand Ying just as nobody understands herself.'

Yet, what does it mean to say that a panda is not understood just as a human is not? If the film conceptualizes a panda's emotional and psychic world in human terms, does it not simply reproduce what Ladino describes as the 'species-ed' perspective? Can we understand the panda's perspective in the documentary as an invitation for humanimal co-worlding? To address these questions, I focus on the motif of TV watching and its uncanny relationship with domesticity. I suggest that the film not only offers a melancholic study of the alienation effects of excessive domestication, but more importantly, gestures beyond the domestic confines through the panda's nonchalant, even vacuous outward gaze. Instead of mapping the panda's sentiments onto his lonely human caregiver, I see the panda's bodily experience in the domestic and institutional environs as a catalyst *and* a puzzle that demand different practices of living and sharing with non-human animals. Rather different from Derek Bouse's critique that facial close-ups in wildlife films only serve 'to ascribe to animals almost whatever feelings and emotions the filmmaker wishes to assign them according to the requirements of the storyline at that moment,'[15] I argue that the panda's facial close-ups in this film point our attention to the animal's gaze that challenges human systems of signification. The meeting of the panda's gaze with our gaze makes us wonder about the animal subjectivity, which simultaneously invites communication and mutual embodiment, *and* frustrates them. This renders becoming-animal and humanimal co-worlding an open-ended experimental practice.[16]

In this documentary, Ying is the world's last show panda, prematurely retired in compliance with regulations in International Trade in Endangered Species of Wild

Fauna and Flora. Incapable of living in the wild due to his long-term training in the human environment, he comes to live in Bai's home as a domesticated animal. The film shows Ying with various identities *vis-à-vis* human institutions (including the home and the circus). As Bai's foster child, he is fed, bathed, instructed to wash his 'hands,' to ride a rocking horse and is perched at a window to look out now and then. As a companion and a family member, he demands and receives caress from Bai that satisfies his physiological and emotional needs. As an ex-show animal employed in Wuhan City Circus in Hubei Province, he has the circus staff to take charge of his health and hygiene.

Most astoundingly, the documentary dispels the audience's oozy sentiment by showing the panda masturbating in the cage. For this voyeuristic gaze, the director offers an apology to the panda for violating his privacy. This, combined with the panda's clinging hugging of Bai, not only undermines the stereotype of infant-like animals, but also foregrounds an unconventional humanimal physiological meshing similar to the Deleuzian notion of contamination.

This multi-layered depiction of the panda as a child, a worker (or show animal), a family member, *and* a male adult/companion underscores the complexity of the panda's experience with the variegated human institutions. This filmmaker's apology to the panda, in particular, is symptomatic of the paradox of making fun of and disavowing the panda's subjectivity *as* a means of affirming it, or conversely, positing the animal subjectivity only to render it metaphorical. This lends significance to his uncanny gaze from behind the bars of the cage and the window. In the exceptional setting of domestication-*cum*-confinement, Ying, Bai and the TV form an impossible trio. By constructing frequent eyeline match shots between the TV and Bai, the TV and Ying, or Ying watching Bai watching TV, the filmmaker seems to indicate a bonding between Ying and Bai around the TV, which would suggest a conventional home environment, with the TV as the new-age hearth. Yet, the fact that Ying's gaze is invariably from behind the cage bars literalizes the confinement inherent in the family and other institutional structures. Furthermore, many shots show the TV image upside down and split by vertical lines, simulating Ying's point of view while lying on his back, glancing through the cage bars. His playful non-engagement, combined with Bai's melancholic disinterest in the TV news, detours the eyeline match shots, converting TV culture into a helpless existential situation in modern society rather than a meaningful experience.

By visualizing the (dis-)interactions between a domesticated wild animal and an icon of modern human civilization, the film poses a conundrum regarding the animal's subjectivity. Even as we strive to understand the panda in human terms (imagining his ability to 'watch' TV), we immediately confront the fact that we do not have access to what the panda sees, and how he processes what he sees, and that the panda's subjectivity inevitably departs from and exceeds our anthropocentric thinking.[17] The impenetrability of the panda's gaze is further played up as he is perched on a stool and looks out of the window. In the long exterior shots capturing the window, we are bemused to see a panda's head sticking out (where we normally expect to see a human, especially a child). The panda's unfathomable gaze makes him a literal anomaly in the human-made environment. His silent, playful and distant gaze introduces an uncanny dimension to this environment and defamiliarizes it, as emblematized in the upside-down TV image.

In failing to accommodate the panda's full lived experience, the domestic setting (as an important human institution) is exposed as a fragment of the ecosystem. Meanwhile, the panda's gaze leads us toward a fuller ecological realm beyond the film's representational domain. This realm out there is deliberately left unspecified and virtual due to the predominantly interior shots.[18] Its power hinges upon our (imaginary) experience of ecstasy (or being out of the current space) and the ex-body existence. Seeing a panda watching TV or looking out of an apartment window, therefore, should not convince us of our hospitality to non-human life forms, nor allegorize the human feeling of loneliness. Rather, it stimulates the sensation of breaking out of one's conventionalized, domesticated body in order to access that extra dimension of humanimal co-worlding or contamination.

Conclusion

I have traced both the quotidian and the remarkable materiality of non-human animal existence in four Chinese-language documentaries made since 1990. In a span of just over two decades, Sinophone documentary has come a long way in institutional setup, funding sources, distribution platforms, technological transformation, aesthetic exploration, thematic concerns and sociocultural interventions. Despite these shifts, the documentaries I study showcase an abiding engagement with non-human animals in various relationships with the human world. Whether explicitly thematized or not, the animal presence undergirds and animates the documentaries, making them docu-ani-mentaries.

Through the lens of docu-ani-mentary, my study participates in the local as well as global eco-criticism, sharing the agenda of deconstructing anthropocentrism and anthropomorphism. In attempting to combat the rampant and destructive poaching and trading in bear bile, elephant tusks, animal fur in China, as well as its networks of cat- and dog-meat production and consumption, I share Ladino's endeavour to 'articulate new kinds of socially just environment practices as we enter into an era where conceiving of a human–nature – or a human–animal – binary is increasingly impossible.'[19] In other words, my study explores more productive modes of humanimal worlding, which, for Donna Haraway, means to 'speculate, imagine, feel, build something better' ethically and politically.[20] Docu-ani-mentary offers a unique contribution to this agenda due to its mediation of and insistence on the ground-level material locations and conditions of the human and non-human animals alike. As 'a form of negotiation' in the 'ecology of connections', it 'is itself ecologically placed as it consumes the entangled world around it, and in turn, is itself consumed.'[21]

More specifically, docu-ani-mentary strives toward a form that can effectively negotiate and mediate the material existence of the animal-ness that permeates the human domain, serves human interests to a great extent, and yet ultimately remains independent of the human perspective. The creation of the form is closely related to film technologies, including the DV camera that facilitates location shooting, improvisational capturing, experimental camera angles and framing, and ultimately, ground-level interventions. Through experimental usage of the technologies, the form of the docu-ani-mentary purposefully or potentially pushes beyond the exclusive human perspective. Thus, it fulfils the ecological function of disclosing a new world.[22] In so doing, it urges China's globalization to take on a new task, namely, to engage with and participate in the project of environmentalism and ecocommunal worlding in the age of global neighbourliness.

Works cited

Adams, Carol. *The Sexual Politics of Meat: A Feminist Vegetarian Critical Theory*. London: Continuum, 1999.
Bousé, Derek. 'False intimacy: close-ups and viewer involvement in wildlife films,' *Visual Studies* 18.2 (2003): 123–32.
Chris, Cynthia. *Watching Wildlife*. Minneapolis, MN: University of Minnesota Press, 2006.
Cubitt, Sean. *EcoMedia*. Amsterdam and New York: Rodopi, 2005.
Deleuze, Gilles and Félix Guattari. *A Thousand Plateaus: Capitalism and Schizophrenia*, trans. Brian Massumi. Minneapolis, MN: University of Minnesota Press, 1987.
Haraway, Donna. *When Species Meet*. Minneapolis, MN: University of Minnesota Press, 2007.
Heise, Ursula. 'From Extinction to Electronics: Dead Frogs, Live Dinosaurs, and Electric Sheep' in Cary Wolfe (ed.), *Zootologies: The Question of the Animal*. Minneapolis, MN: University of Minnesota Press, 2003, 59–81.
Ivakhiv, Adrian. 'An Ecophilosophy of the Moving Image: Cinema as an Anthrobiogeomorphic Machine' in Stephen Rust, Salma Monani and Sean Cubitt (eds), *The Ecocinema Reader: Theory and Practice*. London: Routledge, 2012, 87–105.
Ladino, Jennifer. 'For the Love of Nature: documenting life, death, and animality in *Grizzly Man* and *March of the Penguins*,' *Interdisciplinary Studies in Literature and Environment* 16.1 (Winter 2009): 53–90.
Lippit, Akira. *Electric Animal: Toward a Rhetoric of Wildlife*. Minneapolis, MN: University of Minnesota Press, 2000.
Liu, Jie. 'You'er yuan, yizhong shengshi de fangshi: jilupian biandao Zhang Yiqing fangtan' (*The Kindergarden*, One Kind of Regard: Interview with Documentary Maker Zhang Yiqing,' *Nanfang dianshi xuekan* (Journal of Southern TV) 3 (2004): 81–6.
Lu, Sheldon and Jiayan Mi (eds). *Chinese Ecocinema in the Age of Environmental Challenge*. Hong Kong: Hong Kong University Press, 2009.
MacDonald, Scott. 'Toward an eco-cinema,' *Interdisciplinary Studies in Literature and Environment* 11.2 (Summer 2004): 107–32.
Miyoshi, Masao. 'Turn to the Planet: Literature, Diversity, and Totality' in David Leilei Li (ed.) *Globalization and the Humanities*. Hong Kong: Hong Kong University Press, 2004, 19–36.

Næss, Arne. 'The Shallow and the Deep, Long-Range Ecology Movement. A Summary,' *Inquiry* 16 (1973): 95–100.
Rust, Stephen, Salma Monani and Sean Cubitt (eds). *Ecocinema Theory and Practice*. New York: Routledge, 2012.
Wang, Ban. 'Of Humans and Nature in Documentary: The Logic of Capital in *West of the Tracks* and *Blind Shaft*' in Sheldon Lu and Jiayan Mi (eds), *Chinese Ecocinema*, 157–69.
Zhang, Yiqing. 'Jilu yu xianshi: jiantan jilupian *Ying he Bai*' (Documentation and Reality: on Documentary *Ying and Bai*), *Dianshi yanjiu* (TV Studies) 8 (2001): 54–5.

Notes

I would like to thank the editors for their incisive comments that encouraged me to strength my argument. All errors that may still remain are my sole responsibility.

1 Masao Miyoshi, 'Turn to the Planet: Literature, Diversity, and Totality' in David Leilei Li (ed.), *Globalization and the Humanities*, 35.
2 Cynthia Chris, *Watching Wildlife*, 71.
3 Scott MacDonald, 'Toward an Eco-Cinema,' 109 [emphases original].
4 Sheldon Lu and Jiayan Mi (eds), *Chinese Ecocinema*, 2.
5 Ecofeminist critics such as Carol Adams offer a significant critique of anthropocentrism that reduces animals to 'absent referents' and 'metaphors for describing people's experiences' in cultural representations. See Carol Adams, *The Sexual Politics of Meat*, 53. See also Akira Lippit's deconstructive reiteration of animal as metaphor, 'Animal and metaphor, a metaphor made flesh, a living metaphor that is by definition not a metaphor, antimetaphor – 'animetaphor.' Lippit, *Electric Animal*, 165.
6 Donna Haraway, *When Species Meet*, 301.
7 Haraway, ibid., Chapter 3.
8 Here my agenda both intersects and diverges from 'deep ecology' formulated by the Norwegian philosopher Arne Næss in 1973. See Arne Næss, 'The Shallow and the Deep, Long-Range Ecology Movement.' Næss characterizes deep ecology in terms of principles of diversity, complexity, autonomy, decentralization, symbiosis, egalitarianism and classlessness (95). These principles reject anthropocentrism that evaluates other life forms only in reference to human needs, and instead promotes 'biospherical egalitarianism' (95). My exploration of the docu-ani-mentary shares this commitment, but takes issue with deep ecology's tendency to downplay tension in its emphasis on diversity and co-existence of various life forms. My analysis accentuates the human–animal imbrication that unfolds through tension, conflicts, as well as mutual dependence.
9 Ban Wang, 'Of Humans and Nature in Documentary,' in Lu and Mi (eds), 2009, op. cit., 164 [emphases mine].
10 Ursula Heise, 'From Extinction to Electronics,' 77. In agreeing with Heise on this point, I do not dismiss technology as categorically oppositional to eco-consciousness. In fact, *My Himalayan Vulture* and the whole Yunnna Qinghai Rural Moving Image Project would not have been possible without the DV technology; nor would we have

been able to learn about these local campaigns in the current form. As Sean Cubitt argues, *techne* (the technological) plays a key role in mediating *polis* (the human world) and *physis* (the green world), and I should add, between different zones of *polis*. See Cubitt, *EcoMedia*. Nevertheless, just as we attend to the importance of *techne* in ecocinema, we must simultaneously examine exactly how technology not only enables, but also conditions filmic rendition of non-human animals. Such critical reflection leads us to develop a non-anthropocentric perspective that contributes to deep ecology (*à la* Arne Næss). I am indebted to the editors for encouraging me to engage with Cubitt's work.
11 Jennifer Ladino, 'For the Love of Nature,' 60 [italics original].
12 Gilles Deleuze and Félix Guattari, *A Thousand Plateaus*, 249.
13 Deleuze and Guattari, ibid., 240.
14 Responding to the critique of his subjective framing of the material for the purpose of thematizing loneliness and alienation, Zhang states that he deliberately deployed allusion, symbolism and contrast to create a form that suits the content. This form allows the audience to access a 'downloaded' or processed life, not life *per se*. See Zhang Yiqing, 'Jilu yu xianshi: jiantan jilupian *Ying he Bai*,' 55.
15 Derek Bousé, 'False Intimacy,' 128.
16 Reflecting on his approach in another documentary *The Kindergarten* (*You'er yuan*, 2004), director Zhang emphasizes the importance of 'capturing the unexpected, vivid moments in the flux of apparently mundane life, the moments that are unusual and transitory.' Qt. in Liu Jie, '*You'er yuan*, yizhong shengshi de fangshi,' 83. Zhang's emphasis on the unexpected and unruly moments emerging from the life flow (as opposed to the conventionalized images and the well-rehearsed occasion-specific events) justifies my inquiry into the panda's gaze.
17 Director Zhang affirms that the humans can never know what the panda sees, and that the simulated panda's point-of-view shots from behind the bars are 'anthropomorphic,' as if it were humans looking from an analogous position. This makes the bars a cultural signifier that says more about the human condition than the panda's. See Zhang (2001), op. cit., 28. My analysis emphasizes the unknowability of the panda's gaze as precisely the departure point to go beyond the anthropocentric signifying system.
18 Zhang's comments on his treatment of exterior shots in his documentary *The Kindergarten* is instructive here. He observes that exterior shots tend to be conventionalized, resembling cliché news report that sits poorly with the vivid, concrete shots of children in an interior space. To settle this interior–exterior mismatch, he uses soft focus for the exterior shots to underscore the children's vision of their uncertain future. See Liu (2004), op. cit., 83. The children's blurry view of the outside and future is analogous with the panda's gaze that yields no object of interest, but rather the desire to look.
19 Ladino (2009), op. cit., 58.
20 Haraway (2007), op. cit., 92.
21 Stephen Rust, Salma Monani and Sean Cubitt (eds), *Ecocinema Theory and Practice*, 1.
22 Adrian Ivakhiv develops Heidegger's definition of the human as a world-bearing being and that art works 'open' and 'unconceal' a world from out of a larger self-subsistent milieu. Thus, '[t]o be a work means to set up a world.' See Ivakhiv, 'An Ecophilosophy of the Moving Image,' 92.

10

Working with Rubble: Montage, Tweets and the Reconstruction of an Activist Documentary

Ying Qian

I have taken the title of this essay from the last sequence in Ai Xiaoming and Hu Jie's documentary film *Our Children* (*Women de wawa*, 2009). Completed in April 2009, *Our Children* follows the investigations carried out by grieving parents into poor qualities of public school buildings that may have led to high death rates among school children in the Wenchuan earthquake of 2008. The film ends with a sequence shot in low light by a cheap digital camera. The trembling viewfinder captures blurry images of a group of parents sneaking into collapsed schools at night to retrieve bits and pieces of the debris. During the day, most 'ground-zero' sites such as this one were closely watched by local police with public access restricted. Fearing that soon the site would be cleared and no evidence would remain to hold the government and the construction companies responsible, these parents rolled out concrete columns, sawed off steel frames, and brought bits and pieces of the ruins back home.

Ruins are by now a familiar motif in Chinese documentary cinema. Lu Xinyu began her book-length survey of the 'New Documentary Movement' in 2003 with an introduction chapter entitled 'On the Ruins of Utopia,' tracing the birth of new documentary in early 1990s to a double disillusionment from the socialist ideals in the Mao era, and from the ideals of modernization and democratization in the 1980s.[1] Abé Mark Nornes, writing about contemporary Chinese documentary cinema in 2009, observed that demolition and architectural ruins had become a visual staple for the documentarians.[2] Wang Bing's nine-hour documentary epic *West of the Tracks* (*Tie xi qu*, 2003) portrayed the gradual dissolution and abandonment of a sprawling industrial complex in the Tiexi District of Shenyang in northeastern China, the workplace for about a million workers. Jia Zhangke's feature film *Still Life* (*San Xia Hao Ren*, 2006) and documentary film *Dong* (*Dong*, 2006) were both set in the Three Gorges area, where the building of the Three Gorges Dam led to entire cities and towns being razed before their complete submersion in water. In these films, the filmmakers' auteurial cameras cast long and pensive gazes over ruins and rubble that symbolized the destruction of ideals, certainties and homes. Ruins represented absolute loss, too broken to be incorporated into a new structure of meaning, and the people surviving on them were more or less powerless, unable to change what was happening before their eyes. In *Our Children*, however, one encounters an entirely new engagement with a landscape laid to waste. Ruins became sites of investigation, rubble became evidence, and the melancholic, auteurial long-takes in previous documentaries gave way to vibrant montages of investigative footage made by the involved people themselves. The sequence that concluded *Our Children*, for example, was shot not by a filmmaker but by a participant in the nightly mission of stealing debris out of the school site.

Since around 2004, a new activist documentary cinema has been quietly on the rise in China, and *Our Children* is one of its finest examples. In this essay, I examine a number of films made by this new cinema's most important practitioners, Ai Xiaoming, Hu Jie and Ai Weiwei, in order to understand this cinema's distinct aesthetics, epistemology, and its embedding and intervention in politics. This activist cinema, I further argue, constitutes a new response to China's postsocialist condition. The explorations of cinema into China's postsocialist condition have been observed by a number of scholars. Writing on both feature and documentary cinemas from China, Chris Berry and Mary Ann Farquhar have observed in many films a postsocialist cultural logic of pastiche, ambiguity and play, an 'aesthetic parallel to postmodernism'.[3] In a recently published monograph, Luke Robinson analyses Chinese independent documentary's engagement with the fleeting, the contingent, and the ambiguous, as a response to an uncertain postsocialist environment 'in which all sociocultural forms are semiotically unstable, and where the power to determine their significance is open to outright contestation.'[4]

These observations are insightful and accurate with regard to a large number of independent cinematic productions in China today, yet they do not characterize the strategies and aspirations of the emergent activist documentary. While it is true that the majority of independent documentaries, as Yiman Wang observes, do not seek to alter the social conditions in front of the camera, but only to provide a 'densely textured,' 'historical' experience to alter the way people remember things,[5] activist documentaries do strive for actual social change. Therefore, rather than reflecting and articulating postsocialist experiences such as moral ambiguity, epistemological uncertainty, and loss of security and ideals to the banality of neoliberal-inspired consumerism and state capitalism, activist documentaries respond to them by resurrecting ideals based on moral reasoning at the grassroots and reasserting an epistemology based on evidence and testimony. Aiming for lucidity not ambiguity, activist documentaries deal with contingency not by denial but by understanding what one has reasons to believe.

In this chapter, I begin by discussing Hu Jie's *Searching for Lin Zhao's Soul* (*Xunzhao Lin Zhao de Linghun*, 2004) and Ai Xiaoming and Hu Jie's first collaborative work, *The Vagina Monologue: Backstage Stories* (*Yindao dubai*, 2004). Resurrecting the heroic figure of the political activist calling for social change, and portraying exhilarating experiences of empowerment enabled by activism, these two films, I argue, laid the foundation for the emergent activist documentary. I then proceed to close-read Ai Xiaoming and Hu Jie's film *Our Children*, in which the filmmakers reinvigorated the use of cinematic montage to bring together fragmentary evidence and found footage, and reach for a deeper social reality made visible by the ruins after the earthquake. Finally, as Ai Xiaoming regards her earthquake documentaries as forming a series of tweets and re-tweets with Ai Weiwei's documentaries, I discuss Ai Xiaoming's *Why are Flowers so Red* (*Hua'er weishenme zheyang hong*, 2010) and Ai Weiwei's *Disturbing Peace* (*Lao ma ti hua*, 2009) together as serialized and corroborated cinematic actions, and contemplate the conceptual affinities between montage, serialization and tweeting as means to bring together activist communities, and reconstruct a bottom-up activism that returns epistemological cogency and political salience to cinema.

In search for the political activist: Hu Jie's *Searching for Lin Zhao's Soul* and Ai Xiaoming's *The Vagina Monologue*

Like all new beginnings, China's new activist cinema began with retrospection. In 2004, Hu Jie finished *Searching for Lin Zhao's Soul*, a three-hour documentary film on Lin Zhao, a former Beijing University student condemned as a 'rightist' in the Anti-Rightist Campaign of 1957. A gifted writer and courageous thinker, Lin Zhao never rescinded her right to think independently and critically. Writing in her own blood on scraps of paper and bed sheets in prison, Lin Zhao produced voluminous writings amounting to hundreds of thousands of words, protesting against the ruthless political oppressions during the Anti-Rightist Campaign as well as during the first years of the Cultural Revolution. She was executed in April 1968.

In the 2004 documentary, Hu Jie searched for Lin Zhao's soul by contacting and then interviewing people who knew her and who experienced the same turbulent historical period. By finding everyone who knew Lin Zhao and contacting them for interviews, this former soldier and painter tapped into a close-knit network of memory. For years, Hu travelled all over the country to conduct interviews, which make up most of the film's running time. The film not only resurrected the heroic figure of Lin Zhao from oblivion, but also created a collective portrait for a whole generation of people living through the darkest period of the PRC's history, some of whom had come forward to recount their experiences and offer testimony after forty years had passed.

Hu started to show rough drafts of the film in 2003, four years after the production began. Cui Weiping, a professor at the Beijing Film Academy, wrote in 2004 about the shockwaves generated by the rough cuts of Hu's film: 'The news of the film was passed from mouth to mouth; copies travelled from hands to hands among friends... Many shed tears, even more lost sleep over it.'[6] While the film moved many, it also generated a fair amount of controversy. Cui reported that some criticized the film for its enthusiastic portrayal of Lin Zhao's heroism. Lin Zhao, the suffering heroine, and her eventual martyrdom were considered to bear too much similarity to the heroic figures in China's socialist era. As the documentary discourse in the 1990s had moved away from heroism and favoured narratives about ambivalent characters living with everyday compromises, some felt that Hu Jie's film was nothing other than nostalgia for a lost era.[7]

Cui Weiping defended Hu's film against these critiques. The abandonment of heroism in the 1990s was an 'overcorrection,' Cui argued, and behind the new motto that 'heroes are just human beings' lurked an overly narrow understanding of human experiences and achievements. Furthermore, Cui argued that the heroic picture Hu Jie painted of Lin Zhao was epistemologically different from the reified, abstract and obedient heroic figures featured in the Socialist Realist cinemas of the past. 'Hu Jie spent four years on a journey of tens of thousands kilometres, visited all of those who knew Lin Zhao first-hand,' Cui wrote. 'The film was not created by one individual nor by Hu Jie's own mind. It was a collective creation including the contribution from the heroine Lin Zhao herself.' Likening Hu's film to orally transmitted epic poetry, Cui argued that Hu's film was a true 'people's cinema,' composed of collective testimonies from a large number of people, and expressive of a widespread desire to resurrect heroism in today's Chinese society.

Searching for Lin Zhao's Soul circulated on the internet and university campuses,[8] and soon became a centre of attention thanks to an open letter penned by Lu Xuesong, a lecturer at the Jilin Institute of Art in northeastern China, in the summer of 2005. Lu had learned about Lin Zhao from Hu Jie's film. Deeply moved, she showed the film to her class at the art institute. After a student from her class reported the film screening to the school officials, the school made a decision to transfer Lu from her teaching post to an administrative position. Inspired by Lin Zhao's example, Lu penned an 'open letter' to the president of her school. This letter became a hit on the internet and was reposted in countless discussion forums, arousing discussions on education, freedom of expression and the possibility of living 'authentically' in today's China.

In the letter, Lu argued for a teacher's responsibility to help students become authentic people (*zhenshi de ren*), and questioned whether young people could ever grow to live an authentic life if their social environment 'fetishizes order and unity, while fearing life in its full vitality and freedom.'[9] Lu called on the society to fight against the hypocrisy and indifference that made people willing slaves to arbitrary 'hidden rules' (*qian guize*), and prevented them from living an honest life. Her protests won immediate support from the intellectual community. Both Ai Xiaoming and Cui Weiping were among the many who wrote in support of her, lauding her actions as an example of the everyday heroism needed in today's China.[10] If the making of *Searching for Lin Zhao's Soul* enabled collective testimony in a network of memory about Lin Zhao, then the circulation of the film brought together outspoken intellectuals such as Ai Xiaoming, Cui Weiping and Lu Xuesong as well as millions of netizens in a collective articulation of what it would mean to live an authentic life, and whether heroism remained relevant in today's society.

Encountering Hu Jie and his film *Searching for Lin Zhao's Soul* prompted Ai Xiaoming to go into filmmaking. A professor of comparative literature at Sun Yat-Sen University in Guangzhou, Ai ventured into filmmaking in 2003 when she translated and staged Eve Ensler's *The Vagina Monologues* at her university. Having watched a rough-cut of Hu Jie's *Searching for Lin Zhao's Soul*, and become acquainted with the filmmaker, Ai invited Hu to come and help her record the play. Soon their project expanded from a simple performance recording into a documentary film entitled *The Vagina Monologue: Backstage Stories*. Intercutting the performance together with interviews with actresses, their families and audiences, the film broke the spatial and temporal boundaries of theatre performance, and documented the discussions enabled by the play. In the prologue to *The Vagina Monologue*, Ai added the following lines: 'Things that we don't talk about are not seen, acknowledged, or remembered. What we don't talk about becomes a secret, and secrets cause shame, fear and myth. We talk about [the vagina], because we want to talk about it freely one day, without feeling shame.'

For Ai, *The Vagina Monologue* and the discursive communities it enabled would offer women the transformative experience of speaking the unspeakable, and thereby move closer to an authentic life. The film-in-progress was taken to school campuses and social organizations that dealt with women's issues, and inspired many women to start speaking about what they had kept silent. For example, young women migrant workers, after seeing the film, spoke about sexual harassment from their male supervisors, which they had not dared to speak about in the past for fear of retribution. These testimonies were then edited back into the film, making the film an ongoing, open project documenting the exhilarating experiences of empowerment as the video of the play travelled to university campuses and social organizations, inspiring conversations and changes of mentalities.

Making *The Vagina Monologue* was a transformative experience for Ai Xiaoming as well. Encouraged by the visual medium's ability to reach a wider public, Ai Xiaoming's shift in focus from academic writing to filmmaking seems inevitable. Working on and off with Hu Jie and on her own, she has covered topics including date-rape, village elections and protests, the plight of HIV/AIDS patients in rural China, and citizen investigations around the Sichuan Earthquake.[11] These films have allowed Ai Xiaoming and Hu Jie to further articulate the distinct aesthetics and epistemology of an activist documentary.

Investigating ruins: Grassroots perspectives in Ai Xiaoming and Hu Jie's *Our Children*

On 12 May 2008, an 8.0-magnitude earthquake shook the Sichuan Province of China, leaving close to 70,000 people dead, 37,000 injured and nearly 20,000 missing, according to official statistics.[12] Among the earthquake casualties in Sichuan, and according to the official statistics released a year after the earthquake, 5,335 of the dead were school children.[13]

Ai Xiaoming and Hu Jie's *Our Children*, the documentary chronicling the aftermath of this earthquake, starts with a black screen. In darkness, the viewer hears the soundtrack of people running and screaming, and a man's voice telling everyone to calm down. As the soundtrack gradually fades into silence, the screen lights up. One sees low-resolution video footage shot just minutes after the earthquake, in a small frame about one-quarter of the normal screen size. With three-quarters of the screen entirely black and the soundtrack utterly silent, the frame at the centre of the screen provides a tunnel vision, a flickering window onto a nightmare. One sees grainy images of corpses between cracks, grieving parents searching and wailing in the rubble, and people frantically rushing back and forth, but one feels trapped in a dream-like immobility by the horrendous image-track divorced from sound.

It is not possible to identify who was behind the camera for these images – they were shot with mobile phones and digital cameras, and these fleeting images were all part of 'found footage' from the disaster. Shortly after the earthquake, many homemade DVDs circulated in the earthquake-affected areas, sometimes on sale cheaply on streets, other times passing from hand to hand. They contained video footage and photographs, bits and pieces of visual wreckage preserved by ordinary people with whatever recording devices they had at hand. With these found images filling almost half of the running length of *Our Children*, Ai Xiaoming and Hu Jie's film provides viewers a precious opportunity to see the earthquake from the survivors' perspective and to understand how cameras were used in the earthquake at the grassroots level.

In *Theory of Film*, Siegfried Kracauer compares the film camera with Perseus's shield. Mirroring unspeakable horrors that would in reality paralyse us with blinding fear, the film camera allows the spectator to see image replicas of horror, thus 'incorporating into his memory the real face of things too dreadful to be beheld in reality.'[14] In the aftermath of the earthquake, people immediately began to use cameras as this shield and mirror, to see and understand what had happened. This muted gaze of horror, however, was only the initial reaction after the earthquake. Even at the most devastating moments, people observed carefully and took note of what they saw. 'All of us saw the collapse from afar,' one parent said to Ai Xiaoming in an interview. 'It took the elementary school ten seconds to collapse completely. For the high school, it took longer, fifteen seconds. We realized that it was too short a time. Few children could make it out.' As it became obvious that the school buildings were among the first buildings (and sometimes the only buildings in the vicinity) to collapse, people immediately began to ask why, and people's cameras became fiercely investigative once again.

As many children were buried under the collapsed buildings, parents who participated in the rescue took up the emotionally impossible task of photographing the layout of the corpses in order to discover how and why these children did not make it out safely: 'I saw many children's corpses just at the exit. If the building had held out just ten seconds longer, all these children could have escaped.' Cameras started to record the debris in close-up, as building materials, which had been hidden from public view under layers of paint and structures, were now exposed. Parents measured the thickness and weight of the construction materials, placed cigarettes next to the steel rods before they took a picture, in order to build into the photos a scale of measurement. At one site, parents dug out every piece of steel. 'I was the one responsible for having the steel weighed,' a parent said during an interview. 'Guess how many tonnes of steel were there in the three-storey school building? 4.2 tonnes. It was not enough for a two-storey family house.' Verifying measurements, specifying construction materials, photographing everything including building contracts and school petitions for building repair, these parents and activists treated sites of wreckage as sites of investigation, where they could probe at a deeper reality that the ruins had made visible: the inner materials and structures of social construction.

Parents' investigative endeavours prompted counteractions from the police and the state media. These counteractions were also recorded by cameras, further revealing the various forces operating around the ruins. Parents' video records show that the day after the earthquake, parents returned to one school site to find that police had surrounded the site, prohibiting anyone from entering. Parents whose children were still missing pleaded to be let in, but to no avail. As time went on, some sites were cleared overnight without notice. Others were heavily guarded. Stationed at crossroads, police checked cameras and deleted photos and videos. Yet the recording activities continued. Parents and activists photographed and videotaped every meeting they requested with the authorities, every public demonstration they staged. They made newspaper clippings and recorded television news clips by simply pointing a digital camera at the paper or the television screen. They used the cameras to take notes, photograph documents and keep a record of names and telephone numbers of witnesses. When collected and placed in a chronology, these materials offered an immensely rich record of grassroots organization, protest and negotiations with the government. They also documented the highly inconsistent media responses to the parents' actions, revealing the ongoing negotiations between journalists and the authorities with regard to what could be printed in the news from day to day. The camera became the critical apparatus for the parents and activists to bear witness and share their testimonies. 'We have audio-visual materials' – this was what the parents often would say during interviews with Ai Xiaoming and Hu Jie. Then they took out their small digital cameras to show the images they had taken. In one memorable scene, a mother holds her digital camera, and points to its small LCD screen to show how the police forces stopped demonstrating parents from marching to the provincial capital to petition the government. After pressing a few buttons, she shows her child buried in the ruins, suffocated in the collapsed concrete. Ai's camera captured the mother's hands tightly holding the small screen, as if trying to protect the frame of her testimony.

Piecing together wreckage: Montage over long-takes

Using a large amount of home videos and photographs made at the grassroots level meant that the film *Our Children* had to be constructed in a jigsaw fashion, allowing the narrative to arise from fragments of evidence and testimony. The cinematic montage, then, became indispensible to such a project of piecing together multiple perspectives, voices and found images.

Using montage as the organizing principle for documentary, however, was uncommon for Chinese independent documentary at the time of *Our Children*'s production. Since the beginning of the 1990s, the majority of independent filmmakers have tended to prize long-takes over montage. This was because while montage had been used in the early Soviet Union to represent and explore social realities and contradictions, it became reified in Stalinist Soviet Union and further in China's Cultural Revolution, driven no longer by the spirit of empirical investigation, but by ideologically determined pre-selection of what could and could not be represented. Montage was no longer an exploration of reality, but an imposition of ideology onto reality. Sergei Eisenstein's 1948 writing about montage said it all. Montage, Eisenstein wrote after Stalinism had become firmly established in all aspects of life in the Soviet Union, was the 'destruction of the indefinite and neutral, no matter whether it be an event or a phenomenon, and its reassembly in accordance with the idea dictated by attitude to this event or phenomenon, an attitude which, in its turn, is determined by my ideology, my outlook, that is to say, our ideology, our outlook.'[15]

Chinese filmmakers in the post-Mao era revolted against an ideologically determined reality. In an essay summarizing the theoretical debates on the meaning of 'reality' and 'realism' through the 1980s and 1990s, Wang Xiaolu wrote ironically about the notion of 'essential realism' (*benzhi zhenshi*), which he considered a hallmark of Chinese socialist realist art. 'The social problems we see are all just superficial and secondary. They cannot reflect the "essence" of our society. If you see starvation, you cannot represent it in your work, because it is not really the essence of our society, which is bright. That kids in Western countries seem to have good nutrition doesn't mean anything. In essence they suffer from an evil system, and need us to save them.'[16] This 'essential reality' had nothing to do with what the human eyes saw in the society, nor with empirical investigations. It was determined *a priori* by ideology, and the montage, enabling selective representations of reality, became a powerful tool to fabricate images of an 'essential reality.'[17]

Therefore, it was not surprising that filmmakers looked to André Bazin and his advocacy for long-takes when envisioning a new cinema.[18] When discussing the Italian neo-realist filmmaker Vittorio de Sica, Bazin writes:

> The originality of Italian neorealism as compared with the chief schools of realism that preceded it and with the Soviet cinema, lies in never making reality the servant of some *a priori* point of view. Whether in the service of the interests of an ideological thesis, of a moral idea, or of a dramatic action, realism subordinates what it borrows from reality to its transcendent needs. Neorealism only knows immanence. It is from appearance only. It's a phenomenology.[19]

The idea of 'phenomenological reality' (*biaoxiang zhenshi*) gained momentum among filmmakers in the early 1980s, because this reality was something that one could see with one's own eyes in everyday life. 'Because "phenomenological reality" is what everyone can feel and recognize, everyone can make a judgement based on his or her own feelings. This gives the right of speech to everyone, and breaks the monopoly of political power over the definition of "essential reality", wrote the film scholar Hu Ke.[20]

Meant to debunk political authorities and give the power of judgement back to the observer, the turn away from montage to the long-take in new documentary successfully established respect for the autonomy of the physical and historical world before the camera lens. Yet at the same time, Chinese critics such as Wang Xiaolu have also argued that this approach has curtailed the development of filmmakers' strong subjective positions and political will.[21] Chinese independent documentary, according to Wang, tends to represent 'atomized individuals and inexplicably miserable lives.'[22] Quoting from Alan Rosenthal's *The Documentary Conscience* that 'in one way or another, film should be used as a tool, some would even say, as a weapon, for social change,'[23] Wang believes that the independent filmmakers must learn to strengthen their films' social engagement, question social phenomena, and seek understanding of the social processes that gave rise to social phenomena rather than simply documenting what happens in front of the camera.[24]

Since their collaboration on *The Vagina Monologue* in 2004, Ai Xiaoming and Hu Jie have always prioritized montage over long-take. The reinvigoration of the cinematic montage has been one of the hallmarks of an activist documentary aesthetic. In *Our Children*, montage was used to juxtapose images of official TV reports and government documents with shaky and grainy images from the ruins of the earthquake. The filmmakers then overlaid the soundtracks of official announcements onto footage from the earthquake site, to reveal the inconsistencies between the official rhetoric and the situation on the ground. Montage was also used to bring together documentary images made by different people and cameras at the same event, in order to consolidate truth claims of images. As filmmakers, Ai Xiaoming and Hu Jie's primary role was not to shoot footage themselves, but to gather and edit found images into the most effective montage that could accommodate contending voices, while also establishing what multiple voices had claimed to be true. When gathering and verifying evidence, the filmmakers treated visual and audio materials differently and with a clear hierarchy: in almost every instance, the visual was considered more authentic than the audio, and voices were almost always embodied in order to prove their authenticity – i.e. a speech was almost always made, at least partially, with the speaker in view on camera. The only time when a voice was disembodied was in the cases of 'official voices.' By signing their speech with their faces and bodies, the activists attempted to set apart their testimony and opinion from propaganda. The film could be viewed as a series of visual signatures to a shared open letter, echoing common practices in the citizen rights movement on the internet such as collecting signatures and using one's true name in web posts.

From montage to tweets: Ai Xiaoming 'RT' (re-tweets) Ai Weiwei

In June 2009, Ai Xiaoming submitted *Our Children* to the municipal court of Chengdu as supporting evidence for the trial of Tan Zuoren, an environmentalist and writer from Chengdu whose investigations into school buildings in the earthquake area had led to his arrest. In addition to sending *Our Children* to court, Ai decided to work with Xie Yihui, a collaborator of Tan Zuoren, on another film entitled *Citizen's Investigations* (*Gongmin diaocha*, 2009), using photographs and videos taken by Tan and Xie in their investigations and collecting testimonies in support of Tan.

The Tan Zuoren case brought the Beijing-based avant-garde artist and architect Ai Weiwei into documentary activism. Since 2008, Ai Weiwei had been conducting a separate citizen investigation with a team of volunteers into children death tolls during the Sichuan earthquake. Even though Tan and Ai had worked independently of each other, they were aware of each other and their common concerns and efforts. In August 2009, Tan Zuoren's defence lawyer, Pu Zhiqiang, one of China's leading human rights lawyers, invited Ai Weiwei to serve as a witness in Tan's trial. Ai Weiwei arrived in Chengdu with a group of volunteers the day before the court opened. However, local police forced their way into the hotel rooms where Ai Weiwei's team was staying, and kept everyone illegally at the hotel for 11 hours, preventing them from attending the trial. They also arrested Liu Yanping, one of the volunteers in the team, without any legal procedure.

During Ai Weiwei's trip to Chengdu, the team kept video recordings of their daily activities. When the police broke into Ai Weiwei's hotel room at night, he had also turned on the audio recorder, and thereby managed to record the sound of the police's interrogation and attack, including a blow on his head, resulting in a cerebral haemorrhage that required an emergency operation in Munich a month later. Upon returning to Beijing from Chengdu, Ai Weiwei and his team edited the DV recordings into a documentary film entitled *Lao Ma Ti Hua* (a.k.a. *Disturbing Peace*), taking the Chinese title from the name of a popular Sichuanese dish of braised trotters. The film documented the group's train journey to Chengdu, the nighttime break-in by the police at the hotel, and the group's subsequent dealings with the police in order to find the whereabouts of Liu Yanping. Ai Weiwei, two lawyers and Liu Yanping's husband travelled between police stations and public security headquarters, where they were repeatedly denied any clear account of what had happened at the hotel and where Liu Yanping might be. Having finally gained permission to enter a public security headquarters, the group decided not to leave until the police offered clear information about Liu Yanping's whereabouts. While Ai Xiaoming and Hu Jie's films focused on enabling testimonies of the powerless, Ai Weiwei's film confronted the powerful to the point that their power began to crumble. The camera documented the confrontation between the police and Ai's group, filming Ai hurling angry witticisms at the police, and locking the police party secretary Xu Hui and a police officer Xu Jie in frontal medium shots, watching them growing increasingly embarrassed, self-contradictory and distraught during the confrontation.

Besides making 20,000 DVD copies and sending them via post all over the country, Ai Weiwei and his team also circulated *Disturbing Peace* via the internet, using Twitter to disseminate information on the download site. By that point, Ai Weiwei and Ai Xiaoming were both Twitter users, and the internet had brought human rights activists ever closer as a community. Understanding her own work and Ai Weiwei's work as tweets and re-tweets that build on each other, Ai Xiaoming began to think about making a sequel, or a 're-tweet,' to *Disturbing Peace*. The resulting film was *Why are the Flowers So Red: RT Disturbing Peace* (*Hua'er weishenme zheyang hong: RT Laoma tihua*). The seriality between the two films can also be seen in their respective titles: the Chinese title of *Why are Flowers So Red* begins with the character Hua, or flower, which coincides with the last character in *Lao Ma Ti Hua*, the Chinese title of *Disturbing Peace*.

A portrait of a network of volunteers and activists working as far from each other as Guangdong, Sichuan and Beijing, *Why are the Flowers So Red* began with gatherings of activists in Sichuan, proceeded to document Ai Weiwei and his team's daily activities in Beijing, and ended with a conversation in prison between Tan Zuoren and human rights lawyer Pu Zhiqiang. Ai Xiaoming conducted interviews with members of Ai Weiwei's team who had gone to Chengdu and appeared in *Disturbing Peace*. She also spent time at Ai Weiwei's studio, and documented Ai Weiwei and his colleagues' daily activities, including communicating with government offices to request release of information, providing consultation to people from the earthquake region who sought help in fighting local government's corruption and opacity, and supporting the works of other social activists. Almost an ethnographic film on China's activist community, *Why are the Flowers So Red* portrayed Ai Weiwei's office and home as a nexus for activists, writers and artists to meet and share ideas and probed into the inner workings of this lively community. How did people come together? How did the community sustain itself and expand? How could the activists, especially young ones, be so fearless when dealing with the police? What motivated them? Ai Xiaoming's interviews registered the languages, cultures and prevailing moral reasonings of this community. 'Why do you participate in the citizen investigation?' Ai asked one young volunteer. 'Because it is something warm,' answered the volunteer, metaphorically expressing his humanistic ideals and the community's emotional tonality.

While montage in *Our Children* served to bring multiple testimonies together, in *Why are the Flowers So Red* it created rich intertextuality. Images from *Disturbing Peace* appeared intermittently throughout the film, intercut with viewers' reactions to the film and daily activities at Ai Weiwei's studio. At a semi-private screening of *Disturbing Peace* attended by artists, journalists and film scholars, Ai Xiaoming recorded reactions of the audience during and after the film. Likening interactions between Ai Weiwei and the police to an absurdist play, one viewer observed that Ai Weiwei was a great dramatist capable of soliciting performance from the police, and contemplated on what this absurdist drama had revealed: the utter 'unreality' of the relationship between ordinary people and the state. Another viewer described Ai Weiwei's filmmaking as close-quarters combat, challenging the police in an unprecedented, open manner. Ai Xiaoming's interest in art as a means to initiate conversations and form publics had already manifested itself in her first film, *The Vagina Monologue*, which moved beyond the space of the theatre to explore the play's engagement with a wider society. In *Why are the Flowers So Red,* Ai Xiaoming highlighted the power of film in strengthening an activist community.

Conclusion: Montage, tweets and reconstruction of an activist cinema

Despite Ai Weiwei's pronounced individualism, *Why are the Flowers So Red* revealed the collective nature of citizen activism, and situated Ai Weiwei as one person among a network of people sharing knowledge, information and tactics of citizen action with each other. The film ended with the human rights lawyer Pu Zhiqiang speaking to Tan Zuoren in prison. Pu read out aloud, slowly, the names of a long list of supporters and colleagues, who had wished to pass encouragement and support to Tan. Many of them belonged to the activist communities Ai Xiaoming had portrayed earlier in the film. Behind the iron bars, and hearing the support of so many colleagues, Tan was moved to tears. By ending the film with this long list of names, Ai Xiaoming again brought to the fore the expanding network of citizen activism in China.

To be sure, Ai and Hu's films have not only revived heroic figures able to bear witness and testify out of one's life experiences, but also represented a connected and mobilized community based on shared concerns. Moving beyond phenomenological reality, Ai and Hu use montage to juxtapose different perspectives, corroborate evidences and probe into hidden structures underlying the society made visible in times of fracture and crisis. Combining interviews, recordings of discussions and meetings and observations of everyday activities, these films document political and moral reasoning at the grassroots level in the society, and portray processes of politicization. Mostly circulating on the internet and in activist networks, these films also become serialized as filmmakers work independently but also with each other to provide long coverage of important events that continue to evolve. In 2009, Ai Xiaoming had already instructed me to watch her films together with Ai Weiwei's: 'These films are best watched in sequence. You first watch "Our Children," then "Citizen Investigations." After that, you watch Ai Weiwei's "Laoma Tihua." Finally you come back to me and watch "Why are the Flowers So Red."' This, Ai Xiaoming has acutely observed, is a form of 'retweeting'. As a new media of organizing pluralistic voices, and sharing information, Twitter has indeed influenced the cinematic form, creating more intertextuality and allowing cinema to move more freely between temporal and spatial confines. All these developments help realize a sustained, collective search for a new political cinema.

Works cited

Ai Xiaoming. 'Baowei linghun ziyou de zitai,' [Defending the Attitude of a Free Soul], 2005. http://blog.boxun.com/hero/200801/ziyouhun/25_1.shtml

Bazin, André. *What is Cinema*, vol. 2, trans. Hugh Gray. Berkeley and Los Angeles: University of California Press, 2005, 64.

Berry, Chris and Mary Ann Farquhar. 'Postsocialist Strategies: An Analysis of Yellow Earth and Black Cannon Incident' in Linda C. Ehrlich and David Desser (eds),

Cinematic Landscapes: Observations on the Visual Arts and Cinema of China and Japan. Austin: University of Texas Press, 1994, 81–116.

Cui, Weiping. 'Jilupian "Xunzhao Li Zhao de Linghun" beihou' [Behind the documentary Searching for the Soul of Lin Zhao], Nanfangchuang, April 2004.

Eisenstein, Sergei. Problems of Film Direction. Honolulu: University Press of the Pacific, 2004, 72.

Hu, Ke, 'zhongguo dianying zhenshi guannian he bazan yingxiang' [The Concept of Reality in Chinese Cinema and Bazin's Influence], Dangdai Dianying, no. 4, 2008, 6–12.

Kracauer, Siegfried. Theory of Film: The Redemption of Physical Reality. Princeton, NJ: Princeton University Press, 1997, 305–6.

Li, Tuo, and Zhang Nuanxin. 'Tan dianying yuyan de xiandaihua' [The Modernization of Film Language], Beijing Film Art, no. 3, 1979.

Lu, Xinyu. Ji lu Zhongguo : dang dai Zhongguo xin ji lu yun dong. [Documenting China: Contemporary Chinese New Documentary Movement], Beijing: Sheng huo, du shu, xin zhi san lien shu dian, 2003.

Lu, Xuesong. 'Wo mengxiang zaori huidao wo re'ai de jiangtai – gei jilin yishu xueyuan dangwei shuji de gongkaixin' [I dream of returning to my beloved teaching podium soon – an open letter to the party secretary of Jilin Art Academy], http://bbs.tianya.cn/post-books-64837-1.shtml

Nornes, Abé Mark. 'Bulldozers, bibles, and very sharp knives: the Chinese independent documentary scene,' Film Quarterly, vol. 63, no. 1, 2009, 50–5.

Robinson, Luke. Independent Chinese Documentary: From the Studio to the Street. New York: Palgrave Macmillan, 2013, 34.

Rosenthal, Alan. The Documentary Conscience: A Casebook in Film Making. Berkeley, CA and Los Angeles: University of California Press, 1980, 1.

Wang, Xiaolu. Dianying yu shidaibing [Film and the Diseases of the Contemporary Age]. Guangzhou: Hua Cheng Press, 2008, 40.

Wang, Yiman. 'The amateur's lightning rod: DV documentary in postsocialist China,' Film Quarterly, Summer 2005, vol. 58, no. 4, 16–26.

Notes

1 Lu Xinyu, Ji lu Zhongguo: dang dai Zhongguo xin ji lu yun dong. Beijing: Sheng huo, du shu, xin zhi san lien shu dian, 2003.
2 Abé Mark Nornes, 'Bulldozers, bibles, and very sharp knives: the Chinese independent documentary scene,' Film Quarterly, vol. 63, no. 1, 2009, 50–5.
3 Chris Berry and Mary Ann Farquhar, 'Postsocialist Strategies: An Analysis of Yellow Earth and Black Cannon Incident' in Linda C. Ehrlich and David Desser (eds), Cinematic Landscapes: Observations on the Visual Arts and Cinema of China and Japan. Austin: University of Texas Press, 1994, 81–116.
4 Luke Robinson, Independent Chinese Documentary: From the Studio to the Street. New York: Palgrave Macmillan, 2013, 34.
5 Yiman Wang, 'The amateur's lightning rod: DV documentary in postsocialist China,' Film Quarterly, Summer 2005, vol. 58, no. 4, 16–26.

6 Cui Weiping, 'Jilupian "Xunzhao Li Zhao de Linghun" beihou' [Behind the documentary *Searching for the Soul of Lin Zhao*], *Nanfangchuang*, April 2004.
7 Cui Weiping, 'Jilupian "Xunzhao Li Zhao de Linghun" beihou.'
8 The first places where Hu's film circulated were university campuses. It was screened in March 2004 as part of a retrospective on his documentaries entitled 'Women and Other People on the Margin – Documentary films by Hu Jie' at Zhongshan University's Guangzhou and Zhuhai campuses. Ai Xiaoming, another public intellectual rallying behind Hu's film, organized the event. More than 1,000 teachers and students watched the film and heated discussions ensued. In the relatively liberal atmosphere of Guangdong and with the help of Ai Xiaoming and her local contacts, the film proceeded to screen at the Guangzhou Art Gallery, the He Xiangyin Art Gallery in Shenzhen, and the Foshan Public Library, and travelled in 2004 to Hong Kong, with more than 1500 people attending these screenings altogether. Ai Xiaoming also brought the film into graduate level curriculum in Zhongshan University's programme on comparative literature, where Ai Xiaoming was a professor. Ai Xiaoming, 'Baowei linghun ziyou de zitai' [Defending the Attitude of a Free Soul], 2005. http://blog.boxun.com/hero/200801/ziyouhun/25_1.shtml (accessed 27 February 2013.)
9 Lu Xuesong, 'Wo mengxiang zaori huidao wo re'ai de jiangtai – gei jilin yishu xueyuan dangwei shuji de gongkaixin' [I dream of returning to my beloved teaching podium soon – an open letter to the party secretary of Jilin Art Academy], http://bbs.tianya.cn/post-books-64837-1.shtml (accessed 27 February 2013.)
10 Ai Xiaoming, 'Baowei linghun ziyou de zitai,' 2005.
11 For Ai Xiaoming's filmmaking activities in her own words, see Tieh-Chih Chang and Ying Qian, 'The citizen camera: interview with Ai Xiaoming,' *New Left Review* 72, November–December 2011, 63–79.
12 http://news.cctv.com/china/20090507/108604.shtml, May 7, 2009 (accessed 3 January 2010).
13 http://news.cctv.com/china/20090507/105047.shtml, May 7, 2009 (accessed 3 January 2010).
14 Siegfried Kracauer, *Theory of Film: The Redemption of Physical Reality*. Princeton, NJ: Princeton University Press, 1997, 305–6.
15 Sergei Eisenstein, *Problems of Film Direction*. Honolulu: University Press of the Pacific, 2004, 72.
16 Wang Xiaolu, *Dianying yu shidaibing* [Film and the Diseases of the Contemporary Age]. Guangzhou: Hua Cheng Press, 2008, 40.
17 Ibid., *Dianying yu shidaibing*, 39–50.
18 See Li Tuo and Zhang Nuanxin's seminal article *Tan dianying yuyan de xiandaihua* [The Modernization of Film Language], Beijing Film Art, no. 3, 1979. For an English version, see George S. Semsel, Xia Hong and Hou Jianping (eds), *Chinese Film Theory: A Guide to the New Era*. New York: Praeger, 1990, 10–20.
19 André Bazin, *What is Cinema*, vol. 2, trans. Hugh Gray. Berkeley, CA and Los Angeles: University of California Press, 2005, 64.
20 Hu Ke, 'zhongguo dianying zhenshi guannian he bazan yingxiang' [The Concept of Reality in Chinese Cinema and Bazin's Influence], *Dangdai Dianying*, no. 4, 2008, 6–12.
21 Wang Xiaolu, *Dianying yu shidaibing*, 53.

22 Ibid., 62.
23 Alan Rosenthal, *The Documentary Conscience: A Casebook in Film Making*. Berkeley, CA and Los Angeles: University of California Press, 1980, 1.
24 Wang Xiaolu, *Dianying yu shidaibing*, 63.

11

Provincializing the Chinese Mediascape: Cantonese Digital Activism in Southern China

Jia Tan

The recent events of the Arab Spring have shown some positive applications in the revolutionary potential of digital technology, which suggest that social media such as Twitter and Facebook have found a way to change the world. Such an optimistic view on technology is critiqued in Evgeny Morozov's *The Net Delusion* in terms of 'cyber-utopianism,' which refers to 'a naive belief in the emancipatory nature of online communication that rests on a stubborn refusal to acknowledge its downside.'[1] When it comes to digital contention in China, similar tendencies of techno-utopianism have gained prominence, overpowering any detractors' rumblings. Despite many scholars and opinion leaders outside of China fixating on the ways recent technologies, including the internet and mobile communications have strengthened media control, surveillance and censorship, a point could be made however that researchers are only now beginning to explore the ways in which these newer technologies have empowered individuals and communities through the creation of reimagined social spaces.[2] One such optimistic study would be Yang Guobing's *The Power of the Internet in China*, in which the author argues that the internet provides spaces for 'unofficial democracy,' whereby websites provide openings for continual negotiations based on the lived experiences of millions of online users in China.[3]

This chapter investigates the wave of Cantonese digital activism that can be conceived of as another application of social media and formation of moving image culture that is worth interrogating. My aim is to inquire beyond the techno-utopia/-dystopia binary by locating Cantonese digital activism in its historical, social and industrial contexts against the backdrop of the explosion of various moving image cultures in the new millennium. The present study explores the particularities of Cantonese digital activism by deploying the notion of the *provincial*. I borrow this term from the post-colonial scholar Dipesh Chakravarty who asserts that we can 'provincialize Europe' through deconstructing the myth of 'the West' as an originary site of modernity by revealing the constitutive positions of the colonies in the modernization process. Chakravarty has criticized the developmental logic of many third world countries that subscribe to the linear narrative of modernity. Rather than provincializing a centre, the present study instead *centralizes a province* in order to explore the theoretical potential of 'the provincial' and reconfigure debates on globalization and transnationalism, particularly in the fields of cultural and media studies specific to the Chinese online moving image culture.

This study invokes the term *provincial* in two ways. First, it employs the province as an analytical framework for examining the central–provincial structure in the Chinese media industry. Second, it explores the possibilities and problematics of Cantonese media activism, in the sense that the term functions as a nuanced way of thinking beyond the constraints of cultural dominance versus cultural resistance. In other words, I will argue that Cantonese digital activism seeks to uncover how new communication technologies, e.g. mobile devices and the internet, in conjunction with other mass media such as television, have facilitated new cultural articulations. While some of these articulations have been critical of the state's monolingual policy and developmental logic, others run the risk of reproducing existing social hierarchies such as class-based discrimination. The progressive and reactionary attributes in the same digital activism urges us to move from the question of *whether* certain technologies are revolutionary to the question of *how* technologies are embedded in social relations. In my chapter, I aim to use the *provincial* to demonstrate a more contextual understanding of the relationship between technology and culture beyond the techno-utopia/-dystopia binary.

Cantonese activism and its discontents

On 1 August 2010, thousands of people gathered in and around the People's Park in the city of Guangzhou in southern China. The crowd was disbanded when hundreds of police marched in and dragged away protesters, filing them away on large municipal buses. In front of the confrontational scene between the protesters and the police, nearly every protester held either digital cameras, camcorders, or cellular phones to document that event. Some of these pictures were immediately posted online via telecom networks on Chinese micro-blogs such aso Sina Weib.[4] Videos and pictures would soon be uploaded to the internet, a place to disseminate opinions and organize the street demonstrations, which made the fast mobilization of protesters possible in the first place.

What were the protestors rallying for or against? They had not gathered to voice their discontent over environmental pollution, labour disputes, or land confiscation, all prevalent social problems and popular topics online in China today. Instead, this protest was triggered by a government proposal that the local Guangzhou TV station replace Cantonese primetime shows with Mandarin programming during the Asian Games in 2010. The protests can now be seen as climactic moments where a series of 'flash mob' gatherings, street demonstrations and civil disobediences exploded in metropolitan Guangzhou, all demanding the preservation of Cantonese language and culture.[5]

Cantonese is widely used throughout southern China, Hong Kong and across the diverse Chinese diaspora worldwide. Yet, despite its linguistic importance throughout greater China, Cantonese has been relegated to the status of a Chinese dialect, soon to be expunged in the PRC via a national campaign to promote *Putonghua*, or Mandarin.[6] Article 19 of the Constitution of the PRC proclaims the use of *Putonghua* nationwide. We can trace the promotion of Mandarin in the educational sector back to the mid-1950s, as the Communist Party had an interest in creating a standardized national language. Since that period, the state has championed Simplified Chinese, Mandarin and the pinyin system in its educational institutions. Furthermore, dialects are highly circumscribed within the Chinese mass media. In January 2001, the Law of the Standard Spoken and Written Chinese Language established Chinese as the standard language – officially enforcing Mandarin across the vast public sector, including the broadcasting industry.

Netizens have dubbed such monolingual language policy the 'Mandarin Promotion Machine,' or more crudely 'Language Slaughter.'[7] To express concern over this promotion of Mandarin, netizens organized many street gatherings through social media, gatherings that were accompanied by debates, netizen-made videos, songs and images of dissent online. Such shows of activism have been tactically combined with criticism of urban planning and redevelopment policy, as well as calls for freedom of expression in the country. The activism soon received support from Cantonese speakers in Hong Kong, Macau and throughout cyberspace, as well as in physical spaces within the mainland and beyond. For example, at the same time as the August 1 demonstration in Guangzhou, hundreds of protesters in Hong Kong joined the demonstrations as part of the 'Guangdong-HK Support Cantonese Action,' working in unison from two different Chinese territories connected by digital activists.

The banner term 'Cantonese digital activism' is used here to describe the participatory use of the internet and electronic devices for the articulation of shared language and cultural experiences, as suggested by the name of this activism: 'Support Cantonese language.' Despite the political agency and possibilities fulfilled in this wave of activism from user-generated content online to street demonstrations, such bottom-up cultural expressions also have limitations – chiefly, they have the potential to reproduce social hierarchies. A widely circulated netizen-reproduced propaganda poster points to the discriminatory side of Cantonese digital activism. The caption reads: 'Canton people speak Cantonese. Go back to the countryside if you don't understand Cantonese.' This slogan may be a reference to the millions of migrant workers in China who come from the countryside and work in the city. According to the population census of 2010, more than four million people living in Guangzhou are non-locals, a figure representing more than one-third of the city's total population. Many of these non-Cantonese-speaking, non-locals are migrant workers living on a minimal wage, excluded from social welfare due to China's *hukou* system of citizen registration.

Notably, compared to previous cases of rights-based activism in China, Cantonese activism has a distinguishing cultural dimension, a departure from actions that target specific economic needs and social justice issues. After the Tiananmen social movement of 1989, massive demonstrations disappeared on the street within China due to high levels of state surveillance, intense implementation of the Economic Reform policy, and the de-politicization of politics.[8] The previous notable online rights activism causes were more or less reclaiming rights regarding specific issues, such as labour disputes, legal injustices, corruption and environmental pollution – and these campaigns were usually repressed by the state. Most demonstrations permitted by the state have tended to be ones with strong nationalistic sentiments, such as the anti-American protest after the accidental bombing of the Chinese embassy in Yugoslavia in 1999 and the anti-Japanese demonstrations of 2005. Elsewhere, and after the controversy of Tibet and the 2008 Xinjiang conflicts, the overseas 'support Olympics' has demonstrated how pan-Chinese cyber-nationalism joined forces with street activism abroad.

The most studied cases of culturally associated online activism in Anglophone scholarship have included cyber articulations of nationalism, based solidly on the framework of the nation-state.[9] Where the Cantonese activists depart from these previous studies is how they view the state as a homogenizing mechanism, which cannot be explained easily in the nation-state framework in the study of Chinese media and culture. Cantonese activism, therefore, is a culturally distinct activism that forces us to think beyond the framework of the nation-state and inquire into the centre-provincial dynamic.

Cantonese digital activism is indebted to the development of provincial media industries in Guangdong and the influence of Hong Kong media in the last 30 years. Though Mandarin is forced upon all educational institutions, the local media in Guangdong province enjoy an exceptionally 'liberal' linguistic policy compared to other provinces. This is why Guangzhou TV station, which triggered the Cantonese digital activism, was able to broadcast in Cantonese in the first place. In the next section, I will include a brief history of provincial media industries in Guangdong and the influence of Hong Kong media, which enabled Guangzhou TV station to broadcast in Cantonese when it was founded in 1988.

Provincial media industries in contemporary China

Media apparatuses in China, including the press, radio, film and television, all contain heavily administrative structures. Each media apparatus is carefully supervised by a corresponding department or unit of the Department of Propaganda. Such a view of scale and structure in the media matrix in China is a relevant point to linger on for a moment. In reference to scale in the Chinese media, Sun Wanning has invoked the term 'geographical turn' in order to observe 'how a range of media studies concerns such as media policy, industry, content production and consumption are played out at various sub-national levels – the village, the county, the city, the province, and the region.'[10] So far, this chapter's use of the term *province*, carefully chosen over other similar analytical terms such as *region*, is intended to emphasize the structural hierarchy between the provincial and the national, particularly in the context of the state-sanctioned Chinese media industry.[11]

Regulated under the SARFT, Chinese media companies on different levels have been required to be more and more individually accountable for how they perform and function financially. Such an administrative centralization and financial decentralization points to the 'double properties' of the broadcasting industry in China, demonstrating the neoliberal alliance as well as the friction between the nationalized entities and transnational capitalism. For example, the Pearl River Film Studio has been one part of the highly centralized system of film production. Since its 1958 establishment in Guangzhou, the Pearl River Film Studio has represented the beginnings of a provincial film production centre in a larger wave of development, paving the way for provincial film studios nationwide. Following the neoliberal initiative of the Economic Reform in the post-Mao period, the film industry and broadcast media in China were not only part of the propaganda machine, but were also transforming into commercial enterprises seeking to secure profits – nationally, regionally and globally.[12]

Like radio and film production, the development of television industry in China was also caught up in the Reform. In the 1980s, the growth in Chinese television reached unprecedented levels, both in terms of the expansion of TV networks and the increase in broadcasting hours. The number of TV channels nationwide grew from 35 in 1980 to more than 500 in 1990.[13] As with other provincial and national broadcasting media, radio and TV stations in Guangdong are framed in vertical administration from the old top-down propaganda model, and horizontal commercial links to local or national enterprises. That is to say, while these broadcasters have remained under the purview of the state, they are increasingly self-reliant financially. Obviously, the provincial media may have more leeway to incorporate commercial operations. However, only selected stations at the provincial level may maintain a satellite channel and receive nationwide and international coverage.

Today, China touts more than 3,000 TV channels, most of which are limited to local or provincial coverage. Unlike the film industry in Guangdong, where a singular provincial film studio centralizes virtually all production resources, the expansive infrastructures of the TV networks in Guangdong make this medium a more democratic, decentralized platform. At the same time, however, the decentralized commercial model is constantly at odds with the imposing centralizing impulse of the state. In Lisa Leung's study of local media outlet Hunan Satellite TV's role in the transnationalization of the Korean Wave (*Hallyu*) to the Chinese public, the author observes that the state-level legal and regulatory mechanisms create obstacles for local media to import global media; Leung notes that the state 'legitimizes and perpetuates its political and ideological domination and economic prowess over the local as the periphery through restrictive broadcasting and financial policies.'[14]

In the context of the TV industry, the umbrella term 'provincial media' includes TV networks that (1) are headquartered in provincial and municipal centres; (2) mostly have provincial and local coverage; and (3) closely reflect provincial and local interests and promote national concerns at a local level. In relation to the particularities of provincial media infrastructure in Guangdong, the *provincial* here is not necessarily a counterpart of the national or the global, but rather an integrated part of the national media infrastructure.

Since 1980, in order to compete with the overwhelming popularity of Cantonese Hong Kong TV programmes, several TV channels and radio stations in Guangdong have been permitted to broadcast in Cantonese. By contrast, other provincial TV networks have never been allowed to produce dialect-based programming, despite the occasional appearance of such programming in the 2000s.[15] Four channels in Guangdong TV, four channels in Southern Television, and several municipal-level TV channels (such as Guangzhou Television channels) all broadcast in Cantonese.[16] In 2004, Southern Television (TVS) became the only satellite TV channel with nationwide coverage to broadcast in Cantonese; all other satellite TV channels in China are in either Mandarin or English. Furthermore, Cantonese TV productions are also popular in Guangdong. Guangdong's TV networks began dubbing selected Mandarin TV dramas into Cantonese, thus targeting not only Cantonese speakers in Guangdong, but also Cantonese speakers throughout the diaspora.[17] For example, Guangdong TV's golden programme, Cantonese sitcom *Local Husbands and Migrant Wives*, received high ratings in 2003 and has produced more than 1,000 episodes since its debut in 2000.[18]

In the next section, I will introduce a netizen-produced commentary via a video called 'Rap Guangzhou (Canton)' as a specific example of recent moving image cultures in provincial contexts.[19] The video content is considered against the backdrop of the historical development of provincial media; it is analysed in relation to its textual engagements and its transmedia disseminations.

Rap Cantonese: Netizen 'Vidding'

Among the abundant user-generated content from Cantonese digital activism, 'Rap Guangzhou (Canton)' is a widely circulated, netizen-produced Cantonese video that articulates the consciousness of people who want to preserve Cantonese.[20] The song tactically incorporates criticism of urban planning and redevelopment policy and calls for the preservation of Cantonese. This combination is reflected in its lyrics, which elaborate on the disappearance of Cantonese language in everyday life and the demolition of Cantonese neighbourhoods in the urbanization process. The following excerpt from the song's lyrics delineates the disappearance of Cantonese, both as a language and as a way of life:

> Rap Cantonese line by line, please don't say Cantonese is aging. In this grand epoch full of changes, Cantonese is the seal of the past. Rapping Cantonese beat by beat, seeing the change of Guangzhou second by second. English and Mandarin are often heard in this busy city, but please don't forget Cantonese. I have been living in this city for twenty years; the old restaurants and neighbourhoods are all demolished. The news reportages keep reporting on how much money is spent in

the preparation for the 2010 Asian Games. I don't care how much is spent. Our collective memories are demolished... Now speaking Cantonese is even becoming an issue. I really want to know what is wrong with you. I never say you cannot promote Mandarin, but why are you trying to diminish Cantonese?[21]

The song begins with the mixing of Cantonese and Mandarin audio clips from TV news reporting on Cantonese neighbourhoods facing threats of demolition in the name of redevelopment. Using first-person experience of living in Guangzhou 'for 20 years,' the singer strongly asserts the frustration caused by the demolition of older neighbourhoods. The song has been remade by other netizens into numerous versions of online music videos. A popular version of the song is accompanied by the official video of the 2010 Asian Games held in Guangzhou – an event specifically targeted in *Rap Cantonese*.

The Asian Games' official video, typical of promotional videos for sporting events, showcases corporeal movements in athletic activities such as cycling, gymnastics, marathons, swimming and running. Relying heavily on crane shots and slow motion, the video exhibits athletic bodies on the move. The original Asian Games video is at the same time a city-branding product, featuring unfolding modern interior spaces – including car assembly lines, a music hall and a shopping mall. Intercutting modern architectural space with athletic movements, the video is a visual statement of Guangzhou's modernization and urbanization, asserting it as a desirable city to host the Asian Games. The images in the Asian Games promotional video exemplify the mainstream visual narrative or the branding strategy, which is a recurring formula of promoting Chinese cities on the global stage. The international games demonstrate how the nation-state panders to the discourse of neoliberal globalization and its developmental logic, while also displacing both Cantonese dialect and neighbourhoods to make room for Guangzhou's urban redevelopment.

Replacing the soundtrack in the Asian Games video with the *Rap Cantonese* song, the netizen-produced video sharply points out that the considerable investment in urban redevelopment for the preparation of the Asian Games has led to the demolition of 'our collective memories' as Guangzhouers. Moreover, in the online video *Rap Cantonese*, the creator not only replaces the soundtrack of the original Asian Games video, but also broadcasts the lyrics onscreen in white characters. Here the visualizations in the video deviate from the meaning in the lyrics, which I shall explain later in this chapter. In a typical aerial shot of Guangzhou's cityscape (see Figure 11.1), the modern bridge lies in the foreground while the city skyline anchors the composition nicely in the background. The white characters on the screen recount the demolition of the old Arcade Building, a residential-commercial space whose exterior arcades provided shelter for pedestrians. Visually, for Cantonese readers, the video calls into question the demolition – against the backdrop of the city's new skyline.

Even more importantly, the Arcade Building emphasized in the lyrics points to the lived space of traditional architecture, where people still dwell. In the Asian Games video, traditional architecture is occasionally featured – e.g. the Chan Clan Ancestral Hall and the Sun Yet-San Memorial Hall. However, these places are mostly tourist sites

Figure 11.1 Still of an aerial shot of Guangzhou's cityscape in online video *Rap Cantonese* (2010).

or performance venues, instead of everyday lived spaces. Thus, the Asian Games video favours traditional architecture's symbolic and ritual values over its everyday lived-in quality, a critique presented throughout the *Rap Cantonese* video.

The Asian Games video's celebration of economic development logic, exemplified by the obsession with skyscrapers and modernist architectural spaces, goes hand in hand with the construction of a local identity by showcasing symbols of ethnic culture, such as flower boats, Cantonese opera and historic sites. Another of the ethnic cultural traditions featured in the video is dragon boat racing, an ancient folk ritual common in southern China. The importance of this ancient sport found a place in the 2010 Asian Games; it appears multiple times in the video. However, the video emphasizes the theatricality of the dragon boat. As shown in the picture (see Figure 11.2), the dragon head of the boat, carried by a group of men and centred on the screen, is much larger than those used in real competition.

Again, coupled with the song, the lyrics onscreen complicate the phallic representation of the dragon boat head. While the dragon boat asserts the existence of traditional ethnic culture, the songwriter of *Rap Cantonese* suggests that urban demolition has been happening so quickly and drastically that 'one can easily disorient oneself' wandering in the city, even for someone who grew up in the city.

The superimposition of lyrics on the image is reminiscent of the popular Karaoke culture in China, and an effective way of disseminating the song's messages to Chinese readers. But the fact that the words occupy more than half of the screen creates a visual reinscription of the rap song that negates the 'harmonious' developments of the city. The words appear as a rewriting of the meaning behind the city's urban makeover and

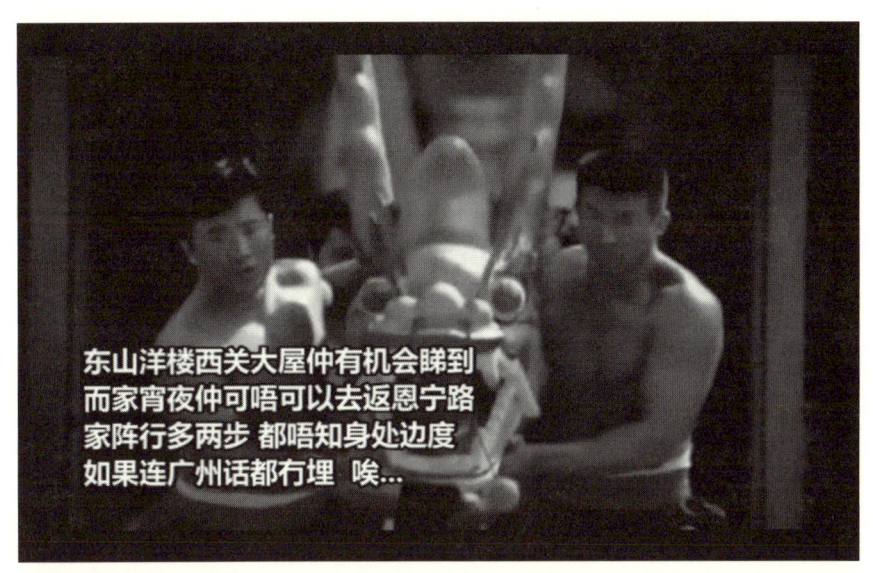

Figure 11.2 Still of men carrying a dragon boat in the online video *Rap Cantonese* (2010).

Figure 11. 3 Still of a smiling woman in online video *Rap Cantonese* (2010).

redevelopment. The video also shows how traditional cultures are 'preserved' in the images, yet are gradually disappearing from people's lived experiences. Here, besides reflecting the conflict of linguistic and regional differences, Cantonese activism engages the preservation of traditional architecture, in response to the vulnerability of historical sites to intensified urbanization and demolition.

The issue of preserving traditional cultures and architectures against aggressive urban planning has been a consistent public concern in contemporary Chinese cinema. For example, Fifth-Generation director Ning Ying's Beijing trilogy [*For Fun* (1992); *On the Beat* (1995); and *I Love Beijing* (2000)] documents urban change in the context of police regulation. As Yomi Braester points out, the trilogy dwells on images of demolition and elevates demolition to a metaphor of the erasure of collective memory.[22] Sixth-Generation director Jia Zhangke's documentary-realist films also incorporate images of demolition as thematic and visual components. Scenes of demolition can easily be found in Jia's *Xiao Wu* (1997), *Still Life* (2006), and *24 City* (2008), featuring urban destruction in the context of small towns as well as major cities such as Chengdu. Despite the popularity of the demolition theme, Guangdong has been underrepresented in cinema regarding China's rapid and intense urbanization. From a grassroots perspective, Cantonese activism fills this void by giving voice to opposition against drastic urban demolition.

At first glance, Cantonese activism might appear to be a sort of provincialism, or an ethno-linguistic articulation challenging monolithic Chinese nationhood. However, the developmental logic of the state, which has led to the demolition of Cantonese neighbourhoods in the name of real estate redevelopment, is also attributable to the state's gradual embrace of transnational capitalism beginning in the late 1970s. In this sense, critiquing the developmental logic of the state, Cantonese digital activism is what Arjun Appadurai has termed 'grassroots globalization,' which 'strives for a democratic and autonomous standing in respect to the various forms by which global power further seeks to extend its dominion.'[23] As demonstrated in Cantonese digital activism, such acts of 'grassroots globalization' are struggles that are situated in the connections and frictions among the provincial, the national and the global. In other words, the notion of the *provincial* clarifies the complicated nature of 'grassroots globalization.'

Transmedia flow and the dissemination of *Rap Cantonese*

While many studies of new media stress the possibilities and specificities of the internet, new media research tends to obscure the transmedia connections as they play out in reality. For online activism in general, issues that have gained broad appeal continue to rely on mass media – e.g. newspapers and television – for in-depth discussion and dissemination of information; at times, activism might also rely on state intervention.[24] The emergence of Cantonese digital activism has been aided by television and press coverage in Guangdong and Hong Kong, which cements Cantonese digital activism as a transmedia phenomenon. State-owned media in Guangdong, particularly Guangzhou media outlets *Southern Metropolis Daily* and *Yangcheng Evening Daily*, were at the centre of the so-called 'battle between Mandarin and Cantonese.' Cantonese digital activism routinely interacts with traditional media, including television and the news media. *Southern Metropolis Daily* was among several newspapers that reported early flash mob gatherings.²⁵ Local television, especially Cantonese broadcasts, also played an important role. As discussed above, the *Rap Cantonese* song has several versions of *vidding*, i.e. different visuals accompanying the same song. The song was also broadcast on Guangzhou TV, accompanied by the quick-changing images of the cityscape, as a prominent example of online activism promoting Cantonese language and culture. It was picked up by the TV station as a pro-Cantonese example, as part of its reportage on the 'battle between Mandarin and Cantonese'.

Broadly speaking, Weibo was one of the most prominent social platforms to promote Cantonese digital activism in early July 2010. Thousands followed the trending topic 'abolishing Cantonese,' which examined a government proposal to change Cantonese primetime programming into Mandarin. The Guangzhou TV station, whose programming was subject to change under the fiat, aired the results of an online survey of the proposal. According to the report, more than 90 per cent of survey participants opposed the proposal. On 10 July, in the People' Park in central Guangzhou, about 30 young people gathered and sang Cantonese songs, including Cantonese-pop classics by the Hong Kong pop rock band Beyond as well as the classic Cantonese nursery rhyme *Rain*. It was the first *kuaishan* gathering,²⁶ which sparked successive street demonstrations. The gathering was organized by users in the *Guangzhou bentu wang*, an online forum dedicated to various aspects of Guangzhou living. The gathering was soon publicized online and by various press and TV news programmes in Guangzhou. *Southern Metropolis Daily* noted that the majority of the participants were '*80 hou*,' a term widely used in mainland China to describe the generation born in the 1980s who share some common characters or habits, due to their experience of growing up in postsocialist China.²⁷

On 25 July 2012, thousands gathered in the Jiangnanxi subway station in Guangzhou to protest the proposed abolition of Cantonese-language primetime broadcasts. Netizens used their cell phones to publicize comments in an almost real-time format as the demonstration kicked off. This July mass action in Jiangnanxi subway station, like the other demonstrations mentioned earlier in this chapter, were all mediated through the use of social media, via computers and mobile devices. The action was praised as a 'perfect victory' for the spontaneous gathering of netizens and the peaceful process by which the activity came together. Describing the convergence of online activism and street activism, outspoken intellectual and film scholar Cui Weipin observed, 'Online is more than online, netizens are more than netizens.'²⁸ Intrigued by these successful internet-facilitated events, provincial television and press outlets joined the public debate. Eventually, Guangzhou's municipal government held a conference and dispelled notions of government's intention to replace Cantonese with Mandarin on Guangzhou TV. After the conference, the proposal to change TV programming language was never implemented.²⁹ Such an official reaction was highly influenced by the transmedia flow of Cantonese activism. In this process, the reportage and discussions on 'traditional' media such as newspapers and local television were much more than auxiliary developments. This transmedia dimension plays an important role in disseminating digital moving image cultures and new cultural articulations.

Conclusion

This chapter has illustrated the ways in which Cantonese digital activism has utilized new communication technologies – such as mobile phones and the internet, in conjunction with other mass media such as television – to facilitate new cultural articulations, as manifested in online media-making and street demonstrations. Such new cultural articulations brought about new formations of moving image cultures in the new millennium. Focusing on Cantonese digital activism, I have attempted to unravel the plurality of *Chineseness*, which is obscured by the national framework in the study of Chinese media industries, particularly within the fields of political science, communications and sociology, while too textually derived in the fields of film and media studies. This is where my deployment of the *provincial* comes in; functioning within the frames of both the conceptual and the organizational, the term is arguably a more productive way to engage with the relationships that span the local, the global and the national.

The provincial, as this chapter has argued, is a nuanced way of engaging Cantonese digital activism as a distinctively cultural activism, both in relation to its modes of expression as well as its *particularness* within the Chinese mediascape. Meanwhile, the provincial offers a new perspective to move beyond the worn techno-utopia/-dystopia binary. As exemplified by the tactical production of the online video, *Rap Cantonese*, the articulations in Cantonese activism are critical of the state's monolingual policy and developmental logic. At the same time, other articulations in the same activism run the risk of reproducing existing social hierarchies such as class-based discrimination. The progressive and reactionary attributes in the same digital activism urge us to move from the question of *whether or not* certain technologies are revolutionary to the question of *how* technologies are embedded in social relations. Deploying the notion of the *provincial*, I offer a more contextual understanding of the relationship between technology and culture beyond the techno-utopia/-dystopia binary. And I believe that this contextual understanding is crucial in decoding emerging articulations and moving image cultures.

Works cited

http://economy.southcn.com/e/2010–07/12/content_13684809.htm (accessed 9 January 2014.)

http://gd.sohu.com/20100729/n273845964_1.shtml

Appadurai, Arjun. 'Grassroots globalization and the research imagination,' *Public Culture* 12, no. 1 (2000): 1–19.

Braester, Yomi. *Painting the City Red: Chinese Cinema and the Urban Contract*. Durham, NC: Duke University Press, 2010.

Chakrabarty, Dipesh. *Provincializing Europe: Postcolonial Thought and Historical Difference*. Princeton, NJ: Princeton University Press, 2000.

Chen, Gang and Jinjing Zhu. 'Behind the "green dam": internet censorship in China,' *EAI Background Brief*, no. 474 (2009).

Guo, Zhenzhi. 'Dialects and Local Media: The Cases of Kunming and Yunan TV' in Wanning Sun and Jenny Chio (eds), *Mapping Media in China: Region, Province, Locality*. London: Routledge, 2012, 47–61.

Harwit Eric and Duncan Clark. 'Shaping the internet in China. evolution of political control over network infrastructure and content,' *Asian Survey* 41, no. 3 (2001): 377–408.

Hong, Junhao. *The Internationalization of Television in China: The Evolution of Ideology, Society, and Media since the Reform*. Westport, CT: Praeger, 1998.

Leung, Lisa. 'Mediating Nationalism and Modernity: The Transnationalization of Korean Dramas on Chinese (Satellite) TV' in Chua Beng Huat and Kōichi Iwabuchi (eds), *East Asian Pop Culture: Analyzing the Korean Wave*. Hong Kong: Hong Kong University Press, 2008.

Mao, Jinqin. *Sheng shi Nanfang: Guangdong guangbo dianshi 60 nian* (*The Audiovisual South: 60 Years of Guangdong Radio and Television*). Guangzhou: Ji'nan daxue chubanshe, 2009.

Morozov, Evgeny. *The Net Delusion: The Dark Side of Internet Freedom*. New York: PublicAffairs, 2011.

Niu, Guangxia. 'Fangyan Guangbo Dianshi Jiemu Xingqi Yuanyin Ji Cunzai Zhuangtai Tanxi (Analysis of the Emergence of Dialect Broadcasting Programming),' *Qilu Yiwan*, no. 2 (2006).

—'Guangzhou ting Yueyu huodong yanshen, heping lixing jidong geng duo wangmin' [Support Cantonese Activities Expanded in Guangzhou, More Netizens were Encouraged Peacefully and Rationally], *Ziyou yazhou diantai putonghua* [Radio Free Asia], 14 September 2011. http://www.rfa.org/mandarin/yataibaodao/yue-07262010093055.html

'RAP.' YouTube, 18 July 2010. http://www.youtube.com/watch?v=s-r556Xb5L8

Shen, Simon and Shaun Breslin. *Online Chinese Nationalism and China's Bilateral Relations*. Lanham, MD: Lexington Books, 2010.

South Metropolis Daily. 12 July 2010. http://economy.southcn.com/e/2010-07/12/content_13684809.htm

Stockmann, Daniela and Mary E. Gallagher. 'Remote Control: How the Media Sustain Authoritarian Rule in China,' *Comparative Political Studies* 44, no. 4 (2011): 436–67. 14 February 2011. http://cps.sagepub.com/content/44/4/436.abstract

Sun, Wanning and Jenny Chio. *Mapping Media in China: Region, Province, Locality*. London: Routledge, 2012.

Wang, Hui and Theodore Huters. *China's New Order: Society, Politics, and Economy in Transition*. Cambridge, MA: Harvard University Press, 2003.

Wu, Xu. *Chinese Cyber Nationalism: Evolution, Characteristics, and Implications*. Lanham, MD: Lexington Books, 2007.

Yang, Guobin. *The Power of the Internet in China: Citizen Activism Online*. New York: Columbia University Press, 2009.

Yu, Deshui. *Zhu ying ren yu zhu ying de lu*. Guangdong: Luyou chubanshe, 1999.

Zhao, Yuezhi. 'Rethinking Chinese Media Studies: History, Political Economy and Culture' in Thussu Daya Kishan (ed.), *Internationalizing Media Studies: Impediments and Imperatives*. London: Routledge, 2008.

Zhou, Minglang and Hongkai Sun. *Language Policy in the People's Republic of China: Theory and Practice since 1949*. Boston: Kluwer Academic Publishers, 2004.

Zhu, Ying. *Chinese Cinema during the Era of Reform: The Ingenuity of the System.* Westport, CT: Praeger, 2003.

Notes

1. Evgeny Morozov, *The Net Delusion: The Dark Side of Internet Freedom.* New York: Public Affairs, 2011, xiii.
2. For how the internet and mobile communication have strengthened media control, surveillance and censorship, see Daniela Stockmann and Mary E. Gallagher, 'Remote Control: How the Media Sustain Authoritarian Rule in China,' *Comparative Political Studies* 44, no. 4 (2011) http://cps.sagepub.com/content/44/4/436.abstract (accessed 18 March 2013); Gang Chen and Jinjing Zhu, 'Behind the "green Dam": Internet Censorship in China,' *EAI Background Brief*, no. 474 (2009); Eric Harwit and Duncan Clark, 'Shaping the internet in China: evolution of political control over network infrastructure and content,' *Asian Survey* 41, no. 3 (2001).
3. Guobin Yang, *The Power of the Internet in China: Citizen Activism Online.* New York: Columbia University Press, 2009, 224.
4. Chinese social networking platform Sina Weibo, or simply Weibo, has been likened to Twitter.
5. The term 'flash mob' translates to *kuaishan* in Chinese, which literally means 'fast flashing,' to describe the instant mobilization, gathering and dissemination of a group of people in public space. The first flash mob gathered in Manhattan in 2003.
6. See Minglang Zhou and Hongkai Sun, *Language Policy in the People's Republic of China: Theory and Practice since 1949.* Boston: Kluwer Academic Publishers, 2004.
7. The term *netizen* is a neologism for 'internet citizen.'
8. See Hui Wang and Theodore Huters, *China's New Order: Society, Politics, and Economy in Transition.* Cambridge, MA: Harvard University Press, 2003.
9. For the study of online nationalism in China, see Simon Shen and Shaun Breslin, *Online Chinese Nationalism and China's Bilateral Relations.* Lanham, MD: Lexington Books, 2010; Xu Wu, *Chinese Cyber Nationalism: Evolution, Characteristics, and Implications.* Lanham, MD: Lexington Books, 2007.
10. Wanning Sun and Jenny Chio, *Mapping Media in China: Region, Province, Locality.* London: Routledge, 2012, 8.
11. This rationale includes derivative terms, e.g. *regionality*.
12. For more on the reform of the film industry on a national scale, see Ying Zhu, *Chinese Cinema during the Era of Reform: The Ingenuity of the System.* Westport, CT: Praeger, 2003.
13. Junhao Hong, *The Internationalization of Television in China: The Evolution of Ideology, Society, and Media since the Reform.* Westport, CT: Praeger, 1998, 78.
14. Lisa Leung, 'Mediating Nationalism and Modernity: The Transnationalization of Korean Dramas on Chinese (Satellite) TV' in *Chua Beng Huat and Kōichi Iwabuchi* (eds), *East Asian Pop Culture: Analyzing the Korean Wave.* Hong Kong: Hong Kong University Press, 2008, 56.
15. With the further commercialization of TV programming, dialect programmes emerged nationwide in the new millennium. Other provincial TV networks such as Sichuan, Hunan and Shandong TV use local dialect in news broadcasting and sitcoms. Municipal TV stations in Hangzhou, Chongqin, Shaoxin and Quanzhou also

incorporate the use of local dialects. For more, see Guangxia Niu, 'Fangyan Guangbo Dianshi Jiemu Xingqi Yuanyin Ji Cunzai Zhuangtai Tanxi (Analysis of the Emergence of Dialect Broadcasting Programming),' *Qilu Yiwan*, no. 2 (2006).

16 The Cantonese TV channels include Zhujiang channel, Sports channel and public channel from Guangdong TV networks; and the four channels of TVS (Southern Television Networks). See Jinqin Mao, *Sheng shi Nanfang: Guangdong guangbo dianshi 60 nian* (*The Audiovisual South: 60 Years of Guangdong Radio and Television*). (Guangzhou: Ji'nan daxue chubanshe, 2009), 208.

17 Ibid., 209.

18 According to CSM Media Research, the major TV and radio audience measurement research company that offers rating information for Hong Kong SAR and China.

19 The song's title translates to 'Rap Guangzhou (Canton)' and its shorthand, 'Rap Cantonese.' Both English translations are used interchangeably in reference to the video.

20 See the song's video, 'RAP.' YouTube, 18 July 2010, http://www.youtube.com/watch?v=s-r556Xb5L8 (accessed 6 March 2014).

21 Ibid.

22 Yomi Braester, *Painting the City Red: Chinese Cinema and the Urban Contract*. Durham, NC: Duke University Press, 2010, 265–6.

23 Arjun Appadurai, 'Grassroots globalization and the research imagination,' *Public Culture* 12, no. 1 (2000): 3.

24 The most famous case is that of Sun Zhigang. Sun, a college graduate in Guangzhou, was beaten to death while in police custody in 2003. His death made a heated discussion topic online and then was reported by the newspaper *Southern Metropolis Daily*. Sun's death triggered wide concern on the media and the system of police custody was abolished later on. In this case, the internet changed the agenda-setting in traditional media and eventually pushed for positive change of the legal system.

25 The flash mob gathering was reported the next day by *Southern Metropolis Daily*. http://economy.southcn.com/e/2010-07/12/content_13684809.htm (accessed 9 January 2014).

26 See note 5.

27 See http://nf.nfdaily.cn/nfdsb/content/2010-07/12/content_13677089.htm (accessed 6 March 2014).

28 See http://www.rfa.org/mandarin/yataibaodao/yue-07262010093055.html (accessed 6 March 2014).

29 See http://gd.sohu.com/20100729/n273845964_1.shtml (accessed 14 September 2011).

Part Four

Platforms and Politics

12

Interpreting *ScreenSpaces* at the Shanghai Expo and Beyond

Jeesoon Hong with Matthew D. Johnson

Introduction

Few visitors to World Expo 2010 Shanghai China (hereafter the 'Shanghai Expo') would have come away unimpressed by the ubiquity of digital screens and billboards dispersed throughout the various exhibition sites and pavilions. As an event, the Shanghai Expo seemed as focused on media as it was on commerce, with streaming video and luxurious imagery playing a key role in captivating visitor attention. This global event was not only a fairly typical industrial exhibition, in the mode of the globally influential 1937 Paris Exposition; instead the Expo's pronounced, almost excessive use of digital display technology suggested broader connections with a primarily urban phenomenon of digital screen proliferation and the ongoing creation of what I call *ScreenSpace*.

Other recent studies of public spectacle in China, particularly those focusing on the Beijing 2008 Summer Olympic Games, have also focused primarily on the role of multimedia-augmented performance in generating collective affect – for example, national pride. This chapter, however, also looks at the geography of screen dispersion within exhibitions, multiplexes and other public and semi-public spaces. In it, I argue that the increasing prevalence of digital screen technology in China's social space, extending all the way down to the local level, means that society itself has become a site of permanent exhibition and screen-mediated collectivity formation.

The themes of this chapter are the spatiality and experience of screens. Its central claim is that a close examination of visual power in contemporary China through the phenomenon of digital screens suggests that trans-regional state and commercial forces have become embedded in urban sites of upper- and middle-class consumption. As a result, screen-mediated experiences are characterized by a distinct uniformity. They are controlled by companies and state initiatives that are national, or even international, rather than regional in character. They are also powerful, both by virtue of their ubiquity and as a result of their deployment as part of multimedia configurations intended to heighten spectator engagement through sensory immersion. By deploying

Figure 12.1 The National Pavilion at the 2010 Shanghai Expo. Source: Lucia Wang, 2010. Available from: Wikimedia Commons.

the term *ScreenSpace*, which is inspired by the term *MediaSpace* as formulated by media studies scholars Nick Couldry and Anna McCarthy, I am connecting this chapter's focus on screens with the *MediaSpace* method, which examines both the spatial forms *of* media and the experiential spaces *created* by media.¹ I am also inspired by Doreen Massey's argument that 'spaces' can be imagined as processes as well as relationships.² In other words, when exploring *ScreenSpace* it is important to consider the production, distribution and consumption of screen-disseminated images, as well as the experiences that screens provide. Ultimately, the comprehension and critique of *ScreenSpace* requires that we be attentive to macro-level questions of political economy and to micro-level questions of bodily-sensory experience. What connects these two sets of questions is the technology of screens.

This chapter begins by considering *ScreenSpace* from the perspective of the Shanghai Expo, prefaced by an account of the relation of this 'screengoing' experience to the urbanizing upper- and middle-class population's encounters with *ScreenSpace* in multiplexes and mega shopping malls, such as Shanghai Stellar Cinema City (*Xingmei zhengda dianying cheng*), located in the Super Brand Mall Shanghai (*Zhengda guangchang*). I attempt to convey something of the rich interface between body and screen that these experiences imply, with particular focus on the animated 'painted scrolls' on display at China's National Pavilion (*Zhongguo guan*, see Figure 12.1) during the Shanghai Expo, as well as on 3D, digital and IMAX screens in other urban settings. Many of these screens – particularly those of the National Pavilion and digital advertising screens found in buses and mass transit systems, elevators, public squares and malls – imply a relationship to what I call a 'mobile audience'. In other words, they are intended to capture and engage the attention of individuals whose visual position, unlike that of the film-goer, is always changing. Many of my observations regarding mobile audiences were formed in the course of fieldwork conducted during the Shanghai Expo in 2010. Additionally, I examine the Jia Zhangke film *I Wish I Knew* (*Hai shang chuanqi*, dir. Jia Zhangke, 2010), which was commissioned by the Shanghai Expo's state planners. This film is significant in the connections it draws between historical and contemporary Shanghai and its incorporation of the Expo itself as a cinematic setting. These aspects of *I Wish I Knew* provide rich examples of how *ScreenSpace* experiences fuse the virtual – the reality of the screen – with the reality of the spectator's surroundings. Lastly, I examine how *ScreenSpace* produced at local levels replicates this logic of fusion, by combining multiple media and representations of past and present, into site-specific media 'events'. Here, I argue that local *ScreenSpace* can be viewed as an alternative to more ubiquitous urban *ScreenSpace* forms, based on evidence for the articulation of personal and community narratives.

The proliferation of *ScreenSpace*: Urban theatres and public screens

The production of *ScreenSpace* in China began with the growth of urban film-going as a cultural practice. Since 2002, China's cinematic exhibition industry has undergone rapid expansion following serious capital depletion during the 1990s. Specifically, exhibition spaces have proliferated at a rapid pace. In 2010, theatrical screens in China totaled 6,200, bringing in box office revenues of approximately CNY 100 billion.[3] By the end of 2011, there were in total 9,266 screens, of which 90 per cent were used for digital projection. Thus, in 2011 more than 3,000 new screens appeared – an average of more than eight new screens per day.

Of these more than 3,000 screens, roughly 60 per cent were built in what are typically called 'second-tier' and 'third-tier' cities; in other words, in cities whose growth and population makes them politically and economically subordinate to global cities such as Beijing and Shanghai. Second- and third-tier cities represented important and 'unoccupied' markets in the wake of China's rapid national economic take-off, markets that were partly captured by locally based theatre chains such as Zhejiang Shidai (Zhejiang Epoch) and Sichuan Taipingyang (Sichuan Pacific). Overall, however, the increase in screen numbers has been led by the expansion of national theatre chains including Beijing Wanda, Zhongying Xingmei and Shanghai Lianhe. These three major chains are the most profitable among China's 40 registered theatre chains as listed in 2011.

The rapid growth of the screen numbers was accompanied by great improvements in theatre quality and comfort. In other words, it was supported by investment in theatre facilities and by increased levels of film-going. Newly constructed, so-called 'five-star' theatres are replacing older venues. National and transnational theatre chains, including multiplexes attached as wings of 'mega malls' – of which Shanghai Stellar Cinema City located in the Super Brand Mall Shanghai is a prime example – helped to set the benchmark for theatre design, floor planning and furnishing. The result was improved leisure experiences for Chinese filmgoers, whose ranks were also growing in terms of numbers and spending power. Audiences were also drawn by on-screen spectacles of an increasingly overpowering and immersive nature. To that end, 3D and IMAX viewing experiences also became an intrinsic part of the new cinematic experience, as exemplified by domestic director Feng Xiaogang's *Aftershock* (*Tangshan da dizhen*, 2010), a film about the catastrophic 1976 Tangshan Earthquake and its effect on the lives of a mother and her children. At the time of its release, *Aftershock* quickly became the highest-grossing film in China's history. This film, which magnified the spectacle of disaster using IMAX technology, managed to attract a record-breaking Chinese audience even following the advent of home film viewing via computer screens. Its success simultaneously signaled the return and evolution of screen culture, both of which were triggered by new technological spectacles and patterns of consumer spending.

In addition to the growth of cinemas in second- and third-tier cities, global cities such as Shanghai are also able to support increasing numbers of screens as their residents' spending power increases. Screen abundance has, in a sense, itself become a symbol of Shanghai's globalization; the city is home to an increasingly international, increasingly diverse film culture, and has reclaimed its former place as China's cinematic capital. Like other East Asian global cities such as Seoul and Taipei, Shanghai now exhibits signs of a second key development in expansion of ScreenSpace – namely, the phenomenon of outdoor and public screens in the form of digital advertisements, displays and billboards. Advertisements on LED and plasma screens in high-traffic locations where affluent people congregate, or where people are predisposed to shop, have become big business in China, especially in large and cosmopolitan cities like Shanghai (see Figure 12.2).[4] Commercial and transport locations in these cities are now saturated with digitally displayed images encouraging consumption and, to a lesser extent, displaying political and public safety messages at the behest of China's Communist Party and subordinate government organs. In short, the number of urban screens is rising rapidly.

The crucial point here is that *ScreenSpace* has moved out of the theatre in China. So what, then, is *ScreenSpace*, when seemingly detached from its cinematic environs and dispersed throughout the wider city? Theorists of architecture and urban spaces can help us answer this question. Robert Venturi's conception of urban architecture as 'communication for the Information Age', echoed in Lev Manovich's description of the city as an 'information surface', suggests that what we are witnessing is a transformation of *all* urban leisure space, and perhaps public space generally, into the 'augmented space' of information and image delivery. *In this respect, the cinematic theatre was but a technological precursor of physical spaces overlaid with communicative 'surface' – the digital screen.*[5] For example, LED screens and digital billboards have become important sites of one-way communication within urban settings.

Figure 12.2 *ScreenSpace* along Nanjing Road, Shanghai. Source: tayloranddayumi, 2008. Available from: Wikimedia Commons.

Urban screens, like the fixed-image advertisements which preceded them, promote consumption and luxury lifestyles. The cityscape has become the imagescape, the *screenscape* and an increasingly information-rich environment. Coupled with the additional dimension of spectator experience, this screenscape becomes the sensory and technological social terrain of *ScreenSpace*.

The use of urban buildings, interiors and public spaces as digital 'skin' has also increased the actual and potential power of cities to serve as sites of political and corporate communication. And as cities are linked by political and corporate entities, the formation of trans-urban and 'new' collectivities becomes possible – not just through the political communication of the Chinese Communist Party, but also through the advertising of Chinese and multinational brandmakers. The virtual space of information has quickly become 'domesticated' (Manovich) by commerce, the suburb made 'electronic' (Norman Klein) and dissolved into to urban space – space filled with commercialized electronic billboards through a process that Otto Riewoldt calls 'brandscaping'.[6] Like politics during the Mao years, brandscaping shapes the urban cultural experience in China. While commerce has not completely eclipsed political mobilization as the most fecund source of signs and symbols in Reform Era-China, the consumerism that it encourages has become integral to China's national political economy. Indeed, the display of material achievement and abundance that characterized the Shanghai Expo was both a major event in the transformation of *ScreenSpace*, as I discuss below, and a symbolic milestone representing the compatibility of a state-sponsored and distinctly 'Chinese' identity with the realization of economic prosperity.

The animated scroll at the Shanghai Expo China pavilion: Spectator immersion and mobile experience

The Shanghai Expo China Pavilion was a symbolic and architectural achievement, a 'gate facing toward the world' as described on *Sina.com* in the months leading up to the Expo's opening.[7] Official statements accompanying the construction insisted that the China Pavilion should represent the distinctiveness of China's civilization and contemporary economic achievements – a 'crown of the East' (*Dongfang zhi guan*). The China Pavilion's intended purpose was thus to encourage domestic Expo-goers and audiences to adopt the identity of politically, economically and culturally confident subjects – national citizens, consumers and bearers of civilization. To this end, it was endowed with a particularly distinctive feature – a massive reproduction of the panoramic scroll painting 'Riverside Scene at Qingming Festival' (*Qingming heshang tu*) by the celebrated Northern Song dynasty artist Zhang Zeduan (1085–145). The digitally produced reproduction was animated, making it one of the largest and most memorable displays at the Expo and portending, perhaps, the creation of a post-industrial, urban exposition aesthetic.

The animated 'Riverside Scene at Qingming Festival' display possessed several qualities, which suggest that the intended *ScreenSpace* experience is ultimately one of spectator immersion, or overload. Within the digitally enhanced panorama, nearly every person and animal is moving or talking. The river flows by. The sky gets darker and brighter. Lanterns fade and are kindled according to whether it is 'day' or 'night'. The effect is that of a magic spell transforming the spectator, who is submerged within the insistent reality of the scroll and its human scene. The screen additionally impresses spectators with its aura of technical mastery. A medieval Chinese painting is infused with ultra-modern technology; for some Chinese spectators, this fusion was undoubtedly a source of great national pride. Finally, the size of the screen-displayed scroll, which dominated the hall-like passageway to the China Pavilion's interior, was also intended to attract and overwhelm spectators' senses. The Pavilion's scroll was 30 times larger than the original, and featured an estimated 1,000 moving figures. As one moved closer to the scroll, it became possible to hear conversation and street noises accompanying the visual impression of motion.

As a manifestation of *ScreenSpace*, the animated scroll can be placed within a global, rather than purely national, context. The relevant trend here not only points toward ubiquity of screens, but also their increasingly gargantuan size, as well as

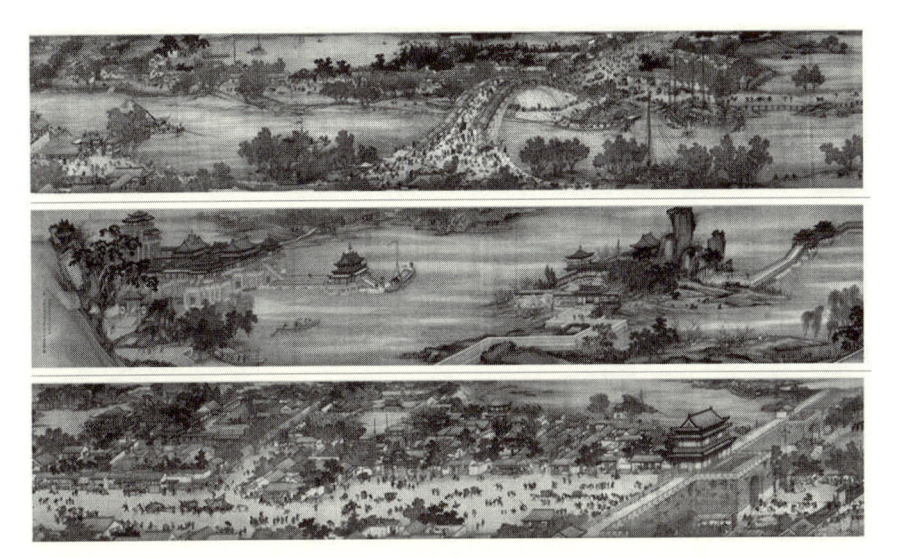

Figure 12.3 Images from Zhang Zeduan, 'Riverside Scene at Qingming Festival', early eleventh century. Available from: Wikimedia Commons.

toward international image projection and technological competition. Taking the Shanghai Expo as an example, the pavilions of numerous other countries also made use of panoramic screens and digital screen displays; in fact, the largest screens at the Expo were those installed in Saudi Arabia's pavilion. The scroll production team, headed by 'Chief Creator' Yu Zheng, was comprised of 70 employees of the Beijing-based multimedia firm Crystal CG, or Crystal Computer Graphics (*Shuijingshi shuzi keji*), which specializes in 'architectural visualization' according to the company's website. By 2010, Crystal CG had already produced work for Olympic Games ceremonies in Beijing 2008 and later, in London 2012. In other words, the animated scroll – and the phenomenon of China's *ScreenSpace* generally – must be seen in the context of China's national advance toward spectacular, screen-based forms of public and urban experience.

In addition to multi-sensory overload and scale, the digitally enhanced 'Riverside Scene at Qingming Festival' also possessed immersive qualities by virtue of its winding shape (see Figure 12.4). The massive size of the China Pavilion and its interior spaces – the main exhibition hall was 6.3 metres high and 130 metres long – was conceived with housing the enormous animated scroll in mind. Combined, the scroll and exhibition hall together created what I personally experienced in the course of my fieldwork as a 'surround spectacle'. Like cognate technologies of 'surround sound', this spectacle totally immerses the spectator, who is potentially anaesthetized, if not annihilated, by the overwhelming size of the art and attention-dominating power of its technologies. In a sense, the world that it depicted brought spectators into a virtual reality, by virtue of the fact that the screen's surface was not flat, nor was its shape

Figure 12.4 The digitally enhanced and animated 'Riverside Scene at Qingming Festival' scroll, located in the China Pavilion. Source: AlexHe34, 2010. Available from: Wikimedia Commons.

square. Rather, it surrounded and enfolded the spectator. Yet ironically, the spectator's experience is not of 'full attention' but rather 'constant distraction', in part because he/she was physically incapable of occupying a vantage point from which viewing the *entire* screen was possible. At any given moment much of the screen was hidden from view, which gave rise to a perceptual experience that was at once concentrated and distracting. One was both captured by the spectacle of the scroll *and* impelled to seek more of the image, to turn the next corner.

It could be argued that the experience of the animated screen was like the experience of the Shanghai Expo in miniature. Both were the products of national, or a range of national, attempts at seizing spectator attention and overwhelming the spectator with an experience of technological prowess and mastery as manifested by screens, commodities and architecture. Unlike national histories, the goal was not to present a grand, unifying narrative but rather to create an impressionistic experience that is – by virtue of the multi-sensory mode of its presentation – partial, distracted and fragmented, but memorable nonetheless. The cavernous space of the China Pavilion's exhibition hall not infrequently provided some respite from the animated scroll inside; the Shanghai Expo experience could easily become one of frustration and fatigue due to the massive scale of the Expo grounds and the seeming endlessness of its queues (see Figure 12.5).

Figure 12.5 Long queues and human crowds in the China Pavilion. Available from: Wikimedia Commons.

Both the China Pavilion and Shanghai Expo experiences draw attention to the strengths and limitations of *ScreenSpace* as a form of immersive spectacle, and to experiences that are becoming increasingly typical in heavily media-'skinned' urban environments. First, *ScreenSpace* is predicated on a presentation of spatial continuity. The 'Riverside Scene at Qingming Festival' animated scroll required simultaneous operation of 12 projectors on a four-minute cycle. Special software was required to coordinate problems related to the overlapping edges of the projected images, so that each segment of the panorama was presented as part of a larger whole rather than a standalone image. Without this software, the scroll would not have appeared seamless, nor would objects have been able to 'move' in a visually uninterrupted way between images. Just as the technology of film is based on the optical illusion of temporal continuity across sequential 'cuts', the technology of the animated scroll is based on the illusion of spatial continuity between projected images. To the extent that such continuity is, or is not, achieved, the immersive effect works, or doesn't.

This brings up a final point in connection with the animated scroll and invites us to contemplate the phenomenon of *mobile audience*. In the case of the China Pavilion, the audience is forced to move around, both in order to see the entire scroll and because spectators are not allowed to remain in the exhibition hall indefinitely. Even away from the main exhibition hall, visitors were conveyed through the structure by means of elevators and mini-trams – it would not be an exaggeration to describe the China Pavilion as a kind of perpetual-motion machine. One can easily imagine parallels between this situation and the conditions of a thronging urban crowd, which must also be engaged with *while in a state of constant motion*. Twenty-first century *ScreenSpace* is thus immersive not only by virtue of its digital augmentation, but also by virtue of its *shape* – its multi-surface, multi-image and, by necessity, its spatially seamless nature.

By way of a conclusion to this section, I would like to invoke Walter Benjamin's notion of 'distraction' in part to suggest that the phenomenon of *ScreenSpace*, while perhaps more immersive than could have been imagined in a pre-digital age, is not wholly new. Instead, its possibility was readily apparent in the context of the urban environment of twentieth-century Europe. Rather than casting solely negative light on distraction, Benjamin sees it as the central characteristic of modern perception and, accordingly, analyses the urban culture of distraction as collective, habitual, everyday and fragmentary. Physical mobility, however, adds greater complexity to Benjamin's conception of distraction. In particular, while film-going audiences are, at least in principle, characterized by immobility and silence, the spectators in the China Pavilion are mobile. This physical mobility enhances the experience of distraction and, as a result, the distracted, mobile audience does not simply receive messages and images in a passive manner, but has the additional option of fleeing the site of reception.

The Shanghai Expo as historical montage: Jia Zhangke's *I Wish I Knew*

In addition to the 'River Scene at Qingming Festival' animated scroll, another notable screen-based outgrowth of the Shanghai Expo was the specially commissioned film by Jia Zhangke, *I Wish I Knew*. To be sure, the choice of Jia as artistic representative seemed jarring due to the director's reputation as a Sixth Generation iconoclast and champion of personal, unvarnished storytelling which deliberately contrasted with official narratives. Though primarily a maker of feature and semi-fictional films, Jia is also celebrated for his documentaries, use of non-typecast actors and preference for local, even peripheral settings. In the end, *I Wish I Knew* was very much a familiar 'Jia Zhangke film', owing to its use of historical montage to challenge festival narratives of industrial and technological progress.

The natures of commercial exhibitions are above all spectacles attesting to the *superiority and stability of industrial society in its myriad, corporeal forms*. Whether held in London (1851), Moscow (1935), Taipei (1936), or Paris (1937) – to name but a few well-known and less well-known examples – exhibitions are devoted to the idea of 'progress' as embodied by architecture, commodities and even entertainment. The Shanghai Expo fits easily into this framework. Under the official slogan of 'Better City, Better Life' (a blatantly pro-urbanization mantra), the entire event was intended to represent the reality of China's own national progress in disparate areas such as construction, technology, arts and culture, public etiquette and, more generally, civilization. Like expos of nineteenth-century Europe, visitors to the Shanghai Expo were predominantly of the working class, and the Expo's focal point was commodities – the fruits of industrial progress and national wealth. The vision of a globalized, urban present and future on display at the Expo was thus directly related to the party-state's ideological project of promising urban lifestyles and elevated living standards.[8]

Along with the Beijing 2008 Olympic Games (the 'Beijing Olympics'), to which it was explicitly compared in official statements and media reports, the Shanghai Expo was portrayed by its official partners and promoters intended to promote globally an image of China as a world-class, techno-cultural superpower. However, one subtle difference existed between the Beijing Olympics vision of China and the Shanghai Expo vision. Whereas the opening ceremony of the former event celebrated China's superiority as a global *producer* of technology, goods and ideas, at the Shanghai event China was recognized as the world's greatest *consumer* market. Both events, however, strove to depict China as having moved on from its economic position as a producer of cheap consumer goods and middle tier within global manufacturing value chains, by putting forward a new national 'brand' of China as the world's greatest past, present and future civilization. Yet despite all of this elevated rhetoric, the steady drumbeat of commerce was never faint. More than 90 per cent of Shanghai Expo visitors were Chinese citizens, and the national pavilions of other countries – unlike China's own national pavilion – served as platforms for making direct appeals asking China's domestic consumers to purchase goods, educational degrees and travel products from abroad.

All of these developments make the decision to include, as one of the Expo's cultural centrepieces, a semi-realistic, semi-fantastic 'documentary' of Shanghai and its history somewhat incongruous. Commissioned by the Expo's planners and screened in the event site's Cultural Center, Jia Zhangke's *I Wish I Knew*, used interviews, urban tableaux and a ghostly (or angelic) figure to deliver a personal meditation on China's complex past. In form, *I Wish I Knew* is both an interview-based documentary and a historical montage; its elements include first-person narratives woven together with images of past and present-day Shanghai. Additionally, Jia employs other cinematic representations of the city, as well as a recurring actor – played by Jia's wife, Zhao Tao – who plays a ghost-like role in the film, 'haunting' the contemporary city by gazing upon its architecture and linking its contemporary urban space to images, sounds and stories associated with Shanghai's history. Other scholars have reviewed *I Wish I Knew* at length, with the basic gist of their comments being that Jia presents a sensitive, polysemic reading of Shanghai's cosmopolitan and tumultuous heritage.[9] Here I would like to draw attention to two critical details: the first scene and the ghostly figure of Zhao Tao.

Critics such as Xu Jing, Dudley Andrew, and Tony Rayns have paid serious attention to the first scene (see Figure 12.6). For instance, in the co-authored review, Xu Jing and Dudley Andrew interestingly juxtapose the 'imperious brass lion's gaze' with Jia Zhangke's own gaze: 'A man lovingly buffs the lion, one of a pair sitting at the entrance to the Bank of Communication. Red lettering announces this to be 'A Film by Jia Zhangke', who thereby adopts the lion's view as his own'.[10]

In contrast to the Expo's official vision of urban development and renewal, Jia meditates at length upon the literal destruction that Shanghai's economic growth has caused. A stunning reverse shot from the vantage point of the lion includes three horizons of Shanghai's skyline: debris of demolished buildings, colonial architecture from the early twentieth century and anonymous, mushrooming skyscrapers (see Figure 12.7). One may even detect in Jia's cinematic 'gaze' a visual manifesto that recalls Walter Benjamin's 'Theses on the Philosophy of History'. As Benjamin writes:

Figure 12.6 Bund, bank, lions and man in Jia Zhangke's *I Wish I Knew* (2010).

Figure 12.7 Reverse shot: surveying urban development and debris. *I Wish I Knew* (2010).

A [Paul] Klee painting named 'Angelus Novus' shows an angel looking as though he is about to move away from something he is fixedly contemplating. His eyes are staring, his mouth is open, his wings are spread. This is how one pictures the angel of history. His face is turned toward the past. Where we perceive a chain of events, he sees one single catastrophe which keeps piling wreckage upon wreckage and hurls it in front of his feet. The angel would like to stay, awaken the dead, and make whole what has been smashed. But a storm is blowing from Paradise; it has got caught in his wings with such violence that the angel can no longer close them. The storm irresistibly propels him into the future to which his back is turned, while the pile of debris before him grows skyward. This storm is what we call progress.[11]

Whether or not Jia had Benjamin's appraisal of the 'Angelus Novus' painting in mind when he directed *I Wish I Knew*, his contrast of Shanghai's urban debris with its ongoing re-construction does call into question the degree to which his film supported the Expo-sanctioned view of progress as desirable and inevitable.

Following the 'lion' scene, the Jia-directed camera moves deeper into the city, buoyed by the natural rhythms of gentle breezes and the lapping waves of the Huangpu River. However, if we apply the logic of the first scene to the entire film, the puzzling presence of the ghostly figure, played by Zhao Tao, can be read as a the lion's avatar (and thus, by extension, a symbol of Jia's own historical gaze), and thus as the angel of history in Klee's painting. In contrast to a similar cinematic figure, Wim Wenders' 'angel of Berlin,' Jia's Shanghai angel is dressed in an unfussy white T-shirt and carries a collapsible fan (see Figure 12.8), whereas the Berlin angel appears in Wenders' films wearing a long black coat and adorned with a pair of white wings. The Shanghai angel is worldly; her modest fan represents a rejoinder to the notion of historical progress, or 'wind,' as progressive or divinely ordained. Toward the end of *I Wish I Knew*, following a series of live interviews arranged as a history of twentieth-century Shanghai, Zhao Tao reaches the Expo site itself, figuratively as well as literally locating her in the present day (see Figure 12.9). Somewhat amazingly, the scene that greets her is not a vibrant image of urban efflorescence, but rather a gloomy ruin littered with debris – the wreckage piled at the angel of history's feet.

Much of the rest of *I Wish I Knew* also conveys Jia's implied skepticism concerning claims for a better future. The film reaches its emotional climax during a heart-rending interview with Wang Peimin, the child of a Communist revolutionary executed at the hands of Chiang Kai-shek's Nationalist Party more than 60 years ago. At the same time, its historically agnostic visual sublime reappears in a scene in which dusty construction workers carry bag after bag of cement. This neo-socialist allegory is minimalist and modernist rather than tragic or heroic. A labouriously slow and repetitive rhythm, conspicuous absence of sound and aestheticization of the construction site's dust, muted hues and debris signal an ambiguous stance toward

Figure 12.8 A ghostly Zhao Tao haunts the rubble-strewn Bund …

Figure 12.9 … and is juxtaposed against the site of the Shanghai Expo. *I Wish I Knew* (2010).

Shanghai's urban transformation. Toward the end of the film, Jia's documentary representations are pushed aside by interviews coupled with strident and colourful 'found footage' from post-revolutionary propaganda films. However, Jia's signature aesthetics of urban detritus and toil is reiterated at the very moment when the Shanghai Expo makes its cinematic appearance. Rather than a festival celebrating technological progress and confidence in the future, Jia's Expo is literally in ruins. Rather than global spectacle of the present, or an idealized vision of China's traditional past (a la the Beijing Olympics), Jia's introduction to the Expo comes in the form of an interview-based, living memory of twentieth-century events and, ultimately, a vision of historically directionless destruction.

According to official Chinese media sources and the Shanghai Expo's own publicity materials, *I Wish I Knew* was simply a 'documentary about Shanghai'. This bland formulation conceals both the complexity of the film's aesthetics and the ambiguity of its stance toward Shanghai's present and future. Yet as I have argued here, its view of the twentieth-century past does not ultimately romanticize 'old Shanghai'. Rather, Jia's 18 interviewees provide a range of cautionary object lessons that are not reflected by the film's visual narrative – one must *listen* for them. With respect to *ScreenSpace*, the example of Jia Zhangke's commissioned work for the Shangahi Expo brings home another important lesson. Just as the ghostly character played by Zhao Tao in *I Wish I Knew* haunts the city of Shanghai, state – artist partnerships are often 'haunted' by the overlapping agendas and meanings with which top international talent like Jia Zhangke regularly infuse their work. The production of *I Wish I Knew* demonstrates that *ScreenSpace* content may be, as in the case of the augmented 'Riverside Scene at Qingming Festival' scroll, technologically and artistically sophisticated. Yet the messages implied by *I Wish I Knew* also demonstrate that experience of *ScreenSpace* is nonetheless rendered 'open' by virtue of artist and audience perspectives. This is a familiar dynamic in the history of political art, with examples ranging from the Roosevelt-era Works Progress Administration in the United States to the production of literature under totalitarian leaders like Stalin and Mao. To the extent that effective and alluring communication depends on talent that state-appointed cultural managers lack, or on audience responses that cannot be assured, ideological control over *ScreenSpace* remains incomplete.

Alternative *ScreenSpace*: Jian Yi and the Qingyuanshe 'memory project'

As I have described, a combination of commercial screens, political screens and cinematic screens are among the major constituent elements of *ScreenSpace* in urban China today. Personal media devices and computers represent another form of *ScreenSpace* technology also deserving of close consideration. However, I believe that studies of personal screens will ultimately support my basic points – that *ScreenSpace* is rapidly proliferating, and that its content is largely determined by powerful social forces such as corporations, governments and well-funded media producers. As my examination of the primary screen attractions of the Shanghai Expo has also shown, the collective experience generated by public *ScreenSpace* is characterized by virtual participation in spectacles of economic abundance, cosmopolitanism, cultural and technological achievement and national progress. However, while such experiences are immersive, they are not fully 'closed'. To return to the example of Jia Zhangke's *I Wish I Knew*, *ScreenSpace* platforms and systems remain open to representational strategies are not entirely 'harmonious' *vis-à-vis* dominant ideologies and interests. And, returning to the site of the Shanghai Expo itself, it is abundantly obvious that that spell of *ScreenSpace* may be perpetually challenged by the sensory experience of long lines, crowds and the restless, jostling circulation of bodies. Ordinary people literally push back against their built environment with its digital 'skin' and thus puncture – if only for a few critical moments – the continuum of seamless *ScreenSpace* immersion.

Another important characteristic of *ScreenSpace*, and its potential, is interactivity between producer, audience, and represented image. Alternatives to *ScreenSpace*'s dominant forms are thus generated both by new technologies (although these may be quickly subsumed into pre-existing hierarchies) and by new social actors. In this section, I examine one example of *ScreenSpace* that reflects one possible alternative to the dominant culture of *ScreenSpace* as it exists in strongholds of political and economic power such as Shanghai. Here my argument is that a truly balanced perspective on *ScreenSpace* requires acknowledgment of the activities of 'amateur' or independent filmmakers and videographers. In my view, the ranks of these individuals are growing due in part to the increasing affordability of image-making technology – digital cameras, editing software and display platforms – and in part due to a corresponding rise in activity related to the archiving and preservation of experience. Neither of these developments are strictly local phenomena. Memory preservation via digital technology is undoubtedly a global practice. However, it is place-based – that is to say, particular to the subjectivities of those whose lives interact with a particular geographic location.

The case I want to highlight here is a regional documentary movement. The primary proponent of this movement is Jian Yi, an independent documentary filmmaker, community organizer and international cultural consultant. Jian Yi's career as a filmmaker began in 2005, when he joined Wu Wenguang's China Villagers Documentary Project (*Zhongguo cunmin yingxiang jihua*) as the project's public communication expert (see Chapter 14). In 2009 Jian Yi completed a documentary on government-promoted 'red tourism' in China titled *New Socialist Climax* (*Hongse zhi lü*, 2007–9). 'Red tourism' (also the Chinese title of Jian Yi's film) is intended to bolster popular support for the Communist Party by encouraging citizens to revisit sites with special significance in the history of the Party's revolution. While producing the film, Jian Yi returned to his home city of Ji'an, in Jiangxi Province, and participated directly in the establishment of the IFCHINA Original Studio and Participatory Documentary Center (hereafter the IFCHINA Studio) on the campus of Jinggangshan University.[12] The studio's Chinese name, *Qingyuanshe* avoids deploying sensitive words like 'documentary' altogether.[13] Like Wu Wenguang's China Villagers Documentary Project, the main activity promoted by *Qingyuanshe* is documentary filmmaking by inhabitants of Ji'an and its surrounding environs – participatory video. In Jian Yi's words, the goal is to make ordinary Chinese 'camera literate'.

The IFCHINA Studio was in full operation at the same time as the Shanghai Expo. If one of the goals of the Expo was to create a new image of China and a unified experience of national unity and pride for Chinese citizens, the goal of the IFCHINA Studio founders was something quite different altogether – to use a second-tier city as a staging ground for a *multimedia memory project* emphasizing individual histories over collective narratives. Because Jinggangshan's position in Communist Party histories as the birthplace or cradle of the revolution, Jian Yi and others have expanded their project to include the memories of 'red tourists' passing through the city. The IFCHINA Studio serves as a repository for photographs collected *from* tourists, which are historical in nature. In short, it is a kind of archive for personal image and memory. Another important aspect of the studio's activities is oral history collection; it also engages in the collection and archiving of historical or local documents. According to Jian Yi, one of the principal goals of these activities is to record the memories of those older than 90 years of age, whose memories are on the verge of passing out of the world. The IFCHINA Studio itself, supplemented by the filmmaking of Jian Yi and a cast of amateur directors, has held regular screenings and exhibitions for the community that make use of these memory materials.

Accompanying this 'memory project' is a parallel architecture project, and this leads me to my final point concerning alternative *ScreenSpace*. With the assistance of foreign architects, *Qingyuanshe* helps local residents to rebuild their houses in the traditional and climatically appropriate architectural style of the region. In return, house owners allow the local community to use a part of the house, such as the front yard or the wall, to display their memorabilia and testimony. In the long term, *Qingyuanshe*'s organizers plan to add recorded oral testimony from the residents, to be replayed by passers-by and tourists at the touch of a button; or, for multi-media displays incorporating image projection. Using these methods, entire villages become information- and memory-rich museums. The architectural goals of the *Qingyuanshe* memory project thus promote *ScreenSpace* of another kind – a localized, individualized experience circulated via multiple 'platforms' within the community and with deep resonance for the members of that community. While the IFCHINA Studio enjoys a global reputation among artists and participatory video advocates, its ideal model is that of an organic, non-didactic relationship with communities within China. Within this alternative *ScreenSpace*, a more profound form of interactivity between individual producers and audiences is taking shape.

Critics might challenge the IFCHINA Studio's claims to collect and re-circulate unfiltered, authentic personal experience. Or they might object to the idea that the open-ended collection of personal testimony represents a convincing alternative to official history and dominant forms of collective identity. Regardless, the IFCHINA Studio is among the vanguard of a new wave of memory projects now on display in China and abroad, and which do seem to differ from the more dominant modes of *ScreenSpace* I have explored in earlier sections. Unlike Jia Zhangke's *I Wish I Knew*, the IFCHINA Studio filmmakers largely eschew montage for more direct videography – the uninterrupted recording of the act of remembrance. This mode of 'individualizing' narration is increasingly popular amongst amateur and independent Chinese filmmakers, as described elsewhere in this volume (see, for example, Chapter 1). Of equal concern, however, is the reliance of such projects on foreign funding. Both Jian Yi and the IFCHINA Studio have received significant support from institutions outside of China, to the extent that the scope of their activities would appear to depend on such support. The future of alternative *ScreenSpace* in China, though promising, appears fragile.

Conclusion

With the advent of new media platforms such as the internet, some scholars have envisioned the corresponding rise of new forms of social organization and subjectivity. What new kind of subjectivities will arise within China's distinctive media environment? Will new, globally networked collectivities emerge to challenge existing orders? How will new media platforms empower urban workers, such as grey-collar (*huiling*) employees who perform repetitive productive tasks within white-collar technology industries? Who will be the new consumers of information delivered via China's expanding *ScreenSpace*? Will constant real-time media engagement result in a digital revolution, or digital paralysis? Who will hold the upper hand in this brave new world – the digital working class, corporations, or the state?

This chapter has not sought to directly address these questions, but it has endeavoured to show that first-, second- and third-tier cities are the most important sites for addressing them. By privileging *only* Beijing on Shanghai, we run the risk of overlooking alternative dynamics taking place in more peripheral locations such as Ji'an. I have focused much of my analysis on Shanghai because of its visibility within the constellation of global urban centres and because it represents one of the densest nodes of urban *ScreenSpace* within China. What we learn from an examination of the Shanghai Expo's screen-based spectacles is that the interface between individuals and screens can no longer be thought of in purely cinema- or television-derived terms – technologies, and built urban environments, are changing too fast. The implication is that looking for evidence of state and commercial power – and challenges to this power – in the movie theatre is no longer an adequate methodology for understanding how the experience of Chinese citizens is mediated through screens, who does the mediating and so on. Investigators into screen culture may need to be less like screen critics and more like urban anthropologists; fieldwork is an increasingly necessary component of research and informed analysis. What we learn from fieldwork is that there is real substance to the Chinese government's efforts to transform its urban and industrial structure toward a *more* urbanized, *more* digital-rich form. China is more connected than ever before, with one of the most recent waves of connectivity emerging from its post-WTO accession 'universal service plan' for public cultural service (*gonggong wenhua fuwu*).[14] The Communist Party-led state takes supremacy in media industries seriously, as part of its agenda to become a comprehensive global power – a superpower. The party-state's power is palpable in *MediaSpace*, not only in *ScreenSpace*. Media technology, including digital screens, is seen as a crucial puzzle to be solved *en route* to resolving a range of issues ranging from macroeconomic dislocation to political atrophy. Commercial enterprise may yet gain strength through advertising and political influence but, as the Shanghai Expo reminds us, the state remains China's pivotal economic and historical actor. This ideology is reproduced in *ScreenSpace*, where the biggest spectacles are essentially state-created, or state-financed.

And yet, just as the spectacles of the Shanghai Expo – its architecture, digital displays and audiovisual content – draw from global reservoirs of technology and human talent, so too have China's alternative and independent media producers nurtured their own transnational linkages with foreign institutions and funding sources. The result is a (still) diverse media mélange which is sometimes rendered globally invisible by China's national branding efforts. Who are the most trusted sources of news? Whose statements will be taken at face value? This question is not China's alone. As evidenced by the recent WikiLeaks 'incident', the dispersion and control of sensitive information flows are globally coordinated. This is not a new issue, but it is an important one when we consider how *ScreenSpace* in China will interact with the insistent tide of network and information sprawl. Alternative media eddies may exist within internet-connected bedrooms, fiscally marginal cities and the production facilities of well-funded entrepreneurs. In such *ScreenSpace*, consumerism quickly asserts itself as the dominant cultural. However, just as digital media ushered in the 'age of the amateur producer' – thus displacing an earlier, top-down 'age of technological reproduction' – evidence for dispersed, participatory modes of public image creation seems to likewise anticipate an unpredictable future for *ScreenSpace*.

Works cited

Benjamin, Walter. *Illuminations*. New York: Harcourt Brace Jovanovich, 1968.
Chan, Yik-Chin and Matthew D. Johnson. 'New Paradigms of Public Service Policy, Regulation, and Reform in China's Television Industry'. In Gregory Ferrell Lowe and Jeanette Steemers (eds), *Regaining the Initiative in Public Service Media (RIPE@2011 Reader)*. Nordic Information Centre for Media and Communications Research, 2012.
Connery, Christopher. 'Better City, Better Life'. *boundary 2*, Vol. 28, No. 2 (2011).
Couldry, Nick and Anna McCarthy. *MediaSpace: Place, Scale, and Culture in a Media Age*. London: Routledge, 2004.
Hempton, John. 'Focus Media: What Happened to the Airports?' *Bronte Capital*, 26 September 2012. http://brontecapital.blogspot.co.uk/2012/09/focus-media-what-happened-to-airports.html
Gumbrecht, Hans (ed.). *Mapping Benjamin: The Work of Art in the Digital Age*. Stanford: Stanford University Press, 2003.
Lock, Margaret M. and Judith Farquhar (eds). *Beyond the Body Proper: Reading the Anthropology of Material Life*. Durham: Duke University Press, 2007.
Manovich, Lev. 'The Poetics of Urban Media Surfaces,' *First Monday* (Special Issue No. 4: Urban Screens), http://journals.uic.edu/ojs/index.php/fm/article/view/1545/1460
Massey, Doreen. *For Space*. London: Sage Publications, 2005.
Rayns, Tony. 'I Wish I Knew,' *Cinema Scope*, 44 (Fall 2010).
Richter, Gerhard. *Walter Benjamin and the Corpus of Autobiography*. Detroit: Wayne State University Press, 2000.
Riewoldt, Otto. *Brandscaping: Worlds of Experience in Retail Design*. Heidelberg, New York, Dordrecht and London: Birkhäuser, 2010.
Xu, Jing and Dudley Andrew. 'The Lion's Gaze: Truth and Legend in *I Wish I Knew*,' *Film Criticism*, Vol. 36, No. 1 (Fall 2011).
Zhongguo dianyingjia xiehui chanye yanjiu zhongxin. *Zhongguo dianying chanye yanjiu baogao* [Research Report on China's Film Industry]. Beijing: Zhongguo dianying chubanshe, 2012.

Notes

1 See Nick Couldry and Anna McCarthy, *MediaSpace: Place, Scale, and Culture in a Media Age*. Routledge, 2004.
2 See Doreen Massey, *For Space*. Sage, 2005.
3 Zhongguo dianyingjia xiehui chanye yanjiu zhongxin, *Zhongguo dianying chanye yanjiu baogao* [Research Report on China's Film Industry] (Beijing: Zhongguo dianying chubanshe, 2012), 40–1.
4 John Hempton, 'Focus Media: What Happened to the Airports?' *Bronte Capital*, 26

September 2012, http://brontecapital.blogspot.co.uk/2012/09/focus-media-what-happened-to-airports.html (accessed 9 January 2014).
5. See Lev Manovich, 'The Poetics of Urban Media Surfaces,' *First Monday* (Special Issue No. 4: Urban Screens), http://journals.uic.edu/ojs/index.php/fm/article/view/1545/1460 (accessed 9 January 2014).
6. See Otto Riewoldt, *Brandscaping: Worlds of Experience in Retail Design*. Birkhäuser, 2010.
7. 'Zhongguo guan jun gong: Shanghai shibohui jijiang kaiqi mianxiang shijie de damen' [The magisterial construction of the China Pavilion: the Shanghai Expo's gate to the world is about to open], Sina.com.cn, 9 February 2010, http://news.sina.com.cn/c/2010-02-09/072917069097s.shtml (accessed 14 March 2014).
8. Christopher Connery, 'Better City, Better Life,' *boundary 2*, Vol. 28, No. 2 (2011): 207–27.
9. See Xu Jing and Dudley Andrew, 'The Lion's Gaze: Truth and Legend in *I Wish I Knew*,' *Film Criticism*, Vol. 36, No. 1 (Fall 2011); Tony Rayns, 'I Wish I Knew,' *Cinema Scope*, 44 (Fall 2010).
10. Xu and Andrew, 'The Lion's Gaze,' 29.
11. Walter Benjamin, *Illuminations* (New York: Harcourt Brace Jovanovich, 1968), 257–8.
12. http://ifchinastudio.wix.com/ifchina#!__home (accessed 14 March 2014).
13. http://ifchinastudio.wix.com/ifchina#!__home-ch (accessed 14 March 2014).
14. See Yik-Chin Chan and Matthew D. Johnson, 'New Paradigms of Public Service Policy, Regulation, and Reform in China's Television Industry' in Gregory Ferrell Lowe and Jeanette Steemers (eds), *Regaining the Initiative in Public Service Media (RIPE@2011 Reader)*. Nordic Information Centre for Media and Communications Research, 2012.

13

Regarding the Grassroots Chinese Independent Film Festivals: Modes of Multiplicity and Abnormal Film Networking

Ma Ran

When the first Beijing International Film Festival (BJIFF, *Beijing Guoji Dianyingji*) kicked off in late April 2011, the eighth Beijing Documentary Film Festival (DOChina) was called off 'due to unexpected reasons' (*yin'gu*). On the BJIFF's official website it is not difficult to find a plethora of celebratory rhetoric that shows off how much this state-sanctioned film festival – one of the major three in mainland China – has achieved, given its unbelievably short preparation period and the glamour it staged with an illustrious line-up of international stars, filmmakers and top film festival directors. Not surprisingly, as one of the leading Chinese independent filmmakers and a festival programmer himself, Ying Liang decided to call it 'the most bizarre film festival' ever.[1]

If such a newborn official festival as BIJFF appears 'bizarre' to acute observers/practitioners who are familiar with the Chinese independent film scene like Ying Liang, then it indeed poses a unique question about how do we approach unofficial, independent film festivals like DOChina in the People's Republic of China. For instance, why are independent festivals in China considered less abnormal if their survival is not only contingent on the overall financial condition needed to produce these cultural venues, but is also constantly haunted by the seemingly whimsical decisions made by the 'relevant bureaus' of the state apparatus to cancel these film events?

In their innovative contribution to film festival studies, Thomas Elsaesser and Marijke de Valck have built up the 'international film festival network' model utilizing Niklas Luhmann's system theory, Manuel Castells' theory of the 'space of flows' and 'space of place,' and particularly utilizing Bruno Latour's 'actor network theory' (ANT).[2] According to de Valck, there are two advantages in deploying the Latourian theory of network to study film festival phenomenon: it presupposes relational interdependence and includes both humans and non-human actors as objects of study.[3] On the other hand, she also admits that one limitation of the ANT approach is that it 'offers few critical tools for assessing power relations.' She articulates that under such a theoretical framework, within the power grid of the network, the differentiation between prestigious, major film festivals and less important, small film festivals can be easily identified as 'task division,' with the major media events as central nodes in the network whereas the smaller festivals perform specific functions 'by supporting new talented directors, paying attention to specific genres or serving as a cultural-political platform for (ethnic) minority groups.'[4] She also proposes that Michael Hardt and Antonio Negri's notion of empire can be deployed to critique how neo-colonial tendencies still lurk in the global festival network – with Western festivals, funding and taste wielding greater influence over world cinemas.[5] Meanwhile, she believes by connecting to Saskia Sassen and Castells' theorization about the 'global space economy,' the spatial and temporal dimensions of film festivals can be further examined 'to assert how power relations on various scales are constituted.'[6] Partially sharing de Valck's view regarding Latourian thinking, I hope my focus on the localized/regionalized, circulatory/exhibition networks of Chinese independent cinema opens up more critical space to engage with the loci of power in the film festival network, given that Chinese grassroots film festivals usually operate semi-underground and raise intricate questions regarding artistic autonomy, state power and marketization of culture in postsocialist China.

Although the ANT approach will still be a major thread in the arguments presented here, it is also important for us to adjust the critical lenses. Take, for example, Wang Shu-jen and Jonathan J. H. Zhu's illuminating piece, 'Mapping Film Piracy in China,' which extends Latour's ANT framework to canvass the film piracy networks in China. By endorsing Sassen's argument that the 'national-global duality' tends to overemphasize the forces of globalization *vis-à-vis* the power of the state, Wang and Zhu believe that globalization should be regarded as 'conceptually reconstituted "in terms of a transnational geography of centrality of multiple linkages and strategic concentrations of material infrastructure."'[7] They agree with the Latourian perspective that the network in ANT should be considered 'as the summing up of interactions through various kinds of devices, inscriptions, forms and formulae, into a very local, very practical, very tiny locus where no interaction is not framed.'[8]

Overall Wang and Zhu highlight the following aspects in re-conceptualizing the loci of power: (1) the links and nodes of the network; (2) the directions, movements, and forces of the lines that connect the nodes and points; and (3) the realignment of spatial organizations and cooperation among various networks and agencies.[9] I will reappropriate these three aspects to structure this chapter. It will accentuate the study of independent cinema-related *minjian*, or grassroots film festivals, as well as several related circulation/exhibition initiatives, entities and other connected networks, which have constituted what I have tentatively proposed as the '*minjian* film festival network' (the significance of '*minjian*' and 'grassroots' will be elaborated further later in this chapter). Though embedded in its local specificities, China's grassroots film festivals and related entities have developed their regional and global linkages by interacting with and counteracting various networks and agencies such as the general public, the party–state, the international film festival circuit and mainstream film industries; specific attention is paid in this chapter to what Wang and Zhu have referred to as directions, movements and mechanisms connecting the nodes and points of these networks.

The research methodology here is underpinned by case studies based on field trips and participant observation. It also involves archival documents including festival catalogues, media reportage and discussions circulating on social media platforms such as the microblog *Sina Weibo* (the so-called 'Chinese Twitter'). In light of this amount of material, this chapter is composed of three sections: first, I attempt to periodize the domestic exhibition history of Chinese independent cinema and to map out related circulatory entities in order to contextualize the evolution of grassroots film festivals in the country. Then the second part of this chapter explores the nodes and points of the '*minjian* film festival network' by focusing on Beijing-based Fanhall Studio, Li Xianting's Film Fund, and the Chongqing Independent Film & Video Festival (CIFVF, since 2007) in western China. In the conclusion, we shall return to the discussion of the significance of '*minjian* film festival network' by rethinking how the network works to engage with the independent film community as well as today's Chinese society.

Two stages of exhibiting Chinese independent cinema

As a veteran curator and dedicated endorser of Chinese independent films, Zuo Jing has suggested that the first stage of circulating Chinese indie cinema domestically lasted roughly from the late 1990s to the early 2000s. Grassroots cinéphile/filmmaking groups were established in several major Chinese cities during this period, and the core activities of such groups revolve around 'film appreciation – discussion – exhibition – filmmaking'.[10] Their exhibition and screening activities generally took place at cafes, bars, or other itinerant venues – and usually emanated from culturally liberal colleges and universities and artist communities. Some of the major cinéphile/film groups still active today include U-theque Organization (*yuanyinghui*) in Shenzhen and Guangzhou, Touchfilm (*shijianshe*) in Beijing, Rear Window (*houchuang kandianying*) in Nanjing, Film 101 Studio (*101 dianying gongzuoshi*) in Shanghai, Free Cinema (*ziyou dianying*) in Shenyang and Kunming Film Study Group (*dianying xuexi xiaozu*) in Kunming.[11] It has been argued that the introduction of Digital Video cameras into PRC and the popularization of DV filmmaking among the public since the late 1990s have partially reshaped the semi-underground screening and exhibition practices of these cinéphile groups.[12] Screening events by such groups had to accommodate more Do-It-Yourself visual productions, among which there were a certain amount of independent documentary films.[13] This trend tightened the pre-existing ties between film groups nationwide, since in required stronger coordination between the groups, filmmakers and so forth, which also laid the basis for the primary organizational format of grassroots film festivals. On the other hand, China's extensive piracy film networks, the timely upgrading and economization of hardware such as the VCD and DVD players, and the expansion of the internet since late 1990s has made it convenient and affordable to collect (download) and consume pirated versions of Euro-American arthouse films that were once the major sources for film groups' screenings. Consequently, it became redundant for such groups to programme and showcase global arthouse cinema. What Jia Zhangke has described as the privatized/personalized film viewing experience underscored by its democratic connotation has also facilitated the collapse of collective viewing activities in the form of cinéphile organizations.[14] Today, most once-active film groups have ceased to exist after a few years of activities, yet unconventional venues and spaces still prove vital in the circulation of Chinese independent cinema.

As Zuo Jing points out, what has characterized the second stage exhibiting practices of Chinese independent cinema is the way several major organizations have cooperatively functioned as 'platforms' or 'interfaces' to facilitate the exhibition, research, publishing, production and distribution.[15] These major platforms, as delineated by Zuo in 2009, are: Fanhall Studio (since 2001), Yunnan Multicultural Visual Festival (YunFest, since 2003), China Independent Film Festival (CIFF, since 2003), Caochangdi Workstation Art Center (CCD, since 2005), Indie Workshop (since 2005), Li Xianting's Film Fund (since 2006) and China Independent Film Archive (CIFA, since 2009). Arguably, the first Unrestricted New Image Festival (hereafter UNIF) in 2001 was the first grassroots film festival held in the PRC. It was collectively organized by three cinéphile groups (Film 101 Club, Free Cinema and U-theque Organization), and was financially supported by the Guangzhou-based liberal newspaper *Southern Weekend* and the Beijing-based IT company *Beida-Online*. With its open call for Chinese independent films produced since 1996, the festival received 109 submissions (including 35 documentaries), which were either filmed with DV cameras or equipment borrowed from TV stations. UNIF went smoothly with its screenings held at the Beijing Film Academy (BFA) until the fourth day of the festival, when the university deemed a queer film called *The Box* (*Hezi*, 2001) inappropriate, and the whole event was suddenly called off. This led the core organizer Du Qingchun, who is also a BFA professor, to complain that 'nobody would give you a reason [for why the festival was cancelled], since in China a film festival is not supposed to be organized by the grassroots.'[16] Though thwarted in Beijing, the festival continued to tour in other cities such as Shenyang, Xi'an, Hangzhou and Shanghai. Unfortunately, UNIF never had a second season. In addition, the First Beijing Gay and Lesbian Film Festival (also China Queer Film Festival), which took place in the winter of 2001, was also forced to cancel its screenings and panels, and it was not until 2004 that the second China Queer Film Festival pulled off an uninterrupted platform to showcase queer-themed works both from China and abroad.[17] Both festivals, through their courageous experimentation with film content as well as organizing format, have provided some early templates for other grassroots film festivals to follow suit. It is quite common that emerging grassroots film festivals take shape from the organization and networking of local/regional cinéphile groups and further rely on their activities to thrive, specifically regarding the latter's leverage at the grassroots level in: (1) film selection and programming; (2) venue management; (3) audience development; and (4) publicity and sponsorship. The two pioneering film festivals are no exception. Such a pattern of cooperation has been repeated with other emerging film festivals, such as with the successful launching of YunFest at Kunming in 2003.[18] Particularly, for the emerging festivals, there are lessons to be learned from dealing with the censors and other potential regulating bodies (such as the National Security Bureau, or even the Ministry of Education, if any university is to take part in these events); they have been cautious about the unstated forbidden zones of the state control. Even if both UNIF and the queer festival were forced to cancel by the authorities, the fact that they were organized in the first place speaks to the evolution of Chinese indie cinema and the independent film community's demand for engaging with the public. Additionally, grassroots film festivals have actually long been considered essential to the global film festival network's circulation and exhibition of Chinese indie films.

I argue that the conceptualizations of '*minjian*' and 'grassroots' and the ideas of being 'independent' and 'alternative' have provided various nuanced sociocultural and political underpinnings to rethink the circulation/exhibition network of Chinese indie cinema: these perspectives can help to map out the intersecting networks and relations among the party–state, Chinese film industry, global film market, international film festival network and the general public. Based on his ethnographic study of film clubs and documentary screening events (such as DOChina) in Beijing during the early 2000s, Seio Nakajima relies on Foucauldian theories of power and agency to approach the relationship between grassroots screening clubs and the Chinese film bureaucracy; he posits that the independently produced Chinese documentaries are 'independent' exactly because 'they engage with the influence emanating from the sphere of the state and the economy.'[19] Nakajima's insights also raise intriguing questions concerning the 'status of independence' for grassroots film festivals, whereas I suppose an understanding of the Chinese word '*minjian*,' which shares a similar meaning with that of 'grassroots,' may help us to switch the critical lens.

The idea of '*minjian*' as a preferred term by the indie film community may be approached in light of both of its literal definitions, namely: (1) 'belonging to the general public,' and (2) 'among the people.'[20] To Judith Pernin, the contextualization of '*minjian*' has opened up the possibility of talking about the circulation of Chinese independent films from the perspective of the 'public sphere' or 'public space.'[21] Yet, in searching for an accurate term to describe the cultural and artistic practices that 'have developed outside the new state-corporate hegemonic culture of China' since the decisive '1989/1992 conjuncture,' Lisa Rofel and Chris Berry have adopted the term 'alternative': they believe 'civil society' and 'public sphere' are not suitable critical phrases to describe the contemporary Chinese context, and also deny the applicability of the term 'independent' since it fails to address 'the foreclosure on a public, visible and organized opposition.' Hence, they posit the word '*minjian*' as being 'civilian or popular' and therefore closely connected with such alternativeness. Arguably, '*minjian*' can be understood as one necessary condition for creating and sustaining the alternativeness that could bring about significant change without recourse to direct opposition.[22] This type of reasoning underscores why I intend to approach my research subject as the *minjian* film festival network rather than simply emphasizing them as being *independent* film festivals.

Hence although it may be true that the democratic implication of '*minjian*' justifies the independent film community's identification and engagement with the public, it does not necessarily signal a confrontation between the community, the (enlightened) public, and the party–state. As indicated earlier in this chapter, films screened at *minjian* festivals are mainly independent films from mainland China, a majority of which would encounter difficulties regarding domestic theatrical distribution partially due to the problematic system, policy and regulations with film distribution and exhibition in the PRC (notorious censorship, lack of film rating system and challenges for privately run arthouse theatre chains, etc.). Sometimes filmmakers or producers just choose not to apply for the screening permit for their films in the first place. Understandably, they primarily rely on *minjian* festivals and the overseas festival circuit, or other niche markets such as Euro-American arthouse chains and TV channels for exhibition and distribution. Also, *minjian* festivals and entities are usually affiliated with grassroots non-governmental organizations and initiatives; some are sponsored by private capital or made possible with donations and cultural funds from both Chinese and overseas institutions such as the European Union, Japan Foundation, Goethe-Institute China, Alliance Française and various film festivals and film commissions.

In other words, it is fair to say that grassroots festivals have negotiated a subtle if not tricky relationship with state authorities, such as the governing body for film exhibition SARFT's (the State Administration of Radio, Film and Television) Film Bureau, and even the national security bureau at various administrative levels. For instance, SARFT's Film Management Regulations (which have been in force since February 2002) and its Notice on Strengthening DV Management in Theater, Television and on the Internet (issued in May 2004) have both laid out legal frameworks regulating film exhibitions, including film festivals in the PRC, with the 'Notice' specifically targeting DV works' circulation and exhibition. It is therefore noteworthy that grassroots film festivals usually do not use the corresponding Chinese phrase for 'film festival' (*dianyingjie*) in their Chinese titles, but opt instead to disguise themselves as events titled (in Chinese) as 'Film Week,' 'Exchange Week,' 'Forum,' or 'Exhibition' to avoid the problematic application procedure and thus to evade censorship. Such situations have prompted Chris Berry to half-jokingly title his festival report on the Nanjing's CIFF as 'When is a Film Festival Not a Festival.'[23] When these film exhibitions do take place, the Chinese authorities seemingly grant a type of silent permission, which equates to a form of passive regulation and intervention toward the (unauthorized) grassroots festival organizers and participants. For the festivals, keeping a low profile and imposing self-censorship, whether voluntarily or unwillingly, has proved to be a way to survive in the post-WTO period.[24] Nevertheless, state supervision and regulation of the *minjian* festivals is unpredictable, non-negotiable and contingent on various sociopolitical factors.

Furthermore, as CIFF's producer Cao Kai once explained, we can draw parallels between the exhibition modes of Chinese contemporary art and those of independent cinema. He suggests that contemporary artworks are circulated on dual-tracks: on the one hand, there is the National Art Exhibition as the top event connecting the various levels of regional governmental bodies of the China Artists Associations (*zhongguo meishujia xiehui*) and the China Federation of Literary and Art Circles (*zhongguo wenxueyishujie lianhehui*); on the other hand, there is also the exhibition mode of the biennial or triennial, initiated by independent curators and independent art institutes. Cao emphasizes that in recent years the independently curated biennials and triennials 'curve to achieve collaboration with the official bodies horizontally,' which to a certain extent illustrates the road map for *minjian* film festivals to 'effectively join force[s] with certain local institutes or governmental bodies'[25] to ensure visibility throughout China and Asia. Finally, while *minjian* festivals differ from state-run film festivals in terms of their programming visions and operational strategies, I argue that the study of '*minjian* film festival network' should also take into account state-sanctioned festivals: official film festivals at Beijing and Shanghai in recent years have started to co-opt the indie film community by programming and promoting legitimized Chinese independent films (i.e. works with screening permits). Essentially, both official and *minjian* film festivals are now embedded in the global film festival circuit. With this said, certain observations about the standard international film festival do not apply to the *minjian* festivals, which as mentioned earlier are often under-resourced and susceptible to government interference. In the next section of this chapter, I attempt to engage with two locally situated film networks in order to better articulate the model of the '*minjian* film festival network.'

Minjian Film Festival Network: Departing from Songzhuang

I propose the framework of the '*minjian* film festival network' (MFFN) to zoom in on the circulation and exhibition of Chinese independent cinema at the local and regional level. Since the MFFN model is formulated to complement the 'international film festival network,' I also argue that it may be applied to localized or regionalized configurations for circulating minor and alternative films in other locales. For example, in Japan and South Korea, indie/arthouse film *minjian* festivals operate in relation to initiatives and entities of a similar nature, initiatives that are distinct from the mainstream, commercial models. I find it helpful to deploy the ANT approach to the framework of the MFFN when approaching the issues of power, as this approach suggests that 'the analysis of power becomes the study of associations.'[26] Yet, as mentioned in the introduction, we also need to realize that film festival circuit 'is no neutral assemblage of sites and events.'[27] My analysis of the MFFN framework has focused primarily on marginalized, under-resourced and localized festivals and entities in China. Intriguingly, situated within the hierarchy of the international circuit, these *minjian* film festivals can leverage their linkages with the networks and mechanisms of Chinese independent cinema to enhance the festivals' cultural and political profile, which has brought out complex issues of art, politics and power.

Established by Zhu Rikun and his friends in 2001, Fanhall Studio (or FS, *xianxiang gongzuoshi*, also known as Fanhall Films) ventured into funding and producing

Chinese independent films at a time when there were few domestic independent entities dedicated to the production and distribution of Chinese independent cinema. FS has played a versatile role, from film production and distribution, archiving and preservation, to social networking, which is central to their business model and cultural ethos. Even though Fanhall Films are available through VCDs and DVDs in domestic market,[28] FS has not bothered to obtain the screening permits for their indie titles. Yet, their indie films could be circulated on the festival circuit, due to FS's connection with various global exhibition and circulation networks. Accordingly, besides working as an independent film producer, Zhu also plays a leading role as a film curator discovering new films, filmmakers and programming for other domestic and overseas film festivals. In addition, the early success of FS was contingent on the thriving cinéphile culture in Beijing – including a series of themed weekly events titled 'In Dialogue with the Filmmaker' (*yudaoyan duihua*) that began in 2002. This venue has not only showcased important (mostly underground) independent films, it has also hosted independent filmmakers and film scholars for Q&A sessions and panel discussions. In 2003, collaborating with the Media School of Beijing Normal University, FS was able to launch the first China Documentary Film Festival (later known as DOChina).

Li Xianting's Film Fund (LFF) was initiated by the Godfather-figure of Chinese contemporary art, independent critic and curator Li Xianting, in October 2006. The festival takes place at Songzhuang in the eastern suburbs (Tongzhou District) of Beijing, with Zhu Rikun serving as the fund's first executive director.[29] In recent years, LFF has incorporated DOChina into its portfolio of activities, and set up other entities such as the Li Xianting (or LXT) Film Archive and the LXT Film School (since 2009). The LXT Film Archive has preserved Chinese independent films (particularly documentaries) with its free online library of Chinese indie films, and the LFF has sponsored another major *minjian* film festival, the Beijing Independent Film Festival (BiFF), which launched in 2006, with Li Xianting as artistic director. Into the 2010s, Fanhall Studio has found its new incarnation as the Fanhall Center for Arts (*xianxiang yishu zhongxin*, henceforth FCA), a self-labelled 'grassroots art institution' composed of entities such as Fanhall Films, Fanhall Cinema (a new screening venue for indie films since 2009), Fanhall Café, and the studio's official website (fanhall.com).

Li's new dedication to Chinese indie cinema has further implications for the MFFN. First of all, Songzhuang is a locale that is best known for its artist commune founded under Li's auspices – it is the largest in Beijing, with around 1,500 artists and professionals in residence. After artists such as Fang Lijun and Yue Minjun migrated to Songzhuang in the mid-1990s and achieved market success, they invested in the community financially and creatively,[30] supporting the establishment of the Songzhuang Art Museum in 2006 and other cultural undertakings. For instance, the RMB 100,000 donation that launched the LFF came from Fang Lijun. At the same time, the fact that the artist community and initiatives such as LFF have gradually gained support from the local government also speaks to the importance attached to the promotion of cultural industries by the party–state, since Songzhuang has been visualized as an emerging creative cluster by the government and corporations.[31] The logic of inscribing *minjian* film festivals into the grand plan of developing the local creative economy has also underwritten the collaboration between local governments and *minjian* film festivals in several other cities.

Nevertheless, independent film community members do not view Songzhuang-based film entities as fitting into the standardized, sanitized rhetorics about Chinese creativity.[32] Instead, Chinese indie cinema engages with the discourse of Chinese creativity by exploring uncharted territory and overlooked alternatives, as best exemplified with the founding of the LXT Film School, with its open-to-all, short-term and non-certificate training courses on filmmaking taught by experienced independent filmmakers. More important than the imparting of filmmaking techniques at this film school is the delivery of certain socially relevant and even radical philosophies on filmmaking, which might not be valued in a classroom tailored for people who want to enter the mainstream filmmaking apparatus. Benny Shaffer points out that the students at Songzhuang 'become a part of a vibrant community of filmmakers and thinkers,' where the hierarchy between the instructor and students is often defied.[33] Ambitious students connect with like-minded peers, find future partners for their own team, and network with talents within and beyond the local community. Today, this film school's alumni often return to Songzhuang to showcase their own work at the *minjian* film festivals there. In this way, the school is contributing to community building for Chinese independent cinema from the pedagogical level.

As the LFF's DOChina and BiFF faced obstacles that threatened their closure, however, both events were absorbed into the 9th Beijing Independent Film Festival in August 2012. Despite interference from local authorities, this festival managed to run its full programme, with the last several days' screenings held at secret venues. It remains to be seen whether the Songzhuang-based film festivals powered up by LFF and FCA are still viable under the new Chinese Communist Party (CCP) leadership, as both the CIFF at Nanjing (scheduled for October 2012) and YunFest in Kunming (scheduled for April 2013) were shut down during a time of political transition. At the same time, independent cinema-centred screenings and related events still continue at FCA. In spite of political pressures, Songzhuang provides a crucial locale to enable the general public to get access to independent films.

Latour believes that if power lies anywhere it is in the resources used to strengthen the bonds between people; in light of Latour's vision, Jonathan Murdoch and Terry Marsden regard structure, society and power as the outcomes that occur 'as actors are associated,' and thus we have to 'analyze how these resources are defined and linked and how actors impose definitions and linkages upon others.'[34] As briefly delineated above, China's indie film community would not have been associated with Songzhuang without the influx and clustering of artists in the area. In addition, Li Xianting's decision to allow the indie film community to appropriate his land ownership at Songzhuang has facilitated the process of association. Moreover, the town tries to leverage state policies on creative industries and urban planning to further boost local economy; the Songzhuang local government conveniently incorporates the infrastructural development of independent cinema into its planning framework. Therefore, at the local level, the indie film community has skilfully navigated state regulations by leveraging its affiliation with the cultural industry policy. With the founding of LFF, the community has started to 'impose definitions and linkages upon others' by carving out its own space and exploring new territories at the periphery of Beijing.

Mapping CIFVF geopolitically

Among the *minjian* film festivals, one thing is distinct: that their 'modus vivendi' negotiating with state power is obviously geopolitically unbalanced and defies any easy generalization. People tend to believe that independent film culture in first-tier cities such as Beijing and Nanjing is better rooted in the local cinéphile culture and benefits from the concentration of film institutions and cinematic resources. It is surprising, therefore, that a hyper-modern place like Shanghai does not host any *minjian* festivals as of this writing.[35] Even though Beijing has the advantage of currently hosting several *minjian* festivals, the regulation of indie film events could become much tighter given the capital city's political sensitivity towards cultural events. By contrast, the film festivals held in 'western region cities' such as Kunming and Chongqing are less subject to political interference, perhaps due to the strategies these festivals have utilized to collaborate with the local official bodies and corporations, and not solely owing to their geopolitical remoteness from Beijing.[36]

While the cancellation of the Songzhuang based *minjian* festivals testifies to the CCP's tightening cultural policy and state surveillance in wake of more subversive acts, 2011 still witnessed the success of the 8th CIFF in Nanjing and the 5th Chongqing Independent Film & Video Festival at Chongqing (CIFVF), which says something about the complexities of power and control between the government and the independent film community. Originally launched to showcase students' film works, CIFVF was founded in 2007. Ying Liang joined the festival's team of producers during its second year, which has considerably facilitated the festival's evolution both culturally and logistically. Compared to the national-scale *minjian* festivals in Beijing, Nanjing, or even Kunming, Chongqing's festival tends to attract more new talents rather than veteran filmmakers and film critics.

For instance, Ying Liang (b. 1977) – generations younger than Li Xianting and Zhang Xianmin (founder of CIFF and the *Indie Workshop*) – and his colleagues aspire to distinguish the CIFVF from other *minjian* festivals by highlighting three aspects, namely: cultivating local consciousness (*bentu*), supporting new talents in independent filmmaking (*chuangzuo*), and nurturing local audiences (*guanzhong*). CIFVF introduced the NETPAC (Network for the Promotion of Asian Cinema)'s 'Asian Film Critics' Awards' at the festival by endorsing one feature and one short film respectively since 2010, though its size remains essentially unchanged. Arguably, the creation of the NETPAC award has enhanced the international profile of CIFVF, making Chongqing the only Chinese city affiliated with such an award that is usually attached to 'international film festivals.' At the same time, however, CIFVF is the only *minjian* festival advocating a local identity (of Chongqing Municipality, and its love–hate connection with Sichuan Province), a discourse often utilized by the international film festivals' city-marketing campaigns. Such a geopolitical focus is underscored by the fact that Chongqing is one of the main cities in China's less developed western region, which is complicated by the controversies over Chongqing as the former notorious 'Red Capital' under the leadership of the once-ambitious and since-disgraced political figure Bo Xilai.

The boldly defined regional and global vision of the CIFVF is particularly apparent in three aspects of the festival's engagement and intersection with the 'international film festival network.' In summer 2011, the CIFVF collaborated with the newly installed Hangzhou Asian Film Festival (HAFF) in organizing a seven-day Film Talent Camp. Even though both *minjian* festivals lacked a presence on the international circuit and could not lure young film talent with large honoraria, they managed to secure sponsors and venue partners, and to run the camp at a reasonable budget to cover the living expenses for its ten trainees and several lecturers. It is both thought-provoking and ironic that the under-resourced CIFVF set up its talent camp to cultivate creative filmmaking skills, with face-to-face consultation with mentors, intensive discussions, location shooting exercises and so forth, while the master class of the Shanghai International Film Festival is more about kowtowing to industry celebrities who give public talks to an unspecified audience. Referred to as 'artivism,' a buzzword hybridizing art and activism, the Talent Camp obviously celebrates the dimension of social engagement characterizing Chinese independent filmmaking, which also distinguishes the camp from other mainstream film educational programmes currently available in mainland China. Later on, the trainees were able to gather at the 5th CIFVF in November 2011 to screen their accomplished works and attend the intensive masterclass with prominent Thai independent filmmaker Apichatpong Weerasethakul.

Another aspect of the CIFVF's expanding film programme is its crowd-funding initiative called 'Co-producer Project' (CPP), which was launched in December 2011. CPP has appropriated the format of South Korea's Jeonju Film Festival's 'Work in Progress' and the International Film Festival Rotterdam's innovative financing plan 'Cinema Reloaded,' the latter of which held that a dedicated film audience could become one of the co-producers of selected short film projects by donating as little as five euros. Whereas the 'Cinema Reloaded' utilized not only its official site – cinemareloaded.com – but also the platforms of Facebook and YouTube for filmmakers to interact with the co-producers/donors, CIFVF predominately relies on Sina Weibo to publicly promote and interact with 'co-producers' for its first round of CPP projects – reportedly three Chongqing-centred shorts respectively by filmmaker Li Ning, Chen Xinzhong and Yutian, with a 50 RMB individual donation limit. According to the CPP regulations, co-producers could have their names included in the credits and were invited to the premiere of the short films at the 2012 CIFVF. On Weibo, the filmmakers regularly update their progress on the short films; they can even get the co-producers involved in script development and so on. As a result of its three-month online campaign (16 January–16 April 2012), CPP raised RMB 29,790 from its 148 co-producers.[37] As promised, the three filmmakers provided online updates about the progress of their works, which received continuous attention and triggered discussion among concerned netizens. I argue that far from a mere replica of the 'Work in Progress' and 'Cinema Reloaded' initiatives, CPP has explored new visions of publicness and sense of community for independent filmmaking in the PRC by mobilizing the public via social media like Weibo.

A third dimension of CIFVF's regional and global engagement is its partnership with other Chinese-language film festivals through the network of 'Chinese Independent Filmmaking Alliance' (cifa), an initiative launched in 2011 for independent films' screening and cultural exchange among art groups from five locales: Hong Kong (*Ying E Chi* and the Hong Kong Independent Film Festival, or HKIFF), Taiwan (South Taiwan Film Festival, or STFF), Chongqing (CIFVF), Shenzhen (Art de Vivre) and Macao. The cifa network has facilitated the circulation of Chinese-language independent works by sharing and co-presenting programmes of new films from across Hong Kong, Macau, mainland China and Taiwan, as could be observed from the cifa-themed programmes at HKIFF 2013 and STFF 2012. Also, rather than aiming at collectively contesting major mainstream regional film festivals such as the Hong Kong International Film Festival, or Taipei Golden Horse Film Festival, the cifa-network is more about strengthening the presence of independent film culture by realigning the indie film communities spatially and conceptually, and thus more emphasis is on the indie film communities' interconnected, cross-regional, socio-political engagement.

Regrettably, at the time of writing Ying Liang cannot return to mainland China from Hong Kong for certain reasons.[38] As a result, the CIFVF was not held in 2012. The three aforementioned CPP shorts were not shown at Chongqing due to the festival's cancellation, yet they have toured several other film festivals during 2012 and 2013. On the other hand, the above-mentioned festival networking models and projects have inspired and found their reincarnation at other *minjian* festivals. For instance, HAFF also experimented with crowd funding to support its 2012 edition. Also in 2012, Ying Liang was able to collaborate with Ying E Chi in launching the 'Chinese Independent Filmmaking Fundraising Project' (CIFFP) to help three young Hong Kong filmmakers make their short film projects.[39] Ultimately, CIFVF has strategically redefined the way Chinese-language indie film culture is connected with the film networks nationally, regionally and thus globally.

Conclusion: The mode of multiplicity and the abnormal festival

In this chapter, I have taken a network-oriented and spatial-oriented approach in canvassing the circulation and exhibition of Chinese independent films on the '*minjian* film festival network' in Beijing and Chongqing. With the foci on translations and transformations, I have repositioned the issues revolving *minjian* film festivals in the dynamic relations among various mechanisms and agencies, as those of the Chinese independent film community, party–state, international film festival circuit, general public and so forth. Meanwhile, I have situated my theoretical framing within the existing literature of film festival studies; particularly the framework of the 'international film festival network' as carefully developed by de Valck and Elsaesser. This framework has lent insight into the questions of network, space and power, which I shall revisit in this chapter conclusion.

Mode of multiplicity

The interrelation between these circulating entities on the MFFN can be approached as a mode of multiplicity. Taking the example of DOChina, it exists in the multiplicity of 'FCA + Lixianting Film Fund + Songzhuang Art Museum + DOChina (or Beijing Independent Film Festival).' In the case of CIFF, it is the configuration of 'Indie Workshop (Fanhall Studio's equivalent) + RCM Museum + Nanjing University + CIFF.' We may extend these observations about the mode of multiplicity to two innovative circulatory networks of indie films that have come into existence since 2011, namely the Cinéphile Collective (qifang) and the Indie Screening Alliance of Art Spaces (ISAAS). In qifang, Indie Workshop collaborates with organizers of cinéphilia groups and managers of cultural space in second- or third-tier Chinese cities to circulate a body of independent films, while ISAAS utilizes independent art galleries and privately run museums to exhibit selected indie works. Both networks have demonstrated how the MFFN have been spatially reorganized and the border between the interlacing organizations and networks redefined – either by engaging with the revived and reshuffled form of the once-active autonomous organizations and cinéphile groups featured in the first stage of circulating independent cinema, or by channelling in-between the exhibition modes of Chinese independent cinema and contemporary art. Presumably, qifang and ISAAS contribute to the community building of Chinese independent cinema by expanding its nationwide network. Accordingly, by referring to the 'mode of multiplicity,' I am also drawing attention to the set of associations devised by the independent film community to achieve its goals. To refer to Murdoch and Marsden, we may approach the 'mode' as ways for 'resources to be defined and linked,' and for 'actors [to] impose definitions and linkages upon others.'[40] Power has been engendered through and within such processes and bonds, which we can associate with Wang and Zhu's argument of viewing power 'in terms of the dynamics of those involved,' namely to view power *in relations* and *as relations*.[41] In this way, we can develop a more flexible view of the contestation between the party–state and the independent film community.

Abnormal festival and public space

Acknowledging that the perspective of 'power as relations' has offered insights into the proclaimed 'status of independence' of grassroots film festivals in the PRC, I still find it necessary to elaborate on the public significance of *minjian* film festivals, which may complement and deepen our discussion about power, control and resistance regarding the circulation and exhibition of Chinese indie films.

In his festival report on the 6th China Independent Film Festival at Nanjing in 2009,

Chris Berry suggests: 'the very particular circumstances of China mean that CIFF can claim to be the most important film festival in the country.'[42] Whereas Berry's observation of CIFF tries to tease out the underlying reasons why a minor film festival like CIFF can be pivotal to Chinese independent cinema and why the clusters of similar independent events are 'crucial to the artistic health of China's film industry,'[43] CIFF's director Zhang Xianmin has pointed out that such perceived importance is 'abnormal' (*bingtai*), since independent filmmakers become heavily dependent on grassroots events such as the CIFF or DOChina to circulate their works and make contact with the public and the market.[44] Yet Fudan University professor Lü Xinyu opposes Zhang by stating that it is the society itself that is 'abnormal,' since it hardly provides channels for individuals to air their opinions. Therefore, Lü argues, independently run film festivals are needed, which constitute 'the outlets for the society to express itself,' and she contends that the independence of events like CIFF is powered by the internal force of the society itself.[45] Zhang and Lü's debate could be related to Nakajima's observations about 'counter-discourses' *vis-à-vis* grassroots film clubs. Nakajima poses that although these clubs might not constitute the Habermasian ideal of the public sphere, they have problematized the status quo in China and facilitated the formation of counter-discourses 'that have important and real consequences in the transformation of state-society relations in contemporary urban China.' In other words, such venues have extended the possibilities that: (1) documentary films are in fact 'as discourse(s)' that are accessible to the public; and (2) discourses on documentary films reflecting upon social realities could be formed.[46]

Similarly, in his study on Chinese independent cinema, Sebastian Veg argues that while applying the Habermasian notion of 'public sphere' to modern China could be somewhat problematic, the conceptualization of 'public space' as 'a discursive space of "shared humanity" or of an "imagined community" in which each individual is free to air an opinion on matters of public significance' is workable within contemporary China's context. He believes Chinese independent cinema has sought to give voice to ordinary individuals by engaging with the public space that is shaping private stories in the country, and such unofficial space is also identified as *minjian*.[47] I agree with Veg in that the emergence and evolution of MFFN are not only of vital importance for circulating and exhibiting Chinese independent cinema; the permeation and extension of this network into the Chinese social texture have testified to the growth of certain 'public consciousness' as integral to building up the civic culture in China.

My proposal for the MFFN is also meant to address and describe the alternative characteristics of Chinese independent cinema's circulation and exhibition practices. Crucially, with the development of social networks such as Sina Weibo and Douban, facilitated by video sharing sites such as Youku, Tudou and 56, the MFFN utilizes these social media connecting with different actors despite the limited freedom of speech (instanced by the blocking of access to Twitter, Facebook and YouTube) and unpredictable censorship in mainland China. Aided with the almighty presence of the internet, especially these social media platforms, Chinese independent films are now rooted in local and regional independent communities and simultaneously engage in the highly fluid global network of image consumption.

In 2012, even with the constrained sociocultural environment for exhibition and screening events of Chinese indie films, reportedly 32 *minjian* film festivals disguised as forums and exhibitions have taken place in 19 cities across China, including locales such as Lhasa, Xi'an, Harbin, Urumqi, Shenzhen and Dalian.[48] It reminds us of what Shelly Kraicer anticipated in his reports on the cancellation of DOChina in 2011: 'DOChina was neither revolutionary nor radical. The organizers are savvy, and know when it's time to press forward, and when it's time to take a temporary step back. A very similar event might reappear later in a somewhat different incarnation, in a less sensitive location (i.e. one far from the capital), with a different name.'[49] Kraicer's observation echoes de Valck's hypothesis that the film festival network is 'capable of self-preservation precisely because it knows how to adapt to changing circumstances.'[50] But as I have attempted to show, the adaptability and self-regeneration of *minjian* film festivals should not simply be examined in the light of film festival network theory; we have to also situate the study of the 'abnormalities' of *minjian* film festivals in their connections with the party–state, the international film festival circuit, film industries and the general public, so we can better understand how the circulation of culture has been transformed by the functioning of MFFN.

Works cited

Berry, Chris. 'When is a Film Festival not a Festival?: The 6th China Independent Film Festival,' *Senses Of Cinema*, issue no. 53 (December 2009). http://www.sensesofcinema.com/2009/festival-reports/when-is-a-film-festival-not-a-festival-the-6th-china-independent-film-festival/

Berry, Chris and Lisa Rofel. 'Alternative Archive: China's Independent Documentary Culture' in Chris Berry, Lü Xinyu, and Lisa Rofel (eds), *The New Chinese Documentary Film Movement: For the Public Record*. Hong Kong: Hong Kong University Press, 2010, 135–54.

Cao Kai and Dai Zhanglun. 'An interview with the Curator Of CIFF, Caokai,' (in Chinese) *Contemporary Art & Investment*, vol. 4 (2009): 16–17

—'Chinese Independent Filmmaking Fundraising Project Short Film Programme & Discussion,' *Cultural Studies, CUHK* (blog). 1 April, 2013. http://culturalstudiescuhk.wordpress.com/2013/04/01/chinese-independent-filmmaking-fundraising-project-short-film-programme-discussion

Elsaesser, Thomas. *European Cinema: Face To Face With Hollywood*. Amsterdam: Amsterdam University Press, 2005.

Guo, Jing. 'Introduction: Dedicated to Documentary Filmmaking in an Age of Image Production,' (*zai yige zhizaoyingxiang de niandai congshi jilu*) *YunFest* (blog), 22 Feburary, 2003. http://www.yunfest.org/last/xu.htm

Ho, Elaine W. 'HomeShop Series Number One: Games 2008 Off the Map,' *Urban China: Creative China – Counter-mapping the Creative Industries*, issue no. 33 (15 November 2008): 70–1

Jia, Zhangke. 'Irrepressible Images: New Films in China From 1996,' trans. Sebastian Veg, *China Perspectives* 2010, no. 1 (March 2010): 46–51. *Academic Search Premier, EBSCOhost.*

Kraicer, Shelley. 'The Film Festival That Wasn't,' *dGenerate Films*, Last modified 12 May 2011 http://dgeneratefilms.com/film-festivals/shelly-on-film-the-film-festival-that-wasnt

Latour, Bruno. 1999. 'On Recalling Actor-Network Theory' in John Law and John Hassard (eds), *Actor Network Theory and After*, 15–25. Quoted in Wang Shujen and Zhu J. H. Jonathan, 'Mapping film piracy in China,' *Theory, Culture & Society*, vol. 20, no. 4 (2003): 97–125.

Liu, Hui. 'Conversation with Mr. Li Xianting on Songzhuang and Songzhuang Art Museum,' *Today*, issue no. 76 (Spring 2007) http://www.jintian.net/fangtan/liuhui4.html

Lü, Xinyu and Xianmin Zhang. 'Dialogue Between Zhang Xianmin and Lü Xinyu: Independent Film Festivals Are The Channels For The Society To Express Itself' (Chinese), CIFF (blog), 16 October 2009. http://view-ciff.blog.163.com/blog/static/127477476200991691158581/

Murdoch, Jonathan and Terry Marsden. 'The spatialization of politics: local and national actor-spaces in environmental conflict,' *Transactions of the Institute of British Geographers, New Series*, vol. 20, no. 3 (1995): 368–80.

Nakajima, Seio. 'Watching Documentary: Critical Public Discourse and Contemporary Urban Chinese Film Clubs' in Chris Berry, Lü Xinyu and Lisa Rofel (eds), *The New Chinese Documentary Film Movement: For the Public Record*. Hong Kong: Hong Kong University Press, 2010, 117–34

Pernin, Judith. 'Filming space/mapping reality in Chinese independent documentary films,' *China Perspectives* 2010, no. 1 (March 2010): 22–34. *Academic Search Premier*, EBSCOhost.

Shaffer, Benny. 'Philosophies of Independence: the Li Xianting Film School,' LEAP 8: the Education Issue, (April 2011). http://leapleapleap.com/2011/04/philosophies-of-independence/

Stringer, Julian.2001. 'Global Cities and the International Film Festival Economy' in Mark Shiel and Tony Fitzmaurice (eds), *Cinema and the City: Film and Urban Societies in a Global Context*, 134–44. Quoted in Marijke De Valck, *Film Festivals: From European Geopolitics to Global Cinephilia*. Amsterdam: Amsterdam University Press, 2007.

de Valck, Marijke. *Film Festivals: From European Geopolitics to Global Cinephilia*. Amsterdam: Amsterdam University Press, 2007.

Veg, Sebastian. 'Introduction: Opening Public Spaces.' *China Perspectives* 2010, no. 1 (March 2010): 4–10. *Academic Search Premier*, EBSCOhost.

Wang Shujen. *Framing Piracy: Globalization And Film Distribution In Greater China*. Lanham, MD: Rowman & Littlefield, 2003

Wang Shujen and Zhu JH Jonathan. 'Mapping Film Piracy in China,' *Theory, Culture & Society*, vol. 20, no. 4 (2003): 97–125

Wang Xiaolu. 'Memoir of Shijianshe' (*Shijianshe wangshi*, in Chinese), *Economy Observer News*, last modified 25 June 2010, http://www.eeo.com.cn/2010/0625/173872.shtml

Ying, Liang. Sina Weibo post, 20 April 2011, 14:01, http://e.weibo.com/cifvf

Zuo, Jing. 'Preface to the Inaugural Exhibition of Chinese Independent Film Archive: what has been Happening here,' *Contemporary Art & Investment*, vol. 4 (2009):7.

Zhu, Rikun. *Feichuban*, issue no. 1 (2012): 58–70

Filmography

Hezi (the Box) DVD. Directed by Ying Weiwei. 2001

Notes

All the English translations of the quotes, publications and transcripts from Chinese are mine, unless indicated.

1. Ying, Liang. Sina Weibo post, 20 April 2011, 14:01, http://e.weibo.com/cifvf (accessed 9 January 2014).
2. See Elsaesser, Thomas. 'Film Festival Networks: the New Topographies of Cinema in Europe,' *European Cinema: Face To Face With Hollywood*. Amsterdam: Amsterdam University Press, 2005, 82–107.
3. De Valck, Marijke. *Film Festivals: From European Geopolitics to Global Cinephilia*. Amsterdam: Amsterdam University Press, 2007, 34.
4. Ibid., 214.
5. Ibid., 214–15.
6. Ibid., 41.
7. Wang Shujen and Zhu JH Jonathan. 'Mapping film piracy in China,' *Theory, Culture & Society*, vol. 20, no. 4 (2003): 100.
8. Latour, Bruno. 1999. 'On Recalling Actor-Network Theory,' in John Law and John Hassard (eds), *Actor Network Theory and After*, 15–25. Quoted in Wang Shujen and Zhu JH Jonathan, 'Mapping Film Piracy in China,' 97–125.
9. Wang and Zhu. 'Mapping Film Piracy in China,' 119.
10. Zuo, Jing. 'Preface to the Inaugural Exhibition of Chinese Independent Film Archive: What Has Been Happening Here,' *Contemporary Art & Investment*, vol. 4 (2009): 7.
11. For the detailed information on U-theque Organization (disbanded in 2004), please refer to their official website (bilingual): http://www.u-theque.org.cn/ (accessed 9 January 2014).
12. Wang, Xiaolu. 'Memoir of Shijianshe' (*Shijianshe wangshi*, in Chinese), *Economy Observer News*, last modified 25 June 2010, http://www.eeo.com.cn/2010/0625/173872.shtml (accessed 9 January 2014). Also see Wang Xiaolu's blog entries that reminiscence about the history of these cinéphile groups. His blog 'weiziyoushu': http://blog.sina.com.cn/wangxiaolu (in Chinese) (accessed 9 January 2014).
13. Refer to Wang Yiman's article 'The *Amateur's* lightning rod: DV documentary in postsocialist China,' *Film Quarterly* 58.4 (2005): 16–26, in which she also talks about the amateur-ship of Chinese independent filmmakers.
14. Jia, Zhangke. 'Irrepressible Images: New Films in China From 1996,' trans. Sebastian Veg, *China Perspectives* 2010, no. 1 (March 2010): 46–51. *Academic Search Premier, EBSCOhost* (accessed 5 May 2013).
15. See note 9 above.
16. Quoted in Wang, Xiaolu. 'Memoir of Shijianshe.'
17. Refer to 'History of Beijing Queer Film Festival (1),' *Beijing Queer Film Festival* (blog), 12 September 2008 (07:40), http://blog.sina.com.cn/s/blog_5aea47cf0100ag83.html (accessed 20 January 2013).

18 Guo, Jing. 'Introduction: Dedicated to Documentary Filmmaking in an Age of Image Production,' (*zai yige zhizaoyingxiang de niandai congshi jilu*) *YunFest* (blog), 22 February, 2003. http://www.yunfest.org/last/xu.htm (accessed May 2013).
19 Seio Nakajima, 'Watching Documentary: Critical Public Discourses and Contemporary Urban Chinese Film Clubs,' in Chris Berry, Lu Xinyu and Lisa Rofel (eds), *The New Chinese Documentary Film Movement: For the Public Record*. Hong Kong: Hong Kong University Press, 2010, 133–4.
20 According to *The Comprehensive Dictionary of Chinese Language* (*hanyu dacidian*), vol. 6 (Shanghai: Shanghai Cishu Press, 1990), 1420, the first definition of 'minjian' is being opposite to that of the official (*guanfang*), signifying the common people, the general public, the grassroots (*minzhong*); and the second definition means 'among the people/general public.'
21 Pernin, Judith. 'Filming Space/Mapping Reality in Chinese Independent Documentary Films.' *China Perspectives* 2010, no. 1 (March 2010): 22–34. *Academic Search Premier*, EBSCOhost (accessed 5 May 2013).
22 Berry, Chris and Lisa Lofel. 'Alternative Archive: China's Independent Documentary Culture' in *The New Chinese Documentary Film Movement*, 137.
23 Berry, Chris. 'When is a Film Festival not a Festival? The 6th China Independent Film Festival,' *Senses Of Cinema*, issue no. 53 (December 2009). http://www.sensesofcinema.com/2009/festival-reports/when-is-a-film-festival-not-a-festival-the-6th-china-independent-film-festival/ (accessed January 2010).
24 Seio Nakajima remembers how the documentary film exchange week in Beijing was cancelled due to 'self-censorship on the part of the venue rather than any explicit political action by the government'. See Seio Nakajima, 'Watching Documentary,' 132.
25 Cao Kai and Dai Zhanglun. 'An interview with the Curator of CIFF, Caokai' (in Chinese), *Contemporary Art & Investment*, vol. 4 (2009): 15
26 Murdoch, Jonathan and Marsden, Terry. 'The spatialization of politics: local and national actot-spaces in environmental conflict.' *Transactions of the Institute of British Geographers, New Series*, vol. 20, no. 3 (1995): 372
27 Stringer, Julian. 2001. 'Global Cities and the International Film Festival Economy' in Mark Shiel and Tony Fitzmaurice (eds), *Cinema and the City: Film and Urban Societies in a Global Context*, 134–44. Quoted in de Valck, Marijke. *Film Festivals*, 40.
28 Since early on Fanhall Studio has utilized its website fanhall.com (launched in January 2002) as an online forum to promote and cultivate the independent film culture. The website was shut down in 2011, and despite its brief recovery in 2012 was shut down a second time in the same year.
29 However, Zhu Rikun resigned in 2011 from LFF and in 2013 he also resigned from his position at the Fanhall Center of Arts.
30 Shaffer, Benny. 'Philosophies of Independence: the Li Xianting Film School,' LEAP 8: *the Education Issue* (April 2011). http://leapleapleap.com/2011/04/philosophies-of-independence/ (accessed 6 March 2014).
31 Liu, Hui. 'Conversation with Mr. Li Xianting on Songzhuang and Songzhuang Art Museum,' *Today*, issue no. 76 (Spring 2007) http://www.jintian.net/fangtan/liuhui4.html (accessed May 2013).
32 Ho, Elaine W. 'HomeShop Series Number One: Games 2008 Off the Map,' *Urban China: Creative China – Counter-mapping the Creative Industries*, issue no. 33 (15 November 2008): 70.

33 Shaffer, Benny. 'Philosophies of Independence.'
34 Murdoch, Jonathan and Terry Marsden. 'The spatialization of politics,' 372.
35 Mecooon Film Festival (*micang dianyingjie*) based in Shanghai was called off in 2008 after its first edition in 2007. Refer to the blog article (Chinese): http://blog.sina.com.cn/s/blog_5540382b010096fr.html (accessed January 2013).
36 The 6th YunFest however was cancelled according to a short notice posted on the festival's official site on 19 March 2013, only two days before its scheduled date of opening, 21 March 2013. No specific reasons are offered.
37 'Chinese independent filmmaking fundraising project short film programme and discussion,' *Cultural Studies, CUHK* (blog). 1 April 2013. http://culturalstudiescuhk.wordpress.com/2013/04/01/chinese-independent-filmmaking-fundraising-project-short-film-programme-discussion (accessed May 2012).
38 In 2012, Ying Liang 's short film 'When Night Falls' for the *13th Jeonju International Film Festival* led to secret visits from the Shanghai policemen and Security Bureau. For more on Ying Liang's political predicament, see Brody, Richard. 'For Yingliang,' *The New Yorker*, 7 May 2012, http://www.newyorker.com/online/blogs/movies/2012/05/ying-liang-james-cameron-chinese-censorship.html (accessed January 2013).
39 For more information on CIFFP, refer to the specific entry on the project at the official blog of *Ying-E-Chi*, http://yingechi.blogspot.com/ (accessed 9 January 2014).
40 Murdoch, Jonathan and Terry Marsden. 'The Spatialization Of Politics,' 372.
41 Wang Shujen and Zhu JH Jonathan. 'Mapping Film Piracy in China,' 117 [emphasis added].
42 See note 22.
43 Ibid.
44 Lü, Xinyu and Xianmin Zhang. 'Dialogue Between Zhang Xianmin and Lü Xinyu: Independent Film Festivals Are The Channels For The Society To Express Itself' (Chinese), *CIFF* (blog), 16 October 2009. http://view-ciff.blog.163.com/blog/static/127477476200991691158581/ (accessed 9 January 2014).
45 Ibid.
46 Seio Nakajima, 'Watching Documentary,' 131–2.
47 Veg, Sebastian. 'Introduction: Opening Public Spaces.' *China Perspectives* 2010, no. 1 (March 2010): 7–8. *Academic Search Premier, EBSCOhost* (accessed 5 May 2013).
48 Refer to Shuiguai's *Douban* blog entry (in Chinese), 'Mapping Out The Visual Image Festivals In Mainland China In 2012' (2012 *Zhongguo dalu yingxiangjie ditu*), http://www.douban.com/note/262624173/ (accessed 16 February 2013).
49 Kraicer, Shelley. 'The Film Festival That Wasn't,' *dGenerate Films,* last modified 12 May 2011, http://dgeneratefilms.com/film-festivals/shelly-on-film-the-film-festival-that-wasnt (accessed 9 January 2014).
50 De Valck, Marijke. *Film Festivals*, 36.

14

Bringing the Transnational Back into Documentary Cinema: Wu Wenguang's *China Village Documentary Project*, Participatory Video and the NGO Aesthetic

Matthew D. Johnson

Chinese cinema is often understood through stark, even extreme contrasts. State against private. Studio-made against independent. Fifth Generation against Sixth Generation. Fiction against documentary. Above-ground against underground. Commercial against avant-garde. Professional against amateur.

To an extent, this method of labelling Chinese films and their creators reflects a certain polarizing of opinion concerning China itself – specifically, the People's Republic of China. China's government is either loved or hated. Authoritarianism is either resilient or brittle. China's rise will either give way to global economic prosperity or to a Third World War. In the cases of both Chinese cinema and China generally, one of the most frequently invoked contrasts is that of the state ('the party-state,' 'the Chinese Communist Party,' 'the Party,' 'Beijing,' 'Zhongnanhai,' and so on) in contradistinction to some non-state counterpart: society, film directors, artists, the people, ordinary Chinese.

This last contrast is telling. It reflects the fact that for many people, whether PRC citizens or those living outside of China, social realities are understood primarily in terms of a state/society dichotomy.[1] In this chapter, I argue that twenty-first-century China, and by extension twenty-first-century Chinese cinema, can no longer be understood as occupied by only two types of forces: state and society (or, perhaps more appropriately, by the party-state and everyone else).

Among the elements missing from this mainstream state/society vision are transnational actors. In political terms, this third group of actors includes transnational civil society organizations and foundations, multinational corporations, international institutions and agencies, and NGOs.[2] As I will demonstrate, all of these actors play a role in the production of moving image culture within China and in the dissemination of that culture abroad. Curiously, however, transnational actors have been effectively written out of accounts of how films made in China, particularly documentaries, are produced and circulated.³ With the exception of an emerging body of scholarship on international film festivals, the state/society dichotomy dominates our understanding of who produces Chinese cinema, how it is produced, and what mechanisms are involved in its exhibition.⁴ The diversity and influence of transnational actors should not be overstated, but, as this chapter shows, their activities further complicate our understanding of what constitutes independent cultural production within the context of twenty-first-century, iGeneration China.⁵ To be clear, my concept of 'the transnational' refers specifically to state and non-state actors whose activities reach across national boundaries; in other words, it is grounded in transnational relations theory.⁶ As I show in this chapter, connections between independent producers and cross-border partnerships and between international organizations and Chinese government actors have promoted documentary activity in ways that connect the state, filmmakers and citizens through development and governance reform.

My case study is the China Village Documentary Project (*Zhongguo cunmin yingxiang jihua*, 2005–8).⁷ To most observers of the Chinese cinema scene, the project was a product of one of the premier centres of independent documentary filmmaking in China – the Caochangdi Workstation, founded by preeminent documentarian and independent, cultural luminary Wu Wenguang. The conventional story is that Wu, under his own initiative and with funding from the European Union–China Training Programme on Village Governance (about which considerably more will be said below), recruited ten villagers from all over China to receive training in digital video filmmaking and then to document life in their home villages. This footage was later edited by a team of younger filmmakers associated with Wu and screened internationally along with another documentary, *Seen and Heard* (Jian Yi, 2006), which detailed the origins of the project and process of recruiting, selecting, and training the villagers. The China Village Documentary Project went on to receive modest international acclaim. Moreover, it solidified Wu's reputation as a filmmaker interested in marginal people and everyday life, and concerned with the question of how artistic 'amateurs' – like the ten villager filmmakers – might be empowered by the use of relatively low-cost digital technology. In subsequent years, Wu has pursued these concerns even further, establishing the Folk Memory Documentary History project to produce an oral history of the 1958–62 Great Leap Forward famine.

One problem with this narrative is that it is not entirely true. Or, to put it another way, its credibility depends more on the abstractions of cinematic auteur theory, which assumes that authorship in film is determined solely by the personal vision of a single director, without examining how the films of the China Village Documentary Project were actually produced.⁸ In the sections that follow, I attempt to lay out more precisely how the project became an addition to Wu Wenguang's rich *oeuvre* by tracing its origins through a complex narrative spanning post-Mao political reform, European Union promotion of China's village democratization and self-government, Ford Foundation-funded development initiatives in Yunnan province, and reviews and promotional materials framing the documentary project as a product of Wu's singular artistic sensibility. To return to my argument, I am trying to show that independent filmmaking in contemporary China is entangled with a range of transnational forces that are rarely accounted for in scholarly appraisals of the independent film scene. NGOs, international programmes linking foreign governments directly to China's citizenry, and cross-border cultural funding have expanded the range of opportunities for independent moving image producers, many of whom had previously relied on the better-documented international film festival circuit for patronage and exposure. They have also influenced the form of independent filmmaking itself, thus giving rise to what I call an NGO Aesthetic – a visual culture of citizen empowerment, if not activism, which privileges the principle that ordinary people should 'tell their own stories' as a means of transforming lower-class society into legible terrain.[9]

With respect to the themes of this volume, the story told here emphasizes the point that China's accelerating internationalization, coupled with technological change, has made it difficult to continue viewing state/society relations in dichotomous terms, or to ignore connections between visual practices in China and avant-garde artistic movements elsewhere in the world. Establishing alternatives to more dated views, however, requires careful sociological and textual analysis and a willingness to get beyond more familiar narratives concerning the recent history of filmmaking in the PRC. In particular, I find that most interpretations of the China Village Documentary Project – including those circulated by Wu Wenguang and by frequently overlooked project co-producer Jian Yi – tend to appeal to a 'bad state, good society' sensibility familiar to observers of contemporary Chinese politics and cinema alike. It is beyond the scope of this chapter to determine whether such a sensibility is justified. But it is possible to demonstrate that by valorizing Wu and his team of villager filmmakers as authors of the China Village Documentary Project, while ignoring or downplaying the project's transnational origins, we are missing something important about the way that state and international forces are transforming the context in which independent culture is produced. Instead, by searching for clues that might allow us to 'bring the transnational back in,' we make it possible to understand how changes in iGeneration moving image culture are not only being driven by engagement with domestic realities, but also by an equally important dynamic of engagement with visual culture and media practices from other, non-cinematic contexts. Transnationalism is thus part of the texture of contemporary Chinese filmmaking, and as such deserves to be considered alongside national politics, temporality, neoliberalism, technology, and other analytics used as launching points for investigations of moving image culture.[10]

The China Village Documentary Project: An overview

The China Village Documentary Project began in 2005. As described on the website of Wu Wenguang's Beijing-adjacent production and exhibition space, Caochangdi Workstation (*Caochangdi gongzuozhan*), the project's purpose was initially to:

> Open a visual channel from the villages by putting video and still cameras in the hands of villagers across the nation. The project represents a new direction for

documentary-making in China. In its first phase, the selected topic for documentation was *village self-governance*.[11]

Several additional details concerning the project are also worth mentioning: it was an outgrowth of EU–China Training Programme on Village Governance; it was coordinated and directed by Wu Wenguang and Jian Yi (the latter as an adviser to the EU programme); the project outputs were documentary films and photographs created by villagers who had joined the project by application; these films and photographs were later exhibited along with a 55-minute documentary film about the project, titled *Seen and Heard*, as well as another planned companion film on the history of village self-governance reform and democratization in China.

My first contact with the China Village Documentary Project came in 2009, when I contributed a review of the now-defunct online China Independent Documentary Film Archive (http://www.cidfa.com, CIDFA) to the scholarly journal *American Anthropologist*.[12] At that time, the CIDFA website's media content consisted of documentaries produced by Wu Wenguang, documentaries produced by younger filmmakers, and documentaries produced by Chinese villagers. As I was already familiar with Wu's earlier work and, within the format of the review, wanted to recommend the CIDFA website to anthropologists interested in issues of rural change, I was primarily drawn to the backstory behind the villager films.[13] A brief period of internet research soon revealed the basic narrative of the China Village Documentary Project: it had begun as a public communication effort to promote the challenges and successes experienced in the course of the China Training Programme on Village Governance; the stated goal of the project was to document village-level democracy; the films were jointly produced by villagers trained in basic camera and documentary technique, and a cohort of young documentary filmmakers recruited by Wu Wenguang and Jian Yi to work with the villagers as technical advisers and editors.

As I also discussed in the review, the China Village Documentary Project had already proven to be surprisingly effective in terms of its production and dissemination strategy. The first phase of the project had yielded ten short villager documentaries in addition to *Seen and Heard* and *Village Documentary Project* (China Village Self-Governance Film Project, 2006), the latter a 95-minute film including all ten villager documentaries as well as brief introductions to each villager filmmaker.[14] The personalities of the villagers were lively and the subjects engrossing to a first-time viewer. Titles like 'A Welfare Council,' 'A Nullified Election,' 'Village Head Wu Aiguo,' 'I Film My Village,' 'Returning Home for the Election,' 'The Spirit Mountain,' 'The Quarry,' 'Our Village Committee,' 'Allocation of Land' and 'Did You Go Back for the Election?' convey something of the thematic focus of the project, as well as the diversity of perspectives provided by the ten villager filmmakers on the overarching subject of self-governance. The villagers themselves were spread across villages within nine different provinces, including a Zhuang ethnic minority village in Guangxi. A second phase of the project generated nearly ten full-length villager documentaries on everyday aspects of village life. Whereas the films of the first phase had focused primarily on village elections and local governance, these second-phase films were primarily records of quotidian experience.

One the most compelling aspects of the China Village Documentary Project was the human element – the villager filmmakers themselves. The ages of the filmmakers ranged from 24 to 59 years. Only one, wedding studio videographer Yi Chujian, had any sort of previous training in image production. Titles of seven of the ten short films referred to elections or village governance, but their depictions included extensive images of the villager filmmakers interacting with co-villagers, scenes of quotidian village life, and abundant dialogue on a range of topics beyond elections. The films appeared novel, rich in sociological data and full of candour, particularly when the villager filmmakers were themselves interviewed by project personnel. For a first-time viewer, it would be easy to see these films – as I did at the time – as a novel experiment in citizen filmmaking funded by the EU–China Training Programme (as described on the CIDFA website), but conceived and produced by Wu Wenguang personally. Because of my own appreciation for the project, I have dug deeper into its origins than others covering the China independent documentary scene. As I describe in subsequent sections, the most striking thing about the China Village Documentary Project which has not already been recounted before is that it is not simply the brainchild of one of China's most celebrated independent filmmakers.[15] Instead, the project's genesis reveals an important and poorly understood history of transnational involvement in China's democratization and development process. This process, in turn, has impacted the production of realist documentary images of China's society and villages.

Situating the NGO Aesthetic: Village elections and the EU-China Training Programme on Village Governance

My basic argument concerning transnational actors in the field of independent documentary image production is that their presence has fostered the development of an 'NGO Aesthetic' – a specific form or mode of staging which characterizes documentaries produced within the space of international organizations and related projects. The list of works exhibiting this aesthetic is not necessarily long, but it includes the China Village Documentary Project and other works of activist or citizen documentary being produced globally.[16] Its presence in these works suggests that transnational actors have played important roles in the development of realist aesthetics within the context of what has elsewhere been called China's New Documentary Film Movement (*Zhongguo xin jilu yundong*), within which Wu Wenguang occupies a prominent position.[17] As I show in this section, the attraction of the NGO Aesthetic for filmmakers in China derives from two sources: first, a shared interest in empowering citizens to serve as recorders of local realities, and second, the recruitment of Chinese cultural producers by NGOs and international development programmes for purposes of audiovisual data collection and publicity.

Films that possess NGO Aesthetic qualities follow a 'logframe' (logical framework, or logical framework approach) strategy of making claims about the necessity of development intervention. Logframe-derived planning is ubiquitous within the world of NGO intervention and management.[18] The visual culture of films bearing the NGO Aesthetic, like logframe strategy and analysis, is distinguished by: (1) an intervention logic based on the need to solve an existing social problem; (2) the proposal of an indicator of achievement (e.g. democratic participation); (3) the introduction of trustworthy sources of information (e.g. informants) for verification of progress; and (4) the highlighting of specific, external conditions necessary for successful intervention. A key point to be made concerning logframe strategy, and thus the NGO Aesthetic, is that it exists within institutional spaces that are created by both state and non-state developmental institutions, as the above reference to 'international organizations and related projects' indicates. In the case of the China Village Documentary Project, the institutional space of production was primarily created by the European Commission and the People's Republic of China Central People's Government Ministry of Commerce and Ministry of Civil Affairs.

The formal *intervention logic* of the EU–China Training Programme on Village Governance (EUCTP), and thus the films produced by Wu Wenguang and Jian Yi within the institutional space of this programme, was that China's villages required democratization and self-governance. The reason why so many of the villager films focused on these themes was that the films themselves were commissioned as evidence of progress in these areas – for example, by positioning villagers as uncensored observers of village-level official institutions, or of the electoral process. As such, their production, selection and editing and exhibition, was part of an effort to promote awareness of village elections in China, but also to draw attention to the efforts of the partners in the EU–China Training Programme on Village Governance, the European Commission and PRC Ministry of Civil Affairs, to deal with rural problems. They were, as Wu Wenguang and Jian Yi acknowledged, part of a general public communication effort.

Understanding why such an effort was deemed necessary by the EUCTP requires a brief foray into the history of China's post-Mao democratization and self-governance reforms. It is not often noted that beginning in the 1990s, the history of village elections in China is partly a history of international (state-to-state) and trans-national (state–private, state–non profit) relations. Village elections themselves go back to the early 1980s, and were part of a larger package of local governance reforms enacted by the Chinese Communist Party with the intention of promoting local stability, economic prosperity, and leader accountability during the fractious post-Mao transition and the dismantling of the commune system of rural governance. The goal of such reforms was to improve relations between villagers and the state, and thus to make more unpopular policies related to taxes and family planning palatable.[19] China's 1982 Constitution made legal the creation of elected villager committees (*cunmin weiyuanhui*) for the implementation of these policies, as well as for the handling of public affairs, management and provision of social services, mediation of civil disputes, maintenance of public order, and communication between the grassroots and upper levels of government.

Creation of village committees required a 'democratic education' process for the public – a key detail in understanding why China Village Documentary Project films were produced in the first place. The 1998 Organic Law on Villager Committees (the 'VC Law') required that committees promote democratic administration and be subjected to fiscal oversight. Villagers were to engage in the nomination and selection process of committee members. Nomination and selection of committee members were carried out under the supervision of the Ministry of Civil Affairs, and the committees represented the lowest level of civil administration within China's state bureaucracy. A prerequisite of the new laws was thus that villagers be taught to behave as if rule of law existed – for example: exercising their rights and responsibilities under the VC Law by electing accountable leaders. The VC Law was seen by some political reformers as a pilot project for implementing competition for committee memberships at higher (e.g. township and county) levels. In more immediate terms, it introduced the system of urban residents' committees (*chengshi jumin weiyuanhui*) for city-dwellers living outside of the work unit (*danwei*) system to village life. In 1999, the urban-to-rural flow of governance reform reversed when experimental elections were held for larger communities (*shequ*) in 20 cities.

Village elections represented a pivotal and contested transformation of local governance in China because they potentially threatened the power of Communist Party members and other political stakeholders during the early years of CCP rule under Deng Xiaoping. While it has become fashionable to deny the existence of support for procedural democracy in China during the 1980s, village committees were first established in February 1980, and in 1987 the Sixth National People's Congress approved the provisional 'Organic Law of the Village Committee of the People's Republic of China,' which preceded the 1998 VC Law by more than a decade. The provisional version of the Organic Law was enacted on a trial basis from 1 June 1988 onward. At the same time, the Ministry of Civil Affairs began organizing democratic training and inter-village collaboration, elements of the 'Four Democratic Components.' By the time the Ninth National People's Congress did finally revise the provisional law to become the new VC Law in 1998, which legalized village elections and required that they be held every three years, village elections had already become a component of village governance in China. In 2004, the Communist Party and State Council granted elections further sanction by jointly issuing a circular titled 'On Completing and Perfecting Village Affairs Transparency and Democratic Supervision.'[20]

Enter, then, the transnational actors. Already by the early 1990s the Ministry of Civil Affairs had begun to build international support for its experiments in limited grassroots procedural democracy in China.[21] Institutions such as the Asia Foundation, Carter Center, Ford Foundation and International Republican Institute (US), the governments of Canada and Finland, other European organizations, and the United Nations Development Program, all supported and observed China's rural self-governance reforms and related economic reforms. Positive press around these developments allowed the Ministry of Civil Affairs to enhance its position within the central government. Foreign participation in the reform process began with the arrival of a Carter Center delegation to China in 1997; subsequent endorsements of the reforms by former US president Jimmy Carter and Vice President Al Gore produced positive international reaction, which was then used internally by the Ministry of Foreign Affairs to boost its democratization programme as a key means of encouraging positive foreign appraisals following a rocky period in relations between China and the international community. *New York Times* columnist Thomas Friedman was allowed to report on village elections by the State Council Information Office in 1998; central leaders like Zhu Rongji appeared pleased with the subsequent positive response from US President Bill Clinton, Vice President Al Gore, and House Speaker Newt Gingrich.[22] US, European, and Japanese leaders toured villages, or requested to observe elections and discuss their significance with Chinese leaders. Noted 'hardliner' Li Peng emerged as a supporter of the reforms, followed later, and cautiously, by Communist Party General Secretary and PRC President Jiang Zemin.

The year 1998 was thus not only a watershed in terms of promulgation of the VC Law, but also in terms of transnational involvement in China's village reforms. Governments on both sides participated to varying degrees in supporting the democratic experiment. Although I use the term 'transnational' throughout this chapter, the less succinct phrase 'national-international-transnational nexus' might more accurately characterize the context of events on the ground, which also drew in political parties, private foundations, NGOs and other non-state actors. According to Qingshan Tan, the focus of non-state efforts with respect to village elections was training of election officials and producing civic education materials:

> Foreign NGOs such as the Ford Foundation, IRI [International Republican Institute], the Carter Center, and the Asian Foundation have all engaged in the provision of training materials and courses for electoral officials and elected village committee chairs and members. These training activities have helped to spread local awareness of village election[s] and improve electoral rules and procedures. Moreover, foreign involvements in exchange programs have enabled civil affairs and local government officials to acquire technical expertise and comparative knowledge in conducting village elections. Furthermore, foreign assistance reinforces MoCA [Ministry of Civil Affairs] commitment to policy implementation and innovation in village election and governance.[23]

Stable self-governance through elections was also tied to the prospect of economic development. The Carter Center was supported by the US–China Legal Cooperation Fund, itself a project of the China Business Forum, Inc., the research and education wing of the US–China Business Council.

It was in this context of political and economic cooperation across national borders that the EUCTP started its operations in China. The EUCTP was a long-term intergovernmental project between the European Commission and the People's Republic of China, with financing from the European Commission and China's Ministry of Commerce. Its origins go back to 1996, when it was first envisioned as one of four programmes to 'nurture local governance in Chinese villages, train young managers to do business with China, boost investment there and help European and Chinese firms understand each other's technical standards.'[24] In 2001 the EU–China Training Programme for Management of Village Affairs was established in Beijing to 'promote self-government by villagers and democracy in rural China.' The Ministry of Civil Affairs and Delegation of the European Commission to China and Mongolia served as executing agencies.[25] The EUCTP's objectives included: (1) long-term cooperation and understanding between the EU and China, (2) enhancing understanding and observance of law by villagers, elected representatives and local officials, and (3) development of village self-governance within the framework of China's laws and regulations.[26] In short, the goal of the programme was establishing civil society capacity.

Support for the EUCTP was buttressed by additional interests on both sides. For China, the development of local governance capacity and improvement of state-to-state relations with foreign trading partners were important concerns that most likely superseded the Ministry of Civil Affairs' stated objective of implementing village elections. For Europe, the EUCTP also represented a 'discreet' channel through which to promote human rights in China.[27] Within the jointly formulated operating guidelines of the project, interventions were focused on capacity-building through the institutionalization of law and of human rights. The EUCTP itself, with its emphasis on promoting citizens' civil rights and the selection of village committee officials, was one of a range of cooperative projects between the EU and China that were devoted to law- and rights-related capacity-building. Others included the EU–China Legal and Judicial Cooperation programme (LJC), the Governance for Equitable Development programme (with the United Nations Development Programme), the EU–China Human Rights Projects Facility, support for the Chinese Federation of Handicapped Persons, and a separate programme to promote economic, social and civil rights in Yunnan province.[28] Within this broader EU–China cooperative scheme, *indicators of achievement* included changes in China's legal system for the better protection of human rights and, perhaps more modestly, progress with respect to legal and electoral procedure, including demonstrable and consistent enforcement of laws.

In addition to institutional development, the second and third major components of the EUCTP were training and human resource development and research. The programme was initially launched in seven pilot provinces before extending to almost all provinces within China; more participants were involved in the EUTCP than any other foreign organization-sponsored project.[29] Related exchange programmes sent Chinese civil affairs personnel and policymakers to Sweden, Germany and France to receive governance training and observe local European elections. The EUCTP also generated copious teaching materials and reports, as well as public communication concerning the *progress of the project*.

This last point is significant. Initially, my assumption after reviewing publicly available EUCTP materials was that the China Village Documentary Project films were conceived as part of a larger programme of electoral observation – in other words, as a means of collecting information about local elections and governance for training, but also for verification purposes. However, it seems that EUCTP planners viewed the project's main purpose as raising public awareness of village elections and issues of village governance generally as demanding sustained intervention. According to one programme report:

Governance and its components were the subject of numerous interventions. The flagship programme in the area was the Village Governance Programme, which promoted democracy at the level of rural villages.[30]

Returning to the final category of logframe analysis raised earlier in this section, what this quotation indicates is that the *specific, external conditions necessary for successful intervention* are none other than the presence of the EUCTP itself, the promoter of 'democracy at the level of rural villages' in the context of 'numerous' interventions, with improvement of law- and rights-based governance as their target.

The China Village Documentary Project may thus be understood as a public communication offshoot of EUCTP efforts to support village democratization according to China's laws. As extensions of EUCTP village-level work, the villager films all possess elements of the programme's own logframe-defined structure – the NGO Aesthetic. The theme running across all nine films – elections and local village politics – reflects the programme intervention logic. The realities depicted in these films provide indications of programme achievement, or lack thereof (and thus potential grounds for future intervention). The villagers themselves represent trustworthy sources of independent verification. Produced and edited by Wu Wenguang and Jian Yi, the films become both documents of the democratization process and evidence of its necessity. As such, they serve to legitimate actors external to the village, such as the EUCTP itself, as the architect of present and future reforms.

This last point is perhaps the most difficult to establish, but I believe that it is confirmed by the wider dissemination of China Village Documentary Project films in settings relatively divorced from the context of independent film. For example, the villager films were each broadcast via CCTV 12, the official law and society channel, as part of a broader programme of public outreach to encourage village-level democratization and villager participation in elections. The broadcasts made clear that these reforms continued to enjoy the sanction of the Ministry of Civil Affairs and had been successfully implemented under the EUCTP. As such, the films represented public communication of a specific sort within China – outreach to government officials and villagers for the purpose of raising awareness of, and validating, EUCTP efforts.[31] In addition, both the making of the films and their dissemination seemed to reflect an assumption that democratization's success depended not only on the programme, but also on a transformation of villager consciousness effected by placing cameras in the hands of villagers and by providing media platforms for sharing results.

The moving image culture of village democratization

Many elements in the China Village Documentary Project films, particularly those exhibited when the project's first phase was screened for an external audience, were inherent to the EUCTP's logframe strategy. The theme of village elections that was particularly notable in the first-phase films was essentially dictated by the fact that the project was paid for and supported by an international cooperative project that framed village democratization as a desirable outcome. The narratives created by the villager filmmakers and project-employed editors focused on the extent to which elections and other governance processes produced satisfactory or unsatisfactory outcomes. At the very least, these films included visual evidence concerning how democratization and development goals were being implemented on the ground. That is to say, the films served to communicate the importance of the role being played by the EUCTP itself in carrying forward the Ministry of Civil Affairs' village democratization experiment. In this sense, the moving image culture of the villager films has, at least from a representational perspective, been defined by what I have thus far called the NGO Aesthetic.

Those who have actually seen the China Village Documentary Project films will note that the EUCTP is for all intents and purposes invisible within the films themselves. As I have noted earlier, the promotional materials related to the project make explicit its connection to the EUCTP, or acknowledge that the planning of the project preceded Wu Wenguang and Jian Yi's involvement. How and why this has become the case is a question that I will take up in just a moment. For now, the more pressing question would appear to be: Where is the justification in referring to an NGO Aesthetic at all, when the actors involved in the EUCTP are clearly very much governmental? First, it is important to acknowledge that the logical framework analysis approach is ubiquitous in international development organizations, and that many NGOs are indeed development- and rights-focused in practice. But this is not a wholly convincing response. Why not, then, use the term 'Logframe Aesthetic' or some more appropriate neologism? The real justification comes from an examination of where the form taken by the China Village Documentary Project films – in other words, the 'villager documentary' – has come from.

The answer, at least according to several scholars who have also researched this question, is the Ford Foundation. According to Siosan Un's 2009 study of independent documentary in China, the practice of putting cameras in the hands of ordinary people has roots in Ford Foundation-supported projects such as Guo Jing and Zhaxi Nima's Yunnan-focused participatory video education project titled 'Learn Our Own Traditions'.[32] According to Un, the China Village Documentary Project followed this precedent of putting video and still cameras in the hands of villagers. The notion that the 'Learn Our Own Traditions' project represented the inspiration for Wu Wenguang and Jian Yi's approach to EUCTP public communication is also raised by Yingjin Zhang, who argued that the 'turn of the Chinese independent documentary to collective activism' began with the Azara Visual Workshop, organized by Guo Jing and the Yunnan Academy of Social Sciences, which aimed to promote 'participatory visual education' as developmental practice.[33] According to Zhang, the Azara Visual Workshop not only preceded Wu Wenguang and Jian Yi's project, but was itself inspired by a 1991 Ford Foundation project, the Yunnan Women's Reproductive Health and Development Program, which included support for 53 rural Chinese women photographing their daily lives, in this case with the goal of promoting awareness and education concerning women's reproductive health.[34] Guo Jing and Zhaxi Nima's 'Learn Our Own Traditions' project was then launched with additional

Ford Foundation funding in 2002. Like the China Village Documentary Project, Guo's method was to recruit villagers from three Yunnan villages to document distinctive local cultural practices. The resulting footage was then edited in Kunming for wider dissemination. The Azara Visual Workshop (reorganized as the BAMA Mountain Culture Institute in 2004) also benefited from NGO support, in this case from the Virginia-based Conservation International and The Nature Conservancy.

Perceptive insiders will be aware that one of China's best-known independent documentary festivals – the Yunnan Multi Culture Visual Festival, or 'Yunfest' – was first organized in 2003 by the Yunnan Provincial Museum, then also under Guo Jing's direction. Since then, additional sponsorship for Yunfest has come from the Ford Foundation, Conservation International, and The Nature Conservancy. A pattern thus emerges: namely, that since 2002-3 independent cultural producers like Guo Jing, Wu Wenguang and others have been increasingly engaged with transnational NGOs and other international actors, and that the form of their projects has been one of participatory video education – what is known in the broader activism and development world as participatory video or citizen media.[35] The NGO Aesthetic, then, is so named because it points to the fact that in addition to the logframe elements that I have already discussed in connection with the China Village Documentary Project, the *most* notable impression generated by the project films, and which has struck observers familiar with the various projects headed by Guo Jing as well, is that they rely on the participation of villagers. This overarching participatory form can be viewed as a product of Ford Foundation activities in China dating back to the early 1990s, specifically via the importation of Ford Foundation developed and funded Photovoice (*yingxiang fasheng*) public health strategies intended to give aid recipients an opportunity to communicate their concerns and coping strategies to policymakers and service providers.[36] The NGO Aesthetic thus has its origins in the international development world, but the means of its transmission into China has been the activities of NGOs in Yunnan province. In this context, Yunfest represents the primary node through which participatory education practices have been further disseminated into the world of independent film and documentary.

What international and NGO-led development efforts in China have created is a 'glocal' space occupied by independent filmmakers and cultural entrepreneurs in the roles of investigators, liaisons, and interlocutors. Without going too deeply into thorny issues of agency, another reason for opting for the term 'NGO Aesthetic' over other alternatives is that while the China Village Documentary Project also exists within this space, its films reveal more of an emphasis on villager participation in the filmmaking process, and less of an emphasis on the EUCTP and its initiatives (for which, again, the project nonetheless served as a form of publicity). In other words, the project closely resembles a participatory video programme of the sort either funded or inspired by the Ford Foundation within Yunnan province.[37] Both the NGO Aesthetic and participatory video form of the China Village Documentary project point to the influence of transnational development projects on independent documentary production in China.

It is worth noting that within China, assessments of the China Village Documentary Project have raised important questions concerning the relationship between the documentary producers, Wu Wenguang and Jian Yi and the villager filmmakers.[38] Wu's reports and interviews concerning the project have stressed the importance of encouraging villagers to 'naturally' create images of their communities, and through this process to develop a sense of their inherent rights to speak and represent.[39] The connection to democratization often goes unmentioned, although participatory video activism generally stresses the inculcation of a sense of citizen empowerment as a prerequisite of sustained political engagement. Links between the China Village Documentary Project and participatory video methods have also been investigated in the context of academic communications research.[40] It seems fair to say that the project is as much an outgrowth of trends in global filmmaking practices as a new iteration of China's independent documentary movement. Nonetheless, as I show below, reception of the project has rendered these parallels and paradigms of mutual influence nearly invisible.

'Their own words': Feeling good about villagers and bringing back independence

NGOs and international development efforts, democratization-focused and otherwise, have thus provided a new, participatory model for documentary and on-the-spot (*xianchang*) filmmaking in China. This participatory model gained traction in Yunnan and, as Siosan Un and Yingjin Zhang have suggested, was most likely emulated and adapted in the context of the China Village Documentary Project. Indeed, even though authorship of the project is frequently seen to reside with Wu Wenguang, co-producer Jian Yi has also been at the forefront of collaborative and community media projects in China since 2005, when he founded the ARTiSIMPLE Studio – a forerunner to the better-known IFCHINA project founded by Jian Yi, Eva Song, and Douglas Xiao in Ji'an, Jiangxi.[41] Notable nodes in Jian Yi's international network include the Kroc Institute for International Peace Studies at the University of Notre Dame; the Appalshop documentary film studio in Whitesburg, Kentucky; the CRASSH programme at Cambridge University; the British Council; and the Starr Foundation and Asian Cultural Council in New York City. Since the China Village Documentary Project's inception, Jian Yi has become a well-regarded documentary filmmaker in his own right; in 2005, however, Jian was also serving as a communication expert and photographer for the EUCTP. Together, Wu Wenguang and Jian Yi brought to the programme a fairly wide range of expertise concerning documentary filmmaking practice and, perhaps just as significantly, international 'best' practices concerning the uses of media in a development context.

What is striking, though, is how promotion and reception of the ten China Village Documentary Project films and the associated *Seen and Heard* documentary have eclipsed the project's origins in the democratization-focused EU-China Programme on Village Governance, the role of China's Ministry of Civil Affairs in that programme, and the documentary project's obvious connections to a range of participatory education and media efforts that emphasize development rather than 'art.' In this section I suggest that the most obvious reason for a lack of precision, or even consensus, concerning the origins and rationale behind the China Village Documentary Project is that many observers of Chinese cinema only see China through the dichotomy of state and society, within which the artist stands on the side of the people and against the powers-that-be. I also argue that while the writings of these observers may help us feel good about what we are watching, they tell us only part of the story about why, how, and by whom the films we are watching were actually made.

Following completion of the first-phase villager documentaries and *Seen and Heard*, Wu Wenguang and Jian Yi hit the road. By April 2006, the films of the China Village Documentary Project had appeared at four US universities (New York University, Yale, Columbia, and Notre Dame), been shown in Beijing on multiple occasions, and appeared at the Hong Kong International Film Festival and Visions du Reel, a film festival in Nyon, Switzerland. A selection of villager photos was also shown during the US tour, in Beijing, and, later that summer, at the House of Cultures in Berlin, Germany.[42] Early coverage of the project did not identify it by name. Instead, considerable emphasis was placed upon the films as evidence of social unrest and Wu Wenguang's concern for China's villagers:

> For all of China's many apparent successes, a certain degree of discontent is bubbling at the edges. Government-released figures state 74,000 "mass incidents" took place in 2004, up from 53,000 in 2003. Many of the protests, most of which center on public outrage for government wrongs, have turned violent, resulting in skirmishes between villagers and police, burned cars, [sic] and damaged property. Recent events involving local residents' bitter land dispute with local officials in Taishi village of Guangdong province only further highlight the precarious nature of local level governance in China. Some of the most engaging responses to these conditions are coming from China's artistic communities. China's pioneer documentary filmmaker Wu Wenguang has shot Chinese social problems since first picking up a camera in the late 1980s. These concerns are evident in his landmark films *Beijing Drifters* and *On the Road*, intimate portraits of people on the fringe. "This project is closely connected to China's rural population," Wu explained. "Most of China's population lives in the countryside; it's the location of some of the biggest problems. I am excited about this because the project is based on people's own ideas and proposals. People need to understand village governance in the broader sense – and not just the associations and committees but what they stand for and what they could achieve in the broader sense. I think this will help more people care for and consider the real conditions among China's peasants. We need to care for the people."[43]

To view the films as an artistic response to rural discontent was perhaps an inspiring angle to take – one perhaps encouraged at the time by Wu Wenguang himself. But, as we have seen, the notion of the films as emerging from 'the people's own ideas and proposals' was only part of the story – albeit a compelling part. Two additional aspects of the story can be seen as particularly notable indicators of how the China Village

Documentary Project was to be received. First, and this is a more minor point, it was unclear what the project was to be called. Second, observers understood the project as a kind of spontaneous outgrowth of villager concerns, for which Wu Wenguang (and the not-yet-visible Jian Yi) served as primary interlocutors.

According to at least one account, the project's title was then still the Visual Documentary Project on China's Village-Level Democracy.[44] At the time of its March 24, 2006 screening at the Center for Religion and Media at New York University, it was being billed as 'The Village Video Project with Wu Wenguang.'[45] Three days later, at Yale University's Henry R. Luce Hall Auditorium, it appeared as the 'Visual Documentary Project on China's Village-Level Democracy: An Introduction.'[46] Comparing these titles, it is clear that promotional emphasis had quickly shifted to the specific issue of democratization; the Yale screening was also notable for having disseminated the project's own English-language press materials online in PDF form. These materials clearly laid out the project's relationship to the EUCTP and gave the project a name – the Visual Documentary Project on China's Village-Level Democracy. Wu Wenguang was identified as the curator, a documentary filmmaker, and visual consultant for the EUCTP; Jian Yi was identified as coordinator, a filmmaker, photographer, and an EUCTP public communications expert. The promotional materials also included a description of project goals: providing a village-level perspective on village self-governance, political decentralization, democratization, and 'bringing together young filmmakers and villagers, and seeing changing realities from the perspective of the young generation and the people whose lives are dependent on the villages.'[47] The materials' brief synopsis of the project described its official role as 'part of the public communication activities of the EU–China Training Programme on Village Governance.' It also claimed that the ten villager DV films provided an 'uncensored' window onto the lives of villagers in remote China, bestowing upon the project an air of exoticism and verisimilitude, if not a vague hint of transgression.

To summarize the story thus far, while some ambiguity existed concerning the title of the project and how it had come into being, by the time of the Yale University screening, three distinct aspects of the China Village Documentary Project had become apparent through its promotional campaign: it was focused on the issue of democracy, it represented a collaboration between the EUCTP and filmmakers Wu Wenguang and Jian Yi, and it provided an unvarnished and unofficial perspective on China's countryside. As predicted by the project's early press coverage, the angles most appealing to subsequent observers were Wu Wenguang's role as project impresario and the focus on villager filmmaking. In almost all of the accounts, connections to the EUCTP were noted, only to be dismissed:

> Chinese documentary director, writer, and educator Wu Wenguang's most recent project, the *China Village Self-Governance Film Project*[,] is entertaining and charming, despite its best efforts to be a public diplomacy collaboration between China and the European Union. The film series, a palette of combined works including video village self-governance reports by rural Chinese and a documentary describing the process of preparing the villagers to take their role

behind the camera, provides a startling and guileless view of the lives of the people most underrepresented in Chinese media. Wu, the central figure in China's "New Documentary Movement" – a cinematic trend that emerged in Beijing in the early 1990s – ably captures the personalities and struggles of his charges with such grace and naturalness that while the representation of village self-governance is poignant, the most lasting impressions from the film are the excitement of the villagers about their exposure to and interaction with the documentary mode. Truthfully, some of the most interesting parts of the story emerged from outside the stated aim of documenting local village self-government. In roughly half of the village documentaries, voting never occurs, or otherwise other topics dominate. Seeing old women get off of their bikes to talk with one another at a dirt road intersection in a Northern Chinese village offers a surprisingly intimate and prosaic view of the side of China that often gets left out in most economic growth rhetoric. Hearing ethnic Tibetans matter of factly [sic] discuss environmental changes in the snowcapped mountains surrounding their village, and what those changes mean in their belief system, provides a surprising alternative discourse to much contemporary discourse on global warming. Hearing a young urban professional talk about how removed his life is from life in his village is more revealing to the audience on a human level than hearing the specific reasons why he failed to go home and fill in his last ballot. More generally, the ten villager documentarians exposed bits and pieces of perspective into the lives of Chinese people by capturing domestic moments through happenstance while attempting to find democracy in China.[48]

Other online promotional materials described the issue of village democratization in more breathless terms, but continued to identify Wu as the project's prime mover:

When China's central government allowed local elections to proceed in 2005, Wu Wenguang, one of the main exponents of the Beijing-based "New Documentary Movement," offered villagers in remote areas of the country DV cameras and technical training so that they could document this historic event. From housewives to peasants young and old, the newly empowered villagers tell stories that are intimate, earnest, revelatory – and uncensored. Shifting between documentary and news exposé, these vivid accounts range from "A Futile Election" in Shaanxi to a housewife observing the everyday life of her community, from a property dispute over a quarry field to the impact of governmental decisions on the livelihood of Yunnan farmers.[49]

The project's own online releases by contrast, continued to emphasize the official EUCTP context while also casting doubt on claims for the impact of democratization on village life:

This project is an activity organized by the EU–China Training Program on Village Governance. We focus on what we call "village self-governance," which refers to the democratic election of the village committee, the democratic management of village affairs, transparency of village affairs, democratic decision making, and supervision of the village committee. Self-governance is now a state policy that is being implemented (regardless of its effectiveness) among all of China's 700,000 odd villages to a rural population of some 900,000,000. A call for documentary film proposal[s] was advertised in September 2005. Some ninety proposals were entered for both competitions: Villager DV-Makers and Young Filmmakers (under 30). From each category, the ten best proposals were retained. The exciting comments written in the proposals entered in by the villagers serve as testimonies of how valuable this unprecedented project is – out there in the countryside, the villagers, who previously had only been the objects of curious cameras, have always had a yearning for expressions of their own.[50]

In all cases, descriptions framed the China Village Documentary Project as an outgrowth of peasant storytelling and testimony.

In my view, there are several reasons why the China Village Documentary Project was reviewed and represented as providing an authentic – that is to say, truthful and uncensored – perspective on village life in China, and why the project's institutional connections to the EUCTP were almost uniformly downplayed. The first is that the producers themselves did not appear particularly interested in addressing the context of the project – namely, grassroots political reform. Instead, the focus of their promotional efforts was primarily to depict the films as works of villager storytelling. Second, names like the European Commission and Ministry of Civil Affairs do not seem to have registered with audiences interested in contemporary cinema coming out of China. Third, for producers and audiences alike, the wider field of independent documentary filmmaking, with its emphasis on individual artistry or auteur-ism, was a more readily available framework for positioning the films than was international civil society capacity-building. Finally, it is difficult to avoid the conclusion that discussions of current, state-led democratization efforts in China are viewed as non-starters outside of official circles. For citizens both inside and outside of China, the topic is more likely to be avoided or treated with incredulity, if not suspicion.

As a result, subsequent packaging and coverage of the China Village Documentary Project oscillated between relatively factual accounts of the project's origins and development and a more pro-independence, pro-society spin that obscured its transnational and government ties. This spin included praiseworthy buzzwords such as 'grassroots humanism' and 'socially engaged art,' while accentuating the role of filmmakers Wu Wenguang and, to a lesser extent, Jian Yi.[51] One particularly daring piece linked the films to debates over the reemergence of a post-Mao public sphere.[52] Where differing perspectives appeared, their origins lay largely outside of the Chinese cinema–focused transcript of festivals, interviews, academic papers, and online reviews. Supporters of activist media placed the China Village Documentary Project within a broader, international spectrum of participatory image-making spanning China, the European Union, Sierra Leone, England, India, Spain, Iraq, and Lebanon.[53] Another perspective included that of the Chinese Communist Party's official English-language website, which reproduced parts of an interview with Wu Wenguang in which Wu was quoted as stating that:

If these villagers are given more channels in which to voice their desires and rural officials handle them with more meticulous care, patience, [sic] and skills, the problems of widespread protests in the countryside will be tackled since the Chinese farmers are the "most lovable."[54]

According to official Party media sources, both the project and the EUCTP had contributed to 'management in a democratic way' in the 'new socialist countryside'. The EUCTP, in particular, was deemed a 'success'.[55] One might note a certain irony in international audiences reading the public communication activities of an EU–China cooperative project as uncensored perspectives on the dysfunction of local governance in rural China.[56] More striking, however, is that the Party itself took a positive view of both the democratization programme and the related villager documentaries. While this response fits into established patterns of the use of grassroots elections to buff the CCP's international image, it is very difficult to place this within the state/society dichotomy that appears in so much writing on Chinese cinema and, by extension, art and culture in China generally. It is not just the transnational which is invisible in accounts of independent documentary filmmaking – the idea that the state itself could play an enabling role must be hidden from sight if the twin fictions of independence and individual authorship are to be preserved.

Conclusion

This chapter has advanced the argument that independent documentary film production in China has been transformed by transnational forces and from unexpected directions. Since the 1990s, international NGOs like the Ford Foundation have cooperated with cultural producers in China as part of broader efforts to integrate audiovisual media into the development process. In the case of Photovoice and related participatory video projects, this cooperation has taken the specific form of empowering citizen-filmmakers to document their own lives. However, these projects are themselves ultimately re-channelled through what I have called the NGO Aesthetic – a mode of representation that reflects development managers' desire to create and sustain an intervention logic through the identification of social problems; establishes indices of progress; identifies reliable and independent sources of verification; and establishes specific conditions necessary for successful intervention. This logframe-derived set of elements has influenced the development of what is called 'participatory' or 'activist' documentary filmmaking in China. While I have focused primarily on the Wu Wenguang- and Jian Yi-produced China Village Documentary Project in my account, the NGO Aesthetic is also discernible in other endeavours that connect dispersed, participatory video methods of production with developmental and rights-oriented intervention goals.

It is not difficult to locate antecedents to the NGO Aesthetic in community and activist media stretching back several decades. However, I would argue that the emphasis on dispersed media production through recruitment of citizen volunteers does constitute a new paradigm within the broader narrative of China's independent documentary cinema – one that can also be seen in Wu Wenguang's more recent oral history-based 'memory project' devoted to the Great Leap Famine. This chapter, however, is less a genealogy of participatory video and the NGO Aesthetic generally and more an attempt to demonstrate that the presence of both of these elements in the films of the China Village Documentary Project signals the presence of transnational networks linking filmmakers in China to state and NGO institutions. It goes without saying that directors in China have hardly been latecomers to transnationally circulating audiovisual practices such as Photovoice (developed in Yunnan province with Ford Foundation support) and participatory video (an emerging field in which Wu Wenguang ranks among the best-known practitioners). While the precise connections between innovations taking place in Yunnan and the China Village Documentary Project are somewhat difficult to confirm, the similarities between the projects are obvious, with Yunfest representing the most likely node linking Yunnan-based Guo Jing to Beijing-based Wu Wenguang. In addition, the EUCTP itself can be seen as one of many authors of the project, not only for its financial support, but also because its activities in the realm of village democratization and elections have dictated the themes and, notably, the aesthetic qualities of the China Village Documentary Project films.

To be sure, Wu Wenguang, Jian Yi, and the villager filmmakers themselves must nonetheless be acknowledged as the project's authors. And yet here again it bears repeating that both Wu and Jian have operated throughout their careers in contexts extending well beyond the boundaries of China and – returning to my final point – are constantly engaging with dynamics that, ultimately, transcend the better-documented (and often misrepresented) struggle between state and society which is depicted as the central concern of China's independent documentary film producers. To speak of the transnational is not only to speak of international film festivals and their attendant critical apparatus of scholars, reviewers, enthusiasts, and programmers, but also of NGOs, state-supported development organizations, and even cultural diplomacy. All of these elements have been present in the history of the China Villagers Documentary Project, with implications not only for how we understand Chinese independent documentary and its origins, but also how we understand authorship within that field of moving image production. With respect to the project, however, there has been a notable trend among observers and even the project's own producers to downplay outside forces in favour of promoting a story about grassroots agency – that the project represents villagers' 'own stories.'

This story about agency is not wholly incorrect, but it is incomplete. Its incompleteness suggests that there are still significant shortcomings in how we view film production in China. The state/society binary is not the only factor responsible for this trend. Another culprit is auteur theory, or the assumption that every cultural object must have an individual human producer – 'the artist' – when in truth markets, institutions, networks, and other forms of social organization play a determining role as well. While democratization in China is not a particularly successful reform in the eyes of the PRC government's many critics, efforts to carry it out have provided support for the China Village Documentary Project and related public communications efforts undertaken by the EUCTP. Likewise, while the Ford Foundation's activities in China are often rendered invisible by the country's authoritarianism, a small number of perceptive scholars have suggested ways in which NGO developmental programmes in Yunnan have presaged what might be called the 'participatory turn' in China's independent documentary cinema. Here I have attempted to build on those insights by showing how they might be leveraged to understand cinema from a transnational, non-auteur-centred vantage point. Independent documentary production in China is not solely a byproduct of some agonistic conflict between state and society – though elements of that conflict are indeed evident – but is a geographically dispersed, aesthetically eclectic cultural field whose existence can be attributed to state, non-state, domestic, and international actors.

Works cited

Alpermann, Björn. An Assessment of Research on Village Governance in China and Suggestions for Future Applied Research (report prepared for the China-EU Training Programme on Village Governance, 14 April 2003). http://homepage.ruhr-uni-bochum.de/david.beckeherm/WiSe%202005-2006/Hausarbeit/Dorfwahlen%20in%20China%20-%20Demokratieansatz%20oder%20Opium%20f%FCrs%20Volk/Quellen/File888.pdf

Asian Cultural Council. *Asian Cultural Council Annual Report 2007–2008*. http://www.asianculturalcouncil.org.hk/upload/annual/ACC_Annual_Report_2007-2008.pdf

Berry, Chris, Lu Xinyu and Lisa Rofel (eds). *The New Chinese Film Documentary Movement: For the Public Record*. Hong Kong: Hong Kong University Press, 2010.

Blakewell, Oliver and Anne Garbutt. *The Use and Abuse of the Logical Framework Approach*. Stockholm: Swedish International Development Cooperation Agency, 2005. http://www.intrac.org/data/files/resources/518/The-Use-and-Abuse-of-the-Logical-Framework-Approach.pdf

Callahan, William A. *Contingent States: Greater China and Transnational Relations*. Minneapolis: University of Minnesota Press, 2004.

Chen, Xiaomei. *Visuality and Identity: Sinophone Articulations across the Pacific*. Berkeley, CA: University of California Press, 2007.

China Daily. 'Democracy Program "A Success" in Rural Areas,' China.org.cn, 6 April 2006. http://www.china.org.cn/english/government/164775.htm

'China Village Documentary Project.' CIDFA website, n.d., http://www.cidfa.com/video/China_Villagers_Documentary_Project_category

'China Village Documentary Project.' CCD Workstation, n.d.. http://www.ccdworkstation.com/english/China%20Village%20Documentary%20Project%20intro.html

Commission to Support the Reform Process in China. Press Release, Europa website, 7 November 1996, http://europa.eu/rapid/press-release_IP-96-994_en.htm

Cooper, Caroline. 'Capturing China's Problems on Film,' Asia Times Online, 29 November 2005. http://www.atimes.com/atimes/China/GK29Ad01.html

The Council on East Asian Studies at Yale University. Announcement for 'Visual Documentary Project on China's Village-Level Documentary,' n.d. [March 2006]. http://eastasianstudies.research.yale.edu/chinesevillagedemocracyfilms.pdf

Cui Weiping. 'Cunmin yingxiang yu shequ yingxiang' [Villager images and community images], *Zhongguo nanfang yishu*, 28 September 2012. http://www.zgnfys.com/a/nfpl-5929.shtml

'EU–China Program to Promote Village Management.' People's Daily Online, August 6, 2001. http://english.people.com.cn/200108/06/eng20010806_76629.html

'EU Helps China Train 14,000 Experts in Village Affairs.' People's Daily Online, 19 May 2005. http://english.peopledaily.com.cn/200505/19/eng20050519_185702.html

'European and Chinese Municipalities Meet at CEMR's.' Council of European Municipalities and Regions website, 18 January 2006. http://www.ccre.org/en/champsactivites/detail_news/686

Evaluation of the European Commission's Co-Operation and Partnership with the People's Republic of China: Country Level Evaluation: Final Synthesis Report, Volume 2 – Annexes, April 2007.

Fewsmith, Joseph. *The Logic and Limits of Political Reform in China*. Cambridge: Cambridge University Press, 2013.

Gallagher, Mark. *Another Steven Soderbergh Experience: Authorship and Contemporary Hollywood*. Austin: University of Texas Press, 2013.

Gallagher, Mark and Julian Stringer. 'Reshaping contemporary Chinese film sound: Dolby laboratories and changing industrial practices,' *Journal of Chinese Cinemas*, vol. 7, no. 3 (2013): 263–76.

Guo, Sujian (ed.). *Political Science and Chinese Political Studies: The State of the Field*. Heidelberg: Springer-Verlag, 2013.

Hong, Han. 'Canyu shi yingxiang yu canyu shi chuanbo – fazhen chuanbo shiye zhong de Zhongguo canyu shi yingxiang yanjiu' [Participatory Video and Participatory Media – Research on China's Participatory Video from the Perspective of Media Developments], *Zhongguo shehui kexue wang*, 20 August 2012. http://www.cssn.cn/66/6603/201208/t20120820_202718.shtml

Haralampieva, Angelina. 'Justifiable Conformity?: Research on the Causality Behind the Disturbances in the EU's Cooperation with China in Priority Area 'Civil Society."' MA thesis, Aalborg University, 2010.

Hirono, Miwa. *Civilizing Missions: International Religious Agencies in China*. New York: Palgrave Macmillan, 2008.

Horsley, Jamie P. 'Village Elections: Training Ground for Democratization,' China Business, March/April 2001. https://www.chinabusinessreview.com/public/0103/horsley.html

Jie, Chen. *Transnational Civil Society in China: Intrusion and Impact*. Cheltenham: Edward Elgar Publishing, 2012.

Johnson, Matthew David. '"A Scene Beyond Our Line of Sight": Wu Wenguang and New Documentary Cinema's Politics of Independence' in Paul G. Pickowicz and Yingjin Zhang (eds), *From Underground to Independent: Alternative Film Culture in Contemporary China*. Lanham: Rowman & Littlefield, 2006.

—'Website review: China independent documentary film archive,' *American Anthropologist*, vol. 112, no. 3. September 2010.

Jun, Li. 'Cunmin yingyiang jihua – duihua Wu Wenguang' [The Villager Documentary Project – A Dialogue with Wu Wenguang], *Yunfest* newsletter, 21 March 2009. http://yishujia.findart.com.cn/25400-blog.html

Keohane, Robert O. and Joseph S. Nye Jr. *Transnational Relations and World Politics*. Cambridge: Harvard University Press, 1971.

Khoo, Olivia and Sean Metzger (eds). *Futures of Chinese Cinema: Technologies and Temporalities in Chinese Screen Cultures.* Bristol: Intellect, 2009.

Kokas, Aynne. 'Finding Democracy, and Other Village Tales: Wu Wenguang's China Village Self-Governance Film Project,' Asia Pacific Arts, 16 February 2007. http://www.asiaarts.ucla.edu/article.asp?parentid=63699

Lu, Sheldon Hsiao-peng (ed.). *Transnational Chinese Cinemas: Identity, Nationhood, Gender.* Honolulu: University of Hawai'i Press, 1997.

Lu, Yiyi. *Non-Governmental Organizations in China.* Abingdon: Routledge, 2008.

Ma, Qiusha. *Non-Governmental Organizations in Contemporary China: Paving the Way to Civil Society?* Abingdon: Routledge, 2006.

Ma, Ran. *Chinese Independent Cinema and International Film Festival Network at the Age of Global Media Consumption.* PhD diss, University of Hong Kong, 2010.

McLagan, Meg and Yates McKee (eds). *Sensible Politics: The Visual Culture of Nongovernmental Activism.* Cambridge: MIT Press, 2012.

O'Brien, Kevin J. and Rongbin Han. 'Path to democracy? assessing village elections in China,' *Journal of Contemporary China*, vol. 18, no. 60 (June 2009): 359-78.

'Participatory Photography,' The Rights Exposure Project – Visual Media for Social Activism website, n.d. http://therightsexposureproject.com/photography-resources/participatory-photography/

'Participatory Video Projects,' *Machik* website, n.d., http://www.machik.org/index.php?option=com_content&task=view&id=34&Itemid=60

Pickowicz, Paul G. 'Independent Chinese Film: Seeing the Not-Usually-Visible in Rural China' in Catherine Lynch, Robert B. Marks and Paul G. Pickowicz (eds), *Radicalism, Revolution, and Reform in Modern China: Essays in Honor of Maurice Meisner.* Lanham: Lexington Books, 2011.

Rudman, Stephen Todd. *The Multinational Corporation in China: Controlling Interests.* Malden, MA: Blackwell, 2006.

Shambaugh, David. 'European and American Approaches to China: Different Bed, Same Dreams?,' Sigur Center Asia Papers No. 15. Washington, DC: The Sigur Center for Asian Studies, 2002.

Tang, Qingshan. 'Foreign NGOs' Role in Local Governance' in Zheng Yongnian and Joseph Fewsmith (eds), *China's Opening Society: The Non-State Sector and Governance.* Abingdon: Routledge, 2008.

Taylor, Jeremy E. *Rethinking Transnational Chinese Cinemas: The Amoy-Dialect Film Industry in Cold War Asia.* Adingdon: Routledge, 2011.

Ting Wai. 'Human Rights and EU-China Relations' in Roland Vogt (ed.), Europe and China: Strategic Partners or Rivals? Hong Kong: Hong Kong University Press, 2012.

Un, Siosan. 'Floating as a Keyword: Independent Documentary Films in Postsocialist China.' MA thesis, University of Toronto, 2009.

Voci, Paloa. *China on Video: Smaller-Screen Realities.* Abingdon: Routledge, 2010.

Wang, Caroline and Mary Ann Burris. 'Photovoice: concept, methodology, and use for participatory needs assessment,' *Health Education & Behavior*, vol. 24, no. 3 (1997): 369-387.

Wang, Caroline C. 'Photovoice: a participatory action research strategy applied to women's health,' *Journal of Women's Health*, vol. 8, no. 2 (1999): 185-92.

Wang, Caroline C., Wu Kun Yi, Zhen Wen Tao and Kathryn Corovano. 'Photovoice as a participatory health promotion strategy,' *Health Promotion International*, vol. 13, no. 1 (1998): 75-86.

Wang, Lingzhen (ed.). *Chinese Women's Cinema: Transnational Contexts*. New York: Columbia University Press, 2013.
Wheeler, Norton. *The Role of American NGOs in China's Modernization: Invited Influence*. Abingdon: Routledge, 2013.
'Wu Wenguang: China Village Self-Governance Film Project,' Roy and Edna Disney/ CalArts Theater (REDCAT) website, 29 January 2007. http://www.redcat.org/event/wu-wenguang (accessed 18 September 2013).
'Wu Wenguang: China Village Self-Governance Film Project,' Yahoo website, 2007. http://upcoming.yahoo.com/event/137374/CA/Los-Angeles/Wu-Wenguang-China-Village-Self-Governance-Film-Project/REDCAT/
Xinhua. 'Grassroots Democracy Shot Forth by Village Photographers,' *News of the Communist Party of China* website, 13 June 2006. http://english.cpc.people.com.cn/66098/4468712.html
Zhang, Yingjin. *Cinema, Space, and Polylocality in a Globalizing World*. Honolulu: University of Hawai'i Press, 2010.
Zhuangzhou, Zheng. 'Situating Socially Engaged Art in China,' *ArtHub*, October 2009. http://arthubasia.org/archives/situating-socially-engaged-art-in-china/

Notes

1. For a recent and thought-provoking set of essays on this theme, see Sujian Guo (ed.), *Political Science and Chinese Political Studies: The State of the Field*. Heidelberg: Springer-Verlag, 2013.
2. See William A. Callahan, *Contingent States: Greater China and Transnational Relations*. Minneapolis: University of Minnesota Press, 2004; Qiusha Ma, *Non-Governmental Organizations in Contemporary China: Paving the Way to Civil Society?* Abingdon: Routledge, 2006; Miwa Hirono, *Civilizing Missions: International Religious Agencies in China*. New York: Palgrave Macmillan, 2008; Yiyi Lu, *Non-Governmental Organizations in China*. Abingdon: Routledge, 2008; Chen Jie, *Transnational Civil Society in China: Intrusion and Impact*. Cheltenham: Edward Elgar Publishing, 2012; Norton Wheeler, *The Role of American NGOs in China's Modernization: Invited Influence*. Abingdon: Routledge, 2013. The literature on multinational corporations is voluminous. See, for example, Stephen Todd Rudman, *The Multinational Corporation in China: Controlling Interests*. Malden, MA: Blackwell, 2006.
3. For one near-exception to this rule, and a brilliant collection of essays on the issue of Chinese cinemas in historical and transcultural context, see Lingzhen Wang (ed.), *Chinese Women's Cinema: Transnational Contexts*. New York: Columbia University Press, 2013.
4. The most comprehensive and anticipated work in this regard is, undoubtedly, Ran Ma, *Chinese Independent Cinema and International Film Festival Network at the Age of Global Media Consumption* (PhD dissertation, University of Hong Kong, 2010).
5. For additional historical and theoretical overviews of transnationalism in Chinese cinemas, see Sheldon Hsiao-peng Lu (ed.), *Transnational Chinese Cinemas: Identity, Nationahood, Gender*. Honolulu: University of Hawai'i Press, 1997, and Jeremy E. Taylor, *Rethinking Transnational Chinese Cinemas: The Amoy-Dialect Film Industry*

in Cold War Asia. Abingdon: Routledge, 2011. For recent research pointing to the importance of transnational and international dynamics in Chinese screen industries, see Mark Gallagher and Julian Stringer, 'Reshaping contemporary Chinese film sound: Dolby laboratories and changing industrial practices,' *Journal of Chinese Cinemas*, vol. 7, no. 3 (2013): 263–76. A key work that looks at transnational cinema from a linguistic perspective is Shu-mei Shih, *Visuality and Identity: Sinophone Articulations across the Pacific*. Berkeley, CA: University of California Press, 2007.

6 For a classic definition and analysis of transnational relations, see Robert O. Keohane and Joseph S. Nye Jr., *Transnational Relations and World Politics*. Cambridge: Harvard University Press, 1971.

7 Here I am adopting what I have found to be the most consistently used title for the project, which in Chinese has also been known as the *Cunmin yingxiang jihua* and *Zhongguo cunmin zizhi yingxiang chuanbo xiangmu jihua*. In English the roughly corresponding translations, all of which have been used in promotional materials and the project's own English-language publicity, are: China Villagers Documentary Project, China Village Self-Governance Film Project, and, less frequently, Visual Documentary Project on China's Village-Level Democracy.

8 On the problem of authorship in film, see Mark Gallagher, *Another Steven Soderbergh Experience: Authorship and Contemporary Hollywood*. Austin University of Texas Press, 2013.

9 On visual culture and nongovernmental sensibilities, see Meg McLagan and Yates McKee (eds), *Sensible Politics: The Visual Culture of Nongovernmental Activism* Cambridge: MIT Press, 2012.

10 On texture in Chinese cinemas and screen cultures, see Olivia Khoo and Sean Metzger (eds), *Futures of Chinese Cinema: Technologies and Temporalities in Chinese Screen Cultures*. Bristol: Intellect, 2009, 19.

11 'China Village Documentary Project,' CCD Workstation, n.d., http://www.ccdworkstation.com/english/China%20Village%20Documentary%20Project%20intro.html (accessed 12 September 2013).

12 See Matthew D. Johnson, 'Website Review: China Independent Documentary Film Archive,' *American Anthropologist*, vol. 112, no. 3 (September 2010): 471–2. According to a recent server message, the site has been temporarily closed for 'policy reasons.' *China Independent Documentary Film Archive* website. http://www.cidfa.com/ (accessed 12 September 2013).

13 See Matthew David Johnson, '"A Scene Beyond Our Line of Sight": Wu Wenguang and New Documentary Cinema's Politics of Independence,' in Paul G. Pickowicz and Yingjin Zhang (eds), *From Underground to Independent: Alternative Film Culture in Contemporary China*. Lanham: Rowman & Littlefield, 2006, 47–76.

14 Like the titles of the project itself, the title of 95-minute compilation film has undergone several changes, with other renderings including *Chinese Villagers' DV Documentaries on Village-Level Democracy*.

15 For an alternative perspective on China Village Documentary Project, which more directly addresses the role of Jian Yi and presence of state involvement – primarily censorship – see Paul G. Pickowicz, 'Independent Chinese Film: Seeing the Not-Usually-Visible in Rural China,' in Catherine Lynch, Robert B. Marks and Paul G. Pickowciz (eds), *Radicalism, Revolution, and Reform in Modern China: Essays in Honor of Maurice Meisner*. Lanham: Lexington Books,

2011, 161–84. A full description of the project's administrative personnel and structure appears at 'Zhongguo cunmin zizhi yingxiang jihua' [China Village Self-Governance Visual Project], *Renmin wang* website, 23 September 2005. http://tv.people.com.cn/GB/40029/43349/3720494.html (accessed 7 November 2013).

16 Other participatory video projects include, for example, workshops hosted by the Tibet-based community engagement organization Machik, whose work includes cooperation with the Columbia University Digital Media Center for Film and Media Arts and Sichuan Provincial Tibetan Institute. See 'Participatory Video Projects,' *Machik* website, n.d. http://www.machik.org/index.php?option=com_content&task =view&id=34&Itemid=60 (accessed 2 October 2013). Other examples include the Participatory Video Project in Sierra Leone; the Kham Film Project in Tibet; Film Africa in Ghana and Zambia; FilmAid in Kenya; Women Educating for Peace; the Rights Exposure Project.

17 For a comprehensive account of the movement and its origins, see Chris Berry, Lu Xinyu and Lisa Rofel (eds), *The New Chinese Film Documentary Movement: For the Public Record*. Hong Kong: Hong Kong University Press, 2010.

18 See Oliver Blakewell and Anne Garbutt, *The Use and Abuse of the Logical Framework Approach*. Stockholm: Swedish International Development Cooperation Agency, 2005. http://www.intrac.org/data/files/resources/518/The-Use-and-Abuse-of-the-Logical-Framework-Approach.pdf (accessed 13 September 2013).

19 Jamie P. Horsley, 'Village Elections: Training Ground for Democratization,' China Business, March/April 2001. https://www.chinabusinessreview.com/public/0103/horsley.html (accessed 17 September 2013).

20 Some might argue that real procedural democracy for China's villages has been more recently tabled, or even fatally thwarted. Engagement with that argument lies beyond the scope of this chapter. For a thorough and empirically grounded assessment of village election outcomes, see Kevin J. O'Brien and Rongbin Han, 'Path to democracy? assessing village elections in China,' *Journal of Contemporary China*, vol. 18, no. 60 (June 2009): 359–78. More recently, see Joseph Fewsmith, *The Logic and Limits of Political Reform in China*. Cambridge: Cambridge University Press, 2013.

21 See Qingshan Tang, 'Foreign NGOs' Role in Local Governance,' in Zheng Yongnian and Joseph Fewsmith (eds), *China's Opening Society: The Non-State Sector and Governance*. Abingdon: Routledge, 2008, 207. See also David Shambaugh, 'European and American Approaches to China: Different Bed, Same Dreams?,' Sigur Center Asia Papers No. 15. Washington, DC: The Sigur Center for Asian Studies, 2002. www.gwu.edu/~sigur/assets/docs/scap/SCAP15-Shambaugh.pdf (accessed 2 October 2013).

22 Tang, 'Foreign NGOs,' 207.

23 Ibid., 215.

24 Commission to Support the Reform Process in China, press release, Europa website, 7 November 1996. http://europa.eu/rapid/press-release_IP-96-994_en.htm (accessed 17 September 2013).

25 'EU–China Program to Promote Village Management,' People's Daily Online, August 6, 2001. http://english.people.com.cn/200108/06/eng20010806_76629.html (accessed 17 September 2013). The majority of funding for the program was provided by the European Union.

26　Angelina Haralampieva, 'Justifiable Conformity?: Research on the Causality Behind the Disturbances in the EU's Cooperation with China in Priority Area "Civil Society"'. MA thesis, Aalborg University, 2010, 6.
27　Shambaugh, 'European and American Approaches to China,' 8.
28　Ting Wai, 'Human Rights and EU–China Relations' in Roland Vogt (ed.), Europe and China: Strategic Partners or Rivals?. Hong Kong: Hong Kong University Press, 2012, 123–4; 'EU Helps China Train 14,000 Experts in Village Affairs,' People's Daily Online, May 19, 2005. http://english.peopledaily.com.cn/200505/19/eng20050519_185702.html (accessed 17 September 2013).
29　Ting, 'Human Rights,' 123–4; 'European and Chinese Municipalities Meet at CEMR's,' Council of European Municipalities and Regions website, 18 January 2006. http://www.ccre.org/en/champsactivites/detail_news/686 (accessed 17 September 2013).
30　Evaluation of the European Commission's Co-Operation and Partnership with the People's Republic of China: Country Level Evaluation: Final Synthesis Report, Volume 2 – Annexes, April 2007, 76.
31　Björn Alpermann, 'An Assessment of Research on Village Governance in China and Suggestions for Future Applied Research' (report prepared for the China-EU Training Programme on Village Governance, 14 April 2003). http://homepage.ruhr-uni-bochum.de/david.beckeherm/WiSe%202005–2006/Hausarbeit/Dorfwahlen%20in%20China%20-%20Demokratieansatz%20oder%20Opium%20f%FCrs%20Volk/Quellen/File888.pdf (accessed 24 September 2013).
32　Siosan Un, 'Floating as a Keyword: Independent Documentary Films in Postsocialist China'. MA thesis, University of Toronto, 2009, 21–2.
33　Yingjin Zhang, Cinema, Space, and Polylocality in a Globalizing World. Honolulu: University of Hawai'i Press, 2010, 134.
34　The original Photovoice projects employed photography rather than video.
35　Perhaps unsurprisingly, participatory video has arisen along with the widespread use of relatively low-cost digital cameras in filmmaking and digitization of film production.
36　See Caroline Wang and Mary Ann Burris, 'Photovoice: concept, methodology, and use for participatory needs assessment,' Health Education & Behavior, vol. 24, no. 3 (1997): 369–87; Caroline C. Wang, Wu Kun Yi, Zhen Wen Tao and Kathryn Corovano, 'Photovoice as a participatory health promotion strategy,' Health Promotion International, vol. 13, no. 1 (1998): 75–86; Caroline C. Wang, 'Photovoice: a participatory action research strategy applied to women's health,' Journal of Women's Health, vol. 8, no. 2 (1999): 185–92.
37　This preliminary history is further complicated by Guo Jing's early experiences with Appalshop, a Kentucky-based media, arts, and education centre with a history of local filmmaking going back to the late 1960s, when it was sponsored by the US government as part of national War on Poverty initiatives.
38　See Cui Weiping, 'Cunmin yingxiang yu shequ yingxiang' [Villager images and community images], Zhongguo nanfang yishu, 28 September 2012. http://www.zgnfys.com/a/nfpl-5929.shtml (accessed 2 October 2013). For a discussion of tensions of ownership between Wu Wenguang and the village filmmakers of the China Village Documentary Project, see Paloa Voci, China on Video: Smaller-Screen Realities. Abingdon: Routledge, 2010, 152–8.
39　See, for example, Li Jun, 'Cunmin yingyiang jihua – duihua Wu Wenguang' [The Villager Documentary Project – A Dialogue with Wu Wenguang], Yunfest newsletter, 21 March 2009. http://yishujia.findart.com.cn/25400-blog.html (accessed 2 October 2013).

40 See Han Hong, 'Canyu shi yingxiang yu canyu shi chuanbo – fazhen chuanbo shiye zhong de Zhongguo canyu shi yingxiang yanjiu' [Participatory Video and Participatory Media – Research on China's Participatory Video from the Perspective of Media Developments], *Zhongguo shehui kexue wang*, 20 August 2012. http://www.cssn.cn/66/6603/201208/t20120820_202718.shtml (accessed 2 October 2013).
41 Asian Cultural Council, *Asian Cultural Council Annual Report 2007–2008*. http://www.asianculturalcouncil.org.hk/upload/annual/ACC_Annual_Report_2007–2008.pdf (accessed 2 October 2013).
42 'China Village Documentary Project,' CIDFA website, n.d., http://www.cidfa.com/video/China_Villagers_Documentary_Project_category. (accessed 9 January 2014)
43 Caroline Cooper, 'Capturing China's Problems on Film,' Asia Times Online, 29 November 2005. http://www.atimes.com/atimes/China/GK29Ad01.html (accessed 18 September 2013).
44 Siosan Un, 'Floating as a Keyword: Independent Documentary Films in Postsocialist China'. MA thesis, University of Toronto, 2009, 21–2.
45 'Ethical Direction: The Village Video Project with Wu Wenguang,' The Center for Religion and Media website, 2006. http://www.crmnyu.org/event/ethical-direction-the-village-video-project-with-wu-wenguang/ (accessed 18 September 2013).
46 The Council on East Asian Studies at Yale University, announcement for 'Visual Documentary Project on China's Village-Level Documentary,' n.d. [March 2006]. http://eastasianstudies.research.yale.edu/chinesevillagedemocracyfilms.pdf (accessed 2 October 2013).
47 Ibid.
48 Aynne Kokas, 'Finding Democracy, and Other Village Tales: Wu Wenguang's China Village Self-Governance Film Project,' Asia Pacific Arts, 16 February 2007. http://www.asiaarts.ucla.edu/article.asp?parentid=63699 (accessed 18 September 2013).
49 'Wu Wenguang: China Village Self-Governance Film Project,' Yahoo website, 2007. http://upcoming.yahoo.com/event/137374/CA/Los-Angeles/Wu-Wenguang-China-Village-Self-Governance-Film-Project/REDCAT/ (accessed 18 September 2013).
50 'Wu Wenguang: China Village Self-Governance Film Project,' Roy and Edna Disney/CalArts Theater (REDCAT) website, 29 January 2007. http://www.redcat.org/event/wu-wenguang (accessed 18 September 2013).
51 See, for example, Zheng Zhuangzhou, 'Situating Socially Engaged Art in China,' *ArtHub*, October 2009. http://arthubasia.org/archives/situating-socially-engaged-art-in-china/ (accessed 3 October 2013).
52 Ibid.
53 'Participatory Photography,' The Rights Exposure Project – Visual Media for Social Activism website, n.d.. http://therightsexposureproject.com/photography-resources/participatory-photography/ (accessed 3 October 2013).
54 Xinhua, 'Grassroots Democracy Shot Forth by Village Photographers,' *News of the Communist Party of China* website, 13 June 2006. http://english.cpc.people.com.cn/66098/4468712.html (accessed 3 October 2013).
55 China Daily, 'Democracy Program 'A Success' in Rural Areas,' China.org.cn, 6 April 2006. http://www.china.org.cn/english/government/164775.htm (accessed 3 October 2013).
56 On the censorship of China Village Documentary Project films, see Pickowicz, 'Independent Chinese Films.'

15

The Cinematic Deng Xiaoping: Scripting a Leader or a 'Traitor'?

Xiaomei Chen

In China's post reform-and-opening cinematic world – where filmmakers have shifted to individualism, commercialism, urbanization and globalization – how did the Maoist filmic tradition survive in post-Mao capitalist China, which had by and large cast doubts on the country's very revolutionary traditions, filmic and otherwise? Did old-fashioned tales of revolutionary leaders of the Chinese Communist Party still matter on the postsocialist screen? If so, what are the underlying themes, images and characters that have continued to draw audiences? This chapter examines a group of films and television dramas focused on the glorious life stories of Deng Xiaoping, who is said to have brought about 'real' happiness to the Chinese people thanks to his prosperity policies. On the one hand, the Deng stories on screen seem to work perfectly well with the ruling regime's propaganda machines in post-reform China. On the other hand, however, when read between texts, across genres, and especially when compared to the most recent scholarship on CCP history, a different Deng emerged: a cautious man with great survival skills who had more than once escaped from the frontline of a war for his own safety. Most significantly, this chapter argues that propaganda films in a capitalist Chinese society with socialist characteristics are alive and here to stay, and should and can be taken seriously in our scholarly research on twenty-first-century cinema.

Similar to performance art versions of Mao's life stories, film and TV dramas about Deng's career frequently premiered on the founding dates of the PRC, the CCP, the People's Liberation Army (PLA), and the birthdays and death anniversaries of their leaders. A 'revolutionary youth idol film' (*lingxiu qingnian ouxiang pian*) entitled *My Years in France* (*Wo de Falanxi suiyuei*) appeared to commemorate Deng's 100th birthday in 2004. This film portrays Deng's five-year experience in France, from the age of 16 to 21, and his participation in the overseas work-study programme (*fu Fa qin gong jian xue*).[1] Uniquely focusing on Deng's adolescent life, the film demonstrates the energy, passion, and inspiring utopian appeal of the socialist movement in the 1920s that turned a group of Chinese diaspora students into determined Communists.

This remembrance of the martyrs echoes Deng's statement at the onset of the film: 'More than four years of living in France tempered my unyielding character with tribulations and hardships. Others deemed the Soviet Union as the cradle of their revolutionary careers; I am, on the contrary, forever grateful to France, and to its miserable realities in the 1920s, and its championship of freedom, all of which had fostered my firm determination to become a Communist. How many former friends of mine have already given up their lives for the establishment of our new motherland!'[2] This mainstream theme of celebrating early CCP leaders could challenge the legacy of Mao on at least two levels: first, other unsung heroes and early martyrs paved the way for Mao's success. Second, the film highlights Deng's will to carry out the unfinished task which appears to be the most challenging.

In the middle of the film, when asked what would he do if he were to be executed as a counter-revolutionary, the teenage Deng states resolutely: 'for my idealism and faith, I have already given them all to the young Communist Party!' An idealistic Deng in his younger days could not have imagined that he would be labelled as an arch counter-revolutionary, or 'an incorrigible capitalist roader' who had 'never really admitted his guilt nor changed his behaviour' (*si bu ganhui de zouzipai*) during the Cultural Revolution in the socialist China he had helped established. His long and problematic career in the PRC, especially during and after the Cultural Revolution, led to his eventual conviction that Mao's socialist approach, and its adherence to the Marxist orthodoxy of waging class struggle, had failed in leading China to prosperity. When he became China's leader, Deng determined that he had to replace Mao's system with his own capitalist approach of a market economy. Ironically, he had personally suffered under this system while working as a steel factory worker in France, an unforgettable experience that had turned him to the Communist cause in the first place.

Another film released to commemorate Deng's 100th birthday, *Deng Xiaoping in 1928* (*Deng Xiaoping zai yi jiu er ba*), became part of a series of movies that followed the model of a Soviet film series on Lenin, which included *Lenin in October* (*Lening zai shiyue*), *Lenin in 1917* (*Lening zai yi jiu yi qi*) and *Lenin in 1918* (*Lening zai yi jiu yi ba*). These Lenin films were all popular in China, especially during the Cultural Revolution, when films from the socialist bloc attracted Chinese audiences due in part to the lack of domestically produced Chinese films. The Deng movies on a single year also paralleled with those of Mao, such as *Mao Zedong in 1925* (*Mao Zedong zai yi jiu er wu*) and *China in 1929* (*Zhongguo yi jiu er yi*).

Whereas *My French Years* featured a young Deng in an exotic, romantic European setting, *Deng Xiaoping in 1928* picks up upon his return to China from the Soviet Union. At that time, Deng served as the chief secretary of the CCP Central Committee (*Zhongyang mishuzhang*), and was in charge of running its daily affairs in Shanghai from autumn 1927, when Deng followed the CCP Central Committee's move from Wuhan to Shanghai, to May 1928, right before the CCP's Sixth Congress.[3] Gu Bai, the film's director, did not just want to make another biographical film about the great leader, so he structured the film entirely as a thriller, a pioneering genre never explored before in the leader films.[4] Gu dramatized Deng's effort to protect Zhou Enlai and other CCP leaders, then being rounded up by the Kuomintang (KMT) after the failure of the 'grand revolution of 1927.' Deng succeeded in eliminating traitors, retained courageous CCP members who had been set up by the KMT secret agents as 'conspirators,' established secure places for the CCP leaders to meet, and provided safe passage for all the representatives from different parts of China to depart from Shanghai to travel to Moscow in 1929 to participate in the CCP's Sixth Party Congress.

These plot details emphasize Deng's remembrance of his fallen comrades, their wisdom and sacrifice. Most significantly, it reflects the hindsight of the filmmakers in contemporary times, as Deng was ousted in his later career thanks to mistrust from his own party leaders, a running theme that we see in subsequent films and TV dramas. The scriptwriter's claim to historical 'truth' can only be appreciated in light of his own perception of history and its relevant lessons for contemporary audiences. The film's director revealed his crew's motivation in producing a movie favourable to Deng's legacy, saying: 'Our generation, and the entire young generation growing up in the Reform Era, all benefited from Deng's policies to open up China to the outside world. We devoted ourselves to the making of this movie with real feeling of gratitude toward Deng Xiaoping.'[5]

Detective story aside, *Deng Xiaoping in 1928* includes the characteristics of the 'significant revolutionary historical film' with a popular love story. Gu wove together a suspenseful thriller with Deng's passionate love for Zhang Xiyuan, whom he first met in the Soviet Union and married in Shanghai in 1928. According to Maomao's biography, *My Father, Deng Xiaoping*, Zhang was 'a rare beauty,' and Deng treasured his memory of her after she died in childbirth in 1929.[6] Similar to *My French Years*, *Deng Xiaoping in 1928* also portrays Deng's deep friendship with Zhou Enlai, his superior to protect and a 'brother' to guide him. To better shield Zhou from the enemy's round-up, Deng and Zhang rented an apartment on the first floor of the same house where Zhou and his wife, Deng Yingchao, lived on the second floor. The two young couples' beauty, passion, friendship, faith and dedication attracted audiences both young and old alike, and the casting itself boosted ticket sales, with the film featuring well-known movie and theatre stars from China, Hong Kong and America.[7]

The next three films and TV dramas I discuss concentrate on one year in Deng Xiaoping's life: 1929, when he established his military career with his leadership of the Baise Uprising in Jiangxi Province, as seen in the film *Baise Uprising* (*Baise qiyi*); a three-part TV drama series, *Tiger Commander Li Mingrui* (*Hujiang Li Mingrui*); and a six-part TV drama series, *The Red River Bank – Deng Xiaoping in 1929* (*Hong'an – Deng Xiaoping zai yi jiu er jiu*).

Before examining these three performance texts, I will briefly discuss the importance of the Baise Uprising in relation to similar events. Previous CCP history gave much credit to the Nanchang Uprising of 1927 as the CCP's first military action against the KMT and the formation of the CCP military force. By the same token, the Autumn Peasant Uprising of 1927, led by Mao, assumed its ultimate significance in having established the first CCP armed base by relying on peasants, a uniquely Maoist approach that supposedly led to the final victory of the Chinese Revolution. Both uprisings were featured in numerous Chinese textbooks, party narratives, literature and art. Seen from this perspective, the rediscovered success story of the Baise Uprising was indeed significant. In comparison to these two uprisings, the Baise Uprising was rarely included in the CCP party narrative, textbooks and public media before and during the Cultural Revolution, or even in the early post-Mao China when party narratives were revised to fully credit other key leaders of the CCP, especially those persecuted during the Cultural Revolution. In the 1990s, however, the Baise Uprising gained prominence as a fruitful event in the Communist Revolution, which established the 'Left and Right Bank River revolutionary armed base' (*Zuoyoujiang geming gejudi*), and was cited as an early triumphant example of 'military occupations by the workers and peasants' (*gongnong wuzhuang geju*).

Released in 1989, the film *Baise Uprising* dramatized Deng's leadership role in this uprising that led to the formation of the Seventh and Eighth Red Amy troops, which joined forces with Mao Zedong and Zhu De's troops in Jingguangshan. Clearly defining it as a 'revolutionary history film with documentary features' (*wenxian xing de geming lishi gushi pian*), the production team dug into historical archives visited with survivors of the Baise Uprising.[8] Based on this solid understanding of 'history,' the film crew focused on creating a 'particular environment' (*dianxing huanjing*) without losing sight of the powerful image of a young, compassionate, resourceful Deng, who, at the tender age of 25, had already established himself as a wise leader in the complex historical circumstances of 1929.

The film *Baise Uprising* presents the intricate situations in Guangxi around June 1929, when KMT leader Chiang Kai-shek appointed Yu Zuobai as the president of the Guangxi government and Li Mingrui as his special agent in Guangxi. Influenced by the CCP's policies, Yu and Li invited CCP members to join their efforts in managing governmental affairs in Guangxi. As a result of this invitation, the CCP sent Deng Xiaoping, Chen Haoren, Zhang Yunyi, Gong Hechun and others to Guangxi. Upon his arrival, Deng made friends with Yu and Li, convinced them to release imprisoned CCP members, developed underground party organizations in Nanning, and carried out land reform in the rural areas to inspire peasants to join the revolution.

The film dramatized a resourceful Deng who makes thoughtful yet swift decisions at crucial moments. Most significantly, it depicted Deng as a rebel against the leftist opportunist policies of the CCP, then under the leadership of Li Lisan, who ordered Deng's troops to seize urban centres first – an erroneous strategy imposed by Stalin, who insisted that the Chinese Revolution should follow the Soviet model of the proletariat dictatorship. One scene, for example, depicts Deng's debate with his radical peers, who called for a quick Communist insurgency (a 'Nanning Uprising'), in imitation of the heroic spirit of the failed Guangzhou Uprising. Deng insisted on the contrary: the CCP forces should quickly move to the remote, rural area to join Wei Baqun's peasant movement for sustained military struggles against the KMT. With thoughtfulness and wisdom, Deng reminded his comrades to honour those 'brave and exceptional comrades, who prematurely died in the abortive Guangzhou Uprising, a painful and profound lesson never to forget.'[9]

Upon receiving the letter sent by the CCP Central Committee, Deng responded indignantly: we had paid heavily for the rightist policies that brought about the failure of the 'grand revolution'; we would pay an even heftier price for the current leftist policies. He dismissed the letter's charge of him as 'having fallen into the mud of opportunism,' and indicated he would not back off even if others accused him as having pursued a 'rightist opportunist approach' of trusting warlords in their efforts to assist revolution. 'I cannot move heaven and earth, but I take to heart eight Chinese characters: "adopt new strategies for different circumstances" (*sui ji ying bian*) and "seek truth in practice" (*shi shi qiu shi*),' Deng declared wittily and firmly (205). These two characteristics defined Deng's unique leadership in his later career, both in the historical record that this film is based on, and in the representations of this record in numerous party narratives and literary works in Dengist China.

Film, after all, is not history. Other survivors' memories can, in fact, be read as having challenged the dominant role of Deng's leadership as it was portrayed in *Baise Uprising*. Yuan Renyuan, for instance, gave more weight in his memoir to the contributions of Yu Zuobai and Li Mingrui, the warlords who had already supported the development of the peasant movement before the CCP leaders' arrival. Most significantly, Yuan pointed to Deng's absence during the Baise Uprising: he left for Shanghai to report to the CCP Central Committee, while Yuan and other leaders threw themselves into preparing for the forthcoming uprising: they reorganized the military units under CCP control; distributed the resolution of the CCP's Sixth Congress; made uniforms, army flags and arm bands for the insurgent troops; and arrested reactionary officers and local authorities to thwart their sabotage (109–10). On 11 December 1929, in honour of the second anniversary of the Guangzhou Uprising, they declared their uprising in Baise and established the Seventh Red Amy and the Soviet Worker-Peasant Government in a mass rally of three thousand participants. Yuan recounted all these events without mentioning of Deng's presence (110–11).[10]

By the same token, Mo Wenhua's memoir emphasized Zhang Yunyi's significant role in leading the 55th Regiment of the Seventh Red Army to reach Jinggangshan after Deng had left his troops to report to work in Shanghai after March 1931. Mo also gave credit to Gong Hecun (Gong Chu), who was instrumental in building up the Seventh and Eighth Red Armies, but who disappeared in PRC history thanks to his switching sides to the KMT in 1935.[11] Gong, in his own memoir, was blunt: with regards to the formation of the Seventh Red Army, Deng was one among many representatives sent by the CCP, and he worked 'only temporarily for a short period of time' 'during Yu Zuobai's appointment by Chiang Kai-shek in presiding over provincial affairs in Guangxi.' Deng 'merely played the role of a liaison between the CCP Central Committee and the Guangxi Soviet areas' without 'any substantial work after the formation of the Seventh Red Army.'[12]

Published in Hong Kong decades after Gong had defected from the CCP, his memoir did not have to toe the CCP party line in celebrating Deng's career, and thus provides a unique perspective on Deng's rôle in Guangxi. Most other party histories and memoirs recorded Deng's leaving his troops to report to the CCP Central Committee in Shanghai, but they differed in the details as to whether or not the Central Committee had indeed asked him to go back or whether he was sent by his own local party committee of the Seventh Red Army.[13] Yang Bingzhang's authoritative account points out inconsistencies in these versions: both the accounts of Maomao, or Deng Rong (Deng's daughter), and the official party history encounter a dilemma: they want to portray Deng as a key leader of the Baise Uprising, which nevertheless failed in its mission to establish a long-standing Soviet area in the region.[14] They had no choice but to scapegoat Li Lisan, who was dismissed from his leadership position in the CCP Central Committee for his leftist opportunist policies; Deng Guang, who died in the war; and Gong Chu, who turned 'traitor,' for their mistakes that had supposedly brought about the defeat of the Guangxi Soviet areas (72). One point is clear, however, according to Yang: Deng decided to leave his troops without a collective decision from his own committee, and he did not receive any directives from the Central Committee to go back to Shanghai. As a smart politician, 'Deng understood that self-protection was the most important factor in one's political career' (78). Seen from this perspective, the film *Baise Uprising* deviated from the survivors' accounts and blurred fictionality with historicity by dramatizing the above-mentioned events without making clear whether Deng was in fact present. The filmmakers, therefore, explored visual images to bypass the complex past by either avoiding narrative details or misleadingly juxtaposing images of various events to manipulate facts.

In 2009 internet bloggers went even further to reveal Deng's so-called crimes of running away from the impending battlefield of the Baise Uprising. In his article entitled 'The Wounds of the Seventh Red Army,' Wang Buyi quoted former leaders of the Seventh Red Army such as Chen Haoren and Mo Wenhua, who had complained to the CCP Central Committee about Deng's fleeing from the uprising, even after his peers had urged him to stay. Understandably, Deng wanted to be with his young wife, who was on the verge of giving birth to their first child, but who, Wang asked, did not have families to look after? Worse still, Deng left the Seventh Red Army for the second time, and this time at an even more dangerous moment: during their 'long march' to the north to join Zhu and Mao's troops in the Jinggangshan, when the Seventh Red Army suffered a series of defeats and was split into two regiments, led by Zhang Yunyi and Li Mingrui, respectively. In his 'My Self-Explanation' (*Wo de zishu*), written in 1968 and submitted to the Central Committee, Deng admitted, 'Now, I realized that at the time when the two regiments lost contact with each other upon their defeats, I, as a key leader responsible for the army, should not have left the troops. This is a serious political mistake.' Wang believed that Deng's 'fleeing event' (*taopao shijian*) added to 'the deep wounds' of the Seventh Red Army, which witnessed other tragedies, such as the execution of Wei Baqun by his own nephew, who handed him over after enemy's torture and the wrongful and brutal execution of Li Mingrui by the CCP as a 'KMT agent,' after he had overcome numerous setbacks to lead the remaining troops of the Seventh Red Army to Jiangxi. Li's calamity resulted from certain CCP members' continuing distrust of his true commitment to the Communist cause because of his distinguished career as a warlord commander.

How to understand the history of the warlord period, which is often interpreted in the PRC history as a chaotic time dominated by greedy, 'reactionary' and power-driven military despots, who were mostly to blame for the suffering of the Chinese people in the 1920s? For whom did they fight, and how should we evaluate their contributions in modern Chinese history? To what extent did they aid the Communist movement, and how should revolutionary history represent them? These questions would find some answers in a three-part TV drama entitled *Tiger Commander Li*

Mingrui, which premiered in 2001 in commemoration of the anniversary of the Baise Uprising.

Most significantly, *Tiger Commander* depicted Li Mingrui's family as having a peasant background, with peasants considered the backbone of the Chinese Revolution. Li's father had no choice but to sell his cows to support Li's career, not unlike Deng's father in *My French Years*, who raised money to send Deng abroad in search of a new life. Li told his family that he joined the military in order to 'end the chaotic world and bring peace for the ordinary people' and because he 'hated those governments who did not place the interests of the people in the first place.' Similar to Deng's love story, Li also bid farewell to his beloved wife upon his graduation from the military academy. From that point on, his wife waited for his return for years, sometimes learning that he was still alive through reading news reports on the war front, while she raised their two children on her own without knowing his whereabouts, even after 1949, long after his execution in Jiangxi in 1931.

Li's military career did not come about without other personal losses. He parted company with his best friend Chen after Chen had led his troops to fight Li in order to wipe out the Communist base Li maintained in Baise. The TV drama presents a moving scene in which two brilliant commanders, who once had promised never to fight each other on the battlefield, now met again by a riverside as agonized friends and mortal enemies. At a tense moment in front of a grief-stricken Li, Chen puts down his gun and kills himself, leaving behind a piece of paper on which he had written these bitter words: 'Why can't we travel on the same road / after twelve years of bloody war and suffering together / as classmates, comrades, and brothers? / Why pursue 'faith' at the expense of friendship? / He who broke his oath must now kill himself. / Let me die, to join our brother Lu Huanxin in heaven.'

Chen's resentful words shed light on the predicaments of Li, who, as the concluding words on the screen reveal, was 'wrongly executed in the autumn of 1931 thanks to the radical policies of Wang Ming,' who had erroneously suspected and murdered a large number of the CCP leaders and commanders as alleged 'KMT agents and spies.' One therefore wonders what Chen would have to say about Li's 'faith' in the Communist cause, if Chen had lived to hear about Li's execution, and how Li would have explained his own choice if asked by his best friend. One potentially powerful theme of *Tiger Commander*, therefore, resides in how CCP ideology made class struggle a core value, and victimized those who had followed its cause as well as those who had fought against it. Furthermore, *Tiger Commander* finally restored the familiar image of 'warlord villains' – popular stereotypes in countless literary and artistic representations of the Chinese Revolution – to their rightful place in history, as committed soldiers and devoted patriots with their own dreams and sorrows. Most significantly, this TV drama explored the same occasion of celebrating the anniversaries of the Baise Uprising, but it presented a missing piece of the historical narratives of the uprising by praising all the famous men – not just Deng, but also Li Mingrui, his 'warlord' colleagues, and their irreplaceable contributions to the Baise Uprising, as well as their leading the Seventh Red Army to the Jiangxi Soviet area, a heroic deed that Deng had failed to follow through with due to his two sudden departures.

One might choose to imagine that, when read against such accusations of Deng's 'fleeing incidents,' an eight-part TV drama series entitled *The Red River Bank – Deng Xiaoping in 1929*, which premiered in 2009, could have raised the issue of possible guilt on Deng's part that might have haunted him in his later years. With the music of 'The Story of Spring' as its theme song, the TV drama began with the elderly Deng, in his 80s, taking a walk with his little granddaughter on a beautiful beach in contemporary China at the peak of his career, hailed as the 'chief architect' of the Chinese reform era (*Zhongguo gaige kaifang de zong shejishi*). Gazing at the ocean waves, however, old Deng suddenly sees the 'ghost' images of Li Mingrui and Wei Baqu from an ethereal past. The youthful, handsome Li and Wei, wearing their Seventh Red Army uniforms, ask the old Deng: 'Do you still remember me?' 'I *do* remember you,' Deng answers humbly. 'You have sacrificed your life heroically for the Chinese Revolution. You will live forever in the memories of the Chinese people.'[15] Through the unique perspective of the old Deng telling his own stories to his granddaughter, moreover, *The Red River Bank* could possibly be interpreted as Deng's 'confession,' in which he defends his 'fleeing incidents' because of his passionate love for his wife.

Part 1 of the series, for instance, presents a tender scene of the young Deng in 1929, at the age of 25 in his Shanghai residence, comforting his pregnant wife, who resents Deng's departure to Guangxi at the time when she needs him the most. She understands, nonetheless, that as devoted members of the CCP they have no choice but to follow the party's order at the expense of personal interests. In another scene aboard a ship from Shanghai to Nanning (by way of Hong Kong), Deng longs for his wife: 'I will always miss you no matter wherever I go – neither high mountains nor distant road will separate us.' Part Three dramatizes Deng's personal pains and frustration in finally returning to Shanghai, only to find his wife in a hospital bed. After his wife's death in childbirth, Deng recalls the image of his beautiful and energetic wife, only to wake up to the harsh reality of an infant daughter, whom he has no choice but to entrust in the care of his wife's sister, before departing for Guangxi without being to take care of his wife's burial.

If Deng's love for his wife justifies his 'fleeing' from the immanent Baise Uprising, *The Red River Bank* took a bold step further to 'turning historical memory into personal memory in order to recreate the life stories of revolutionary leaders,' in the words of script writer and director.[16] It in fact portrayed Gong Chu, historically known as the 'number one traitor of the Red Army (*hongjun zhong di yi panjiang*),' as a protagonist who contributed significantly to the Baise Uprising in 1929, long before he turned a traitor in 1935.

Presenting the historical figure of Gong Chu in the dramatic character of Gong Hecun – another name Gong Chu actually used in real life – *The Red River Bank* depicts him as a vital player. As an underground CCP leader, Gong Hecun manages to become the police chief of the city of Nanning and helps Wei Baqun and others escape from KMT secret agents. Some critics praised *The Red River Bank*'s effort 'not to avoid Gong Chu' but to give him credit where it was due for his proper place in history. Internet bloggers went further, contextualizing Gong's betrayal in the bloody history of the 'Red Army' period, which witnessed the largest number of betrayals, including seven or eight division and regiment commanders. Wang Buyi, for example, named two reasons for this massive betrayal. First, the CCP's radical campaign up to 1933 to eliminate the 'rich landlords,' 'KMT agents,' and other 'counter-revolutionaries' even within their own ranks alienated many Red Army commanders and soldiers alike. Second, after the Red Army embarked on the Long March north, the units ordered to persevere in the south suffered from the relentless crusades of the KMT to eliminate them, which resulted in the largest number of traitors among the CCP ranks. Among a series of party secretaries and political commissars on the provincial level, Gong Chu ranked the highest in his capacity as the chief staff officer of the Central Military Area (*Zhongyang junqu canmou zhang*).

Nevertheless, Gong had a distinguished career and played a significant role at almost every critical moment during the early revolutionary period: he was a veteran of Dr. Sun Yat-sen's Guangzhou troops in 1917; joined the CCP in 1925; and led the peasant movement in Guangdong Province. Gong led his peasant troops from the Beijiang areas to participate in the 1927 Nanchang Uprising, and was appointed as the party representative of the Tenth Division of the Fourth Red Army after he joined Zhu De and Mao Zedong in Jinggangshan. Most significant for our current discussion, Gong pioneered and was chiefly responsible for instigating the defection and mutiny of 'new warlord' troops led by Yu Zuobai and Li Mingrui in Guangxi, which resulted in the Baise Uprising, and was appointed the chief staff officer of the Seventh Red Army thereafter. Despite his critical contributions, the film *Baise Uprising* unfairly erased Gong from history, Wang Buyi contended;[17] the film mentioned Gong's name just once, without presenting him even as a minor character, while giving credits to others for having led the uprising.

After Li Mingrui's wrongful execution in 1931, Gong was appointed as Li's replacement as commander of the Seventh Red Army. Like many others, Gong became increasingly disillusioned by the persecutions and executions of numerous colleagues in the Soviet area of his unit's operations. In his memoir published years later, Gong bitterly narrated a tragic story of a close friend named Yang Yucun, a brilliant division commander in Jiangxi, whose parents were rounded up as rich landlords and had their house and properties confiscated; as a result, Yang risked his life to flee from the Soviet area and thereafter faithfully served the KMT cause for the rest of his life. After Gong expressed his doubts about this massive persecution against one's own rank and file, he was demoted and even accused of having followed the 'rightist opportunist line of the party,' which gave in to the demands of the people's enemy. All these occurrences led to Gong's betrayal in 1935 upon the KMT's brutal campaign to wipe out the remaining Red Army troops in Jiangxi.[18]

Despite internet bloggers' attempts to rehabilitate Gong, however, *The Red River Bank* was only 'safe' in depicting Gong's earlier career around 1929, before his betrayal. Gong's history as a traitor nevertheless can be linked to the end of this TV drama, when the young Deng finally climbs onto his horse, bidding farewell to the people of the Right Bank River areas, and eventually reaches Chongyi in Jiangxi Province before he leaves the Seventh Army for the second time (known as the second 'fleeing incident') to 'report to the CCP Central Committee in Shanghai.' Interestingly, *The*

Red River Bank ends its flashbacks at this point. Deng's little granddaughter in a red dress asks him, 'What happened to Wei Baqun after the Seventh Red Army left?' The ensuing black-and-white scene depicts the brutal murder of Wei by his nephew in a cave. The next scene concludes *The Red River Bank* with a happy image of Deng climbing down from his horse to greet Mao for the first time in the Jiangxi Soviet area, with Mao's welcoming remark: 'Let's walk together, forward!'

On the one hand, one might argue that the optimistic ending of Deng following Mao reinforces the official line of both Mao and Deng as invisible leaders. On the other hand, however, the parallel scenes of Wei Baqun's murder by a traitor and Deng's survival of the same war period – all narrated from the perspective of Deng's possible guilt over his 'fleeing incidents' – can be seen as serving multiple functions: to honour a martyr 70 years after his death and to condemn a traitor who brought about this catastrophe, without eliminating the possibility of having fused the line between the two by dramatizing a brilliant leader who had a distinguished career precisely because he was not willing to be a martyr. Seen in this light, the concluding remarks of old Deng, as he stares at the ocean waves, make perfect sense: 'Some say I am brave and smart. In reality, I am a practical man. I love my motherland. I serve my people forever.' As we have seen in both party history narratives and in their screen representations, this 'practical man' has finally led China to an economic prosperity without carrying out a political reform, which he had promised when he returned to power in 1978,[19] but which, for 'practical reasons,' he never realized in his lifetime.

Deng was not the only practical leader in the Chinese revolutionary narrative. *Persevering with Blood and Sacrifice* (*Yu xue jianchi*), a 22-part TV drama series that premiered in 2008, presents a startling contrast between two practical men: Chen Yi, the renowned leader of 'the three-year guerrilla warfare in the South,' and Gong Chumin, another name used by Gong Chu, the 'arch traitor' in the CCP history discussed above. The media fanfare celebrating the release of *Persevering with Blood and Sacrifice* reiterated the new party narrative of the twenty-first century, which has finally granted 'the three-year guerrilla warfare in the South' a significant status equal to that of the Long March. Different from the Red Army's main force of 185,000 soldiers on the Long March, which fought their way out of the enemy's elimination campaigns, Chen Yi, Gong Chumin (Gong Chu) and their units were left with only 16,000 troops and 30,000 wounded soldiers, and entrusted with the almost impossible task of luring the enemies away from the Red Army main force. As the first piece in the film and TV dramas to represent this most difficult episode of the revolutionary war period, *Persevering with Blood and Sacrifice* demonstrates that being 'practical' does not simply lead to acts of escape, desertion, or betrayal.

On the contrary, a practical spirit proved to be the best approach for a great leader such as Chen Yi, who knew to retreat when the enemy posed overwhelming threats, and when to 'stand his ground' when others doubted the future of the Chinese Revolution. Together with Xiang Ying, the head of the branch bureau of the CCP Central Committee (*Zhongyang fenju*), Chen encourages soldiers to persevere behind enemy lines against starvation, cold weather, brutal battles and betrayals by one's own comrades. The practical man is also equally emotional: Chen kneels down in front of the local peasants and begs them to take wounded soldiers into their homes before the Red Army's withdrawal: 'Some of your sons were killed by the KMT; others had already joined the Long March. Please take a son, or a son-in-law, from our troops. After you nurture them back to health, you will gain an extra farmhand, or a seed of the revolution to avenge the enemies!' One by one, these wounded soldiers are taken home by the local peasants, who shelter them in the most treacherous circumstances, with some even giving their own lives to protect them. For obvious reasons, the TV series apparently omitted a brutal fact: almost all the wounded soldiers and those local peasants associated with the Red Army were slaughtered by the 'white army,' as recounted in several biographical accounts.[20]

Amid this 'white terror,' the practical Chen needed to be at his strongest, as depicted in *Persevering with Blood and Sacrifice*. At the lowest point after Gong Chumin's betrayal, when Gong leads the enemy's campaign to eliminate Chen's unit, some soldiers dismiss their own thoughts of leaving the units after they witness Chen's display of indomitable will; as he says: 'I have many rich friends in Shanghai and Hong Kong, and I could have sought their help and become a big-shot official for the KMT government, but I chose to suffer here because I chose not to betray revolution, nor my own faith!'[21] Chen's unswerving determination proves particularly touching to his soldiers because Chen himself is a wounded man, with a severe injury to his leg – the key reason he was appointed for this challenging job, for it was assumed that he could not endure the Long March. In this even more exigent job, however, Chen's personal charm, good humour and tenaciousness wins the hearts of his soldiers, who follow him to the very end against all odds. In the fateful moment when they had no choice but to eat rats, snakes and wild berries to survive, the practical Chen also turned 'poetic' to inspire his dwindling troops: he recited poetry to describe their most unromantic existence as well as his faith in the eventual victory of the Communist cause.[22]

The loathing of traitors permeates the history, culture and literary and artistic representations of China's revolutionary past, and finds expression in *Persevering with Blood and Sacrifice* with the film's depiction of Gong Chumin. Portrayed as another kind of 'practical man,' Gong switched to the enemy's side in May 1935, sharing his inside knowledge of the Red Army in order to capture Chen Yi and Xiang Jing. By casting Wang Ban – the gorgeous, rising star from the Beijing People's Art Theater who had successfully played protagonist roles such as Zhou Ping in Cao Yu's *Thunderstorm* – as Gong, director Hu Mei attempted to portray the 'humanistic spirit of early revolutionaries' through contrasting antagonists. Familiar to his audiences as the striking hero in other TV war dramas, Wang hesitated to take the role at first, but he decided to portray Gong not as a 'bad man,' but as a 'waverer in his faith.' To depict Gong as a compassionate lover, Wang added a scene in which he gently kisses his wife. After the warm reception of the television drama upon its release in a CCTV prime-time programme, Wang became the centre of audience attention for his multi-faceted portrayal of Gong, whose treacherous acts Wang 'had defended as if [he were] his lawyer,' in Wang's own words. Wang's good looks and his prior roles as striking protagonists further blurred the otherwise clearly cut line between hero and traitor, embodying in one character a complex and rich historical past that resists distinctions between good and evil.

Indeed, the storyline more than defended Gong Chumin. At the beginning of the TV programme depicting the CCP's defeat at Laoyingpan (*Laoyingpan zhanshi*), Chen Yi and Gong Chumin, the division commander, were both blamed for having lost the front gate to the Soviet Republic, even though it was the result of the erroneous military strategy of Li De, a Soviet adviser assigned to oversee Chinese military affairs without any prior knowledge of Chinese society, geography and history. The ensuing long episodes focusing on Li De, Bo Gu and Zhou Enlai's debate over which high-ranking leaders to leave behind – including Li's insistence on leaving Mao Zedong behind and Zhou's resolve to bring Mao along on the Long March – further explain Gong Chumin's resentment at being ordered to stay behind to lead an almost impossible war after the departure of the main force. Gong's sense of having been deserted by the top leaders of the CCP seems to mitigate, to some extent, his decision to betray his comrades. One cannot forgive Gong, nor did the TV drama portray him entirely as a positive figure, but enough is presented to depict him as a human being who followed the revolution in its early days and made undeniable contributions, but in the end had become a practical man pressed by extraordinary circumstances. The TV drama, therefore, followed the tradition of the 'red classics' by portraying heroes such as Chen Yi, but they also presented 'grey characters' that are neither heroes nor antiheroes, but merely products of their own time and place.

Contemporary media's continuing fascination with the legend of Deng Xiaoping and other revolutionary-era leaders prompted more films and TV drama series, as seen in the 2009 film entitled *The Seventh Red Army* (*hong qijun*) and in the 2010 film *The Seventh Red Army and Me* (*Wo he Hong qijun*), which commemorated the founding of the PLA and the eightieth anniversary of the Baise Uprising. *The Seventh Red Army and Me* presented a particularly interesting perspective, because the first-person narrator's voiceover came from a former KMT commander who had first fought against the Seventh Red Army, but who subsequently defected and fought alongside the Seventh Red Army because of his admiration for the CCP commanders and their 'just cause'. The storyline of a KMT commander who converted to the CCP cause presented a traitor story in reverse, in which the CCP won a 'traitor' who was nevertheless as talented and resourceful as Gong Chumin in *Persevering with Blood and Sacrifice*. In the first decade of the twenty-first century, therefore, the party line between the vicious KMT and the victorious CCP became even more blurred; what remained unchanged, however, was the everlasting legend of Deng, who leads key battles to defeat the KMT, a contribution he made as part of the first generation of Chinese leaders under Mao. Deng was portrayed as more practical than Mao, even on the verge of being a defeatist escapee from the war front; it is this practical man, nevertheless, that finally brought China to its successful transformation to capitalism in the reform era.

It is therefore no wonder that a spoken drama entitled *Deng Xiaoping* begins with an Italian journalist questioning Deng in 1986: 'when you meet Mao in heaven, how do you answer Mao if he accuses you of having carried out a capitalist restoration, and regrets that he did not expel you from the CCP membership when he struck you down for the second time after the April Fourth movement of 1976?' Deng replied with pride and confidence: 'Mao would have congratulated me because he had always wanted the Chinese people to live a happy and comfortable life!' Situated in this dramatic conflict between Mao and Deng, however, one might indeed wonder if Mao was right in distrusting Deng as his successor for the socialist cause. One might also wonder if Cultural Revisionary films such as *Spring Sprouts* (*Chunmiao*) might have prophetically described what would indeed happen to the rural poor if Deng had succeeded in his attempt to restore capitalism: as the film describes, the rural poor would never afford medical treatment in a county hospital, whose doctor lets a poor peasant's child die without any treatment because he was busy developing special health regiments for high-ranking officials of the CCP. As a typical Cultural-Revolutionary film, *Spring Sprouts* criticized hospitals in socialist China that did not serve the peasants, but only the 'urban overlords,' as Mao had once criticized the revisionist and capitalist orientations of the Ministry of Public Health right before the start of the Cultural Revolution. Denounced in post-Mao China as a 'Gang of Four film' to attack Deng Xiaoping's attempt to restore capitalism, *Spring Sprouts* takes on a new significance in contemporary China when the rural population has paid the heaviest price in Deng's push for capitalism, and when China's income inequality and the growing disparity between the rich and poor have become one of its biggest economic problems.

All in all, the history of dramatic representations of the life story of Deng in the past 40 years – from the anti-Deng films during the Cultural Revolution, to the reform period that featured Deng as the greatest reformer, and finally to the urgent reflections on the pitfalls and consequences of the reform period – reveals contradictions and grey areas in our usual representations of 'revolutionary' and 'counterrevolutionary,' 'socialist' and 'capitalist,' leaders and traitors, and everyday life and theatricality. These depictions of Deng present a miniature history of the twists and turns of the 40 years after Mao's era, and the performance artists' efforts at interpreting and participating in the social and political events that defined much of the contemporary Chinese reality as well as their reflections on the heritage and debts of both the Mao and Deng eras.

In the larger scheme of things, I argue that in a socialist state with 'capitalist characteristics' such as the PRC, 'propaganda performance' can no longer be simply dismissed as a monolithic, top-down and meaningless practice characterized solely by censorship and suppression of freedom of expression in a totalitarian regime. Instead, propaganda performance can be studied as a complex, dialogic and dialectical process, in which multiple voices and opposing views collide, negotiate and compromise in forming what looks like a mainstream ideology – and indeed functions as such – to legitimize the powerful state and its right to rule.

Works cited

'Baise Qiyi (Baise Uprising)'. http://club.xilu.com/emas/msgview-821955-271909.html?PHPSESSID=

Chen, Yi and Zhang Qian. *Chen Yi shici xuanji*. Beijing: Renmin wenxue chubanshe, 1977.

Geng, Biao. *Geng Biao huiyi lu* (A memoir of Geng Biao). Beijing: Jiefangjun chubanshe, 1991.

Gong, Chu (Gong Hecun). *Huiyi* (A memoir), 2 vols. Hong Kong: Mingjing yuekanshe, 1971.

Gu, Bai. 'Yong jingxian xingshi suzao qingnian Deng Xiaoping xingxiang' (Use a suspense genre to create a young Deng Xiaoping) in *Deng Xiaoping dianying juben xuan*.

—'Hong'an – Deng Xiaoping zai yi jiu er jiu' (The Red Riverbank – Deng Xiaoping in 1929). http://www.hudong.com/wiki/

Hou, Yuzhong. 'Ba lishi de neirong huan gei lishi' (Return the content of history to history) in *Deng Xiaoping dianying juben xuan*.

Li, Bochi. *Hong'an* (The Red Riverbank). Beijing: Huaxia chubanshe, 1998.

Maomao (Deng Rong). *Wo de fuqin Deng Xiaoping: ji qing nian hua* (My father Deng Xiaoping: the passionate years). Beijing: Zhongyang wenxian chubanshe, 2010.

Mo, Wenhua. *Mo Wanhua huiyi lu* (A memoir of Mo Wenhua). Beijing: Jiefangjun chubanshe, 1996.

Yang, Benjamin. *Deng: A Political Biography*. Armonk, NY. M. E. Sharpe, 1998.

Yang, Bingzhang. *Xiaoping da zhuan* (A big biography of Xiaoping). Hong Kong: Shidai guoji chuban youxian gongsi, 2004.

Yuan, Renyuan. 'Cong Baise dao Xiangjiang' (From Baise to the Xiang River), in Zhang Yunyi et al. (eds), *Xing huo liao yuan wei kaigao* (Unpublished articles from the original versions of *The Spark That Sets the Prairie Afire*), 10 vols. Beijing: Jiefangjun chubanshe, 2007.

Zhao, Baohua. 'Zoujin Deng Xiaoping qingnian shidai', in Li Mengxue (ed.), *Deng Xiaoping dianying juben xuan* (Anthology of film and drama script on Deng Xiaoping). Beijing: Zhongguo dianying chubanshe, 2004.

—'Zhiyong chuangquan de Deng Xiaoping' (A brilliant and brave Deng Xiaoping). *Guangming Ribao*, 11 August 2004. www.gmw.cn.

Zuoyoujiang geming genjudi (Zuoyoujiang Revolutionary Base Areas), edited by Zhonggong Guangxi quwei dangshi ziliao zhengweihui (Committee on collecting party history materials organized by the district committee of the CCP in Guangxi Province), 2 vols. Beijing: Zhonggong danshi ziliao chubanshe, 1989.

Notes

1 Zhao Baohua, 'Zoujin Deng Xiaoping qingnian shidai', in Li Mengxue (ed.), *Deng Xiaoping dianying juben xuan* (Anthology of film and drama script on Deng Xiaoping). Beijing: Zhongguo dianying chubanshe, 2004, 313–16.

2 Quoted from the film version, which differs from the script published in *Deng Xiaoping dianying juben xuan*.

3   Gu Bai, 'Yong jingxian xingshi suzao qingnian Deng Xiaoping xingxiang' (Use a suspense genre to create a young Deng Xiaoping), in *Deng Xiaoping dianying juben xuan*, 317–19.
4   Gu Bai, 317.
5   'Zhiyong chuangquan de Deng Xiaoping' (A brilliant and brave Deng Xiaoping). *Guangming Ribao*, 11 August 2004. www.gmw.cn (accessed 10 July 2010).
6   Maomao (Deng Rong). *Wo de fuqin Deng Xiaoping: ji qing nian hua* (My father Deng Xiaoping: the passionate years) Beijing: Zhongyang wenxian chubanshe, 2010, 186. For an English version, see Maomao, *Deng Xiaoping: My Father*. New York: BasicBooks, 1995.
7   'Zhiyong chuangquan de Deng Xiaoping' (A brilliant and brave Deng Xiaoping). *Guangming Ribao*, 11 August 2004. www.gmw.cn (accessed 10 July 2010).
8   Hou Yuzhong. 'Ba lishi de neirong huan gei lishi' (Return the content of history to history) in *Deng Xiaoping dianying juben xuan*, 320–5, 320–3.
9   Hou Yuzhong and Zhu Xuming. *Baise qiyi* (Baise Uprising) in *Deng Xiaoping dianying juben xuan*, 147–244, 90.
10 For a similar article, see Yuan Renyuan, 'Cong Baise dao Xiangjiang' (From Baise to the Xiang River), in Zhang Yunyi et al. (eds), *Xing huo liao yuan wei kaigao* (Unpublished articles from the original versions of *The Spark That Sets the Prairie Afire*), 10 vols. Beijing: Jiefangjun chubanshe, 2007, 2:4–15.
11 Mo Wenhua, *Mo Wanhua huiyi lu* (A memoir of Mo Wenhua). Beijing: Jiefangjun chubanshe, 1996, 48.
12 Gong Chu (Gong Hecun). *Huiyi* (A memoir), 2 vols. Hong Kong: Mingjing yuekanshe, 1971, 1:265.
13 For example, a 1989 publication recorded that 'the CCP Central Committee sent a telegraph asking Deng to report work.' See *Zuoyoujiang geming genjudi* (Zuoyoujiang Revolutionary Base Areas), ed. Zhonggong Guangxi quwei dangshi ziliao zhengweihui (Committee on collecting party history materials organized by the district committee of the CCP in Guangxi Province), 2 vols. Beijing: Zhonggong danshi ziliao chubanshe, 1989, 1:14. The same publication also claimed that the local party committee decided that Deng should go to Shanghai to report for work for the second time (36). *Deng Xiaoping Nianpu* (Chronology of Deng Xiaoping's life) simply lists early December 1929, as the time when 'Deng left Longzhou for Shanghai' (1:56), and 7 March 1931, as the date when Deng 'proposed to go to Shanghai, which was approved by members of the local party committee' (1:80). In contrast, among Western publications, David Evans believed that Deng 'most likely' 'decided to go of his own volition' (*Deng Xiaoping*, London: Hamish Hamilton, 1993, 51). Uli Frantz noted that 'Two years after the Guangxi mission, a commission reopened the "desertion affair," but "the case was closed" shortly after' (*Deng Xiaoping*, Boston: Harcourt Brace Jovanovich, 88). David Goodman stated: 'It is an event which has resurfaced historiographically to embarrass Deng. Apparently, at the 7th CCP Congress in 1945,' Mo Wenhua 'spoke out about Deng's action in 1931.' *Deng Xiaoping and the Chinese Revolution*. London: Routledge, 1994, 33.
14 Yang Bingzhang, *Xiaoping da zhuan* (A big biography of Xiaoping). Hong Kong: Shidai guoji chuban youxian gongsi, 2004, 249. For an English version, see Benjamin Yang, *Deng: A Political Biography*. Armonk, NY: M. E. Sharpe, 1998, 72.
15 Li Bochi, *Hong'an* (The Red Riverbank). Beijing: Huaxia chubanshe, 1998. The television drama was directed by Mao Lujian and produced by Zhonggong Guanxi qu

dangwei xuanchuan bu (The propaganda department of the district committee of the CCP in Guangxi), et al.
16 '*Hong'an* – Deng Xiaoping zai yi jiu er jiu' (The Red Riverbank – Deng Xiaoping in 1929) http://www.hudong.com/wiki/ (accessed 21 April 2012).
17 Wang Buyi, 'Hong Qijun de shangkou – xie zai Baise Qiyi bashi nian zhi ji' (The scar of the Red Seventh Army – on the occasion of 80th anniversary of Baise Uprising) http://blog.sina.com.cn/s/blog_563dbf410100fznz.html (accessed 24 June 2013).
18 'Baise Qiyi' (Baise Uprising) http://club.xilu.com/emas/msgview-821955-271909.html?PHPSESSID= (accessed 24 August 2013).
19 In his speech entitled 'Jiefang sixiang, shishi qiushi, tuanjie yizhi xiang qian kan' (Liberate our thought, seek truth in practice, and unite with a forward-looking perspective) at the working session of the CCP Central Committee on 13 December 1978, Deng emphasized the importance of a legal system and institutionalized democracy. As Yang Bingzhang has pointed out, Deng's advocacy for democracy changed soon after Wei Jingsheng and others challenged Deng's new authority; Deng's practical concern with his own political power resulted in Wei's 15-year imprisonment. See Yang, *Xiaoping dazhuan*, 245–6.
20 Geng Biao, *Geng Biao huiyi lu* (A memoir of Geng Biao). Beijing: Jiefangjun chubanshe, 1991, 196; Wang Shuzheng, *Changzheng* (The Long March). Beijing: Renmin wenxue chubanshe, 2006, 80.
21 See part 16 of the television series.
22 The television drama uses Chen Yi's depiction of their hard life from his poem titled 'Gannan youji ci' (Poems on guerrilla war in southern Jiangxi) in Chen Yi and Zhang Qian, *Chen Yi shici xuanji*. Beijing: Renmin wenxue chubanshe, 1977, 13–16. 'Meiling san zhang' (Three verses written in Meiling) in Chen and Zhang, *Chen Yi shici xuanji*, 20–1.

Part Five

Online Audiences

16

Zhang Yimou's Sexual Storytelling and the iGeneration: Contending *Shanzhashu Zhi Lian* (*Under the Hawthorn Tree*) on *Douban*

Ralph Parfect

Since at least the start of the twenty-first century, China's internet users have increasingly been turning to the public, interactive spaces of the web, not only to review and debate new film releases, but also to discuss the broader political, economic and cultural environment for film in China.[1] Particularly active in this rise of web-based film commentary is the generation that grew up with the internet, China's iGeneration. Discussion of film and moving image culture, and of individual films, has appeared on a profusion of online spaces, from bulletin boards (BBS) and dedicated review or database sites such as www.douban.com (hereafter *Douban*), to more individualized blogs and microblogs. So far, however, little research has appeared on how exactly these new spaces are being used to address issues relating to film in China, or on what the broader implications of their rising prevalence and visibility may be for China's film culture.

To the extent to which this online universe can be mapped, Sabrina Qiong Yu has taken a notable lead by examining the role of a variety of websites and of individual netizen (internet user) voices in constructing the transnational celebrity of Jet Li and in the debate on Zhang Yimou's film *Yingxiong* (*Hero*) (2002).[2] This chapter aims to contribute further to this new research area through focused analysis of a single review website, *Douban*, and the reviews hosted there of Zhang's later film *Shanzhashu Zhi Lian* (*Under the Hawthorn Tree*, 2010, hereafter *Hawthorn*).[3] In examining how Chinese netizens have used *Douban* to express conflicting views of *Hawthorn*, the chapter makes reference to Guobin Yang's concept of 'contention' in Chinese internet culture, and to some of the characteristic genres and styles of this culture.[4] This chapter pays special attention, as has China's iGeneration itself, to *Hawthorn*'s representation of teenage romance and sexual behaviour during the Cultural Revolution; in this regard, netizens' responses to the sexual politics, both of the film itself and of its much-criticized marketing campaign, are read as assertions of 'sexual citizenship' that variously resist and approve the 'sexual storytelling' of the film.[5] The chapter thus argues that online reviews, as with much online film commentary, can be seen as part of a broader culture of internet contention that Yang terms an 'unofficial democracy,' albeit one still constrained by the dynamics of both the state and the market.[6] Although a certain freedom of expression prevails in such online spaces, writings that contravene government-imposed limits on internet content may find themselves 'harmonized;' meanwhile the anti-commercial stance of many reviewers has limited power to resist, and may even contribute to, the 'hype' for certain products above others in an entertainment-driven cultural industry.

Douban, the marketization of culture and online contention in China

Douban was launched in March 2005, and at the time of writing ranks as the twentieth most popular website in China, with 68 million registered users and over 150 million visits each month.[7] Its core function is as a place to find and share information and views on three kinds of cultural product: books, films and music. In its film section, *Douban Dianying* (*Douban Film*), users can rate a film with from one to five stars, or post a review of any length, on which any *Douban* user can then comment; these comments in turn can be responded to, hence allowing multi-party discussions to develop. Over time, *Douban* has added further functions such as live music streaming, city events listings and interest-based 'communities' or 'groups' with social media features. Its parent company emphasizes the website's interactivity, describing it not only as 'a cultural resource database' with 'high quality' reviews, but also as 'a creative community with cultural events and life-sharing.'[8] Its audience is characterized as 'urban youth': 80 per cent of users live in one of 12 major cities, including Beijing, Shanghai, Tianjin and Chongqing, while 92.5 per cent are aged 18–35. The audience is 'well-educated': more than 80 per cent of users have or are taking 'a bachelor's degree or above,' and '17 per cent have or are taking a Master's degree.' They are also relatively prosperous: '42.8 per cent have more than 3000 RMB monthly income.'[9] This demographic is not fully coterminous with China's iGeneration, but the two clearly overlap significantly.

As a space for cultural commentary, *Douban* is characteristic in at least two ways of the broader Chinese cultural landscape of the early twenty-first century: first, it participates in a commodity culture with retained elements of state control; and secondly, it belongs to a culture of the internet in post-WTO China. Just as film production and consumption have become strongly commercialized in the reform period in China, with films increasingly forced to compete as products in a globalized, consumerist cultural marketplace, while remaining subject to state controls including censorship,[10] so too has the nature of published comment on film changed dramatically. The marketization of culture since the early 1980s, and particularly in the 1990s and 2000s, has seen a proliferation of new cultural forms, including forms of commentary.[11] Facilitating this has been the rapid advance since the late 1990s of the internet, and, in particular, of web 2.0 capabilities, enabling a more participatory culture of film criticism and commentary to take shape.

While this culture may appear more 'democratic,' however, online commentary on film is still subject to state-imposed restrictions, just as film itself is. In common with much of the Chinese internet, *Douban* self-censors in order to retain its government-granted permission to operate. Furthermore, like other sites hosting online film commentary, *Douban* belongs to a cultural marketplace and is subject to its logic, for instance obtaining income from advertising and attracting new users by prominently displaying new cinematic releases on the home page. *Douban* users often comment on whether or not films are worth the ticket price. Reviews themselves can become commodities of a kind; one *Douban* reviewer of *Hawthorn* comments of his own popularity: 'I didn't expect that this film review would become so *hot*' [my italics].[12]

While being rooted in China's state-capitalist culture, *Douban*, again like much of the Chinese internet, can nonetheless share in what Yang Guobin calls a 'culture of contention.'[13] It is misleading, Yang argues, for the Chinese internet to be seen merely in terms of its two most reported aspects, government control and popular entertainment. Chinese internet culture rather has a contentious character, in which 'authority of all kinds is subject to doubt and ridicule,' and in which a culture of 'online activism' has been born.[14] Among other scholars, David Herold has similarly described a 'carnivalesque' quality to the Chinese internet which often makes it a place of subversion.[15] While this chapter will not look at activism *per se*, it does find Yang's concept of a culture of contention applicable to the case of user-generated content on *Douban*. In 2011, for instance, *Douban* users posted such negative reviews of the film *Jian Dang Wei Ye (The Founding of a Party)*, which had been released to mark the nineteenth anniversary of the founding of the Chinese Communist Party, that the ratings facility for this film was disabled.[16] *Douban* users moreover have a history of playfully protesting at the site's self-censorship on sexual issues. In March 2009 users mocked *Douban* for deciding as part of an anti-pornography campaign to remove images of Renaissance oil paintings featuring nudity; a satirical counter-campaign was organized by users to post clothed images of the nude figures.[17] A year and a half later, *Douban* users would again be making fun of perceived sexual censoriousness, this time in relation to a new film by Zhang Yimou.

Under the Hawthorn Tree: Synopsis, marketing campaign and internet reception

Hawthorn was Zhang Yimou's twenty-second film as director, and was released cinematically in mainland China on 16 September 2010.[18] It is based on a popular internet novel of the same title by Ai Mi, itself reportedly based on a true story.[19] Set in Hubei province in the mid-1970s, it narrates the tragic teenage romance of its two protagonists, Jingqiu and Lao San, which ends with the latter's death from leukaemia. Several factors hinder the two lovers: the stigmatization and poverty of Jingqiu's family, her father being absent from the home for unspecified political reasons; an acute need for secrecy in conducting the relationship, given Jingqiu's wish to become a teacher, like her mother, for which she must show exemplary behaviour, particularly avoiding any taint of *zaolian* or 'premature love'; and the suspicious gaze of the mother herself, who is desperate to improve the chances not only of Jingqiu but also two younger children. Lao San, the son of a People's Liberation Army area commander, by contrast, is relatively carefree, enjoying the deference and material benefits accruing to his family background. He works in a geological survey team, a prestigious occupation which also evidently allows him ample time and freedom to pursue a romance. The couple meet and subsequently fall in love after Jingqiu, as a *zhiqing* or 'educated youth,' is sent down temporarily from her provincial city of Yicheng to learn from the peasants in the nearby village of Xiping, which is also where Lao San's geological team happens to be stationed. The film's action subsequently alternates between city and village, according to Jingqiu's varying commitments. In spite of Lao San's gradually worsening illness, caused by the handling of radioactive materials during his geological survey work, an illness that he tries to conceal from Jingqiu, he takes the lead in an increasingly physical intimacy. The two lovers end up in bed together; however, Lao San's attempt to initiate sexual intercourse with a professedly willing Jingqiu stops short when she reveals her actual uncertainty and fear. The film ends with Lao San on his deathbed surrounded by his grieving family and a hastily summoned Jingqiu. In the closing credits it is stated that Jingqiu ended up years later leaving China for the United States, and that the hawthorn tree on a hillside near Xiping remained a symbol of Jingqiu and Lao San's everlasting love.

The promotional campaign for *Hawthorn* was based on the slogan '*lishishang zui ganjing de aiqing gushi*' [the purest love story in history], a line recycled from the marketing of the popular novel on which the film script was based.[20] Several Chinese words connoting purity and cleanness, for example *chunjie* and *qingchun*, were used in the various forms that the marketing campaign took. This included posters, print and broadcast advertisements, media interviews and even a televised launch ceremony, at which the film was previewed and discussed and cast members appeared and sang songs. At one point in this event, the teenage actress Zhou Dongyu, who plays Jingqiu, is asked by the presenter, 'What is pure love?' and she answers, shyly, '*Ganjing*' [clean].[21] A television advertisement further embellished the theme of purity, quoting the film's producer, businessman Zhang Weiping, as saying: 'in this commercialized society, I haven't felt this unadorned simplicity for a long time.'[22]

Pre-release publicity for the film and for the 'purity' concept of its marketing campaign was boosted, albeit with unintended consequences, by two incidents. First, at the Hong Kong Film Festival in April 2010, breaking the news of his forthcoming film, Zhang Yimou complained to the media of the difficulty of finding actors who appeared 'innocent' enough to play ordinary people from the Cultural Revolution era.[23] Secondly, during filming, the production team reinforced Zhang's complaint by releasing to entertainment media a comical five-minute *huaxu* ('bits of news') video that showed the casting panel for *Hawthorn* auditioning a long series of young actresses, but rejecting all of them; the implication being, again, that none seemed 'pure' enough.[24] Following these two incidents, comments started to circulate on internet bulletin boards, complaining that, through his new film, Zhang wished to attack the sexual morals of contemporary youth. Zhang, it was argued, was endorsing a traditional morality of innocence and restraint inappropriate to a China characterized by increasing sexual openness and acceptance of premarital sex.[25] Discussion of *Hawthorn* quickly became somewhat polarized, as we shall see reflected in later comments found on *Douban*. Those who took 'pure love' to mean premarital chastity, and saw the film as trying to reinforce this traditional norm, typically attacked *Hawthorn*, whereas those reading 'pure love' merely as undiluted romantic love tended to welcome *Hawthorn*'s perceived romantic idealism, as against the more pragmatic, materialistic form of courtship taken to be the undesirable social norm of the reform period.

Zhang himself insisted in interviews that he had not intended to promote traditional sexual morality, and that he lamented the damaging consequences that sexual ignorance could have; he dismissed the key marketing slogan 'the purest love story in history' as 'brought over from the novel.'[26] This is consistent with his early films, which are associated with transgressive representations of eroticism and sexuality.[27] However, some of Zhang's comments suggested an ambivalence around contemporary sexual morals. In one interview he confirmed that he did think young people's sexual knowledge was too great: they were growing up too fast and 'a third year high school student is not like a third year high school student.'[28] He also suggested there could be a quaintly comic quality about the sexual ignorance of the Cultural Revolution period, in which many people thought that if a couple simply held hands that could lead to pregnancy.[29] This comic potential is indeed exploited in several scenes of the film, in which the naïve assumptions of Jingqiu, her mother and her friend Hong Wei are implicitly mocked.

Before the film's release, then, the controversy over the meaning of its 'purity' had made *Hawthorn* a 'hot topic' on the internet. Reviews of the film on *Douban*, while far from being the first internet comments on the film (even if many appeared rapidly, arriving online from the evening of the pre-release premiere on 14 September 2010) are indicative in their range and variety of the wider debate about the film, in spite of the reportedly rather homogeneous demographic of *Douban* users. According to *Douban*'s own statistics, of the 1891 full-length reviews posted by April 2013, 11.8 per cent had awarded five stars, 30.6 per cent four stars, 44.8 per cent three stars, 10.0 per cent two stars and 2.8 per cent one star. The average rating cited by *Douban* for the film is 6.4.

Methods, terms and contexts

This chapter is informed by the well-established tradition in reception/audience studies of seeing audiences as active makers of meaning, rather than being passively 'acted on' by cultural texts.[30] It uses a sample of 21 reviews, with accompanying comments, published on *Douban* in 2010–11. To obtain a spread of positive, balanced and negative reviews, seven five-star, seven three-star and seven one-star reviews were read. In each category, the reviews selected were those rated as 'useful' by the greatest number of fellow *Douban* users. To analyse the reviews a form of close reading is used, informed by Yang Guobin's concepts of 'style' and 'genre' in internet contention; both content and form in the material are examined with a view to observing significant patterns and meanings. It is conceded that no perfect methods of selection and analysis exist in audience/reception studies, particularly when dealing with material as profuse and diverse as internet film criticism. For example, for demographic reasons already made clear, *Douban* users are clearly not representative of the whole audience for *Hawthorn*, which was ostensibly pitched partly at an older generation. Nor are precise demographic data on individual reviewers such as age, gender and location available from *Douban*, although some users do choose to reveal this. Further illuminating discussion of the issues involved in examining the reception of films using internet reviews may be found in Sabrina Qiong Yu's work.[31]

Before moving on to analysis of the *Douban* reviews, certain important terms and contexts should be briefly discussed. First, two terms, namely *styles* and *genres* of contention, are borrowed from Guobin Yang's theorization of Chinese internet contention.[32] A key point of Yang's is that, in contrast to the sometimes 'epic' style of contention of protest movements in China's past, and a residual tendency towards 'emperor-worship' (that is, pinning hopes for reform onto strong leaders), China's internet age has seen a 'new sensibility towards power and authority' emerge, in which 'mockery and satire' play a prominent part.[33] At the same time, alongside this more 'playful' style of contention, which can also be 'insulting' and 'angry', contention of a more 'prosaic' quality has also appeared; this style can be down-to-earth or even technical, again in contrast to more 'grandiose' modes of the past.[34] Yang further argues that, as well as styles, genres of contention have changed. There has been a notable 'flourishing of diverse speech genres,' which in itself constitutes a 'challenge to power', given that 'political authorities everywhere tend to employ a narrower range of speech types.'[35] Among the genres that Yang identifies as especially popular on the Chinese internet are the 'confessional and autobiographical' and the 'parodic-travestying.' The latter includes 'jokes, doggerel [and] satire.'[36]

As Yang makes clear, it is above all an 'irreverence towards power and authority' that characterizes the use of these styles and genres of contention.[37] As this chapter argues with reference to the *Douban* reviews, the notion of a resisted 'authority' applies to *Hawthorn* in a number of ways: to the authority of Zhang Yimou as an established cultural figure; to the authority of the marketplace in an era of commercialization; to the authority of the notion of 'purity' with all its connotations of a still-influential traditional morality; and to the authority of historiography with reference to the Cultural Revolution period. It is *Hawthorn*'s very relationship with all of these forms of authority that ostensibly drives *Douban* reviewers to apply diverse genres and styles of contention to the film.

A further key context for *Hawthorn*'s reception is the proliferation of sexuality discourses in reform-era China. While it has been well established that discourses of sexuality were far from being entirely suppressed in Maoist China, even during the Cultural Revolution,[38] the reform period has seen an explosion of representations of and public comment on love and sex, as part of an 'opening up' to increasingly liberal forms of sexual thought and behaviour.[39] Particularly relevant to the current discussion, research on changing sexual attitudes in China has demonstrated the increasing acceptance of premarital sex.[40] In contemporary Chinese literature, film and popular culture, much-discussed manifestations of a greater openness towards sex in recent decades have included the cause célèbre of Wei Hui's sexually explicit *Shanghai Baobei* (*Shanghai Baby*); the more pessimistic work of Mian Mian, which emphasizes grotesque and nightmarish aspects of 'open' sexuality; the films of Andrew Cheng, which have adapted Mian Mian's work; and the rising prevalence of online pornography.

In interpreting such new sexuality discourses in China, the concepts of 'sexual storytelling' and 'sexual citizenship' have been productively deployed; and in this chapter these are likewise applied to *Hawthorn* and to the online responses to the film. Sexual storytelling can be defined as 'narratives of the intimate life, focussed especially around the erotic, the gendered and the relational.' [41] Sexual citizenship indicates 'a cluster of rights and responsibilities [...] around issues of sexual partner choices, control over the body, reproductive rights, intimate bonds and sexual identities.'[42] Both terms are taken here from James Farrer's ethnographic work on youth sexual behaviour in Shanghai in the early 2000s, with reference also to a theoretical source of Farrer's, namely sociologist Ken Plummer's *Telling Sexual Stories* (1995). Writing about youth sexuality in Shanghai, Farrer finds not only that 'Chinese youth have pursued the rights to engage in sexual relations before marriage,' but also that 'loose communities of discourse have emerged around prominent stories shared through the internet and other media.'[43] These findings correspond to my own view of *Hawthorn* and its internet reception in two particular respects. First, just as Farrer's youthful respondents use their own sexual stories and concepts of sexual rights to resist the authority of social norms, in particular the intolerance of 'premature love' (*zaolian*) in Chinese schools, so too do some viewers of *Hawthorn* contend the authority of the film's perceived disapproval of premarital sex. Secondly, Farrer finds that 'youth in present-day China have developed their own more permissive sexual standards primarily based on a code of romance'; Farrer calls this 'romance as resistance.'[44] In the analysis that follows, we will see that 'romance as resistance' is a tendency visible in many responses to *Hawthorn*: some viewers value the romance of the film as implicitly critiquing the materialism of present-day Chinese society, and they reject the perceived sexual cynicism of the film's critics.

Contextually *Hawthorn* should also be seen as one of a significant body of retrospective representations of sexual behaviour during the Cultural Revolution. As Wendy Larson and Emily Honig have shown, a large body of literary works and films have used the Cultural Revolution as a space for exploring issues, not only of citizenship in a broad sense, but of sexual citizenship in particular.[45] Larson discusses the many negative consequences of the period's equation of sex with bourgeois ideology, and details examples of actual sexual abuses that took place, such as the sexual exploitation of sent-down youth by rural cadres.⁴⁶ However, she also demonstrates that many Chinese, including memoir-writers and filmmakers, have found it valuable to speak out about the era's sexual histories, in revisitings of the past that shed light on the present. While these accounts often emphasize the many sexual horrors of the time, others, such as Jiang Wen's film *Yangguang Canlan De Rizi* (*In The Heat of the Sun*) (1994), have portrayed the sexual freedoms that became available to many in the relative absence of parental supervision.⁴⁷ As Honig argues, both types of account can illuminate the present in exposing continuities as well as ruptures. In the case of *Hawthorn*, it is precisely the nature of sexual morality in the present that comes into question through reviewing of a Cultural Revolution 'sexual story.'

Negative reviews: Contention of *Hawthorn*'s sexual storytelling

In my analysis of reviews of *Hawthorn*, I start with negative reviews for the simple reason that these perform contention most obviously, even if positive reviews will also be found to be contentious too in important ways. The aim here is to analyse not only the content but also the manner of this questioning of the film's sexual story. Above all, it can be found that these reviews closely match Guobin Yang's account of popular styles and genres of contention on the Chinese internet. Irreverence and playfulness are immediately apparent. The most popular review of *Hawthorn* on *Douban* (receiving the greatest number of 'useful' ratings) is an extended *e'gao* (parody) that mocks the perceived implausibility of the film's plotline.⁴⁸ Another parodic review incorporates a spoof interview with Zhang Yimou.⁴⁹ Light-hearted irreverence can be seen in many reviews through how Zhang Yimou himself is referred to, such as, in one review, 'old Mouzi,' and, with tongue in cheek, '*guoshi*' [educator of the nation].⁵⁰

A feature special to the irreverence of *Hawthorn* reviews, however, is the way in which graphically or suggestively sexual language and imagery in particular is used to contend *Hawthorn*'s perceived pretence of coyness. A pattern emerges of such language being used satirically to undermine or unmask the supposed inauthenticity of the sexual story. The most popular non-parodic review of *Hawthorn* on *Douban* at the time of writing, by 'Gongyuan1874', is entitled 'Freshness and Purity Coming out of the Clothes of a Prostitute.'⁵¹ This begins in rather startling fashion by graphically describing the range of sexual gratifications available in many Chinese cities, including domination and school uniform fetishism. The latter is particularly emphasized in the review, the point being that *Hawthorn* is analogous with the sex industry in contemporary China, through amounting to little but a commercially packaged version of schoolgirl-style innocence designed to titillate and exploit a paying audience. Gongyuan1874 also complains that the emotive ending of *Hawthorn* is a kind of pornography; if we cry at seeing characters losing a loved one to leukaemia (as many audience members reportedly did), it is merely a physiological reaction, no different in essence to 'getting an erection.' The review links these points firmly to a critique of commercialism, attacking in particular the hypocritical producer Zhang Weiping for making money from (covert) pornography while claiming his own product to be above the commercialism of the times.

Several other reviewers attack *Hawthorn*, albeit playfully, using similarly graphic or suggestive sexual language. Some of these borrow from the rich lexicon of sexual Chinese internet slang; 'Lv Jiaozhi,' for example, pokes fun at the purity concept of the film by saying that Lao San is a 'YY' [*yiyin*, sexual fantasist], who really just wants to 'fry rice [*chaofan*] with Jingqiu,' but is forced to settle for masturbation ('DIY').[52] Other kinds of sexual discourse are also deployed: for example, pop psychology in 'Shale De Mao's' accusation that Zhang Yimou has a 'virgin-complex' (*qunv qingjie*), and literary allusion in the same review, with its claim that 'the couple in one shot look like a "big uncle" and his Lolita' (*dashu he luolita*). For 'Nalanmiaoshu,' *Hawthorn* is like a pornographic film with a 'strange uncle' (*guai shushu*), or a doctor seducing a patient; but at the same time Zhang Yimou is 'like court eunuch trying to tell a pornographic story'; he cannot 'hit the spot', because he is lacking the correct 'organ' to tell such a tale.[53] Similarly, in criticizing the supposed unsubtleness of the bedroom scene in which 'Lao San reaches straight for Jingqiu's private parts [*sichu*],' another reviewer exclaims: 'Fuck! [*wo cao*] Zhang Yimou, what kind of depravity are you thinking of?'[54]

What this sexually frank style highlights is the claim to sexual citizenship that these reviews effectively make by contending the pretence of purity in *Hawthorn*'s sexual story. By bringing sexual content to light, and moreover doing so in sexualized language, they implicitly wrest authority over sexual morals and rights from the film and its director. They demonstrate not only their facility with sexual language but also their knowledge of other kinds of sexual stories: one, as we have seen, is *Lolita*; another, cited by Gongyuan1874 as truly exemplifying the 'purity' that *Hawthorn* merely pretends to have, is the Italian film *Malèna*, for its depiction of a kind-hearted prostitute.[55]

Perhaps the most playfully inventive of the negative reviews is one which combines a sexually frank style with verse. Yang Guobin has noted that verse has played a venerable role in cultures of contention in Chinese history.[56] Updating this tradition, the review entitled 'Great Master, the People Present You with a Pair of Pants' is an elaborate 'shape poem' in triangular form, intended to resemble a pair of underpants (see figure 16.1).[57] It makes much play with rhyme; every line ends in the 'ang' sound, leading to rhyming of '*angzang*' [dirty], '*selang*' [lustful wolf] (applied to Lao San) and 'Yimou Zhang' (Zhang Yimou's name mockingly inverted with reference to his international fame, taken here as a sign of inauthenticity).

As against all of this irreverence and profanity, some negative reviews adopt a more serious tone, even using more formal, literary, or academic style and answering Yang's identification of a 'prosaic' and even technical style of Chinese internet contention. The review by 'Baisange Feiyun' advances a scholarly argument as to why *Hawthorn* should not be considered a 'pure love' film; it transgresses the rules of this genre, the proper features of which are described in some detail.[58] A review by 'andrew' uses formal language to make a series of statements on moral responsibility, somewhat in the matter of a letter to a newspaper, such as that 'A reputable filmmaker has a duty to

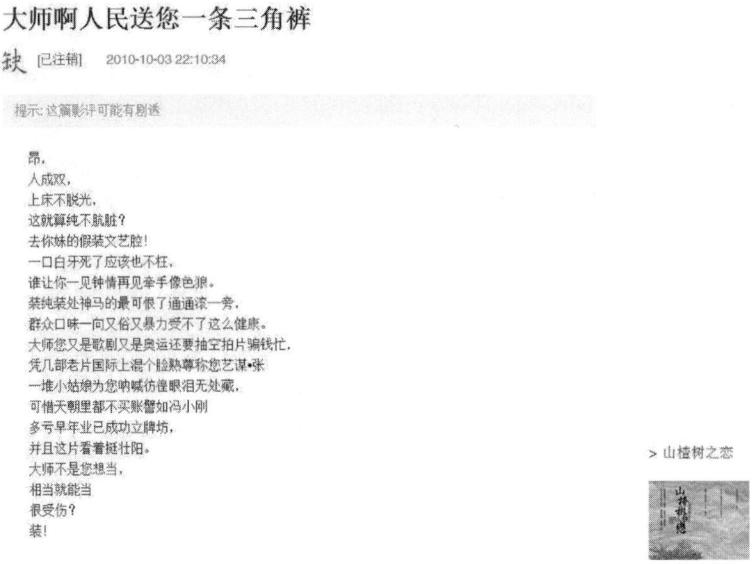

大师啊人民送您一条三角裤

钬 [已注销] 2010-10-03 22:10:34

提示: 这篇影评可能有剧透

昂,
人成双,
上床不脱光,
这就算纯不肮脏?
去你妹的假装文艺腔!
一口白牙死了应该也不枉,
谁让你一见钟情再见牵手像色狼。
装纯装处神马的最可恨了通通滚一旁,
群众口味一向又俗又暴力受不了这么健康。
大师您又是歌剧又是奥运还要抽空拍片骗钱忙,
凭几部老片国际上混个脸熟尊称您艺谋•张
一堆小姑娘为您呐喊彷徨眼泪无处藏,
可惜天朝里都不买账譬如冯小刚
多亏早年业已成功立牌坊,
并且这片看着挺壮阳。
大师不是您想当,
相当就能当
很受伤?
装!

> 山楂树之恋

Figure 16.1 Screenshot of the review 'Great Master, The People Present You with a Pair of Pants' on douban.com.

follow the laws of filmmaking, and protect the good name and the value of cinema,' and that 'we make ourselves complicit by going to see these films.'[59] Nalanmiaoshu, whose blog reveals her to be a published author with a doctorate in literature,[60] demolishes *Hawthorn* via a series of numbered points and language full of literary allusion.[61]

As well as academic and literary styles, negative reviewers also make use of confessional and autobiographical genres, which, as mentioned above, Yang has found to be widely used in Chinese internet contention. Family histories are used to add veracity to their reviews; Gongyuan1874, for example, cites his own family's experiences to argue that the Cultural Revolution was a period of sexual exploitation, far from the era of comic sexual innocence portrayed by the film.[62] Another more mundane kind of 'autobiographical' veracity is provided by reviewers who offer first-person narratives of their experience of watching the film, for example Nalanmiaoshu's wearied account: 'Ten minutes in, my friend and I were looking at each other in dismay, and saying "What shall we do? Stay or leave?"'[63] Negative reviews thus use a variety of approaches, styles and genres to subvert the authority of the film's sexual storytelling, to assert youthful sexual knowledge and rights and to reference sexual stories of their own.

Positive reviews: Romance as resistance

In contrast to the irreverent, playful and sexually frank styles used to critique the film, positive reviews of *Hawthorn* have two notable features: first, while not necessarily precluding a certain inventiveness, they tend to make use of more earnest styles of contention; and secondly, they frequently exemplify the notion of romance as resistance. These reviews often deploy a romantic language, and experiment with genres that can accommodate such language. The most popular positive review of *Hawthorn* on *Douban* is not a really a review at all, but rather a kind of polemic on romantic love in the form of a prose poem. Entitled 'You Must Believe There is Such a Person in This World,' this brief (277-character) text repeatedly apostrophizes the reader with the words 'You must believe,' making for a more strident appeal to romantic sentiment than *Hawthorn* itself. Using cinematic imagery, the review urges readers to persevere in their search for a lover 'whether right now you are surrounded by light and drowning in applause, or all alone crossing the cold street, soaked by the heavy rain.'[64] *Hawthorn* itself is not mentioned; it is merely implied that film and review share the same spirit of romantic resistance.

Another review that uses stylized prose and a distinct genre to find resistance in romance is that of 'Joyuan.' This review takes the form of rhetorically patterned prose, a series of eight short paragraphs all beginning with the phrase 'the we of then' (*na shi de women*) and formulaically comparing past with present.[65] The spartan lifestyles and naïve romantic behaviours of 'then' (the Cultural Revolution) are contrasted with the supposed evils of the present day, from mobile phones to 'sweet words and honeyed phrases.' Items such as 'lovers' adornments and rings' and 'man-eating beauty' respectively invoke the supposed materialism and exploitation of today's more cynical romantic narratives. The review concludes, breaking its rhetorical pattern, with a statement that the film's protagonists 'teach us how to believe in love and persevere with love' and that the 'callow writings' of the reviewer are offered up 'to the pure Jingqiu and Lao San and to a pure life.' Thus the very language of *Hawthorn*'s marketing campaign, that of 'purity,' is reappropriated in a context of defiance and resistance to perceived anti-romantic tendencies in contemporary society.

As with negative reviews, an academic or pseudo-academic style may be used to support the film. 'Zhongyuan,' for example, claims that *Hawthorn* embodies what he calls 'Love as Metaphysics.'[66] This review positively contends the value of *Hawthorn*'s romantic narrative through a rather rambling and unclear assemblage of philosophical quotes and ideas: the Daoist philosopher Zhuangzi's idea of 'free and easy wandering' (*xiaoyaoyou*), for example, is cited in support of the claim that what matters is the romantic 'mood' (*xinqing*) of the film, rather than consideration of its truth-status; while Kant is quoted as saying 'even if reality is this way, I still believe,' ostensibly in support of the notion that love should be an article of faith, and act as an index of virtue.

Autobiographical and confessional modes may also be used in positive reviews, just as in their negative counterparts. A review entitled 'About the Era My Mother Remembers,' as well as incorporating a first-person narrative of the act of movie-going ('I just went to see *Hawthorn* with my mother'), details at some length the Cultural Revolution history of the reviewer's family.[67] At times these reminiscences are explicitly linked to *Hawthorn*: 'Jingqiu volunteers to repair the sports ground. Similarly my mother sprayed pesticide over a large tree. She would work voluntarily until dead tired. That was the mindset of the time.' But memoir far outweighs film commentary in this review, the very excess of the former thereby seeming to testify to the film's historical resonance and veracity. The review ultimately uses its praise of *Hawthorn*'s truthfulness to endorse the romantic storytelling of the film: 'People who haven't experienced sincere first love and young love won't understand this film.'

As with negative reviews, then, positive reviews make use of a range of styles and genres of contention, eschewing playfulness, irreverence and sexually frank language, while deploying rhetorically patterned 'poetic' prose, pseudo-academic discourse and autobiographical reflections. Above all, they praise love and romance, producing the discourse of romance as resistance in support of *Hawthorn*'s variety of sexual storytelling. The sexual citizenship assertion in these reviews, more implicit than explicit, consists in their upholding the right to 'believe in love,' to pursue romance, and to enjoy and praise sexual stories such as *Hawthorn* where these are found to be in keeping with a self-consciously contentious belief in anti-materialistic 'purity.'

Counter-contention

As has already been observed, the capabilities of *Douban* allow for user-to-user interactive dialogue on films. Accordingly, a key characteristic of the commentary on *Hawthorn* is precisely its interactivity, chiefly in the form of comments directly supporting or criticizing reviews. Comments, like reviews themselves, contain a range of meanings and express these in a range of styles, variously approving, echoing, extrapolating, mocking and insulting the reviews to which they are attached.

Hawthorn's supporters, for example, frequently deplore negative reviews as forming part of the very culture of anti-romanticism that they see themselves as contending. In response to Gongyuan1874's notion that *Hawthorn* fetishizes schoolgirls, one commenter responds: 'I think you are just the kind of virgin-defiler and male supremacist you talk about. Maybe you have never experienced true love and don't know how it feels.'[68] Answering Nalanmiaoshu's structured, literary and sexually frank review is the comment: 'Your remarks are not very broad, and perhaps just suit today's society and taste. Kind of lamentable.'[69] Not only comments, but also some reviews are written in response to other reviews, for example Zhongyuan's 'Love as Metaphysics.' Quoting earlier, negative *Douban* reviewers' critical comments, such as that *Hawthorn* merely shows us 'rich kids picking up girls' (*fu'erdai paoniu*), Zhongyuan remarks: 'Seeing the comments on the web, I really want to curse: "You evil moths, so ignorant, please do not bawl mercilessly everywhere."'[70] Conversely, *Hawthorn*'s supporters often approve one another's romantic contentions. The review entitled 'You must believe that there is such a person in the world,' for example, receives the response: 'I do ultimately believe these things, even though I understand what kind of society this is.'[71] Putting the same sentiment more strongly, one commenter on Zhongyuan's review supportively remarks that it's 'tragedy for this society' that so many people despise and mock a film like *Hawthorn*.[72]

In contrast to this positive-spirited interactivity, however, negative reviewers too use *Douban*'s interactive spaces to counter-contend positive reviewers' meanings and styles. Zhongyuan's pseudo-academic essay, for example, is variously refuted as an argument for *Hawthorn*'s handling of 'love as metaphysics' (rather, it is claimed that the film's representation of love is superficial), and criticized for its haphazard and unclear use of philosophical terms and quotations.[73] As a final point on the interactivity of the *Douban* space, it should be noted that, while some reviewers, such as Gongyuan1874, thank and praise the website for its services in allowing a culture of contention to flourish, *Douban* itself (through its editors) at times suppresses this culture through censorship.[74] One review calls itself a 'harmonized version,' and explains that it is a reposting in edited form of a highly rated and much-commented-on review that was deleted from the site, ostensibly for using sensitive words blacklisted by China's internet authorities.[75] Drawing attention to the limits of internet contention, commentors on this review find little to do but complain at *Douban* for its capitulation to state power, via comments such as '*Douban* is really evil.'[76]

Conclusion

Online spaces for film criticism are a relatively new and under-researched part of film culture in China. Such spaces have proliferated rapidly and provide rich and diverse content for the understanding of this culture. Although online film commentary may be circumscribed by both the commercial logic of the market, with its 'hyping' of certain films, and by state power, with its restrictions on freedom of expression, it nevertheless allows for strongly contending meanings and forms of criticism to circulate and mutually interact. In spite of what might be supposed to be the limitations of the film review format, comments may borrow from a range of genres and styles of contention, even including forms that might appear incongruous within established practices of film criticism. Characteristic of such contention are, on the one hand, playfulness, jokes, parody and irreverence towards authority, and, on the other, the use of more serious or deadpan styles and genres, from prosaic description and analysis to autobiographical narrative. The forms of authority challenged by reviewers may include the status of established, state-endorsed filmmakers and the power of the commercial film market. Film commentary may in addition contribute to wider social debates around matters such as sexual citizenship and historical representation, challenging the influence of mainstream popular culture in determining meanings around issues of sexual citizenship, and weighing conflicting claims and counter-claims towards sexual stories in the public realm, for example those set during the Cultural Revolution. In the contestation of *Hawthorn*'s variously suspected and approved sexual storytelling, special modes of contention include, on the one hand, explicit or suggestive sexual language and imagery, and, on the other, a romanticism that sees itself as a form of resistance to crassly anti-romantic social norms and tendencies in contemporary China. While this chapter necessarily makes only a small contribution to analysing internet cultures of contention in China, considering the implications of participatory spaces of film commentary for film culture, and investigating the use of such commentary as a means of intervention into social debates on sexual citizenship, it is hoped that subsequent research will go further in investigating these and related issues.

Works cited

andrew [username]. 'Cong *Shanzhashu Zhi Lian* Kan Zhang Yimou De Jian'e' [From *Under the Hawthorn Tree* We Can See Zhang Yimou's Evil], *Douban*, 16 September 2010. http://movie.douban.com/review/3768409/
Anon 1 [username deleted]. 'Zhang Yimou Zui Cha Zuopin' [Zhang Yimou's Worst Film], *Douban*, 16 September 2010. http://movie.douban.com/review/3693650/
Anon 2 [username deleted]. 'Dashi A Renmin Song Nin Yi Tiao Sanjiaoku' [Great Master, The People Present You with a Pair of Pants], *Douban*, 3 October 2010. http://movie.douban.com/review/3803722/
Baisange Feiyun [username]. 'Bu Zuo Ai, Ru He Ai?' [What Kind of Love Is Not Making Love?], *Douban*, 26 September 2010. http://movie.douban.com/review/3738147/
Braester, Yomi. 'Contemporary Mainstream PRC Cinema' in Song Hwee Lim and Julian Ward (eds), *The Chinese Cinema Book*. Basingstoke: Palgrave Macmillan, 2011, 176–84.
Brooker, Will and Deborah Jermyn (eds). *The Audience Studies Reader*. Abingdon: Routledge, 2003.
CNTV. 'Yinxiang Zhang Yimou' [An Impression of Zhang Yimou]. *CNTV*. 24 October 2010. TV broadcast, available at http://news.cntv.cn/society/20101024/102457.shtml
Deppman, Hsiu-Chuang. *Adapted for the Screen: The Cultural Politics of Modern Chinese Fiction and Film*. Honolulu: University of Hawai'i Press, 2010.
'Douban Introduction 2011Q3.' PDF, *Douban*, 2011.
'Douban.com Site Info.' *Alexa*. http://www.alexa.com/siteinfo/douban.com
Evans, Harriet. *Women and Sexuality in China: Dominant Discourses of Female Sexuality and Gender Since 1949*. Cambridge: Polity Press, 1997.
Farrer, James. *Opening Up: Youth Sex Culture and Market Reform in Shanghai*. Chicago: University of Chicago Press, 2002.
—'Sexual Citizenship and the Politics of Sexual Storytelling Among Chinese Youth' in Elaine Jeffreys (ed.), *Sex and Sexuality in China*. London: Routledge, 2009, 102–23.
Garibaldi [username]. '*Shanzhashu Zhi Lian*: Qiancang Zai Chun'ai Beihou De Shenghua Weiji' [*Under the Hawthorn Tree*: The Biochemical Crisis Hidden Behind Pure Love], *Douban*, 6 October 2010. http://movie.douban.com/review/3831763/
Gongyuan1874 [username]. 'Maiyinnv Zhuang Chulai De Qingchun' [Freshness and Purity Coming out of the Clothes of a Prostitute], *Douban*, 21 September 2010. http://movie.douban.com/review/3710644/
Herold, David and Peter Marolt (eds). *Online Society in China: Creating, Celebrating, and Instrumentalising the Online Carnival*. Abingdon: Routledge, 2011.
Honig, Emily. 'Socialist Sex: The Cultural Revolution Revisited,' *Modern China* 29, no. 2 (2003): 143–75.

Jiang Wen. *Yangguang Canlan de Rizi* [*In the Heat of the Sun*]. DVD. 1994.
Jiao Xiao A De Xiangyu [username]. 'Ni Yao Xiangxin Zhei Ge Shijieshang You Zheme Yige Ren' [You Must Believe There Is Such a Person in This World], *Douban*, 16 September 2010. http://movie.douban.com/review/3692708/
Jiushi Xihuan Yijianzhongqing [username]. 'Zaoshang Kan Xinwen Laomouzi Shuo *Shanhashu Zhi Lian* Xuanbudao Qingchun de Nvsheng, Benren Maosi Tuijian Yige Qingchun' [This Morning I Saw the News That Old Mouzi Can't Find a Fresh and Pure Actress for *Under the Hawthorn Tree* – I Will Brave Death to Recommend One], *Tianya*, 24 March 2010. http://www.tianya.cn/publicforum/content/funinfo/1/1899273.shtml
Joyuan [username]. 'Na Shi De Women' (Xiegei Jingqiu Laosan Yiji Chuncui De Shenghuo) [The We of Then (Dedicated to Jingqiu, Lao San and the Simple Life)], *Douban*, 20 September 2010. http://movie.douban.com/review/3709640/
Kan, Michael. 'Web Ratings Disabled for Chinese Communist Party Film,' *PC World*, 22 June 2011. http://www.pcworld.com/article/230858/article.html
Lü Jiaozhi [username]. 'Rang Wo Gaosu Ni Shenme Cai Jiao Chunjie De Aiqing' [Let Me Tell You What Pure Love Is], *Douban*, 17 September 2010. http://movie.douban.com/review/3699174/
McGrath, Jason. *Postsocialist Modernity: Chinese Cinema, Literature, and Criticism in the Market Age*. Stanford: Stanford University Press, 2008.
Nalanmaioshu [username]. 'Nalan Meijiu Yeguang Bei' [blog title], *Sina*, http://blog.sina.com.cn/wisely1229
—'Luanlun Zhi Ge Yi Hao, Chun'ai Zhi Qu Nangong' [It's Easier to Sing of Immorality Than of Pure Love], *Douban*, 24 September 2010. http://movie.douban.com/review/3727860/
Shang, Qing. 'Nima Zhan Hexie: Caoben Dou Quanwei' [The Mud Horse Battles the River Crab: The Grassroots Struggle Against Authority], *BBC*, 17 March 2009. http://news.bbc.co.uk/chinese/simp/hi/newsid_7940000/newsid_7948300/7948369.stm
'*Shanzhashu Zhi Lian* Shouying Qingdian' [*Under the Hawthorn Tree* Première Celebration], *CCTV-6*, 14 September 2010. TV broadcast, available online at http://ent.cntv.cn/enttv/shouying/classpage/video/20100914/100986.shtml
Xiunian [username]. 'Guanyu Wo Ma Huiyi De Nage Shidai' [About the Era My Mother Remembers], *Douban*, 6 October 2010. http://movie.douban.com/review/3837918/
Yang, Guobin. *The Power of the Internet in China: Citizen Activism Online*. New York: Columbia University Press, 2009.
'Yimou Zhang – IMDb.' *IMDb*. http://www.imdb.com/name/nm0955443/
Yu, Juping. 'An overview of the sexual behaviour of adolescents and young people in contemporary China,' *Australasian Medical Journal* 3, no. 7 (2010): 397–403.
Yu, Sabrina Qiong. 'Camp Pleasure in an Era of Chinese Blockbusters: Internet Reception of *Hero* in Mainland China' in Gary D. Rawnsley and Ming-Yeh T. Rawnsley (eds), *Global Chinese Cinema: The Culture and Politics of Hero*. Abingdon: Routledge, 2010, 135–51.
—*Jet Li: Chinese Masculinity and Transnational Film Stardom*. Edinburgh: Edinburgh University Press, 2012.
Zhang Yimou. *Shanzhashu Zhi Lian* [*Under the Hawthorn Tree*]. DVD. Fortune Star. 2010.
—'Zhang Yimou Huo Dianying Jiechu Gongxian Jiang – Xinpian Nanmi Qingchun "Shanzhanv"' [Zhang Yimou Wins Outstanding Contribution Award – Difficult to

Find a Fresh and Pure 'Hawthorn Girl' for His New Film], *Ifeng*, 24 March 2010. http://ent.ifeng.com/movie/news/hk/detail_2010_03/24/403391_0.shtml
— 'Zhang Yimou Tan *Shanzhashu*: Wo Shi "Hei Wu Lei" Chengfen Bi Jingqiu Hai Cha' [Zhang Yimou Talks About *Under the Hawthorn Tree*: I Was One of the 'Five Black Categories'; My Status Was Lower Than Jingqiu's], *Nanfang Daily*, 13 September 2010. http://news.nfmedia.com/nfrb/content/2010-09/13/content_15824419.htm
Zhongyuan [username]. 'Zuowei "Xingershangxue" De Aiqing: *Shanzhashu Zhi Lian*' [Love as 'metaphysics': *Under the Hawthorn Tree*], *Douban*, 25 September 2010. http://movie.douban.com/review/3734533/

Notes

1. On the extent of internet film criticism in China by the early 2000s, see Sabrina Qiong Yu, 'Camp Pleasure in an Era of Chinese Blockbusters: Internet Reception of *Hero* in Mainland China' in Gary D. Rawnsley and Ming-Yeh T. Rawnsley (eds), *Global Chinese Cinema: The Culture and Politics of Hero*. Abingdon: Routledge, 2010, 137.
2. See ibid. and Sabrina Qiong Yu, *Jet Li: Chinese Masculinity and Transnational Film Stardom*. Edinburgh: Edinburgh University Press, 2012.
3. Zhang Yimou, *Shanzhashu Zhi Lian* [*Under the Hawthorn Tree*], DVD, Fortune Star, 2010.
4. Guobin Yang, *The Power of the Internet in China: Citizen Activism Online*. New York: Columbia University Press, 2009, 1–3.
5. These terms are borrowed from James Farrer, 'Sexual Citizenship and the Politics of Sexual Storytelling Among Chinese Youth' in Elaine Jeffreys (ed.), *Sex and Sexuality in China*. London: Routledge, 2009.
6. Yang, *The Power Of The Internet In China*, 220.
7. 'Douban.com Site Info,' *Alexa*, http://www.alexa.com/siteinfo/douban.com (accessed 8 April 2013).
8. 'Douban Introduction 2011Q3,' PDF, *Douban*, 2011.
9. Ibid.
10. Yomi Braester, 'Contemporary Mainstream PRC Cinema' in Song Hwee Lim and Julian Ward (eds), *The Chinese Cinema Book*. Basingstoke: Palgrave Macmillan, 2011, 180.
11. Jason McGrath, *Postsocialist Modernity: Chinese Cinema, Literature, and Criticism in the Market Age*. Stanford: Stanford University Press, 2008, 3.
12. Gongyuan1874 [username]. 'Maiyinnv Zhuang Chulai De Qingchun' [Freshness and Purity Coming out of the Clothes of a Prostitute], *Douban*, 21 September 2010, http://movie.douban.com/review/3710644/ (accessed 9 January 2013).
13. Yang, *The Power Of The Internet In China*, 82.
14. Ibid., 1–2.
15. David Herold and Peter Marolt (eds), *Online Society in China: Creating, Celebrating, and Instrumentalising the Online Carnival*. Abingdon: Routledge, 2011.
16. Michael Kan, 'Web Ratings Disabled for Chinese Communist Party Film,' *PC World*, 22 June 2011, http://www.pcworld.com/article/230858/article.html (accessed 9 January 2013).
17. Qing Shang, 'Nima Zhan Hexie: Caoben Dou Quanwei' [The Mud Horse Battles the River Crab: The Grassroots Struggle Against Authority], *BBC*, 17 March 2009,

http://news.bbc.co.uk/chinese/simp/hi/newsid_7940000/newsid_7948300/7948369.stm (accessed 9 January 2013).
18 'Yimou Zhang – IMDb,' *IMDb*, http://www.imdb.com/name/nm0955443/ (accessed 8 April 2013).
19 CNTV, 'Yinxiang Zhang Yimou' [An Impression of Zhang Yimou], *CNTV*, 24 October 2010, TV broadcast, available at http://news.cntv.cn/society/20101024/102457.shtml (accessed 9 January 2013).
20 Ibid.
21 '*Shanzhashu Zhi Lian* Shouying Qingdian' [*Under the Hawthorn Tree* Première Celebration], *CCTV-6*, 14 September 2010, TV broadcast, available online at http://ent.cntv.cn/enttv/shouying/classpage/video/20100914/100986.shtml (accessed 9 January 2013).
22 Gongyuan1874 [username], 'Maiyinnv Zhuang Chulai De Qingchun.'
23 'Zhang Yimou Huo Dianying Jiechu Gongxian Jiang – Xinpian Nanmi Qingchun "Shanzhanv"' [Zhang Yimou Wins Outstanding Contribution Award – Difficult to Find a Fresh and Pure 'Hawthorn Girl' for His New Film], *Ifeng*, 24 March 2010, http://ent.ifeng.com/movie/news/hk/detail_2010_03/24/403391_0.shtml (accessed 9 January 2013).
24 CNTV, 'Yinxiang Zhang Yimou.'
25 One example of an early negative bulletin board comment on *Hawthorn* is Jiushi Xihuan Yijianzhongqing [username], 'Zaoshang Kan Xinwen Laomouzi Shuo *Shanhashu Zhi Lian* Xuanbudao Qingchun de Nvsheng, Benren Maosi Tuijian Yige Qingchun' [This Morning I Saw the News That Old Mouzi Can't Find a Fresh and Pure Actress for *Under the Hawthorn Tree* – I Will Brave Death to Recommend One], *Tianya*, 24 March 2010, http://www.tianya.cn/publicforum/content/funinfo/1/1899273.shtml (accessed 9 January 2013).
26 CNTV, 'Yinxiang Zhang Yimou.'
27 See for example Hsiu-Chuang Deppman, *Adapted for the Screen: The Cultural Politics of Modern Chinese Fiction and Film*. Honolulu: University of Hawai'i Press, 2010, 34–60.
28 'Zhang Yimou Tan *Shanzhashu*: Wo Shi "Hei Wu Lei" Chengfen Bi Jingqiu Hai Cha' [Zhang Yimou Talks About *Under the Hawthorn Tree*: I Was One of the 'Five Black Categories'; My Status Was Lower Than Jingqiu's], *Nanfang Daily*, 13 September 2010, http://news.nfmedia.com/nfrb/content/2010-09/13/content_15824419.htm (accessed 9 January 2013).
29 CNTV, 'Yinxiang Zhang Yimou.'
30 For discussions and examples see Will Brooker and Deborah Jermyn (eds), *The Audience Studies Reader*. Abingdon: Routledge, 2003, 91–126.
31 Yu, *Jet Li*, 22–8.
32 Yang, *The Power Of The Internet In China*, 64–102.
33 Ibid., 85.
34 Ibid., 85–94.
35 Ibid., 77.
36 Ibid.
37 Ibid., 82.
38 Harriet Evans, *Women and Sexuality in China: Dominant Discourses of Female Sexuality and Gender Since 1949*. Cambridge: Polity Press, 1997.
39 See James Farrer, *Opening Up: Youth Sex Culture and Market Reform in Shanghai*. Chicago: University of Chicago Press, 2002.

40 Juping Yu, 'An overview of the sexual behaviour of adolescents and young people in contemporary China,' *Australasian Medical Journal* 3, no. 7 (2010).
41 Ken Plummer, *Telling Sexual Stories: Power, Change and Social Worlds*. London: Routledge, 1995, 5.
42 James Farrer, 'Sexual Citizenship and the Politics of Sexual Storytelling Among Chinese Youth,' in Elaine Jeffreys (ed.), *Sex and Sexuality in China*. London: Routledge, 2009, 102–3.
43 Ibid., 103.
44 Ibid., 108.
45 Emily Honig, 'Socialist sex: the cultural revolution revisited,' *Modern China* 29, no. 2 (2003).
46 'Socialist sex: the cultural revolution revisited,' *Modern China* 29, no. 2 (2003): 162.
47 Jiang Wen, *Yangguang Canlan de Rizi* [*In the Heat of the Sun*], DVD, 1994.
48 Garibaldi [username], '*Shanzhashu Zhi Lian*: Qiancang Zai Chun'ai Beihou De Shenghua Weiji' [*Under the Hawthorn Tree*: The Biochemical Crisis Hidden Behind Pure Love], *Douban*, 6 October 2010, http://movie.douban.com/review/3831763/ (accessed 9 January 2013).
49 Lü Jiaozhi [username], 'Rang Wo Gaosu Ni Shenme Cai Jiao Chunjie De Aiqing' [Let Me Tell You What Pure Love Is], *Douban*, 17 September 2010, http://movie.douban.com/review/3699174/ (accessed 9 January 2013).
50 Nalanmiaoshu [username], 'Luanlun Zhi Ge Yi Hao, Chun'ai Zhi Qu Nangong' [It's Easier to Sing of Immorality Than of Pure Love], *Douban*, 24 September 2010, http://movie.douban.com/review/3727860/ (accessed 9 January 2013).
51 Gongyuan1874 [username], 'Maiyinnv Zhuang Chulai De Qingchun.'
52 Lü Jiaozhi [username], 'Rang Wo Gaosu Ni.'
53 Nalanmiaoshu [username], 'Luanlun Zhi Ge Yi Hao.'
54 Anon 1 [username deleted], 'Zhang Yimou Zui Cha Zuopin' [Zhang Yimou's Worst Film], *Douban*, 16 September 2010, http://movie.douban.com/review/3693650/ (accessed 9 January 2013).
55 Gongyuan1874 [username], 'Maiyinnv Zhuang Chulai De Qingchun.'
56 Yang, *The Power Of The Internet In China*, 77–9.
57 Anon 2 [username deleted], 'Dashi A Renmin Song Nin Yi Tiao Sanjiaoku' [Great Master, The People Present You with a Pair of Pants], *Douban*, 3 October 2010, http://movie.douban.com/review/3803722/ (accessed 9 January 2013).
58 Baisange Feiyun [username], 'Bu Zuo Ai, Ru He Ai?' [What Kind of Love Is Not Making Love?], *Douban*, 26 September 2010, http://movie.douban.com/review/3738147/ (accessed 9 January 2013).
59 andrew [username], 'Cong *Shanzhashu Zhi Lian* Kan Zhang Yimou De Jian'e' [From *Under the Hawthorn Tree* We Can See Zhang Yimou's Evil], *Douban*, 16 September 2010, http://movie.douban.com/review/3768409/ (accessed 9 January 2013).
60 Nalanmaioshu [username], '*Nalan Meijiu Yeguang Bei*' [blog title], *Sina*, http://blog.sina.com.cn/wisely1229
61 Ibid.
62 Gongyuan1874 [username], 'Maiyinnv Zhuang Chulai De Qingchun.'
63 Nalanmiaoshu [username], 'Luanlun Zhi Ge Yi Hao.'
64 Jiao Xiao A De Xiangyu [username], 'Ni Yao Xiangxin Zhei Ge Shijieshang You Zheme Yige Ren' [You Must Believe There Is Such a Person in This World], *Douban*,

16 September 2010, http://movie.douban.com/review/3692708/ (accessed 9 January 2013).
65 Joyuan [username], 'Na Shi De Women' (Xiegei Jingqiu Laosan Yiji Chuncui De Shenghuo) [The We of Then (Dedicated to Jingqiu, Lao San and the Simple Life)], *Douban*, 20 September 2010, http://movie.douban.com/review/3709640/ (accessed 9 January 2013).
66 Zhongyuan [username], 'Zuowei "Xingershangxue" De Aiqing: *Shanzhashu Zhi Lian*' [Love as 'metaphysics': *Under the Hawthorn Tree*], *Douban*, 25 September 2010, http://movie.douban.com/review/3734533/ (accessed 9 January 2013).
67 Xiunian [username], 'Guanyu Wo Ma Huiyi De Nage Shidai' [About the Era My Mother Remembers], *Douban*, 6 October 2010, http://movie.douban.com/review/3837918/ (accessed 9 January 2013).
68 Comment on Gongyuan1874 [username], 'Maiyinnv Zhuang Chulai De Qingchun.'
69 Comment on Nalanmiaoshu [username], 'Luanlun Zhi Ge Yi Hao.'
70 Zhongyuan [username], 'Zuowei "Xingershangxue" De Aiqing.'
71 Comment on Jiao Xiao A De Xiangyu [username], 'Ni yao xiangxin.'
72 Comment on Zhongyuan [username], 'Zuowei "Xingershangxue" De Aiqing.'
73 Comments on ibid.
74 Comments on Gongyuan1874 [username], 'Maiyinnv Zhuang Chulai De Qingchun.'
75 Lü Jiaozhi [username], 'Rang Wo Gaosu Ni.'
76 Comments on ibid.

17

From the Glaring Sun to Flying Bullets: Aesthetics and Memory in the 'Post-' Era Chinese Cinema

Xiao Liu

How do we remember the past in a post-medium era in which our memories of a previous era are increasingly reliant upon, and thus continually revised by, the ubiquitous presence of media networks? Writing about the weakening historicity under late capitalism, Fredric Jameson sharply points out that the past has been reduced to 'a multitudinous photographic simulacrum,' 'a set of dusty spectacles.'[1] Following Guy Debord's critique of the spectacle as 'the final form of commodity reification' in a society 'where exchange value has been generalized to the point at which the very memory of use value is effaced,' Jameson reveals the ways in which the past appropriated by what he calls 'nostalgia films' is 'now refracted through the iron law of fashion change and the emergent ideology of the generation' for omnivorous consumption that is an outcome of neoliberalism and its cultural motor – post-modernism. Implicit in Jameson's argument is how the crisis of historicity is tied to the commercialization of media and the repetitious production of media simulacra. Jameson's argument generally follows the line of the critique of the mass media as laid out of the Frankfurt School critics, focusing on the ideological function of the cultural industry. How has the post-medium, networked society of control changed this milieu diagnosed by Jameson?

I use 'post-medium' on the one hand to refer to the state of media saturation in our current moment, and on the other hand, to illustrate the conditions of media convergence that challenge the modernist notion of media specificity.[2] First raised by art critic Rosalind Krauss (2000) to address the increasing threat to the notion of media specificity by the pervasive power of electronic and digital media, the term 'post-medium' has become part of a contentious discourse for rethinking the relationship between cinema and other forms of media, as well as the socio-economic and political powers that shape and are in turn reshaped by a network society. Pertinent here is Friedrich Kittler's observation of the convergence of media in the form of digital coding and computer processing. Henry Jenkins furthers Kittler's notion of 'convergence culture,' and adds to the technical definition with 'the flow of content across multiple media platforms, the cooperation between multiple media industries, and the migratory behavior of media audiences who would go almost anywhere in search of the kinds of entertainment experiences they wanted.'[3] While convergence culture involves a technological process of 'bringing together multiple media functions within the same gadgets and devices,' this hybrid media experience, above all else, also represents a shift in the cultural logic 'as consumers are encouraged to seek out new information and make connections between dispersed media content.' While affirming the increasing role of consumers, Jenkins also points out that this convergence culture is 'shaped by the desires of media conglomerates to expand their empires across multiple media platforms.'

Here Jenkins's elaboration of convergence culture raises several pertinent issues. First, cultural production has shifted from a producer-controlled mode of mass culture to a more distributed mode of networks. Consumers are no longer just at the end of the commodity chain, waiting to consume the products provided to them by an industry, but are also today increasingly incorporated into the very production of these commodities. Second, while the emergence of 'prosumers' becomes a crucial issue among current network theories, in this chapter I ask what pressures are placed on 'auteurs' to replicate and be reflexive to new media platforms and distributed 'prosumers'? What are the aesthetic choices of 'auteurs' in this networked society? Finally, I relate this former question to the eclipse of historicity raised by Jameson: has the increasing participation of the audience in media culture broken down the repetitious spectacularization of historical memories, as Jameson suggests?

An examination of the media repercussions of Jiang Wen's 2010 film *Rang zidan fei* (*Let the Bullets Fly*) may address this question in the context of contemporary Chinese cinema. Loosely set in the 1920s (a time of 'revolutions' against warlords and imperialism) and with references to real historical figures, the film seems uninterested in providing a serious historical backdrop for narration: its characters mouth buzzwords from current social media, pulling the audience out of the film's constructed past; any references to historical facts in the film are seemingly ridiculed and dismissed by its characters as insignificant, as *Let the Bullets Fly* comes to construct a past which is reduced to filmic bricolage.

Despite the commercial success of the film with its domestic box office take of 700 million RMB, *Let the Bullets Fly* also generated heated discussion in Chinese tabloids and on online social media sites. Instead of reading the film as a historical account, its audience read each segment of the film's various media incidents in relation to their own postsocialist experiences. This anachronistic juxtaposition of the past and the present compels a critical reflection on the intertwined relationship between cinematic representation of history and social media networks. Most online discussion centred upon the notion of 'revolution,' as the protagonist of the film, Zhang Muzhi (Jiang Wen), is simultaneously a bandit who fights for the poor against the warlords and a cynical revolutionist who belittles the masses as self-interested and politically apathetic. The online debate around 'revolution' also has to do with the ambiguity of the overloaded word in postsocialist memories of twentieth-century China.

With the end of the Cultural Revolution and the Mao era, official historical narratives of Chinese Revolutions gradually lost their ideological coherence and credibility under the drastic process of marketization led by the CCP. Though the memories associated with 'revolution' are repeatedly remediated in literature and cinema, the ideology and sentiments behind these narratives and representations are often fuzzy and self-contradictory. Without serious historical reflections, these narratives often slip into commercialization of the past. Thus any film that evokes the 'revolutionary past' has to address the existing media stereotypes and the danger of reducing history for nostalgic consumption.

In the latter part of this chapter I will examine the ways in which the intermedia flows between cinema and the internet have transformed the textuality of *Let the Bullets Fly*, placing the film amid the economy of exchanges of social media and creating an experience of temporality that is aligned with what Jameson describes as the eclipse of historicity. I use 'economy' here because accompanied with flows of media contents is the flow of money, and the box office of the film affirms again that the production of cinema today still follows the rule of commodity production. Yet before that, I will draw attention to Jiang Wen's previous film made in 2007 – *Taiyang zhaochang shengqi* (*The Sun Also Rises*). Aesthetically distinct from *Let the Bullets Fly*, *The Sun Also Rises* shows Jiang Wen's almost modernist efforts to construct a self-enclosed cinematic world, and his self-conscious interrogation on the narrative possibilities of the revolutionary past in a postsocialist and post-medium era. To read the two films in tandem promises to reveal not only the pressure of social media networks on the autonomy of cinema, but also their shared social conditions of production behind their disparate aesthetics.

Starting with a close reading on *The Sun Also Rises*, I will elucidate the multiple temporalities implicit in the elliptical narrative of the film, which I regard as Jiang Wen's reflections on the representability of the past: how to tell the stories of the past when the existing narratives are either hollow official ideology or commodification of reified nostalgia? Jiang, in his efforts to eschew media stereotypes, created exquisite sensuous images to evoke historical memories. Though my analysis of this film does not directly involve its reception on social media, I argue that the narrative and aesthetic of the film self-consciously address the issue of media and representability in a media-saturated society. The relation of cinematic images to existing media stereotypes is implicit in Jiang's choice of aesthetic.

I will then come back to *Let the Bullets Fly*, examining its audience reception and the role of social media in that reception, and conclude with a parallel reading of the two films in terms of their shared dilemma of representing the past. In other words, I read both films symptomatically as revealing the crisis of historicity and representability in a post-medium, postsocialist era. The seemingly self-enclosed aesthetic of *The Sun Also Rises* displays Jiang's arduous effort to preserve the autonomous space of an 'auteur' film amid constant flows of media, and to bring attention to the entangled relations between media and historicity. *Let the Bullets Fly* serves as a counterpoint in this sense, as its open textuality lends itself to the dissemination of media and the networked media effect of simultaneity that eclipses the historicity of 'deep time.'

Focusing on one auteur's two films of very different aesthetics, this chapter analyses the dilemma of 'writing' memories in the postsocialist, post-medium milieu.

Elliptical remembrance and erotic memories

From his directorial debut *In the Heat of the Sun*, Jiang Wen has always been fascinated with exploring the ambivalent experiences of his generation and their growing up during the Cultural Revolution as 'eggs under the red flag'.[4] To Ma Xiaojun and his playmates, the days 'in the heat of the sun,' often in the absence of their physical fathers, are thrilling and restless, full of adventures and disillusionment. In *The Sun Also Rises*, his third feature-film, Jiang revisited the ambivalent experiences of his generation again, this time in a more elliptical way. There are four fragments loosely woven together, with the first three set in the year 1976, the last in 1958. In the first fragment of the narrative, we find a son (Fang Zuling) who is eager to trace the whereabouts of his absentee father from his 'mad' yet mysterious mother (Zhou Yun), who secretly builds a white stone house in the forest – in effect, her own museum which holds pictures of opera heroes and other nostalgic items from the Maoist era. The second vignette is about the affair between Tang (Jiang Wen) and Dr. Lin (Joan Chen) and the suicide of their friend Liang (Huang Qiusheng). The third vignette is about another affair, of Tang's wife (Kong Wei) with Fang. The fourth vignette is about two women, the mad mother and Tang's wife, whose life paths crisscross with Xin Jiang, on her way to claim a few items left behind by her deceased husband, the other marrying Tang, an overseas intellectual who returns to 'support the construction of the new China.'

To straighten out the plot, Jiang Wen clarified in an interview in 2007, that: 'At the beginning everyone comes together from all directions, everyone is in love. The mother is, so are Tang and his wife, and they all meet in Xinjiang. Decades later, husbands and wives are split, Tang betrays his wife, his wife also has an affair and the son is killed.'[5] In Jiang's half-joking accounts, the film becomes a cluster of stories about the fragmentation and deterioration of human ties across the initial decades of the 'new China.' However, the commotion and significance of political events are all removed from the film. Instead, the film on the surface is simply diffused with unaccountable erotic desires and love affairs that take up the majority of running time of the film. Why does Jiang strenuously reconstruct the memory of his generation as such a drama of erotic desires?

To move to *In the Heat of Sun*, Jiang Wen consciously mediates the narrative of his film through the voiceover of the desire-stricken protagonist Ma. His erotic desire drives and manipulates the narrative, which makes him an unreliable narrator. In this coming-of-age story, the absence of the biological father alludes to the ubiquitous presence of the symbolic father – the Party, which authoritatively demands the son's total submission and devotion. In this sense, the 'illicit' erotic desire of Ma in the film symptomatically indicates a love–hate relationship of the son with his symbolic father. In *The Sun Also Rises*, the story of 'the son's generation' continues as that of the disoriented Fang, who desperately seeks any traces left by his never-seen father. The plot of the film invites an allegorical reading, as it is set in 1976, the year of the end of the Cultural Revolution and the Mao era, and therefore also serves as an indicator of the shaken authority of the symbolic father. The son's journey of seeking starts exactly at the point when the traces of the symbolic father begin to fade. The face-effaced photo of his parents, a bunch of unreadable letters and self-contradictory accounts by other people, all fail to give him a coherent story. Moreover, Jiang Wen's reversed order of narration from the point of deterioration already suggests an impossible task of recuperating the past, for any such recuperation reflects the desire for intact memories in an era of deterioration. Along with the two temporalities of the recalling 'now' and the elusive past in the film, there is also the phenomenological present of viewing (and making) the film: the son's difficulty in recuperating the past is parallel to the tough task of the audience (and the filmmaker) to reconstruct the past. Thus the reverse order of storytelling in the film becomes a self-referential gesture: is it possible for us who live during the post-medium, postsocialist 'now' to recuperate the memory of the past? Self-consciously addressing this tension between the present and the past, forgetting and remembering, the stories in the film become elliptical fragments. It is this aesthetic of ellipsis that Jiang employs to salvage the grains of memory.

In an interview, Jiang Wen was frank to describe the effects of his film as a 'flirtation with the audience,' as he claimed: 'I am not content with a narration of a crawling speed.... I want it to be spinning and dancing, to be high and intoxicating. Only in this way can the film evoke the audience's feelings and emotions.' He also mentioned his fascination with the 'red' ballet classic *The Red Detachment of Women*: 'As a boy, every time I watched *The Red Detachment of Women*, I was dazed by the dozen pairs of women's legs on the stage, their toes, their revolutionary will and the music, all full of sensations. That is truly an extraordinary show.'[6] From the young Jiang Wen's perspective, the Chinese revolutionary drama could be both sensational and erotic.

In *The Sun Also Rises*, Jiang reinvigorates his erotic memories of the red classic. The audience is provided with a scene that takes place at an outdoor film screening, in which the character Liang walks into an amorous field of soft, rosy light surrounding the screen. The next shot reveals, instead of the images on the screen, their 'electronic shadows' in a rippling pond, glittering yet blurry. An oblique vision of a corner of the screen soon shifts to the intoxicated audience depicted in the film, whose bodies involuntarily dance to the brisk music. Then the camera slowly pans to the projector, gently caressing its beams of blue light before shifting to the 'pixelated' screen, which finally reveals the movie to be *The Red Detachment of Women*. In this scene, the revolutionary film is no longer about iconic images and storytelling, but rather about sensuous light and rhythm visually abstracted. The field of the film screening becomes a field so infused with erotic desires that Liang cannot but help reaching out his hand toward a girl before him. As if to poke fun at the now-erotic ambience accumulated through the previous shots, an outburst from the audience 'Catch the hooligan!' turns the film screening into a comic chase scene: hundreds of flashlights mimic the projector, pursuing the running Liang as they project beams of light on him. The projector, originally facing the screen, also turns around, joining the flashlight search, chasing Liang. As it sweeps across the frenzied crowd in sprint, it becomes a machine gun, shooting its 'bullet-like' beams of light toward the exhilarated crowd. The scene at this moment transforms itself into a mimetic reference to a war scene in so many of the revolutionary period films, only this time the bullets are the sensuous beams of cinematic light that double as reified political energies. The chase scene becomes a type of mass euphoria, in synch with the rhythmic movement of the sweeping light. Here, in Jiang Wen's own words, revolution and erotic desires are ironically entangled. The diegetic and the extradiegetic spaces are blurred in this playful turn. The images, with no fixed, sharp shapes, become affective and fluid-like, transcending the frame of the screen and making the audience themselves erotic and heroic subjects.

Jiang Wen is not alone in discovering the erotic power of revolutionary film. Recent scholarship has contributed helpful insights on this issue. In his 'Communists Have More Fun' (2009), Jason McGrath examines the sublimation thesis in Chinese revolutionary films – whereby he posits that the sublimation of 'libidinal drives towards the object of revolution' – first advanced by Chris Berry, and fully developed by Wang Ban, who, against the repression thesis that revolutionary films repress individual desires and emotions, discovers 'an intense emotional exuberance' in revolutionary films. McGrath exquisitely pinpoints the ways in which the conventions of Hollywood romance are adopted and appropriated to show 'the growing bond between the female protagonist and the communist cause.'[7] It is through the conventions of romance that libidinal energy is aroused and re-channelled for revolutionary cause. Given this confluence of ideas, McGrath further proposes 'the possibility that audiences may have enjoyed (mis)reading the visual cues of Hollywood romance according to their "original," unsublimated meanings and taken pleasure in the implied love stories featuring attractive actors whether or not the political meanings had much effect on their consciousness.' His investigation of post-Mao era films shows 'a reverse sublimation in which the public and political passions of the prior narrative mode are quickly channeled into the private, masochistic libidinal trajectory.' One example

Figure 17.1 The amorous screen of revolutionary ballet in *Let the Bullets Fly* (2010).

he gives is *Letter from an Unknown Woman* (2004), which happens to feature Jiang Wen as the male lead. It replaces revolutionary narrative with the erotic desire of individuals, and its historical setting plays only a marginal role.

McGrath's investigation highlights the intimate dynamics between revolutionary narrative and erotic desires. The attempts to write or rewrite contemporary Chinese history through the dynamics between revolution and erotic desire can also be found in Wang Xiaobo's Foucauldian take on the Cultural Revolution. In his widely read stories such as 'The Golden Age' (*Huangjin shidai*) and 'Love in an Era of Revolution' (*Geming shidai de aiqing*), Wang provides a witty narrative in which libidinal energy is generated and dispersed around the sadistic mechanisms of political interrogation. A similar scene appears in *The Sun Also Rises*, in which the interrogation process to decide who committed sexual harassment during the film screening turns out to be an erotic field for the female character Lin to satisfy her own sexual desire. However, if Wang Xiaobo's ironic narrator keeps his readers at a reflective distance, the sensuality found in *The Sun* absorbs its audience into an intense, erotically charged *mise-en-scène*. Jiang Wen intoxicates himself with the memories of erotic desires, and 'flirts' – in his own words – with his audience through the erotic power of his film. The aforementioned scene of the film screening, where the cinematic apparatus becomes the erotic object for the camera to caress, therefore, self-referentially points back to the role of cinema in producing erotic desire and mediating historical memories.

Jiang's eroticization of the past on the one hand exposes the channelling of libidinal energy in revolutionary films, while on the other hand revealing that when revolutionary narratives hollow out with the official ideology, it is the fragments of erotic memories that connect his generation to the past. In other words, historical memories now exist merely as remnants of bodily experience.

A textual reading of the invisible

Just as the son in *The Sun Also Rises* who desperately seeks the traces of his inaccessible father in order to approach the inapproachable, Jiang develops his own aesthetic of 'gesturing' beyond the visible images. The first section of the film is made of numerous chase scenes, in which the camera has to desperately 'run' or 'track' its subject in order to follow the same desperately running son who is after his crazy mother. The *mise-en-scène* is activated and animated as the camera sweeps across a bucolic countryside. As if the camera is too engrossed in the single-minded chase game, it no longer gives a clear vision of the world. Moreover, the camera is always forced to turn from its headlong horizontal movement toward the vertical axis, as the mother often disappears from the horizontal view and suddenly reappears in a tall tree or in a cave beneath the roots of a tree. What can she see from atop the tree? The camera never follows her closely enough to provide us with her point of view. It can only mimic her movement, and through its 'bodily' mimicry induces the bodily movement of the audience, but also always reminds us of its own (and the audience's) historically situated and thus limited perspective on the world around us. The rhythmic repetition of the chase scenes conveys the pulsating movement of the camera, pushes the bodily experience of the audience beyond the visible, and, by calling attention to the restricted perspective of the camera, indicates the existence of another reality, a world beyond our familiar vision.

This world beyond our familiar vision is further suggested by the mother's floating slab of riverbank and her mysterious stone house in the forest. A patch of riverbank that can be unanchored from the riverbed gestures toward an alternative topography that cannot be accessed through banal perceptions of the world around us. Following this floating riverbank, the son is led to a white stone house. As if in dream, a hidden world is suddenly revealed to him. Yet at this moment when this other world begins to take its shape, the son shivers and his several sneezes leaves everything in ruins. The magic has suddenly disappeared, and the dream of the other world is as flimsy as cinematic images that can easily become blurry and filmy when the light disperses. The abrupt appearance and disappearance of this other world leaves the son (and the audience) oscillating between reality and illusion, this world and the dream world.

The haunting oscillation cracks open the solid surface of the world we thought we understood, revealing the rich textuality and layered traces left by the hand of time. Thus images are no longer realistic but contingent on both personal experiences and historical memories that are evoked by the images. Jiang Wen describes his experience being haunted by the images as such:

> I saw the film in my mind when I closed my eyes. Once I started shooting, I was fascinated with the feeling of fluidity, and tried to capture the images as I had seen. Their colours were always there. As if they were beams of light, the images sometimes jumped beside you, sometimes dwelled above your head. When you finally captured them, you felt that they were not your creation. They were already there (even before you made the film).[8]

In Jiang's account, the content of these scintillating images no longer matters. It was the sensuality of the images that fascinated Jiang Wen and provided him a secret access to his innermost experience and buried memories. The images are glittering – intangible yet animated with their own life. It may not be a coincidence that Jiang requested his cinematographer Zhao Fei to overexpose the film in order to create a dreamy atmosphere. Overexposure brings in the glaring sunshine: everything is bathed in light, yet also rendered surreally nebulous. Jiang Wen's apparent fascination with the sun persistently appears in the titles of his films, from *In the Heat of the Sun* to *The Sun Also Rises*. To people familiar with contemporary Chinese history, the sun in the Cultural Revolutionary years cannot be severed from its political and symbolic implication. Yet Jiang Wen, through his highly stylized cinematic language, transforms the symbol into a hallucinatory experience of his individual take, as well as the euphoria and confusion of his generation growing up in the glaring sunshine. Their ambivalent experience of the years to be buried soon in history, their intoxication and disillusioned wakening, now can only appear as the sensual images and light.

The inalienable possessions and the production of cinema

While reconstructing lost memories through sensual images, Jiang Wen is well aware that any reconstruction is necessarily incomplete and mediated. To a certain extent, the crazy mother signifies the incomprehensibility of the past from the perspective of the son, as Jiang Wen explains:

> Why does the mad mother sing poems on the roof of her house? [That is because] she has an inner world that cannot be easily conveyed to her son. Any parents have their own stories of being thrown into mad love, and for some reason, they seldom tell their own love stories to their children. Their narrations are always broken. *Their love stories may be conveyed around various objects passed down*, but even so, the story the father told might be different with the one from the mother.[9] (my italics)

Here 'madness,' instead of being perceived as abnormal, indicates unavoidable incomprehensibility and limited accessibility of latter generations to recover and recapitulate the past they scarcely knew. And stories are contingent upon objects passed down by their parents and inevitably fragmentary. The centrality of objects in the recollections of the past brings our attention to the various particular objects in *The Sun* that connect subtly to the innermost world of the characters: the deceased husband's dilapidated copy of *What is to be Done?*, a utopian novel on the subject of reforming the institutions of marriage and work by the Russian writer Nikolai Chernyshevsky; a stone house in the forest that holds items from an eclipsed era; and letters full of broken sentences and inexplicable jokes. These objects are posited at the boundary of reality and the realm of dream, blurring the line between the two.

This is best seen in the pair of shoes that emerge directly from the mad mother's dream: beside the shining rail tracks among flowers lies a pair of exquisitely embroidered cloth shoes in the shape of fish. Next, the bare feet of a woman emerge from rippling water, and soon the feet are walking on a damp stone lane. As the camera shifts to focus on the pair of shoes in the woman's hands, it gradually reveals the face of the woman to be the mad mother. These shots are fluidly bound together, with no distinction between dream and 'real' life, as if the mother retrieves the shoes directly out from her oneiric world, as she tells her son: 'I dreamed the shoes. When I opened my eyes, I saw them.' When she stands in front of a shop counter, the camera focuses on the hands on the table. Instead of those of the salesman or saleswoman, the hands on the other side of the table are a pair of infant's hands, innocently knocking at the table as if impatiently waiting for the mother to pick up her shoes. The capricious joke Jiang Wen plays here immediately distances the scene from the buying-and-selling transactions of commodities. The pair of shoes is an inalienable possession[10] with its own particularity, invested with the mother's fantasies and innermost feelings. They are also inalienable because they are not exchangeable and replaceable commodities. After their mysterious disappearance, the son is never able to buy a similar pair for his mother.

However, this luscious world made of inalienable possessions cannot be severed from the industrial production of cinema today. The lush, colourful world in the cinematic space is in fact a composite of Jiang's aesthetic pursuit as well as the economic rules that govern cinematic production, each reinforcing the other. Rather than being inalienable, objects used in the films are often transferred to the filming site from other remote areas. For *The Sun Also Rises*, hundreds of birds and beasts were shipped from thousands of miles away, and even the lustre of the their feather and fur was produced by manual labourers who literally painted them with dream-like colours. Tibetan-style houses that appear in the film were moved from Tibet to the filming site in Yunnan, but their roofs were replaced with Hani-style thatched roofs, typical of the dwellings of ethnic minorities in southwestern China. Even the pebbles used to build the stone house and the particular type of red earth in the film were shipped from elsewhere. Such a large scale of removal and recombination demands a huge amount of money to throw into the production of the film. This tension inside and outside of the film text is finally dramatically reflected in the film's box office earnings: with an investment of 80 million RMB, the film gained merely less than 30 million RMB. The film's inalienable objects and the memories tied to them, which Jiang Wen invested great efforts to preserve, had to endure cruel economic pressures in an era when everything has become exchangeable commodities.

Exchangeable bullets

Jiang Wen's 2010 film *Let the Bullets Fly* displays many similar 'Jiang Wen' elements, such as luscious *mise-en-scène*, a fascination with revolutionary history, and the remembrance of the past. But this time the film is set in the 1920s, in the aftermath of the 1911 Revolution led by Sun Yet-sen. It is also no coincidence, then, that the film was released on the occasion of the centenary of the 1911 Revolution. The film tells the story of Zhang Mazi (Jiang Wen), a previous revolutionary and now a head bandit committed to robbing the rich, who finds himself the enemy of a local landlord named Huang Silang (Chow Yun-Fat), and finally succeeds in his self-invented 'revolution' and distributes the landlord's wealth among the masses.

However, without the self-conscious reflection on its own narrative that occurs in *The Sun Also Rises*, *Let the Bullets Fly* is a facetious drama soaked with frolicking 'lightness': the landlord Huang Silang has a stand-in, and the real and the stand-in often mimic each other; the bandits are revolutionaries at the start of the film, but become 'legitimate' government officials in the second half; prostitutes are revolutionary heroines, and sometimes the propaganda team of the government; a caricature of the bandit leader Zhang Mazi shows no resemblance to the one who claims himself to be Zhang Mazi; a fake head of the county assumes the role of another fake head of the county; even the name Zhang Mazi is a farcical double of Zhang Muzhi. Every name and identity is a mask that anyone can try on for size; every individual appears with a different face each time. By wearing masks – in the film, characters wear literal masks imprinted with abstract mah-jong signs – everyone becomes a bandit, or a hero from the revolution. The travesty of the role-playing game hollows out any identities. In the end, the narration of the film makes itself a mass entertainment in which everyone can imagine himself playing a role, and can release his libidinal energy in laughter.

In this sense, *Let the Bullets Fly* assumes quite a different relationship with its audience. If *The Sun* keeps reminding its audience through meticulous narrative structure and *mise-en-scène* of the difficulty of recuperating the past, the participatory festivity of *Let the Bullets Fly* invites its audience members to replace history with their own 'eternal present.' In addition, fans were eager to match every detail of the film with recent media incidents. For example, netizens read one graphic scene in which one character opens up his own stomach to verify his unsullied character as a reference to the media explosion around a case in 2009 of a person 'opening up the chest to examine his infected lung.'[11] Jiang Wen's bold imagination of having several galloping horses pulling a train was read as a play on the homonyms of 'Marxism' and 'horses' in Chinese, an insinuation to the CCP's forced 'Marxist control' over China. *Let the Bullets Fly* became an open text that dissipated into constant flows of media; its emptied signifiers provided a bit of everything for everyone, however different meaning each 'prosumer' gave to each bit. One amateur reviewer jumping on the historical discordance at the end of the film, in which the characters are going to the Pudong District of Shanghai, developed the following interpretation of the film:

> The Pudong district fell under the jurisdiction of Shanghai only from 1958. It is totally anachronistic to have those guys by the end of the film announcing they're leaving for Pudong of Shanghai. Why is this? Of course this is because Jiang Wen ambitiously made the film a parable of our time. Echeng and Pudong are two poles, one a closed, primitive inland small town, the other a coast city in the process of marching towards an open civil society.[12]

This reviewer believed that this anachronistic detail suggested Jiang Wen's allusions to contemporary politics rather than his adherence to historical exactitude. Here 'revolution' is equated with the reforms starting in Deng's era. Placed within the simultaneity created by social media networks, the text of the film becomes a cluster of random hyperlinks, to which historical time becomes irrelevant.

In contrast to *The Sun*'s miserable box office performance, *Bullets* won acclaims from its audience and was a box office smash. The different fates of these two films might testify to Henry Jenkins's (2009) dictum, that: 'If it doesn't spread, it's dead.' Jenkins shows that 'spreadable media' involves a collaboration between the gift economy and commodity culture, where corporations' best strategy for engaging consumer participation is to distribute 'long tail' content and reach niche markets with lower promotional budgets. The box office triumph of *Bullets* obviously relied on such spreadability. One reviewer on the Chinese social media website Douban demonstrates the economy of fandom:

> If you are a rich man, you should treat all your friends with the movie. If you are unfortunately a poor guy, skip your meals and save the money for a forty-yuan

daytime screening. If even that won't work, get a (pirated) DVD. Ok, at least get the film through E-Mule or Bi-Torrents. Even a person as stingy as me decided to join the fandom of Jiang Wen after watching *Let the Bullets Fly*.[13]

Corresponding to the flood of money flowing into the box office for *Let the Bullets Fly*, inside the film text itself, tonnes of silver and gold fill in *the mise-en-scène*. The streets of the fictive ECheng city are covered with tonnes of silver, as if the silver were mere pebbles to pave the road. Such forms of visual extravagance undoubtedly assault the eyes with an ostentatious display of the fetishism of money, but also deride the value of otherwise (and de-commodified) useless metal. Reflecting on this scene, one blogger amusingly described the Chinese state's fetishism of money, writing with half-hearted seriousness that: 'What's the use of dispensing money among the masses? Does that help them at all? … Silver is the currency, merely a medium in circulation. It can neither be eaten nor drunk. It is only useful when exchanged for commodities and services…. The dispensing of a large amount of money would not lead to wealth, but inflation.'[14] His comments connected the visual fetishism of money inside the text with the economy of the currency outside of the text, skewering the high inflation behind the prosperous scene of high GDP growth in China. What is of interest to my argument here is the ways in which exchangeable currency replaces inalienable objects in *The Sun*. If every object in *The Sun* is always connected with memories and innermost emotional investment of an individual, silver and gold in *Bullets* are homogenous and impersonal. As currency for exchange, they have no history, or ignore history, and substitute standardized measurability for individual needs and sentiments. Thus, dispensing money among the masses symptomatically becomes a panacea in *Bullets*. After all, money is assumed to be exchangeable for everything.

There is another layer of exchangeability surrounding the film. The reception of the film is deeply embedded in a media network, especially facilitated by the internet. The space films share with other media flows places a film in simultaneity with news and instant messages. Spoof videos on Tudou, Youku and other YouTube-like video sharing websites often appropriate clips from films as mimicry of recent political and

Figure 17.2 Paving the street with gold and silver in *Let the Bullets Fly* (2010).

social incidents. This blending of different genres and media cultures seeps into the production of commercial movies. A conscious incorporation of recent eye-catching incidents and catchphrases into the textuality of a film becomes a marketing strategy to solicit responses from the media-savvy audience. Therefore, the consumption of films also becomes to a large extent a type of information processing. The compact information in *Bullets* – its fast-paced and often abrupt transition between scenes, as if no second should be lost in pushing forward the plot – never gives the audience a break in the three-hour film, a pace that follows the rhythm of our information age with its bombardment of simulacra. If we examine the ways in which the film was dispersed in the media network and gained exchangeability with other media flows, it is always some catchy lines or phrases from the movie that gained the most frequent circulation. For example, lines such as 'Let the bullet fly!' and 'Be patient! Let the bullet fly for a few more seconds!' soon spread widely as catchphrases. Phrases such as 'let the oil price fly,' 'let the real estate price fly,' 'let the stock fly' – all playing with the double meaning of 'fei' in Chinese as both 'to fly' and 'to skyrocket' – soon went viral in Chinese media. Crucial to the circulation of the phrases was their brief form, and their mutability, so that they became 'meta-phrases' that could flow to fit into different contexts. *Let the Bullets Fly* thus is a pastiche that can be taken apart and thrown into circulation with its easy exchangeability.

So far my readings of Jiang Wen's two recent films adopt quite different approaches. This is because *The Sun Also Rises* and *Let the Bullets Fly* are stylistically distinct texts that demand different approaches. The self-enclosed cinematic world of *The Sun*, with its unconventional narrative and its exquisite sensuousness, demands a phenomenological reading to reveal its subtlety, and even more importantly, the historical conditions that exert pressure on its aesthetic form. *Bullets*, meanwhile, invites mass participation through easy exchangeability of its particles with media flows in the network, and therefore the film *per se* is decentred in the constant exchanges of media flows. However, despite these films' aesthetic differences, they do share certain commonalities. My parallel reading of the two may reveal the similar conditions of post-medium and postsocialism that shape their textuality and aesthetic. Though both films are set in historically specific years, they encounter immense difficulty in presenting the past: in *The Sun*, this difficulty is acknowledged by its integration of the very act of remembrance into its own textuality, through which fragmentary memories are evoked as affective images; *Bullets* circumvents the problem by replacing the past with stereotypical images of the present. In both cases, the past becomes a myth reinvented through contemporary imagination.

Such eclipse of historicity is considered by Jameson as a symptom of our postmodern era. Jameson, in his *Postmodernism, or The Cultural Logic of Late Capitalism*, states that the past in films and historical novels of our era has 'become a vast collection of images,' and even a seemingly realistic novel like *Ragtime* by E. L. Doctorow becomes 'a nonrepresentational work that combines fantasy signifiers from a variety of ideologemes in a kind of hologram.'[15] He thus concludes that a historical novel in our postmodern era 'can no longer set out to represent the historical past; it can only "represent" our ideas and stereotypes about that past (which thereby at once becomes "pop history").' But 'postmodern' should neither be regarded as teleological replacement of 'modern,' nor as innate to capitalism of the West. The notion of 'postmodern' is further complicated in the Chinese context with its postsocialist conditions. As Zhang Xudong argues, Chinese postmodernism since 1992 is closely related to 'the surplus of commodities and capital' as well as 'a bubble economy of images, signs, and discourses,' which reinforce 'the impression that daily life in China today is an integral part of *timeless now* of global capitalism' (italics mine).[16] He also points out that Chinese postmodernism means not only the dissolution of Maoism as a utopian ideology, but also of a monolithic, capitalist notion of 'modern.' With disillusion of both socialist utopianism and the capitalist mode of 'modern,' the postsocialist subjects' need for a new collective identity and social ideal can be read from the efforts to recuperate and appropriate previous revolutionary memories, as demonstrated both in Jang Wen's films and by the audience's enthusiastic reactions to them. Such efforts, however, are also conditioned by the postmodern, consumerist culture.

Conclusion

The ambivalent memories of Jiang Wen and his generation as 'eggs under the red flag' cannot be separated from the images and stereotypes of history in postsocialist conditions. The references to Wang Xiaobo's stories, the theme of 'madness,' as well as revolutionary narratives entangled with erotic desires are recycled in *The Sun*. Thus, *The Sun* is a tension-ridden text that on the one hand strives to reserve a space for memories in an era of forgetting, and on the other hand has to address the 'holograms' of the past in our media-saturated postmodernist age. The experience of seeing the film also becomes an unstable process of moving through its sometimes deliberately stilted performance and ambiguous images to a sudden encounter with fragments of memory. However, the hybridity of the film is aesthetically smoothed out in its assumedly autonomous world. Such a striving for autonomy may resemble the pursuit of aesthetic autonomy in modernism. Yet the high investment involved in the production of the film that was finally reduced into the figures of its box office receipts only confirms once again the whip of capitalist logic on artistic production, and the precarious autonomy of art under certain postmodern conditions. In this context, *Let the Bullets Fly* is the other side of the same coin: by submitting itself to the reproduction of spectacles in accordance with Hollywood conventions, the film makes history appear as a game of travesty and exchangeability. Audience participation through social media networks did not help bring back 'authentic' history, but instead dissembled the film into flows of exchangeable bits, to which history is no different from clusters of hyperlinks. Perhaps, the numerous deaths in the film, both fake deaths and revived corpses, may serve as a best trope for the violence inflicted on memory by our time: any living memories of history are inextricably entangled with the corpses of stereotypical images of the past in the Chinese mediascape of a postsocialist era.

Works cited

Dai, Jinhua. 'Severed Bridge: The Art of the Sons' Generation,' trans. by Lisa Rofel and Hu Ying, in Dai Jinhua, *Cinema and Desire: Feminist Marxism and Cultural Politics in the Work of Dai Jinhua*, Jing Wang and Tani Barlow (eds). London: Verso, 2002, 13–48.
Jameson, Fredric. *Postmodernism, or The Cultural Logic of Later Capitalism*. Durham, NC: Duke University Press, 1991.
Jenkins, Henry. *Convergence Culture: Where Old and New Media Collide*. New York: New York University Press. 2006.
—'If It Doesn't Spread, It's Dead: The Value of Spreadable Media.' 2009. See http://henryjenkins.org/2009/02
Krauss, Rosalind. *A Voyage on the North Sea: Art in the Age of the Post-medium Condition*. London: Thames and Hudson, 2000.
Kim, Ji-Hoon. 'The Post-media Condition and the Explosion of Cinema,' *Screen* 50:1 (Spring 2009): 114–23.
—'Jianying de Jiang Wen' (Hard-boiled Jiang Wen) in *Sanliang shenghuo zhoukan*, no. 30, 2007. http://tieba.baidu.com/f?kz=553331576
—'*Wo yishi shuo wo shi ge yeyu daoyan*' (I Always say I am an Amateur Director), interview with *Nanfang Zhoumo*, last modified 6 September 2007. http://www.infzm.com/content/9822
McGrath, Jason. 'Communists Have More Fun,' *World Picture* (Summer 2009). http://www.worldpicturejournal.com/WP_3/McGrath.html
Weiner, Annette. *Inalienable Possessions: The Paradox of Keeping-While-Giving*. Berkeley, CA: University of California Press, 1992.
Zhang, Xudong. 'Epilogue: Postmodernism and Postsocialist Society – Historicizing the Present' in Arif Dirlik and Xudong Zhang (eds), *Postmodernism & China*. Durham, NC and London: Duke University Press, 2000, 399–442.

Notes

1 Fredric Jameson, 18–19.
2 The notion of 'post-medium' comes from art critic Rosalind Krauss. For a critique of Krauss, see Kim (2009).
3 Henry Jenkins, 2–16.
4 This phrase comes from a 1994 album of the famous Chinese songwriter named Cui Jian. It is an ironic self-reference of the generation who were born in the early PRC years, grew up during the Cultural Revolution and lived through the drastic sociopolitical changes from the Mao era to the post-Mao Reform and Opening.
5 'Jianying de Jiang Wen (Hard-boiled Jiang Wen),' in *Sanliang shenghuo zhoukan*, no. 30, 2007. http://tieba.baidu.com/f?kz=553331576 (accessed 20 March 2012).
6 '*Wo yishi shuo wo shi ge yeyu daoyan*' (I Always say I am an Amateur Director), interview with *Nanfang Zhoumo*, last modified 6 September 2007. http://www.infzm.com/content/9822 (accessed March 2012).
7 Jason McGrath, 'Communists Have More Fun.' *World Picture* (Summer 2009).

8 'Jianying de Jiang Wen' (Hard-boiled Jiang Wen), *Sanliang shenghuo zhoukan*, no. 30, 2007. http://tieba.baidu.com/f?kz=553331576 (accessed 20 March 2012).
9 Jiang Wen, '*Wo yishi shuo wo shi ge yeyu daoyan*.'
10 The term 'inalienable possessions' comes from anthropologist Annette Weiner's studies of Melanesian societies, referring to the items that possess 'absolute value rather than exchange value' that places them 'above the exchangeability of one thing for another,' because they are 'symbolic repositories of genealogies and historical events' and 'imbued with intrinsic and ineffable identities of their owners.' However, the boundary between the inalienable and alienable can be much more complicated and porous. That's why I continue in the essay to list the alienable objects (or commodities, such as birds and beasts as well as Tibetan-style houses) appropriated from elsewhere to the filming site in order to construct in the film an alternative world composed of inalienable possessions.
11 A young migrant worker called Zhang Haichao was diagnosed with pneumoconiosis after working in a nocuous environment in a factory for three years, but could not get compensation from the factory. In 2009, the desperate Zhang opened up his own chest in order to verify the disease he got was pneumoconiosis, rather than tuberculosis as the factory claimed.
12 See http://movie.douban.com/review/4531090/ (accessed 1 May 2013).
13 See http://movie.douban.com/review/4542206/ (accessed 1 May 2013).
14 See Analytical Beep: 'Echeng Jingji' (The Economics of Echeng). http://beeplin.blog.163.com/blog/static/1725441602010112964312876/ (accessed 1 May 2012).
15 Fredric Jameson, 18–25.
16 Xudong Zhang, 422–4.

Notes on Contributors

Chris Berry is Professor of Film Studies at King's College London. He has published widely on Chinese cinema and media, of note: *Public Space, Media Space* (2013), *The New Chinese Documentary Film Movement: For the Public Record* (2010), *Electronic Elsewheres: Media, Technology, and Social Space* (2010), *Cultural Studies and Cultural Industries in Northeast Asia: What a Difference a Region Makes* (2009).

Xiaomei Chen is Professor of Chinese literature in the Department of East Asian Languages and Cultures at University of California, Davis. She is the author of *Occidentalism: A Theory of Counter-Discourse in Post-Mao China* (Oxford University Press, 1995; second and expanded edition, Rowman and Littlefield, 2002), and *Acting the Right Part: Political Theater and Popular Drama in Contemporary China* (University of Hawai'i Press, 2002). She is the co-editor, with Claire Sponsler, of *East of West: Cross-Cultural Performances and the Staging of Difference* (Palgrave, 2000), and with Julia Andrew, of *Visual Culture in Contemporary China* (Ohio State University Press, 2001), she is the editor of *Reading the Right Texts* (University of Hawai'i Press, 2003), and *Columbia Anthology of Modern Chinese Drama* (Columbia University Press, 2010; abridged edition, 2014). She has authored 40 journal articles and book chapters, and her book, entitled *Performing Chinese Revolution: Founding Fathers, Red Classics, and Revisionist Histories of Twentieth-century China*, is forthcoming from Columbia University Press.

Bingfeng Dong is the artistic director of the Li Xianting Film Fund Beijing and an independent curator.

Dan Gao is a PhD candidate in the Department of Cinema Studies at New York University. She has written essays, book reviews and criticisms on Chinese language cinema, independent film, popular TV drama and mass culture. Her forthcoming work includes an anthology essay on the digital distribution of Chinese independent films, encyclopaedic entries on early Chinese cinema by Routledge, and an article about the representation of madness in new Chinese documentary in a special issue of *Duli Dianying Pinglun* by Li Xianting Film Foundation. As an active translator, she has also been introducing cutting-edge academic work written in English (including Zhen Zhang's *Amorous History of the Silver Screen: Shanghai Cinema, 1896–1937*) to readers in China.

Jeesoon Hong is Assistant Professor of Chinese media culture at Sogang University, Seoul, South Korea. Before joining Sogang, she worked as a Lecturer in the Department of Chinese Studies at the University of Manchester, UK; as an Adjunct

Professor in the Department of Media Studies and Film at the New School, New York; in the Department of Comparative Literature at Korea University, Seoul; and the East Asian Studies Institute, Sungkonghoe University, Seoul. She completed her PhD in Chinese Studies at the University of Cambridge, UK and carried out post-doctoral research at J. W. Goethe-Universität Frankfurt, Germany and Columbia University, USA. She has published on Chinese media, stereotypes, martial arts films, translation and Chinese women's literature. She is currently working on media spaces in East Asia such as commercial spaces, big screens and online gaming spaces.

Matthew D. Johnson is Assistant Professor of East Asian History at Grinnell College. His research and teaching examine intersections of politics, culture and transnational relations with a focus on modern and contemporary China. He has written on topics ranging from early cinema to present-day cultural and economic soft power, and is a member of the editorial board of *Journal of Chinese Cinemas* (Routledge).

Xiao Liu received her PhD from the University of California at Berkeley in 2013. She was a post-doctoral fellow at Brown University, and began teaching as an Assistant Professor at McGill University in 2014. Her recent work examines the information fantasies and new media aesthetics in the post-Mao 1980s China. Her essay on parody videos appears in the *Journal of Chinese Cinemas*.

Ran Ma is Associate Professor for the Global-30 'Japan-in-Asia' Cultural Studies Program at the Graduate School of Letters, Nagoya University, Japan. She received her MA degree from the University of Amsterdam in Film Studies in 2005 and PhD degree from the Department of Comparative Literature, the University of Hong Kong in 2011. Her doctoral project examined the impact of Chinese independent cinema on global film festival networks, while her postdoctoral research (2010–13) has extended this research to also explore participatory art projects in Asian cities. Currently, her research project focuses on the grassroots-level, independent film-oriented film festival network in East Asia. Her publications include essays, reports and interviews on China's film festivals and Chinese independent cinema.

Ralph Parfect is a Teaching Fellow in the Lau China Institute at King's College London. He works broadly on the consumption of Chinese cultural goods, including film, literature and visual art, both in China and the West, and in both the early twentieth century and the contemporary period. He is currently working on British modernists' championing of Chinese art after 1900, and on recent Western rewritings of the life of the short story writer Ling Shuhua. He is also working on two book projects, the first examining aspects of Chinese cultural production and consumption in relation to the concept of soft power, and the second, co-authored with Xinzhong Yao, entitled *Tradition, Transformation and Globalization – A Discourse on China in the 21st Century*. His doctoral thesis, at King's College London, was in English Literature, and was entitled *Hell's Dexterities: The Violent Art of Robert Louis Stevenson*.

Ying Qian is a Post-doctoral Fellow with the Australian Centre on China in the World, Australia National University. She received her doctoral degree from Harvard University in Chinese history, with a secondary field in Film and Visual Studies. She is now revising her dissertation *Visionary Realities: Documentary Cinema in Socialist China* for book publication, while starting a new research project on the history of photography and cinema in China's multi-ethnic border regions. Her research interests include modern Chinese cultural and social history, cinema, visual art and image ethics and historiography and memories of socialism. She has written extensively on documentary in China, including a survey of independent Chinese documentary titled 'Power in the Frame' in *New Left Review*, and articles in *Oxford Handbook of Chinese Cinemas* and *China Heritage Quarterly*.

Jia Tan is Assistant Professor in the Academy of Film, Hong Kong Baptist University. She holds a PhD from the Division of Critical Studies in the School of Cinematic Arts at the University of Southern California. Her ongoing work engages television and media, popular culture, gender and sexuality and documentary. She is a recipient of Social Science Research Council Fellowship Award and Harold Lloyd Foundation Award. As a filmmaker, her short film was selected for Davis Feminist Film Festival and nominated for Best Gay/Lesbian Film in Great Lakes International Film Festival.

Paola Voci is a Senior Lecturer and Program Coordinator in Chinese Studies at the University of Otago in New Zealand. Her area of study combines East Asian Studies (in particular, Chinese language and culture), film and media studies and visual culture. In particular, her recent research has focused on documentary film/videomaking in contemporary China and the media of the Chinese diaspora. She has published in *Modern Chinese Literature and Culture*, *Senses of Cinema*, *Screening the Past*, *New Zealand Journal of Asian Studies*, and contributed to the *Encyclopaedia of Chinese Cinema*. Her work appears in several edited collections of essays. She is the author of *China on Video* (Routledge 2010), a book that analyses movies made and viewed on smaller screens (i.e. the DV camera, the computer monitor – and, within it, the internet window – and the cellphone display).

Luke Vulpiani is currently completing his PhD on China's Sixth Generation at King's College London in the Department of Film Studies, supervised by Dr Victor Fan. His interests are in Chinese film, film aesthetics and film philosophy, as well as the work of Alain Badiou.

Keith B. Wagner is an Assistant Professor of Film Studies and Social Theory in the Graduate School of Film and Digital Media at Hongik University in Seoul, South Korea. He is the co-editor of *Neoliberalism and Global Cinema: Capital, Culture and Marxist Critique* (Routledge 2011) and has published in a variety of journals, most recently with *Inter-Asia Cultural Studies* and *Third Text*. He is currently completing a manuscript titled *Living with Uncertainty: Precarious Work and Labor History* and co-editing two special journal issues: one on Korean independent cinema that goes beyond the Hallyu syndrome and the other on financial crises and Hollywood. Before taking up his post in Korea, he completed his PhD at King's College London and received his MPhil degree at the University of Cambridge.

Yiman Wang is Associate Professor of Film and Digital Media at University of California Santa Cruz. She is author of *Remaking Chinese Cinema: Through the Prism of Shanghai, Hong Kong and Hollywood* (University of Hawai'i Press, 2013). She is currently working on two book projects, one on Anna May Wong as a transnational 'minor' star, the other on animals and cinema. Her articles have appeared in *Quarterly Review of Film and Video, Film Quarterly, Camera Obscura, Journal of Film and Video, Literature/Film Quarterly, Positions: East Asia Cultures Critique, Journal of Chinese Cinemas, Chinese Films in Focus* (Chris Berry ed. 2003, 2008), *Idols of Modernity: Movie Stars of the 1920s* (Patrice Petro ed. 2010), *The New Chinese Documentary Film Movement: For the Public Record* (Chris Berry, Lü Xinyu and Lisa Rofel [eds] 2010), *Cinema at the City's Edge: Film and Urban Networks in East Asia* (Yomi Braester and James Tweedie [eds] 2010), *Engendering Cinema: Chinese Women Filmmakers Inside and Outside China* (Lingzhen Wang ed. 2011), *The Chinese Cinema Book* (Julian Ward and Song H. Lim [eds] 2011), *A Companion to Chinese Cinema* (Yingjin Zhang ed. 2012), and *The Oxford Handbook of Chinese Cinemas* (Carlos Rojas and Eileen Chow [eds] 2013).

Weihua Wu is Head of the New Media Division in the Faculty of Journalism and Communication, Communication University of China, where he specializes in visual and cultural studies, media sociology, research methodologies and health communication. He has published widely on problems from contemporary Chinese postmodern culture, animation culture and new media, and is the author of *Reading Notes on Visual Narrative* (China Broadcast, 2010) and *The Ambivalent Image Factory* (Routledge, 2014).

Tianqi Yu is a filmmaker, and Assistant Professor of Film and Media Studies, University of Nottingham, China campus (Ningbo). She received an MPhil in Sociology from the University of Cambridge, and a PhD from the Centre for Research and Education in Arts and Media, the University of Westminster, London. Her research focuses on documentary, amateur cinema culture, cinema and memory, Chinese cinema and visual arts. Currently she is completing her monograph *'My' Self On Camera – First Person Documentary Practice in Twenty-first Century China*. As a filmmaker, she explores documentary and essay film, and her works include *Photographing Shenzhen* (2007, Discovery), and *Memory of Home* (2009, collected by DSLCollection). Yu is also a member of the editorial board of the *Journal of Contemporary Chinese Art* (Intellect).

Ling Zhang is a PhD candidate in the department of the cinema and media studies at the University of Chicago. She is working on her dissertation on film sound, urban space and transmediality in 1920s–1940s Chinese cinema. She has published articles in both English and Chinese on contemporary Chinese independent cinema, Taiwan new cinema and Chinese opera film.

Index

3-D 16, 216, 218
24 City 24, 89–96, 99, 101, 120n., 122n., 206
85 New Wave 78, 85n.
798 Art District 14
2008 Global Financial Crisis 15

acoustic space 112, 116
activist vi, 38, 79, 85n., 154, 181–3, 185, 187, 189–92, 199–200, 259, 271–2
activist documentary vi, 85, 181–2, 185, 189, 272
activist movement 235, 250n., 251n.
Adobe Flash, 4, 11, 13, 57–8, 62–8, 69–71n., 80
aesthetic, v, vi, 5, 7–8, 11–12, 14, 16–17n., 20n., 23–4, 28, 59, 64, 66–9, 71n., 75–6, 82–4, 87, 89, 90, 92–3, 96, 101, 105–6, 108–11, 116–17, 119–20n., 124n., 133, 150–2, 171, 173, 175, 177, 182, 185, 189, 220, 227–8, 255, 273–4, 321–5, 327, 330, 333–4
affect ix, 12, 17–18n., 20n., 85n., 90, 92, 102–3n., 111, 119n., 122n., 135, 174, 186, 215
affective economy 174
Aftershock 218
Ai, WeiWei 3, 36–8, 76n., 182–3, 189, 190–2, 251n.
Ai, Xiaoming 5, 181–92, 194n.
alternative(ness) 28, 45, 64, 78, 82, 107, 117–18, 121n., 130, 139, 141n., 145n., 160–2n., 168, 217, 229–32, 239, 241, 243, 248, 249n., 252n., 257n., 266, 270, 275n., 278n., 328, 336n.
amateur 4, 8, 10, 12–13, 16, 28, 34, 38–9, 40n., 50, 58, 60, 69, 132, 139–40, 150, 152, 193, 229–31, 233, 251n., 255–6, 331, 335n., 340n.

Andrew, Dudley xi, 225, 233n., 234n.
animal-ness 168–9, 172, 174, 177
architectural space, 83, 109, 112, 116, 203–4
  as imagined processes
artist viii, 2, 11,13, 16, 26, 36, 38, 48, 57–8, 64–6, 68–9, 73--82, 84, 85n., 124n., 147–9, 168, 190–1, 220, 228–9, 231, 236–7, 241–3, 255, 268, 273, 295
art criticism
art galleries 2, 11, 45, 50, 75, 81–3, 124n., 247
artist film 74, 76–7, 82
artistic movements 149, 257
Asian Games 198, 203–4
audience vi, 5–6, 9, 13, 16, 18–19n., 23, 25–6, 36–8, 50, 51, 57, 59, 62–3, 68–9, 77, 82, 109–10, 122n., 125–7, 130, 132–4, 154–5, 158–9, 173, 176, 180n., 185, 191, 211n., 217–18, 220, 223–4, 229, 231, 238, 244–5, 264, 270–2, 283–5, 293, 299, 302, 305–6, 308, 314n., 317n., 322–3, 325–8, 331, 333–4
auteur theory (critique of), 256, 273
autobiography 26–7, 233
avant-garde 51, 65, 67, 69, 78, 105, 119–20n., 124n., 168, 190, 255, 257

B&T Studio 68
banality 6, 182
Bauman, Zygmunt 2, 24–5, 41–2n.
Bazin, Andre 188, 192n., 193–4n.
Beck, Ulrich 2, 24, 40–1n.
Beijing Film Academy 38, 60, 70n., 138, 183, 238
Benjamin, Walter 118n., 120n., 127, 131–2, 137, 140n., 146n., 224–6, 233–4n.

Berry, Chris v, vii, xi, 17–20n., 40n., 43n., 51, 52–3n., 155, 160–2n., 182, 192n.–3n., 239–40, 248, 249n.–50n., 252n., 274n., 279n., 326
Berry, Michael 97, 100, 101n., 103n.
black market criminality 3
BlackAnt Animation Studio, xv, 61, 70
Blockbuster(ization) 1–2, 9, 50, 61, 315–16n.
blogs or micro-blogs (*weibo*) 4–5, 13, 162n., 198, 207, 210n., 233–4n., 237, 245–6, 248, 250–1n., 253n., 301
box office ix, 1, 10, 17–18n., 217, 322–3, 330–2, 334
Braester, Yomi xi, 35, 40n., 43n., 90, 101–2n., 206, 208, 211n., 314n., 316n.
Brandscaping 219, 233–4n.
Bristow, Rebecca Jean 60, 69–70n.
Bruno, Giuliana 108, 119–23n.
Bumming in Beijing 6, 79, 147, 149, 161–2

Cantonese vi, xv, 2, 5, 49, 121, 128, 197–200, 202–8, 209n., 211n.
Cao, Fei 74, 106, 109, 119–4n.
Caochangdi Workstation 238, 256–7
Castells, Manuel 16n., 20n., 235–6
CCTV 11, 51, 65, 70n., 148, 153, 194n., 264n., 293n., 315n., 317n.
Celebration of heterogeneity 114
Chengdu Upriver Gallery 81
Chengzhongcun 107, 119n., 121n.
China Film Group 8
China National Pavilion 220–4, 234n.
China Village Documentary Project, The 256–60, 263–9, 271, 273, 280n.
Chinese contemporary art v, 14, 73–86, 240, 242
Chinese Independent Animation Festival 60
Chinese independent cinema 85, 137, 140, 145n., 236–8, 241–3, 247–8, 276–7n.
Chinese independent documentary 1–55, 147–63, 167–97, 215–55, 265, 273
Chineseness 208
Chow, Rey 59–60, 69–70n.

Chris Marker 26
Cinema of exhibition 73–7, 81–4
Cinephilia xi, 10, 13, 126–46, 150, 247, 250–1n.
Closer Economic Partnership Arrangement 7
collective vii, 5, 25–6, 29, 34–7, 39, 51, 52n., 55n., 74, 79–80, 92–3, 95, 100, 107, 113–14, 118, 121n., 123n., 129, 143n., 145n., 174, 183–4, 192, 203, 206, 215, 224, 229–31, 238, 246–7, 265, 288, 334
collectivity 215
commodified leisure 16
communal screen 4
Communicative Practice v, 23, 25–6, 30
Communism 131
Communist Party 2, 29, 58, 199, 218–19, 230, 232, 243, 255, 260–2, 271, 277n., 281n., 283–4, 303, 315–16n.
consumption vii, ix, x, 1–5, 9–10, 14, 30, 41n., 93–5, 125, 129, 133, 141–3n., 145n., 168, 174, 177, 200, 215–16, 218–19, 248, 276–7n., 302, 321, 323–3
corporeal landscape 111
corruption 2, 156, 191, 200
cosmopolitanism 229
Couldry 216, 233n.
co-worlding 175, 177
CRASSH program, The (Cambridge University), 267
Cui Weiping 183–4, 193–1n., 275n., 280n.
cultural rescaling 2
cultural revolution 36, 61, 143n., 183, 188, 284, 286, 295, 301, 304–8, 310–12, 313, 314n., 318n., 323, 324–5, 327–8, 335n.
Curtin, Michael 16, 18–19n.

D-generation 129, 141n., 145n.
decollectivization 39
Deleuze, Gilles 16n., 20n., 174, 178n., 180n.
democracy 2, 6, 143n., 197, 258, 261, 263–4, 269–70, 274n., 276–9n., 281n., 298n., 302

democraticization of the digital image 117
Deng, Xiaoping vi, 4, 24, 261, 283–6, 290, 294–5, 296–8n., 331
deprivation 3, 171
dialectical process 126, 295
digital vii–x, 11–13, 23–86, 167–211, 215–83, 301–19
    activism vi, 2, 5, 197–200, 202, 206–8
    augmentation 223
    contention 197
    film 11
    technology 1, 4, 12, 53n., 59–60, 62–3, 90, 125, 197, 230, 256
Digital City Symphony film v, 9, 105–24
disorder 107, 113, 122n., 140, 152
dispersion vii, 1, 101, 215, 232
Dissanayake, Wimal, 3, 18n.
distorted motion 110
distribution channels 1, 45
DOChina 139, 235, 239, 242–3, 247–9
docu-ani-mentary vi, 167–8, 172, 177–8, 179n.
documentary ethics 158–9
domestic violence 35
domesticity 169–72, 175
Douban vi, xvi, 84–5n., 248, 253n., 301–3, 305–6, 308, 310–13, 314–16n., 318–19n., 331, 336n.
Du, Qingchun 75, 84n., 238, 304, 314–19n.
DV 11, 28, 30, 37, 39, 43, 45, 50–1, 54n., 79, 106, 133, 138, 140, 145n., 247, 159, 160n., 162n., 172–5, 178, 179n., 190, 193n., 237–8, 240, 251, 269, 270–1, 278n.
    camera 11, 28, 30, 37, 39, 43n., 140, 147, 172–3, 178, 238, 270
    documentary 43n., 193n., 251n.
    dynamism 109–10
    filmmaking culture 237
    individualized writing 30

ecocinema 167–8, 178–80n.
eco-community 170–1
eco-criticism 167, 177
ecology 175, 177, 179, 180n.
engagement vi, 16, 26, 38, 60, 73, 97, 129, 161–2n., 165, 176–7, 182, 189, 191, 202, 215, 231, 240, 245–6, 257, 267, 279n.
enterprising 93
entrepreneurial 2
Environmentalism 167, 178
erotic 83, 128, 136, 305, 307, 324–7, 334
ethical relationship 35
ethnic 25–6, 42, 106, 112, 142–3, 158, 172, 204, 236, 258, 270, 330
ethnographic films 24, 191
E-TOON Creation Co. 68
E.U.-China Training Program 256, 258–60, 262, 269–70, 274n., 280n.
European Union-China Training Programme on Village Governance (EUCTP) 43, 256, 258–61, 263–4, 267–70, 274n., 280n.
expose–style 13
exhibition v, viii, ix, x, 2, 7–8, 10, 13–14, 73–78, 80–4, 85n., 111, 117–18, 158–9, 215, 217, 221–4, 230, 236–42, 246–51, 256–7, 260

familial 3, 5, 23, 26–7, 29–31, 34, 37–9, 138, 158
    trauma 26
female directors 24
film (classifications)
    independent 38, 65, 73–6n., 79–80, 82, 121–2n., 126, 128, 137, 140, 141n., 145n., 168, 188–9, 229, 235, 237–48, 249–53n., 256–7, 259, 264, 266
    internal reference films 128
    kamikaze documentaries 150
    mini films 5, 11
    NGO aesthetic vi, 6, 255, 257, 259–60, 264–6, 272–3
    passerby films 128
    pirated films 135, 137
    reckless documentary 148–9, 152–3
film censorship
film circulation 143n.
film industry 1, 7–8, 18–19n., 23, 57, 82, 140n., 144n., 201n., 210n., 233n., 239, 248, 276–7n.
film quotas 8
first person documentary v, 5, 23–8, 39, 340

female first-person documentary v, 23–43
Feng Xiaogang 9, 50, 218
Fifth Generation 4, 8–9, 15, 138, 206, 255
flâneurs 108
flash mob 198, 207, 210–11n.
Ford Foundation, The 256, 261–2, 265–6, 272–4
found footage 2, 13, 27, 183, 186, 228
fragmentation 324
Fulian 29
Funding of a Republic, The 9

generational 8, 15, 39, 167
Giddens, Anthony 2, 24–5, 41n.
global vii, x, 1, 3–4, 6, 9–10, 12, 14–15, 16n., 18–19n., 30, 51, 52n., 54n., 57–8, 60, 63–4, 68, 76, 79, 90, 101, 102n., 105–8, 112, 115, 117–18, 119n., 121n., 123–4n., 125, 130, 141–2n., 145n., 160n., 162n., 167, 172–3, 177–9, 198, 201–3, 206, 208, 211n., 215, 217–18, 220, 224–5, 228, 230–2, 236, 238–9, 241–2, 245–6, 248, 250–2n., 255, 259, 267, 270, 276–7n., 280n., 283, 302, 315–16n., 334
global economic system 1
goutong (communication) 30
grassroots vi, 10, 74, 137, 140, 158–9, 173, 175, 182, 185, 187, 192, 206, 208n., 211n., 235–40, 242, 247–8, 252n., 260–1, 271–3, 277n., 281n., 315–16n.
Grassroots Chinese independent film festivals vi, 235
Grassroots perspectives 185
Great Fire Wall 3
grim real v, 89, 92–3, 95, 99–102
Guangdong Art Museum 73, 81
Guo Jing 10, 249n., 252n., 265–6, 273, 280n.
Guo, Jingming 10

Harvey, David 107, 114, 118, 119–21n., 123–4n.
He Dihe 68
He Yi 68
Heart 12, 36, 66, 69, 71n., 95, 131, 227, 287, 293, 308–9, 332

heterogeneity 114–15
HIV/AIDS 185
Hollywood 8–9, 11–12, 43, 45, 128, 144, 249n., 251n., 275n., 278n., 326, 334
home movies 27
Home Video xv, 23, 28, 30–2, 35, 37, 49, 187
Hong Kong 7–8, 17n., 19–20n., 40n., 43n., 49, 70n., 93, 96, 128, 133, 141–5n., 160–2n., 178n., 194n., 199–200, 202, 206–7, 209–11n., 246, 249–50n., 252n., 268, 274n., 276–7n., 279–80n., 285, 287, 290, 293, 296–7n., 304
Hu, Ge 5, 17n., 19n., 48–9
Hu Jie 181–7, 189–90, 194n.
Hu Xinyu 38
Hukou 114, 199
humanimal 6, 167–72, 174–7

identity 3, 5, 16, 17–19n., 25–8, 37, 39, 41–2n., 64, 69, 113, 126, 130, 134, 136, 138, 142n., 146n., 204, 220, 231, 244, 274n., 276–8n., 330, 334
identity construction 16
ideological superstructure 12
ideology 2, 11, 29, 35, 52n., 54n., 57, 69, 188, 209–10n., 232, 289, 295, 307, 321, 323, 327, 334
I Wish I Knew xv, xvi, 24, 217, 224–9, 231, 233–4n.
If You Are the One I&II (feicheng wurao I and II) 9
iGeneration v, vi, vii, viii, ix, x, xi, xii, 1, 3–6, 8–16, 17–18n., 23–4, 38, 57–8, 60, 69, 73, 76, 84, 89–90, 92, 95, 99, 101, 107, 148, 159, 257, 301–2
IMAX 7, 16, 98, 216, 218, 227, 230
immersive spectacle 223
immobility 114, 286, 224
individualization (*gerenhua*) 1–4, 17–18n., 23–5, 40–2n.
individualization process 24, 29
individualized writing 29–30
industrial capitalism 113
industrial democracy 2
Information flow 232
international film festival network 235, 239, 241, 245, 247, 276–7n.

Internet vii, ix, 3–5, 10–11, 45, 48–9, 51, 54–5n., 57, 60–4, 76, 80, 90, 99, 101, 146n., 184, 189–90, 192, 197–9, 206–8, 209–11n., 231–2, 237, 240, 248, 258, 288, 290–1, 301–3, 305–10, 313–14, 315–18n., 323, 332
iPhones 4

Jia, Zhangke xv, 8–9, 24, 53n., 74, 89–91, 96, 102n., 120n., 122n., 127–8, 133, 141n., 144n., 151, 181, 206, 217, 224–6, 228–9, 231, 238, 249n., 251n.
Jian Yi 229–31, 256–8, 260, 264–5, 267–9, 271–3, 278n., 315n., 317n.
Jiang, Zemin., 14, 262
Jiangxi 28, 142n., 144n., 230, 267, 285, 288, 291–2, 298n
Juvenile crime v, 147, 150, 157, 159

kinship trauma 5
Knight-errant (*wuxia*) films 9, 95

labyrinthine 108
landscape (types of) 62, 80, 107–8, 111, 114, 140n., 143n., 151, 169–71, 182, 193n., 302
  corporeal 111
  logframe 259–60, 264–6, 272
  physical 107
LCD- and plasma-screen technology 13
Lenin in October 284
Let the Bullets Fly xvi, 10, 322–3, 326, 330–4
LGBT 3
Liu, Jiayin 5, 38
Local consciousness 76, 244
Lost in Thailand 10
Lou Ye 89, 96, 99, 127

Main-melody films 9
Man with a Movie Camera 105–6, 109, 117–18, 120–3n., 131, 142n., 146n.
Manovich, Lev 7, 17n., 20n., 218–19, 233–4n.
marginalization, 153
marriage, 28–30, 34–6, 39, 307, 329

Massey, Doreen 216, 233n.
Massumi, Brian 17n., 20n., 178n.
materiality vii, 17n., 20n., 78, 169, 172, 177
Matrix 113, 200
Matrix, The 11, 49
McGrath, Jason 17n., 20n., 315–16n., 326–7, 335n.
me culture (*ziwo wenhua*) 5, 18–19n., 27, 42n.
media xi, 1-5, 8, 10–16, 17n., 20n., 39, 45, 48, 51, 52–5n., 58, 60, 63–5, 69, 71n., 73–7, 79–82, 84–5n., 111–12, 117, 125–7, 129, 132, 140, 141n., 145–6n., 148, 153, 16–9, 178n., 187, 192, 197–202, 206–8, 209–11n., 215–17, 223, 225, 228–9, 231–2, 233–4n., 236–7, 242, 246, 248, 257–8, 264, 266–2, 275–7n., 279–81n., 285, 292, 294, 302, 304, 307, 316–17n., 321–4, 327, 329, 331–4, 335n.
MediaSpace, 216, 232, 233n.
Meishu film 57, 69–70n
metrical montage 108, 112, 116–17
Miaoyin Motion Pictures 68
middle-class consumption 215
mini films (*wei dianying*) 5, 11
Ministry of Civil Affairs (*Minzheng bu*) 260–5, 267, 271
minjian independent 10–11, 74, 236–7, 239–49, 252n.
missing period 13
mobile audience 217, 223–4
mode of multiplicity 246–7
modernism 26, 131, 182, 321, 333–4, 335n.
modernist impulse 106
modernity 17n., 20n., 25, 40–1n., 52n., 54n., 68, 105, 107, 118, 119–21n., 123n., 157, 160n., 162n., 197, 209–10n., 315–16n.
montage v, vi, 96, 105–6, 108–10, 112, 114–17, 119–20n., 122n., 131, 181–3, 187–9, 192, 224–5, 231
mother-daughter 30
multi-platform 1
multiple layers of movement 115

neo-formalism 2

neoliberalism vii, 2, 17–19n., 101, 102n., 153–4, 157, 159, 257, 321
  globalization 10, 18–19n., 106, 203
  "Neoliberalism with Chinese characteristics" 2, 4
  reality 2
  underdevelopment 150, 153, 158
neo-nationalism 3
Netizens 13, 49, 126, 184, 199, 203, 207, 209n., 246, 301, 331
New Documentary Movement 8, 40n., 48, 52–3n., 79–80, 147, 161–2n., 181, 193n., 270
new media art 71n., 73, 75, 79–82, 111
New Socialist Climax 230
new women 29, 37, 42n.
NGO-aesthetic vi, 6, 255, 257, 259–60, 264–6, 272–3
Nichols, Bill 26, 42n., 148, 160–1n.
Nick and Anna McCarthy 216, 233n.
Nostalgia 38, 59, 62, 66, 71n., 184, 321, 323

Ong, Aihwa 3, 18n.
Online audiences vi, 16, 299
Ou, Ning 106, 111, 117, 119–24n.
Our Children 5, 181–2, 185–92

Pearl River Film Studio 201
Peng, Laikwan 17n., 19n., 125, 141n.
performance 26–8, 36, 39, 43n., 76, 78, 93, 109, 114, 121n., 137, 185, 191, 204, 215, 283, 285, 295, 331, 334
performativity 27, 30, 167, 169
personal cinema 27
photovoice 266, 272–3, 276n., 280n.
Pickowicz, Paul 40n., 141n., 145n., 148, 160–2n., 275–6n., 278n., 281n.
Pixar 13, 61
Planetarianism 167–8
platforms vi, vii, 1, 3, 9, 16, 74, 130, 177, 207, 213, 225, 229–31, 237–8, 245, 248, 264, 322
plasma screens 13, 218
Pleasant Goat and Big Bad Wolf 59, 68
pluralism 6, 155
popular culture 64–5, 67, 133–4, 137, 307, 313

post-cinematic 1, 4, 6, 12, 17–18n., 20n., 101, 102–3n.
post-Mao 10, 24, 37, 188, 201, 256, 260, 271, 283, 286, 295, 326, 335n.
post-medium 321, 323–5, 333, 335n.
post-reform 38, 283
post-socialism 10, 40n., 52–4n., 333
  postsocialist primitives 137
  postsocialist subjects 126, 132–3, 334
  repressive social structures of sexuality 136
  transitional society 139
post-WTO society 1, 2, 3, 13, 15, 64, 84, 126, 147, 158, 232, 240, 302
power relations 235–6
private 3, 5, 7–9, 12–13, 24, 26, 30–1, 38, 41n., 81, 120n., 123n., 128–9, 139, 141n., 143–4n., 150, 153, 158–9, 191, 240, 247–8, 255, 260, 262, 309, 326
production vii, ix, x, xi, xii, 2–16, 18n., 24, 27, 39, 43n., 45, 50–2, 58–60, 66, 75, 77–82, 90, 106, 117, 126–7, 131, 133, 140, 150, 155, 158, 161n., 174, 177, 182–3, 188, 200–2, 208, 216–17, 220–1, 229, 232, 233, 237–8, 242, 249n., 252n., 255–60, 266, 272–4, 280n., 286, 302, 304, 321–3, 329–30, 333–4
provincialization vi, 151, 197–8, 208n.
  province 28, 106–7, 115, 128, 154, 176, 185, 198, 200, 209–10n., 230, 245, 256, 258, 263, 266, 268, 273, 285, 291, 296–7n., 303
  provincial media 200–2
public sphere 30, 82, 141n., 145n., 239, 248, 271

quality (*sushi*) viii, x, xi, 6, 48, 74, 114, 116, 118, 124n., 127, 131–2, 134, 138–9, 204, 217n., 302–3, 305–6

Rap Guangzhou 2, 202, 211n.
realism 12, 45, 48, 53n., 94–5, 188
  essential realism 188
  (mode of) cinema verite 131, 148
  neorealism 188
  socialist realist 184, 188

Reception theory 2, 5
Renov, Michael 26–7, 40n–2n., 52n., 54n.
Reform Era 13, 69, 127–8, 140, 145n., 220, 285, 290, 294, 306
regional 2, 9, 11, 13, 119n., 121n., 150, 152–3, 155, 158–9, 160n., 163n., 201, 205, 210n., 215, 230, 236, 238, 241, 245–6, 248
relational self 34
relying on oneself (*kao ziji*) 4, 58
remembrance 6, 114, 231, 283, 285, 324, 330, 333
representation v, 4, 12–14, 26, 45, 48, 57, 60, 69, 81–2, 90–93, 95–6, 99, 105–6, 110–11, 117, 132–3, 137, 139, 177, 179n., 188, 225, 229, 265, 270, 272, 287, 293, 295, 305, 307, 313, 322–3, 333
  of crime v, 9, 112, 147, 150, 152–3, 155–9, 160–2n., 288
  documentary forms of 137
  of a post-socialist reality 11, 126, 147
  of subjectivity 26, 89, 93, 111
  of urban space 89, 91, 93, 108, 218–19, 225
reviewing 263, 308
Revolution xvi, 36, 41–3n., 60–1, 77, 92, 131, 142–4n., 146n., 160n., 162n., 183, 188, 197–8, 208, 227–8, 230–1, 249, 276n., 278n., 283–95, 296–7n., 301, 304–8, 310–11, 313, 314n., 318n., 322–8, 330–1, 334, 335n.
Riverside Scene at Qingming Festival xv, 220–3
Rodowick, D. N. 11–12, 17n., 20n.
Rofel, Lisa 17n–18n., 20n., 40n., 43n., 160–2n., 239, 249–50n., 252n., 274n., 279n., 335n
romance 137, 301, 303–4, 307, 310–12, 326
ruins 181–3, 185, 187, 189, 228, 328
rural migrants 107, 113

San Yuan Li v, 105–18, 119–24n
screens viii, xi, xv, xvi, 4, 13, 16–17n., 19–20n., 83, 123n., 215–22, 229, 232, 233–4n

ScreenSpaces vi, xv, 7, 215–24, 228–33
Seaworld 59
second-tier city 230
Seen and Heard 256, 258, 267–8
self-expression 4, 6, 64
self-institutionalization 77
sex vi, 3, 5, 29, 38, 40n., 42–3n., 48, 95, 99–100, 112, 129, 133, 136–7, 178–9n., 185, 276n., 281n., 301, 303–5, 307–10, 312–14, 315–18n., 327
sexuality 3, 17–18n., 26, 29, 38, 40n., 42n., 46, 69–70n., 136, 305–7, 314n., 316–18n.
Shu Haolun 38
shadow economy 129, 145n.
Shanghai vi, viii, xv, 3, 7, 8, 11, 14, 48–9, 53n., 62, 70n., 77, 80–1, 96, 134, 141–5n., 152, 154, 157–8, 161n., 215–32, 234n., 237–8, 241, 244–5, 252–3n., 284–5, 287–8, 290–1, 293, 297n., 302, 307, 314n., 317n., 331
Shanghai Art Museum 81
Shanghai Expo vi, xv, xvi, 7, 215–17, 220–5, 228–30, 232, 234n.
Shanghai Film Group 8
Shanghai Tianzi Fang 14
Shaviro, Steven 12, 17–18n., 20n., 102–3n.
Shenzhen OCT LOFT 14
Shih, Shu-mei 6, 17n., 19n., 278
Sichuan earthquake 2, 5, 152, 185, 190
Sinodoor Animation 68
Sixth Generation v, 4, 24, 50–1, 63, 69, 82, 89–92, 95–7, 99, 101, 102n., 134, 206, 224, 255
Snail Studio 68
social media 4, 11, 13, 197, 199, 207, 237, 246, 248, 302, 322–3, 331, 334
sociological methodologies, 2
Solar Tree 79
solipsism 4, 5, 10, 26, 148
Song, Fang 5, 23
space ix, 1, 6, 10–15, 23–4, 26, 30–1, 34, 37–9, 51, 57–8, 62–3, 65, 68, 73–5, 78, 80, 82–4, 85n., 89–91, 93, 97, 101–3n., 105–9, 112–13, 115–18, 119–23n., 126, 129, 131, 134, 146n., 148, 151, 154, 158–9, 168, 170–3,

177, 180n., 191, 197, 199, 203–4, 210n., 215–19, 221–2, 225, 233n., 235–6, 238–9, 244, 247–8, 250n., 252–3n., 257, 259–60, 266, 277n., 280n., 301, 302, 307, 313–14, 323, 326, 330, 332, 334
  acoustic 112, 116
  architectural 83, 109, 112, 116, 203–4
  digital augmentation 223
  immersive 57, 68, 218, 221, 223–4, 229
  "of flows" 235
  pedestrian-oriented 113
  physical 109, 112, 199, 218
  public ix, 1, 15, 26, 38, 109, 129, 168, 210n., 215, 218–19, 239, 247–8, 250n., 253n.
spatial construction v, 105–7
State Administration of Radio, Film, and Television (SARFT) 7–8, 19n., 201, 240
Stella, Bruzzi 26, 42n.
streaming and P2P 9, 77, 125, 215, 302
subjective 6, 27, 30, 34, 40n., 48, 66–7, 83, 112, 116, 123n., 174, 180n., 189
subjectivity 12, 23, 26, 27n., 89, 92–3, 111, 161n., 174–6
Summer, Cat 66
Summer Palace 89, 92, 95–7, 99–101
Sun Also Rises, The 323–5, 327–8, 330, 333
surface 116–17, 151, 218, 221, 223, 233–4n., 297n., 324, 328
surveillance 16, 197, 200, 210n., 244

Tan, Beilin 68
Tao, Gan 68
techno-utopianism 197
temporal v, 16n., 19n., 43n., 53–4n., 60, 67–8, 75, 91–92, 96, 105–14, 117–18, 122, 130, 170, 185, 192, 223, 236, 257, 276n., 278n., 323, 325
They Are Not the Only Unhappy Couple 23, 28, 34–5, 37
third world, the 106
Three Small Animals II 7, 150–5, 157–9, 161–2n.
Tiananmen 95–101, 102–3n., 156, 199
Tiger Commander Li Mingrui 285

transition viii, 3–4, 28, 37–9, 83, 89–90, 92, 95–6, 99, 101, 102n., 107, 109, 113, 115, 119n., 121–4n., 139, 141n., 146n., 160n., 162n., 209–10n., 243, 260, 333
transmedia flow 206–7
transnational connoisseurship 16
transnational perspectives 2
transnationalism 198, 255–81
Tweets vi, 181, 183, 189, 191–2

ubiquity 4, 12–13, 215, 220
UltraGirl Studio 61, 63
Under The Hawthorn Tree vi, 301, 303, 314–19n.
Urban Generation 3, 8–9, 15, 40n., 102n., 107, 129, 142n., 145n.
urban xvi, 1, 3, 6, 8–9, 15, 17, 20n., 24, 38–9, 40n., 48, 51, 62, 89–93, 101–2n., 105–9, 112–18, 119–22n., 128–9, 141–3n., 145–6n., 151–2, 155–6, 172, 199, 202–6, 208n., 211n., 215–21, 223–9, 231–2, 233–4n., 243, 248, 249–50n., 252n., 261, 270, 275n., 280n., 283, 286, 295, 302
  urban poverty 113
  village 107, 109, 112–18, 119n., 121n.
urbanization 24, 39, 106–7, 113, 118, 119n., 121n., 202–3, 205, 224, 283

Vagina Monologue 182–5, 189, 191
Vertov, Dziga 105–6, 109–10, 117–18, 120n., 122n., 126–7, 131–2, 134, 142n., 146n.
Vidding 202, 207
video art 45, 52–4n., 73, 75–82, 85n., 122n.
violence 13, 35, 100, 153, 156, 159, 226, 334
Visual *aides–memoires* 4

Wan Brothers 57, 70
Wang, Ban 17–18n., 173, 179n.
Wang, Bing 6n., 151, 167, 171, 181
Wang, Fen 5, 23–4, 28, 36–9, 42–3n.
Wang, Hui 2, 149, 155, 157, 160n., 162n., 209–10n.

Wasson, Haidee 13, 17n., 20n.
Web-based Flash animation 57–8
Webber, Andrew 115, 119n., 123–4n.
Wen, Jiang 10, 308, 315n., 318n., 322–34, 335–6n.
Wenchuan earthquake 181
Wilson, Rob 3, 18n.
Women filmmakers 25, 27–30, 38–9, 340
Wu, Wenguang vi, 6, 8, 39, 43n., 79, 84–5n., 89, 147, 149–50, 154, 160–2n., 230, 255–60, 264–73, 275–8n., 280–1n.

Xi'an Film Group 8
XOYTO Comic 68, 71
Xu, Zheng 10
Xue, Jianqiang v, 7, 39, 147, 149, 151, 153, 155, 157, 159, 161n.

Yan, Yunxiang 2–3, 18n., 24, 41n.
Yang, Fudong viiii, x, 74, 76, 80–3

Yang, Lina 5, 23, 28, 36–8, 42–3n., 80
Yi, Jian 229–31, 256–8, 260, 264–5, 267–9, 271–3, 278n., 315n., 317n
YunFest 3, 11, 238–9, 243, 249n., 252n., 253n., 266, 273, 275n., 280n.

Zhao Tao xvi, 225, 227–8
Zhang, Li 3, 18n., 161–2n.
Zhang, Yimou vi, 5, 8, 49–50, 301, 303–4, 306, 308–9, 314–18n.
Zhang, Yingjin 125, 141–3n., 145n., 148–9, 153, 160–2n., 227n., 265, 267, 275n., 278n., 280n., 340
Zhang, Zhen xi, 40n., 85n., 89, 102n., 134, 142n., 337
Zhaxi Nima 265
Zhou, Dongyu 5, 304
Zhu, Zhu 75, 84n.
zoom 31, 34, 98, 115–16, 158, 170, 173, 241
zooming shots 115, 173